Beiträge zum ausländischen und internationalen Privatrecht

146

Herausgegeben vom

Max-Planck-Institut für ausländisches
und internationales Privatrecht

Direktorium:

Holger Fleischer, Ralf Michaels, Anne Röthel

Abdruck mit freundlicher Genehmigung der Niedersächsischen Staats- und Universitätsbibliothek Göttingen (Handschriften und Seltene Drucke).

Mathias Reimann

Rudolf von Jhering

From Roman Law to Modern Jurisprudence

Mohr Siebeck

Mathias Reimann, Legal education at the University of Freiburg i.Br.; 1978 1st, 1981 2nd State Exam; 1982 Dr. iur. utr., University of Freiburg; 1983 LLM University of Michigan; since 1985 Professor of Law at the University of Michigan; 1995–99 Professur für Zivilrecht, Rechtsvergleichung und Rechtsgeschichte at the University of Trier; regular visiting professor at University of Freiburg; currently Hessel E. Yntema Professor of Law at the University of Michigan.

ISBN 978-3-16-164001-8 / eISBN 978-3-16-164002-5
DOI 10.1628/978-3-16-164002-5

ISSN 0340-6709 / eISSN 2568-6577
(Beiträge zum ausländischen und internationalen Privatrecht)

The Deutsche Nationalbibliothek lists this publication in the Deutsche Nationalbibliographie; detailed bibliographic data are available at *https://dnb.dnb.de.*

Printed on non-aging paper.

Mohr Siebeck GmbH & Co. KG, Wilhelmstraße 18, 72074 Tübingen, Germany
www.mohrsiebeck.com, info@mohrsiebeck.com.

For Max

“Zuerst blendet und überwältigt er, dann erkennt man die zahlreichen Schwächen und auch mancherlei Blendwerk und lässt sich dadurch abstossen bis man schliesslich doch wieder zum eigentlichen Kern und Dauergehalt durchdringt und dessen hohe Bedeutung einsieht.”

“At first he dazzles and overpowers, then one recognizes the many weaknesses and a good deal of flashiness and is taken aback, until finally, one penetrates to the essential core and lasting substance and understands its great significance.”

Max Rümelin, Rudolf von Jhering (1922) 4.

Foreword

The idea to write this book arose in the context of a summer school I taught on Jhering, jointly with Professor Nils Jansen (University of Münster), for the Studienstiftung des Deutschen Volkes in July of 2016. Thus I owe a debt of gratitude to both my fellow-teacher and the students in that course. The weeks we spent together in St. Johann (in the Italian province of Südtirol/Alto Adige) provided not only an occasion to engage with Jhering and his ideas but also to undertake many vigorous hikes into the breathtaking mountain scenery of the surrounding Dolomites. I am also indebted to Bruce Frier and Reinhard Zimmermann for reading various parts of the manuscript and for reviewing my analyses of Jhering's engagement with Roman law. Michael Kunze, the author of a forthcoming (German) biography of Jhering, hosted me for an afternoon of discussion at his home in Hamburg and provided many valuable insights both on this and other occasions. Dr. Christian Eckl (Max-Planck-Institut, Hamburg) patiently provided diligent and invaluable editorial assistance. Sunita Ganesh carefully reviewed the manuscript and proofread the page-proofs. Last, but not least, I am deeply indebted to Keith Lacey from the University of Michigan Law Library for his tireless and unfailingly efficient help with finding even arcane sources and for speedily providing every piece of bibliographical information I requested.

Ann Arbor, December 2024 *Mathias Reimann*

Table of Contents

Introduction: About This Book

1. Why Jhering?

Rudolf von Jhering (or Ihering)[1] was, by any standard, one of the "great jurists of the world."[2] Certainly in terms of influence on nineteenth and twentieth century legal thought, he should be on anyone's list of the top ten – along with Savigny and Windscheid in Germany, Bentham and Maine in England, Holmes and

---

[1] Both of these spellings have been used. There is some debate over which spelling is correct, or rather, more appropriate. The issue arises in part because there was often no difference between (capital) "J" and "I" in the Gothic (Fraktur) font prevalent in German printing until the later nineteenth century. When his works began to be printed in the more modern Latin font, some publishers used "Ihering" (as in Der Kampf ums Recht, 1872) others "Jhering" (as in both volumes of Der Zweck im Recht, 1877/1883), both presumably with the author's approval. Apparently, the matter was not considered very important. Ultimately, however, "Jhering" must win out because Jhering himself signed in that fashion, as *Rückert*, Methodenorakel (2019) 460, has pointed out; see the facsimile in *Pleister*, Persönlichkeit, Wille und Freiheit im Werke Rudolf von Jherings (1982) (before the title page). It also makes more sense because it is commonly accepted that the name is pronounced, as Jhering himself stated, in two syllables, Jhering in Briefen (1913) 217 (i.e., "Je-ring," in English "Yeah-ring," instead or "Eering"). In any event, in the last couple of decades, "Jhering" has become broadly accepted (a major exception is *Fikentscher*, Methoden des Rechts III (1976) and this book adopts this now more common version. In a similar vein, the first name is sometimes spelled "Rudolf" (e.g., as the author of Der Kampf ums Recht (1872) and of Scherz und Ernst in der Jurisprudenz (1884), sometimes "Rudolph" (e.g., as the author of Geist des römischen Rechts (1852–1865) and of Der Zweck im Recht (1877/1883). Again, it was apparently not important. Since Jhering himself typically signed as "Rudolf" (see, e.g., his curriculum vitae, Jhering in Briefen (1913) 214; Jhering, Scherz und Ernst (1884) VI), this spelling is adopted here as well.

[2] See *MacDonell and Mason*, Great Jurists of the World (1914). The essay on Ihering (sic) was written by *MacDonell*, id. 590–599. His earliest German biographer, Ludwig Mitteis, himself a highly prominent and accomplished jurist, agreed; *Mitteis*, Jhering (1905) 664 ("one of the greatest of all times"), as did others, see *Jenkins*, Rudolf von Jhering (1960) (counting Jhering among "the giants of legal thought"); *Lange*, Die Wandlungen Jherings (1927); *Rümelin*, Rudolf von Jhering (1922) 80. Already during his lifetime, Jhering received a long list of honors including honorary doctorates (Dr. h.c.) from prestigious universities, memberships in learned societies, such as the Royal Dutch Academy of Sciences (where he succeeded Savigny), see *Heutger*, Rudolf von Jhering (2023) 46–47, and even the Japanese "Order of Merit of the Rising Sun" bestowed by the Tenno in 1892; for a more complete list, see *Behrends* (ed.), Jhering, Beiträge und Zeugnisse (1993) 80–81, 86–90.

Pound in the United States, Gény and Saleilles in France, and Kelsen in Austria. While reasonable people can of course differ about exactly who should be on such a list, no history of legal thought and no survey of jurisprudence can afford to bypass Jhering, and I know of none that does.[3]

Jhering was also a great jurist in terms of his impact on, and popularity with, a broader lay audience. Like Holmes, he was one of those rare jurists who have been widely read and quoted even by non-lawyers.[4] As in Holmes' case, his popularity has been due in no small part to his style as a writer which has captured the public imagination through aphorisms and wit – as well as through reckless simplification and exaggeration. In addition, unlike Holmes' typically sardonic, often cold, and bleak pronouncements, Jhering's writings are often playful, satirical, and hilarious – and thus much more fun to read.

What makes Jhering's work particularly fascinating is that it deeply engages *both* of the two most basic perspectives on law.[5] On the one hand, he took the internal point of view, dealing with law as a realm of fundamental principles and positive rules. Here, he *worked in* the law, so to speak. This side shows him as a great master of legal doctrine and an enthusiastic theoretician of legal method who was second to none even in nineteenth century Germany where such qualities were not in short supply. On the other hand, Jhering took the external perspective, dealing with law as a cultural and social phenomenon evolving throughout history. Here, he *looked at* law from the outside in order to explore its relationship with society and economy.[6] This side shows him as an audacious pioneer who broke vast new ground and arguably became the most important founder of modern legal thought.[7]

Jhering's long term significance is mainly due to his work according to the second, external, perspective. In particular, his view of law as a result of the struggle between social interests and as a "means to an end," i.e., an instrument for social governance and control, has become a dominant jurisprudential paradigm in the twentieth century and beyond. This was most clearly visible in socialist legal ideology, which is now largely defunct. It is also particularly pronounced in modern American legal thought since Holmes and Pound, in the

---

[3] In a book written for an educated general audience, American author William Seagle (1898–1977) even listed Jhering in the august company of, inter alia, Hammurabi, Solon, Gaius, and Justinian; *Seagle,* Men of Law (1947).

[4] This has, of course, been noted by others, see, e.g., *Wieacker*, Gründer und Bewahrer (1959) 197; *Wieacker*, Privatrechtsgeschichte (1967) 450.

[5] See *Jansen and Reimann*, Begriff und Zweck in der Jurisprudenz (2018) 90–91.

[6] Roscoe Pound considered the transition from the internal to the external perspective the crucial progress of jurisprudence in the late nineteenth century; *Pound*, Spirit of the Common Law (1921) 212; see infra chapter VII.3., note 222 and text.

[7] In a similar vein, Wolfgang Fikentscher considered a jurist "great" if he combined work in positive law with the invention of a new methodology which has been accepted by posterity; *Fikentscher*, Methoden des Rechts III (1976) 101. As we will see throughout this book, Jhering passes this test with flying colors.

wake of legal realism, and especially under the dominance of law and economics.[8] It is palpable in European Union law as well where legal rules are almost exclusively employed to promote political agendas. More generally, today, an instrumental use of law is probably the prevalent approach in most legal systems of the Westernized world. It was Jhering more than anyone else who, a century and a half ago, first decisively pointed in that direction. Thus, Jhering stood, as Joachim Rückert aptly put it, "at the beginning of modern jurisprudence."[9]

Like Marx's economics, Nietzsche's philosophy, and Weber's sociology, Jhering's jurisprudence casts a long shadow. In Jhering's case, this is also true because during the last century or so, we have learned that conceiving of law primarily as a means to political ends can be both a blessing and a curse, depending on who gets to use it and for what purpose.

2. Goals and Limitations

Despite his great importance both for the history of jurisprudence and for our current understanding of law, access to Jhering and his ideas has been difficult for a global audience. While most of his important works have been translated into several languages,[10] trying to understand Jhering's writings on their own is anywhere from challenging to impossible. Not only are they written against the backdrop of a particular time and embedded in the larger context of nineteenth century German legal scholarship, their often poor organization, inconsistent terminology, and idiosyncratic style also tend to confound even the determined reader. Of course, there is an extensive literature on Jhering in German, and there are numerous publications about him in several other major languages[11] but most of these writings are linguistically inaccessible to most readers in most jurisdictions. The main exception is the literature in English as the current global lingua franca in legal scholarship. The English-speaking literature on Jhering, however, is either fragmentary, dated or both. What has been missing is an up-to-date, book-length, study of Jhering that can be read by most legal (and other) scholars in the world today.

This book seeks to make Jhering and his work more accessible to a worldwide audience by providing an English introduction to the man and his work. It is primarily aimed at the reader who is no expert on Jhering but wants to learn about him and his ideas, but who lacks the mastery of German required to read the pertinent legal scholarship.[12] It will also be helpful to those who can actually

---

[8] See infra chapter IV.2., note 367 and text.

[9] *Rückert,* Methodenorakel (2019) 457.

[10] See infra chapter VII.2.

[11] See the extensive bibliography in *Kunze*, Lieber in Gießen (2018) 63–85

[12] Some of the essays about Jhering written two generations ago by German scholars such as Franz Wieacker and Erik Wolf (in the 1950s and 1960s) are brilliant in their own right and

read German but who are, for lack of training in German jurisprudence and legal history, insufficiently familiar with the background and context of Jhering's work. Yet, in order to forestall false expectations, three particular limitations of this enterprise need to be clearly stated.

First, while this book provides a broad and wide-ranging portrait of the man and his work, it is in no sense a fully comprehensive study. Jhering's *oeuvre* was so rich and varied that a complete rendition and assessment would require a multi-volume effort. Nor does the book attempt to refer to, never mind integrate, all the existing publications about him. Such an undertaking would get bogged down in a mass of literature and quickly lose sight of the forest before the trees. While not limited to bare essentials, this book should be read as an introduction that highlights its topic's most salient aspects. It focuses only on Jhering's most significant works, and even with regard to those, it emphasizes mainly the elements that are of continuing interest today.[13]

Second, the book does not claim to present an entirely new interpretation of the man and his work. To be sure, in many respects, it presents profiles which sometimes deviate from the existing ones. It not only proffers ideas and arguments that go beyond what other authors have written but sometimes also challenges established views. Yet, more often than not it builds on existing scholarship. In short, the book's primary goal is not originality but accessibility.

Third, the book does not attempt a single, overarching, interpretation of Jhering's work. Given the multifaceted character of the man, the extreme diversity of his scholarship, and its significant shift of focus over time, it is a serious question whether a coherent interpretation of the whole is feasible. Some scholars have claimed that it is or have even attempted such a feat,[14] others have rejected the

have attained quasi-classical status, but they are scarcely suitable as a first introduction because they assume that the reader is already familiar with Jhering's work at least in great outline; they also do not make for easy reading – even for a German native speaker. While this is less true for the slightly more recent work of Wolfgang Fikentscher (published in 1976), its inherent complexity still makes digesting it a challenge. In a similar vein, much of the most recent German scholarship on Jhering (written in the late twentieth and early twenty-first century), especially by Okko Behrends, Christoph-Eric Mecke, Wolfgang Pleister, and Joachim Rückert, is not cast in simple language. The forthcoming biography by Michael Kunze, entitled "Das unsichtbare Recht" ("The Invisible Law"), promises to become the most accessible work on Jhering in German but the book is aimed primarily at a German readership, i.e., an audience familiar with much of the background information many foreign readers will lack, and its primary goal is a personal biography and portrait, not an academic interpretation of Jhering's scholarship.

[13] It does not directly focus on the essays which Jhering published (mostly anonymously) in the Literarische Zeitung 1842–1846; many of his smaller doctrinal articles which appeared in the Jahrbücher für die Dogmatik des heutigen römischen und deutschen Privatrechts as well as in other periodicals; *Jhering*, Plaudereien eines Romanisten, a series of about a dozen essays in Juristische Blätter 1880, republished in *Jhering*, Scherz und Ernst (1884) 21–243; as well as the plethora of occasional pieces about a broad range of legal and non-legal subjects which Jhering published throughout his life in various venues.

[14] The most important examples are *Behrends*, Durchbruch zum Zweck des Rechts (1987)

idea[15] or at least remained highly skeptical.[16] As we shall see, Jhering himself was ambivalent; while he loved to announce all-encompassing theories with great fanfare, he also often unabashedly recognized the tensions and contradictions in his thought. This book does not take a position on the issue whether a single, coherent reading of Jhering's work is possible. Instead, it is based on the view that even if that were the case, constructing such a reading would miss much of what is most valuable. What makes engagement with Jhering's *oeuvre* so fascinating and rewarding is exactly that it is riddled with tensions and contradictions which, ultimately, reflect the very tensions and contradictions within law itself. Jhering constantly forces the reader to think about the law from different perspectives – as a system of doctrines and a political instrument, as a theoretical construct and a practical craft, as a product of history and a reflection of present-day conditions, as a construct of power and a search for justice.

3. A Roadmap and a Summary

Jhering's work is virtually impossible to grasp without am understanding of the man, both as an individual and as a scholar. The book thus opens, in chapter I, with a biography and a portrait. It sets the stage by looking at the environment in which Jhering lived and worked, i.e., nineteenth century Germany, especially the prevailing trends in jurisprudence, philosophy, society and economy, as well the dominant political questions of the time. It then traces the waystations of Jhering's academic life which was divided into three major periods, each spent at a different university (Gießen, Vienna, Göttingen) and each associated with an emphasis on a particular kind of jurisprudence (doctrinal/methodological, po-

---

and *Fikentscher*, Methoden des Rechts III (1976) 274–279; Rückert also appears to find considerable overall coherence in Jhering's theory of law and method, *Rückert*, Geist des Rechts (2004); id., Methodenorakel (2019). Others have at least emphasized pervasive themes, see, e.g., *Smith*, Four German Jurists XII (1897) 41 (law as an expression of social utility); *Schelsky*, Das Jhering Modell des sozialen Wandels ((1971) 59 ("law as a guideline and essential social factor for social change"); see also *Dreier*, Jherings Rechtstheorie (1996) 232; *Hurwicz*, Rudolf von Jhering und die deutsche Rechtswissenschaft (1911) IX. Wieacker found "internal unity" ("innere Einheit") in Jhering's overall *oeuvre* – though not in an objective manner but in the subjective sense of being rooted in a "mighty will" and a consistent personal experience, see *Wieacker*, Jhering (1969) 12; what exactly that means remains unclear, however.

[15] See, e.g., *Wolf*, Große Rechtsdenker (1963) 661; *Jenkins*, Rudolf von Jhering (1960) 169–170; Larenz (justly) emphasized Jhering's tendency to "oscillate between extremes," *Larenz*, Rudolf von Jhering (1970) 141 – a habit that Jhering himself openly admitted, see his letter to Windscheid of July 29, 1856, Jhering in Briefen (1913) 64, 65.

[16] See, e.g., *Wieacker*, Rudolf von Jhering (1969) 11; *Helfer*, Rudolf von Jhering als Rechtssoziologe (1978) 560–561 (pointing to multiple contradictions in Jhering's work most of which appear irresolvable).

lemical, sociological). Along the way, it briefly touches on Jhering's most important works, all of which are then discussed in greater depth in the following chapters. We will also consider two of Jhering's most important professional friendships which shed additional light on the man and the scholar. The chapter concludes with a close-up-and-personal portrait of Jhering as a private individual, a thinker in general, and a jurist in particular, including a look at his station in society and his political convictions.

The rest of the book is organized mainly by following Jhering's path as a scholar through his three major phases rather than by focusing on particular substantive themes in a cross-sectional fashion. One could, of course, provide chapters that discuss his views of Roman law, historical evolution, the nature and function of law, legal methodology, theory and practice, Darwinism, etc., and readers looking specifically for such aspects might find that helpful. Yet in these, as well as in many other, regards, Jhering's views constantly evolved and sometimes changed so substantially over time that each of these chapters would have to revisit his intellectual development in its particular context. It thus seemed more advisable to look at Jhering's dozen or so signature works in roughly chronological order; each is used as a platform for discussing that element of Jhering's thought and that stage of his intellectual development for which the respective work is most representative. In that regard, the core of the book has features of a field guide to Jhering's principal publications.[17] While these chapters are not entirely free-standing, they are sufficiently self-contained to be read separately by those interested (only) in a particular aspect of Jhering's work. Making such a separate reading possible sometimes required repeating information and arguments discussed in other chapters and to provide numerous cross-references.

As mentioned, Jhering's academic life and work can be divided into three major phases: an earlier period (ca. 1845–1860) marked by an emphasis on an internal, i.e., doctrinal and methodological, perspective; a transition characterized by polemical attacks on the very methodology developed in the first phase and by a reorientation towards a new approach (ca. 1860–1870); and the development of that new, external and sociological, jurisprudence (ca. 1870–1890). An overarching topic, running through all these periods, is Jhering's historical perspective on law.

Chapter II explores the first of Jhering's jurisprudential modes, i.e., his internal perspective on law. Here, we see him engaged with law as a field of doctrine (*Dogmatik*) which lay at the very core of nineteenth century German legal scholarship. Jhering's engagement with legal doctrine had five dimensions. In his first *magnum opus*, "Geist des römischen Rechts auf den verschiedenen Stufen seiner

---

[17] For reasons of authenticity, I frequently quote, rather than paraphrase, the language in his books and essays. Thus, the reader can often hear Jhering speak in his own voice, albeit of course in (my own) English translation. Where it is difficult to capture his (nineteenth century) German in English, or where he uses key terms with connotations that a translation cannot fully convey, I provide the original German as well.

Entwicklung" ("Spirit of the Roman Law at the various Stages of Its Development") (1852–1852), Jhering sought to lay the foundations for a new jurisprudence. Here, his ultimate goal was to extract the essence from Roman law to then transcend its substance, i.e., to proceed, in his own, famous words, "through the Roman law beyond the Roman law" ("durch das römische Recht über das römische Recht hinaus"). This, however, meant no less than replacing the dominant Historical School founded by Savigny with its focus on the classical Roman sources with a new, more up-to-date, legal science. Second, in pursuit of this project, Jhering presented a specific methodology. His (in)famous "natural-historical method" ("naturhistorische Methode") was a peculiar technique that took the conceptual and logical approach, which dominated German jurisprudence at the time, to new heights, as illustrated by Jhering's essay "Unsere Aufgabe" ("Our Task," or "Mission") (1857). Third, as part of his project, and seeking to demonstrate his method, Jhering produced several important law review articles of doctrinal scholarship. By way of example, we will take a close look at an article that demonstrates his doctrinal mastery with particular force, i.e., his essay on *culpa in contrahendo* (1861). The piece has not only had a lasting influence on private law doctrine but has also become a classic in its own right. Fourth, despite his high-flying methodology, Jhering always kept a keen eye on the concerns of legal practice. That was true not only in his academic work but also a busy advisor to courts as well as an expert consulted by parties to high-profile legal disputes. Last, but not least, Jhering had to focus on doctrine when he was in the classroom. He was a devoted and highly successful teacher who employed an interactive teaching-style long before Christopher Columbus Langdell introduced the "Socratic method" in the United States, and who pushed for clinical education long before it became fashionable in our own age. Chapter I concludes by situation Jhering in relation to the Historical School that he followed in some regards while fighting it in others.

Chapter III then discusses Jhering's famous "conversion" from the internal to the external perspective. Around the late 1850s, Jhering developed increasing doubts about his own "natural-historical method." When he had to advise a court in a concrete dispute involving the allocation of risk in a contract of sale, these doubts finally became overwhelming. Jhering was faced with a situation in which a strictly logical application of prevailing doctrine led to an outcome that was totally unacceptable to his sense of justice. As a result, Jhering lost faith in the highly abstract conceptual and logical method that he himself had celebrated up to that point. Almost suddenly, he felt the need to distance himself radically from this approach, attacking and ridiculing it in a series of articles published in the early 1860s. These pieces were later included in a book which also contained a satirical description of Jhering's fictitious but famous visit in the "Heaven of Concepts" ("Begriffshimmel"). The term nicely captured Jhering's mockery of "conceptual jurisprudence" ("Begriffsjurisprudenz") and became common coinage in the twentieth century. The chapter concludes by asking how decisive Jhering's turn away from his own erstwhile method really was. Some earlier scholarship regarded it as a radical experience and termed it Jhering's "Damascus."[18] A closer look, however, reveals that this overstates the case. As the modern literature has largely recognized, there was much continuity in Jhering's work: he significantly modified, but never entirely abandoned, his earlier approach, and he continued to publish doctrinal work. Thus, Jhering's internal perspective survived, though it was increasingly overshadowed by the external view which came to predominate his later work.

This later work, tackling law from the external perspective, is the object of chapter IV. It begins with a discussion of the slender volume in which Jhering first openly embraced a sociological approach: his world-famous 1872 tract "Der Kampf ums Recht" ("The Struggle for Law"). Jhering loudly proclaimed, against the great and late Savigny, that law did not evolve quietly on its own but is rather the result of constant (and often violent) struggle between competing (social) interests. From here, it was but a small step to a view of law as an instrument for social purposes. Jhering spent most of his later years exploring this instrumental conception, especially in what became his most influential work: "Der Zweck im Recht" (literally "The Purpose in Law," translated, however, as "Law as Means to an End"[19]) (1877/1883). Beyond its simple – and simplistic – motto: "purpose is the creator of all law" ("der Zweck ist der Schöpfer des ganzen Rechts"), the book covers an immense terrain reaching far beyond law proper. Fascinating in its vast range and originality of insights, but also maddening in its lack of focus and logical organization, the book is a tour de force of exploration and imagination but a disaster as an exposition of a coherent theory of law. Chapter IV finally turns to a key concept that had intrigued Jhering for decades: "das Rechtsgefühl" ("the feeling of justice"). Jhering tackled it in both "Der Zweck im Recht" and in a lecture he gave in 1884. Here, he struggled mightily to identify a normative perspective from which the justice of positive law could be judged – an endeavor in which he largely, and in a sense tragically, failed.

After tracing Jhering's work through its three major phases, chapter V turns to the overarching topic of Jhering's Historical Perspective. As a "Romanist," Jhering delved deeply into the (early) history of Roman law. While he proffered some original and thought-provoking insights, his writing on ancient Roman law in and of itself is not the most interesting part of his historical work. What is more noteworthy from a long-term perspective is his critique of contemporary historiography and his (quasi-Hegelian) conception of history as a process of progress. The latter idea was part of a larger fashion at the time, also involving scholars from other countries, especially Henry Sumner Maine in England and Oliver Wendell Holmes in the United States.

---

[18] *Wieacker*, Privatrechtsgeschichte (1967) 451. Wieacker later revised his views, see infra chapter III.3., note 103.

[19] *Jhering*, Law as a Means to an End (Isaac Husik transl., 1921).

In his later years, Jhering increasingly strayed beyond jurisprudence in order to satisfy broader interests. Chapter VI looks at the two main topics he tackled in his last decade – as well as at the price he paid for pursuing them. The first topic was custom. It was the object of his ire in the 1882 essay "Das Trinkgeld", a diatribe, more entertaining than profound, against the custom of tipping. Custom also become a major focus of the second volume of "Der Zweck im Recht" (1883); here, Jhering left jurisprudence almost completely behind and delved into a hodgepodge of non-legal topics, especially social norms such as custom, decency, and courtesy. The second, very different, topic of his last years was the pre-history of the Indo-European race. In his "Vorgeschichte der Indoeuropäer" (translated as "The Evolution of the Aryan")[20] (1894) Jhering sought to trace and define some of the earliest foundations of European culture, especially, of course, of Roman law. Jhering's explorations of both social norms and of pre-history bring his strengths and weaknesses as a scholar into sharp relief. On the one hand, he was an endlessly curious mind and a creative thinker who courageously ventured beyond his field of expertise. On the other hand, he got himself involved in tasks for which he admittedly lacked the requisite training. In that sense, his non-legal work illustrates the boon and bane of amateurism. Ultimately, Jhering set himself up for failure: both "Zweck" and "Vorgeschichte" remained amateurish – as well as unfinished.

Chapter VII moves beyond Jhering's lifetime and explores his impact on twentieth century legal thought. That influence was profound in his homeland, i.e., Germany, especially through the "Interessenjurisprudenz" ("jurisprudence of interests") emerging in the century's early decades. Yet, Jhering's influence is also notable in many other jurisdictions in the world as the more than 150 translations of his work into more than a dozen languages illustrate. Jhering's impact was particularly strong in the United States, where he became the recognized "father of sociological jurisprudence," i.e., of one of major strands of twentieth century American legal thought. We will also take a look at Jhering's influence on three particular sub-disciplines of jurisprudence, i.e, Roman legal history, legal sociology, and modern comparative law.

The Conclusion returns to the claim discussed in this Introduction, i.e., that Jhering's work is best understood not by squeezing it into one comprehensive theory but by acknowledging how riddled it is with inherent tensions and inconsistencies. The Conclusion does, however, highlight some pervasive features that seek to clarify the kaleidoscopic nature of Jhering's *oeuvre*. In particular, it shows how Jhering worked in a variety of basic modes which can be grouped into five sets of opposite perspectives: an internal versus an external form of jurisprudence, an individualist versus a social conception of law, a strictly juristic method versus a variety of other approaches, a scientific versus a philosophical outlook, and a positivist versus an idealist stance. At the end of the day, most of the resultant contradictions remained unresolved.

---

[20] *Jhering*, The Evolution of the Aryan (A. Drucker transl. 1897).

What makes engaging with, and perhaps even reading, Jhering so timely is his intrepidity: he always had the courage candidly to speak his mind and openly to state what he saw as the truth – no matter how unpopular or even upsetting that truth might be. With his combination of personal fortitude and intellectual honesty, Jhering provides an important model in times when public discourse is becoming ever more inhibited by the demands of political correctness and restricted by the erection of social taboos.

Chapter I

The Bon Vivant Law Professor – A Biography and a Portrait

It is a truism that a legal scholar's ideas are influenced by his environment, life experience, and personality. In some cases, this influence is so strong that one cannot really grasp these ideas without knowing the man behind them and the world he inhabited. Jhering is one of these cases. The remarkable shift in his perspective from his earlier to his later years, his passionate, provocative, and often humorous style, his frequent tendency to proceed in leaps and bounds, the many contradictions in his work, as well as the failure to complete his most important projects are closely interwoven with his environment, career path, temperament, and ambition. Beyond all that, looking at Jhering's life and personality provides his opus with a human face.

We devote a whole chapter to a biography and portrait of the man mainly because there is, as of yet, no substantial rendition of Jhering's life, character, and times in English.[1] There is, however, a wealth of material in German providing close-up-and-personal views of Jhering, inter alia, in form of the many letters which he wrote throughout his life and in which he often spoke straight from the heart.[2] His biography and portrait are also interesting in their own right because Jhering's was a life fully lived and often greatly enjoyed.

[1] As mentioned in the Introduction, 2., there is a fair amount of scholarship about Jhering published in English, but the biographical sketches available in that language are fairly basic, see, e.g., *MacDonnell*, Great Jurists (1914) 590–91. Nor is there, as of yet, a comprehensive biography in German. Michael Kunze has been working on filling that gap for some time and written a book, entitled "Das unsichtbare Recht," which is scheduled to be published in the fall of 2025; unfortunately, the manuscript could not be made available in advance. For the time being, the most extensive biographies are provided by *Fikentscher*, Methoden des Rechts III (1976) 101–163; *Kunze*, Rudolf von Jhering (1995); *Kunze*, Ein großer Jurist (2023), and in a general essay on Jhering and his work, by *Wolf*, Große Rechtsdenker (1963) 622–668. The best of the shorter accounts is still the brilliant essay by *Wieacker,* Gründer und Bewahrer (1959) 197–202*;* see also *Jansen and Reimann*, Begriff und Zweck (2018) 92–94; *Rückert*, Der Geist des Rechts (2004) 128–132*; Kleinheyer and Schröder*, Deutsche und europäische Juristen (2017) 233–234. Some periods of Jhering's life have been documented and discussed in greater depth: his life in Gießen (1852–1868) by *Kunze*, Lieber in Gießen (2018), and his Viennese years (1868–1872) by *Hofmeister*, Jhering in Wien (1995). A close-up-and-personal view is also provided in the essay by his son *Hermann von Jhering*, Erinnerungen (1913).

[2] See Bibliography C. The most significant collection was edited posthumously by his daughter, *Helene Ehrenberg* (ed.) Jhering in Briefen (1913). It contains almost 150 letters written over the whole course of Jhering's academic career and covering more almost half a

We begin with a sketch of Jhering's world and look at some of the features that provided the framework for his life and work (1.). We then follow Jhering's academic waystations which are related to the phases of his intellectual development (2.). We briefly consider his friendships with other leading legal scholars of the day, especially Carl Friedrich von Gerber and Bernhard Windscheid, who both played significant roles in his life (3.). We finally take a closer personal look at Jhering – as a private individual, intellectual in general, jurist in particular, member of society, and at his political views (4.). Some of what is laid out here will be revisited in context of discussing Jhering's specific works.

1. Jhering's World: Jurisprudence, Philosophy, Society, and Politics in Nineteenth Century Germany

To understand Jhering as a person and a scholar, one must have a sense of the environment in which he lived and worked. Simply put, Jhering's world was nineteenth century Germany – he was born 18 years after its beginning and died 8 years before its end – a contemporary of Karl Marx (1818–1883), Theodor Mommsen (1817–1903), and Otto von Bismarck (1815–1898).[3] Beginning with the aspects closest to Jhering's work as a jurist, we first look at nineteenth century German jurisprudence and then radiate gradually outward to the broader picture, i.e., the major philosophical teachings at the time, the rapidly changing economy and society, and the most significant political developments of his lifetime.[4]

Jurisprudence: The Historical School. Nineteenth century German jurisprudence was dominated by the Historical School which thus inevitably provided the background and context of much of Jhering's work. Founded by Gustav Hugo (1764–1844) and the more famous Friedrich Carl von Savigny (1779–1861) just before Jhering's birth, the Historical School was a multifaceted phenomenon. Here it suffices to call attention to four major aspects.

To begin with, the Historical School is sometimes understood in two different ways. A narrower conception encompasses only Hugo, Savigny, and their immediate successors. Thus understood, the Historical School was limited to the

---

century, as well as the reminiscences of his son Hermann. The volume is cheaply available in a modern reprint at <https://www.forgottenbooks.com/>. In his letters, Jhering wrote mostly about himself and his work, rather than about the concerns of his addressees – a feature that has been noted by others who have sometimes seen it as evidence of unshakable self-confidence and even self-love; see, e.g., *Wolf*, Große Rechtsdenker (1939) 498.

[3] As well of the Englishmen John Stuart Mill (1806–1873), Charles Darwin (1809–1882), and Herbert Spencer (1820–1903) who all came to play roles in Jhering's thought after ca. 1860; see infra chapter IV.2., notes 316–340 and text.

[4] For a pithy sketch of Jhering's intellectual environment, see *Rückert*, Methodenorakel (2019) 462–466.

first half of the nineteenth century and concerned only with Roman Law.[5] It ended around 1850 when Savigny retired from academic life and when his successor Puchta (1798–1846) had died. Throughout this book, we will refer to the Historical School in this, narrower, sense – as a movement which prevailed in German legal academia when Jhering was a student and a fledgling scholar, but which was already in decline when he published his first major works. A broader conception encompasses the developments in the second half of the century (as well as the Germanist side). Thus understood, the Historical School was essentially the mainstream of nineteenth century German legal science;[6] Jhering was very much a part of that mainstream during the first phase of his academic work (i.e., until ca. 1860) and in some respects even beyond. This, broadly conceived, Historical School ended when the codification of German private law finally terminated the reign of the received Roman jurisprudence.[7]

Second, as the name suggests, the adherents of the Historical School (conceived in the narrower sense), focused on law as a product of historical development. Reacting against the rationalism of the natural law school that prevailed in the seventeenth and eighteenth centuries, the historical jurists denied that law was a product of (or could be meaningfully constructed from) reason. True to the spirit of the Romantic era, they postulated that law, like language, evolved slowly and organically over time. This evolution expressed the inner consciousness of the nation – what Jhering's teacher Puchta eventually called the *Volksgeist* (spirit of the people).[8] *Volksgeist* was not, however, understood as a social or psychological reality but rather as the innate cultural tradition of a nation. It is important to note that in the eyes of the historical jurists, at advanced stages of society this cultural tradition was not represented by the common people but by the professional class of learned lawyers. Since the law's organic development should thus lie in the hands of the jurists (i.e., the members of the Historical School themselves), legislative interference was in principle an undue disturbance and thus an evil to be avoided as far as possible. For that reason, among others, Savigny famously (and successfully) opposed the early nineteenth century plans of a German civil code.[9] While Jhering was not a member of the group advocating these tenets, he did share some of the Historical School's credos in his early years, only to turn against most of them over time.

---

[5] *Haferkamp*, Die historische Rechtsschule (2018).

[6] *Reimann*, Nineteenth Century German Legal Science (1990).

[7] In a sense, a third way to look at the Historical School, not directly relevant here, is to see it as an international, especially transatlantic, phenomenon, see *Reimann*, Historical Jurisprudence (2018); *Rabban*, Law's History (2013).

[8] *Puchta*, Das Gewohnheitsrecht vol. I (1828) 144, 152, 154. While the term is usually ascribed to Savigny, he originally spoke of "das gemeinsame Bewußtsein des Volkes" ("the common consciousness of the people"), *Savigny*, Vom Beruf unserer Zeit (1814) 11. He adopted Puchta's term in 1840, *Savigny*, System des heutigen römischen Rechts I (1840) 14.

[9] *Savigny*, Vom Beruf unserer Zeit (1814).

Third, if one conceives of the Historical School broadly (i.e., as the mainstream of nineteenth century German legal science), it consisted of two major branches. The *Romanists* under Savigny's leadership considered the Roman law, adopted (first by scholars, then in practice) in Germany in the late Middle Ages and early modern period, the legitimate tradition in German (private) law. They focused on the jurisprudence created by the classical Roman jurists in antiquity, seeking to clarify and refine it, and to adapt it for modern use. The *Germanists*, by contrast, looked to the indigenous tradition, especially to the medieval sources, sometimes in cooperation with, sometimes in opposition to, the *Romanists.*[10] As a scholar of Roman law, Jhering was concerned only with the former side, i.e., with the use of classical Roman law for modern purposes and needs.

Last, but certainly not least, it is important to note that from the very beginning, the historical jurists, chiefly among them Savigny, saw the task of contemporary jurisprudence not only in the historical exploration of the law, but also in its organization according to its inner logic. The final goal was, in Savigny's terms, a "System of Modern Roman Law."[11] In fact, since the 1840s, the historical jurists' emphasis shifted increasingly from the historical to the systemic endeavor, resulting in the *Pandektenwissenschaft* (Pandectist legal science) which then dominated mid- and late nineteenth century German jurisprudence. As we shall see, during the first half of his academic career (ca. 1845–1865), Jhering propounded a closely related agenda, i.e., the distillation of the Roman law's fundamental features and concepts and their organization into an internally logical system, although in contrast to many prominent contemporaries, he never produced one.[12]

Thus, as we will see throughout the subsequent chapters, Jhering's relationship with the Historical School was complex. On the one hand, he still operated within its tradition in his earliest phase; on the other hand, he sought to overcome the Historical School through his own work, especially in his "Geist des römischen Rechts" ("Spirit of the Roman Law") (1852–1865) before he finally veered off in a completely different direction after 1870. Eventually, we will have to discuss Jhering's position vis-à-vis the Historical School in greater detail and

---

[10] These two branches reflected two main intellectual movements in early nineteenth century Germany. Savigny's return to the Roman law of antiquity was a variation of the classicist theme so prominent in the contemporary work of Goethe (especially his plays) and Schiller (especially his ballads). The *Germanists'* turn to the indigenous past was a variation on the Romantic search for the deep roots of the popular culture as also captured in the songs collected by *Achim von Arnim and Clemens Brentano* in Des Knaben Wunderhorn (1805–1808) and in *Jacob and Wilhelm Grimm's* Kinder- und Haus-Märchen (first published in 1812, then much expanded in subsequent editions).

[11] This was the title of one of Savigny's principal works, i.e., *Savigny*, System des heutigen römischen Rechts (8 vols., Berlin 1840–1849).

[12] See infra chapter II.1.

depth; yet, that has to wait until we have explored his agenda and methodology for the treatment of Roman law.[13]

Philosophy and Science: From Idealism to Positivism. During Jhering's formative years, German philosophy was dominated by the idealism of Immanuel Kant (1724–1804) and Georg Friedrich Wilhelm Hegel (1770–1831) with Johann Gottlieb Fichte (1762–1814) and Friedrich Wilhelm Joseph Schelling (1775–1864) also playing significant roles. Whether or not one had actually read (much of) these philosophers' works, during the first half of the nineteenth century, their ideas almost inevitably shaped the worldview of the educated class in Germany, including its jurists.[14]

It is important to note, however, that the direct impact of philosophy on jurisprudence was surprisingly limited. This was because in early to mid-nineteenth century Germany, mainstream legal thought was largely divorced from philosophy – not by accident but by design. In part as a reaction against the amalgamation of philosophy and law in seventeenth and eighteenth century natural law thinking, the doyen of nineteenth century German jurisprudence, Friedrich Carl von Savigny, had established a "geschichtliche Rechtswissenschaft" ("historical legal science") that was supposed to deal only with the historically given sources and thus with the positive law they contained. It rejected philosophical speculation and, by and large, renounced normative claims. Jurisprudence, Savigny wrote, did not require philosophy,[15] and his successor Georg Friedrich Puchta (1798–1846) essentially agreed.[16] As a result, mainstream nineteenth century German jurisprudence became a "science" of positive law (only), leaving metaphysics and questions of justice to the philosophers. As a jurist trained and operating in this environment, Jhering thus neither had nor needed specific training in philosophy.[17] Thus, in his capacity as a strictly legal scholar, Jhering was, like the vast majority of his colleagues, a positivist in the sense that at

[13] See infra II.6.

[14] For a thorough and thoughtful discussion of Jhering's intellectual trajectory in the context of the contemporary natural and social sciences, see *Mecke*, Jherings Rechtsdenken (2023). In particular, Mecke shows how the change of Jhering's conceptions and methods tracked the development various disciplines beyond law.

[15] *Savigny*, Juristische Methodenlehre (1802/03) 50 ("Even as merely preparatory knowledge philosophy is not at all necessary for a jurist."). Savigny did not, however, disparage philosophy, quite to the contrary: he thought that mastering it required serious commitment, not just dabbling in it. ("He who is not driven to [study] philosophy should leave it alone. Its study requires not just half-a-year but a whole life." Id.)

[16] Puchta claimed that "a developed system of philosophy is by no means a precondition for jurisprudence," and that a jurist does not have to be "a philosopher by profession." Yet, he also argued that "without philosophical views [a jurist] will not be able fully to meet the demands of his profession." *Puchta*, Cursus der Institutionen I (1841) § 32 (quoted after the 10th ed., Leipzig 1893, 56).

[17] Jhering himself repeatedly noted that with regret, see *Jhering*, Geist I (1852) 301 note 224; *Jhering*, Zweck I (1884), ix–x. On Jhering's knowledge of contemporary philosophy, see *Rümelin*, Rudolf von Jhering (1922) 17.

least at the outset, his primary focus was on the (private) law actually in force – which meant the (modernized) Roman jurisprudence as the common private law in pre-unification Germany.[18]

Still, certain elements of German idealist philosophy inevitably undergirded early and mid-nineteenth century German legal science. Kantian ideas informed Savigny's conception of law as separate from morality as well as his definition of law as the "invisible boundary" that demarcated the spheres of individual liberty in society.[19] His successor Puchta's scholarship betrayed the influence of Hegel in its focus on abstract concepts and strictly logical reasoning, and it endorsed the Hegelian notion of law as a manifestation of individual will.[20] More generally, idealism in the sense of focusing on (more or less abstract) ideas, rather than realities, strongly shaped mainstream legal reasoning in the 1830s and 1840s, when Jhering was a student and young scholar.[21]

As a member of the educated class, Jhering was of course roughly familiar with contemporary idealist philosophy, especially of the Kantian and Hegelian variety.[22] Direct and indirect references to the ideas of Kant and Hegel are scattered widely throughout his writings, and we will encounter them in various contexts when looking more closely at his work.[23] Jhering's engagement with these ideas is marked by three pervasive features. The first is a lack of real expertise: Jhering did not command a thorough understanding of Kant's and Hegel's thought. As he himself repeatedly admitted, as a scholar of Roman law, he was essentially an amateur in matters of (legal) philosophy. While he sometimes bemoaned that deficiency, it did not keep him from venturing into the terrain where a thorough understanding of philosophy was necessary or least helpful.[24] As his critics often pointed out, Jhering's lack of philosophical training seriously weakened his work on many occasions.[25] The second pervasive feature is randomness:

[18] On the complex issue of Jhering's positivism, see infra chapter IV.3.

[19] *Kant*, Metaphysik der Sitten (1797) 239–241 (Einleitung in die Rechtslehre, C.); *Savigny*, System vol. I (1840) 331 ("unsichtbare Gränze"). On the, in part very significant, differences between Kant's and Savigny's conceptions of law, see *Nörr*, Eher Hegel als Kant (1990) 22–24.

[20] *Hegel*, Philosophie des Rechts (1821) Einleitung §§ 5–16. On Puchta, see *Haferkamp*, Georg Friedrich Puchta (2004). When Puchta attended the *Gymnasium* in Nürnberg (1811–1816), Hegel was its principal (*Rektor*) and gave lectures on philosophy.

[21] Despite its title, the short tract by *Nörr*, Eher Hegel als Kant (1990), is not primarily an inquiry into these philosophers' influence on nineteenth century Germany jurisprudence; instead, it is, as its subtitle indicates, mainly a (very thoughtful) study of the idea of private law during that period.

[22] By contrast, Jhering paid little attention to the ideas of Fichte and Schelling because he was apparently not very familiar with them. Jhering had, however, read his share of Johann Wolfgang von Goethe (1749–1832) who was of course the towering figure in German literature at the time. As we will see, Jhering liked to refer to Goethe on various occasions, usually quoting language that he could assume to be familiar to his audience.

[23] See, e.g., *Jhering*, Geist III (1865) 299–305.

[24] See, e.g., *Jhering*, Zweck I (1884), ix–x.

[25] See infra chapter VII.1., note 9.

Jhering did not engage with Kantian or Hegelian ideas in a systematic, never mind in-depth, fashion. Instead, he brought them up wherever and whenever it suited his purposes – or just struck his fancy. On many occasions, the references are so indirect or outright opaque that it is not clear whether he was fully conscious of what he was doing. Finally, there was a pervasive ambivalence: even without going into detail, clearly Jhering's relationship with these philosophers was anything but monolithic or consistent. In part, Jhering's ambivalence was a result of the change in his thought over time; in part, however, it was also hardwired into his mind. On the whole, the superficiality of Jhering's philosophical understanding, the scattered nature and frequent opacity of his references, and his ambivalence vis-à-vis Kant's and Hegel' philosophy suggest that an in-depth analysis of Jhering's relationship with these thinkers is probably not a worthwhile undertaking.[26] This book does not attempt such an analysis but for purposes of overall orientation, a few general remarks are in order.

Jhering's reaction to Kant was essentially negative – in two regards. First, Jhering came to reject all "metaphysics" (without explaining what exactly he meant by that), and since he regarded Kantian philosophy as a prominent manifestation of that evil, he considered Kant's whole approach (at least in his legal philosophy) fundamentally misguided.[27] Second, Jhering's eventual turn to an empirical approach as well as to (social) utilitarianism[28] was at loggerheads with Kant's *a priori*, often categorical, and thus decidedly anti-utilitarian, positions. None of this, however, kept Jhering from invoking, or at least relying on, a variety of more specific Kantian ideas with apparent approval.[29] All in all, Jhering's understanding of Kant was amazingly superficial and in fact, sometimes plainly wrong – which, on some occasions, caused Jhering to commit outright blunders.[30]

---

[26] For a fairly thorough discussion of the relationship between some of Jhering's and Hegel's ideas, see *Pleister*, Persönlichkeit, Wille und Freiheit (1982) 148–158, 295–338. On the influence of Puchta and Friedrich Julius Stahl (1802–1861) on Jhering, see id. 170–192.

[27] While Jhering referred to Kant on several occasions, he did not cite any particular works. His references show, however, that he was familiar at least with Kant's legal philosophy which constitutes the first part of *Kant's* Metaphysik der Sitten (1797); in that work, Kant had clearly rejected an empirical approach, id. 230 (Einleitung B.). In fact, Kant had famously made fun of it: "A merely empirical jurisprudence is (like he the wooden head of Phädrus' fable) a head that may be pretty, but alas, it has no brain," id. It is not clear whether Jhering had also read *Kant's* Grundlegung zur Metaphysik der Sitten (1985); apparently, that book was not part of Jhering's library, see *Pleister*, Persönlichkeit, Wille und Freiheit (1982) 21 n. 95.

[28] See infra chapter IV.2., notes 317–340 and text.

[29] For example, Jhering's postulate that law had to protect an individual's "personality," see infra chapter VI.1., notes108–120 and text, had Kantian (as well as Hegelian) roots; his (at least occasional) insistence that law must be categorically respected, see infra chapter IV.1., smacked of Kant's "fiat justitia, pereat mundus" (which Kant, however, postulated less categorically than is often assumed, see infra chapter IV.2., note 218); and on several occasions, Jhering presented ideas apparently derived from Kant's categorical imperatives, see, e.g., infra chapter IV.1., note 82 and text.

With regard to Hegelian philosophy, Jhering reacted differently to different elements. On the one hand, there was Hegel's highly abstract form of (legal) reasoning and his reliance on the individual will as the foundational concept of private law;[31] as mentioned, both these features were incorporated into mainstream Romanist jurisprudence by Hegel's disciple and Jhering's early model, Puchta. As we will see, Jhering first enthusiastically embraced these elements and then later vehemently rejected them. It is but a slight caricature to say that in this regard, Jhering turned from a quasi-Hegelian into a determined anti-Hegelian.[32] On the other hand, there was Hegel's conception of history as a sequence of developmental stages moving towards higher states of civilization, as well as the idea that this process was driven by a progressive force (*Weltgeist*). This (idealist) understanding of history became widely popular in early nineteenth century Germany and was incorporated into legal historiography by Hegel's disciple Eduard Gans (1797–1839).[33] Jhering subscribed to it by and large as well, some differences and modifications notwithstanding.[34] Simply put, Jhering came to reject the technique and foundations of Hegel's *Rechtsphilosophie* while he essentially came to accept, and built on, Hegel's *Philosophie der Geschichte*.[35] As a result, whenever Jhering invokes Hegel, the reader has to consider which of these two sides Jhering had in mind.

---

[30] Examples are provided by *Pleister*, Persönlichkeit, Wille und Freiheit (1982) 25, see especially n. 25.

[31] *Hegel*, Philosophie des Rechts (1821) 50–87 (sec. 34–81).

[32] See infra chapter III.3. and chapter IV.2., notes 138–157 and text. It is interesting to note that Hegel and Jhering shared some personal character traits, such as the love of good company and wine, pig-headedness, and strong sense of independence, as well as a tendency to explode into sudden rage; for Jhering, see infra 4; for Hegel, *Wiedemann*, Hegel (1965) 100–101, 103–104.

[33] *Gans*, Das Erbrecht in weltgeschichtlicher Entwickelung (4 vols., 1824–1835).

[34] See infra chapter V.3. Jurisprudence in its historical dimension, Jhering explained in 1868, follows law "auf all seinen Wegen, die es genommen hat,um sich von Stufe zu Stufe zur höchsten Vollkommenheit zu erheben." ("on all the paths it has taken to elevate itself from level to level towards the highest perfection"), *Jhering*, Ist die Jurisprudenz eine Wissenschaft (1868) 92. In contrast to Hegel, however, Jhering did not see the historical development as by and large complete in his own time but as wide open towards a largely uncertain future, see infra chapter VI.2. note 74 and text. Jhering's view of history as a progressive development of mankind was also shaped by his early exposure to Gotthold Ephraim Lessing's (1729–1781) tract Die Erziehung des Menschengeschlechts (1780; engl. The Education of the Human Race, 1858); see infra chapter V.2., notes 104–111 and text.

[35] *Hegel*, Philosophie des Rechts (1821); *Hegel*, Philosophie der Geschichte (1837, 1840, 1848). These were apparently the only two works by Hegel that Jhering was at least somewhat familiar with. As a jurist, he had no reason to deal with Hegel's work on phenomenology and logic. This is, of course, a simplified rendition of Jhering's relationship with Hegel's philosophy; for a much more sophisticated and in-depth discussion (in particular with regard to Jhering's Der Zweck im Recht), see *Pleister*, Persönlichkeit, Wille und Freiheit im Werke Jherings (1982) 316–338.

While Jhering's formative period was marked by German idealism (as well as classicism and romanticism), his middle and later years saw fundamental changes in philosophy and science.

Around the middle of the nineteenth century, Kantian and Hegelian idealism was increasingly questioned and lost much (though not all) of its influence in Germany, and Jhering openly welcomed the decline of Hegel's prominence (sometimes almost sounding like Hegel's arch-enemy Arthur Schopenhauer, 1788–1860).[36] At the same time, a new, scientific, positivism was on the rise, notably in the wake of the work of Auguste Comte (1798–1857).[37] The older foundations of human knowledge, philosophy and history, gave way to the emerging modern sciences as most famously represented by the work of Jhering's contemporary Charles Darwin (1809–1882).[38] For example, evolution – a concept central to nineteenth century thought – was no longer understood mainly as a historical unfolding of ideas but increasingly as a biological, and eventually also a political and social, process.[39] While Jhering was neither an explicit follower of Comte nor a full-fledged Darwinist,[40] he responded to their ideas, as we will see, with a fundamental re-shaping of German legal thought after the middle of the century. His turn from an essentially idealist to a thoroughly sociological view of law was fully in line with the ascendancy of scientific positivism and realism. Especially in the first volume of "Der Zweck im Recht" (1877), Jhering sought to establish a jurisprudence based not on fundamental ethical precepts nor on abstract legal concepts, but on the observation of psychological forces and social facts.[41]

The rise of positivism was intimately related to the meteoric rise of the natural sciences as fact-based and experimental disciplines. Throughout the nineteenth century, enormous progress was made in chemistry, physics, biology, and, as a result, human medicine. Justus Liebig (1803–1873) laid the foundations for modern organic chemistry; Hermann von Helmholtz (1821–1894) worked on the conservation of energy and revolutionized the treatment of eye problems with the invention of the ophthalmoscope (1851); Robert Koch (1843–1910) made the break-through discoveries in microbiology which hugely advanced the treatment of infectious diseases, to name just a few of the developments that were close to home for Jhering in one way or another.[42] Like many of his contemporaries,

---

[36] Jhering's sarcasm, humor, overblown criticism of others, and occasionally excessive confidence in the veracity of his own views, were often reminiscent of Schopenhauer's writing, as noted by Jhering's friend and eulogist Adolf Merkel, see *Merkel*, Jhering (1893) 19. There were some similarities, but also some fundamental differences between Jhering's and Schopenhauer's ideas, see *Pleister*, Persönlichkeit, Wille und Freiheit (1982) 20–23, 301–304.

[37] *Comte*, Cours de philosophie positif (1830–1842).

[38] *Darwin*, On the Origin of Species (1859).

[39] *Spencer*, Principles of Sociology (1874–1875).

[40] See infra chapter IV.1., notes 39–57 and text; chapter IV.2., notes 310–315, 342–345 and text.

[41] See infra chapter IV.2.

[42] When Jhering arrived in Gießen in 1852, Justus Liebig had just left the university after

Jhering was utterly fascinated by the progress and discoveries of the natural sciences. As we will see, they had a direct and powerful influence on his early jurisprudence which imported the terminology and to some extent even sought to mimic the methodology of chemistry and biology.[43]

Thus, Jhering's work was not only embedded in, and shaped by, the transition from early nineteenth century philosophical idealism to mid- and late nineteenth century scientific positivism and realism; his work was itself very much part of that development: it constituted the jurisprudential side of this larger process. It was in large part this connection with the epistemological and methodological developments of his time that gave his work such great significance.

Society and Economy: Urbanization and Industrialization. During Jhering's lifetime, German society and economy underwent massive changes. The society of his childhood was still largely rural (though no longer feudal); the society of his old age was substantially urban (though not yet predominantly so). In the second half of the century, Germany began a process of belated but now particularly rapid industrialization which entailed the large-scale replacement of artisan work by industrial mass production. Fast developing technology also changed people's lives. As a young man, Jhering had to travel by stagecoach, but in his later years, he could take trains to all major destinations in Germany and beyond, reaching them in hours rather than days.[44] Long-distance communication increased at even greater speed when the use of the telegraph became common around the middle of the century.

Industrialization, and in its train the rise of full-fledged capitalism, also entailed the emergence of a proletariat, labor unions, and socialist ideology. It brought questions of social justice, especially with regard to the working class, into sharp relief. Karl Marx published "Das kommunistische Manifest" when Jhering was a young man[45] and wrote "Das Kapital" when Jhering was approaching old age.[46] To be sure, there was no lack of class conflict before the middle of the century,[47] but it became much more prominent and visible in its closing dec-

---

almost three decades, and Liebig's (now former) laboratory was across the street from Jhering's first apartment, see *Kunze*, Lieber in Gießen (2018) 14. Jhering probably experienced Helmholtz' ophthalmoscope first hand when he was diagnosed with a retina detachment in 1880; letter to Windscheid of June 19, 1880, Jherings Briefe an Windscheid (1988) 49. Jhering's second wife died of tuberculosis, and Robert Koch was the first to detect that the disease, hitherto considered hereditary, was actually caused by a bacterium.

[43] See infra II.2.

[44] The first travel by railway in Germany occurred in 1835, i.e., when Jhering was a teenager. When he was an old man (in 1890), there were almost 10,000 locomotives in Germany running on more than 40,000 km (25,000 miles) of railroad tracks.

[45] *Marx and Engels*, Manifest der kommunistischen Partei (1848).

[46] *Marx*, Das Kapital (1867–1894).

[47] The perhaps most notorious conflict was the uprising of the Silesian weavers in 1844, i.e., at a time when Jhering stood at the beginning of his academic career; it became the theme of (1912 Nobel Laureate) Gerhard Hauptmann's (1862–1946) play "Die Weber," published in 1892, i.e., the year of Jhering's death.

ades, entailing increasing challenges to the existing social and legal order. The Savignian notion of law developing slowly and peacefully in line with a nation's culture may have been a romantic illusion even in 1815, but by 1870, reality made a mockery of it, and Jhering was eager to point that out.[48]

At the same time, social life became less dominated by religion. Important areas of the law, such as the rules governing marriage, were secularized,[49] and the Church lost most of its legal power over (though not necessarily its influence on) people's lives. In this regard as well, Savigny and Jhering, though both Lutherans, symbolized different eras. Savigny was a fairly pious man for whom religion was an important basis for state and society; his jurisprudence was embedded in a Christian culture.[50] In Jhering's life, by contrast, religion played a more marginal role.[51] Jhering's conception of the state and of law owed almost nothing to it.

Politics: Power Struggles and National Unification. Jhering lived through a period of relative political stability; unlike previous or later generations, he was not directly exposed to bloody revolutions, devastating wars, major social unrest or famine. This does not mean, of course, that all was quiet on the German political front. During Jhering's lifetime, German politics revolved around two major issues: the struggle for power between the old nobility and the rising bourgeoisie, and the question of national unity. Jhering showed relatively little interest in the former but much enthusiasm for the latter.

In early nineteenth century Germany, the nobility was still the ruling class. While the *ancien régime* had ended in the French Revolution across the border, in Germany, aristocratic rule staged an impressive comeback after the Napoleonic wars at the Congress of Vienna in 1815. Born three years later, Jhering thus grew up during the period of "restauration" (of the old order). Aristocratic rulers often oppressed liberal movements through censorship, political prosecution, and incarceration. After a period of gradually increasing unrest, known as *Vormärz*[52], frustration with restauration finally boiled over in the German (and to some extent European) 1848/49 Revolution, which, however, ended in failure: the aristocracy defeated the republican rebellion as well as the project of a liberal constitution for all of Germany. Jhering took no active part in these developments and remained in the position of an observer.[53]

The other burning political issue during Jhering's lifetime was German national unity. The German Federation (*Deutscher Bund*), founded at the Congress

---

[48] See infra III.1.

[49] An important marker was the introduction of obligatory civil marriage in Prussia in 1875.

[50] For an in-depth discussion of Savigny's relationship with religion, see *Rückert*, Religion und Recht bei Savingy (2020).

[51] See infra notes 191–196 and text.

[52] Literally: "pre-March" because it preceded a revolution that eventually broke out in the month of March (1848).

[53] On Jhering's political activities and views, see infra 4.

of Vienna in 1815, was not a nation state but a fairly loose confederation of some 40 more or less sovereign political entities – kingdoms, duchies, cities, etc. Efforts to unite Germany under a liberal constitution failed in the 1848/49 revolution. In subsequent years, the rivalry between the German Federation's two largest members, Prussia and Austria, became ever more acute. The score between them was settled in 1866 when Prussia decisively defeated Austria in a brief war. The German Federation was dissolved and replaced, for the time being, by the North German Federation (*Norddeutscher Bund*) in 1867 under Prussian leadership. German unification was finally achieved by Bismarck in the wake of Prussia's victory in the Franco-Prussian war with the foundation of the (second) German Empire in 1871.[54] The Empire was dominated by Prussia, excluded Austria, and lasted beyond Jhering's lifetime (until 1918). In light of his otherwise limited political engagement, it may seem surprising that Jhering followed these events with growing emotional engagement and outright enthusiasm for German unification.[55] This time, however, he was directly concerned in various ways. As we shall see, shortly after the separation of Austria from the rest of Germany in 1867, Jhering became a professor at the University of Vienna, the capital of the Austro-Hungarian Empire. And when, after a few years in the Habsburg metropolis, he began to yearn for small town life again and received an offer from the University of Göttingen in 1872, the recent unification of Germany provided an additional reason to leave Vienna and return to his – now finally united – homeland.

2. Waystations: A Nineteenth Century Academic's Life

Jhering's childhood, education, and early academic appointments were the prelude, so to speak, to three major periods of his adult life. He spent these periods at the universities of Gießen, Vienna, and Göttingen. Over the course of his career, Jhering produced radically different kinds of work which can be put into three major categories: scholarship on Roman law, provocative writings aiming to upset established views, and historical-sociological inquiries into the origin and nature of law.[56] Each of these kinds of work can roughly be associated with one of his three major waystations. To be sure, there was much overlap and even considerable continuity, and the lines are far from sharply drawn. Still, as he moved from one of these venues to the next, the emphasis shifted from one kind of work to another.

[54] The Wilhelmine *Reich* was "second" in the sense that it succeeded the Holy Roman Empire which dated back to AD 962 when Otto the Great was crowned emperor, and which had ended in 1806, largely as a result of military defeat in the Napoleonic wars.

[55] See infra 4., notes 258–262 and text.

[56] In addition, Jhering wrote – with great enthusiasm – about various non-legal topics, see infra chapter VI.

Prelude (1818–1852): The (Not So Straight) Path to Legal Academia.[57] Jhering was born on August 22, 1818, in the small town of Aurich in East Frisia, a province in the far north-west corner of the (then) Kingdom of Hanover, close to the Dutch border and the North Sea. He came from old Frisian stock – his family could be traced back in the region to the fifteenth century. The Frisians have long had the reputation for being strong-willed, combative, outspoken, freedom-loving, and thus inclined to question authority. Jhering clearly evinced these character traits, attributed them to his Frisian origins, and was proud of them. They heavily influenced how he thought, worked, and argued.[58]

Jhering also came from a prominent family of jurists. For many generations, his ancestors had been members of the region's patriciate, and most of his forefathers had been lawyers or government officials. Legal historians keep pointing in particular to Hermann Conring (1606–1681), one of the most influential German jurists of the early modern period.[59] Jhering's father, who died when Rudolf was still a boy, was not only a practicing attorney but also legal counsel to the Frisians estates.

Given this pedigree, it is tempting to consider Rudolf destined from the very beginning to become a lawyer as well. That, however, was not clear at all. It is true that after completing the *Gymnasium* in his hometown in 1836, he enrolled as a law student first at the University of Heidelberg, then at the University of Munich (changing universities was fairly common at the time). Yet, in his first few semesters, Jhering showed much more interest in becoming a writer than in studying law. Seeing himself as a future author of humorous literature, he wrote several essays on non-legal topics, authored a "comical novella," and sketched a comedy[60] – and eventually gave up attending law lectures altogether. For a while, it seemed as if the aspiring writer in him was about to prevail. Yet, when he sent one of his pieces home, his mother decided to put an end to her son's literary antics: she promptly ordered him to return and then to transfer to the University of Göttingen. Situated, like Aurich, in the Kingdom of Hannover, that institution was much closer to home and provided much less opportunity to stray from the path of duty. Her plan worked. In Göttingen – where Jhering would eventually spend the last and longest period of his life – his interest finally turned to law. Now, he pursued his legal studies with rigor and ambition, determined to become a successful jurist. And yet, decades later, he would rekindle his literary

---

[57] For a more detailed and nuanced account of Jhering's early life, see *Kunze*, Rudolf von Jhering (1995) 127–138.

[58] Letter to Auguste von Littrow-Bischoff of August 28 , 1877, Jhering in Briefen (1913) 326. Both contemporary and modern commentators endorsed the idea that these character traits were ethnically conditioned, see *Smith*, Four German Jurists (1895) 685; *Wieacker*, Gründer und Bewahrer (1959) 200–201; *Wolf*, Große Rechtsdenker (1963) 630; *Fikentscher*, Methoden des Rechts III (1976) 108 also hints at that.

[59] See *Stolleis* (ed.), Hermann Conring (1601–1681) (1983).

[60] Letter to Windscheid, dated "beginning of 1864," Jhering in Briefen (1913) 162.

ambitions and indulge in producing satirical, provocative, and stylistically idiosyncratic essays – which became his most famous and most widely read works.[61]

Given that Jhering devoted his life to legal academia, it is also tempting to assume that he was destined from the very beginning to become a professor. Yet, that was not clear at all either. Nearing the completion of his studies, Jhering aimed at legal practice rather than a university post. Much to his chagrin, his plan to become an attorney-at-law or a government official in his home state failed because it was blocked by the King of Hanover: Jhering's older brother was already admitted to the bar in the kingdom, and the regent did not want to have two family members in legal positions in his realm[62] – possibly to keep the Frisians' influence and independence under tight control.

Thus for Jhering, an academic career was, at least at this point, merely a second best. Even after he took that path, he maintained a life-long interest in legal practice which left its mark on much of his work.[63] To explore his academic options, he moved to Berlin in 1840. The university in the Prussian capital was the premier institution of higher education in Germany at the time. Influential friends helped the 22-year old to make connections with prominent members of the law faculty; as a result, Jhering was admitted as a doctoral student. In 1842, he defended his dissertation on a topic of Roman law[64] with brilliant results. A mere year later, he completed – again with excellent marks – the postdoctoral requirements for his *Habilitation*. He was now a *Privatdozent*, licensed to teach at a law faculty, and qualified as a candidate for a full professorship.

At the University of Berlin, Jhering encountered some of the most famous legal academics of his time. In the winter term of 1847/48, he attended the last lecture of Friedrich Carl von Savigny, founder and leader of the Historical School of Law and the most celebrated legal scholar of his age. He also came under the influence of Savigny's successor, Georg Friedrich Puchta, the father of what Jhering himself later called *Begriffsjurisprudenz* (Conceptual Jurisprudence), who was actually one of the examiners at Jhering's *Habilitation*. And he absorbed ideas of the late Eduard Gans (1797–1839), the Hegelian representative of universalist ideas and the perhaps leading opponent of the Historical School. Yet, none of these luminaries, nor in fact anyone else in Berlin, became Jhering's actual mentor. Unlike most budding legal academics in Germany, Jhering was not a *Schüler* (disciple) of an older, established professor, nor was

[61] See chapter III.2., IV.1 and V.2. Eventually, however, he acknowledged that his talent was too weak to produce serious literature; letter to Windscheid, "beginning of 1864," Jhering Briefe (1913) 162. Still, even in 1872, Jhering claimed that he would gladly trade the authorship of his (then) magnum opus, "Geist des römischen Rechts," for that of a "a good German comedy," see *Ermacora*, Vorrede (1992) 24.

[62] See Jhering's (semi-serious) *curriculum vitae*, Jhering in Briefen (1913) 214–215.

[63] See infra II.4.

[64] *Jhering*, De hereditate possidente (Berlin 1842), reprinted in *Jhering*, Vemischte Schriften Juristischen Inhalts (1879 1–46. The tract was written entirely in Latin.

there any single scholar who may be called his overall model.[65] Evincing his strong sense of independence, Jhering developed his ideas largely on his own, albeit initially within the academic traditions and boundaries of his time. Jhering was, as his eulogist would later call him, "an original thinker who always sailed under his own flag."[66]

He gave his first lecture at the University of Berlin in May of 1843, several months before his 25th birthday, on "Prinzipien des römischen Rechts" ("Principles of Roman Law"). In Jhering's early lectures and publications, one can already recognize the emerging features of his later thinking: a decidedly forward-looking perspective; thus an incipiently critical attitude towards the then dominant, and largely backward-looking, Historical School; and the enduring conviction that legal science must serve the practical needs of life.

After teaching in Berlin for about two years, Jhering obtained his first professorship, at the University of Basel (Switzerland) where he succeeded Johann Jacob Bachofen (1815–1887) (who was to become famous as the author of "Das Mutterrecht", 1861), on the chair of Roman law.[67] The year after, however, Jhering moved back north to take a chair at the University of Rostock on the Baltic Sea. The move had largely private reasons. Jhering was engaged to a young women from Northern Germany whom he eventually married when he began teaching at Rostock. He later remembered his years at this small and remote university as a very happy time, both professionally and in his private sphere. In 1848, however, disaster struck: his wife died in childbirth; two months later, he also lost his baby son.[68] Grief-stricken, he wanted to leave Rostock behind and thus accepted an offer from the University of Kiel two hundred kilometers to the northwest, where he began to teach in the summer of 1849. Longing for a new family, he remarried, settled in, and was once again content with his life and his work.

At his early academic stage, Jhering published a variety of articles in legal journals and (sometimes anonymously) in newspapers. In 1844, some of his scholarly pieces were collected in a small volume.[69] This early work established

---

[65] The most plausible candidate for that position would be Puchta whose methodology Jhering followed and refined during the first phase of his academic career; but even with regard to Puchta, Jhering maintained his distance and independence in many important respects, see infra chapter III.3.

[66] *Kuntze*, Rudolf von Jhering (1892) 616.

[67] Bachofen, who had been a student of Savigny, recommended Jhering for the appointment. Jhering and Bachofen became friendly during Jhering's brief stay at Basel and also remained in touch thereafter. Their scholarship developed in different directions, however, with Jhering focusing largely on the Roman law's utility for the present and Bachofen seeking to explore antiquity in its own right; see *Gossman*, Basel in the Age of Burckhard (2002) 135–136

[68] Letter to Frölich May 7, 1849, Jhering in Briefen (1913) 4–6. In 1846, he had already lost twins who died at birth, id. at 5.

[69] *Jhering*, Abhandlungen aus dem römischen Recht (1844).

Jhering as a promising young scholar of Roman private law but it remained otherwise inconsequential; today, it belongs into the museum of legal history. All of Jhering's important work was done after his wandering years had ended, during the three major waystations that were to follow.

Gießen (1852–1868): Roman Law in the Boondocks.[70] In 1852, Jhering took a professorship at the University of Gießen, a small provincial capital in the farthest northwest corner of the Grand Duchy of Hesse. Here, he would remain for sixteen years. The decision to move to Gießen had not come easy. On the one hand, Jhering was increasingly unhappy about the situation at the University of Kiel, and the University of Gießen had wooed him for some time. Also, while provincial, Gießen had its attractions. It was the home of Justus Liebig, the founder of organic chemistry and at the time the most admired natural scientist in Germany, if not the world. Perhaps more importantly, Jhering hoped to be joined at the law faculty by Carl Friedrich von Gerber (1823–1891), a good friend and kindred spirit with whom he wanted closely to collaborate. On the other hand, Jhering shuddered at the thought of having to live in an unremarkable town of merely 9,000 souls, proffering little sophistication and even less cultural life. He ultimately decided to roll dice: he demanded an unusually high salary, part of him hoping that the University would refuse and thus make the decision for him. Yet, the University accepted, Jhering was committed, and packed his bags. In the end, things turned out almost exactly opposite to Jhering's hopes and expectations. On the one hand, Liebig left for Munich in the year of Jhering's arrival and Gerber accepted a professorship in Tübingen. On the other hand, Jhering did eventually settle down in Gießen; he used his generous salary to acquire a beautiful house and to live in style; he raised a growing family; and he helped to create and then enjoyed a lively musical culture.[71]

In Gießen, Jhering was at mid-life and full of energy. He found satisfaction in his teaching even though he lamented the small number of students he had, was highly productive as a scholar, and enjoyed a growing reputation as one of Germany's leading Roman lawyers. Signs of recognition included his own government granting him the rank of *Geheimer Justizrat* (privy counsellor), a title that in mid-nineteenth century Germany carried greater prestige than that of a mere professor. Even collaboration with Gerber eventually worked out. In 1857, they co-founded a new legal periodical: the "Jahrbücher für die Dogmatik des heuti-

[70] Jhering's time in Gießen is described by his son, see *Friedrich von Jhering*, Zur Gießener Wirksamkeit Rudolph von Jherings, Briefe und Erinnerungen (1907) 79–90. A particularly detailed and vivid picture in painted by *Kunze*, Lieber in Gießen (2017). For shorter accounts, see *Kunze*, Rudolf von Jhering (1995) 138–142, and *Fikentsche*r, Methoden des Rechts III (1976) 103–106.

[71] Jhering became involved in the local musical society (Musikverein) and, as its president, turned it into a highly active and successful association. It organized concerts on a regular basis and invited performers from outside of Gießen who frequently stayed with Jhering during their visits; see *Kunze*, Lieber in Gießen (2018) 26.

gen römischen und deutschen Privatrechts" ("Yearbooks for the Doctrine of Modern Roman and German Private Law") which they jointly edited for several years.[72] In addition, Jhering actively participated in the law faculty's work as a *Spruchfakultät*, i.e., the then common practice of drafting decisions for courts on difficult legal questions.[73]

Gießen represents what is often called the early period of Jhering's work, i.e., his first major phase as a mature scholar. During this period Jhering focused almost entirely on Roman law which, at the time, was the centerpiece of legal theory and practice in German speaking lands and beyond. His work in Roman law was of two kinds.

Jhering spent much of his energy on a series of doctrinal studies – published in his own "Jahrbücher" – in which he deftly developed solutions to concrete practical problems: the distribution of risk between seller and buyer when the object of sale perishes before delivery; the liability for damages when contracts fail to materialize through the fault of one party; the limitations of real property rights in the interest of a neighbor; etc.[74] This was doctrinal scholarship, working with the established Roman sources, reasoning from fundamental concepts, and interpreting or developing positive rules. Such work was fairly traditional – it was what many mid-nineteenth century Roman lawyers produced much of the time. Jhering was just particularly good at it, and he paid an unusual amount of attention to the practical side of things.[75]

At the same time, Jhering worked in Roman law more broadly to deconstruct and thus overcome it. He pursued that agenda on two fronts: history and methodology. On the historical side, there was the major book project that he had worked on since the 1840s, and that came to fruition only once he had settled down in Gießen: "Geist des römischen Rechts auf den verschiedenen Stufen seiner Entwicklung" ("Spirit of the Roman Law at the Various Stages of Its Development"). Between 1852 and 1865, Jhering published the first and second volumes as well as the first part of the third. "Geist" is a strange, multifaceted, book which defies easy characterization. In a sense, it is a history of Roman law. Yet, it traces this history not for its own sake but rather in order to find the "spirit" of Roman law, i.e., its ultimate character. In another sense, it is a work on legal methodology in part tied to, and in part reaching beyond, Roman law. Ostensibly, the purpose of the enterprise was not to affirm the greatness of Roman law in order to maintain it; instead it was to put that law into proper perspective in order to liberate the present from its spell. Since "Geist" is one of Jhering's signature works, we will take a much closer look at it in the next chapter.

---

[72] See infra 2., notes 130–132 and text.

[73] See infra 4.

[74] *Jhering*, Beiträge zur Lehre von der Gefahr beim Kaufcontract (1859); *Jhering*, Culpa in Contrahendo (1861); *Jhering*, Zur Lehre von den Beschränkungen des Grundeigentümers (1863).

[75] Infra chapter II.4.

On the methodological level, Jhering pursued a similar goal which he explained inter alia in an essay entitled "Unsere Aufgabe" ("Our Task" or "Our Agenda") The essay was a core element of his methodological writings and published in 1857 as an introduction to the newly established "Jahrbücher."[76] The article is, again, too complex to be summarized in a few sentences. Suffice it to say here that Jhering called on legal science to identify those ideas of the Roman lawyers that were of timeless and universal validity, including their unique method. At the same time, he urged his contemporaries to purge modern Roman law of all elements that were idiosyncratically Roman or otherwise unsuitable for present-day purposes.[77]

In other words, with regard to both history and method, Jhering wanted modern jurisprudence to absorb the valuable essence of Roman law while freeing the present from its grip. The agenda of his Gießen years was to proceed, as he famously put it, "durch das römische Recht über das römische Recht hinaus" ("through Roman law beyond Roman law").[78]

Yet, Gießen was not only the period when Jhering developed his own scholarly program with great confidence; it was also time when he eventually suffered his greatest intellectual crisis. It is the amazing story of a scholar who almost suddenly loses faith in his own convictions. In order to distill the timeless essence from the Roman sources, Jhering had previously developed his own, specific, approach. Driving his model Puchta's highly abstract version of doctrinal work, later known as "Begriffsjurisprudenz" ("conceptual jurisprudence") to extremes, Jhering announced a "Konstruktionsjurisprudenz" ("jurisprudence of construction"). Drawing heavily on methods and imagery from natural sciences, especially from chemistry, Jhering labelled his approach "naturhistorische Methode" ("natural-historical method") – and expanded it with great enthusiasm in the second volume of "Geist."[79] Yet, while writing the successive volume, his trust in this method gradually gave way to doubt. Then, in 1859, when faced with the consequences his approach generated in an actual case before him, Jhering had to recognize that his method could produce results that struck him as patently unjust. The experience triggered a significant reorientation of this thinking.[80] In the early 1860s, he published a series of "Vertrauliche Briefe über die heutige Jurisprudenz" ("Confidential Letters on Present-Day Jurisprudence") in which he suddenly levelled scathing criticism at, and openly made fun of, not only Puchta's but also his very own approach.[81] Whether Jhering's apparent *volte-face*

[76] *Jhering*, Unsere Aufgabe (1857).

[77] For a fuller discussion, see infra chapter II.2.

[78] Jhering, Unsere Aufgabe (1857) 52.

[79] Jhering, Geist II.2 (1858) 334–414; for a more detailed analysis, see infra II.2.

[80] This "conversion" is the topic of chapter II.3.

[81] The letters were published anonymously though their author soon became known. Decades later, in 1884, he republished them in a small book entitled Scherz und Ernst in der Jurisprudenz which, in the long run, became one of his two most widely read works; see infra chapter III.2.

really evinced as sudden and radical a change of his methodological convictions as he loudly claimed has been a matter of some debate.[82] Be that as it may, his diatribe signaled the end of his unbridled enthusiasm for a purely logical approach to law – and thus the end of his "early period." It was time for reorientation – and for another change of venue.

Wien (1868–1872): Fame and Reorientation in the Habsburg Metropolis. The reasons for Jhering's long sojourn in Gießen were in part personal, in part professional. On the personal side, the long illness of his (second) wife, who suffered from tuberculosis, strongly counseled against another move. A professional reason was Jhering's hope (indeed expectation) to succeed the famous Adolph von Vangerow (1808–1870) as holder of the prestigious chair for Roman law at the University of Heidelberg. In 1867, however, his wife died; at the same time, his hope to obtain the coveted chair in Heidelberg vanished (it was eventually given to his friend Bernhard Windscheid). Thus ready to leave Gießen after all and longing for a more prestigious position, Jhering quickly accepted an offer from the University of Vienna in 1868, at age 50. Vienna was attractive in part because two scholars with whom Jhering had long been in close and friendly contact – Joseph Unger (1828–1913) and Julius Glaser (1831–1885) – were already at that university, and in part also because his salary would be far higher than in Gießen.

Going to Vienna was not only a move from the Hessian province to the capital of the Habsburg empire; from a quiet town of a few thousand souls to a noisy metropolis of nearly a million, and from a smallish university where one could know every (law) student to a mighty institution populated by a largely anonymous crowd. It was also, politically speaking, a move abroad because as of 1866, Austria was no longer part of the federation of German states, a fact that would later play a role in Jhering's next and final relocation.

Vienna was a new phase in Jhering's life both personally and professionally. In his private life, he found new happiness when he married the governess of his children who were now rapidly growing up. He was lavishly paid and could afford a lifestyle unusually luxurious for a professor. He socialized a lot, moved in prominent circles, and enjoyed the status of an academic celebrity. He was particularly fond of the Viennese women with whom he loved to socialize and flirt.[83] On the professional side, he finally felt fully appreciated. He was hugely

---

[82] Infra III.5.

[83] "My need for women friends ["Freundinnen"] has also found the richest satisfaction here. Since the Viennese women are easygoing, one quickly becomes intimately acquainted with them, and I already have six... What an agreeable contrast with the [...] bland Gießen where one must search for ladies, who can elicit one's interest, with a lantern." Letter to Windscheid, March 1, 1869, Jhering in Briefen (1913) 237. The German term used by Jhering for his relationship with the Viennese women is "vertraut" which means more than "familiar" but unlike "intimate," does suggest physical involvement. In a similar vein, letter to Windscheid, November 17, 1868, Jhering in Briefen (1913) 235; letter to Auguste von Littrow-Bischoff, December 30, 1884, Jhering in Briefen (1913) 381.

successful in the classroom. Students attended his lectures not, as in Gießen, by the dozens but by the hundreds. Thus, as a teacher, Jhering soon ranked among the top guns at one of the oldest, largest, and most prestigious universities in all of Europe.[84]

As a scholar, however, Jhering had a hard time finding the ground under his feet again. Having lost faith in the purely logical approach announced in the introduction to "Geist" and expounded in "Unsere Aufgabe," he found himself at a methodological impasse. He put the completion of "Geist" on hold, though he published the existing volumes in new editions whose modifications sometimes reflected new ideas and hinted at future directions.

Jhering missed an opportunity to develop future methodological directions in his inaugural lecture – despite the fact that he tackled the fundamental question of whether jurisprudence is a "science"[85] – and what, if anything, makes it one. The topic had been much discussed in early and mid-nineteenth century Germany; Savigny and his followers had emphatically claimed the scientific character and value of their discipline[86] while others had vigorously denied it.[87] Not wasting any time on trying to define "science," Jhering's principle answer was that, aside from legal history and philosophy, jurisprudence as a science consisted of the doctrinal work of digesting, clarifying, and organizing the material produced by legal practice. Its purpose was to bring the principles underlying judicial decisions to light thus providing future guidance for judges (and perhaps legislatures). In other words, the task of legal science was to cooperate with practitioners in developing the law as doctrine.[88] As he openly admitted, Jhering essentially postulated the kind of doctrinal scholarship he had produced in Gießen and published in the *Jahrbücher*. To be sure, admonishing legal academics to end their glass bead games and to turn their attention to real-world problems was both appropriate and timely. Nothing in his lecture, however, advanced Jhering's own methodological ball one inch.

Nor did Jhering otherwise make much methodological headway. He published several essentially doctrinal pieces, inter alia on the law of possession as the then most fashionable Roman law topic, but they showed him in something like an extended holding pattern. That ended only, and almost suddenly, at the very end of his Viennese period when Jhering gave a farewell lecture that became his

---

[84] On Jhering as an academic teacher, see infra II.5.

[85] *Jhering*, Ist die Jurisprudenz eine Wissenschaft? (1868); for a more detailed analysis, see infra chapter II.4.

[86] For an extensive discussion and analysis of the concept of legal science in early and mid-nineteenth century German jurisprudence, see *Schröder*, Recht als Wissenschaft (2012) 193–277.

[87] The most notorious attack was *von Kirchmann*, Die Werthlosigkeit der Jurisprudenz als Wissenschaft (1848).

[88] Jhering's summary defined Rechtswissenschaft in a fashion that was so all-encompassing as to be virtually useless; *Jhering*, Ist die Jurisprudenz eine Wissenschaft (1868) 92.

most famous, widely read, and frequently quoted work: "Der Kampf ums Recht" ("The Struggle for Law").[89]

"Kampf" was not a work of academic scholarship but a talk given to, and directly aimed at, an audience mainly of practitioners.[90] It was a polemic, presented in a flamboyant style, full of provocative statements and catchy phrases. Its Darwinian title was somewhat misleading because Jhering did not propagate ideas of evolution, natural selection or survival of the fittest.[91] Instead, his foundational argument was that law is a struggle, i.e., that by its very nature, it is, must be, and should be, a reflection of social conflict. Jhering also passionately demanded that citizens fight for their rights. Such a fight, he claimed, was every man's ethical duty both towards himself and towards society as a whole. When viewed in the broader context of Jhering's intellectual development, however, the most significant feature of "Kampf" was that Jhering now openly embraced a functional and sociological approach to jurisprudence. Rejecting the Historical School's concept of law as a result of peaceful growth in the form of custom, as well as his own, earlier, conception of law as a logical phenomenon, Jhering now viewed law a means for the enforcement of individual and social interests.[92] This view had gradually ripened during his Viennese years, and it was to determine his future course as a scholar. Thus, "Kampf" signaled the open acknowledgement of Jhering's shift from his earlier to his later jurisprudential convictions.

Jhering left Vienna after a mere four years. His initial enthusiasm for the city and its society had waned quickly. Soon, he began to complain about the bad "climate;" in particular, Jhering frequently bemoaned the unbearable air in the old university buildings and stuffy lecture halls which he felt put his health at risk.[93] "Climate" also had a social dimension, however, as Jhering felt increasingly uncomfortable in Viennese society.[94] In part, this was for political reasons. In 1871, after the Franco-Prussian war, Bismarck united Germany under Prussian leadership. Jhering became an enthusiastic supporter of the new nation as well as of its chief architect.[95] This put him at odds with many of his Viennese colleagues

[89] *Jhering*, Der Kampf ums Recht (1872); for a more detailed discussion, see infra III.3.

[90] Jhering gave the talk to the *Wiener juristische Vereinigung*, an association of practicing lawyers. The occasion shaped his argument and style. The association revered Jhering and was dear to his heart, see Hofmeister, Jhering in Wien (1995) 20–25. More than a decade later, it was the venue of another important lecture, i.e., *Jhering*, Das Rechtsgefühl (1884).

[91] *Darwin's* The Origin of Species had been published in 1859, and Jhering could assume that the notion of the "struggle for live" was familiar to his audience.

[92] "Das Recht ist kein logischer, sondern es ist ein Kraftbegriff." ("Law is not a logical conception but one of power.") *Jhering*, Kampf (1872) 9.

[93] In his letter to Windscheid of Mach 26, 1870, Jhering in Briefen (1913) 246, Jhering complained about the "infernal stench that almost made me faint." See also letter to Bülow, October 28, 1871, Jhering in Briefen (1913) 267.

[94] Letter to Windscheid of December 18, 1871, Jherings Briefe an Windscheid (1988) 28, 29 ("The moral air here is not for me either, one has to be native Austrian to tolerate it.").

[95] Infra 4.

who resented Prussian hegemony and the exclusion of Austria from the new nation. It was also, however, German unification in and of itself that made him want to return to his fatherland as he approached old age.[96] In addition, Jhering increasingly felt that life in the big, bustling city distracted him from serious academic work.[97] Being a celebrity was nice, and Jhering was not above enjoying it, but ultimately, being a scholar was more important. Having found his new scholarly groove, he longed for the quiet of a smaller city and university where, for the remaining years of his life, he could pursue his new agenda of exploring the functional and social dimension of law. Rejecting an offer from the University of Strasbourg, in 1872, he thus quickly accepted an offer from the University of Göttingen, his alma mater.

Shortly before his departure, the Austrian emperor knighted Jhering, granting him hereditary nobility. This was not an attempt to bribe him into staying in Vienna but a sign of recognition and a token of gratitude for services rendered. He thus returned to his fatherland as "von Jhering."

Göttingen (1872–1892): Sociological Jurisprudence in Provincial Germany. When Jhering arrived in Göttingen, it was a homecoming in several regards. He returned to Germany (i.e., the newly united German Empire), to the province of Hanover (until 1866 its own kingdom, now a province of Prussia) and to the very university where he had been a student more than a generation ago. It was also a return to the small-town life Jhering had come to miss in Vienna. While Göttingen was more substantial than Gießen, it was by no means a big city,[98] and while it was situated in a beautiful environment, it was a provincial town hours away from the great centers of late nineteenth century Germany.

Jhering, now in his mid-fifties, quickly settled in. In 1874, shortly after his arrival, he received offers from two of Germany's very top universities with a prestige far greater than Göttingen, but he had decided not to move again and thus rejected even the invitation to take the chair in Heidelberg which he had coveted so much some years before.[99] Thus Jhering lived out his years in Göttingen. It was a period of relative tranquility, occasionally interrupted by travel, as well as of contentment with his personal life,[100] various physical ailments notwith-

[96] "If only I could be in Germany now!", Jhering wrote to Bülow from Vienna on February 1, 1871, Jhering in Briefen (1913) 262.

[97] Letter to Bülow October 28, 1871, Jhering in Briefen (1913) 267.

[98] In 1870, Göttingen had a population of about 17,000; Encyclopedia Britannica vol. 12, 278 (11th ed. New York 1910); it was thus about twice as large as Gießen and must be considered a mid-size town by the standards of the time.

[99] Jhering always remained wistful that Heidelberg had never panned out. It was a pity that the offer had not come earlier, but at least it gave him some satisfaction that he did finally receive it (and with it the recognition) and that he could now turn it down; letter to Bülow August 9, 1874, Jhering in Briefen (1913) 296–297. The other offer came from Leipzig, which was not only one of the oldest and most prestigious German universities but also the seat of the Reichsgericht (Imperial Supreme Court).

[100] Jhering did, however, find Göttingen "ledern langweilig" ("very boring") and some-

standing.[101] Though he had taken a big pay-cut, he could afford a large and comfortable house with a beautiful view and a substantial plot of land which catered to his interest in gardening and farming. As gregarious as ever, he frequently hosted gourmet dinners and other social events, and after a day's work, he often enjoyed long evenings of conversation, playing music or card games with family and friends or simply smoking a cigar.

The academic harvest of Jhering's Göttingen years is large, varied, and complex.

The principal fruit of his labors was the book he became so widely known for: "Der Zweck im Recht"[102] ("Law as Means to an End"). Upon his departure from Vienna, Jhering had touched on some of the law's sociological dimensions in his "Kampf ums Recht." Now, he explored these dimensions at much greater length and in much greater depth. The position of "Zweck" in Jhering's *oeuvre* requires some explanation.[103] Jhering was painfully aware that the book he considered his definitive work, "Geist des römischen Rechts," was still unfinished, and his main goal when moving to Göttingen was to finally complete it. Yet, having lost his faith in his initial approach, and having come to regard law as a means to the pursuit of social interests, Jhering felt that he must first fully understand the instrumental character of law before he could finish "Geist". He thus plunged headlong into an exploration of the law's social origins and functions. Soon he convinced himself that all law ultimately emanates from purpose. As the book's motto stated: "Der Zweck ist der Schöpfer allen Rechts." ("Purpose generates all law.") Of course, the implications of that approach were daunting. Jhering struggled mightily with the rapidly proliferating issues for many years but he never gained full control of the project. The first volume of "Zweck" was published in 1877 and already laid out a vast terrain populated by often poorly defined concepts and terms; the second volume followed in 1883 and wandered off in all sorts of directions, way beyond the province of law proper; a third volume was planned but never written. Thus, after many years of torturous effort, "Zweck" ultimately remained unfinished. As a result, so did "Geist" – to which Jhering never managed to return. At the end of the day, then, both of his major works were not only monumental undertakings but also, at least in terms of completion, monumental failures.

In the context of writing "Zweck," Jhering engaged with a concept that had intrigued him for decades, first as a corrective to results reached by doctrinal analysis, now as a crucial element in the evolution of law: the human sense of justice. When in 1884, he once again gave a talk before the *Wiener juristische Gesellschaft*, where he had discussed the "Kampf ums Recht" a dozen years

---

times regretted having left Vienna with its much more attractive social life – and women!, letter to Auguste von Littrow-Bischoff August 10, 1879, Jhering in Briefen (1913) 353.

[101] Infra 4., notes 171–172 and text.

[102] *Jhering*, Der Zweck im Recht (2 vols. 1877/1883).

[103] For a more detailed discussion, see infra chapter IV.2.

before, he ruminated "Über die Entstehung des Rechtsgefühls" ("On the Origin of the Sense of Justice").[104] Jhering now presented an understanding of the sense of justice that was outright heretical: it is not the sense of justice that shapes the law, he postulated, but the law that shapes the sense of justice.[105]

Perhaps surprisingly, even after having spent years on "Zweck" and having explored the role of "Rechtsgefühl," Jhering also continued to engage with doctrinal scholarship. In the 1880s, he published two books dealing with legal doctrine, albeit in such radically different manners that they appear to be at loggerheads. On the one hand, in 1884, Jhering presented "Scherz und Ernst in der Jurisprudenz" ("Humor and Seriousness in Jurisprudence").[106] This collection of essays reprinted, inter alia, the attacks he had launched against Puchta's as well as his own "jurisprudence of concepts" in the 1860s; to this Jhering added a satire that was destined to become his perhaps most famous piece: a fictitious visit "Im Begriffshimmel" (in "The Heaven of Concepts") – an environment free from air and light where the late champions of "juristic constructions" like Puchta could work with hairsplitting machines, hydraulic concept presses, and the like, unconcerned with reality or practicality. On the other hand, Jhering published an extensive treatise on an eminently doctrinal (and much debated) subject: "Der Besitzwille," an analysis of the role of the (individual) will in the concept of possession.[107] Yet, the contradiction between these two works was more apparent than real: Jhering did abjure (once again and in most dramatic terms) the "conceptual jurisprudence" of old because of its *l'art pour l'art* aberrations and its lack of practical orientation; at the same time, he tried to demonstrate what an analysis of the concept of possession informed by practical considerations and modern needs looked like. In other words, the de-constructive diatribe of "Scherz und Ernst" was counter-balanced by the sober constructive effort of "Der Besitzwille."

Towards the end of life, Jhering had apparently abandoned all hope to complete either "Geist" or "Zweck." Instead, he turned, yet again, to new projects, i.e., two new books. Predictably, he finished neither though what he had written was eventually published posthumously by his son in law. One was a study of the pre-historic origins of the Indo-European civilizations: "Vorgeschichte der Indoeuropäer" ("Pre-History of the Indo-Europeans")[108] The book is a cultural-anthropological study seeking to understand the origins of the eventual European

---

[104] The essay was published almost a century after it had been written, *Jhering*, Über die Entstehung des Rechtsgefühls (1884).

[105] *Jhering*, Über die Entstehung des Rechtsgefühls (1884); for a more detailed analysis, see infra chapter IV.3.

[106] *Jhering*, Scherz und Ernst (1884); for a more detailed analysis, see infra chapter III.2.

[107] *Jhering*, Der Besitzwille (1889).

[108] *Jhering*, Vorgeschichte der Indoeuropäer (1894). The English translation was entitled "The Evolution of the Aryan" (A. Drucker transl., New York 1897); for a discussion of the work, see infra chapter VI.3.

cultures of antiquity. While Jhering did not manage to complete it, he did produce a multi-chapter volume of around 400 pages. Though professedly amateurish, is an interesting read even today. By contrast, his effort to write a history of the development of the Roman law, "Entwicklungsgeschichte des römischen Rechts," returned him to the subject of "Geist." The book never proceeded beyond the very early parts which were also published after Jhering's death. Its introduction contains some new and interesting thoughts on legal historiography which are worth exploring in the context of Jhering's work in that area.[109]

When Jhering was in his final years, the reign of Roman law as the positive private law in Germany was finally coming to an end, just as Jhering had predicted and demanded decades before. In the 1880s, the preparations for a German Civil Code got underway,[110] and a first draft was published 1887. It is not clear whether Jhering had any ambition to be involved in the project. Be that as it may, he was not invited, perhaps because his views were considered too unorthodox. It was certainly easier to work without him (and with his friend Windscheid instead[111]), though Jhering's commitment to the practical side of law could have softened the much criticized rigidity and abstract nature of the Civil Code's first draft (and to a somewhat lesser extent even of the final version).

In the early 1890s, Jhering repeatedly contemplated his death. He looked back at a full life. In the usual Christmas letter to the widow of his late friend and colleague Julius Glaser, he wrote in 1891 that if she did not receive another letter next year, she could tell herself that Jhering did "not find it hard to leave this life." He was not at all bitter but simply at ease: "I have enjoyed so many good things," he added, "and I have also accomplished quite a bit, so that I can tell myself that my life has paid off for myself and for the world." With so many relations and friends having died all around him, he himself felt increasingly "ready for departure."[112]

In August of 1892, the 50th anniversary of obtaining his doctorate provided the occasion to celebrate the famous scholar for one last time. The extensive festivities took place in Kassel-Wilhelmshöhe, in the very hotel where the imperial family often spent its vacations.[113] Most of Jhering's family as well many friends gathered, and representatives from universities near and far made their appearances, showering Jhering with *Festschriften* (collections of writings in his honor),

---

[109] *Jhering*, Entwicklungsgeschichte des römischen Rechts (1894); see infra chapter V 1. and 2. Beyond the introduction, it contains only one, albeit fairly substantial (draft) chapter on the constitution of the Roman household, id. 49–124.

[110] The Civil Code (*Bürgerliches Gesetzbuch, BGB)* was completed in 1896 and entered into force in 1900, i.e., after Jhering's death.

[111] Windscheid was a member of the first drafting commission and had huge influence on what came to be known as "Erster Entwurf" ("First Draft") of 1887.

[112] Letter to Minna Glaser, December 24, 1891, Jhering in Briefen (1913) 432.

[113] The events are beautifully portrayed and touchingly narrated based on the original sources by *Kunze*, Jherings Jubiläum (1991).

congratulatory toasts, and laudatory speeches. Jhering undoubtedly felt greatly honored, but he also reacted to the lavish praise with considerable irony and a dose of self-deprecation.[114] Unfortunately, at the time of the festivities, Jhering was already a terminally ill and largely bedridden man. Yet, he repeatedly managed to get up and participated in the proceedings as best he could. During the breaks between events, his family pushed him through the extensive park around the hotel in a wheelchair.

The celebration of Jhering's doctoral anniversary was the last major event in his life. Six weeks later, on September 17, 1892, Rudolf von Jhering, now back in Göttingen, succumbed to an illness not clearly defined by the sources.[115] He was 74, a very respectable age by the standards of the time.[116] A ten-foot monument marks his grave at the entrance of the old municipal cemetery in Göttingen.[117]

3. Professional Friendships: Gerber and Windscheid

Given Jhering's sociable character, it is no surprise that friendships with other legal scholars were an important part of his life, both on the personal and professional level. While he was fairly close to some of his faculty colleagues when teaching in Gießen, Vienna, and Göttingen, his most important academic friends taught at other universities. At the time, long-distance relationships were maintained by mail, and since Jhering was an eager correspondent, his friendships with faraway colleagues are well-documented in an abundance of letters. Of particular interest are his, essentially life-long, friendships with two German academics, Gerber and Windscheid.

Jhering's correspondence with these men was often very personal. At a time when interaction among German academics was even more formal than it is today, these scholars addressed each other using the informal "Du" (rather than the formal "Sie").[118] They wrote about their work, plans, families, health, moods, hopes, and fears. Jhering's letters to both Gerber and Windscheid (sometimes addressed as "my dear friend") are very frank and often mince no words, but they also express deep and lasting affection.

---

[114] See infra 4., note 224 and text.

[115] According to *Kunze*, Ein großer Jurist (2023) 21–22, Jhering had intestinal cancer and eventually died of heart failure.

[116] In 1890 Germany, the average life expectancy was around 42 years. Of course, that figure reflects a high degree of child mortality. It was thus much higher for people who reached adulthood. Still, few people lived into their 70s.

[117] A marble bust had already been put on display at the University of Göttingen in 1888 where it still adorns the hallway of the building housing the Institute for Roman Law.

[118] Earlier letters still used the more formal "Sie;" in both cases, the writers eventually switched to the informal "Du."

The friendship with these scholars is illuminating because on the professional level, Jhering related to Gerber and Windscheid in almost opposite ways. Gerber was a methodological fellow traveler but focused on different sources. Windscheid worked with the same material but often did not share Jhering's evolving jurisprudential approach.[119]

Carl Friedrich von Gerber: The Germanist Fellow Traveler. Jhering's friendship with the slightly younger Carl Friedrich von Gerber (1823–1891)[120] played an important role in the early part of Jhering's career:[121] when Jhering taught in Gießen, the two men maintained a close working relationship. That relationship was based not only on mutual admiration[122] but also on shared methodological ground. Like Jhering, Gerber was strongly influenced by Puchta and also pursued a form of "Konstruktionsjurisprudenz;" like Jhering, he embraced the idea of legal evolution and a systematic organization of the law.[123] Gerber, however, applied this method not to the Roman sources, but to indigenous German law.[124] Jhering and Gerber were thus kindred spirits in their approaches but represented

[119] Jhering also maintained a close friendship with Joseph Unger (1829–1913) who was his faculty colleague in Vienna and who, after Gerber's resignation from the project, became Jhering's co-, and later the sole, editor of the "Jahrbücher." Yet, at least from today's perspective, Jhering's friendship with Unger is less interesting because as scholars, the two were more similar than different. Like Jhering, Unger was an heir to the Historical School, a scholar of Roman law, and an author of several highly influential doctrinal essays, see, e.g., *Joseph Unger*, Die Verträge zugunsten Dritter, Jahrbücher 10 (1871) 1. As the most influential Austrian legal scholar of his generation, Unger's main accomplishment was the reconnection of Austrian jurisprudence with German Romanist legal scholarship. In contrast to Jhering, he became the head of a large and influential school of scholars as well a notable politician and reformer of legal education. Jhering dedicated the second volume of "Zweck" to Unger and another friend from his time in Vienna, Julius Glaser (1831–1885). For Jhering's correspondence with Unger and Glaser, see *Losano*, Der Briefwechsel Jherings mit Unger und Glaser (1996). Among Jhering's many (professional) friendships, Oskar (von) Bülow (1837–1907) also deserves mention. A Romanist like Jhering, he joined the law faculty of the University of Gießen (in 1867) where he befriended the older Jhering shortly before the latter left for Vienna (in 1868). Von Bülow dedicated his first major book to Jhering and maintained and extensive correspondence with him. Through his most widely known work, Gesetz und Richteramt (1885), von Bülow became a forerunner of the "Freirechtsschule" ("School of Free Law"); see infra chapter VII.1., note 13 and text.

[120] On Gerber, see *Jelowik*, Gerber, Carl Friedrich von (2012).

[121] On the friendship between Jhering and Gerber, see *Losano*, Studien zu Jhering und Gerber (1984) 174–185. Jhering's correspondence with Gerber was published by *Losano*, Der Briefwechsel zwischen Jhering und Gerber (1984); id., Carteggio Jhering–Gerber (1977).

[122] Jhering was often tormented by self-doubt and envious of what he saw as Gerber's superior intellectual powers and stylistic elegance, see, e.g., his letters to Gerber of "Sept. 53," Briefe und Erinnerungen (1907) 24, 25.

[123] See *Gerber*, Das wissenschaftliche Prinzip des gemeinen deutschen Privatrechts (1846).

[124] In 1848/49, Gerber had published an admirably clear and fairly systematic account of German private law, i.e., *Gerber*, System des deutschen Privatrechts (2 parts 1848–49). While the book was an enormously important contribution to the development of private law at the time, it is merely of historical interest today.

the two different branches of mid-nineteenth century German legal academia: Jhering was a *Romanist*, Gerber a *Germanist*.[125] To be sure, the *Romanists* and the *Germanists* had often been at each other's academic throats – the former extolling the reception of Roman law in late-medieval and early modern Germany, the latter decrying it as a "Nationalunglück" ("national disaster").[126] Jhering and Gerber, however, were largely unconcerned by this ideological battle because neither was committed to the respective mainstreams' views. The *Romanist* Jhering ultimately wanted to free German jurisprudence from the spell of Roman law, and the *Germanist* Gerber had no interest in reviving the indigenous medieval sources.[127] Instead, they both looked to distill from their respective materials the underlying principles and systematic order inherent in all law[128] – thus eventually putting the dichotomy between Roman and German law to rest.[129] This made the combination of their efforts particularly auspicious.

As mentioned, in 1857 Jhering and Gerber jointly founded a new legal periodical: the "Jahrbücher für die Dogmatik des heutigen römischen und deutschen Privatrechts." The title was carefully selected: the focus was on Dogmatik (doctrine), i.e., concepts, rules, and systematic order, not on historical research;[130] on the heutigen (modern) law, not on that of antiquity or the middle ages; and it was to encompass both römisches and deutsches Privatrecht (Roman and German private law). The editors themselves, especially Jhering, published frequently in the Jahrbücher, but they also managed to solicit contributions from prominent colleagues. As a result, the journal soon established itself and acquired a solid reputation. After jointly publishing the first six volumes, Jhering's and Gerber's editorial cooperation ended in 1863, largely because Gerber embarked on an administrative and eventually political career.[131] Jhering, however remained committed to the journal until his death.[132] As of 1897, the periodical was published as

---

[125] On the Historical School and its two branches, see supra 1., note 9 and text.

[126] *Beseler*, Volksrecht und Juristenrecht (Leipzig 1843) 42.

[127] In fact, Gerber's "System," supra note 124, strongly resembled the contemporary Romanist treatises in its approach, terminology, and structure.

[128] A key text expressing this belief is Jhering's letter to Gerber on May 22, 1854, Briefe und Erinnerungen (1907) 31–34.

[129] For a more detailed and nuanced discussion of their methodological approaches, see *Wolf*, Große Rechtsdenker (1963) 636–637, as well as *Fikentscher*, Methoden des Rechts III (1976) 134–137.

[130] It was in particular this emphasis on *Dogmatik* that distinguished the journal from a famous counterpart which had almost certainly inspired Jhering and Gerber: the "Zeitschrift für geschichtliche Rechtswissenschaft" ("Journal for Historical Legal Science") founded in 1815. It was also a joint venture by a *Romanist* and a *Germanist*, i.e., Friedrich Carl on Savigny and Karl Friedrich Eichhorn (1781–1854).

[131] Gerber became *Rektor* (president) of the University of Leipzig in 1865 and 1866 and eventually minister of culture in the Kingdom of Saxony in 1871. Gerber's interests also shifted towards public law which he also presented in a clear and systematic fashion, see *Gerber*, Grundzüge eines Systems des deutschen Staatsrechts (1865).

[132] As of 1871, Jhering was assisted by his Viennese colleague Joseph Unger who continued the project after Jhering's passing.

"Jhering's Jahrbücher für die Dogmatik des bürgerlichen Rechts" until it was discontinued in 1942. For almost a century it was one of the most prestigious venues for the publication of scholarship on the doctrine of private law – and thus one of Jhering's lasting legacies.

Bernhard Windscheid: The Romanist Friend and Opponent. Jhering's relationship with Bernhard Windscheid (1817–1892)[133] is particularly noteworthy because it was a close and lasting friendship between two towering, but in many ways very different, figures.[134] Jhering and Windscheid were the two jurisprudential giants of their age. Just like their forerunner Savigny had dominated jurisprudence during the first half of the nineteenth century, Jhering and Windscheid were the preeminent German jurists in its second half – a period when German legal scholarship was widely regarded as leading the world. Their relationship, which is also well-documented in Jhering's letters,[135] was complex. It is helpful to distinguish four dimensions: their similar doctrinal *work in* Roman law, their different *attitudes toward* Roman law, the eventually radical divergence in their basic scholarly approaches, and their dissimilar personalities.

Jhering and Windscheid shared some important ground: they both produced path-breaking doctrinal work in Roman (private) law. In this regard, they were both representatives of the *Pandektenwissenschaft* that dominated mid- and late nineteenth century German legal scholarship. In his early period, Jhering devoted most of his energy to this kind of work[136], and he admired the similar scholarship that Windscheid was producing around the same time.[137] It was also during the 1850s, that their friendship was established.[138] In subsequent decades, that common ground diminished but it never completely vanished. Windscheid fully stayed on course: he devoted his entire life and career to doctrinal work in Roman law and became the leading representative of the Pandectist era. He authored the most influential legal treatise in late nineteenth century Germany; his "Lehrbuch des Pandektenrechts"[139] dominated academic scholarship as well as forensic prac-

[133] The literature on Windscheid is also extensive, though not as vast as on Jhering. Classic, albeit by now somewhat dated, portraits are *Wolf*, Große Rechtsdenker (1963) 591–621, and *Wieacker*, Gründer und Bewahrer (1959) 181–196; for more recent assessments, see *Falk*, Ein Gelehrter wie Windscheid (1989); *Rückert*, Windscheid (2017); for a brief summary, see *Kleinheyer and Schröder*, Deutsche und europäische Juristen (2017) 472–476.

[134] For a detailed discussion, see *Fikentscher*, Methoden des Rechts III (1976) 137–151; for a much briefer assessment, see *Wolf*, Große Rechtsdenker (1963) 637–638.

[135] Jherings Briefe an Windscheid (1988); many letters from Jhering to Windscheid are also collected in Jhering in Briefen (1913).

[136] Supra 2.

[137] Jhering's admiration for *Windscheid*, Die Actio des römischen Civilrechts vom Standpunkte des heutigen Rechts (1856), is expressed in his letter to Gerber of Oct. 29, 1858, Briefe und Erinnerungen (1907) 69, at 71; see also Windscheid, Die Lehre des römischen Rechts von der Voraussetzung (1850).

[138] See supra 1., notes 74–75 and text.

[139] Windscheid, Lehrbuch des Pandektenrechts (3 vols., 1862–70). Windscheid published six subsequent editions during his lifetime. After his death, two further editions were pub-

tice for decades. In the absence of a code, it enjoyed quasi-statutory authority, and it eventually became something of a blueprint for important parts of the Civil Code (Bürgerliches Gesetzbuch) of 1900.[140] While Jhering eventually turned his attention increasingly to other topics,[141] he never completely abandoned doctrinal work either. To the extent he continued to engage in it, both in occasional articles and in his 1889 treatise on possession, "Der Besitzwille," Jhering remained Windscheid's fellow traveler in Roman law doctrine – even though he deviated from, and indeed by now sharply criticized, his friend's methodology.[142]

Jhering's and Windscheid's *basic attitude* towards Roman law was another matter. Again, there was considerable common ground. Both men admired the classical Roman jurists' method, and both of course recognized the current authority of substantive Roman law. Their reaction to that status quo, however, differed. Windscheid essentially followed Savigny, who had been one of his academic teachers, in wanting to preserve Roman jurisprudence as the positive law of his country.[143] Windscheid understood, of course, that the Roman law of the Pandects needed decluttering, modernization, and, especially adaptation to the practical needs of the present. In fact, these were exactly the tasks he so masterfully performed in his treatise. Still, for Windscheid, the Roman material remained the present and future bedrock of the private law in Germany (and beyond). By contrast, Jhering wanted to overcome Roman law. More in the wake of Puchta than of Savigny, he analyzed the Roman material in order to distill – through "Konstruktionsjurisprudenz" – the generally valid principles and concepts of all law. Thus he wrote to Windscheid in 1856 that he had "no interest in Roman jurisprudence" [in and of itself] and that modern jurisprudence had a "duty […] to go beyond it."[144] It is not entirely clear whether at this, relatively early, point, Windscheid and Jhering fully understood the difference between their attitudes. Jhering justly regarded Windscheid as a comrade in arms in the

lished by Theodor Kipp. The book became increasingly obsolete after the German Civil Code ended the reign of Roman law in 1900.

[140] As mentioned, Windscheid was a member of the legislative committee that produced the civil code's first draft (1881–1887) and as such had a strong influence on the project.

[141] In 1878, Jhering wrote to Windscheid that he was hardly reading any law books anymore; instead, he turned to "philosophical and sociopolitical" works; letter to Windscheid of January 23, 1878, Jherings Briefe an Windscheid (1988) 44.

[142] In 1888, Jhering openly told Windscheid that the critique of the prevailing method expressed in Jhering's "Besitzwille" was also directed against Windscheid' approach. Nonetheless, Jhering wanted to dedicate the book to his friend; letter to Windscheid of August 5, 1888, Jherings Briefe an Windscheid (1988) 62–63 (when the book was published in 1889, it bore no such dedication).

[143] It is important to note, however, that Windscheid did not continue Savigny' historical agenda. While Jhering's "Geist" sought to understand Roman law from a historical perspective, Windscheid's "Pandekten" essentially cut modern Roman law off from its past and used the Roman sources as material for present-day purposes – much to the chagrin of many contemporary legal historians, see *Wieacker*, Gründer und Bewahrer (1959) 186–189.

[144] Letter to Windscheid of July 29, 1856, Jhering in Briefen (1913) 65–66.

fight against the status quo of Roman law as a sacrosanct body of principles and rules[145] but he may have overrated Windscheid's determination to overcome it. Windscheid, in turn, was perhaps not sure exactly how Jhering wanted to go "beyond" Roman law. The difference between their attitudes was subtle but significant: with regard to the enduring validity of Roman law, Windscheid essentially still operated in the tradition of the Historical School[146] while Jhering wanted to leave that tradition completely behind.

When it comes to the fundamentals of their jurisprudential approaches, we see, of course, a radical divergence. Their respective perspectives on law were marked by *some* differences from the very beginning: in his work on "Geist," Jhering already showed considerable interest in the function and purpose of law, although for the time being, this interest was not front and center. As long as Jhering focused on doctrinal work in his articles in the "Jahrbücher," he and Windscheid could see themselves on the same page: both the "early" Jhering and Windscheid worked not only on, but within Roman law. Then, however, Jhering veered off in an entirely different direction when he first attacked his own "Konstruktionsjurisprudenz" in the 1860s and finally embraced an early form of sociological jurisprudence in the 1870s and beyond. Jhering now looked at law from the outside. That, however, was not Windscheid's cup of tea.[147] As a scholar, Windscheid never embraced an instrumental or sociological view of law; in his opinion "ethical, political, economic considerations" were not the business of the "jurist as such."[148]

In a sense, then, Windscheid was still looking to the past – preserving, refining, and perfecting the tradition of Roman law for the presence, with his magisterial treatise closing its era as the common (private) law of German speaking lands. His contemporary Johannes Emil Kuntze (1824–1894) thus justly compared him to Accursius (1182–1236) whose work on the rediscovered Roman law brought the project of the glossators to perfection.[149] Jhering, by contrast, was looking to the future – still within the established paradigms in "Geist" and his doctrinal essays, then decisively in his "Kampf" and "Zweck," opening new vistas for the coming century.

---

[145] See Jhering's letter to Windscheid of December 21, 1856, Jhering in Briefen (1913) 74 ("that we essentially pursue the same objective"); letter of November 10, 1861, Jhering in Briefen (1913) 147; letter of April 6, 1865, Jhering in Briefen (1913) 174.

[146] See *Windscheid*, Die Aufgaben der Rechtswissenschaft (1884/1904) 107–109.

[147] This was already apparent at the very beginning of their friendship. In 1852, Jhering sent Windscheid the – just published – first volume of "Geist." While Windscheid's reaction was by and large positive, he criticized Jhering's discussion of, and emphasis on, "purposes" (in Roman law); *Fikentscher*, Methoden des Rechts III (1976) 139.

[148] *Windscheid*, Die Aufgaben der Rechtswissenschaft (1884/1904) 112. It is true that this famous statement was made in the context of discussing legislation and thus directly concerned only the role of the jurist in the making of law, see *Rückert*, Windscheid (2017) 666. Still, at least as a scholar, Windscheid showed scant interest in the sociological dimensions of law that commanded most of Jhering's attention after 1870.

[149] *Kuntze*, Rudolf von Jhering (1892) 616.

Yet, despite all these rather fundamental and openly acknowledged differences, Jhering kept Windscheid in the highest regard.[150] Even the "late" Jhering who pushed far beyond Windscheid's more limited jurisprudential horizon, always deeply respected Windscheid's work for what it was. In fact, one can almost sense a touch of envy. Jhering was smart enough to realize that Windscheid's work of systematizing Roman law was essential, and that he himself lacked perhaps not the intellectual horsepower, but certainly the discipline and patience, to do it. Jhering also repeatedly, and perhaps somewhat anxiously, assured Windscheid (as well as himself) that their jurisprudential differences did not diminish their friendship.

Last, but not least, Windscheid and Jhering had remarkably different temperaments. Windscheid was consistent, disciplined, unassuming, and reserved, and it is difficult to imagine him joking or laughing. His thought was doctrinal, logical, and systematic but not wildly creative. Especially as the author of his "Pandekten" treatise, he strove to conserve, organize, and incrementally improve the law, largely leaving innovation and change to the legislature. He was a meticulous, diligent, and circumspect craftsman with no ambition to be a genius. He avoided overstatements and extreme positions and aimed at balance and compromise. As we will see in a moment, in virtually all these regards, Jhering was almost exactly the opposite.[151]

It is amazing that despite all these differences between their scholarly convictions, despite the exchange of unabashed criticism,[152] and despite their respective personalities, Jhering and Windscheid remained lifelong friends.[153] At one time, it seems that their friendship could have been in jeopardy. As mentioned, Jhering long coveted the prestigious Roman law chair at Heidelberg which had been informally promised to him – only to discover that the chair would be given to Windscheid. Jhering, however, put his disappointment aside and congratulated

[150] In 1871, Jhering openly acknowledged how their paths had diverged and considered their differences "irreconcilable," but he saw that as a benefit for jurisprudence, letter to Windscheid of July 21, 1871, Jherings Briefe an Windscheid (1988) 27. Their methodological differences notwithstanding, in 1886, Jhering wrote to Windscheid that he considered him more important for Romanist jurisprudence than anyone else (including Jhering himself). If a student asked him, Jhering stated, whether to study with him or with Windscheid, he would always respond: "with you", because "I am not capable of presenting the whole, and even with regard to the parts that I do present, not a complete picture of today's legal science, I just present myself, and the I in legal science has narrow limits […]," letter to Windscheid of March 18, 1886, Jherings Briefe an Windscheid (1988) 57.

[151] For portraits of, and perceptive comparisons between, these two scholars, see *Eck*, B. Windscheid and R.v. Jhering (1893), especially 8–26.

[152] See Jhering's letter to Windscheid of July 29, 1856, Jhering in Briefen (1913) 66–67 (Jhering apologizing to Windscheid for the excessive force of his criticism); letter to Windscheid of November 12, 1861, Jhering in Briefen (1913) 159–160 (thanking Windscheid for his frank – and devastating – criticism).

[153] Apparently, Jhering was the godfather of one of Windscheid's daughters, see letter to Windscheid of December 18, 1871, Jherings Briefe an Windscheid (1988) 28, 29.

Windscheid. There is no reason to doubt that he meant it. After all, he knew that his friend was just as worthy of the position as he had considered himself.[154]

And yet, for the development of legal thought, Jhering was the more important figure. As Jhering's Hungarian fan and follower Gusztáv Szászy-Schwarz (1856–1920) pointed out, without Windscheid, the Pandectist legal science could have been developed by other prominent Romanists of the time (albeit perhaps not to the same perfection); without Jhering, however, one of the most original thinkers in the history of jurisprudence would be missing.[155] In other words, there were potential substitutes for Windscheid but not for Jhering.

Eventually, death parted them – but not for long. Windscheid had planned to attend Jhering's funeral but then had to cancel because of illness. He was to survive his friend by a mere 39 days.

4. A Closer Personal Look: Tensions and Conflicts

A closer look at Jhering as a person is not only interesting in its own right, it is also important because without understanding Jhering's personality, it is extremely difficult to understand his *oeuvre*. A reader who faces the publications themselves will be perplexed, for example, by the wild disparity of Jhering's writings: some are tightly reasoned and clearly structured while others are strangely rambling and poorly organized. The reader will also wonder why Jhering sometimes strikes at the heart of the matter with the insight of a genius while on other occasions, he seems to go off on tangents for a hundred pages. Much of Jhering's later work, especially, is both captivating in its originality and imagination but also maddeningly prolix, ambiguous, and at times almost capricious. To be sure, a personal and intellectual portrait of the author does not eliminate these issues. Yet, at a minimum, understanding their roots allows the reader to face them with greater equanimity. Perhaps more importantly, cognizance of Jhering as a person and a scholar struggling with multiple contradictions opens up some of the most intriguing dimensions of his work.

We will first look at Jhering as an essentially private individual, then consider him as thinker and writer in general, and finally focus on him as a legal scholar in particular. The portrait will be completed by taking cognizance of his societal position and his political views.

Private Life: Much Light, Some Shadow. As a private individual, Jhering experienced much happiness. The external circumstances of his existence were fairly typical for a nineteenth century German law professor. He was financially secure, lived in relative comfort, and participated in cultural life. Jhering appreciated a spacious and pleasant home; especially in Göttingen where he was very

[154] For details, see *Fikentscher*, Methoden des Rechts III (1976) 146–148.
[155] *Földi*, Aspekte der Jhering-Rezeption in Ungarn (2023) 95.

happy to own a large house situated on a substantial piece of land "with the best view one can have."[156] He walked to the university, ate lunch at home, and took afternoon naps. While he was committed to his work, much of what was important to him lay beyond the law.

Jhering was a family man whose private life centered around his loved ones. He was happily married three times[157] (twice widowed), a devoted father to five children,[158] and later in life happy to have several grandchildren.[159] His letters are full of reports on his family life, expressions of hope and sadness, and inquiries about the families of his friends. Yet, family life also inflicted much pain. His first two wives died when they were still quite young. He lost several children at, or shortly after, birth. His oldest son emigrated to Brazil which disappointed Jhering so deeply that at some point, he vowed never to speak of him again[160] although he was reconciled with him later. To be sure, death struck early more often before the birth of modern medicine, children often defy their parent's wishes, and Jhering seems to have overcome these blows in due course. Yet, they ensured that he was no stranger to suffering and despair.

Jhering had a strong affection for farm life: in Gießen and Göttingen, he was an avid gardener tending to vegetable beds and a keeper of pigeons, geese, chickens, and on occasion, even a pig and a calf. He never tired of emphasizing how much he enjoyed his "rural paradise,"[161] and at times, the farmer in him eclipsed the jurist.[162] In 1866, he wrote to Windscheid, half seriously: "And you poor fellow are still torturing yourself with literary productions? Become a farmer like me, it is much better for the mind and your health."[163] Jhering simply loved nature. He relished time out in the open, e.g, in a hammock under a shady tree where he retreated to think creatively. From the study and lecture hall he often escaped to the outdoors for short strolls or long hikes through the countryside.

Liking to travel, Jhering availed himself of the rapidly growing railway networks. He attended conferences in other cities, spend vacations in fashionable spas, and repeatedly went to Austria, the Netherlands, Switzerland, and Italy – a

[156] Letter to Windscheid of March 31, 1872, Jherings Briefe an Windscheid (1988) 31.

[157] As reported by his son Hermann, Jhering wrote a letter to his third wife in which he considered "the love which he had received so greatly from his wifes the highest good he had experienced in a life so full of success and enjoyment," *Hermann von Jhering*, Erinnerungen (1913) 464.

[158] Jhering had four sons (Hermann who became a zoologist and emigrated to Brazil, Friedrich who became a judge, Albrecht who became a civil engineer, and Rudolf who became a pastor) and one daughter (Helene who married a Jewish academic, Viktor Ehrenberg, see infra note 285 and text).

[159] Letter to Lotte Hegewisch of September 19, 1888, Jhering in Briefen (1913) 410.

[160] Letter to Windscheid of June 10, 1880, Jherings Briefe an Windscheid (1988) 49.

[161] Letter to Windscheid of August 19, 1866, Jhering in Briefen (1913) 207.

[162] "These things have completely occupied my spirit, for the spirit of the Roman law, there is no space left at all." Letter to Windscheid of March 26, 1866, Jhering in Briefen (1913) 193.

[163] Letter to Windscheid of March 26 1866, Jhering in Briefen (1913) 194.

country for which he had particular affection. His trips took him, inter alia, to Florence, Bologna, Rome, Naples, and as far south as Palermo.[164] Although Jhering had never studied Italian, he spoke it well enough to give dinner talks, albeit only haltingly and with much effort.[165]

Throughout his adult life, Jhering knew how to savor many of the finer points of human existence, though in a way that was often more raw than refined. In marked contrast to his aloof and self-restrained forerunner Savigny and to his austere and unadventurous contemporary Windscheid, Jhering heartily enjoyed wine, women, and song. "Wine, smoked eels, partridges, woodcocks, whist, piano, wife, [and] female friends" were the ingredients of a good life.[166] At the Jherings, friends, colleagues or houseguests were often treated to opulent dinners which lasted late into the night. A connoisseur of fine wine, he once ordered a huge vat that was to last for his "children and their children" – but was emptied in a couple of years.[167] He not only enjoyed (and often carefully prepared) a good punch but even worked on a – not entirely serious – "theory" (or "philosophy") of mixed drinks.[168] And then there were cigars, Havannas, which Jhering continued to smoke even when he was virtually on his deathbed.[169] Jhering fully embraced his epicurean side, and he was grateful that as the years advanced, he still had his "old ability to enjoy life in undiminished fashion."[170] Yet, again, there were significant dampers. While his stout physique and forceful presence created an appearance of strong health,[171] he frequently complained about a wide range

---

[164] See his enthusiastic reports to Windscheid of July 2, 1871, Jherings Briefe an Windscheid (1988) 25; to Oskar Bülow of May 21, 1871, Jhering in Briefen (1913) 263–264; and to Auguste von Littrow-Bischoff of April 6, 1884 (sent from Palermo), Jhering in Briefen (1913) 371–374. Jhering could afford such trips because of the high salary he received in Vienna. On Jhering's travels in Italy, see *Vano*, Itinerari italiani di Rudolf von Jhering (1993).

[165] See letter to Bülow of May 21, 1871, Jhering in Briefen (1913) 264; letter to Auguste von Littrow-Bischoff of April 6, 1884, Jhering in Briefen (1913) 373–374. Jhering also read French and cited French scholarship on occasion though he indicated that his spoken French was not fluent, see *Heutger*, Rudolf von Jhering (2023) 40. He also read Dutch (which was close to the dialect spoken in his home region) but he did not speak it; id. 33, 40. By contrast, his English was apparently poor so that he read and cited English literature mostly in translations.

[166] Letter to Lotte Hegewisch of November 9, 1888, Jhering in Briefen (1913) 411.

[167] Letter to Windscheid of December 15, 1858, Jhering in Briefen (1913) 106; *Hermanm von Jhering*, Erinnerungen (1913) 468. The vat contained 1330 liters (ca. 350 gallons) and was so big, that a wall had to be taken down to get it in the basement of the house, id.

[168] The work was never completed. Fragments of a draft were published by *Helfer*, Prolegomena zur Theorie der gemischten Getränke (1968). Deploring how thoughtlessly most people drank (and ate), Jhering sought to develop a "science" of enjoying fine alcoholic beverages. The enterprise was part persiflage, part serious analysis. It was supposed to be a counterpart to a book on the art of eating which Jhering owned, praised, and recommended, i.e., *Antonius Anthus*, Vorlesungen über die Eßkunst (Leipzig 1838); see Helfer, id 20, note 5.

[169] "[A] good Havanna cigar – oh what feelings it triggers in me!" Letter to Gustav Baur, April 17, 1861, Jhering in Briefen (1913) 135; Kunze, Jherings Jubiläum (1991) 3.

[170] Letter to Windscheid of Dec. 31, 1873, Jherings Briefe an Windscheid (1988) 35, at 36.

[171] *Kunze*, Lieber in Gießen (2018) 27.

of ailments. Perhaps a result of too much good food, drink, and smoking, Jhering often suffered from stomach pain, indigestion, tooth aches, general indisposition, and states of utter exhaustion. At times, he comes across as a hypochondriac with a vivid imagination of all sort of ills.[172] Thus, his *joie de vivre* often fell victim to crappy moods and questionable self-pity.

Jhering had what he called "a definite inclination towards the female sex."[173] "Freundinnen" (women friends) were an important ingredient of a good life. For the most part, that simply meant the pleasure of the company of women – "but definitely not boring ones"![174] As his correspondence shows, Jhering was attracted to women who were educated and spirited and especially to women with whom he could have intelligent and interesting conversations.[175] Yet, there certainly were flirtatious elements, and it is fair to say that Jhering was something of a womanizer.[176] Even though he was (thrice) happily married, "one woman is by far not enough," as he confessed to a former girlfriend.[177] How far these flirtations went, is not entirely clear but there are indications that his interaction with "Freundinnen" was not always completely platonic.[178] There is no reason to believe, however, that Jhering engaged in any full-fledged extra-marital affairs, and his strong sense of moral duty makes that highly unlikely.[179]

[172] *Kunze*, Lieber in Gießen (2018) 27–28.

[173] Letter to Lotte Hegewisch of September 19, 1888, Jhering in Briefen (1913) 409. In conversation with me, Michael Kunze pointed out that in his youth and young adulthood, Jhering displayed homosexual inclinations, which, however, seem to have subsided later in life; for details, see Kunze's forthcoming biography of Jhering, Das unsichtbare Recht (2025).

[174] Letter to Lotte Hegewisch of September 19, 1888, Jhering in Briefen (1913) 409.

[175] The collection of his letters edited posthumously by his daughter Helene Ehrenberg contains numerous letters written to women. His ideal was his Viennese friend Auguste von Littrow-Bischoff whom he visited on several occasions, and for whom his letters expressed much admiration and affection. "With all due respect for the German men, whom I certainly do not wish to disparage," Jhering wrote to her, "but a conversation as stimulating as with you I have had with very few members of my own sex." Letter to Auguste von Littrow-Bischoff of "March and May" 1885, Jhering in Briefen (1913) 383.

[176] Apparently, at least his second wife was aware of that. When Jhering received a letter from his friend Bernhard Windscheid's wife that was full of praise for Jhering, he responded with a somewhat flirtatious letter that he concluded "with best regards from my wife, who is proud of every conquest I make – your most sincere admirer…", letter to Lotte Windscheid of April 15, 1865, Jhering in Briefen (1913) 172.

[177] Letter to Lotte Hegewisch of September 19, 1888, Jhering in Briefen (1913) 409.

[178] In a letter to his erstwhile love, he mentioned (speaking in the third person) "one [woman friend] in Göttingen whom he always embraces tenderly – kindred souls – occasionally also a good-bye kiss under the moon;" letter to Lotte Hegewisch of September 19, 1888, Jhering in Briefen (1913) 409. At the time, Jhering was 60 years old and (apparently happily) married to his third wife. Lotte Hegewisch (1822–1903) was no wallflower; at the time of Jhering's letter, she was a well-known "salonière," benefactor of the arts, and political activist.

[179] Jhering's letter to Lotte Hegewisch does indicate a romantic involvement in 1849–1852, i.e., at the time after the death of his first wife (Helene Hoffmann) in 1848 but after he had

Personality: A Battlefield of Forces.[180] Jhering's personality was a veritable battlefield of opposite forces, perhaps as a result of, or at least reinforced by, the ups and down in his life. He was subject to mood swings so extreme that today, he might be diagnosed as bi-polar. Times of great happiness and exuberance alternated with periods of deep depression and utter despair.

His character traits were also wildly divergent. On the one hand, Jhering had many positive qualities. Many of those who still knew him personally emphasized his "great personal amiability."[181] He was charming, witty, and engaging. Endowed with a healthy dose of personal self-worth,[182] he could be magnanimous, generous, and tolerant. He was forgiving and empathetic, deeply honest and fiercely loyal, and he had that pronounced sense of duty owned by the best public servants at the time. As people expected from a man of Frisian origins, he was driven by a strong need for liberty and independence.[183] He followed his own convictions with courage and determination, even at the risk of conflict with, and condemnation by, others – sometimes, as he recognized, to a fault.[184] In striking contrast to the Northerners' reputation for being phlegmatic, introverted, and somber, Jhering was (mostly) vivacious, extroverted, and passionate.[185] His powerful presence, his intellectual fervor, and his enormous will power struck all those he encountered. "The dominant impression was that of a pulsating, full-blooded and warmth-giving life, of inexhaustible inner richness," wrote Max

---

married his second wife in 1849. The letter does not say how far that involvement went but it is a wistful trip down memory lane that laments the "bad fortune" that separated them and that culminates in a touching confession of lasting affection after more than a generation, id. 411.

[180] For a vivid and subtle portrait of Jhering's personality, see *Rümelin*, Rudolf von Jhering (1922) 1–27.

[181] *Mitteis*, Jhering (1905) 663 ("große persönliche Liebenswürdigkeit"); *Ehrenberg* (son in law), Vorwort (1894) ("the endless goodness of his heart"); see also *Dove*, Rudolf von Jhering (1893) 152 ("The bellicose fighter was a benevolent and affable man.").

[182] He did not, as he wrote to his friend Windscheid's wife, worry much about feelings of unworthiness; "in my life, I should often have been embarrassed if I had asked whether I was worthy of what I have received. For love, veneration, and respect I have an almost unlimited capacity, and I have never been shy about accepting them." Letter to Lotte Windscheid of April 15 1865, Jhering in Briefen (1913) 170.

[183] Supra notes 57–58 and text. Hermann Kantorowicz, one of Jhering's great admirers, also attributed the hit-or-miss nature of some of Jhering's scholarship to his Frisian origins. Clearly tongue-in-cheek, he explained that Jhering's arrows were often a little off the mark because the Frisians went out to hunt and seek adventure only at night; *Kantorowicz*, Jherings Bekehrung (1914) 14.

[184] "I have had rather too much courage in my life than too little; personally, I would have fared better if I had added a bit more caution." Letter to Heinrich von Poschinger of April 22, 1890, *Poschinger*, Bismarck und Jhering (1908) 6, at 7–8.

[185] His acquaintance, the Romanist legal scholar Ernst Immaniel Bekker (1827–1916), aptly observed that while Jhering was from Northern Germany, "his unique mixture of a sanguinic and choleric temperament is not in line with the typical Northern mentality, his imagination was more powerful, the heart more passionate." Quoted after *Fikentscher*, Methoden des Rechts III (1976) 113.

Rümelin, who had still met Jhering in person, in 1922. "The spring of formative and creative power bubbled incessantly [...]. This abundance of perspectives was combined with a mighty personal energy. He took on every task with the full warmth of his heart and the full force of his will."[186] In society, he was the center of attention, "interested in everybody and everything, well-read and quick-witted, full of charisma, self-confident, sociable, free from arrogance, and incapable of deceit. Where he appeared, there was no boredom."[187] Jhering's energetic and magnetic all-round personality accounts for much of the impression he made on his contemporaries and his posterity.[188]

On the other hand, Jhering surely had his foibles. As he well knew and openly admitted, he could be feisty, combative, and obstinate, and thus often difficult to get along with.[189] To make matters worse, he was impulsive and irascible; contemporaries feared his episodes of sudden rage, even though they were often followed by deep regret and honest apology. He could be sarcastic and brutally direct, unintentionally hurting other people's feelings.[190] He did not suffer fools gladly and often took no mercy on those whom he considered intellectually inferior.

Jhering was neither agnostic nor pious. He went to church on Christmas eve[191] and sometimes said prayers with his children at bedtime, but these were not signs of deep religiousness. Concerning himself mainly with what he could observe on Earth, Jhering was happy to leave what lay beyond that to theology.[192] In the *curriculum vitae* mentioned before, Jhering designated his religion as "Romanist!"[193], i.e., believer in Roman law; this was not entirely facetious: for Jhering, the Romanist (legal) tradition was the perhaps ultimate ethical bedrock and framework.[194] It is true, however, that in both his scholarship and his private letters, references to God do occur; in particular, Jhering saw him as the guide of historical development and as the ultimate source of ethics.[195] Yet, at the end of the day, Jhering's belief in God as the architect of the physical and moral universe

---

[186] *Rümelin*, Rudolf von Jhering (1922) 11; see also *Mitteis*, Jhering (1905) 663.

[187] *Kunze*, Ein großer Jurist (2023) 9.

[188] *Mitteis*, Jhering (1905) 655.

[189] Jhering was self-critical at length, though without being bitter, in his letter to Lotte Windscheid of April 15, 1865, Jhering in Briefen (1913) 171–172; see also his – half-serious – self-portrait (1867), Jhering in Briefen (1913) 217.

[190] *Kunze*, Lieber in Gießen (2018) 28 ("honest to the point of cruelty").

[191] See letter to Bülow of December 25, 1884, Jhering in Briefen (1913) 375. The letter suggests that this was the only time of the year that Jhering attended church.

[192] "In my life, I have believed, and have had to believe, many things, but since I am not a theologian, I am not under any obligation to believe the impossible." Letter to Luise Gleim of May 20, 1881, Jhering in Briefen (1913) 363.

[193] Jhering, Rudolf Jhering, Jhering in Briefen (1913) 214. Jhering's self-portrait is a self-deprecating caricature that illustrates his strong sense of humor which he applied not only to others but also to himself.

[194] See *Behrends*, Rudolf von Jhering (1987) 243.

[195] See infra chapter V.2., notes 103–111 and text.

had little influence on his jurisprudence as he developed it in "Geist," "Kampf," and "Zweck." For Jhering, law was decidedly a product of human society and thus an essentially secular matter.[196]

Three character traits deserve special mention because they strongly shaped his thought and are visible in much of his work: his enduring need to break with conventions, his irrepressible humor, and his pronounced sense of honor and justice.

In many ways, Jhering lived well within the conventions set by his station and his age: a dutiful civil servant, learned professor, devoted family man, and conscientious citizen. Yet, there was a part of him that needed to break out of all this normality; that hungered for "adventures and extravagancies of all sorts."[197] Even as a seventy-year old, he still felt "something of the old craziness" in him and (speaking about himself in the third person) confessed that he "never feels better than when he can occasionally commit some profound nonsense."[198] Indeed, he often did – be it by engaging in horseplay with professorial colleagues in a Budapest public bath[199] or by dressing his dog in a militia uniform.[200] His belief that "full enjoyment requires a dose of craziness"[201] also shaped his work time and again: every so often, he simply broke with academic tradition and took intellectual risks that made his colleagues shake their heads in disbelief. Then he pursued a course of thought that took him far away from conventional wisdom, leading to brilliance or nonsense, as they case might be.

A closely related character trait was Jhering's notorious sense of humor and, more or less subtle, irony – an American commentator aptly called him the "Mark Twain of German jurisprudence."[202] Jhering greatly enjoyed making fun of people and things with few holds barred. It is true that sometimes he showed perhaps too little regard for other people's feelings or the limits of good taste, but he also often targeted himself; much of the *curriculum vita*e he penned in 1867 was

---

[196] Religion did play a major role for Jhering as a cultural phenomenon shaping the evolution of law, especially in antiquity, see *Jhering*, Geist I (1852) 256–281.

[197] Letter to Gerber of August 30, 1859, Jhering in Briefen (1913) 117.

[198] Letter to Lotte Hegewisch of September 19, 1888, Jhering in Briefen (1913) 409.

[199] During an academic visit to Budapest, Jhering and a handful of colleagues visited the famous Ofener Baths where Jhering incited this group of honorable law professors to some horseplay in the pool, with the slimmer ones climbing on the backs of their stouter colleagues. It was amazing, his eulogist Kuntze wrote, "how German representatives of a serious science could have so such fun beyond all measure. Among all those having fun, however, Jhering had the most." *Kuntze*, Rudolf von Jhering (1892) 609–610.

[200] As a young professor in Kiel, Jhering was greatly annoyed that he had to participate in military drill. In protest, he had a militia uniform made for his dog. When the canine escaped the house in that outfit, the public authorities were all but amused, and Jhering escaped potentially serious consequences only because shortly after the incident, he left Kiel. The episode is described in some detail by (his son) *Hermann von Jhering*, Erinerungen (1913) 446–447.

[201] Letter to Lotte Hegewisch of September 19, 1888, Jhering in Briefen (1913) 407.

[202] *Seagle*, Rudolf von Jhering (1945) 71.

written tongue-in-cheek.[203] In all this, he had a knack for word-games, as when he addressed his friend Windscheid in a letter as "Dear father" – because Windscheid had just become one,[204] or when after having been knighted by the Austrian emperor, he titled himself "the Knight of the Spirit" (of the Roman law) and even, alluding to Cervantes' Don Quixote, as "the knight of the sorrowful countenance."[205] Jhering's irrepressible sense of humor and his penchant for irony also left their mark on much of his work, as when he mocked the jurisprudence of his day, including his own pursuit of it, in the starkest terms,[206] or when he made fun of the absurd overproduction of (senseless) academic publications he observed all around him.[207]

Last, but certainly not least, Jhering had an unusually strong sense of honor and justice. If he felt insulted, he would at minimum complain bitterly about it. When he received an award from his government that put him on par with people he considered below his rank, he decried that "in many years, nothing has hurt my feelings so deeply," vowed that he would defend his honor by filing a complaint with the authorities, and threatened to resign from his position if need be.[208] It was not only his own dignity he cared about, however, but also that of others, including Shylock's who, in Jhering's eyes, had been degraded by the Venetian tribunal.[209] In a similar vein, Jhering was loath to tolerate perceived injustice. In several instances, he fought for his presumed rights in court because he strongly believed that a man must not take a violation of his rights lying down. He lost every time[210] – and lamented that the courts had failed him.[211] Reasonable people can differ whether to admire his determination to enforce his (presumed) entitlements or to lament his unwillingness to seek compromise and conciliation, but nobody could call him a pushover. His strong commitment to honor and justice pervaded his scholarship as well. Its most visible manifestation was of course his

[203] Jhering in Briefen (1913) 214–217.

[204] Letter to Windscheid, September 14, 1859, Jhering in Briefen (1913) 118. In his letters to friends, Jhering often gave free reign to his need for fun and absurdity; see his letter to Bülow of October 25, 1868, Jhering in Briefen (1913) 230 ("Greetings to the devil and his grandmother"); letter to (professor) Binding of July 9, 1879, Jhering in Briefen (1913) 346–347 (addressed to "My Dear Tiger!" and signed "Your Victim").

[205] Letter to Bülow of June 16, 1872, Jhering in Briefen (1913) 283–284 ("Ritter vom Geist," "Ritter von der traurigen Gestalt").

[206] See infra chapter III.2.

[207] Infra chapter III.2., notes 57–70 and text.

[208] Letter to Auguste von Littrow-Bischoff of "early" 1877, Jhering in Briefen (1913) 319.

[209] See infra chapter IV.1., notes 117–122 and text.

[210] In Gießen, Jhering sued his landlord several times – and lost on each occasion. He was also sued by his maidservant (for three-months wages) and again suffered a stinging defeat. The latter litigation is vividly recounted and closely analyzed by *Hanewinkel and Linder*, "Ein Mann von kräftigem Rechtsgefühl" (2020).

[211] Jhering complained about the injustice he had suffered in his talk on "Der Kampf ums Recht" but the respective part was omitted in the published version; *Hanewinkel and Linder*, "Ein Mann von kräftigem Rechtsgefühl" (2020) 62.

ultimately most famous work, "Der Kampf ums Recht."[212] Yet, even beyond that outburst, the belief in the value and the dignity of the person was one of Jhering's most fundamental credos and a foundational pillar of his whole jurisprudence.[213]

The Scholar and Author: The Jurist and the Artist. As a thinker and author, Jhering had a dual nature: he was a jurist by training and profession, but he was also an artist by mentality and inclination.[214]

On the one hand, he was plainly an unusually gifted legal scholar – "a jurist by the grace of God."[215] He commanded superb analytical skills enabling him to produce first-rate doctrinal work with enviable surefootedness.[216] His knowledge of Roman law was formidable, and he engaged in its study with determination and passion.

On the other hand, as he often emphasized and as has often been observed by others, he related to the world and to life at least as much through his senses and imagination as through his intellect.[217] On the private side, Jhering's artistic mentality expressed itself most obviously in his love of music. Jhering was a knowledgeable, enthusiastic, and skilled pianist. He mastered difficult pieces by his favorite composers, Bach, Beethoven, Mozart, and especially Schubert, whose music could move him to tears.[218] Jhering once even filled in at a public performance when the invited pianist could not appear.[219] He forced his children to learn an instrument, and many evenings in his home were devoted to playing trios or quartets. The artistic, emotional, and intuitive element in Jhering's character was not merely a matter of private pleasure, it also shaped his scholarship. It was, he wrote, "the artistic element in law" that lay at the root of his love for his field.[220] "In every intellectual work," he considered "beauty [...] just as necessary as

---

[212] See infra chapter IV.1.

[213] *Pleister*, Persönlichkeit, Wille und Freiheit (1982) 31–67; see also infra chapter IV.1., notes 64–68, 107–116 and text.

[214] This, artistic, side of Jhering has been noted by others as early as in 1892 by an anonymous eulogist, *Anon.*, Review (1892); later by *Stintzing and Landsberg*, Geschichte der deutschen Rechtswissenschaft III.2. (1910) 792–793; *Rümelin*, Rudolf von Jhering (1922) 14; *Gibert*, Jhering in Espana (1970) 53 ("el artista del derecho").

[215] *Eck*, B. Windscheid und R.v.Jhering (1893) 11.

[216] See infra chapter II.3.

[217] Letter to Gerber of September 19, 1853, Jhering in Briefen (1913) 33–34; *Wieacker*, Privatrechtsgeschichte (1967) 451; *Wieacker*, Gründer und Bewahrer (1959) 201; *Kroppenberg*, Die Plastik des Rechts (2015) 37.

[218] In 1865, Jhering hosted a noted violinist who practiced parts of Beethoven's violin concerto at Jhering's house in anticipation of a public performance next day. "[A] marvelous composition and superbly performed," Jhering commented. "And all the while, I am supposed to grade papers on the interdictum quod vi aut clam!" – which he finally threw into a corner in order to just listen to the music; letter to Windscheid of September 10, 1865, Jhering in Briefen (1913) 185.

[219] See *Fikentscher*, Methoden des Rechts III (1976) 122.

[220] *Jhering*, Unsere Aufgabe (1857) 12. The third volume of "Geist" contained a chapter entitled "Die juristische Kunst" ("The Art of Law"), *Jhering*, Geist III (1865) 1–11 (§48).

truth."[221] Some of his work, Jhering himself pointed out, was probably best explained as a result of his "drive for artistic formation."[222] Thus, Jhering's approach to his work often differed markedly from that of his colleagues: in legal constructs, he looked not only for logical consistency but also for "Durchsichtigkeit," "Plastik," und "Schönheit" ("transparency," "plasticity," and "beauty");[223] in explaining the evolution of law, he focused not only on historical tradition or political power but also assigned a crucial role to an emotional element: the sense of justice (Rechtsgefühl); and in exploring the deep nature of the law, he employed not only knowledge and reason but also, and at times predominately, imagination and intuition. The artist in Jhering also came to the fore with his humorous, jocular, and often sardonic style.

As a result, the jurist and the artist lived in constant, and often productive, tension. It is interesting to note that at the end of his life, Jhering himself emphasized the artist (and the *bon vivant*) over the academic and the jurist. Shortly before his death, during the celebration of his doctorate's 50th anniversary, Jhering requested that the speakers refrain from extolling him as a scholar. But, he said, if they wanted to celebrate him as a card player, musician and connoisseur of wine, that would be most welcome.[224] Even if he spoke partially in jest, he was also partially serious.

The tension between the jurist and the artist shaped Jhering's style. When the jurist took command, Jhering's writing was analytically sharp, carefully guarded, and sober. This is particularly true for his doctrinal work.[225] Even there, however, the artist injected a measure of liveliness which make his doctrinal pieces quite pleasant and rewarding to read. When the artist took over, Jhering turned into the writer he had once wanted to become in his youth.[226] Then his style was passionate and provocative, captivating and satirical, bristling with memorable aphorisms and stirring images;[227] but his writing also tended to become careless and imprecise, boisterous and riddled with exaggerations and cheap shots. This is true, for example, in his attacks on conceptual jurisprudence, his glorification of the "battle for law," and his diatribe against the social custom of tipping.[228] In much of his later scholarship, especially in "Der Zweck im Recht," the jurist and the artist were jointly at work. The former displayed broad knowledge and pursued an honest search for truth which could generate deep insight. The latter

[221] Letter to Gerber of September 19, 1853, Jhering in Briefen (1913) 33.

[222] Remark in Jhering's talk at the dinner of the *Wiener Juristische Gesellschaft* following his talk "Der Kampf ums Recht" in 1872, reprinted in *Ermacora*, Vorrede (1992) 24.

[223] See *Möller*, Die juristische Konstruktion im Werk Rudolf von Jherings – vom universellen Rechtsalphabet bis zur juristischen Schönheit (2017).

[224] *Kunze*, Jherings Jubiläum (1991) 17.

[225] Infra chapter II.3.

[226] Supra 2. notes 60–61 and text.

[227] Jhering's eulogist Alfons Merkel compared Jhering's style with that of Arthur Schopenhauer; *Merkel*, Jhering (1893) 10.

[228] Infra chapter III.2. and chapter VI.2.

infused the discourse with originality and imagination, but also with occasional naiveté, speculation, and a spontaneity that entailed a loss of direction and focus.[229]

The Legal Scholar in Particular: Self-Confidence and Self-Doubt. As a legal scholar Jhering was also riddled with tensions. Perhaps the most obvious issue was the conflict between self-confidence and self-doubt. Most of the time, Jhering had great trust in his intellectual capabilities, his "Frisian toughness,"[230] and his potential to revolutionize the jurisprudence of his age. He was pretty sure that he was smarter than most of his colleagues and that his work was much better than theirs (his close academic friends excepted). On other occasions, however, he was tormented by self-doubt and despair over the imperfections in his work, his inability to make sufficient progress ("there must a snail in my brain"[231]), and even, dramatizing the situation, his "sick mental state."[232] "Am I not one of those many people," he asked himself, "who have illusions about their own accomplishments, who see the latter through a magnifying glass?" Thus, he constantly oscillated between enthusiasm and optimism on the one hand, and anguish and pessimism on the other.

These tensions reflected a serious underlying problem, i.e., a mismatch between ambition and ability:[233] Jhering's ambition and his determination to generate deep and original insight drove him – with a "Faustian urge pushing him beyond his limits"[234] – to take on projects the successful completion of which lay beyond his power. Especially in his two great works, the "Geist des römischen Rechts" und "Der Zweck im Recht," he desperately wanted to get to the bottom of what law was ultimately all about. Unfortunately, he lacked the discipline to keep his inquiries within manageable limits, the synthetic skills to integrate the vast amount of material, and the philosophical training to generate a coherent theory. After many years of often heroic struggle to gain control over these formidable projects, Jhering increasingly realized that he had bitten off more

[229] This was already obvious to the author of a chapter on Jhering published more than a century ago in the United States; see *MacDonnell,* Rudolf von Jhering (1914) 592 ("rhetorical and diffuse," "ingenious and prolific in brilliant conjectures," "fantastic, putting little constraint on his ingenuity").

[230] "[O]stfriesische Zähigkeit," letter to Gerber of March 26, 1854, Briefe und Erinnerungen (1907) 29.

[231] Letter to Windscheid of December 21, 1856, Jhering in Briefen (1913) 74.

[232] "[K]rankhafte geistige Verfassung;" letter to Windscheid of December 30, 1883, Jherings Briefe an Windscheid (1988) 50.

[233] Or, in Erik Wolf's words, "a mismatch between the self-imposed tasks and his powers," *Wolf,* Große Rechtsdenker (1963) 663. As he got older, Jhering became increasingly aware of the problem, see, e.g., his letter to Windscheid of December 30, 1879, Jherings Briefe an Windscheid (1988) 47, at 48 ("I am constantly reminded of the mismatch between my power and the magnitude and scope of the tasks, and the slowness of production is getting worse from one year to the next.")

[234] *Kantorowicz,* Jherings Bekehrung (1914) 14.

than he could chew. Yet, by then, it was too late to change course. Even then, however, he took on new challenges, resigning himself to the fact that the old ones would not be fully met.

A related tension existed between Jhering's unbridled curiosity, which often led him from one idea to the next in leaps and bounds, and his desire to present his ideas in a form that satisfied his standards of clarity and consistency. Thus he often indulged in collecting vast amounts of empirical observations while desperately seeking, like Goethe's *Faust*, the formula that captures how it all makes sense.[235] The realist' openness towards the richness of social life constantly struggled with the idealist's search for a conclusive account.

The combination of self-confidence and self-doubt, search for perfect exposition of his ideas, and confrontation with vast amounts of material turned writing his major works – especially "Geist" and "Zweck" – into a war with himself.[236] Draft followed upon draft, one organization of the material was abandoned in favor of another, and almost nothing truly satisfied the author. "What I have made today, is discarded tomorrow. Penelope, Penelope!"[237] Jhering exclaimed; "my production is a massacre of the innocents at Bethlehem."[238] When the books were finally in print, Jhering was often embarrassed by this chapter or that, wanted to revise this part or that, but also knew that he had to stop himself because otherwise, the struggle would never end. Yet, he refused to be defeated; he continuously took intellectual risks, acknowledged the possibility of failure, and invited others to criticize him – and to do better.[239]

It did not help that Jhering at times oscillated between enthusiasm for and disenchantment with jurisprudence. Sometimes, being a legal scholar struck him as a blissful existence,[240] but at other times, "the mere sight of a law book" stressed him out,[241] and he could simply not make himself "consume legal food" at all, preferring to "indulge in Goethe."[242] In such moments, he wished he had

[235] "[D]aß ich erkenne, was die Welt im Innersten zusammenhält;" *Goethe*, Faust. Der Tragödie erster Theil. Nacht (first scene) (1829). The phrase is difficult to translate. It expresses the desire to understand the innermost connectedness of "the world" in the sense of all of creation.

[236] See, e.g., letter to Auguste von Littrow-Bischoff of May 28, 1876, Jhering in Briefen (1913) 315.

[237] Letter to Windscheid "beginning" of 1854, Jhering in Briefen (1913) 160 (referring, of courses, to the "Odyssee" where Ulysses' wife undoes at night what she has woven during the day to keep the crowd of suitors at bay).

[238] Letter to Bülow of December 24, 1880, Jhering in Briefen (1913) 363 (referencing, of course, the gospel of Matthew 2:16–18). The "massacre" is vividly illustrated by Jhering's handwritten drafts and notes. Paragraphs are crossed out and rewritten on the margin – and often crossed out again, notes are inserted all over the place, headers are repeatedly changed, the result being a frightening mess which is entirely impenetrable to an outsider, see, e.g., his manuscript in COD MS Jhering 2:2.

[239] See, e.g., *Jhering*, Zweck I (1884) vi (Preface).

[240] *Jhering*, Unsere Aufgabe (1857) 12–14.

[241] Letter to Rudolf Gneist of August 12, 1858, Jhering in Briefen (1913) 96.

[242] Letter to Windscheid of December 15, 1858, Jhering in Briefen (1913) 105.

never studied law in the first place, stating that if he could choose again, he would not become a jurist, "at least not a Romanist and certainly not a theoretician."[243] As he grew older, dissatisfaction with jurisprudence grew stronger[244] so that he increasingly ventured beyond it – first beyond its traditional boundaries, then beyond its realm altogether.[245]

Societal Positions: Aristocrat, Bourgeois, Citoyen. Jhering's societal position was also marked by tensions, but they were not full-scale conflicts that tormented him. They simply entailed occasional ambivalence that bothered him little, however. They resulted mainly from the interaction between three sides of his character: aristocrat, bourgeois, and citoyen (i.e., a citizen).

By birth and pedigree, Jhering was an aristocrat, though merely on a provincial level. While not nobility, his forebears belonged to the patrician class in their city and region. They were privileged, influential, and highly respected. As a result, Jhering was quietly confident of his status as a person worthy of respect. He had no need for arrogance or condescension and rarely displayed either. In fact, he carefully avoided to appear vain or self-promoting.[246]

In lifestyle and outlook, however, Jhering was a bourgeois. This should not be taken in a negative sense. It simply means that he lived the life, and by and large shared the views and values of, the upper middle class in mid- and late-nineteenth century Germany. He was not as highly educated in literature, philosophy, and the classics as the elite of Savigny's generation had been, and he evinced no deep affection for, nor any profound understanding of, the tradition of Weimar.[247] But he was of course trained in history, Greek and Latin, and he quoted Goethe and Hegel when it suited his purposes. His financial security resulted not from landownership or family wealth but from his income as a university professor. He had house servants but not an entourage, a sense of family tradition but not of dynasty.

The interplay between the aristocrat and the bourgeois is illustrated by Jhering's ambivalent stance vis-à-vis his elevation to nobility upon his departure from Vienna. Jhering was not indifferent to recognition through official titles. The title of "Geheimer Justizrat" (which can perhaps be translated as "senior judicial counselor"), which he received as a professor in Gießen, designated merely an elevated rank within the state bureaucracy; it was nothing very special and amused Jhering (as well as his wife) more than it flattered him.[248] When he came to

[243] See, e.g., letter to Gerber of October 15, 1858, Jhering in Briefen (1913) 103.

[244] "Between us: I find jurisprudence increasingly boring." Letter to Oskar von Bülow of October 28, 1871, Jhering in Briefen (1913) 268.

[245] See infra chapter VI.

[246] He staunchly refused to publicize his visit and exchange of letters with Bismarck because he did not want to use the great man for self-advancement, and "he feared the reproach of vanity." Letter to Heinrich von Poschinger of April 22, 1890, *Poscher*, Bisrmarck and Jhering (1908) 6–8.

[247] See *Wieacker*, Gründer und Bewahrer (1950) 200.

[248] "My senior judicial counsellor has been enormously amusing […], together with my

Vienna, he also became a "Wirklicher Geheimer Hofrat" ("Senior Privy Counsellor"), a respectable rank in the hierarchy of the monarchial system.[249] Eventually, he was knighted by the Austrian Emperor, which entailed hereditary nobility. The bourgeois in him downplayed the matter, writing that he really did not much care for that status and even disparaging it.[250] The aristocrat, however, immediately filed the requisite application, showing a certain eagerness to avail himself of the opportunity. He claimed that he did it mainly for the benefit of his children,[251] which may very well be true, and yet, he signed as "von Jhering" for the rest of his life, even in correspondence with friends.

The citoyen in Jhering played a fairly modest role in his younger years but grew to sizeable proportions over time. Until about mid-life, Jhering followed public events with interest but did not engage in political action.[252] When he was a law student in Göttingen, seven professors (including the brothers Grimm of fairy-tale fame) were summarily dismissed and expelled from the kingdom by the ruling monarch in retaliation for their political opposition. The treatment of the *Göttinger Sieben* caused an outcry among liberals all across Germany, but Jhering did not participate in any protests and evinced little interest in the affair at the time,[253] although he later stated that it did not exactly endear him to the monarchy.[254] When the 1848/49 Revolution shook Germany to the core, Jhering, now a law professor, remained on the sidelines as well.[255] In 1851, he still claimed political innocence: "I know of politics and its heroes as much as a child."[256]

wife, I nearly died from laughter about the idea [...], and besides me, surely a lot of others will have laughed as well." Letter to Windscheid of December 22, 1860, Jhering in Briefen (1913) 129.

[249] *Hofmeister*, Jhering in Wien (1995) 11, suspects that this was part of what attracted Jhering to the position in Vienna.

[250] "[D]as wenigste wäre in meinen Augen der Baron, den ich morgen haben könnte, [...] der hier bekanntlich sehr vulgär und billig ist," ("[T]he least, in my eyes, would be the title of *Baron*, which I could get tomorrow, [...] which is well known to be quite common and cheap."), letter to Windscheid of January 21, 1872, Jhering's Briefe an Windscheid (1988) 30, 31.

[251] In particular, he thought that it would help them in their careers; letter to Bülow of June 16, 1872, Jhering in Briefen (1913) 283. In late nineteenth century Germany, that expectation was entirely plausible.

[252] *Kunze*, Lieber in Gießen (2018) 29–30.

[253] *Kunze*, Rudolf von Jhering (1995) 130.

[254] Letter to Bismarck of September 15, 1888, Jhering in Briefen (1913) 442. Jhering characterized the king's action as an "Umsturz des Staatsgrundgesetzes" ("overthrow of the constitution"), id. – which it was indeed.

[255] *Kunze*, Rudolf von Jhering (1995) 135. Jhering rejected the radical claims of the "Democrats" who wanted to overthrow the monarchy; he preferred the liberalism of a constitutional monarchy, see *Kunze*, Ein großer Jurist (2023) 15. This, moderate, program was defeated in the 1848/49 Revolution but eventually prevailed in later nineteenth-century Germany, especially after unification under Bismarck in 1871. Jhering the patrician was deeply skeptical via-a-vis popular action. He had attended various popular gatherings – but only with a flask of Eau de Cologne! "all due respect for the sovereign people," Jhering opined, "but they smell bad;" quoted after *Kunze*, Rudolf von Jhering (1995) 135. Kunze plausibly attributes Jhe-

Jhering's political engagement was eventually triggered by the question of German unification – a development in which he took an immense interest and which aroused his patriotism. During the Prussian (and Austrian) conflict with Denmark about the border provinces between the realms (Schleswig-Holstein) in 1864, Jhering engaged in public agitation for the German cause and helped to organize a society that recruited and trained militiamen to send them into the war, calling it his duty to participate actively in the movement.[257] Two years later, he followed the Prussian-Austrian war of 1866 with feverish excitement;[258] after the Prussian victory and the foundation of the North German Federation, he ran for membership in its legislature, now trumpeting his political engagement although it is not clear how seriously he took the matter.[259] (In any event, he was – most narrowly – defeated and never ran for political office again.) Finally, in the Franco-Prussian war of 1870–71, Jhering was an ardent supporter of the German cause, though only in words. His nationalism almost spun out of control: like many Germans at the time, he wished "all bad things upon the French" and "relished their humiliation,"[260] though when he came to his senses, he was embarrassed to have felt that way.[261] Yet, when after the Prussian victory, Germany was finally united in 1871, Jhering's enthusiasm continued unabated. He glorified the event in exuberant language that, while not uncommon in its day, strikes today's reader as hopelessly over the top.[262]

In the course of these events, Jhering suddenly became a great admirer of Bismarck. In the spring of 1866, Jhering had still accused Bismarck of utter shamelessness and notorious lies in provoking the war with Austria,[263] condemning "the evil game Bismarck is playing with all notions of law and truth."[264] Three month later, after the decisive Prussian victory over Austria (at the battle of Königrätz on July 3, 1866) condemnation turned into veneration almost overnight because Jhering thought that only now he understood what had really

---

ring's inaction during the revolution mainly to the personal tragedy that struck him at the time, i.e., the death of his (first) wife and newborn child, which "made him blind and deaf to everything else," *Kunze*, Ein großer Jurist (2023) 16.

[256] Letter to Gerber of August 8, 1851, Jhering in Briefen (1913) 11.

[257] Letter to Windscheid, "Early" 1864, Jhering in Briefen (1913) 159–160.

[258] See his letter to Hermann Fitting of November 18, 1866, Jhering in Briefen (1913) 209–210.

[259] The ironic tone in the curriculum vitae which Jhering wrote at the time, suggests that he took the matter rather lightly (presenting himself as "also a politicus!" who "whenever public and common interests are at stake is always at the forefront – especially with his mouth if a speaker is needed"); Jhering in Briefen (1913) 216.

[260] Letter to Windscheid of January 31, 1871, Jhering in Briefen (1913) 23; see also his letter to Bülow of August 5, 1870, Jhering in Briefen (1913) 248–250.

[261] Letter to Windscheid of January 31, 1871, Jhering in Briefen (1913) 23.

[262] Letter to Windscheid of January 31, 1871, Jhering in Briefen (1913) 23.

[263] Letter to Glaeser of May 1, 1866, Jhering in Briefen (1913) 196

[264] Letter to Windscheid of June 14 1866, Jhering in Briefen (1913) 199–200.

happened: "I bow before the genius of a Bismarck who has delivered a masterpiece of political combination and action as is rarely seen in history," Jhering wrote to Windscheid. "I have forgiven the man everything he has done, in fact more than that, I have completely convinced myself that what appeared to us, the uninitiated, as evil craziness then turned out as an indispensable means to an end. The man is of one of the greatest men of our century."[265] Jhering's *volte-face* shows yet another feature of his character: he was ready unabashedly to revise his opinion if new evidence suggested to him that he been wrong.

In the spring of 1885, Jhering's longstanding dream of a personal encounter with the man to whom he "owed a fatherland"[266] was fulfilled when he spent a few hours with Bismarck at his residence in Berlin – an event Jhering counted among the highlights of his life.[267] When Bismarck sent congratulations to Jhering on his 70th birthday, Jhering felt greatly honored and replied in a letter full of praise and devotion.[268] Jhering even gave Bismarck's *Realpolitik* credit for inspiring him in his jurisprudential efforts to replace "the formalistic with the realistic method."[269] Yet, Jhering's admiration for the "Iron Chancellor" as a "man of action,"[270] also indicated that he could be attracted to power and its decisive exercise.[271]

It has been argued that in his later years, Jhering became more politically conservative and even authoritarian.[272] That view is supported not only by Jhering's eventual veneration of Bismarck but also by his references to Heinrich von Treitschke (1834–1896), a German historian famous for his extreme nationalism, support of colonialism, and at times outright chauvinistic views.[273] It is even more plausible in light of the essentially Hobbesian conception of the state that Jhering developed in the first volume of "Zweck" (1877).[274] Now, Jhering appeared as a supporter of sheer political power[275] and at times expressed support for aggressive

[265] Letter to Windscheid of August 19, 1866, Jhering in Briefen (1913) 206–207.

[266] Letter to Otto von Bismarck of September 15, 1888, Jhering in Briefen (1913) 443.

[267] Jhering recounted his visit in great detail in *Jhering*, Drei Stunden im Hause des Fürsten von Bismarck; *Poschinger*, Bismarck und Jhering (1908) 9–41. The occasion arose when the University of Göttingen granted Bismarck, who had studied in Göttingen in 1832–33, a *doctor iuris honoris causae* on the occasion of his 70th birthday (1885). At the time, Jhering was dean of the law faculty and thus had to compose and sign the diploma. Instead of mailing it, Jhering traveled to Berlin at his own expense to deliver it in person. There, he carefully arranged to be invited to a private dinner with Bismarck and his family. Jhering felt that he was encountering not only a great man but an incarnation of history itself.

[268] Bismarck's letter to Jhering was short and to the point, Jhering in Briefen (1913) 445; Jhering's response was so long and rambling that Jhering felt the need to apologize at its end for tiring the reader, Jhering in Briefen (1913) 441–444.

[269] Jhering in Briefen (1913) 444.

[270] Letter to Windscheid of August 19, 1866, Jhering in Briefen (1913) 207.

[271] See infra chapter IV.2. notes 209–221 and text.

[272] *Giaro*, Jhering and Politics (2023).

[273] *Giaro*, Jhering and Politics (2023) 64–66.

[274] Infra chapter IV.2., notes 267–281 and text.

[275] For a discussion, see *Wieacker*, Rudolph von Jhering (1969) 9–10.

Western trade measures vis-à-vis other nations as well as negative views of primitive peoples – of whom he actually knew very little.[276] At the time, such views were widely shared in Jhering's environment and thus unlikely to raise many eyebrows. Still, they strike a modern reader as disconcerting, especially since in other contexts, Jhering displayed a liberal and humanist attitude as well as a fairly keen social conscience, as we will see in a moment. Ultimately, we must accept that here as well, Jhering was full of contradictions.

Political Convictions: Monarchist, Democrat, Liberal, Socialist. Even though Jhering's active engagement in politics was very limited, he did have political convictions. These convictions were largely matters of observation and opinion, not of advocacy or action. While their impact on the content of his work was, for the most part, neither heavy nor obvious, they influenced his assumptions and colored his views. Perhaps more importantly, they established an implicit baseline which must be kept in mind when considering his writings' implications. This is particularly true for the obvious dangers inherent in his view of law as a means to an end.

Unsurprisingly, Jhering's political views were as multifaceted as his societal positions.[277] He was – simultaneously – a monarchist, a supporter of limited democratic rule, a late nineteenth century liberal with a strong preference for equality, and even a moderate socialist.

With regard to the form of government, Jhering ended up as an avid monarchist. As mentioned, witnessing the expulsion of the *Göttinger Sieben* as a student had made him "not exactly devoted" to the monarchy,[278] although that did not mean that he supported its overthrow in favor of a republic. In his later years, however, he became an enthusiastic supporter of the constitutional monarchy in Prussia. This was largely due to his admiration for *Kaiser Wilhelm I,* the first emperor of the newly united nation (1871–1888), a personally modest and unassuming monarch who left important political decisions largely to the Empire's chancellor (head of government), Jhering's eventual idol Otto von Bismarck.[279]

Jhering supported a limited form of democratic rule: the voice of the people must be heard, the popular sense of justice respected, and an elected legislature must enact the laws necessary in a modern, industrializing society. Yet, he did not support a system of equal voting power for all. Voting power should be weighted, he thought – though not, as was actually the case, according to the amount of

---

[276] *Jhering*, Geist I (2d ed. 1866) 7 (on the native Indians in North America).

[277] Jhering discussed his political views very frankly with his son Hermann during a walk together in 1887 (at age 69). Hermann provided a detailed summary, *Hermann von Jhering*, Erinnerungen (1913) 445–472; reprinted in part also in *Fikentscher*, Methoden des Rechts III (1976) 159–161.

[278] Letter to Otto von Bismarck of March 30, 1890, Poscher, Bismarck und Jhering (1908) 46–48, at 43.

[279] Wilhelm was also King of Prussia 1861–1888. He was widely popular, especially among the educated middle class.

taxes paid,[280] but rather according to the voters' dedication to the common weal and their ability to understand politics. For *that* reason, the vote of the educated class (i.e., his own) should enjoy greater weight than that of peasants and workers.[281]

At the same time, Jhering was a fairly progressive mid- to late nineteenth century German liberal. Accepting inequality of social status and wealth as inevitable, and happily enjoying the privileges and comfortable life-style of the upper middle class, he was an ardent supporter of equality before the law. He supported tolerance in matters of religion (which had largely been practiced in Prussia since days of Frederick II., i.e., the mid-eighteenth century). In an environment where antisemitism was quite common,[282] Jhering made it clear that he had nothing against Jews.[283] In fact, he signed a petition for an association against Antisemitism.[284] His son-in-law Viktor Ehrenberg (1851–1929) was Jewish, fully integrated into the family, and always treated with great respect by Jhering, especially since Ehrenberg also became a recognized legal scholar.[285] Jhering was equally open-minded with regard to the "Frauenfrage," i.e., the then emerging issue of women's rights, which Jhering considered one of the most important social questions of the future. In settling it, he predicted, law will not play much of a role at first; instead social change will take the lead, law will then follow.[286] While full gender equality in all regards was largely beyond the imagination of his generation, his correspondence with several women outside of his family indicates that he took women of his class intellectually seriously. Also, at least his third wife was certainly no wallflower but a self-confident, intelligent, articulate woman.[287]

---

[280] The "Dreiklassenwahltrecht" ("three tier-voting system") prevailing in Prussia 1849–1918 (as well as in some other states and countries at the time) was a regime of general (though male only) franchise in which voting power was weighted according to the amount of tax paid.

[281] *Hermann von Jhering,* Erinnerungen (1912) 464.

[282] See *Massing*, Rehearsal for Destiny (1949); *W. Michael Blumenthal*, The Invisible Wall. Germans and Jews (1998) 200–235.

[283] Jhering recommended a young scholar to his friend Windscheid, adding: "It will matter to you as little as it matters to me that he is Jewish." Letter to Windscheid of December 30, 1883, Jherings Briefe an Windscheid (1988) 50, at 52.

[284] *Dove*, Rudolf von Jhering and Bernhard Windscheid (1893) 149.

[285] Jhering spoke of Ehrenberg as "my magnificent son-in-law," letter to Minna Unger of December 24, 1891, Jhering in Briefen (1913) 430, 432; in a similar vein, letter to Karl Binding of July 9, 1879, Jhering in Briefen (1913) 347. After Jhering's death, Ehrenberg edited and published two of Jhering's (unfinished) works, i.e., "Vorgeschichte der Indoeuropäer" (1894) and "Entwicklungsgeschichte des römischen Rechts" (1894).

[286] Letter to Auguste von Littrow-Bischoff, May 28, 1876, Jhering in Briefen (1913) 317.

[287] Still, there are indications that Jhering subscribed to the traditional and then prevalent notions concerning the respective positions of men and women in society, see, e.g., *Jhering*, Zweck II (1886) 614–615 (men are more truthful then women because that is a prerequisite for participation in public affairs and commerce, while women are more loving than men, largely because of their role as mothers).

As a liberal, Jhering complained about excessive regulation by the state (such as requiring a passport for travel![288]) and particularly about censorship.[289] Regulation of property and limitation of wealth, however, was not only acceptable but even desirable. While Jhering considered property, inheritance and other private rights important to a liberal order, he saw them by no means as something "eternal or unchangeable."[290] Instead, they were subject to limitation by legislation in the public interest: "Our civilization does not want the liberty, but the limitation of [the power of] the individual, the protection of the weak against the strong, equal law, equal welfare ('Fürsorge') for all."[291] Jhering supported a free-market economy (he had no kind words for "communism"[292]), but he also emphasized the need to "reign in the excesses of capitalism."[293] Thus Jhering's ideal of "liberty" was not unbridled (economic or personal) freedom but an ordered liberty that imposed the restrictions necessary for the common good, i.e., with due respect for the interests of all members of society.

As these utterances already indicate, Jhering even voiced support for ideas associated with the socialism much in ascendance at the time.[294] While he counseled against considering wealth as per se evil, he expressed sympathy for the suffering of the masses[295] and advocated a "fairer distribution" of goods and obligations in general[296] and of the tax burden in particular (e.g., through a progressive inheritance tax). He expressly supported the "improvement of the social conditions of the working class"[297] – not through revolution but through political reform.[298] A model of such reform was the introduction of state-mandated health

[288] *Jhering*, Kampf (1872) 76. See also *Jhering*, Geist I (1852) 116–117 ("Wahn, als müsse alles durch den Staat geschehen;" the "delusion that everything must be done by the state"); see also *Jhering*, Geist II.1. (1854) 130; In this regard, Jhering was quite in agreement with Savigny who, two generations earlier, had complained about the "Regierungssucht" ("obsession to regulate") of the times, lamenting "die unglückliche Richtung, alles zu regieren, und immer nur regieren zu wollen" ("the infelicitous direction to regulate everything, and always to want to just regulate"), *Savigny*, Stimmen für und wider neue Gesetzbücher (1816) 250.

[289] *Jhering*, Kampf (1872) 76–77.

[290] *Hermann von Jhering*, Erinnerungen (1913) 456.

[291] *Hermann von Jhering*, Erinnerungen (1913) 456.

[292] "Communism flourishes only in the swamp in which the idea of property has gotten completely lost," *Jhering*, Kampf (1872) 41.

[293] *Jhering*, Zweck I (1884) 134–139.

[294] When his son Hermann asked him (in 1887) whether he "by and large held a positive attitude towards the socialist propaganda," Jhering said yes; *Hermann von Jhering*, Erinnerungen (1913) 455.

[295] *Jhering*, Zweck II (1886) 172–173.

[296] *Jhrering*, Zweck I (1884) 532–535.

[297] *Hermann von Jhering*, Erinnerungen (1913) 456–457.

[298] *Hermann von Jhering*, Erinnerungen (1913) 455. See also *Jhering*, Zweck II (1886) 173 ("We will only defend ourselves against the errors and exaggerations of which [socialism] is guilty, if we acknowledge the truth which it can also claim for itself. To do so in practice is the task of politics and almost surely one of the most difficult ones we have had to face in the course of history. […] our time is a period of change.")

and social insurance for workers in the 1880s, which moved the Wilhelmine empire in the direction of a welfare state, and which Jhering considered a blessing.[299]

Jhering did not regard these quasi-socialist ideas as incompatible with the existing order and the monarchial constitution.[300] Instead, he emphasized the importance of striking the right compromises between the interests of the various classes. In fact, he saw these compromises either already at work or as possible under the constitutional monarchy of Wilhelmine Germany. At least later in life, part of the reason why Jhering was not more politically active was simply that he, by and large, supported the existing order.

All these contradiction, tensions, and facets of his person are reflected in Jhering's scholarship, in one way or another. They are perhaps the main reason why his writings are of such a puzzling diversity with regard to their topics, ambition, approach, and style. In some cases, it is actually difficult to believe that his works were produced by the same person. In fact, one can fairly argue that they were not because in a sense, there were several Jherings: the enthusiast and the pessimist, the jurist and the artist, the empiricist and the theorist, the realist and the idealist, the aristocrat and the bourgeois, the monarchist and the socialist, etc. These various Jherings often took positions that are difficult (or outright impossible) to reconcile. Thus, in looking at his scholarship, it is important to remain cognizant of which Jhering, or rather which combination of Jherings, was involved in producing a particular work.

---

[299] *Hermann von Jhering*, Erinnerungen (1913) 454; see also *Jhering*, Zweck II (1886) 174. The system was a brainchild of Bismarck who sought to appease the working class in order to weaken its support for the rising social democratic party (then called Sozialistische Arbeiterpartey Deutschlands).

[300] *Hermann von Jhering*, Erinnerungen (1913) 455.

Chapter II

Jhering's Internal Perspective – The Method and Doctrine of Law

For much of his life, Jhering, like most legal professionals, looked at law from what may be called an internal perspective: he concerned himself with the substance and method of positive law. For Jhering, that meant the Roman law as the foundation of private law in nineteenth century Germany (and beyond) – a time when private law constituted the core of the legal system and the primary object of legal theory.[1] His work thus focused, like that of most contemporary legal scholars in continental Europe, on *Dogmatik* which can roughly be translated as "doctrine." We use the term here in a broad sense that includes the structure of law, the proper technique of legal analysis, and the positive law's apparatus of rules, principles, and concepts.[2] This, "internal," perspective dominated Jhering's professional activity for roughly the first half of his career, i.e., the 1840s through the 1860s.

During that period, Jhering's work had several interconnected dimensions. The core was his overarching agenda to initiate a new jurisprudence that would lead beyond the contemporary use of Roman law; this agenda was the principal motivation for Jhering's multi-volume "Geist des römischen Rechts" (1852–1865) (infra 1.).[3] A crucial element of this agenda, in turn, was the development of

---

[1] See *Nörr*, Eher Hegel als Kant (1990) 11–15.

[2] *Dogmatik* is, of course, a complex concept with different shades of meaning in different contexts; for an extensive discussion, see *Herberger*, Dogmatik. Zur Geschichte von Begriff und Methode in Medizin und Jurisprudenz (1983). The meaning and function of *Dogmatik* has continued to occupy the minds of German scholars; see *Bumke*, Rechtsdogmatik. Eine Disziplin und ihre Arbeitsweise (2017); *Stürner*, Das Zivilrecht der Moderne und die Bedeutung der Rechtsdogmatik (2012). Unlike, e.g., in theology, *juristische Dogmatik* is not dependent on dogmas in the sense of timeless or unquestionable truths. Instead, it mainly denotes the technical side of legal reasoning. This kind of *Dogmatik* provides conceptual and structural clarity and consensus. It thus enhances the uniformity and stability of legal reasoning which German jurists (and many of their colleagues in the civil law tradition) have long considered indispensable for an ordered and predictable administration of law. For a narrower definition of *Dogmatik*, distinguishing and separating it from *Methode*, see *Fikentscher and Himmelmann*, Rudolph von Jherings Einfluß auf Dogmatik und Methode des Privatrechts (1995) 96–97.

[3] In his early years as a scholar, Jhering had also published several articles on a variety of topics which, however, had no lasting impact; for an overview, see *Mecke*, Rudolf von Jhering: Anonym publizierte Frühschriften (2010) 11–30.

a specific methodology that built on, but also pushed beyond, the ideas of his predecessors Savigny and Puchta; this methodology was also developed in "Geist" but most provocatively presented in Jhering's essay "Unsere Aufgabe" (1857) (infra 2.). In addition to these general projects, Jhering created a large body of specific doctrinal scholarship on particular issues of private law; the respective studies were published mainly as law review articles some of which became classics in the civil law tradition, most famously his piece on "*Culpa in contrahendo*" (1861) (infra 3.). Jhering was also involved in legal practice with some regularity, both as an expert and a quasi-appellate judge; he demanded that doctrinal work prove its mettle in practical application, an aspect he foregrounded in his talk "Ist die Jurisprudenz eine Wissenschaft?" (1868) (infra 4.). Finally, Jhering was of course not only a scholar but also an academic teacher who spent much of his time in the classroom imparting legal doctrine; he did so with great enthusiasm, success, and originality, as exemplified by his course materials, "Die Jurisprudenz des täglichen Lebens" (1870) (infra 5.). Having explored all these dimensions of Jhering's work during the first half of his academic life, we will conclude this chapter by situating Jhering's ideas in relation to the Historical School; the key text in this regard is Jhering's eulogy "Friedrich Karl von Savigny" (1861) (infra 6.).

1. Jhering's Jurisprudential Agenda: "Geist des römischen Rechts auf den verschiedenen Stufen seiner Entwicklung" (1852–1865)

Jhering's principal jurisprudential agenda during the first half of his career (and to some extent also beyond[4]) was the pursuit of a new jurisprudence which was to build on Roman law but ultimately lead beyond it. It was this agenda that drove him to write the magnum opus of the first twenty-some years of his academic life, the three-volume monograph on the "Geist des römischen Rechts auf den verschiedenen Stufen seiner Entwicklung" ("Spirit of the Roman Law at the Various Stages of Its Development").[5] The book laid the foundation for his fame not only among his German-speaking contemporaries but also, inter alia in multiple translations,[6] within the civil law orbit more generally. We will approach it in

[4] See infra chapter III.3.

[5] The idea to write a book about "the spirit of the Roman law" may have originated in Gustav Hugo's call for such a work in the introduction to his translation of Edward Gibbon's famous 44th chapter of "The Decline and Fall of the Roman Empire" (6 vols, London 1776–1789), see *Kunze*, Ein großer Jurist (2023) 14. The magnum opus of the second half of Jhering's academic life was of course his – equally monumental – two-volume "Der Zweck im Recht" (1877/1883) (literally "The Purpose in Law" but typically translated as "Law as a Means to an End"). It is the signature work of his external perspective on law, and we will turn to its two volumes in chapters IV.1. and VI.1., respectively.

[6] "Geist" was translated into all major Western languages (French, Italian, Portuguese,

several steps. For starters, the reader must be frankly informed about some of the work's general characteristics that make it difficult to access and grasp. We can then examine the jurisprudential agenda that it was supposed to promote. In this context, we need to recognize the crucial premise on which this agenda was based, i.e., the universality of Roman law. We will also take stock of the most important results generated by Jhering's search for the definitive features of Roman law – regarding the Roman mentality, the law itself, and the legal method. In closing, we will consider the academic reactions to the book – both by Jhering's contemporaries and by Jhering himself.

Approaching "Geist": Reader Beware! "Geist" is a monumental work,[7] a classic in the history of jurisprudence as well as a testament to Jhering's formidable learning, perceptiveness, and imagination. Yet, it is also an enormously difficult book. In approaching it, one should be aware of several features that can easily cause misunderstanding and confusion. A reader not interested in the general features of the work is invited to skip this section.

To begin with, the title's reference to "Roman law at the Various Stages of Its Development" can lead a reader to expect a book of legal history. That expectation is only partially justified. While the lion's share of the work is devoted to an historical portrait of law in antiquity, Jhering's objective was not to present a legal history in and of itself. Instead, he canvassed the "stages" of ancient Roman law only to find its "spirit" and then to use his findings to build a new jurisprudence. As Jhering himself emphasized (in the foreword to the second edition): the purpose of the work was not "essentially historical" but "rather of a legal-philosophical and doctrinal kind."[8] Thus, Jhering did not provide a full chronological account of the Roman law's development but rather a discussion of select elements that he thought revealed its characteristic features.[9] In addition to the historical material, much of the book consists of several, in part lengthy, methodological discourses. Jhering repeatedly switched back and forth between the historical and the methodological parts, and it is sometimes not easy for the reader to understand when and why. To be sure, for Jhering, both elements went hand-in-glove because he wanted to mine the Roman law, inter alia, for insight into the proper technique of law *tout court*; in the end, however, the methodological parts took on a life of their own. Since the historical and the methodological elements were not fully integrated, it is but a slight exaggeration to say that the book is two works in one – a (selective) history of ancient Roman law and

---

and Spanish) except English; there is, however, an English translation of the preface to the second edition of volume I (1866) which appeared in the Virginia Law Journal 4 (1880) 453–464, under the title "The Value of the Roman Law to the Modern World." "Geist" was also translated into Japanese in abbreviated form; for a list of translations, see *Kunze*, Lieber in Gießen (2018) 55–84.

[7] The first edition already contained a total of ca. 1400 pp.

[8] *Jhering*, Geist des römischen Rechts (1866) IX.

[9] On these features, see infra pp. 78–89.

a tract on legal method. Indeed, the historical and methodological parts have often been read more or less independently.

Even more generally, "Geist" is far from a monolithic and consistent work. It comprises three volumes published in four installments (Volume II has two parts) and written over a twenty-year period.[10] During that time Jhering's views changed in significant regards. This created internal tensions and even some inconsistencies between its earlier and its later parts. To make matters worse, Jhering published new editions of the various volumes at different times, sometimes rewriting the text to reflect new positions, sometimes not, thus often creating further contradictions.[11]. As a result, ascertaining Jhering's views often entails chasing a moving target. Franz Wieacker, one of Jhering's greatest admirers but also most astute critics, aptly remarked that exploring the book can be like walking on "quicksand."[12]

In addition, the book's architecture leaves a lot to be desired. Volumes I and II.1 still followed the overall plan announced in the Introduction, but in subsequent parts, Jhering increasingly departed from that plan and veered off in various directions, until, at the end of Volume III, he left the Roman sources largely behind and turned to constructing of a general theory of law. Thus, over time, the book's emphasis shifted from (Roman law) history to (general) methodology. Consistency of organization and faithful execution of a project were never Jhering's forte because sticking to a game plan was less important to him that pursuing new ideas. The resulting book was a "magic witches' brew"[13] – an eclectic, often rambling, frequently redundant, and sometimes outright self-contradictory work.[14]

---

[10] Some authors thus refer to four volumes. This is correct in the sense that there are four physical, separately bound, tomes. The second and the third books, however, constitute one volume (II); they have one table of contents and are consecutively paginated. Jhering himself spoke of the last volume as the third, letter to Windscheid of March 20, 1864, Jhering in Briefen (1913) 164, 166.

[11] Eventually, there were, depending on the volume, five or six editions, the last published posthumously. The citations in this subchapter are to the first edition unless otherwise marked. For present purposes, i.e., to understand the nature and scope of the Jhering's project, the first edition is a solid foundation. When looking at the development of Jhering's thought over time, however, additions and changes in later editions will have to be considered in several contexts.

[12] *Wieacker*, Rudolph von Jhering (1968) 11 ("Treibsand").

[13] *Stintzing and Landsberg*, Geschichte der deutschen Rechtswissenschaft III.2. (1910) 792 ("magischer Hexenbräukessel").

[14] It did not help that Jhering sought to address two different audiences at the same time. Surprisingly, he claimed to write principally for readers not versed in Roman law, specifically for law students and educated laymen, *Jhering*, Geist I (1852) Vorrede, VIII, 4–5. At the same time, however, he wanted to address specialists, i.e., his fellow-scholars of Roman law. As a result, the book oscillated between general discussions about the nature, development, and method of law on the one hand, and specific inquiries into the intricacies of ancient Roman law on the other. Jhering recognized the difficulties inherent in trying to serve two masters but

Last, but not least, the book remained woefully incomplete. Jhering set out to explore Roman law on three "levels of development."[15] Unfortunately, his discourse got stuck in the second level; before Jhering reached the third, he put the book aside to finish it later[16] – which he never did. Thus, the book fulfilled its promise to distill the "spirit" of Roman law from its history and sources only in part. Jhering largely failed to formulate final conclusions about the Roman law's essence – because he never got that far.[17]

In Jhering's defense, it must be acknowledged that he struggled mightily and for decades with the material, and that he acknowledged many of the book's problems. The scope of the project was so vast, and Jhering's ambition so high, that he repeatedly despaired of the difficulties he faced. In the Preface to the first volume, he lamented: "The more I believe to approach my goal, the more it vanishes from my view [...]; the more I work, the less I feel satisfied."[18] With his typical sense of irony, Jhering even claimed that he regretted having become involved with the wretched "spirit" at all, because it had soon become more like a demon ("Quälgeist" – "tormenting spirit"). It had acquired so much power over him, he quipped, that the only way to escape its grip was to take the plunge and publish a first volume, even though it was just a beginning and thus imperfect.[19] That, however, did not really solve the problem – even at later stages, Jhering lamented that "a subject like mine is inexhaustible."[20] To a significant extent, however, Jhering had himself to blame: while he surely did not lack the erudition, intelligence, nor the determination, to complete the task, he did lack the intellectual discipline to stay on course, stick to a coherent plan, and avoid biting off more than he could chew.

As a result, reading "Geist" is not only difficult, it can also be frustrating. It severely taxes its readers' patience with digressions, tests their tolerance for incoherence, and often requires their forgiveness for abrupt changes. It is true that the work rewards its readers with much penetrating insight, a lively style, and the fruits of a vivid imagination; in fact, there is scarcely a boring page. Still, at least today, studying the entire book is hardly worth anyone's time and effort, except for authors writing about Jhering, and even for them, ploughing through the whole work requires considerable grit.

---

believed that it would actually benefit the project. It would require the book to be clear and straightforward enough to be intelligible to a lay audience but also sufficiently grounded in expert knowledge to be acceptable to specialists. The success of Jhering's dual strategy is open to doubt. Much (though not all) of the book is of little interest to, and very difficult to understand by, readers without legal training. In sense, the book ended up being neither fish nor fowl.

[15] See infra notes 71–77 and text.

[16] See infra chapter IV.2.

[17] Jhering did, however, define a long and impressive list of fundamental features of (early) Roman law; see infra pp. 78–89.

[18] *Jhering*, Geist I (1852) VI.

[19] Jhering, Geist I (1852) V–VI.

[20] *Jhering*, Geist II.2. (1858) IV; see also *Jhering*, Geist III (1865) IV–V.

Jhering's Agenda: "Through the Roman Law Beyond the Roman Law." Fortunately, Jhering's overall agenda that motivated the book is more coherent than much of the rest of the work. Jhering laid out that agenda in the introduction to the first volume in about 80 pages and in a (by his standards) relatively clear and straightforward fashion: he was looking for the Roman law's "spirit" in order to make it the foundation for a new jurisprudence; that jurisprudence would eventually overcome the Roman law's reign as the positive (private) law in Germany (and beyond).[21]

This agenda was a reaction to the situation in which German private law found itself around the middle of the nineteenth century. Since its re-discovery and reception in the Middle Ages and early modern period, Roman law had been repeatedly modified over time, most recently by the *usus modernus pandectarum*, i.e., the scholarship and practice of the seventeenth and eighteenth centuries.[22] In that form it had become the *ius commune* of much of continental Europe (subject to local statutes and customs), including Germany.[23] In early nineteenth century Germany, Friedrich Carl von Savigny had initiated something like a second reception of Roman law: he had (dubiously) justified its adoption as an emanation of the spirit of the people (eventually termed *Volksgeist*), and successfully advocated a return to the purity of its classical sources, in particular the *Digest* (in Greek: *Pandects*) and the *Institutes*, i.e., the most important parts of Justian's early sixth century compilation of Roman law. Thus, in the early decades of the nineteenth century, Savigny (and his immediate successors) had fortified the – classical – Roman law's role as the bedrock of German private law in both theory and practice. This was the environment in which Jhering had been trained – and had thus become a "Romanist."

When Jhering began his academic career in the 1840s, however, these Savignian foundations were crumbling, both as a matter of legal theory and with regard to practical needs. With the end of the Romantic era, the concept of the *Volksgeist* had lost much of its appeal; the idea that the *Roman* law emanated from the spirit of the *German* people had increasingly come under attack; and the Historical School's conception of law as resulting from spontaneous organic growth and custom began to appear quaint, backward looking, and misguided.

---

[21] Jhering also discussed his program in his introductory article to the "Jahrbücher," i.e., "Unsere Aufgabe" (1857), though the emphasis there is much more on the requisite method(s) than on the fundamental notions of the project itself; see infra 2.

[22] As Reinhard Zimmermann remarked in his comments on this chapter, *the* Roman law as a consistent body of jurisprudence does not really exist; instead, there are multiple iterations over long periods of time. Still, Jhering (and his contemporaries) consistently spoke of "the Roman law" ("das römische Recht") – by which they by and large meant the classical sources.

[23] The term is commonly understood to also include the canon law (of the Catholic Church). Yet, as a result of ongoing secularization, in nineteenth century Germany, that element played a minor role in both theory and practice. Jhering and his Romanist colleagues paid it little, if any, attention.

On the practical side, the classical Roman law became increasingly unsatisfactory as well. It is true that as the law of the (largely) free market society of Roman antiquity, it had served much of early-modern continental Europe quite well. By the middle of the nineteenth century, however, the rapid industrialization and the rise of modern capitalism presented questions for which the Roman law had no answers – it had nothing to say about corporations, banks, insurance companies, letters of credit or intellectual property rights. Change was clearly needed. In the 1850s, there were growing calls for renewal in German legal academia. More and more scholars pushed for a deeper understanding of the classical Roman law's essence and for a re-thinking of its utility for present-day needs.[24] In the opinion of many, especially younger, scholars, the Roman law would eventually have to be replaced by a more modern system.[25] An additional impetus for change came from the political upheaval at the time, especially the 1848/49 Revolution that challenged the conservative order prevailing since the Congress of Vienna in 1815.[26]

Jhering was not only part of that broader movement, he was, and saw himself, at its forefront: he did not just want to re-think the inherited Roman law, he wanted to overcome it. His opening volley in "Geist" was unequivocal: "The current generation of jurists must be prepared to bid farewell to the Roman law in its current form."[27] At a time when – modernized – Roman law had long been, and continued to be, the foundation of positive (private) law, such a call for its abandonment bordered on heresy and caused outcries from more traditional quarters.[28] Jhering's blunt statement, however, masked a fairly sophisticated agenda.

Jhering did not advocate simply dumping Roman law – which, he emphasized, he held in extremely high esteem.[29] Notably, it was to be discarded only "in its

[24] For an overview of the contemporary movement to renew the jurisprudence of Roman law, see *Kuntze*, Wendepunkt der Rechtswissenschaft (1856). Kuntze knew not only the first volume of Jhering's "Geist" (published in 1852) but also Jhering's programmatic article "Unsere Aufgabe" (even though its official publication date was 1857). Kuntze's book describes the context in which Jhering's project must be situated. Viewed in this context, Jhering's agenda, as well as his methodological discourse, was somewhat less original than it appears when viewed in isolation. Jhering recognized that many of his ideas were shared by others, *Jhering*, Geist II.2. (1858) III–IV.

[25] See *Mecke*, Der Begriff des Rechts und die Methode der Rechtswissenschaft bei Rudolf von Jhering (2018) 193–194.

[26] See *Geib*, Die Reform des deutschen Rechtslebens (1848).

[27] *Jhering*, Geist I (1852) 2.

[28] See *Stintzing and Landsberg*, Geschichte der deutschen Rechtswissenschaft III.2 (1910) 793. Jhering's heretical position was probably part of the reason why he had to remain in Gießen for so long (1852–1868) before he finally received offers from larger and more prestigious universities.

[29] "Gefühl der höchsten Bewunderung und Verehrung, das ich vor dieser grandiosen Schöpfung empfinde" ("Feeling of utmost admiration and veneration that I have for this terrific creation"), *Jhering*, Geist I (1852) VIII. Jhering's language should be taken with a

current form"! Thus, he explained, discarding Roman law will "primarily concern its form, rather than its substance. It will no longer have the power of a code of law, but...it will provide a significant part of the material which we can use to build our new legal edifice, and thus a large sum of Roman legal principles will continue to exist in altered form."[30] Jhering later captured this program in one of his most famous phrases: he wanted to proceed "through the Roman law [...] beyond the Roman law" ("durch das römische Recht [...] über das römische Recht hinaus").[31] For Jhering, a true science of law could only begin when jurisprudence transcended the Roman sources.[32]

How was this to be accomplished? For starters, it required a critical "account" ("Abrechnung") of Roman law. In particular, Roman law would have to be examined from three different perspectives: a specifically historical view of Roman law itself; a "universal" assessment of its contribution to the development of law in general; and, finally, a legislative evaluation of its utility for present-day purposes.[33] Jhering hoped eventually to perform all these steps. In writing "Geist", however, he originally limited himself to the first, historical, inquiry: thus the book's specific goal became to illuminate the "spirit" of the Roman law at the various stages of its development.

Jhering's "Geist": The Essence of Roman Law. Yet, what exactly did Jhering mean by "spirit"? As so often, he did not provide a definition of his key term and used it rather haphazardly. He also used it in a variety of contexts in which it then took on different meanings. The resulting complexity can be somewhat disen-

---

grain of salt. There is no doubt that he admired many things about Roman law. Yet, his hyperbole here also served to assuage his Romanist colleagues who could well feel threatened by Jhering's call eventually to put the Roman law as such to rest. Jhering recognized that he was provoking harsh criticism from his colleagues which, he stated, he had no reason to resent since he was not mincing words himself, id. VIII. As time went on, Jhering became increasingly dismissive of Roman law as the current foundation of (German) private law. In 1872, he opined that "Roman law has long been surpassed by the German [i.e., modern legislative law]; all brave young people have turned to the latter, for Roman law only the residue is left, cripples and handicapped which are of no other use;" letter to Bülow of April 12, 1872, Jhering in Briefen (1913) 280, 281. He came to see Roman law scholars "in the process of proper petrification," and he predicted that "in 30 to 50 years", they would be "comical characters, antediluvian animals to be put into a museum;" id. 280. He concluded that "[o]ne should turn one's back to the whole nonsense," id.

[30] *Jhering*, Geist I (1852) 2.

[31] *Jhering*, Unsere Aufgabe (1857) 52; Jhering repeated that motto on various occasions, see, e.g., Geist I, 5th ed. 1891, 15. The idea was not as revolutionary as is often believed and as Jhering made it appear. A full generation earlier, Friedrich Carl von Savigny had already stated that once legal science had developed to the point where it has become the "common property of the jurists" ("das Gemeingut der Juristen") [...] Roman law can then be handed over to history," *Savigny*, Vom Beruf unserer Zeit (1814) 133.

[32] "Some claim [...] where the sources end, there also ends science. I, for one, claim that's where it properly begins." *Jhering*, Scherz und Ernst (1884) 126.

[33] *Jhering*, Geist I (1852) 3.

tangled by distinguishing three dimensions: the origin of the book's title, the strategy of Jhering's endeavor, and the nature of his ultimate quest. The first was rooted in Montesquieu's *Esprit*, the second in Hegel's *Weltgeist*, and the third in Savigny's *Volksgeist*.

The book's title of course immediately evokes Montesquieu's (1689–1755) "De'l esprit des loix" (1748)[34] with which Jhering was of course familiar.[35] Since his own choice of title capitalized on the by then century-old classic, it is tempting to assume that he also adopted an equivalent agenda. Yet, the many similarities between the two books notwithstanding,[36] they pursued different objectives. Montesquieu's point was to show the relationship between the laws of a nation and their environment (and to demand that the lawgiver tailor the laws to the respective conditions). Thus the "spirit" of the laws consisted of their specific *rapport* with a nation's constitution, customs, climate, religion, commerce, etc.;[37] as such, *esprit* was essentially an empirical concept. It is true that Jhering followed in Montesquieu's footsteps when he not only agreed that the law was shaped by its environment, but also repeatedly demonstrated how that was the case in ancient Rome. Still, that demonstration was not Jhering's primary objective but merely incidental to it. His main goal was to elucidate what was so special about Roman law that it was worth preserving for a modern jurisprudence. In short, the similarities of the books' titles masked fundamentally different orientations: Montesquieu's focus was on the law's relationship with its environment, Jhering's on its inherent qualities.

---

[34] Apparently, the first German translation was "Des Herrn von Montesquiou [sic] Werk von den Gesetzen" (Abraham Gottlieb Kaestner transl., Frankfurt and Leizpig 1753); modern German tranlations are entitled "Vom Geist der Gesetze."

[35] See, e.g., *Jhering*, Kampf ums Recht (1872) 38.

[36] Like Jhering, Montesquieu was a jurist who took a broad look at law in order to understand its essence, an endeavor in which Roman law played a major role for Montesquieu as well. Like Jhering, Montesquieu despaired over the project and lamented that his powers were insufficient for the task; *Montesquieu*, De' Esprit (1748) Preface xiii; it is quite possible that Jhering's own laments were (probably unconsciously) influenced by Montesquieu's. Also, like Jhering, Montesquieu had reason to despair because like "Geist", "Esprit" remained unfinished as well as fragmented and often quite chaotic. There are many parallels also with regard to the works' substance, such as their view of legislation as the most important source of law, their emphasis on self-preservation as a major influence on the shape of the legal order, their commitment to equality before the law, their aversion against excessive state regulation, their often overly favorable views of English society and law, and even their appreciation of the brevity and poignancy of the Roman XII tables. A full analysis of these (and various other) parallels would require a study in its own right. The extent to which these parallels evince an influence of Montequieu on Jhering will be difficult to fathom, however, because many of these ideas and themes were more broadly shared by eighteenth and early nineteenth century thinkers.

[37] The full title of the work was "De'l esprit des loix ou du rapport que les Loix doivent avoir avec la Constitution de chaque Gouvernement, les Moeurs, le climat, la Religion, le Commerce, e&." This relationship then shaped the *esprit general des loix*. As has often been noted, that idea was among the predecessors of the later (German) conception of *Volksgeist*.

The strategy of Jhering's endeavor, i.e., to demonstrate how the "spirit" of the Roman law had gone through several "stages of development," had nothing to do with Montesquieu but was essentially Hegelian. The idea that history (in general) went through such stages, guided by reason, was of course the core of Hegel's Philosophy of History.[38] In the specifically legal context it was employed by Hegel's disciple Eduard Gans (1797–1849) in his four-volume work on "Das Erbrecht in weltgeschichtlicher Entwickelung" ("The Law of Succession in its Universal-Historical Development") (1824–1835). Jhering was closely familiar with both these works. His own book betrayed the direct influence of their central idea that history (and law as part of it) evolved in an ordered and progressive fashion.[39] Thus Jhering endeavored to trace the Roman law's development from its earliest and primitive forms to its later and more sophisticated ones. That said, tracing the evolution of Roman law in a quasi-Hegelian fashion was not the ultimate objective of Jhering's work either but, like his demonstration of the law's relationship with its environment, incidental to it. We must remember that Jhering analyzed the development of Roman law not for its own – historical – sake but in order to distill its enduring qualities. In other words, for Jhering, the quasi-Hegelian perspective was just the medium through which the Roman law's essence revealed itself over time.[40] History itself had chosen the Romans to fulfill its mission with regard to the development of law.[41]

Jhering's ultimate quest for the essence of the Roman law was still partially rooted in Savigny's *Volksgeist* theory.[42] We will have to explore Jhering's changing views of that theory in greater depth below.[43] Here, it suffices to recognize that when Jhering's book project took shape in the 1840s, he still subscribed to Savigny's idea, in the sense that he regarded the law as shaped by the character traits of a particular people. It is interesting to note that in contrast to the title of Jhering's book, the text itself talks not about the "spirit" of the Roman law (as law), but rather (virtually consistently) about the "Roman spirit" i.e., the "spirit" of the Romans as a people.[44] The *Geist* of the Roman people determined the *Geist*

---

[38] *Hegel*, Philosophie der Geschichte (1840/48) 108, 117, 136.

[39] See, e.g., *Jhering*, Geist I (1852) 61 (a priori assumption that in the history of the law there is a "successive unity"); id. 99 ("the huge progress of history"). See also the discussion by *Rückert*. Der Geist des Rechts (2004) 136–140; and *Rückert*, Das Methodenorakel (2019) 467–469, 480–481.

[40] While "the Roman law cannot be understood without considering its history," Jhering, Geist I (1852) 11, the task of understanding it is ultimately "a matter of the philosophy of history" ("geschichtsphilosophischer Art"), *Jhering*, Geist II.2. (1858) v.

[41] "The reason why the Romans were so much in need of law was... that history needed *them* for law. Their own interest forced them to fulfill the mission which had been assigned to them with regard to the law; living for themselves, they served the world." *Jhering*, Geist I (1852) 304.

[42] Jhering occasionally used that very term, see, e.g., *Jhering*, Geist I (1852) 293; see also infra 6., note 482 and text.

[43] Infra 6, notes 486–499 and text.

[44] See *Jhering*, Geist I (1852) 77, 161, 215, 257, 265, 291; *Jhering*, Geist II.1. (1854) 49, 121, 122; etc.

of the Roman law.[45] Still, when Jhering used the term *Volksgeist*, he did not mean exactly the same thing as Puchta and Savigny. The former had been referring to cultural tradition, whereas Jhering looked at psychological make-up: what shaped the Roman law were the basic features of the Roman people's mentality.[46] Thus, when Jhering looked for "the true essence" ("das wahre Wesen"), "the leading ideas" ("die leitenden Ideen") or, more vaguely still, "the psychological organism" ("den psychischen Organismus") of the Roman law,[47] his quest was to identify its defining features as shaped by the Roman character. What these features are will be discussed below.[48]

Even if we distinguish *Geist* in the potentially misleading title, *Geist* as a feature of historical evolution, and *Geist* as the sum of the characteristic properties of the Roman people and its law, there remains a fair amount of overlap, imprecision, and thus confusion. In early and mid-nineteenth century Germany, *Geist* was a popular term that was employed in many contexts and meanings. Jhering's sloppiness in using it came at the expense of his readers who were left with much vagueness and ambiguity. Jhering himself also increasingly recognized the inherent perils of this multifaceted expression, especially the danger of being led astray by one's own imagination.[49] Later in life, he actually regretted having used the term in the book's title at all.[50]

Still, Jhering's ultimate objective in "Geist" was clear: he wanted to understand and demonstrate exactly "what distinguishes Roman law so favorably from other laws"[51] – something that he thought had not been done yet.[52] More-

[45] At one point, Jhering actually presented them as identical, *Jhering*, Geist I (1852) 34.

[46] See infra notes 79–90 and text.

[47] *Jhering*, Geist I (1852) 11; *Jhering*, Geist II.1. (1854) 3.

[48] Infra pp. 78–89.

[49] Jhering addressed the problem right away in the preface (*Vorrede*), *Jhering*, Geist I (1852) VII. He returned to the matter later in the text: "With some who ventured out to search the spirit of a matter, that spirit has played its tricks [...]." ("Schon mit Manchem, der ausging, den Geist einer Sache zu suchen, hat dieser Geist ein neckisches Spiel getrieben [...]"). Id. 38. Jhering, was perhaps inspired by *Goethe's* poem "Der Erlkönig" ("The Elf-King", 1782) and playfully alluded to the will-o'-the-wisp luring travelers off their path to perish in bogs and swamps, id. 37.

[50] *Jhering*, Geist I (5th ed. 1891) VIII.

[51] *Jhering*, Geist I (1852) 8. This was not quite true as Jhering must have known. In one of the Historical School's foundational texts, Savigny had explained at least one of the Roman law's virtues: the exactitude of its concepts which allowed the jurists to use them almost as in mathematics ("gleichsam mit ihnen rechnen"), *Savigny*, Vom Beruf unserer Zeit (1814) 29. This was probably what Jhering referred to when he argued that praising the ability of the Roman *jurists* was not the same as determining the superior quality of Roman *law*, *Jhering* 1852, Geist I (1852) 8. This is true enough, of course; Jhering failed to explain, however, how to distinguish one from the other.

[52] To be sure, Jhering admitted, there was no lack of lavish praise for Roman law, but much of it was mainly emotional and most of it was quite nebulous; *Jhering*, Geist I (1852) 6. This was, he argued, because jurists always looked at Roman law with a microscope; thus they observed it only on a the level of minute detail – "they could see the blood circulating, so to

over, he wanted to elucidate the essential features of Roman law in particular to then define the desirable characteristics of law in general. Once the true and enduring qualities of Roman law were understood, they could be evaluated and used to shape a modern jurisprudence overcoming it.

Jhering's Crucial Premise: The Universality of Roman Law. In "Geist," there is a pervasive tension between Jhering's ultimate goal of a new jurisprudence and his engagement with Roman law in antiquity. On the one hand, Jhering's goal was general and theoretical: he sought to contribute to the development of a "general theory of the nature of law" ("allgemeine Naturlehre des Rechts").[53] On the other hand, his approach was specific and historical: he reminded the reader that the present task, i.e., the inquiry in "Geist," had to be historical in nature "because Roman law cannot be evaluated without engaging with its history."[54] The connection between these two dimensions lay in a crucial premise on which Jhering's whole project was based: the centrality of Roman law in particular for jurisprudence not only in Germany but throughout the (Western) world in general. That premise is easily overlooked because Jhering did not clearly state it when he first published "Geist." He did, however, explain it at some length in an expanded introduction to the second edition.[55]

For Jhering, Roman law was far more than merely the product of an ancient society (as such, it was just an historical phenomenon). It was also far more than merely the current common private law of Germany (as such, it could, and should, soon be abandoned). Instead, Roman law was a repository of universally valuable features of law *tout court*, and as such a proper starting point for a general jurisprudence.[56] To be sure, at the time, that view was nothing out of the ordinary. It had already been propagated by Puchta[57] and was widely shared by his Romanist colleagues who continued to regard Roman law as *ratio scripta*. They had not, however, provided much of a reason for that view. It was Jhering who went beyond that simple, idealist, assumption and based his view of the Roman law's universal significance on two central aspects: its development from a national to a universalist stance in antiquity, and its unifying effect on law throughout the civilized world in the early modern period.

---

speak, through the smallest and most insignificant parts of the Pandects or Gaius;" *Jhering*, Geist I (1852) 9. What was needed instead was a view through a telescope, i.e., a view of the whole, id. 10.

[53] *Jhering,* Geist I (1852) 11.

[54] *Jhering*, Geist I (1852) 11.

[55] *Jhering*, Geist I (2d ed. 1866) 1–16.

[56] Even though Jhering was keenly aware of the variations of law across time and space, and even though he strongly believed that its content depended entirely on the respective societies' social conditions and historical stage of development, see infra chapter IV.2., he also believed in certain universally shared features. The Roman jurists had captured at least some of these features in their concepts and discussions of a law common to all peoples, i.e., a *jus gentium*; see *Jhering*, Zweck II (1886) 400–401.

[57] *Puchta*, Gewohnheitsrecht I (1828) 202 (Roman law as "Weltrecht").

Jhering saw Roman law as originally developed in the specific national context of early Rome; since the late Republic, however, it had taken a universalist turn because now it had to govern not only Rome itself but an empire populated by both citizens and aliens and marked by enormous diversity.[58] This shift had destined Roman law for lasting glory because its newly acquired universalism made it suitable for other nations and cultures as well.[59]

Through its universalist character, Roman law had unified the law of continental Europe when it was adopted in the late Middle Ages and early modern period through the process commonly termed "reception". Together with law of the (Catholic) Church, it had become the *ius commune* – the common basis of learning internationally shared by European jurists, leading to the "pinnacle of European universality."[60] Like Christianity, and like Greek and Roman literature and art, Roman law had become "a *cultural element* of the modern world."[61] This gave it a broad and lasting significance overarching regional and local laws.

This view led Jhering to reassess the "reception" of Roman law in continental Europe. He mocked the Historical School's attempt to explain it through the notion of the *Volksgeist*: it obviously made no sense to justify the prevalence of the *Roman* law as a reflection of the spirit of the *German* people.[62] Instead, the reception was justified as a bequest of the Roman law's universality to most of modern Europe. Jhering opened the later editions of *Geist* with a powerful assertion of Rome's cultural heritage.

"Thrice Rome dictated laws to the world, thrice it unified the peoples, first when the Roman people was still in full vigor, establishing the unity of the State, a second time, after it [the Roman people, M.R.] had already vanished, creating the unity of the church, a third time as a result of the reception of the Roman law in the middle ages, producing the unity of law. In short, the global historical significance and the mission of Rome is the overcoming of the nationality principle through the idea of universality."[63]

As a result of this history, Roman law was not just one law among others but *the* law at the very center of (at least continental) European civilization.[64] It was the

[58] *Jhering*, Geist I (1852) 81–82; *Jhering*, Geist I (2d ed. 1866) 84.

[59] In this regard, Jhering even compared it with the natural law of the previous centuries, *Jhering*, Geist I (2d ed. 1866) 11.

[60] *Jhering*, Geist I (2d ed. 1866) 10. "This community, what an uplifting feeling, and generally, how enviable the then-existing state of jurisprudence!" id. Jhering lamented that in his own time, the period of the *ius commune* had come to an end with the return of the nationality principle in Savigny's teachings (and also with the advent of national codifications); this motivated him to call for more comparative studies in search of a new universality, id. 14–15. On Jhering's role for the development of comparative law as a discipline in its own right, see infra chapter VII.4., notes 369–397 and text.

[61] *Jhering*, Geist I (2d ed. 1866) 4, 14. Jhering was largely right: Roman law has been the foundation of private law on a truly global level, very much so in the civil law orbit, and to a considerable extent even in common law realm.

[62] *Jhering*, Geist I (2d ed. 1866) 3–5.

[63] *Jhering*, Geist I (2d ed. 1866) 1.

[64] Jhering did not tackle the question to what extent the Roman law had also influenced

law that had "changed our legal thought entirely."[65] Thus, understanding the Roman law's essence promised recognition of features that "have a claim to universal truth."[66] This required separating what was peculiarly Roman from what was universally valid – the former would have to be discarded, the latter preserved.[67]

The Quest for the Roman Law's Spirit: An Unfinished Mission. Jhering thus went to work and examined early Roman law in search of its "spirit." He focused primarily on private law and procedure, which occupied the bulk of the Roman sources. He did touch on criminal law (e.g., its origins in revenge)[68] and public law (e.g., the power of the Roman magistrates)[69] as well, but his thinking was guided by, and geared towards, the paradigm of private law which he considered the most significant heritage of the early Roman period.

What did Jhering find? Surprisingly, that question has rarely been asked, and to my knowledge, has never been substantially answered in the voluminous literature on Jhering. Several books and many more chapters and articles have been written about his methodology, and historians of Roman law have discussed several of his more particular points and interpretations.[70] But Jhering's quest for the Roman law's "spirit", that lay at the very heart of the book, has enjoyed disappointingly scant attention.[71]

It is tempting to assume that because Jhering failed to complete the work, he also failed to reach any interesting conclusions. That assumption, however, would be dead wrong. Jhering did present a large variety of features that for him expressed the "spirit" of Roman law and, thus, presumably gave it lasting value.

Before we turn to these features, however, we must recognize an important limitation: "Geist" deals only with the early period of Roman law. As mentioned,

---

the common law of England – an issue much debated on the other side of the Channel and the Atlantic at the time; see *Reimann*, Historische Schule und Common Law (1993) 147–155; *Graziade*i, Changing Images of the Law in XIXth Century English Legal Thought (1993).

[65] *Jhering*, Geist I (2d ed. 1866) 3.

[66] *Jhering*, Geist I (1852) 11.

[67] "It is crucial to recognize what is specifically Roman, then its power over us, its spell, is broken," letter to Gerber of February 12, 1854, Jhering in Briefen (1913) 39.

[68] See, e.g., *Jhering* Geist I (1852) 197–201.

[69] *Jhering*, Geist II.1. (1854) 267–303.

[70] Infra Ch. VII.4., notes 320–336 and text.

[71] An exception of sorts is *Schulz*, Prinzipien des römischen Rechts (1934; Prinziples of Roman Law, 1936); see infra chapter VII.4., note 333. In a slim volume published in 1995, Alan Watson also undertook to identify "The Spirit of the Roman Law." Watson's account not only significantly overlaps with Jhering's, in many parts it is so similar that it strongly suggests an adoption of Jhering's insights. Watson, however, gives Jhering virtually no credit other than calling him his "hero" in the Preface, *Watson*, Spirit of the Roman Law (1995) XI. In fact, in all of Watson's copious endnotes, id., 209–235, "Geist" is mentioned only once, and just in a most general fashion, id. 209. Thus Watson creates the impression that his ideas are all original whereas most of them had already been presented by Jhering more than a century earlier.

Jhering had planned to discuss three "stages of development"[72] but covered only the first two: "The Origins of Roman Law" ("Die Ausgangspunkte des römischen Rechts"), which he found in the conditions and ideas that the Romans brought with them from their Indo-Germanic past, when they first settled in central Italy (discussed in the first volume of "Geist"),[73] and "The Specifically Roman Legal System" ("Das spezifisch römische Rechtssystem"), which Jhering saw evolving in the first four centuries of Rome (addressed in volumes II and III but left incomplete). Since the first system was essentially a prelude to the second, which absorbed many (though not all) of its fundamental features, one can (with some caveats) look at them together.[74] Thus, even though Jhering avoided clear temporal markers, it is fair to say that "Geist" deals with Roman law roughly from the sixth through the late third centuries B.C.

Jhering never reached the third "system" which he envisaged as the stage that transcended the "national" orbit and developed a "cosmopolitan" and "international" law, served an empire, and was destined to regulate human interaction in a global context.[75] "Geist" thus failed to cover what most scholars have traditionally considered the most important and influential parts of Roman law, i.e., the "classical period," which generated the work of the most important Roman jurists (ca. 30 B.C. to 250 A.D.), as well as Justinian's compilation (528–534 A.D.) through which Roman law was eventually bequeathed upon the middles ages and early modern times. While this omission was a severe shortcoming, it by no means rendered Jhering's account nugatory, however. Jhering himself was convinced that many of the most intriguing features of Roman law emerged in the second system, which then laid the lasting foundations for the third stage.[76] Still, the book, as actually written, should have been entitled "The Spirit of the Roman Law during the Early Stages of Its Development."[77]

---

[72] *Jhering*, Geist I (1852) 77–82.

[73] Jhering increasingly developed an interest in exploring the earliest states of legal development at the very dawn of history; towards the end of his life, he eventually devoted a whole book to that endeavor, i.e., "Vorgeschichte der Indo-Europäer" (posthum 1894); see infra Ch. VI.3.

[74] Jhering did not envisage the various "stages" in a strictly chronological sequence. While he portrayed them as successive phases, he conceived of the systems as layers that were piled on top of each other, see *Jhering*, Geist I (1852) 76. The earlier system were thus not necessarily abrogated by the later ones but rather absorbed and altered by them. As a result, there was much overlap: some of the older features persisted, some were gradually modified, some disappeared. In the end, Roman law was an amalgamation of all these "systems," displaying features of each.

[75] *Jhering.* Geist I (1852) 81. A convenient marker for the beginning of the third system would thus be the emergence of the *praetor preregrinus* in 242 B.C.

[76] *Jhering*, Geist II.1. (1854) 6; *Jhering*, Geist III (1865) 7. Note that a generation earlier, Savigny had already claimed, in a somewhat similar vein, that the material of classical Roman jurisprudence (for Jhering the "third system") was largely a product of the time of the free republic, Savigny, Vom Beruf unserer Zeit (1814) 31.

[77] Of course, the more than three centuries covered by "Geist" brought enormous changes:

When asked about the defining elements of these early stages, most Roman law scholars would point to the Twelve Tables, i.e., the foundational codification of private and procedural law (449 B.C.); the rigid process of the *legis actio* under which all claims had to be based on some statutory ground; and the overall strictness of law (*ius strictum*) that favored categorical rules and predictability of results over judicial discretion and justice in the individual case. Of course, Jhering discussed these features as well but for him, they were still external elements that lay easily visible on the surface. Jhering sought to drill considerably deeper and sweep significantly broader in order to catch the "spirit" that animated these and other phenomena.

A full discussion of Jhering's multifaceted findings (spread out over hundreds of pages) would require a book-length study in its own right; here, a brief summary must suffice. The character traits Jhering presented can be grouped into three clusters: the features defining the Roman mentality with regard to law (outlined mainly in vol. I), those pertaining to the law itself (discussed in volumes I and II.1), and those concerning the technique by which it was handled and developed (covered mainly in volumes II.2. and III).[78]

The Spirit of the Roman Law Determined I: The Underlying Mentality. As mentioned, for Jhering, the Roman law's "spirit" was rooted in the Roman people's "character" ("Volkscharakter")[79]. Looking at Jhering's ideas on that topic is important not only because they directly shaped his understanding of the Roman law's "spirit;" it also matters because here, Jhering already introduced two ideas which would eventually become dominant themes in his later, sociological, jurisprudence: egoism and purposefulness.

According to Jhering, the basic Roman character trait ("Grundzug des römischen Wesens")[80] was egoism ("Selbstsucht"); it was even more important than

from monarchy to republic, from smallish city-state to major Mediterranean power, from primitive and largely agrarian to sophisticated and diversified economy, etc. While Jhering alluded to all these changes on various occasions, on the whole, he emphasized not change but continuity. After all, his project was to define the "spirit" that animated Roman law at each of its stages in their entirety. He thus concentrated on the enduring features that gave each "system" its particular profile. His model in this regard was the famous 44th chapter of *Edward Gibbon's* Decline and Fall of the Roman Empire (1776–1789); see *Jhering*, Geist I (1852) 48 (fn. 26). In addition, Jhering considered continuity one of the most important hallmarks of early Roman law. He repeatedly emphasized how the law of the Twelve Tables endured as the cornerstone of the Roman legal system for centuries, see, e.g., *Jhering*, Geist II.2. (1858) 35, 64–69. Jhering regarded that tenacity as a virtue because it showed the law's moral force, *Jhering*, Geist I (1852) 63, and it bred and ensured respect for the law, Jhering, Geist II.2. (1858) 22–23.

[78] In addition, "Geist" presents a portrait of the early Roman social and political order which, however, is highly idealized; see *Reimann*, Jhering's "Geist des römischen Rechts" as a Study of Ancient Social Order (2022).

[79] *Jhering*, Geist I (1852) 291. Its description and interpretation is the subject of a special chapter in Volume I, entitled "Das Wesen des römischen Geistes," (which could be translated as "the essence" or "the gist of the Roman spirit"), *Jhering*, Geist I (1852) 201–314 (sec. 20).

[80] *Jhering*, Geist I (1852) 292.

will power, courage, and the sense of honor. Jhering did not, however, mean individual, selfish, short-term egoism but rather a "disciplined," collective, and "farsighted" ("weitsichtig") version: it subordinated momentary individual desires and wants to the long-term needs and well-being of the state.[81] The Romans' egoism thus meant that they always pursued the advantage of their own community. Decades later, Jhering would again foreground egoism as the ultimate driver of *all* human action, as well as the need to harness it (inter alia through law) to make it socially useful.[82] In a similar vein, Jhering praised the ancient Romans for being able to combine their love of liberty with the acceptance of necessary limitations; they understood that "in order to become power, liberty must impose limits upon itself."[83]

The second major feature of the Roman character was "purposefulness" ("Zweckmäßigkeit"). It was the "prism of the Roman perception,"[84] the inescapable perspective from which they saw the world and acted in it, consciously or unconsciously. "The Romans [...] cannot do anything that is inexpedient ('zweckwidrig'); they automatically hit on what is purposeful."[85] In other words, they were a deeply pragmatic people in all their undertakings. Eventually, "pupose" ("Zweck") would of course become the lodestar of Jhering's later, sociological, theory of law.[86]

With egoism providing the driving force and purposefulness of the direction, the Romans created a law that was designed to advance the goals of their community: a strict law free from emotions or concerns of individualized justice.

"The Romans have succeeded from early times, to move the law from the realm of emotions to that of calculating reason, to turn it into an external mechanism free from momentary subjective ethical views [...] thus law becomes explainable and readable. It signifies the triumph of purposefulness over subjective ethical feelings."[87]

---

[81] *Jhering*, Geist I (1852) 292, 296–297, 299.

[82] Infra chapter IV.2., notes 234–247 and text. Jhering also provided an explanation why of all peoples (in antiquity) the Romans were the ones to develop such a sophisticated legal system and culture. Beyond the factors already mentioned, i.e., egoism and pragmatism, he attributed their penchant and talent for law to their will power, endurance, and moral fibre (rather than their sheer intelligence which Jhering rated below that of the Greeks); their ability not only to tolerate tensions and contradictions but also to turn them into a source of strength and unity (rather than strife and division); their collective egoism, i.e., their relentless pursuit of advantage for their state and society; and their pragmatism, i.e., their eye for practical purposes and effects; *Jhering*, Geist I (1852) 285–314. These explanations are thought-provoking and have a certain psychological and sociological appeal. Still, even a casual knowledge of Roman history and law reveals that Jhering idealized the Republican Romans in an often (though not entirely) uncritical and speculative fashion.

[83] *Jheing*, Geist I (1852) 160 ("dass die Freiheit, um Macht zu sein, sich selbst Schranken auferlegen muss").

[84] *Jhering*, Geist I (1852) 295.

[85] *Jhering*, Geist I (1852) 295.

[86] Infra chapter IV.2.

[87] *Jhering*, Geist I (1852) 301.

This entailed casting the law into the form of abstract norms.

"The individual case is being subordinated, and sacrificed, to the general rule. This subordination is a postulate of purposefulness, it provides social interaction ('Verkehr') with the necessary security by proffering legal decisions which are uniform and predictable in advance."[88]

In short, as a result of the combination of egoism and purposefulness, the strict law in early Rome was not about ethics or justice but merely about ensuring the functioning, and promoting the well-being, of society through a set of clear and predictable rules.

While Jhering's description of the Roman character often suggests admiration, he was quite frank about the downsides: egoism and purposefulness had their strengths, but they also exacted a steep price.

"The insatiable demon of the Roman egoism sacrifices everything to its purpose, the happiness and blood of its own citizens and the nationality of other peoples. Emotions and fantasy recoil from its icy breath, and the graces flee its presence. For it [i.e., egoism, MR], only purpose or means to an end have any value. Its world is one without soul, bereft of the most beautiful things."[89]

Once again, we see two Jherings. The intellectual Jhering was bound to describe what he saw – and, thus, had to give egoism and purposefulness their due; but the artistic and emotional Jhering reacted with horror to the bleakness he confronted.[90]

Jhering's rendition of the Roman people's character, and of its influence on the character of their law, was largely a result of his own thinking. He did not adduce any empirical evidence or reference any sources. In other words, it was not solid "science" but creative interpretation. Yet, it deeply informed his view of the basic features of early Roman law and legal method.

The Spirit of the Roman Law Determined II: The Law Itself. Jhering characterized the law of early Rome by highlighting a long list of pervasive and often interrelated features. Some of them are fully developed in their own chapters,[91] others are mentioned in various contexts throughout the book, often in a haphazard fashion. Once again, Jhering's account is not always fully coherent, his organization is frequently flawed, and his readers must often assemble the bits and pieces as best they can. Although Jhering did not divide the various features of law itself in that fashion, close inspection reveals that some of them pertained to

---

[88] *Jhering*, Geist I (1852) 301.

[89] *Jhering*, Geist I (1852) 300.

[90] Jhering also repeatedly cautioned – others as well as himself – not to judge ancient institutions and attitudes by modern standards, *Jhering*, Geist I (1852) 192–194; *Jhering*, Geist II.1. (1854) 123.

[91] Alluding (as he often did) to biology and psychology, Jhering called the most significant ones "Triebe" which can be translated as (instinctive) "drives," *Jhering*, Geist II.1. (1854) 20–320.

the law's general nature – autonomy, rationality, formalism, strictness, publicity, and plasticity, while others involved ideas that affected the law's substance – power, liberty, equality, and purposefulness. Beyond all that lies what one may call the centrality of law in early Rome.

Pride of place among the first set of features belongs to the law's autonomy. Law was autonomous because over time, it had emancipated itself from other kinds of normative orders – first from religion (*ius* separated from *fas*), then from morality (as well as from custom and other, merely social, norms)[92]. Leaving the former to the priesthood, the latter in the hands of the *censors,* law thus became the domain of specialized professionals (eventually the jurists).[93] For Jhering, this autonomy entailed something like a minimalist conception of the discipline: early Roman law was not meant to enforce religious precepts, moral norms, nor ideas of a good life; its function was merely to protect private rights and guarantee public order.

Law was rational and formalistic. Cast in the form of general and abstract statutory rules, it transcended the individual case.[94] Its rules stated clear commands based on simple facts and were easy to apply. Since they excluded personal feelings or considerations of individualized justice, their application and interpretation largely turned on the operation of logic. The law's autonomy vis-a-vis religion and morality, its reduction to abstract rules, and the focus on their logical operation, entailed formalism in the sense that the law disregarded substantive notions of right and wrong. Law operated in an essentially mechanical fashion.[95] As a result, legal analysis resembled solving a mathematical problem.[96] Thus law became calculable, predictable, and equal for all – a development Jhering counted among the most important accomplishments in the law's evolution.[97] Half-a-century later, these features would of course reappear in Max Weber's (1864–1920) concept of (formal) "logical rationality."[98]

The law's formalism, however, also entailed rigidity – not only in the analysis of law but also in its application. Legal commands were strictly enforced, if need be to the point of mercilessness and cruelty.[99] Justice could cry out against such

[92] *Jhering* 1854, 20–86 ("Selbständigkeitstrieb"); at the earliest (first) stage, these normative orders had still been merged, id., 78.

[93] For a more thorough analysis and discussion of this feature of Roman law, see *Frier*, Autonomy of Law and Origins of the Legal Profession (1989).

[94] *Jhering*, Geist II.1. (1854) 20–86.

[95] Jhering saw the roots of the law's formalism in the Roman tradition of military discipline, *Jhering*, Geist I (1852) 255. To be sure, this was, once again, speculation but it was quite plausible.

[96] *Jhering*, Geist I (1852) 300, 302. Jhering discussed the methodological side of formalism extensively in Geist II.1. (1858) 496–695.

[97] *Jhering*, Geist I (1852) 300–301; Jhering, Geist II.1. (1854) 30–35.

[98] *Weber*, Economy and Society (1978, orig. 1922) 656–658; see infra chapter VII.4., notes 348–357 and text.

[99] *Jhering*, Geist I (1852) 79 ("unerbittliche, grausame Konsequenz").

enforcement – but usually in vain. It must be remembered that the law's function was not to do equity in the individual case but to lay down and enforce clear and simple rules that actors broke at their peril.

Jhering also emphasized the early Roman law's "publicity" ("Őffentlichkeit") and "plasticity" ("Plastik") both of which made the operation of law observable. Law took place largely in public. Courts sat under the open sky, transactions were made in the public space, and the execution of law was a public affair, showing that law had a good conscience and, thus, nothing to hide. In addition, the creation of legal effects required visible, often symbolic, acts or at least openly spoken and often highly specific formulas. In early Rome, law could be seen and heard.[100]

Among the features that shaped the law's substance, Jhering's central idea was its rootedness in personal power: rights were first acquired through the sheer will and initiative of the individual (e.g., by taking property in conquest).[101] This origin in force (if not violence) was a major reason why the early Romans conceived of law essentially as a matter of power, rather than of justice or morality (a conception which Jhering would later forcefully endorse in "Zweck"[102]). It was also the substantive reason underlying the rigid enforcement of rights in early Rome.[103]

Even more importantly, for Jhering, this factor led directly to one of the most significant features of early Roman law: liberty. Since "the original source" ("Urquell") of law was individual power, not the state,[104] "the whole sphere of private law [lay] outside of the state's domain."[105] Private rights were the realm of "autonomy of the individual,"[106] and thus of freedom from state authority. State power came into play only to enforce private rights, when self-help was ineffective. The original independence of private rights from the state had three major implications. First, for Jhering, it signified nothing less than the "discovery of private law" which Jhering counted among the Roman law's most important and enduring contributions to jurisprudence; it was "an accomplishment that every people can and should make use of, even if it is otherwise not in the least similar to the Romans."[107] Second, since the state had not granted private rights, it lacked unbridled power to limit them.[108] Finally, and in the grand scheme of things perhaps most importantly, the independence of private rights from the state laid

[100] *Jhering*, Geist II.1. (1854) 9–19.

[101] *Jhering*, Geist I (1852) 103–115.

[102] See infra chapter IV.1, notes 194–221 and text.

[103] *Jhering*, Geist I (1852) 123–161.

[104] *Jhering*, Geist I (1852) 146.

[105] *Jhering*, Geist I (1852) 206. Of course, Jhering recognized the affinity between this understanding and traditional natural law theory, id. 218.

[106] *Jhering*, Geist I (1852) 79.

[107] *Jhering*, Geist II.1. (1854) 305.

[108] *Jhering*, Geist I (1852) 205–206. Jhering recognized, however, that private rights could be limited in the well-defined public interest, see infra chapter IV.2., notes 248–266 and text.

the foundation for the general, basic Roman "drive for liberty" ("Freiheitstrieb").[109] That instinct transcended the realm of private rights and eventually pervaded all law governing citizens' lives. The Romans built a republic that respected its citizens' freedom from undue state regulation and coercion – a "system of liberty."[110]

At the same time, Jhering saw early Roman law as characterized by a penchant for equality ("Gleichheitstrieb").[111] Before the law, all citizens were equal (of course, this excluded slaves and foreigners, and it applied to women and children only to a limited extent). In contrast to many other societies, where even the ability to hold certain private rights (e.g. to own certain kinds of property) depended on class or status, under Roman law, all citizens could hold all rights, exercise all professions, and eventually also occupy all public offices. There certainly was much de facto inequality – of wealth, power, merit or prestige. According to Jhering, the Romans accepted these inequalities ungrudgingly as a fact of life. They did not, however, admit them into the precincts of law: before its commands, such differences played no (official) role. Thus it was one of the Romans' most significant accomplishments to have created a law that treated all citizens as – formally – equal.[112]

Beyond all these specific features, Jhering repeatedly emphasized a more general phenomenon that was not strictly speaking a property of early Roman law as such but is nonetheless an important aspect of its "spirit:" its centrality in Roman life, culture, and consciousness.[113] It was eventually evinced by the "omnipresence of jurists" who were crucial for regulating social and economic interaction ("Verkehr").[114] Of course, nineteenth century German jurists had long recognized the importance of law in ancient Rome, but Jhering foregrounded its significance with particular emphasis and enthusiasm. As he pointed out, law played not only a major role in safeguarding private rights, the liberty of citizens vis-a-vis the

---

[109] *Jhering*, Geist II.1. (1854) 123.

[110] *Jhering*, Geist II.1. (1854) 137, 142; 303–320. That claim was of course an idealization even with regard to the early Roman republic. Jhering saw the Roman penchant for liberty counterbalanced by a deeply-rooted ability for self-discipline; the combination of these character traits made the Romans superior to, and thus destined them to rule over, other peoples; *Jhering*, Geist I (1852) 303.

[111] *Jhering*, Geist II.1. (1854) 86.

[112] *Jhering*, Geist II.1. (1854) 86–123.

[113] In addition, Jhering alluded to a "drive towards centralization" ("Centralisierungstrieb") – in a geographic sense. It ensured that even in times of rapid territorial expansion, the capital remained the center of political power, intellectual life, and law. This centralization preserved the unity of law which provided important benefits to the people. Jhering mentioned this aspect almost in passing, did not discuss it in any detail, and apparently considered it a fairly minor point; *Jhering*, Geist I (1852) 312–313. It was of considerable contemporary relevance, however, because at the time (i.e. before 1871), Germany was not a unified nation, lacked a central law-making authority, and thus suffered from a costly fragmentation of its law.

[114] *Jhering*, Geist II.2. (1858) 443–444.

state, and the public peace; it was also an "object of national pride." It was revered and respected because it was more than a set of commands – it had "moral power over the minds."[115] All this evinced that the Roman people had a "particular predestination for the culture of law."[116] Its development was their "historical mission."[117] For Jhering, law was the most defining feature of ancient Roman culture – "the pinnacle of the Roman world,"[118] and its history an "unsurpassed work of art."[119]

If these aspects were the features that defined the (early) Roman law's "spirit," which of them were worth preserving with a view to a future jurisprudence superseding the reign of Roman law? Jhering did not expressly answer that question because his overall project never came to full fruition. Yet, in reading "Geist," the lessons Jhering drew from his investigations for the present (and future) become fairly clear.

Jhering presented most of the defining features of early Roman law in highly favorable, and often in outright enthusiastic, terms, implicitly recommending them for preservation or even augmentation. The law's autonomy as a discipline, its rationality, its relative simplicity, and its publicity were clearly considered virtues (by and large realized in Jhering's own time), as was its strict enforcement (which Jhering often found lacking around him[120]). Jhering also approved of the law's emphasis on individual power and will, the independence of private rights from the state,[121] the resultant autonomy and liberty of its citizens, as well as of the law's commitment to (at least formal) equality. And the law's purposefulness, i.e., its instrumental use for societal interests, began to emerge as Jhering's primary credo that would later lead him to regard law (merely) as a means to an end.[122] In all these regards, the spirit of early Roman law appeared as a model to be followed.

Jhering was not, however, an uncritical admirer of early Roman law in all its dimensions. In some important regards, his attitude was ambivalent and, at times, outright critical. On the one hand, Jhering praised the early Roman law's "exemplary order and simplicity, methodical regularity and exactitude, [and] merciless follow-through ('Consequenz')." On the other hand, he also found it unduly rigid, laborious, clumsy, pedantic, and displaying "a certain stiff, schoolmasterish ('schulmeisterlich') character." "It is not exactly difficult," he

---

[115] *Jhering*, Geist I (1852) 302, 304.

[116] *Jhering*, Geist I (1852) 288.

[117] *Jhering*, Geist I (1852) 289.

[118] *Jhering*. Geist I (1852) 300 ("Der höchste Punkt der römischen Welt").

[119] *Jhering*, Geist I (1852) 55.

[120] See infra chapter IV.1., notes 103–123 and text.

[121] For his own time, Jhering was not, however, advocating unbridled *laissez faire* but rather advocated reasonable regulation of private rights in the public interest, see *Jhering*, Zweck I (1884) 532–535.

[122] See infra chapter IV.2., notes 207–221 and text.

admitted, "to point to the risible side of this picture."[123] Jhering was particularly critical of the early Roman law's formalism and rigidity. While he lauded its clarity and durability, he lamented its inflexibility and lack of attention to individual justice. Writing in the age of rapid industrialization, he repeatedly compared it to a machine.

"The law leaves the impression of a machine magnificent by virtue of its ingenious simplicity. Exactly because of its simplicity, it works with utmost sureness and evenness, but woe to the careless person who does not understand its operation and gets too close: its iron wheels crush him. Its evenness is also based on an imperfection; there is no device to adjust it, it produces always exactly identical pieces, i.e., the law is incapable of adjusting to the individual situations and needs, the equality it seeks and effects is purely mechanical, external, of the kind captured in the saying: *Summum jus, summa injuria.*"[124]

Thus by looking at early Roman law, Jhering saw that clarity, predictability, rigor, and even a certain degree of formalism were necessary conditions for good law – but not sufficient ones. These features provided a solid jurisprudential basis, but especially in his later years, Jhering increasingly recognized that they needed to be counterbalanced by flexibility, attention to the circumstances of the case, and considerations of justice.[125] For Jhering, these virtues would eventually come to the fore in the *ius honorarium* and the work of the classical jurists during the "third system"[126] – which "Geist" never reached.

The Spirit of the Roman Law Determined III: The Method of Law. "Geist" deals not only with early Roman law but also, extensively, with the methodological side of jurisprudence. This reflected Jhering's preoccupation, and at times outright obsession, with methodological issues in the first half of his academic life. Jhering's discussions of these issues in "Geist" were of two kinds. On the one hand, there were discourses on "the nature of technique in general"[127] that were essentially timeless and abstract; we leave these discourses to the next section which will look beyond "Geist" as such and focus on Jhering's own methodology of law.[128] On the other hand, "Geist" contained inquiries into "the technique of

[123] *Jhering*, Geist III (1865) 9–10. It is interesting to note that this criticism was voiced in volume III, i.e., more than a decade after Jhering had written about early Roman law in volumes I and II.1. in more admiring terms. It probably evinced a gradual disillusionment with, and turning away from, his earlier position – though he did not significantly change his account in later editions.

[124] *Jhering*, Geist I (1852) 79; in a highly similar vein id. 300.

[125] "True justice requires a little more than such mechanical equality, [...] the true, inner justice [...] cannot be reached in this manner. The unencumbered feeling of justice rebels against solving a legal issue like a mathematical problem," *Jhering*, Geist I (1852) 302.

[126] *Jhering*, Geist I (1852) 81.

[127] "Das Wesen der Technik im Allgemeinen", thus the title of the most extensive and thorough discussion of the topic in *Jhering*, Geist II.2. (1858) 321–414. In addition, vol. I also contained a substantial methodological discourse, *Jhering*, Geist I (1852) 12–50, as did *Jhering*, Geist III (1865) in various places and contexts.

[128] Infra 2.

early [Roman] law,"[129] especially of its "analysis" and its "economy of law." These inquiries were (largely) historical and concrete; they belong in the present context of assessing the results of Jhering's quest for the Roman law's "spirit." Jhering's inquiries into the early Roman legal method were lengthy (comprising hundreds of pages), complex, often inchoate, and at times ambivalent. As a result, they are difficult to summarize. Thus the following account is, by necessity, selective, rudimentary, and debatable.[130]

For Jhering, the predominant feature of early Roman jurisprudence was its formalism ("Formalismus")[131] which went hand-in-glove with its verbalism ("Haften am Wort"). After he had discussed this formalism, rather incidentally, as a character trait of law (in volumes I and II.1.), he then analyzed it explicitly and extensively under the heading "the technique of law" ("Die Technik des Rechts") (in Volume II.2.).[132] The respective 200-page chapter dealt with both specific descriptions of early Roman jurisprudence[133] and provided a broader discussion of formalism in law. It is a fascinating, at times deeply perceptive, tract in its own right, and among the parts of "Geist" still worth reading today. Inter alia, Jhering pointed out that formalism is, to some extent, inherent in the law itself,[134] explained its necessity at the early stage of the law's development,[135] and recognized that this "product of the juristic spirit" reflected great intelligence and analytical rigor.[136] He discussed its downsides, appreciated its many benefits (especially as a shield against arbitrariness and thus as a protection of liberty[137]), and carefully weighed its advantages against its disadvantages.[138] Ultimately, however, he rejected the strict version of formalism characteristic of early Roman law (as well as its verbalism) as ill-suited for present-day jurisprudence.[139] Here was a

[129] "Die Technik des älteren Rechts", *Jhering*, Geist II.2. (1858) 415–605.

[130] We leave aside here several features of early Roman law addressed by Jhering in vol. II.2, such as the jurisprudential style of the *pontifices*, *Jhering*, Geist II.2. (1858) 415–445, or the law's "fixation on externality" ("Haften an Äußerlichkeit"), id. 446–495. While Jhering's discussion of these features is often extremely interesting from an historical perspective, it turned out not to be directly relevant for his overall agenda of assessing the Roman law's value for present-day jurisprudence.

[131] *Jhering*. Geist II.2. (1858) 546. Jhering recognized that formalism was a pervasive character trait not only in monarchial and republican Rome but of all early forms of law as well as of religion, *Jhering*, Geist II.2. (1858) 545.

[132] *Jhering*, Geist II.2. (1858) 321, 415.

[133] See, especially *Jhering*, Geist II.2. (1858) 554–587.

[134] *Jhering*, Geist II.2. (1858) 505.

[135] *Jhering*, Geist II.2. (1858) 590.

[136] *Jhering*, Geist II.2. (1858) 589.

[137] "Die Form ist die geschworene Feindin der Willkühr, die Zwillingsschwester der Freiheit." ("Form is the sworn enemy of arbitrariness, the twin sister of liberty."), *Jhering*, Geist II.2. (1858) 497. Jhering was fascinated by the interplay between "Form" and "Freiheit" and discussed it at considerable length, id. 498–545.

[138] *Jhering*, Geist II.2. (1858) 503–531.

[139] *Jhering*, Geist II.2. (1858) 682.

major feature of the Roman law's "spirit" that should be left behind – or, at least, should be heavily modified.

Of much greater immediate relevance for Jhering's own project were the features of "The Art of Law" ("Die juristische Kunst"), a label Jhering used to denote the Romans' specific methods of legal analysis and reasoning.[140] For Jhering, these features constituted the heart of Roman jurisprudence: "Now we are finally transported into the innermost workshop of jurisprudence" and thus have "the opportunity to observe its most secret essence."[141] In other words, these methods lay at the core of the (early) Roman law's "spirit." Their discussion constituted the bulk of Volume III. Jhering first turned to "The Analytical Side of Law" ("Die Analytik des Rechts"), then to "The Juristic Economy" ("Die juristische Oekonomie").

The "Analytical Side of Law" referred to the perhaps most important hallmark of early Roman jurisprudence: its method of dissecting legal phenomena into their most elementary parts through a process of "disaggregation" ("Zersetzung"), a term borrowed from the natural sciences.[142] Civil procedure (the *legis actio*) rigorously separated causes of action (allowing only one at a time) as well as the elements of the plaintiff's versus the defendant's case.[143] Matching this procedural disaggregation, legal transactions were split up into simple acts or events, such as the making of a promise (e.g., *stipulatio)* or the transfer of ownership (e.g., *in iure cessio*), each of which could have only one legal effect. In the same vein, jurists developed a legal doctrine that reflected these practical forms of separation ("Scheidung") on the theoretical level by creating elementary legal concepts ("Rechtsbegriffe"). An example was the breaking up of a sales transaction into the obligation to sell, the obligation to pay, and the actual transfer of title to the goods and to the money; these elements were kept separate so that, e.g., the invalidity of the obligation to sell had no direct effect on validity of the transfer of title.[144] For Jhering, the all-important result of this "juristic-analytic spirit"[145] was a law consisting of a multitude of elementary building blocks[146] which Jhering likened to the letters of the alphabet.[147] They were utterly clear, simple, and precise, inviting neither doubt nor debate. In such a system, parties

---

[140] *Jhering*, Geist III (1865) 1–11.

[141] Our discourse "versetzt uns erst jetzt in die innereste Werkstatte der Jurisprudenz und verschafft uns Gelegenheit, sie in ihrem geheimsten Wesen zu belauschen," *Jhering*, Geist III (1865) 2. For Jhering, this "art of law" was not the result of spontaneous legal evolution, as the Historical School propagated, but a product of conscious human action, id. 6.

[142] *Jhering*, Geist III (1865) 12–228.

[143] *Jhering*, Geist III (1865) 16–125. Jhering called the process of the *legis actio* a "machine for juristic separation" ("juristische Scheidemaschine") invented by the Romans, id. 21.

[144] See *Jhering*, Geist III (1865) 199–206; see also id., 134–143.

[145] *Jhering*, Geist III (1865) 14.

[146] Jhering sometimes called them "Rechtskörper" ("law bodies"); e.g., *Jhering*, Geist III (1865) 169; see also infra 2., notes 229–233 and text.

[147] *Jhering*, Geist III (1865) 12; see also infra 2., note 265 and text.

and jurists could focus on one act, effect, or concept at a time. This not only clarified legal transactions but also greatly facilitated the assertion, proof, and adjudication of claims.[148]

The pursuit of "juristic economy" entailed the "art to make do with the given means."[149] Early Roman law sought to satisfy the needs of life by creatively using the existing building blocks, rather than by inventing new ones. Jhering termed this approach "the law of logical economy" ("Gesetz der logischen Sparsamkeit")[150] and considered it one of the most characteristic features of early Roman jurisprudence. If new needs arose (as they obviously did with the expansion of Rome and the transformation of its economy), jurists creatively interpreted and combined the legal material at hand (and if need be resorted to fictions which, however, could get out of hand[151]). Having to create new solutions with the (limited) existing toolkit pushed the jurists' capacity for logical ingenuity. "Necessity is the mother of invention." ("Die Noth macht erfinderisch.")[152] In the discovery of such solutions, Roman "perspicacity ('Scharfsinn') was enormously inventive and has produced examples astounding in their subtlety and genial simplicity."[153]

While Jhering raved about this juristic brilliance, he once again also recognized its dark side: sometimes, the Romans drove their ingenuity too far. They could get so caught up in their logical creativity that it took on a life of its own and made them lose sight of all ethical values.[154] Jhering recognized the dangers of a highly developed technical method: it could be employed for any purpose, good or bad, and thus result in "formalistic nihilism."[155]

These misgivings notwithstanding, Jhering presented many aspects of the early Roman law's methodology as a model for future jurisprudence. He admired

---

[148] Jhering astutely observed the connection between the procedural requirements of proof and the value of substantive rights: complicated and difficult proof makes the enforcement of a substantive right costly and uncertain and thus diminishes its value. "The most precious goods are worthless if the cost of obtaining them devour the [potential] gain," *Jhering*, Geist III (1865) 195. Jhering thus demanded that the lawgiver keep proof as simple as possible, id. In effect, he provided a mini-lecture on the importance of what modern law-and-economics theory terms "transaction costs." In this regard, Jhering opined, present-day law was much inferior to that of the early Romans, *Jhering*, Geist III (1865) 195–196. Indeed, in most modern legal systems, the proof and enforcement of rights is so costly that small- or even medium-sized entitlements are often de facto worthless unless the debtor fulfills the obligation voluntarily. That is particularly true in legal systems which do not provide for cost-shifting to the losing party, as is largely the case in the United States.

[149] *Jhering*, Geist III (1865) 229–292, 230.

[150] *Jhering*, Geist III (1865) 229.

[151] *Jhering*, Geist III (1865) 292 fn. 425.

[152] *Jhering*, Geist I (1852) 307.

[153] *Jhering*, Geist III (1865) 231–232. Jhering presented a multitude of concrete, and often impressive, examples, id. 232–247.

[154] *Jhering*, Geist III (1865) 247–260.

[155] *Jhering*, Geist III (1865) 251.

the analytical sharpness and creativity of the early Roman jurists and envied the resultant clarity and simplicity of the law's procedure, transactions, and conceptual apparatus. To be sure, that jurisprudence was still crude and often overly rigid; it thus had to be modified, especially by injecting more flexibility and paying more attention to notions of justice. Still, as we shall see, the specific features Jhering found in the early Roman law's "technique" and "art" provided a blueprint for the methodology he developed for jurisprudence in general.[156]

Reactions to "Geist": Critique and Self-Critique. As this – fairly short, crude, and incomplete – summary indicates, "Geist" is an amazingly multi-dimensional work, a perplexing concoction of descriptions, interpretations, theories, ideas, and opinions. Yet, the weaknesses described above[157] were also apparent. Reactions by others to the work, and especially to the early volumes, were mainly negative. To be sure, as Jhering noted, there were some positive reviews, and he even received lavish praise from a few colleagues,[158] but on the whole the book had "found a dubious reception."[159] Jhering once quoted from the letter of a friend (!) who lamented: "My dear friend! What stuff have you thrown together here? [...] I had higher expectations of you."[160] Critics saw "Geist" as a strange mixture of historiography and philosophy, "but neither properly so."[161] "The work as a whole," Johannes Emil Kuntze aptly opined in his eulogy of Jhering, "has the effect of a thunderstorm or hurricane, fertile, but it suffers from countless superficialities in the details; it is enormously stimulating, but too much is unreliable."[162]

Jhering himself at times tried to shrug it all off, claiming that he was writing the book following an inner need, not for the sake of praise.[163] He thus vowed to soldier on even if he was "pushed, warned, beaten, etc."[164] If some critics even

---

[156] Infra 2.

[157] Supra notes 10–17 and text.

[158] See, e.g., letter from Joseph Unger (who later became Jhering's colleague in Vienna) of July 18, 1860, Behrends (ed.), Briefe von und an Jhering (1993) 112; see also letter to Ludwig Lange of January 27, 1853, Jhering in Briefen (1913) 21–24.

[159] Letter to Windscheid of January 29, 1853, Jhering in Briefen (1913) 25. See also letter to Gerber of Juli 17, 1852, Jhering in Briefen (1913) 16; letter to Windscheid of Juli 11, 1857, Jhering in Briefen (1913) 80; see also *Eck*, R. Windscheid und R.v.Jhering (1893) 26 (with further references).

[160] Quoted after *Ermacora*, Vorrede (1992) 25; see also *Fikentscher*, Methoden des Rechts III (1976) 219–220; *MacDonell*, Rudolf von Jhering (1914) 593.

[161] *Kuntze*, Rudolf von Jhering (1992) 612. Kuntze found Jhering's historiography "arbitrary" and his philosophy "narrow," id. 613.

[162] *Kuntze*, Rudolf von Jhering (1992) 613; see also *MacDonell*, Rudolf von Jhering (1914) 593 ("I know of no book of jurisprudence more stimulating or suggestive.") MacDonell likened "Geist" to Henry Sumner Maine's contemporaneous "Ancient Law" (1861) and concluded that "it does not suffer from comparison." Yet, MacDonell also noted the book's "imperfections," id.

[163] Letter to Gerber of July 17, 1852, Jhering in Briefen (1913) 15; letter to Windscheid of July 11, 1857, Jhering in Briefen (1913) 80; *Ermacora*, Vorrede (1992) 24–25.

[164] Letter to Gerber of July 17, 1852, Jhering in Briefen (1913) 17.

misunderstood the very nature of his endeavor, Jhering wrote, that was their problem, not his.[165] Yet, he was too astute and self-critical to overlook the book's weaknesses. "Geist" had "quite a few good, indeed superb, parts," he wrote to a friend and colleague in 1873, but is also contained "quite a bit of lame stuff – mush and blahblah."[166] On the whole, he opined, the work did not meet his own standards.[167] In times of crisis, it even seemed to him that the whole project was a grand illusion: "I feel as if my great intellectual edifice, that I am working on and of which I have been so proud, is built on thin air – my whole realm a magic castle which is created by my fantasy and which delights merely a few friends and myself."[168] Fixing the problem would require a more thorough reworking of the book than Jhering was willing to undertake.[169] He thus left it at limited revisions for successive editions – and focused on the hope of finishing the work someday.

2. Jhering's (Natural-Historical) Method: "Unsere Aufgabe" (1857)

Jhering's observations on the defining features of (early) Roman law (i.e., its "spirit") were interesting in their own right, but they were not the main reason why his work became famous in the 1850s and 1860s. Scattered throughout the several volumes of "Geist", these observations were never presented in the concentrated fashion that would grab widespread attention. Instead, Jhering's fame as a Romanist rested on two other pillars: his methodology and his doctrinal essays. We will look at the former here and at the latter in the next section.

Jhering developed his methodology at length and in depth in "Geist"; of all the work's many elements, he considered its methodogical sections the most successful and important.[170] He also discussed his methodology in his introductory essay to the first volume of the "Jahrbücher," entitled "Unsere Aufgabe" ("Our Task" or "Mission") (1857); here he presented his methodological credo with such unbridled enthusiasm and exuberance that this essay became something like his signature work in this regard. To grasp Jhering's methodology, the discourses in "Geist" and "Unsere Aufgabe" must be read together even though this is, as we shall see, not free from difficulty.[171]

For contemporary readers, Jhering's methodology was intriguing because it presented the first comprehensive description and in-depth analysis of the technique that characterized mainstream Romanist legal science. For a modern read-

---

[165] *Jhering*, Geist II.1. (1854) 23, fn. 1.
[166] Letter to Bülow of March 21, 1873, Jhering in Briefen (1913) 286.
[167] *Jhering*, Geist III (1865) iv.
[168] Letter to Gerber of January 6, 1859, Jhering in Briefen (1913) 111.
[169] See his letter to Windscheid, "beginning" of 1864, Jhering in Briefen (1913) 161.
[170] Letter to Windscheid of August 15, 1860, Jhering in Briefen (1913) 123.
[171] See infra notes 201–212 and text.

er, it is interesting mainly because it expresses the extreme form of the logical and conceptual jurisprudence in vogue in mid-nineteenth century Germany.[172] Jhering's methodology drives this approach to the point of near-absurdity, providing almost a caricature. At the same time, it also highlights the considerable benefits of such an approach for both legal theory and practice. Along the way, Jhering's methodological discourses demonstrate his vivid imagination as well as his tendency to get carried away by his own enthusiasm.

While Jhering presented much of his methodology in a book about Roman law, the connection between the former and the latter was not entirely straightforward. Jhering implied that the legal methods he saw at work in early Rome were closely related to the ones he now propounded, but he did not clearly demonstrate that connection.[173] Instead, the connection between the Roman methodology and Jhering's own was more subtle. Jhering found that the Roman jurists possessed "a specifically felicitous natural talent to distill from legal rules the basic constitutive elements"[174] – a process that Jhering considered, as we shall see, an essential feature of any highly developed jurisprudence. At the same time, he admitted that the Roman jurists had not actually taken that step on any significant scale (which is obvious even to the casual observer).[175] Thus, Jhering postulated, it was left to later generations "to bring to consciousness what had remained closed" to earlier ones.[176] In other words, Jhering called upon his own age to complete what the Romans themselves could have done but did not accom-

---

[172] In a sense, one can thus consider Jhering the founder of modern *Dogmatik* German style, see *Fikentscher*, Methoden des Rechts III (1976) 228, although Jhering takes it to extremes no longer widely accepted today. A standard, by now somewhat dated, but still very useful, account of Jhering's methodology is provided by *Larenz,* Methodenlehre (1983) 24–27. The classic essay on nineteenth century German legal methodology is *Wilhelm*, Zur juristischen Methodenlehre im 19. Jahrhundert (1958). Though more than half-a-century old, it is still worth reading today; specifically on Jhering's (and Gerber's) legal methodology, see id. 88–117.

[173] According to the table of contents of Geist II.2., Jhering's extensive (80 pp.) methodological discourse was merely a prolegomenon to the subsequent discussion of the "Technique of the Older [Roman] Law," id., XIX–XX. Yet, the methodological essay soon took on a life of its own and eventually became the most widely noted and influential part of the whole work.

[174] *Jhering*, Geist I (1852) 31.

[175] Franz Wieacker agreed, however, that there was a close connection between the method of the classical Roman jurists and Jhering own version in "Geist"; *Wieacker*, Römische Rechtsgeschichte vol. I (1988) 324.

[176] *Jhering*, Geist I (1852) 32. Jhering also believed that beneath the legal rules we know, there are latent rules the discovery of which is the task of modern jurists, *Jhering*, Geist II.2. (1858) 22. He provided an impressive example when he used a few, somewhat obscure, Roman sources to tease out a general rule that a party who is responsible for the invalidity of a contract is liable to the other for *culpa in contrahendo*. No such general rule was openly recognized in classical Roman law but one could argue that it was hidden beneath its surface; see infra 3.

plish: to transform the rules of private law into a scientific system of concepts.[177] Jhering presented his method as the proper tool for precisely that purpose. While Roman law was the backdrop which provided almost all his illustrations and examples, Jhering considered his approach valid beyond it – it was part of his general theory of law.[178]

On the Shoulders of Giants: Pushing Beyond Savigny and Puchta. Before we turn Jhering's methodology in and of itself, we need to recognize that it was not all his own invention. Instead, it was a substantial continuation of, but also a significant variation on, some of his predecessors' work. In particular, Jhering stood on the shoulders of two giants who had laid many of the foundations on which he now built.[179]

One of these giants was Savigny. A generation earlier, Savigny's agenda had already included capturing the essential building blocks of Roman law (which Savigny mostly conceived of as "institutions").[180] Savigny had stated that the Roman jurists could operate with legal "concepts" almost like mathematicians.[181] He had also famously presented the Roman law in the form of a scientific system that allegedly reflected the law's internal coherence and that provided a basis for contemporary jurisprudence.[182] In addition, Savigny had already claimed that legal science could produce new law[183] – an idea that eventually became the core of Jhering's much more elaborate "productive jurisprudence."[184] In all these regards, Jhering followed in Savigny's footsteps, and for the most part gave him credit for the foundations he had laid.[185]

[177] The idea that the contemporary generation of (German) jurists was destined to complete the work of the classical Roman jurists was widely shared, see *Kuntze*, Der Wendepunkt der Rechtswissenschaft (1856) 67.

[178] *Jhering*, Unsere Aufgabe (1857) 51; *Jhering*, Geist II.2. (1858) 323.

[179] For a more subtle, as well as original, rendition and interpretation of the relationship between the legal thought of Savigny, Puchta, and Jhering, see *Behrends*, Jhering heute! (2023) 188–198. Inter alia, Behrends explains the different and changing role of religious elements in these scholars' conceptions of law in a most interesting manner. Delving into the matter would lead us too far astray here, however.

[180] *Savigny*, System des heutigen römischen Rechts (8 vol. 1840–1849).

[181] *Savigny*, Vom Beruf unserer Zeit (1814) 29.

[182] *Savigny*, System des heutigen römischen Rechts (8 vol. 1840–1849). As Karl Larenz observed, Savigny's conception of a "system" was organic (and related to the Romantic tradition), his successor Puchta's was abstract and strictly logical (and more closely related to mathematics); see *Larenz*, Methodenlehre (1983) 19–20.

[183] *Savigny*, System I (1840) xxvi.

[184] See infra notes 244–245 and text.

[185] For a more thorough analysis, see *Behrends*, Rudolf von Jhering (1987) 246–252; *Wilhelm*, Zur juristischen Methodenlehre im 19. Jahrhundert (1958) 117–121.

The other (only slightly smaller) giant was Savigny's successor Puchta[186] whom the early Jhering regarded as his principal teacher.[187] In the two decades before Jhering began his academic career, Puchta had developed, and become the leading representative of, what Jhering, much later and derisively, called "Begriffsjurisprudenz" ("conceptual jurisprudence")[188]. Largely unmooring the Roman sources from their historical context, Puchta had distilled from them a set of fundamental and essentially abstract legal concepts. Puchta organized these building blocks according to their "genealogy"[189] into what Karl Larenz later called a "pyramid of concepts":[190] a hierarchical order with the most general concepts at the top and increasingly particular ones towards the bottom until one reached the actual rules of positive law.[191] Puchta presented this system not only as strictly logical and gapless but also as capable of discovering new concepts and rules through the induction or deduction from, or the combination of, existing ones. This process of "juristic construction" eventually became central to Jhering's approach.[192]. Thus learned jurists (i.e., Puchta and his Romanist colleagues) could go beyond "customary law" ("Gewohnheitsrecht"), as well as legislation, and employ legal science to produce "jurists' law" ("Juristenrecht").[193]

The relationship between Puchta's approach and Jhering's subsequent methodology is not only complex, it is also difficult to pin down because both scholars

[186] Puchta succeeded Savigny both as the holder of the chair for Roman Law at the University of Berlin and, more generally, as the leader of the Historical School in the 1840s. The definitive modern work on Puchta is *Haferkamp*, Georg FriedrichPuchta und die Begriffsjurisprudenz (2004). For an older, shorter, but highly perceptive discussion of Puchta's methodology, see *Wilhelm*, Zur juristischen Methodenlehre im 19. Jahrhundert (1958) 70–87; see also *Bohnert*, Über die Rechtslehre Georg Friedrich Puchtas (1975). For very concise portraits, see *Wieacke*r, Privatrechtsgeschichte (1967) 399–402.

[187] While Jhering never attended any of Puchta's lectures, he came under Puchta's direct influence as a doctoral and post-doctoral student, and then as a junior faculty colleague, in Berlin in the early 1840s. For more than a decade, Jhering based his main course on Roman law on Puchta's "Pandekten"(1838); see *Jäde*, Jhering als Rechtslehrer (2008) 21–32, In the mid-1870s, Jhering finally switched over to his friend Bernhard Windscheid's new treatise which had become leading in the field, i.e., *Windscheid*, Lehrbuch des Pandektenrechts (3 vol., 1862–1870).

[188] Jhering coined the term in 1884 as a moniker for a jurisprudence he by then had lost trust in, *Jhering*, Scherz und Ernst (1884) 337.

[189] *Puchta*, Cursus der Institutionen (1841) 36 (sec. 16).

[190] "Begriffspyramide", *Larenz*, Methodenlehre (1983) 21–22.

[191] At the very top, this pyramid was anchored to Hegel's concept of individual will which thus pervaded the whole system, even though it was increasingly diluted as one descended from the top towards the lower levels. Puchta's method is reminiscent, of course, of the great systems presented by the natural lawyers of of the seventeenth and eighteenth centuries. Puchta's material, however, was much more limited: it consisted only of classical Roman sources, i.e., a form of positive law. For a pithy description and perceptive analysis of Puchta's approach, see *Larenz*, Methodenlehre (1983) 19–24.

[192] See infra notes 235–245 and text.

[193] *Puchta*, Das Gewohnheitsrecht vol. I (1828) 161–167.

changed their views over time, and because they left many details unclear. As a result, a full-scale analysis requires a study in its own right, which lies beyond the scope of this book.[194] Suffice it to point to Jhering's fundamental ambivalence vis-a-vis Puchta's views. On the one hand, the early Jhering built directly on Puchta whose work already contained almost all the methodological basics later expounded by Jhering. Jhering openly acknowledged his indebtedness to his late model and thus dedicated the first volume of "Geist" to "the Memory of the Great Master Georg Friedrich Puchta."[195] In the 1850s, Jhering largely endorsed, further developed, but also modified Puchta's strictly logical approach; the result was Jhering's methodological theory (to which we will turn in a moment). On the other hand, Jhering also provided a critique of Puchta's work. Already in the mid-1850s, he attacked *some* of its features, often in the harshest terms.[196] Beginning in the mid-1860s, Jhering then vilified Puchta more generally as an advocate of a rigid logic who was blind to the needs of real life. Jhering's eventual turn away from Puchta (and to some extent also from his own, original, approach) requires a more nuanced analysis which is the topic of chapter III.

Thus, Jhering's most important methodological accomplishment in the 1850s was not that he invented an entirely new theory but, instead, that he fully developed what Savigny had touched on and Puchta had outlined.[197] In this manner, Jhering became the first scholar to provide the Romanist jurisprudence of his day with a full-blown methodological apparatus. Despite its problems,[198] this undertaking significantly advanced the jurisprudential ball at the time. Jhering's theory became the methodological manifesto of contemporary Romanist legal science and, as such, famous among his contemporaries and later generations.

For Jhering, this methodology was not limited to any particular kind of jurisprudence. His goal was rather to state a universally valid approach and "to make jurisprudence conscious of itself."[199] Jhering considered it his most lasting contribution in "Geist" to have brought to light how not only the Roman jurists

---

[194] A considerable part of such an analysis has been undertaken by *Haferkamp*, Georg Friedrich Puchta und die Begriffsjurisprudenz (2004) 26–46; see also *Wilhelm*, Zur juristischen Methodenlehre im 19. Jahrhundert (1958).

[195] *Jhering*, Geist I (1852) xiii.

[196] See infra chapter III.2., notes 119–123 and text.

[197] See *Wilhelm*, Zur juristischen Methodenlehre im 19. Jahrhundert (1958) 117–121. According to Wilhelm, id. 119–120, much of what Jhering presented had already been developed by a jurist largely forgotten today, i.e., Johannes Friedrich Martin Kierulff (1806–1894) in his "Theorie des gemeinen Civilrechts" (1839). Jhering was clearly familiar with the work of Kierulff (whom he had succeeded on the chair of Roman Law at the University of Rostock) but barely mentioned it; see *Jhering*, Geist III (1865) 309. This is strange since Jhering typically took great care to acknowledge the ideas of others. Another influence on Jhering was Friedrich Julius Stahl (1802–1861), see *Wilhelm* id.

[198] See infra notes 201–211 and text.

[199] Letter to Gerber of January 2, 1855, Jhering in Briefen (1913) 52 ("die Jurisprudenz zum Bewußtsein ihrer selbst zu bringen"). The phrase rings Hegelian.

worked, but how "jurists in general operate." In his view, the method he described and explained was the one "used by every capable jurist."[200]

A Fair Warning to the Reader: Four Sources of Confusion. Before we delve into Jhering's methodological discourse, the reader must also be advised that we will encounter a fair amount of confusion and vagueness. It is not clear whether Jhering himself considered his theory clear and coherent but it is clear that for most readers it is not.[201] The problem has four causes.

First, Jhering discussed his methodology for doctrinal work in three main instances: in Volume I of "Geist" (1852), he presented a first, still fairly rough, outline in a few dozen pages.[202] Six years later, in Volume II.2. of the same work (1858), he proffered a greatly refined and expanded "Theorie der juristischen Technik" ("Theory of Juristic Technique)."[203] In between, he propounded his methodology in particularly crisp and provocative form in his essay "Unsere Aufgabe" (1857). In a sense, this essay is the apotheosis of his methodology because here he exalted his approach in the most extreme, and in part outright fantastic terms. While Jhering made some effort to coordinate these texts, there is significant overlap,[204] some inconsistency, and, as a result, considerable room for

[200] Letter to Windscheid of September 14, 1859, Jhering in Briefen (1913) 120.

[201] For a succinct and perceptive critique, see *Rüemelin,* Rudolf von Jhering (1922) 45–52. Whether Jhering's methodology is ultimately a consistent and coherent body of thought (see, *Fikentscher*, Methoden des Rechts III (1976) 202–204) is debatable. Observers with a strong urge to find coherence and endowed with the requisite forgiveness for inconsistent language can plausible embrace such a view. Those more tolerant of incoherence and determined to take Jhering at his word will relegate such "unity" to the realm of wishful thinking. The following discussion takes no sides. It is merely an attempt to present the essential features of Jhering's methodology in comprehensible terms and in a plausible sequence. Readers who feel the need can make up their own minds whether to regard Jhering's methodology as a consistent whole or a moderately coordinated collection of interrelated ideas.

[202] *Jhering*, Geist I (1852) 12–50. Along the way, Jhering's made a variety of interesting observations about the nature and development of law in general. Looking at them in detail would lead us to far astray but they deserve at least brief mention because they demonstrate Jhering's intellectual curiosity and perceptiveness. His observations about the relationship between legal rules and legal reality, *Jhering*, Geist I (1852) 20, 22, anticipated the basic tenets of American legal realism, see infra hapter VII.3., notes 253–260 and text. His remarks about the existence of legal rules that are hidden from view ("latente Rechtssätze"), id. 18, amounts to the discovery of what Rodolfo Sacco, more than a century later, famously termed "cryptotypes", see *Sacco*, Legal Formants (1991). Jhering's insight that the essential features of law are often harder to discern by contemporaries than by future generations, *Jhering,* Geist I (1852) 20, anticipates the teachings of twentieth century comparative studies that one's own law is often better understood when perceived from an outside perspective. Jhering also already pointed out very clearly that legal systems constantly borrow from one another, id., 2–3, – a discovery much trumpeted by, and today commonly associated with, Scottish-American comparatist Alan Watson; see *Watson*, Legal Transplants (1974).

[203] *Jhering*, Geist II.2. (1858) 334–414.

[204] For example, Jhering's discussion of "lower" and "higher jurisprudence" in his introductory essay in "Unsere Aufgabe" (1857) is partially replicated, but also much expanded, in the second volume of "Geist," though with considerable modifications, see *Jhering* Geist II.2. (1958) 385–414.

confusion.[205] To make matters worse, even within the individual texts, Jhering often presented his ideas in a haphazard fashion, thus confounding the reader.[206]

Second, as we shall see repeatedly, Jhering' use of key terms lacked consistency and precision. It is difficult, if not impossible, exactly to determine what he meant by "juristic bodies" ("juristische Körper") or "beings" ("Wesen"), "institutions" or "construction." Jhering rarely provided precise definitions, be it because he could not come up with any or because he simply did not care. In his methodological discourses, Jhering-the-jurist was sometimes dominated by Jhering-the-artist[207] who presented fireworks of ideas, metaphors, and claims rather than a clearly stated theory. As a result, a reader trying to understand what exactly Jhering meant will often be puzzled – and is well-advised not to despair when faced with obscurity.

Third, as we shall also see, Jhering exacerbated the terminological confusion by importing terms and concepts from the natural sciences, especially from biology and chemistry, and to some extent also from human medicine. To be sure, we must not overrate these references. As Jhering later noted, jurisprudence had entered a "natural-science phase."[208] Toying with the idea that law was, or at least could be studied like, a phenomenon of the natural world, was very fashionable at the time.[209] At least in Jhering's case, invoking images from the natural sciences scarcely meant that he seriously intended to apply their methods (which he probably did not thoroughly understand anyway) or that he really ascribed a physical existence to legal relations and concepts. His references are best regarded as metaphors and illustrations invoked to explain and vivify his ideas.[210] Yet, for the most part, these metaphors and illustrations are more confounding than enlight-

---

[205] The least confusing rendition of his methodological credos is probably the discussion in *Jhering*, Geist II.2. (1858) 334–414, even though it is plagued by many obscurities and digressions.

[206] In "Unsere Aufgabe" (1857), for example, Jhering first presented the dichotomy of "receptive and productive jurisprudence" with regard to legal doctrine, id. 3–4, then spent several pages on a – quasi-Hegelian – discourse on the search for the "abstract [i.e., general, MR] elements" in legal history, id. 3–7, before returning to legal doctrine, admitting that this is what the article is really about, id. 7 (and implicitly admitting that the discourse about legal history was really a digression). Then, he finally introduced the distinction between what he calls "lower" and "higher" jurisprudence. This is, of course, directly related to "receptive" and "productive" jurisprudence as should have been made clear right at the outset. It is this frequent lack of proper organization that make Jhering's texts, while fascinating, often so hard to grasp.

[207] See supra chapter I.4., notes 214–229 and text.

[208] *Jhering*, Scherz und Ernst (1884) 80.

[209] See *Kuntze*, Der Wendepunkt der Rechtswissenschaft (1856) 30, 40,41, 49, 76, 90, etc.

[210] Jhering himself justified them as "images and comparisons" ("Bilder und Vergleiche") intended to help especially his broader audience (including students and laymen) understand his ideas, *Jhering*, Geist II.2. (1858) X–XI; see also *Wieacker*, Rudolph von Jhering (1969) 21–22. For a different interpretation, see *Viehweg*, Rechtsdogmatik und Rechtszetetik bei Jhering (1970) 214.

ening. Jhering used them as fancy struck him, again without explaining exactly what he had in mind. The numerous references to the natural sciences did, however, vest jurisprudence with the aura of a real "science" – a point to which we shall have to return[211].

Finally, Jhering's methodology has two major structural features whose interplay is not entirely clear. First, Jhering distinguished between two basic forms jurisprudence: a "lower" and a "higher" version. Second, he presented several basic methodological steps: analysis, concentration, and construction; in addition, he also discussed the arrangement of the law into a logical system (while he did not explicitly designate this as a separate step, functionally it clearly is one).[212] His sequence of presentation suggests that the first two steps (analysis and concentration) belong to "lower," and the second two (construction and systematization) to "higher," jurisprudence.[213] Yet, this is dubious in light of what these forms of "jurisprudence" are actually about. It seems preferable to discuss all four methodological steps in the context of "higher jurisprudence," especially since that was Jhering's main focus and principal interest. But let us first get lower jurisprudence out of the way.

"Lower Jurisprudence:" The "Receptive" Mode of Legal Reasoning. The most fundamental feature of Jhering's methodology was his distinction between "lower" and "higher" jurisprudence. While Jhering discussed both (repeatedly),[214] he related to them in very different ways. He was interested in "lower jurisprudence" mainly as a prerequisite for the higher form.[215]

The hallmark of "lower jurisprudence" ("niedere Jurisprudenz") is that it deals with law as it appears in its "original and immediately practical form:" it looks at law as a rule ("Rechtsregel"), be it in the narrow sense of a legal command ("Rechtssatz") or in the broader form of a legal principle ("Rechtsprinzip"). For Jhering, "lower jurisprudence" was essentially concerned with the interpretation of law as a given set of norms. The task of interpretation is to explicate the material ("den Stoff (auseinander) zu legen"), to eliminate seeming contradictions, to remedy obscurities and ambiguities, to bring to light the whole content of the legislative will – in particular to extract from the individual provisions their underlying principle and, vice versa, to deduce from the principle its consequences.[216] Jhering did not develop a specific methodology for "lower jurisprudence" because it was simply not his primary focus.

---

[211] See infra notes 286–288 and text.

[212] At one point, he lists analysis, concentration and then "the systematic ordering of the material," *Jhering*, Geist II.2. (1858) 343.

[213] In "Geist," Jhering first discussed analysis, then concentration, and it is only in the context of then discussing construction that he introduces "higher jurisprudence," *Jhering*, Geist II.2. (1858) 359–389.

[214] The presentation of this distinction was first published in *Jhering*, "Unsere Aufgabe" (1857) 7–21, then in *Jhering*, Geist II.2 (1858) 385–414. The following discussion here tries to integrate both these texts.

[215] *Jhering*, Unsere Aufgabe (1857) 7–8.

[216] *Jhering*, Geist II.2. (1858) 386.

Jhering's label of "lower" jurisprudence was not meant to be derogatory – Jhering was sufficiently engaged in legal practice[217] to appreciate the necessity and utility of its basic operations. In fact, his discourse on legal method in the second volume of "Geist" begins with an extensive discussion of the overwhelming practical importance of proper methods[218] – a point which we shall also consider below.[219]

While "lower jurisprudence" was undeniably important in practice as well as an indispensable basis for "higher jurisprudence," it wasn't really anything out of the ordinary. For Jhering, it was essentially what most jurists do most of the time. In Jhering's eyes, the main problem with "lower jurisprudence" was that its potential was severely limited. In particular, it was merely "receptive" in the sense that it dealt only with the existing rules and principles; thus it could never progress beyond the current material. The true glory lay in a jurisprudence that could actually become "productive."

"Higher Jurisprudence:" The "Construction" and "Production" of Law. For Jhering, "higher jurisprudence" ("höhere Jurisprudenz") was an entirely different matter. What he developed here lay far beyond what Savigny had ever envisaged, though not that far beyond what Puchta had already developed two decades earlier. This approach looked at law in a very different way, i.e., as a universe of concepts. These concepts could be used for "juristic construction," and they could be organized in a system capable of generating new law out of itself. "Higher jurisprudence" alone fully engaged Jhering's methodological ambition and imagination because it, and only it, turned jurisprudence into a true science.[220]

To state Jhering's theory of "higher jurisprudence" in a reasonably intelligible fashion requires proffering more coherence and consistency than there really was. The matter is perhaps best approached by following the basic methodological steps mentioned above. The first two – analysis and concentration – lay the groundwork by distilling the law's basic elements; the second pair – construction and systematization – then exploit the potential of the resulting order.

First, "legal analysis" ("juristische Analyse") must break the various legal relationships ("Rechtsverhältnisse") down through "decomposition" ("Zersetzung") into their constitutive elements. While the terminology was, again, borrowed from chemistry,[221] Jhering explained this step primarily by reference to the alphabet: just like all written language is composed of a finite number of letters, so all legal relationships are composed of a finite number of basic "bodies." Thus, jurisprudence thus has to create an alphabet of law.[222] What do these basic el-

[217] Infra 4.

[218] *Jhering*, Geist II.2. (1858) 335–359.

[219] See infra notes 252–273 and text.

[220] *Jhering*, Geist II.2. (1858) 389.

[221] *Jhering,* Geist II.2. (1858) 361 ("Chemie des Rechts"). The term was also quite popular in the jurisprudential discussions at the time, see *Kuntze*, Der Wendepunkt der Rechtswissenschaft (1856) 22, 76, 79, 97.

[222] Jhering could have explained the matter just as easily by reference to chemistry: all

ements of law look like? Jhering provided several examples and put them into two categories. Some are "concrete" and can exist "independently," for example a contract of sale, an easement, or a testament; others are abstract and always need a concrete partner, such as error, nullity, or delay (of performance). Thus, what Jhering had in mind were the basic elements of private law. The "abstract" elements are, of course, much more versatile because they can apply in combination with a multitude of concrete ones (e.g., error in concluding a contract of sale, the granting of an easement, or the making of a testament).[223]

The second "operation" was the "logical concentration" ("logische Concentration"), yet another term borrowed from chemistry. Here, the jurist had to distill from the multitude of particular legal elements their underlying general principles. By doing so, he could achieve a massive compression of the volume of the legal material.[224] This allowed the jurist to operate with a limited number of elements and principles rather than a myriad of rules.[225]

---

matter is composed of a finite number of elements which analysis can identify. Once we know these elements, we can not only understand the composition of all matter but also combine the elements to create new varieties. Thus, jurists need to create the juristic equivalent of the periodic table of elements. Jhering alluded to chemistry so often to make it almost odd that here, he did not; see *Jhering*, Geist II.2. (1858) 377 (the jurist dissolves "an organic whole" "with great effort into single atoms and reassembles them again"), 378 ("the beautiful flower is gone, and its stead, we have nitrogen, oxygen, etc."); see also *Jhering* 1852, 30 (speaking of "Reagentien").

[223] *Jhering*, Geist II.2. (1858) 372–373. Jhering recognized that the metaphor of a "juristic alphabet" had its limits. The most important caveat was that the (letter) alphabet was universally applicable and timeless while the line-up of the law's basic component parts was contingent on place and time. Different jurisdictions had different "legal alphabets," which also evolved over time, shedding some elements and adding new ones. This, of course, raised the question how Jhering could then hope, in his overarching project, to distill any universally valid essence from the Roman law. Jhering's response was subtle – and perhaps not entirely convincing. There were, he argued, indeed some legal concepts of universal validity, such as the concept of error, and from them, a "universal legal alphabet" could indeed be assembled. Yet, these concepts were of a "merely formal kind" ("abstract" may have been a better term). In order to become applicable in practice, they always had to be fleshed out in the context of a concrete legal order which had to determine, for example, which kinds of errors were legally relevant, and which were not. In this manner, the abstract concepts turned into "positive" ones – and *as such*, they were contingent on time and place; Jhering, Geist I (1852) 374–375. For Jhering, Roman law was no exception. Of course, its amazing longevity made it understandable that it was often regarded as *ratio scripta*, i.e., universally and eternally valid. And its utility even under modern conditions was indeed impressive. But as positive law, i.e., in its concrete manifestations, it was nonetheless Roman, not universal; Jhering, Geist II.2. (1858) 376.

Another caveat was that the language alphabet could tolerate much more inaccuracy than its equivalent in law. If the letters did not always accurately reflect pronunciation, that would not cause great harm. In law, however, "congruence" between the alphabet's elements and their application was of the utmost importance. As a result, the legal alphabet would have to be much more extensive and much more nuanced than its counterpart in language; Jhering, Geist II.2. (1858) 374.

[224] "Zusammendrängung des äußeren Volumens einer Masse Rechtsstoff," *Jhering,* Geist II.2. (1858) 380.

Once analysis and concentration had identified a roster of basic juristic building blocks, "higher jurisprudence" could really get to work. Its defining feature was that it dealt with law no longer in its common form as a set of rules but in "a higher state of aggregation" ("höherer Aggregatzustand"). Jhering's explanation of what that means is not only idiosyncratic but quite fantastic, and it is best to let him speak for himself:

"The transformation that is now happening means, on its *negative* side, that the material completely sheds its immediately practical and imperative form, on its *positive* [side] that it takes on the form of a *juristic* body (eines *juristischen* Körpers). The sum total of law no longer appears as a *system of rules, ideas*, but as an incarnation of juristic *beings* (juristischen *Existenzen*), live creatures (lebende Wesen), servient spirits (dienende Geister), so to speak [...]."[226]

"Higher jurisprudence" looks at law as a universe populated by a specific kind of entities which are envisaged like live beings in nature. Jurisprudence thus becomes "a natural science in the realm of ideas."[227] Borrowing a term from the organicist philosophy of nature fashionable in late eighteenth and early nineteenth century Germany, Jhering famously – and somewhat strangely – named his approach the "natural-historical method" ("naturhistorische Methode").[228]

---

[225] As with regard to "analysis," Jhering was quite aware of the inherent limitations and difficulties of performing "concentration." Of course, it makes sense only if there actually is an underlying principle to begin with, but Jhering was optimistic that this would normally be the case, *Jhering*, Geist II.2. (1858) 381. And of course, that principle may have been hidden to the original maker of the rule(s); in that case, its discovery was the task of later generations, id. Here, Jhering of course thought of Roman law which he, like most of his contemporaries, considered imbued with such principles many of which still remained to be unveiled. He also acknowledged that divergent legal rules may make it difficult to determine what is the principle and what is the exception; id., 383–384. Mastering these difficulties was the mark of a good jurist, and in his own doctrinal articles, Jhering showed his colleagues how it was done, see infra 3.

[226] *Jhering*, Unsere Aufgabe (1857) 16 (emphases in the original). This nomenclarture was less original than it appeared at first glance: as Jhering must have known, a full generation earlier, Savigny had already claimed that to the classical Roman jurists, the concepts and rules of their jurisprudence had been "real beings" ("wirkliche Wesen"), Savigny, Vom Beruf unserer Zeit (1814) 29.

[227] *Jhering*, Geist II.2. (1858) 389; on the consequences, see infra notes 286–288 and text.

[228] *Jhering*, Geist II.2. (1858) 385. Again, in the context of the jurisprudential debates at the time, the term was not as strange as it appears to a modern reader. It was also used by Jhering's contemporary Alois von Brinz (1820–1887), see *Kuntze*, Der Wendepunkt der Rechtswissenschaft (1856) 50. Jhering did not, however, explain exactly what made his method "natural-*historical*." Given the popularity of the term as well of the idea of importing the method(s) of the natural sciences into jurisprudence, Jhering was actually nervous that someone else might preempt his methodology before he could publish it; see *Mecke*, Jherings Rechtsdenken im Kontext der zeitgenössischen Natur- und Sozialwissenschaften (2023) 263–265.

To denote the objects of this juristic science, Jhering used a variety of terms but ultimately settled on "juristic bodies" ("juristische Körper").[229] While such imagery strikes the modern reader as strange, it was not at all unusual at a time when jurists often thought of law as a "world of organic, plastic types and forms"[230] and of jurisprudence as a "biology of law."[231] Nonetheless, understanding Jhering's "higher jurisprudence" requires understanding what he means by such "bodies." This is by no means easy.[232] Jhering's examples suggest that he was thinking of the fundamental notions of private law that find their expression in basic "concepts" ("Begriffe")[233] such as property, obligation, contract, usufruct, possession or *patria potestas*.[234] Thus "higher jurisprudence" is a "jurisprudence of concepts."

Grasping law as a world of concepts turned jurisprudence from a merely "receptive" business dealing with existing rules into a "productive" activity. Again, Jhering was far from clear exactly how this production worked but it seems that he envisaged two main forms: "construction" and extracting new law from a logical system. These two modes should be envisaged as interrelated and are perhaps even flipsides of the same coin.[235]

---

[229] He would have preferred the term "beings" ("Wesen") but feared that it would be considered too contrived, *Jhering*, Geist II.2. (1858) 387. A generation earlier, Savigny had already stated that for the Roman jurists, legal principles and rules were "real beings" ("wirkliche Wesen);" *Savigny*, Vom Beruf unserer Zeit (1814) 29; and Puchta had used the term "living being" ("lebendige Wesen") as well.

[230] *Kuntze*, Der Wendepunkt der Rechtswissenschaft (1856) 102.

[231] *Kuntze*, Der Wendepunkt der Rechtswissenschaft (1856) 90.

[232] Even though Jhering devoted an entire subchapter to "juristic bodies", *Jhering*, Geist II.2. (1858) 389–396, he provided anything but a clear definition. In addition, there is considerable terminological confusion. "Bodies" are closely related to "concepts" though apparently not identical with them: it seems like the "body" is the object whose essence is then captured by the "concept," id., 390–391. Note that in other contexts, Jhering seems to assume that "bodies" and "concepts" are identical, e.g., when he defined the ultimate system of law as the "family tree of concepts" ("Stammtafel der Begriffe"); id. 396. Confusingly, Jhering also speaks of "institutions." The context suggests that it is just another term for the entity otherwise labeled "juristic body," id. 391; see also *Jhering*, Geist I (1852) 25 fn. 12. Jhering may have considered that clear because, as at least his colleagues at the time knew, the term "institutions" has a long history in the civil law tradition, reaching all the way back to *Gaius*' "Institutes" (ca. 130 AD), meaning something like "basic elements." Throwing around all these labels without telling the reader whether they are the same of different again evinces Jhering's, unfortunately almost habitual, terminological carelessness.

[233] This is confirmed by various other remarks: Jhering tells us that "bodies" are the basic elements identified by "analysis," *Jhering*, Geist II.2. (1858) 390; see supra notes 221–225 and text; that they can have purposes (Zwecke), id. 392; that they have a "life" and can thus come into being as well as perish; id. 393; etc.

[234] *Jhering*, Geist II.2.1858) 395–396.

[235] "Construction" was perfectly possible without regard to any system, as Jhering himself demonstrated in his famous article on *Culpa in Contrahendo*, see infra 3.; but it was also possible within the system, i.e., by extrapolating from the internal logic of the arrangement.

For Jhering, the potential for "construction" was the hallmark of his "higher jurisprudence" – the "natural-historical method" was a "jurisprudence of construction" ("Konstruktionsjurisprudenz").[236] What exactly that meant is, again, not easy to pin down. Jhering lamented that although the term "construction" was widely popular in contemporary jurisprudence, nobody had really presented a theoretical foundation – and so he was compelled to provide one himself. What he presented, however, was more a deluge of words than a clear theory.[237] It is perhaps best to say that "construction" meant productively working with the existing "juristic bodies."[238] By combining them or extrapolating from them jurists can devise new solutions for yet unresolved problems. In short, "construction" means dogmatic work on a high level and in a productive fashion. What Jhering had in mind will become somewhat clearer when we see how he employed it in a concrete instance below.[239]

"Higher jurisprudence" also allowed, indeed required, to bring the existing concepts into a logically systematic order. Jhering again further developed Puchta's approach by importing ideas borrowed from the natural sciences. The "natural-historical method" classified the "legal bodies" according to their nature,[240] just like a biologist classifies animals according to their genus, species, etc. This created a system which was, "so to speak, the family tree of concepts" ("die Stammtafel der Begriffe").[241] It put each concept (representing a "body") in its proper place and reflected the relationships between them.[242] In this manner, the system allowed the "recognition of the true nature of law."[243]

Perhaps most importantly, through construction and systematization, "higher jurisprudence" could actually produce new law. Jhering elaborated on that point in vivid language and with his usual enthusiasm.

"Higher jurisprudence is not only the sculptor (Bildnerin) of the material, it is also its creator (Schöpferin); and it is the only one because only it can produce new material with certainty and consciousness (Sicherheit und Bewußtsein)."[244]

---

[236] *Jhering*, Geist II.2. (1858) 397.

[237] His definitions of this crucial concept are either tautological or vacuous: "shaping the legal material in the sense of the natural-historical method," "the creative art of jurisprudence;" etc., *Jhering*, Geist II.2. (1858) 397. For an in-depth discussion of the meaning of "juristic construction" in nineteenth century jurisprudence, see *Hommes*, Der Begriff der "juristischen Konstruktion" (1976).

[238] This basic idea had already been expressed by Savigny a generation before when he compared the extrapolation of new concepts from the existing material to the construction of a triangle from two given sides and one angle; *Savigny*, Vom Beruf unserer Zeit (1814) 22.

[239] Infra 3.

[240] *Jhering*, Geist II.2. (1858) 396.

[241] *Jhering*, Geist II.2. (1858) 396.

[242] *Jhering*, Geist I (1852) 29; again, this was not an original idea; Savigny had already propagated it more than a decade earlier, see *Savigny*, System I (1840) xxxv–xxxvi.

[243] *Jhering*, Geist I (1852) 31.

[244] *Jhering*, Unsere Aufgabe (1857) 14 (emphasis in the original).

In one of his most often quoted sentences, Jhering actually invoked the natural process of procreation.

"Through combination of various elements [legal] science can create *new* concepts and legal rules; the concepts are productive, they mate and beget new ones."[245]

Yet, exactly how "higher jurisprudence" generated new law Jhering did not say. Nor did he create any system, relying instead on the work of Puchta (and later Windscheid).

Abstract Logic and Practical Utility: A Tale of Two Jherings. Jhering's "higher jurisprudence" shows him as an enthusiast of abstract logic. It is thus easy to overlook that he was also a dedicated advocate of his methodology's practical utility. In a sense, there were two Jherings at work at the same time.

Jhering the enthusiast of abstract logic waxed eloquent and at great length about the importance and beauty of "legal bodies" and "juristic construction" and particularly about the importance of the law's systematic order.

"This importance is not due to the fact that law cannot be understood without its systematic coherence, because that is true for all objects of knowledge. It also goes without saying these days that the system, of law as of any other object, must not be one that is *imposed upon* the material but rather an order that is *elicited from* it [....The] system is identical with the internal order of the matter itself [...].

With regard to law [...] the formal process of systematization has a substantive rebound effect on the material, so that it [...] causes an inner transformation. The legal rules enter a higher state of aggregation, shed their form as commands and prohibitions and turn into elements and qualities of institutions."[246]

"To the trained eye, law appears as a logical organism of legal institutions and legal concepts, to the untrained eye, it is a complex of legal rules; the former is the inner nature of law, the latter its external side facing practical life."[247]

Jhering sang the praises of purely logical reasoning with unbridled force and flourish, in terms that even Puchta might have found a bit overdone: "if there is any place in a practical science which offers the human spirit the enjoyment to roam, entirely independently, the world of ideas and to return loaded with multiple treasures, it is to be found in jurisprudence."[248] The "logic of the system," he

---

[245] *Jhering*, Geist I (1852) 29 (emphasis in the original). Again, this did not necessarily sound ridiculous in the context of the jurisprudential writings of the time, which were full of vivid references to "organisms" and "procreating powers" ("zeugende Kräfte"); *Kuntze*, Der Wendepunkt der Rechtswissenschaft (1856) 47, 75. In modern legal theory, this phenomenon could be described as self-reference (Selbstreferenz) and, more specifically, self-production (Selbstproduktion); see *Teubner*, Recht als autopoietisches System (1989) 28–34.

[246] *Jhering*, Geist I (1852) 26.

[247] *Jhering*, Geist I (1852) 51. Most of Jhering's colleagues probably found that latter statement fairly unremarkable.

[248] "[W]enn irgendwo in einer practischen Wissenschaft dem menschlichen Geiste der hohe Genuß bereitet ist, rein auf sich selbst angewiesen in der Welt des Gedankens umherzuschweifen und mit vielen Schätzen beladen heimzukehren, so ist es die Jurisprudenz," *Jhering*, Unsere Aufgabe (1857) 19.

claimed, was not only "the flower" of the legal rules, it also took on a life of its own: a legal rule could exist even if devoid of any practical utility – "just for its own sake, it exists because it cannot not-exist."[249]

By idealizing a spiritual realm of "legal bodies" and investing systematic logic with law-producing power Jhering pushed the jurisprudence of concepts and construction to its extreme – and, as we shall see, to the breaking point.[250] For jurists near and far, this Jhering, even more than Puchta, became the symbol of purely abstract legal reasoning, be it as a model and a hero or, eventually more often, as a caricature and a villain.[251]

The Needs of Practice. Yet, as mentioned, there was also another Jhering: a dedicated and persistent advocate of serving the needs of legal practice. That Jhering actually subjected his whole methodology to the objective of practical utility. He also explained in great detail what practical benefits his approach promised to deliver. Let us first look at his overall framework and then turn to the various practical advantages he claimed.

With all the rage about Jhering's "natural-historical method," it is typically overlooked that he presented his "technique" not as an end in itself but as a means to improve the actual operation of law. At the very outset, i.e., in the introduction to Volume I of "Geist," Jhering divided his methodological discussion into two parts. The first deals with the "anatomy" of law, and it is here, i.e., in the context of structure and texture, that he developed the outlines of his logical and systematic approach.[252] The second part of the chapter, by contrast, discusses the "physiology" of law;[253] here, Jhering focuses on the law's "function in life"[254] – which is to be "realized", i.e., to be put into action.[255] For Jhering, everything that was said about the law's "anatomy" (i.e., structure) must be ultimately be judged in light of its "physiology" (i.e., function). As a result, the whole abstract-logical approach was only as valuable as the practical utility it produced.

"Thus, nothing could be more wrong than to judge a law, like a philosophical system, only from the perspective of its intellectual content, its logical structure and unity. Even if, from this point of view, it appears as a master-piece, that says nothing about its true value because the latter consists entirely of its functions, i.e., of its practical utility."[256]

---

[249] Jhering, Geist I (1852) 18.

[250] See infra chapter III.1. and 2.

[251] Franz Wieacker, again, aptly captured the upsides and downsides of Jhering's logical approach by saying that it "signifies both the naivité and the fertility of this vivid [style of] thinking;" *Wieacker*, Privatrechtsgeschichte (1967) 451.

[252] "Anatomische Betrachtung des Rechtsorganismus," *Jhering*, Geist I (1852) 12–39.

[253] *Jhering*, Geist I (1852) 39–50.

[254] *Jhering*, Geist I (1852) 39

[255] While others had also used ideas of "anatomy" (analysis of structure) and "physiology" (function), see *Kuntze*, Der Wendepunkts der Rechtswissenschaft (1856) 67, 76, Jhering was apparently the first who juxtaposed these ideas in a clear and helpful fashion, id. 52.

[256] *Jhering*, Geist I (1852) 40.

In other words, the logic of law is important only because of the purposes it serves. After all, "what good is a machine that looks like a work of art, if it is useless as a machine?"[257]

In a similar vein, Jhering's extensive methodological discussion in Volume II.2. of "Geist" begins by emphasizing the primacy of the law's (practical) "realization".[258] The crucial issue guiding the entire discussion of legal "technique" was how the law should be "organized and shaped" in order to "facilitate and secure its application to the concrete case."[259] Thus, the "whole theory of technique is nothing but the recognized and realized utility for performing the above mentioned task."[260]

So far, so good. But if "behind the externally unpractical form [of 'higher jurisprudence'], there lies an infinitely rich practical content,"[261] what exactly were the concrete practical benefits of this methodology? Jhering's idea of an "amalgamation of science with life"[262] had two main dimensions: his jurisprudence facilitated operating within existing law, and it could produce answers to new practical problems.

Facilitation is important, Jhering explained, because "realizing" law (i.e., its application) must be "inescapable, thus certain, and uniform on the one hand, and easy and speedy on the other."[263] This requires that law be easy to grasp (i.e., to learn and understand) as well as easy to apply (in practice).[264] Thus a major goal of jurisprudence is to shape the material in a way that facilitates mastering it, in particular that avoids having to memorize a plethora of individual rules. This can be accomplished through the basic methodological steps of analysis, concentration, and systematization.

As mentioned, analysis breaks the law down into its basic constitutive elements, like the alphabet breaks down words into letters. The number of the law's basic elements was considered quite limited, just like the number of letters in the alphabet. Once identified, these elements allow the jurist to de-compose and re-compose every legal relationship with relative ease, just like the alphabet allows us to decompose and recompose every word we can think of.[265]

---

257 *Jhering*, Geist I (1852) 40.

258 *Jhering*, Geist II.2. (1858) 334–335.

259 *Jhering*, Geist II.2. (1858) 336–337.

260 *Jhering*, Geist II.2. (1858) 337; see also id. 393 ("our science is merely a theory of the means...which law proffers for the ends of life.").

261 *Jhering*, Geist I (1852) 20.

262 *Jhering*, Unsere Aufgabe (1857) 27.

263 *Jhering*, Geist II.2. (1858) 335.

264 *Jhering*, Geist II.2. (1858) 340.

265 *Jhering*, Geist I (1852) 50. Jhering provides a – fairly impressive – example by analyzing the lien (Pfandrecht, i.e., the civil law version based on the Roman *pignus*), id. 28. Jhering surmised that laypeople (which were part of his audience, see supra note 14) would not like such an analytic approach because they typically preferred a more holistic view of legal problems. Their sense of justice would rebel against dissecting "an organic whole" into single

Concentration then identified the principles underlying the legal material. This not only massively reduced its volume, but it also made it possible to transition from a "casuistic" to a "principle-based" approach:[266] the jurist would no longer have to learn and memorize a vast number of rules and details but could work with a limited number of basic ideas from which decisions in individual cases could be derived.

In addition, the systematic organization of the law greatly facilitated the jurist's task – in three particular ways. On the most basic level, such a system helped to find the existing rules: if they were all put into their proper place, someone grasping their order could quickly locate them and also be certain not to overlook anything of importance, thus avoiding the constant risk inherent in a casuistic regime. On a more sophisticated level, the law's organization in a logically systematic fashion helped jurists to understand the nature and scope of legal rules. For example, Jhering's distinction between "abstract" and "concrete" juridical bodies[267] is reflected in the structure of most modern civil codes: these codes separate the general rules that apply across the board from the specific ones that govern particular problems, and then put the former before the latter.[268] As a result, a code's user can glean the scope of a rule from its place in the system. Finally, by presenting the law in a highly concentrated form, the system made the jurists' work more efficient: since each of the system's "bodies" incorporates a variety of legal rules, it lets us deal with the material with increased "alacrity, certainty, and ease" ("Raschheit," "Sicherheit," "Leichtigkeit").[269]

Beyond mere facilitation of the jurists' work, Jhering's "higher jurisprudence" also benefitted legal practice by producing new material that could be used to solve new problems. Existing concepts could be combined to create new ones. At first glance, the idea may seem fanciful but it is not difficult to think of instances in modern law where "concepts mate and beget new ones."[270] Just as important,

atoms and then putting them back together again; *Jhering*, Geist II.2. (1858) 377. At this point, Jhering apparently attributed little weight to the feeling of justice; that would change in short order, see infra chapter IV.3.

[266] *Jhering*, Geist II.2. (1858) 380. A notorious illustration of these approaches – which Jhering could have invoked but didn't – is the contrast between two famous codifications: the Allgemeines Preußisches Landrecht of 1794 provided detailed legal rules for every eventuality its makers deemed important, resulting in a code of nearly 20,000 provisions. The French Code civil 1804 relied heavily of broader principles, resulting in about 2300 articles.

[267] See supra note 223 and text.

[268] The perhaps most extreme version of this practice is the (highly abstract) "Allgemeiner Teil" ("General Part") constituting the first "Buch" ("book," i.e., part) of the German Civil Code (*BGB*) (arts. 1–240). It can also be observed, however, in civil codes across the world and even, though in less extreme form, in modern US-American codifications, such as Article One of the Uniform Commercial Code.

[269] *Jhering*, Geist II.2. (1858) 410.

[270] Supra note 245. In German law, for example, courts combined the concept of property with those of a fiduciary duty and a (monetary) obligation to create a (non-statutory) security interest (Sicherungseigentum) that avoids the impracticalities of the statutory lien (Pfand-

new solutions could also be extrapolated from the systematic organization of law. A true follower of Puchta, Jhering assumed that the system was gapless – not because it had a rule for every occasion, but because it contained all the building blocks and reflected all the principles needed from which the rules required for novel cases could be constructed.[271] To worry that the system had no place for a newly arising problem, Jhering claimed, was as pointless as worrying that the existing zoological classifications provided no place for a newly discovered animal.[272] "A jurisprudence at work for millenia has already discovered all the fundamental forms of the world of law [...] Such a jurisprudence, cannot not be embarrassed (in Verlegenheit bringen) by history."[273] To be sure, later generations largely debunked the dogma of gaplessness as an illusion. This does not mean, however, that the system is useless for the solution of legal issues not considered by its builders. As every civil lawyer worth his or her salt knows, the system indeed has the potential to help solve novel problems, even though that potential has its limits.

Thus, the Jhering committed to practical utility justified the use of abstract logic and the pursuit of systematic ordering not by its sheer intellectual appeal but, rather, by its benefits for learning, understanding, developing, and actually applying the law.

In the end, there was a tension between the scholar intoxicated by the "natural-historical method" and the jurist soberly seeking practical improvement. It is tempting to ask which was ultimately the "real" Jhering. The answer is that they both were. Here, as well as in many regards, Jhering was a multifaceted thinker, often marked by opposite inclinations, and for the most part quite happy to live with them.

The Ultimate Goal: The Simplification of Law. At this point, the reader may think that Jhering's methodology aimed at a complex system consisting of concepts difficult to grasp, principles hard to understand, and "constructions" arduous to perform. In fact, however, Jhering's overall objective was precisely the opposite: the ultimate goal of defining basic concepts, formulating general principles, and systematic ordering was the overall clarification and simplification of law.[274]

---

recht). In Italy, courts combined the concepts of *causa* and motivations to create the concept of presupposizione. And even in US-American law, strict liability for breach of warranty was combined with direct action in tort to create strict liability for defective products regardless of privity; Restatement Second of Torts, § 402A (1965).

[271] *Jhering*, Geist I (1852) 18–19. By charging legal science with the discovery of solutions to newly arising problems, Jhering assigned legal science the role of leading practice; being a mere follower, he opined, would an undignified fate, id. Note that 16 years later, he upgraded legal practice to the point where he saw it just the other way around: now jurisprudence had to assist legal practice and to process its results, infra 4, note 559 and text.

[272] *Jhering*, Unsere Aufgabe (1857) 16.

[273] *Jhering*, Unsere Aufgabe (1857) 16.

[274] *Jhering*, Geist II.2. (1858) 341–346. The idea was neither unique nor completely origi-

From today's perspective it is easy to forget how badly such a clarification and simplification was needed in mid-nineteenth century Germany. As a result of the Historical School's return to the classical Roman sources, the common private law of Germany (and beyond) was based mainly on Justinian's *Digest*, a compilation from the early sixth century (530–533 A.D.). This compilation consisted of over 9,000 excerpts from about 300 works authored by several dozen Roman jurists over roughly three centuries; the material was divided according to subject matter into 50 "books" and filled thousands of pages.[275] This vast "casuistic" material could not possibly be mastered by all but a very few highly specialized scholars. Its sheer mass and frightening complexity were badly in need of streamlining. To be sure, the Pandectist literature, Puchta's works prominently among it, had already beaten it into much more manageable shape. Jhering, however, developed a methodology designed to reduce it further to its fundamental concepts, leading principles, and to bring it into a coherent logical system that would greatly facilitate learning, applying, and adapting it.

Time and again, Jhering emphasized the need to minimize both the complexity and the mass of law as well as the concomitant need to strive for clarity, simplicity, and proper organization. He emphasized the "law of parsimoniousness" that required to "do as much as possible with as little as possible."[276] Disregarding that maxim, had dire consequences: "A jurisprudence that has not understood it, that does not know how to economize with the material, will be defeated by the growing mass of material and become a victim of its own richness."[277] In a similar vein, a lack of systematic ordering was a fatal weakness: "as long as [legal] science has not found the proper place for a matter, it has not truly understood it, because understanding means not only comprehending the matter in and of itself but also comprehending its connection with others."[278] Moreover, "a sharply defined and richly developed terminology is of utmost importance [because it] facilitates control and overview […]. Even in science, giving birth [to material] is not sufficient, it must also be christened [i.e., given a proper name]."[279] Last, but not least, "construction," Jhering's pet idea, was to be plain, graphic, and lucid.[280] It should result in a "simple rule" that can be stated in one short sentence,[281] just like the fundamental laws of nature discovered by the hard sciences.[282] In a manner reminiscent of Occam's razor, for Jhering, the most highly developed meth-

---

nal, see, e.g., *Kierulff*, Theorie des Gemeinen Civilrechts (1839) xxi–xxii, xxv. Jhering just brought in into particularly sharp relief.

[275] For a modern English edition, see *Watson* (ed.), The Digest of Justinian (4 vols., 1998).

[276] *Jhering*, Geist II.2 (1858) 342.

[277] *Jhering*, Geist II.2. (1858) 342.

[278] *Jhering*, Geist II.2. (1858) 344, fn. 480.

[279] *Jhering*, Geist II.2. (1858) 344

[280] *Jhering*, Geist II.2. (1858) 406.

[281] *Jhering*, *Culpa in Contrahendo* (1861) 32. In this essay, Jhering provided a powerful demonstration; see infra 3.

[282] Jhering, Das Schuldmoment im römischen Privatrecht (1867) 40.

odology was the one that produced the greatest simplicity.[283] In other words, Jhering pursued the ideal of a legal system that rationalizes and organizes its material in order to make operating with law more user-friendly. He considered a casuistic approach relying on a multitude of rules a "sign of weakness," i.e., of a lack of intellectual power to extract the logical essence from the mass of provisions.[284]

All this continues to resonate deeply with lawyers in the civil law orbit. Even in an age of legislative deluge, for civil lawyers, knowing the law's fundamental elements (captured by a precise terminology), grasping its underlying principles, and understanding its systematic order remains at a premium, especially, though not exclusively, in private law. Someone trained in the common law tradition with its penchant for looking at individual cases and reasoning by analogy will meet Jhering's ideas with greater skepticism. Yet, even there, distilling fundamental principles from precedent is not unknown,[285] though putting these principles into a systematic order reflecting their inherent logic is rarely pursued and even more rarely attained.

Beyond Legal Technique: "Higher Jurisprudence" as Science, Art, and Passion. Jhering's "higher jurisprudence" cannot be fully appreciated if it is regarded merely as a form of legal technique in the service of practical ends. For Jhering, it was much more than that: a version of true science; a form of art; and, last but not least, a personal passion.

"The natural-historical method," Jhering claimed, was "natural science in the realm of ideas" ("Naturwissenschaft im Elemente des Geistes").[286] This claim had three important implications. First, it upgraded legal academia: presenting jurisprudence as a true "science" entitled it to the same prestige enjoyed by biology, chemistry, and physics at the time. By letting jurisprudence bask in the bright light of these fast-progressing disciplines, Jhering (and others) improved its image in the public eye.[287] Upgrading his profession may also have been personally important to Jhering as there were several natural scientists among his friends.[288]

---

[283] *Jhering*, Geist II.2. (1858) 406.

[284] *Jhering*, Geist I (1852) 30.

[285] See *Goff*, In Search for Principle (1984). A famous example is MacPherson v. Buick Motor Co., 111 N.E. 1050 (N.Y. 1916) where Judge Cardozo masterfully reviewed a line of precedents and then extracted from them the principle at the heart of modern product liability law: the seller has a duty of care to the buyer even in the absence of privity if the defective product was foreseeably dangerous to others than the immediate buyer.

[286] *Jhering*, Geist II.2. (1858) 389.

[287] Jhering received credit for this increased prestige of jurisprudence from his early biographer, see *Mitteis*, Jhering (1905) 652. As a highly prominent legal historian in turn-of-the century Austria and Germany, Mitteis was in a good position to judge the matter.

[288] *Klippel*, Rudolf von Jhering (1993) 34; *Klippel*, Juristischer Begriffshimmel und Funktionale Rechtswelt (2000) 125. In Gießen, Jhering actually audited a university colleague's course on physical-chemical problems and on metereology, *Hermann Jhering*, Erinnerungen, Jhering in Briefen (1913) 463.

Second, conceiving of law as a true "science" eliminated, or at least greatly reduced, the dependence of jurisprudence on the legislative will. At the time of Jhering's writing, this was a very sore point. While Jhering was working on "Geist," a prosecutor from Berlin, Julius von Kirchmann, gave a talk entitled "Die Werthlosigkeit der Jurisprudenz als Wissenschaft" ("The Worthlessness of Jurisprudence as a Science") which was widely noted (and has since become a classic).[289] Von Kirchmann charged that a discipline could not be a science if its material was subject to change at the whim of the lawgiver: "Three corrections by the legislator, and whole libraries go to the pulpmill."[290] This, of course, put the dignity of jurisprudence into serious question.[291] Jhering proffered a powerful rebuttal: at least in its "higher" form, jurisprudence did *not* deal with positive legal rules, which the legislator could change at will, but rather with essential "legal bodies," over which the legislator had little or no sway. In short, as Jhering stated very clearly, legal science in the form of "higher jurisprudence" was the learned jurist's escape from the vagaries of positive law.[292] Moreover, Jhering's claim that "higher jurisprudence" itself was actually capable of producing legal material challenged the legislator's monopoly of law production. Higher jurisprudence, Jhering wrote, thus "raises itself from the status of a porter for the legislator, a collector of positive details, to the status of a true art and science."[293] It stands to reason that Jhering's defense of jurisprudence strongly appealed to his academic colleagues. Third, the status of "higher jurisprudence" as an independent science also implied that the legislator should leave it, and thus the work of academic jurists, alone. Here, Jhering echoed Savigny whose claim that jurisprudence was a true science had also led him to protest against excessive legislative interference.[294] There was an important difference, however: Savigny resisted legislative meddling with (private) law in principle (though allowing exceptions); Jhering only argued for a division of labor. He never denied that the legislature needed to make law as required by a fast-changing society, nor did he oppose private law codification,[295] but he demanded that the lawgiver not interfere with inherently scientific business, especially issues of "construction."[296]

---

[289] *Von Kirchmann*, Die Werthlosigkeit der Jurisprudenz als Wissenschaft (1848).

[290] *Von Kirchmann*, Die Werthlosigkeit der Jurisprudenz als Wissenchaft (1848) 23.

[291] The role of von Kirchmann's talk as a trigger for Jhering's methodological response, especially in "Unsere Aufgabe" (1857), is discussed in greater detail by *Mecke*, Jherings Rechtsdenken im Kontext der zeitgenössischen Natur- und Sozialwissenschaften (2023) 266–277.

[292] *Jhering*, Scherz und Ernst (1884) 342.

[293] *Jhering*, Geist II.2. (1858) 389. The natural-historical method, Jhering added, is "the whole dignity and honor" of jurisprudence" ("ihre ganze Würde und Ehre"), id.

[294] *Savigny*, Stimmen für und wider neue Gesetzbücher (1816) 250.

[295] See infra 6., notes 508–516 and text.

[296] *Jhering*, Geist II.2. (1858) 399. Paraphrasing Luther, Jhering demanded: "Legal science should leave to the emperor what is his, but the latter should also leave to legal science what belongs to it," id.

Jhering repeatedly called – higher – jurisprudence an "art and a science" in the same breath,[297] and he was as serious about the former as he was about the latter. This was in part because he considered "higher jurisprudence" creative like art. It "artistically forms the material, shapes it, and breathes life into it"[298](i.e., the jurist as Pygmalion). Conceiving of "higher jurisprudence" as an art also had its implications. Successful "construction" was less a matter of "industriousness and erudition than of talent and intuition."[299] Perhaps more importantly, "construction" was subject to "the law of juristic beauty" ("Gesetz der juristischen Schönheit")[300] It should thus not only be correct and functional but also fulfill certain aesthetic criteria, such as "naturalness, transparency, simplicity, vividness" ("Natürlichkeit, Durchsichtigkeit, Einfachheit, Anschaulichkeit")[301] – of which simplicity was the most important.[302] It was even subject to the changing artistic styles of consecutive epochs.[303] Like art, it offered not only intellectual satisfaction but also pleasure (Genuß).[304]

Finally, for Jhering, "higher jurisprudence" was not merely an intellectual endeavor; it was also an – at times intense – emotional experience. This is important to note because it will help to explain the violence of his later reaction against it.[305] Again operating more in the mode of the artist than of the jurist, Jhering's enthusiasm for his own ideas sometimes worked like a drug that put him in a state of ecstasy. In flowery language, he explained that dealing with this higher state of law "is the true home of the jurist, to it he feels constantly drawn."[306] A layman had no idea of this "ideal, and to him invisible, creation of art." For almost two pages in "Unsere Aufgabe," Jhering waxed eloquent about the "order and harmony, the simplicity and beauty," the "ideal forms, the miracles of this higher world," and "the inexhaustible richness that comes to light" wherever the jurist digs beneath the surface of positive law. Jhering proclaimed that "delving into *this* world is not work, but an enjoyment and capable of filling the soul and the whole life of even the intellectually most demanding human being" (supposedly Jhering himself). Then, almost suddenly, and as if awaking from a trance, he asked: "Did I perhaps idealize the matter?"[307]

---

[297] See, e.g., *Jhering*, Geist II.2. (1858) 389.

[298] *Jhering*, Geist II.2. (1858) 389.

[299] *Jhering*, Geist II.2 (1858) 398 fn. 514. Jhering considered the success rate very low (he rated it at 1/100 though that should not be taken literally), perhaps (unconsciously?) to claim greater glory for his own (successful) endeavors on that field.

[300] *Jhering*, Geist II.2. (1858) 405; for further discussion, see *Möller*, Die juristische Konstruktion im Werk Rudolf von Jherings – vom universellen Rechtsalphabet bis zur juristischen Schönheit (2017).

[301] *Jhering*, Geist II.2. (1858) 406.

[302] *Jhering*, Geist II.2. (1858) 406.

[303] *Jhering*, Geist II.2. (1858) 406.

[304] *Jhering*, Unsere Aufgabe (1857) 13.

[305] Infra chapter III.2.

[306] *Jhering*, Unsere Aufgabe (1857) 12.

[307] *Jhering*, Unsere Aufgabe (1857) 13–14. Jhering essentially said no, he did not. He

A Final Assessment: Reactions to Jhering's Methodology. While skeptical about his accomplishments in "Geist" in general, Jhering himself thought very highly of its methodological parts in particular. "In my opinion," he wrote to his friend Windscheid, "the general theory of juristic technique is the most significant element of the whole book."[308] He considered it pioneering work and was openly proud of it.[309] Even after his turn away from a purely logical approach to law around 1860[310] he did not significantly change his methodological discourses in later editions, showing that he still stood by them – or at least considered them too important to be deleted.

Many of his contemporaries were not so sure of the merits of Jhering's "naturhistorische Methode." In a much noted book, Jhering's contemporary Johannes Michael Kuntze (1824–1894) spoke of "a civilistic artificiality resulting in a transcendental spiritualism."[311] An anonymous reviewer of Jhering's "Aufgabe" sarcastically wished that Jhering had included a few samples of his "legal bodies," to illustrate what he really meant by that.[312] And to the surviving adherents of Savigny's Historical School, this was all blue smoke and mirrors anyway.[313] Thus for some, Jhering had proven himself to rank among the foremost legal theorists of his time; for others, his tendency to go to extremes was out of line with the ethos of moderation widely embraced in German legal academia, both then and now.

3. Doctrinal Scholarship at Work: "*Culpa in Contrahendo*" (1861)

One could justly consider Jhering's big project of going beyond Roman law overambitious, his "natural-historical method" overdone, and his case in favor of both overstated. Yet, when Jhering worked with legal doctrine to solve concrete problems, his mastery was virtually undisputed. He combined a formidable knowledge of the sources with powerful analytical and argumentative skills, enviable creativity, and an unfailing instinct for proper solutions. Since these solutions were geared towards the needs of practice, his doctrinal work generated

explained that of course he had not been talking about the colleagues "whose minds had never opened up to an understanding of this invisible world because they directed their attention from the very beginning only to the lower matters," id. 14. Apparently, these foot soldiers were beyond redemption.

[308] Letter to Windscheid of August 15, 1860, Jhering in Briefen (1913) 23.

[309] Id. See also letter to Gerber of October 14, 1854; *Losano*, Der Briefwechsel zwischen Jhering und Gerber (1984) part I, 118–122.

[310] Infra chapter III.

[311] *Kuntze*, Der Wendepunkt der Rechtswissenschaft (1856) 25.

[312] This reaction was discovered by *Mecke*, Jherings Rechtsdenken im Kontext der zeitgenössischen Natur- und Sozialwissenschaften (2023) 261.

[313] See *Mecke*, Jherings Rechtsdenken im Kontext der zeitgenössischen Natur- und Sozialwissenschaften (2023) 261.

much interest and had significant influence. On the field of Romanist *Dogmatik* – the pride of nineteenth century German jurisprudence – Jhering was second to none.[314]

Jhering left a large and diverse body of doctrinal scholarship, spanning half a century – from his dissertation on the Roman law of inheritance (1842)[315] to a posthumously published article on the law of possession (1893).[316] In about two dozen articles, most of them published in the "Jahrbücher," as well as in a few books,[317] Jhering covered a wide range of private law topics including agency, contracts of sale,[318] lease, violation of personal rights, joint liability, transfer of movables, and real property rights. Even if he had written nothing else, his numerous lasting contributions to the doctrine of private law would have made him one of the great jurists of nineteenth century Germany.[319]

There was one particular topic to which Jhering returned time and again: the law of possession. Beginning with Savigny's pathbreaking treatise "Das Recht des Besitzes" (1803), possession became the most popular bone of contention in nineteenth century German doctrinal scholarship.[320] This was not because of any overwhelming practical relevance, but because *possessio* raised several issues considered fundamental at the time – for example, whether it was a right or merely a fact, why (and to what extent) it needed protection, and whether it required a particular will (*animus possidendi*). Jhering was in the fray for decades, penning about half-a-dozen articles and two monographs on the topic.[321] In his last major work, "Der Besitzwille," a 500-page tome published when he was past 70, he set out to demolish Savigny's (by then 86 year-old) theory[322] and also, though more

---

[314] Ludwig Mitteis opined that "the domain of doctrinal work ("des Juristischen") was always Jhering's true strength," *Mitteis*, Jhering (1905) 658. While Mitteis praised Jhering's doctrinal work in glowing terms, he was openly critical of his "philosophical" and historical scholarship.

[315] *Jhering, De heriditate possidente* (Berlin 1842)

[316] *Jhering*, Der Besitz (1893).

[317] *Jhering*, Über den Grund des Besitzschutzes (1869); *Jhering*, Der Besitzwille (1889); three early articles were collected in *Jhering*, Abhandlungen aus dem römischen Recht (1844); the most important articles are collected in *Jhering*, Gesammelte Aufsätze (3 vols. 1881–1886).

[318] See infra chapter III.1.

[319] For a more detailed discussion of Jhering's most important doctrinal contributions, see *Fikentscher*, Methoden des Rechts III (1976) 167–186.

[320] During the nineteenth century more than a dozen monographs and many more law review articles and doctoral dissertations were published on the subject. Meanwhile, Germanist legal scholars debated the indigenous counterpart to the Roman *possessio*, see *Heusler*, Die Gewere (1872). Possession was also a major issue in the common law orbit where scholars frequently referenced German scholarship, including Jhering's work, see *Link*, Possession, Possessio und das Schicksal des Common Law (2002).

[321] A fairly detailed and very lucid summary of the nineteenth century debate about possession, and of Jhering's contribution to it, is provided in English by one of Jhering's former students, Munroe Smith (1854–1926); *Smith*, Four German Jurists II (1896) 278–290.

[322] *Jhering*, Der Besitzwille (1889). Jhering delved deeply into the sources and went to war

as an afterthought, to critique the provisions on possession in the first draft of the German Civil Code (Bürgerliches Gesetzbuch, BGB).

While working on doctrinal topics consumed much of Jhering's energy, took much of his time, and earned him much of his fame, very little of it has much relevance for a broader audience today. Most of Jhering's contributions were absorbed into twentieth century private law, although some were rejected by future generations. In either case, his doctrinal publications are of lasting interest only to specialists in the genesis of private law.

We will thus look at Jhering's doctrinal work merely to provide an example. The most suitable exemplification is his longish article on "*Culpa in Contrahendo,*" published in the "Jahrbücher" in 1861.[323] The reason for this selection is not so much that "*Culpa*" is Jhering's most famous piece of doctrinal scholarship – at least in the civil law world, even jurists who have never heard of Jhering otherwise, will associate his name with it. It is not even mainly that "*Culpa*" is Jhering's most influential doctrinal essay – it effected a major expansion of liability in modern German law and had an influence in other jurisdictions as well.[324] The main reason for focusing on this article is rather that a close look allows us to watch Jhering at work in the field of *Dogmatik*.[325] Here, we can observe him as a nineteenth-century Romanist scholar who, before private law codification, was still working directly with the Roman sources. As Ludwig Mitteis put it, Jhering was one of the last German jurists "preaching straight from the Bible."[326]

Jhering's doctrinal essays are usually much less concerned with abstract concepts, juristic constructions, and systematic ordering than his methodological program suggests. Instead, they typically tackle concrete problems, are guided by

---

with the prevailing (essentially Savignian) claim that possession required a "will to possess" (as Stintzing and Landsberg remarked, Jhering's "Der Besitzwille" was written against the Besitzwille, *Stinzing and Landsberg*, Geschichte der deutschen Rechtswissenschaft III.2. (1910) 823. On another occasion, Jhering had already shown how this requirement could generate absurd results, *Jhering*, Scherz und Ernst (1884) 63–69. Yet, the book's primary purpose was a – final – critique of the dominant jurisprudential method, as indicated by the book's subtitle ("Zugleich eine Kritik der herrschenden juristischen Methode"). Thus, the book was Jhering's last – and most extensive – assault on the "formalistic" (or "dialectical") method and also his final demonstration of the "realistic" (or "teleological") method, *Jhering*, Der Besitzwille (1889) VIII–XI. That, latter, approach is the subject of chapter IV.

[323] Reprinted in *Jhering*, Gesammelte Aufsätze I (1881) 327–426. The article (including an addendum) has 112 pages, though in fairly large font. For our present purposes, however, the important substance is contained in its first half (pp. 1–56). For an exhaustive analysis, see *Choe*, Culpa in Contrahendo bei Rudolf von Jhering (1988).

[324] Infra notes 376–385 and text.

[325] We will look at another example, though more briefly, in chapter III.1. Many observations presented in the following pages also apply, *mutatis mutandis*, to *Jhering*, Zur Lehre von den Beschränkungen des Grundeigentümers im Interesse des Nachbarn (On the Doctrine of Limitations of a Property Owner in the Interest of the Neighbor) (1863). That article also strongly demonstrates Jhering's attention to practical needs and interests.

[326] *Mitteis*, Jhering (1905) 664.

practical considerations, and often proceed in a fashion that is surprisingly down-to-earth. This is also true for his article on *Culpa in Contrahendo*. Still, the piece does show Jhering in pursuit of his overall project, i.e., to proceed "through the Roman law beyond the Roman law."[327] We can see him engaged in "higher jurisprudence," constructing new law from the existing sources.

The Strengths of Style: The Jurist at His Best. Already on the first few pages, the reader can make some interesting observations about Jhering's style. As in his methodological writings, it is spirited, lively, and engaging. But in stark contrast to his theoretical discourses, it is also disciplined, measured, and precise. There are no rhetorical fireworks, no terminological confusion, no wild exaggeration, and very little redundancy. In his methodological pieces, Jhering often sounds like an orator in a public venue who is trying to capture and entertain his audience. Here, he writes as a scholar in his study who seeks to convince a readership of experts through careful argumentation.

Even though Jhering is writing about a doctrinal issue, presents intricate arguments based on the Roman sources, and diligently explores all dimensions of the problem, his style is plain and pleasant. The discourse is well-paced; it neither lingers nor rushes. Jhering always talks to his audience, never to himself. He does not lecture readers from high above but rather guides them on a tour exploring the problem and developing a solution. At times, he confesses to doubt and flags issues that remain open for now. As a result, the article is a pleasure to read – which may well be part of the reason for its success.

The Problem: Roman Law vs. "Sense of Justice". Jhering captures the reader's attention by beginning with a practical problem that is easy to understand: a party rescinds a contract due to error, e.g., regarding the quantity of goods; as a result, the other party suffers a loss, e.g., the costs of shipping. Since one party's mistake has caused its counterpart harm, there should be a remedy. Yet, established Roman law, and thus the common private law of Germany at the time, provided none. This followed from some of its fundamental features. Roman law allowed actions for breach of specific contracts, such as a contract of sale (*actio emti*, sic[328]), but since there is no contract in our case (whether we treat it as void *ab initio* or voided with retroactive effect) a contractual remedy seems impossible. Roman law also allowed extra-contractual actions – but only in two general forms: where the defendant had caused the harm intentionally, i.e., through fraud or misrepresentation (*actio doli*) or where he had caused physical injury to property (*actio legis Aquiliae*); obviously, these do not help in our case either. In short,

[327] Supra 1., notes 29–32 and text. A close look at this, by now classic, article is also warranted because in the absence of an English translation, it is linguistically inaccessible most readers in the world. For a French translation, see *Rudolf von Jhering*, Oeuvres choisis, vol. 2 (de Meulenaere transl., Paris 1893) 1; an Italian translation is *Rudolf von Jhering*, Della culpa in contrahendo, ossia Del risarcimento del danno nei contratti nulli o non guinti a perfezione (Federica Procchi transl., Napoli 2005).

[328] The more common form is *empti* but Jhering uses *emti* throughout the article.

an action for damages under Roman law normally required either a contract, intent or physical harm,[329] and since none of these requirements were fulfilled in our case, Roman law left the harmed party out in the rain. Jhering surveyed the existing literature and found that indeed, this was pretty much the general consensus. He duly noted the exception of one scholar, but his position in favor of a remedy had largely been forgotten.[330] Thus Jhering faced a situation in which fairness suggested one solution while Roman law seemed to command another.

At this point, most contemporary Romanists would have resigned themselves to the fact that Roman law just did not help the injured party, especially since even the great Savigny had said so.[331] Jhering, however, did exactly the opposite. He found the situation patently and depressingly unfair[332] and appealed to the reader's sense of justice: "Who does not feel that we need an action for damages here?" Jhering then refused to surrender that sense of justice to the dictates of positive Roman law as then understood. If established Roman law did not provide a remedy, it obviously suffered from a lacuna – which needed to be filled.[333] Jhering here followed his general conviction that the literal commands of Roman law were not the final answer to a practical problem. Instead, it was the task of modern jurists to find solutions that satisfy practical needs as well as the prevailing sense of justice. The question then became how to go about that.

Inventing a New Cause of Action: Fault in Contract-Formation. Today, we would probably suggest leaving the existing rules behind and simply fashioning a new one that better satisfies our sense of justice (or makes better policy sense). For Jhering, however, that was not an option. He could not just suggest overruling Roman law. It was not only that the legal community in which he operated (and for which he wrote) felt bound by that law and would not have taken any such suggestion seriously. Jhering himself was far too immersed in, and had far too much respect for, Roman law to just write it off in that fashion. We must remember that he had not advocated sending Roman law to the dustbin altogether; he just wanted to free the present from the dictates of its positive rules while still building on its inherent principles and ideas. This required developing solutions for which Roman law provided the seeds, but which it had not yet brought to fruition. In short, whatever solution he was going to proffer, he had to go "through the Roman law."[334]

---

[329] There were various exceptions none of which, however, came into play in our case.

[330] Jhering fully acknowledged that almost a generation before, an author by the name of (Heinrich) Richelmann had found an entirely correct solution, *Jhering*, Culpa (1861) 3, citing *Richelmann*, Der Einfluß des Irrthums auf Verträge (Hannover 1837). Jhering noted that with negligible exceptions, Richelmann's suggestion had been ignored, and that it had come to Jhering's own attention only after he had begun to think in the same direction, *Jhering*, Culpa (1861) 3–4.

[331] *Jhering*, Culpa (1861) 2 fn. 1, 4 fn. 4.

[332] *Jhering*, Culpa (1861) 2.

[333] *Jhering*, Culpa (1861) 3.

[334] Supra 1., note 31.

One possibility was to expand the extra-contractual actions to cover the current situation. Jhering considered that clearly inadvisable because it would entail bad results. Loosening the restrictions of these actions (i.e. the requirements of either intent or physical harm) and basing extra-contractual liability on mere negligence would mean, for example, that one could be liable to a complete stranger for negligently giving wrong advice.[335] The Roman jurists were wise enough to avoid such results.

Thus the only viable option was to allow a contractual remedy. That would help because within a contractual relationship, mere *culpa* (herein the fault of the offeror) could support a damage action.[336] The problem was, of course, that in our case, there was no valid contractual relationship. Yet, as Jhering keenly observed, the parties were not complete strangers either. By engaging in contract-formation, they had entered some kind of special relationship. Perhaps one could impose liability for mere negligence in that specific context, i.e., for *culpa in contrahendo*.[337]

Constructing Roman Law: From Examples to "Simple Rule." Perhaps. So far, *culpa in contrahendo* was just an idea (Jhering was on page 7 of a 112-page article). It would never find acceptance – neither with Jhering's audience nor, for that matter, with himself – if it could not be grounded in, or at least derived from, Roman law. Jhering thus turned to the Roman sources.

The problem presented by Jhering (a party's mistake about the quantity of goods) was just one possible reason among others for the invalidity of a contract. The classical Roman jurists had discussed a whole variety of scenarios, especially cases in which the performance was impossible *ex ante*, i.e., for reasons that existed already when the agreement was made (such as the sale of an object previously destroyed, of a thing already belonging to the buyer, or of a free person mistaken for a slave). In such cases, the prevailing view was that the contract was invalid (which then raised the follow-up question whether the buyer had any remedy).[338] Jhering was of course keenly aware of the respective sources. For present purposes, we can leave most of them aside, however, because in developing his concept of *culpa in contrahendo*, Jhering focused more narrowly on two specific ones.[339] They were of particular interest to him because here, the Roman jurists had clearly opined that the buyer indeed had an action for damages.

[335] *Jhering*, Culpa (1861) 12–13.

[336] The existence of *culpa*, i.e., some kind of actual fault, was a potential stumbling block; Jhering addressed that issue later in the article, see infra notes 358–366 and text.

[337] *Jhering*, Culpa (1861) 7.

[338] For a summary with ample citations to the Roman sources, see *Kaser*, Das römische Privatrecht I (1971) 349; for a discussion, see *Frier*, A Casebook on the Roman Law of Contracts (2021) 215–217.

[339] Jhering drew on these sources in various other regards, especially in part III of his article where he provided a typology of reasons for a contract's invalidity, discussing them in considerable detail, *Jhering*, Culpa (1861) 56–106.

One involved a "sacred, religious or public" object which, as a *res extra commercium*, could simply not be sold. Even though the contract was thus invalid on grounds of impossibility, the late-classical jurist Modestinus (third century A.D.) opined that the buyer had an action for damages; Justinian's Institutes (533 A.D.) adopted that view; and there was some support for it in the praetorian edict.[340] The other case involved the sale of a non-existing inheritance. Again, while the contract was invalid, the early classical Roman jurist Javolenus (first century A.D.) supported an action for damages here as well.[341] To be sure, these were only two specific instances – and only a total of four sources out of many others. They did show, however, that classical Roman law at least occasionally allowed an action for damages even when the contract was invalid.

Thus, Jhering had demonstrated that his idea was not entirely alien to Roman law. Yet, he still had to show that from these examples, one could derive some kind of rule. In this process, his first step was to "analyze" the "relationships" involved in these sources. He dissected them into five constituent elements which a modern lawyer might call the elements of a cause of action: 1. the apparent[342] conclusion of a contract of sale; 2. its invalidity; 3. a problem in the sphere of the seller (in the first case with the object's salability, in the second with its existence); 4. ignorance of the buyer (knowledge would render him unworthy of protection); 5. a contractual action for damages.[343] This set-up pointed in the direction of a possible rule: according to Roman law, if these five requirements were fulfilled, an injured party might be endowed with a damage action.

Such an action for damages, Jhering claimed, was indeed a contractual one even though the envisaged agreement had failed. In support of that position, he proffered two arguments. First, apparently, the Roman jurists had not considered failed contracts to be completely without effect: a contract's "invalidity" meant only that nobody could demand performance, but that did not exclude liability for *culpa* in their making.[344] Second, this position was justified because the problem did not arise between complete strangers but rather in direct connection with the business of contracting; this connection was not just an external one (of occasion) but an internal one: the *culpa* here is of the kind we normally see in contractual relationships.[345] Jhering thus wrapped the two scenarios discussed into a "simple sentence:"

---

[340] Jhering cited "62 § 1 de contr. emt. (18,1) (Modestinus)" (i.e., D. 18.1.62.1.); "§ 5 J. de emt. et vend. (3.23)" (i.e. Inst. 2.23.5.); and "1. 8 § 1 de relig. (11.7 Ulpianus)" (i.e., D. 11.7.8.1.); *Jhering*, Culpa (1861) 9.

[341] Jhering cited "I.8. und 9 de hered. vend. (18.4) (Javolenus and Paulus)" (i.e. D. 18.4.8. und 18.4.9.); *Jhering*, Culpa (1861) 9–10.

[342] *Jhering* used the term "external" ("äußerer"), Jhering, Culpa (1861) 10.

[343] *Jhering*, Culpa (1861) 10–15.

[344] *Jhering*, Culpa (1861) 29–30.

[345] *Jhering*, Culpa (1861) 26.

"The conclusion of a contract creates not only an obligation to perform it, but also, if this effect is excluded because of a legal obstacle, under some circumstances a liability for damages; the expression 'nullity' of contract means only the absence of the former effect, not of all legal effects whatsoever."[346]

From Simple Sentence to General Principle: Liability for Culpa in Contract Formation. It may seem as if Jhering had now solved the initial problem – but he was not quite there yet: the Roman sources from which he derived a contractual damage action involved problems with the nature of the goods while Jhering's initial case involved a seller's error about their quantity. Jhering was far too careful a doctrinal jurist to simply lump these problems together. If the solution derived from the Roman sources for some cases was to cover other cases as well, it had to be broadened from a "simple sentence" to a general principle applicable to all contractual relationships.

Jhering constructed that principle from what he saw as the underlying reason for the defendant's liability: his fault. Since liability was justified by fault, he argued that *culpa* could serve as a basis for a general principle: "If liability for damages is based on *culpa* in these two cases [addressed in the Roman sources], this inevitably requires creating the same effect in all cases involving the same *culpa*. It would make no sense to consider the *culpa* limited only to the concrete form in which it appears in these cases."[347] Since (according to Jhering) such *culpa* exists whenever a party makes a contract without being able to fulfill the requirements for its validity (e.g., by selling something that could not be sold) or when the contract turns out to be invalid because of a party's mistake (in whatever form), that party must generally be liable for damages.[348] To be sure, reaching this conclusion required a somewhat adventurous construction of – some might even say: tinkering with – the Roman sources, but it was not outside the bounds of plausibility.

Jhering provided two further arguments that went beyond Roman law itself. One invoked spheres and degrees of duties:

"Someone who makes a contract exits the extra-contractual interaction (Verkehr) with its merely negative duties and enters the sphere of contract with its positive obligations; he transitions from the mere *culpa in faciendo* to that of positive *diligentia*, and the first and most general obligation he thus assumes is to comply with the requisite *diligentia*. Not only the contracts already existing, but also the just emerging contractual relationship must come under the protection or the rules based on *culpa*."[349]

---

[346] *Jhering*, Culpa (1861) 32.

[347] *Jhering*, Culpa (1861) 41. Jhering's drive for a general principle made, and continues to make, obvious sense for jurists trained in the civil law where broad rules and general principles are considered essential. A common lawyer may beg to differ and decline to consider the difference between problems with the object of sale on the one hand, and error regarding their quantity on the other, irrelevant.

[348] *Jhering*, Culpa (1861) 41.

[349] *Jhering*, Culpa (1861) 41–42.

As a result,

"[t]he requirement of contractual diligence applies to both completed and incipient contractual relationships, in both cases, its violation entails a contractual action for damages. *Culpa in contrahendo* is merely contractual culpa in a particular dimension."[350]

The other consideration pertained to the nature of the parties' promises. By entering a contract, Jhering explained, a party tacitly promises that on its side, there are no grounds for rendering the contract invalid.

"Whether he assures [the other party] by words or by the fact that he is able to conclude this contract makes no difference; the assurance is inherent in the act of contracting."[351]

Since all these considerations apply to all types of contracts as well as to both parties,[352] the scope of liability for *culpa in contrahendo* is broad: it covers all instances in which one party is responsible for the invalidity of a contract if that causes a loss to the other side.[353] In other words, Jhering's principle applies not only to his initial scenario of (unilateral) mistake but to all the other cases discussed by the Roman jurists in this context as well.[354]

Life, Jhering had claimed at the outset, "will not accept the naked invalidity of the contract according to Roman law."[355] With his construction of a solution from the Roman sources, it no longer had to.[356] Jhering had gone "though the Roman" law and then "beyond it."[357]

---

[350] *Jhering*, Culpa (1861) 52.

[351] *Jhering*, Culpa (1861) 43.

[352] *Jhering*, Culpa (1861) 41.

[353] Jhering's principle was limited in an important regard, however: *culpa in contrahendo* applied only once a contractual agreement had been reached. Jhering clearly stated that it did not cover cases in which a party simply relies on the offer of another before accepting it – a party who is careless enough to do so is itself *in culpa* because it must reckon with the offer's withdrawal; *Jhering*, Culpa (1861) 43. While Jhering used the example of a party relying on the *other* party's offer before acceptance, his argument applies with even greater force to the reverse situation, i.e., if a party relies on its *own* offer before it has been accepted by the other side. In both instances, a party moving towards performance before perfection of the contract does so at its own risk.

[354] Jhering discussed these (and other) cases in the second part of his article. He divided them into those involving problems with the subject (i.e., the contracting parties), with the object (of the contract), and with the parties' will (both its declaration and the will itself); *Jhering*, Culpa (1861) 56–106. While this discussion proffers sophisticated analyses of a broad range of issues, inter alia of various kinds of mistake in contract formation, it is relevant only for a reader specifically interested in the doctrinal ramifications of Jhering's basic concept.

[355] *Jhering*, Culpa (1861) 7.

[356] Jhering also discussed various legislative provisions supporting his position, *Jhering*, Culpa (1861) 44–51. He found them in two of the most important codifications of the time, the Allgemeines Landrecht für die preußischen Staaten (ALR, General Landlaw for the Prussian States) of 1794, and the Austrian Allgemeines bürgerliches Gesetzbuch (ABGB, General Civil Code) of 1811. These codifications were of great practical importance: when Jhering wrote his article, they applied in large parts of the German Federation, and as specific legislation, they provided the positive law for probably the majority of its population, trumping the (residual) Roman sources and doctrine. It may thus seem odd that Jhering did not

Jhering at His Limit: The Problem of "Fault." Thus Jhering had developed a general principle of liability for *culpa* leading to the invalidity of a contract. But what exactly did *culpa* mean? A direct translation would be "fault" which, in turn, suggests blameworthiness. Since this is not, however, how Jhering understood it, we need to take a closer look at his construction of the term. This is important not only to complete our understanding of Jhering's invention but also because his discussion of the matter shows the limits of his project.

As mentioned, for Jhering, the *doctrinal* basis of an action for *culpa in contrahendo* was not protection of the innocent plaintiff but the fault of the defendant. After all, it was a fundamental principle of Roman contract law that liability for damages was based on fault.[358] That, however, raised the question how to treat cases in which the defendant had no knowledge of the problem that ultimately rendered the contract invalid.[359] To be sure, in many instances he was still clearly at fault because *diligentia* required that he should have discovered (or avoided) the problem. But what if the defendant truly had no chance to do so, i.e., if he was "completely innocent" ("vollkommen entschuldigt")?[360] Jhering was convinced that even in such a case, the defendant should be liable because the reason for the contract's invalidity was his mistake. Jhering thus argued that even an "innocent" defendant was *in culpa.*

---

put them at center stage. Yet, relegating such statutory provisions to a fairly minor role was neither inappropriate nor uncommon. It was not inappropriate because Jhering was, after all, a professor Roman law which was the primary (and in many cases the only) subject of private law teaching at the universities, providing the common jurisprudential basis for all German lawyers. Thus, as an academic, Jhering was not tasked with writing about (or teaching) particular statutes. It was not uncommon because the Romanists, who considered themselves the elite of German legal academia, often failed to pay any attention to such local legislation; see *Zimmermann*, Roman Law, Contemporary Law, European Law (2001) 6–8. In fact, it was rather unusual for someone like Jhering to dedicate several pages of an article on *Dogmatik* to specific statutory rules in this or that part of the country. Yet, even though Jhering paid considerable attention to these rules, they were clearly of secondary importance for his project. He turned to them only after having reached his result based on the Roman sources, and he invoked them mainly for two ancillary purposes: they could be read to imply (though "obviously in an unconscious manner", *Jhering*, Culpa (1861) 44, the principle he had found; and their enactment confirmed Jhering's claim that damage actions in cases of failed contracts were an urgent practical need; id.

[357] Jhering warned those limiting themselves to "lower jurisprudence" (see supra 1., notes 215–219 and text) that they may well find his whole argument pointless: "Someone who sees the vocation of jurisprudence merely in explaining obscure legal provisions with the aid of a hermeneutic lamp may dismiss my whole theory with the simple argument that the expression *culpa in contrahendo* does not appear anywhere in *corpus Juris*." *Jhering*, Culpa (1861) 52. In other words, his discourse was addressed to those interested in, and capable of, "higher jurisprudence."

[358] *Jhering*, Culpa (1861) 34.

[359] Knowledge would amount to *dolus* and would thus be ground for an *actio doli.*

[360] *Jhering*, Culpa (1861) 36.

Jhering was smart enough, of course, to recognize that such a form of *culpa* was essentially a fiction.[361] He clearly saw that its effect was to shift the cost of a mistake to the mistaken party: since a defendant's error could never be excused, "he errs at his own expense, not at that of the other side."[362] In other words, Jhering fully understood that his construction of *culpa* amounted to strict liability justified by policy considerations of risk allocation. It would seem, he even conceded, that this kind of *culpa* is "just a different *expression* for the strict liability (gesetzliche Haftungspflicht) of the seller."[363]

Jhering found some support in the Roman sources for considering even an innocent defendant's mistake *culpa*,[364] but that was not the principal reason for his position. It was rather that Jhering considered sticking to *culpa* necessary to maintain the integrity of the Roman system of actions: liability for a failed deal was a proper contract action only if it required *culpa*. Without such a requirement, it could no longer be part of contract law; instead, it would become "a completely isolated positive rule,"[365] i.e., an anomaly. Jhering was not willing to create such an anomaly because an isolated and exceptional rule would lie completely outside of the Roman system of civil actions.[366]

We can see here what Jhering was willing to do and not willing to do. He was quite ready, indeed eager, to push beyond the specific cases discussed by the Roman jurists for *some* contracts, to derive from them a "simple rule," and even to create a "general principle," of liability for causing the invalidity of contracts across the board. He was not ready, however, to create an exception from a defining structural feature of Roman law. Jhering admitted that such a step could be justified on grounds of equity.[367] Taking it, however, would have led him not just "beyond Roman law" but would have put him in open contradiction to it,

---

[361] *Jhering*, Culpa (1861) 36.

[362] *Jhering*, Culpa (1861) 39.

[363] *Jhering*, Culpa (1861) 40 (emphasis in the original).

[364] *Jhering*, Culpa (1861) 35–36. Jhering admitted that the Roman sources were not unambiguous: sometimes they required actual blameworthiness under the circumstances, sometimes they did not; for Jhering the latter was good enough because it showed that the Roman jurists were willing to speak of *culpa* even without actual fault in the individual case when that was needed for the desired result; id. 35–36. Jhering was not quite convinced, however, that such liability without blameworthiness was appropriate if the responsible party lacked the capacity to contract. Regarding persons under guardianship, he suggested to deny an action; against a drunk person, he wanted to allow it ("in such a state, one should not contract"); regarding minors, he was not sure; id. 57–62.

[365] *Jhering*, Culpa (1861) 40.

[366] *Jhering*, Culpa (1861) 40–41. There was probably another, unstated, reason why Jhering was reluctant to give up the *culpa* requirement. As he explained a few years later, he considered the development from strict to fault-based liability one of the defining features of Roman law as well as an important sign of progress, *Jhering*, Das Schuldmoment im römischen Privatrecht (1867); see infra chapter V.2.

[367] *Jhering*, Culpa (1861) 40. Jhering would presumably have had no problem with the legislature creating a rule of strict liability.

and this is where he balked. Jhering understood not only the need sometimes to elicit new rules and principles but also the importance of keeping them compatible with the larger framework of traditional doctrine.

Ultimately, Jhering wanted to have his cake and eat it too. On the one hand, he wanted to maintain the fundamental principles of Roman civil actions. which required fault for a contractual remedy. On the other hand, he wanted to satisfy his sense of justice which required shifting the risk of contract failure to the party causing it, even if innocently. To accomplish the former, he stuck to the *culpa* requirement; to accomplish the latter, he stretched it to the point of strict liability – if necessary by hook or crook.[368]

Limitation of Damages: "Positive" vs. "Negative Interest." The fact that, according to Jhering, a defendant was liable not only for breach of a valid contract but also for causing a problem that led to an invalid contract, does not mean that both cases were treated entirely alike. Instead, the scope of liability varied depending on the validity of the contract *vel non*. In the context of developing his principle of *culpa in contrahendo*, Jhering also expounded the difference between liability for what he termed the "positive" and the "negative interest,"[369] and Jhering is often referenced in connection with these concepts. It is true that the

[368] Squeezing "innocent" mistakes into the concept of *culpa,* was still fairly plausible with regard to the two examples found in the Roman sources, i.e., non-salable objects: "Someone who is not sure of his object, should not sell [it];" *Jhering*, Culpa (1861) 36. Here, Jhering also had the Roman jurists on his side because they had indeed allowed damage actions without making exceptions from the *culpa* requirement. The assumption of *culpa* became distinctly more difficult in other cases, however. Assume an absent party sent out an offer and then promptly died; ignorant of the offeror's death, the offeree accepted and proceeded to perform, incurring expenses. Since the death of the offeror had rendered his offer invalid and thus the completion of the contract impossible, clearly the offeree could not require performance damages for breach of contract, but could he still sue for his expenses? It seems that the answer should be no because, as Jhering recognized, "[o]ne cannot possibly consider dying a form of culpa," id. 92. He openly admitted that here, his theory was facing a hurdle "which cannot be overcome without a forced effort" ("gewaltsame Anstrengung"). Yet, since his sense of justice required that the offeree be compensated (presumably because he had a right to trust in the validity of the contract), Jhering was willing to consider even the death of the offeror a form of *culpa.* Thus, he admitted, "I have no choice but to construe *culpa* in the following manner:" since the offeror had chosen not to go to the offeree but rather to send the offer from afar, he had chosen a means of communication that was convenient for him but riskier for his business partner. Consequently, he had to take responsibility for problems arising from this choice; id. 92–93. One must assume in Jhering's favor that he understood the dubious nature of such a construction. (What if the parties were located on opposite sides of an ocean and had both routinely sent offers and acceptances so that neither could be considered responsible for the long-distance nature of their relationship?)

[369] In his article, Jhering discussed the distinction between the "positive" and the "negative" interest before developing the principle of *culpa in contrahendo*, i.e., in order to set the stage for the subsequent discourse; *Jhering*, Culpa (1861) 15–22. We discuss it at the tail end here because postponing this element makes it easier to follow Jhering's development of his basic argument.

distinction had already been introduced a few years earlier by Friedrich Mommsen, whom Jhering duly cited in a footnote.[370] But it is also true that it was Jhering who fully explored and lucidly explained the distinction so that his fame in that regard is not undeserved.[371]

Jhering put it very succinctly: the foundation of a claim for the "positive interest" is the contract's validity;[372] the basis for recovery of the "negative interest," its invalidity. In other words, if the action is based on (the seller's breach of) a valid contract, the buyer is entitled to the damages resulting from the breach – he must be put in the (financial) position he would be in if the contract had been performed. If, however, the action is based on the invalidity of the contract, the buyer is only entitled to the damages he suffered by relying on the contract's validity – he must be put in the position he would be in if the agreement had never been made. Jhering artfully teased this distinction out of the Roman sources and anchored it in the purposes of the respective remedies. As he explained, what exactly these kinds of damages amount to depends on the circumstances;[373] and as he pointed out, the "negative interest" can be as high as the "positive interest," for example, if through reliance on the contract the buyer loses another profitable deal.[374]

Modern Times: Some Remarks on Culpa in Contrahendo post-Jhering.[375] As mentioned, *culpa in contrahendo* was Jhering's most influential doctrinal discovery. The contemporary reaction, however, was ambiguous, and it was only in the early twentieth century, i.e., after the enactment of the German Civil Code (BGB), that the doctrine became generally accepted.[376] Writing its history from the late nineteenth century to the present would require a monograph in its own right, and a thick one at that. Here, some remarks on the development and influence of the doctrine must suffice to put Jhering's accomplishment into a somewhat broader perspective.[377]

Jhering's discovery had its greatest success in his home country. His idea that a party responsible for the invalidity of a contract (by virtue of mistake or impossibility) should be liable for the other side's reliance damages was codified in the

---

[370] *Jhering*, Culpa (1861) 16 fn. 17, citing (via reference to a previous footnote, i.e., 9) (Friedrich) *Mommsen*, Beträge zum Obligationenrecht I, 107 (1853).

[371] See, e.g., the now classic article by *Fuller and Purdue*, The Reliance Interest in Contract Damages (1936) 86–87 (fns. 54–55); see also *Smith*, Four German Jurists III (1897) 43–48; *Patterson*, Equitable Relief for Unilateral Mistake (1928) 98–101. On Jhering's (rather limited) influence on the concept of "reliance interest" in US-American law, see infra chapter VII.3., notes 123–125 and text.

[372] *Jhering*, Culpa (1861) 16.

[373] *Jhering*, Culpa 1861) 15–23.

[374] *Jhering*, Culpa (1861) 21.

[375] For a study of the historical development and enduring significance of *culpa in contrahendo*, see *Benedict*, Culpa in Contrahendo (2018).

[376] *Schanze*, Culpa in Contrahendo bei Jhering (1978) 355–356.

[377] For an overview, see *Hondius*, Pre-contractual Liability (1990) 129.

German Civil Code of 1900, though without mention of Jhering's catchy term.[378] Perhaps more importantly, in the course of the twentieth century, German scholars and courts fashioned a version of *culpa in contrahendo* that went far beyond anything Jhering had ever contemplated: even at the pre-contractual stage, the (potential) parties are subject to the general principle of good faith (Treu und Glauben, § 242 BGB) and thus owe each other a panoply of duties, almost as if the contract had already been concluded;[379] breaching any of these duties can render a party liable, inter alia for pure economic loss resulting from failure to negotiate in good faith.[380] While this extremely broad version of *culpa in contrahendo* is a far cry from Jhering's original concept, it is still based on his core idea: parties at the contracting stage are no longer to be treated as mere strangers; they have already entered into in a special relationship that creates duties of care beyond those owed to the rest of the world and sanctioned merely by the law of delict (i.e., torts).

Several other civil law jurisdictions have adopted liability for *culpa in contrahendo* in various forms and to varying degrees (e.g., Austria,[381] Switzerland,[382] and Italy,[383]) while in other countries, the doctrine's influence has been more muted or non-existent. Modern European law provides a variety of pre-contractual obligations, especially duties to warn and to inform owed by businesses to consumers.[384] They are, however, mostly based on particular pieces of legislation rather than on any general principle. European and international "soft" law have embraced pre-contractual liability mainly for negotiating in bad faith.[385]

---

[378] § 122 (liability for reliance damages resulting from rescinding a contract on account of error); §§ 306–307 (liability in case of objective impossibility of performance or illegality of the contract if the responsible party knew or should have known the problem). See also § 179 sec. 2 (liability of an agent unknowingly lacking agency power).

[379] The development and expansion over time is analyzed by *Schanze*, Culpa in Contrahendo bei Jhering (1978); for a summary, see *Zimmermann*, Roman Law, Contemporary Law, European Law (2001) 89–92; *Wurmnest*, Contract Law (2018) 255.

[380] Today, liability for misconduct during contract negotiations is codified in § 311 sec. 2 BGB.

[381] See Rechtssatz (legal principle, formulated by the Austrian Supreme Court, Oberster Gerichtshof, OGH) No. 0014855.

[382] (Swiss) Obligationenrecht (1888) Art. 26 (party rescinding a contract for error is liable for reliance damages if he/she was negligent); Swiss courts have also imposed far-reaching duties of information, etc., on the parties during the negotiation stage, see *Peter Gauch, Victor Apri and Hubert Stöckli*, Präjudizienbuch OR, Vorbemerkung zu Art. 1–40, 12–14 (Zürich 2016).

[383] The Italian Codice civile of 1942 codified the doctrine in arts. 1337 (responsibilità precontrattuale) and 1338.

[384] For background and details, see *Lehmann*, Die Zukunft der CIC im Europäschen Vertragsrecht (2009).

[385] UNIDROIT Principles of International Commercial Contracts 2.1.15 (1984/2016); Principles of European Contract Law (1995–2002) 2:301; Principles, Definitions and Model Rules of European Private Law, Draft Common Frame of Reference 3:301 (2008/2009). For an overview and analysis, see *Jansen and Zimmermann* (eds.), Commentaries on European

The concept of *culpa in contrahendo* has also been discussed in the common law orbit, especially in connection with the debate about the duty to bargain in good faith.[386] While common law jurisdictions have not adopted the concept as such, they have devised many functional equivalents, such as promissory estoppel and detrimental reliance, to provide remedies for a party harmed by the other side's conduct at the stage of contract formation.[387] For the most part, these developments not are due to any direct influence by Jhering but they validate his fundamental insight that modern commerce sometimes requires (quasi-)contractual remedies even if the envisaged contract fails to materialize for one reason or another.

4. The Importance of Practice: "Ist die Jurisprudenz eine Wissenschaft?" (1868)

When Jhering gave his inaugural lecture at the University of Vienna in 1868, he tackled a hotly debated question[388] that would surely capture the attention of his audience: "Is Jurisprudence a Science?"[389] As is to be expected, his answer was yes. Yet, to tease out what exactly he meant requires a closer look.[390] Jhering

---

Contract Laws (2018) 348–373 (Introduction before Art. 2:301; Negotiations Contrary to Good Faith Art. 2–301; specifically on Jhering's work see marginal notes 4–6).

[386] *Kessler and Fine*, *Culpa in Contrahendo*, Bargaining in Good Faith, and Freedom of Contract: A Comparative Study (1964); see also *Patterson*, Equitable Relief for Unilateral Mistake (1928). Jhering was also cited in *Williston and Thompson*, A Treatise on the Law of Contacts, revised ed., vol. 1, 186 (§ 63A) (New York 1936) (in the context of revoked offers) and vol. 5, 4470–1 (§ 1600B) (in the context of rescission on grounds of mistake).

[387] The *locus classicus* for that proposition is the article by *Kessler and Fine*, *Culpa in Contrahendo*, Bargaining in Good Faith, and Freedom of Contract (1964); see also *Lehmann*, Die Zukunft der CIC im europäischen Vertragsrecht (2009) 696–698. For modern US-American contract law, see Restatement of Contracts (Second) § 90 (1979/1981). A well-known Australian example is Walton Stores (Interstate) Ltd. v. Maher and Another, 76 Australian Law Reports (ALR) 513 (High Court of Australia 1987).

[388] See supra 2., notes 290–291 and text.

[389] *Jhering*, Ist die Jurisprudenz eine Wissenschaft? (1868).

[390] Jhering's discourse is, once again, poorly organized; it is also bristling with exaggerations, trivialities, and digressions which are hard to forgive in a talk designed to showcase the intellectual prowess of a new appointee to a chair in one of the world's most prestitious law faculties. It is fair to say that Jhering's talk would have sunk his chances of a job at a modern German (or, for that matter, Austrian) law faculty. Perhaps it was recognition of these weaknesses that kept Jhering from publishing the talk. His discourse was published only more than a century after his death in a volume edited by Okko Behrends; *Jhering,* Ist die Jurisprudenz eine Wissenschaft (1998, orig.1868).The volume also contains not only a helpful summary of Jhering's main points but also several interpretive essays. The text of Jhering's talk itself is supplemented by numerous footnotes which proffer highly valuable explanations of many aspects otherwise unintelligible to a modern reader. Behrend's overall view of the talk is apparently less critical than mine.

defined legal science vaguely, and somewhat tautologically, as "the scientific consciousness regarding matters of law"[391] and divided it into three branches. The first was legal philosophy about which Jhering had very little (and nothing of significance) to say;[392] we can safely leave that aside. The second branch was legal history, which Jhering discussed at some length, both defining its proper objective and criticizing it for having become too self-absorbed and impractical;[393] we will leave that aside here as well because his discourse on legal history is better discussed in other contexts.[394] The third branch was *Dogmatik* of the positive law of the present. This aspect turned out to be the principal theme of Jhering's talk, and it is the only one relevant for our present purposes.

Jhering's central claim was that "legal science" consisted of the doctrinal work that processed what had been done by practitioners, especially judges. *Dogmatik* needed to take stock of the work done by the bench and then "put it to use" by "elevating what the judicial decision presented in a concrete form to the generality of a concept."[395] In essence, legal science was the process described by Jhering in his methodological discourses and practiced by him in his doctrinal essays. So defined, jurisprudence could avoid the two pitfalls that had bedeviled it time and again throughout history: it neither fell prey to pure positivism (in the sense of operating with the existing rules in an uncritical fashion – "the mortal enemy of jurisprudence"[396]) nor did it lose itself in abstract speculation devoid of practical utility.[397] The model for a true legal science was, once more, provided by the work of the classical Roman jurists.[398]

To be sure, Jhering had demanded that legal theory must ultimately serve the needs of practice already in his methodological writings.[399] Now, however, he made that function his central postulate and indeed the very hallmark of legal science as a concept.[400] He envisaged a division of labor between the practitioner,

---

[391] *Jhering*, Ist die Jurisprudenz eine Wissenschaft? (1868) 92 ("das wissenschaftliche Bewußtsein in Dingen des Rechts")

[392] All that Jhering had to say about legal philosophy was that it was a necessary element of jurisprudence because "the forces that drive the law are not to be found only on its practical side, instead, there is also the ethical perspective," *Jhering*, Ist die Jurisprudenz eine Wissenschaft (1868) 76; and that legal philosophy had to "explore the ultimate grounds to which law on earth owes its origin and force," id. 92.

[393] *Jhering*, Ist die Jurisprudenz eine Wissenschaft (1868) 68–77.

[394] See infra chapter V.1.

[395] *Jhering*, Ist die Jurisprudenz eine Wissenschaft (1868) 90 ("verwerthen," i.e., "was der Richterspruch ihr in concreter Gestalt entgegen getragen hat, zur Allgemeinheit des Begriffs erheben").

[396] Jhering, Ist die Jurisprudenz eine Wissenschaft? (1868) 52.

[397] The former was the sin of post-classical Roman law and of the late-medieval post-glossators, the latter the sin of the glossators, the natural lawyers, and many contemporary Romanists of the Puchta variety; Jhering, Ist die Jurisprudenz eine Wissenschaft? (1868) 54–66.

[398] *Jhering*, Ist die Jurisprudenz eine Wissenschaft? (1868) 54–55.

[399] See supra 2., notes 252–273 and text.

[400] Note that Jhering thus merely defined what legal science does and for what purpose; he did not explain how that actually made it a "science."

especially the judge, who operated on the concrete level of deciding real cases, and the theoretician (i.e., the academic), who operated on the abstract level of developing and maintaining the conceptual and systematic doctrinal framework. They were co-equal workers in the law's vineyard, and neither should look down on the other.[401] In fact, Jhering now assigned the practitioners the leading role in the law-making process. He no longer waxed eloquent about the productive capabilities of "construction" and of the system of concepts but rather envisaged "practice as acting and progressing, and theory following and bringing what the former has won, into the proper form."[402] The judge was in the driver's seat, and the professor rode along. *Dogmatik* was merely legal practice "made conscious."[403]

Jhering's demand that "theory and practice operate harmoniously next to each other"[404] was not just cheap talk. He put his money where his mouth was – he not only undertook to solve practical problems in his doctrinal articles, but he also showed his regard for practical work by consistently engaging with the practical side of law in a variety of ways.

Observing Real Cases: Inspiration, Motivation, Reconsideration. In his scholarship, Jhering was often informed by real cases[405] to which he sometimes referred in either the text or the footnotes of his work.[406] Occasionally, such disputes provided the inspiration to write about a problem to begin with; the most famous example is a case in which the seller had sold the object twice before it perished.[407]. More generally, many of his doctrinal essays were motivated by the wish to contribute to the solution of practical problems he had noted.[408] At the same time, observing an abstract rule in the context of a concrete dispute could change Jhering's view of the rule itself. "Used to regard it in a state of inertia, so to speak, and to limit myself to the examination of its legitimacy according to the sources, the practical case showed it in motion, in its effect on real life."[409] The case of the double-sale (Doppelverkauf) just mentioned had exactly that impact on Jhering: it lead him first to reconsider, then to reject, and finally to develop an alternative to, the established rule.[410]

---

[401] *Jhering*, Ist die Jurisprudenz eine Wissenschaft? (1868) 91.

[402] *Jhering*, Ist die Jurisprudenz eine Wissenschaft? (1868) 91.

[403] Jhering, Ist die Jurisprudenz eine Wissenschaft? (1868) 91 ("die Praxis zur Form des Bewußtseins erhoben").

[404] *Jhering*, Ist die Jurisprudenz eine Wissenschaft (1868) 91.

[405] "I have always owed my best ideas for doctrinal work to practical cases," he told his Viennese audience, *Jhering*, Ist die Jurisprudenz eine Wissenschaft? (1868) 85.

[406] See, e.g., *Jhering*, Culpa (1861) 64 (fn. 68).

[407] *Jhering*, Gefahr beim Kaufcontract (1859).

[408] See, e.g., *Jhering*, Zur Lehre von den Beschränkungen des Grundeigentümers (1863).

[409] *Jhering*, Ist die Jurisprudenz eine Wissenschaft? (1868) 86.

[410] Jhering's experience with this case also caused him first to question, then to doubt, and finally to reject, some of his most firmly held beliefs, see infra chapter III.1.

Deciding Real Cases: The Professor as a Quasi-Judge. Jhering not only received impulses from legal practice, but he actually participated in it. He believed that "one truly gets to know a practical science only by applying it,"[411] and he had ample opportunity to do so during his sixteen years in Gießen. This was due to the peculiar institution of "Aktenversendung" ("dispatching of the record") which still survived in some German lands at the time. Since the sixteenth century, it had gradually become more and more common for courts to seek the assistance of law faculties in deciding legally complicated cases. After the proceedings (then almost exclusively written) had run their course, the court would wrap up the file (Akte) and send it to the designated "judgment faculty" ("Spruchfakultät") for its opinion. While these faculties were not formally sitting as courts, they usually drafted a judgment (decree, order, etc.) that the court seized with the case then pronounced.[412] As a member of the law faculty at the University of Gießen, it was therefore one of Jhering's duties to participate regularly in the collective resolution of the legal issues involved in actual disputes and to draft the pertinent decisions. This, of course, kept him (and his colleagues) constantly in touch with problems arising in the real world – a pretty powerful antidote to a life in a jurisprudential ivory tower.[413]

Jhering's attitude towards the institution of Aktenversendung was ambivalent. On the one hand, he lamented that it could further complicate and delay the resolution of disputes, especially since the involvement of several university faculties could entail divergent opinions.[414] On the other hand, in his inaugural lecture in Vienna, as well as on other occasions,[415] he expressed regret about the gradual decline of Aktenversendung and the concomitant loss of an important connection between academic theory and forensic practice.[416] In any event, the institution gave him the opportunity to do the practical work which, after all, had once been his preferred career choice.[417]

That the cases could be challenging is vividly illustrated by Jhering's most widely known opinion, rendered in the "Lucca-Pistoia Eisenbahnstreit" ("Railroad Litigation"). Despite the reference to two Italian cities, the case involved a

---

[411] *Jhering*, Ist die Jurisprudenz eine Wissenschaft? (1868) 81.

[412] A major reason for this emerging practice was the reception of Roman law: local judges were often not (sufficiently) trained in it and thus relied on the expertise of the learned jurists teaching at the universities. In the mid-nineteenth century, the practice had been in decline for some time; it was formally abolished when the united German Reich's newly enacted codes of procedure entered in force in 1879. For an overview, see *Dawson*, The Oracles of the Law (1968) 198–206; see also *Oestmann*, Aktenversendung (2008).

[413] In order to keep academic theory and forensic practice in close contact, it is a continuing practice in Germany today for some professors of private law and procedure to serve as part-time judges on appellate courts.

[414] *Jhering*, Der Lucca-Pistoia Eisenbahnstreit (1867) 226.

[415] *Jhering*, Scherz und Ernst (1884) 39.

[416] *Jhering*. Ist die Jurisprudenz eine Wissenschaft? (1868) 81.

[417] Supra chapter I.2., notes 62–63 and text.

classic example of securities fraud, allegedly committed by a German private bank and a commercial agent.[418] The litigation comprised various lawsuits which came before a number of German courts and dragged on for years. Part of the litigation was referred to the Gießen law faculty by a court of third instance. Jhering considered the problems discussed to be of general interest and thus published his opinion (in slightly modified form) as a 128-page article in a legal periodical.[419] Jhering decided the case entirely according to Roman law,[420] against the lower courts, and in favor of the plaintiff. The opinion is a veritable tour de force. Jhering dissected the complex case into its essential elements, quickly identified the crucial issues, discussed them thoroughly from both sides, and resolved them with a combination of doctrinal mastery, respect for commercial reality, and unerring common sense. The flow of the analysis and the clarity of the discourse make for easy reading despite the opinion's length and complexity. The reader can observe a jurist at work who is not only a superb legal scholar but also displays all the qualities of an excellent appellate judge.

Assisting in Real Cases: The Professor as an Expert. Around mid-life, Jhering had become not only a famous Romanist legal scholar, but he had also acquired a reputation as an expert for hire in ongoing disputes. Apparently, this was particularly true in Switzerland,[421] perhaps because Jhering had once been a professor in Basel, perhaps because Swiss parties preferred support from a foreign (though German speaking) jurist who was not a member of the close network pervading much of the Helvetic republic. Writing expert opinions (Gutachten) offered a combination of benefits: it was a considerable source of additional income;[422] sometimes, the opinions could be published as scholarly articles that fostered Jhering's academic reputation; and of course, involvement in live disputes kept Jhering in touch with the real world. His popularity as a legal expert also indicates

---

[418] The shares at stake had been issued by an Italian company to finance the construction of a railroad in Tuscany.

[419] *Jhering*, Der Lucca-Pistoia Eisenbahnstreit (1867).

[420] As of 1861, the member states of the German Federation had a General Commercial Code (Allgemeines Deutsches Handelsgesetzbuch, ADHGB) but the events underlying the litigation had preceded its enactment.

[421] See the opinions listed in *Behrends* (ed.), Beiträge und Zeugnisse (1993) 82–83; for a detailed study of one Jhering's expert opinions, see *Bachmann*, Das Gäubahn-Gutachten (2023).

[422] In one case, Jhering earned 2,000 Reichsmark (in addition to 300 Reichsmark for a quick oral consultation) for an opinion he wrote in four days, *Behrends* (ed.), Beiträge und Zeugnisse (1993) 82. In the 1880s, this was a very significant sum of money (in 1872, Jhering had bought a very large house with a substantial piece of land in Göttingen for 10,000 Reichsmark; letter to Windscheid of March 31, 1872, Jherings Briefe an Windscheid (1988) 31). In other words, his fee amounted to 20% of an expensive house in a German university town – the equivalent of several hundred thousand dollars today. Jhering was jubilant about the unexpected additional income as well as proud to have a name for which parties were willing to pay "about 100 Marks an hour;" letter to his son Friedrich Jhering of September 8, 1887; *Behrends* (ed.), Beiträge und Zeugnisse (1993) 105.

that parties saw him as a scholar who could relate to actual cases, understood the interests at stake, and possessed the requisite common sense – in short, as a jurist with practical skills and qualities.

Mingling with Practitioners: Jhering in Professional Organizations. In pursuit of his interest in legal practice, Jhering often stepped outside of his academic environment to mingle with lawyers and judges. He was a founding member of the Deutscher Juristentag (German Lawyers Conference),[423] an association established in 1860 and still going strong today. Jhering served on its executive committee (ständige Deputation) and often attended its bi-annual meetings.

Jhering stayed in particularly close contact with legal practitioners in Vienna. Notably, his most famous lecture, "Der Kampf ums Recht,"[424] was not an academic exercise but primarily addressed to an audience of practicing lawyers – in both form and substance. Jhering gave it before the "Wiener Juristische Gesellschaft" ("Vienna Law Society") an association of practitioners. The lecture was also expressly tailored to members of the bar. In recognition, the Society made Jhering an honorary member.[425] Twelve years later, he addressed the association in another talk, again on a subject also of particular interest to practitioners, i.e., "Über die Entstehung des Rechtsgefühls" ("On the Origins of the Sense of Justice").[426] Jhering's eventual critique of purely abstract jurisprudence, his persistent calls for a jurisprudence serving the ends of "life," and the practical exercises in Roman law that he offered at the University,[427] made him "the hero of a whole generation of Austrian practitioners."[428] They recognized Jhering as an academic ally and as someone who genuinely cared about legal practice, rather than looking down upon it as a mere craft and business.

5. The Importance of Teaching: "Die Jurisprudenz des täglichen Lebens" (1870)

If you sat in one of Jhering's classes in the 1870s, you might be asked to analyze the following case.

"A mother sends her six-year-old child to the butcher shop to get 1/4 pound of sausage, but the child gets 4 pounds which a large dog snatches from him on the way home. The mother refuses to pay for the sausage – first, because she could not be legally bound by [the actions of] a child; second, because she had asked for only 1/4 pound; third, because she never received the sausage; [also] is the dog's owner liable?"

[423] *Behrends* (ed.), Beiträge und Zeugnisse (1993) 68–69; *Fikentscher,* Methoden des Rechts III (1976) 119.

[424] See infra chapter IV.1.

[425] *Behrends* (ed.), Beiträge und Zeugnisse (1993) 75.

[426] See infra chapter IV.3.

[427] *Hofmeister*, Jhering in Wien (1995) 24.

[428] *Hofmeister*, Jhering in Wien (1995) 22.

One of Jhering's most popular books was a collection of such hypotheticals, aptly entitled "Die Jurisprudenz des täglichen Lebens"[429] – "The Jurisprudence of Daily Life".[430] Each of its twenty-one chapters covered a particular sphere of quotidian existence – "To and on the Railroad," "At the Inn," "In the Rental Apartment," "Domestic Life", etc.[431] Each of these chapters contained dozens of carefully composed hypotheticals, and sometimes more general questions, for a total of nearly 500 problems. Their pedagogical purpose was to make students look not only at big cases that may be litigated, but also "at incidents occurring in normal life from a legal perspective."[432] Despite the lightness of touch, the purpose of the books was very serious: the hypotheticals forced students to analyze daily events that were factually simple but often raised tricky legal questions. One can easily imagine spending a whole hour on the story of the lost sausage.

Enthusiasm and High Standards: Jhering in the Classroom. When we look at legal scholars, we tend to focus entirely on their publications, be it because academics live on through their published work (or at least hope to), or be it because we assume that an academic life's most valuable legacy is its paper trail. In Jhering's case, that would produce a badly incomplete picture. Jhering was not a legal scholar who also taught law on the side. Instead, the classroom was as important an element of his life as the study. He was eagerly engaged in teaching from his first days as a Privatdozent in Berlin to his very last weeks as a professor in Göttingen. Teaching was, as his biographer Erik Wolk put it, "an essential part of his accomplishment."[433]

Jhering taught a lot. Most days of the week, he had to be in the classroom both mornings and afternoons. During the semester, that left precious little time for scholarly production; during the examination periods, none. Moreover, Jhering

---

[429] *Jhering*, Die Jurisprudenz des täglichen Lebens (1870/1889); for the hypothetical, see id. 36. The text's publication history is peculiar. Early in his career, Jhering published a collection entitled "Civilrechtsfälle ohne Entscheidungen" ("Private Law Cases without Decisions") (Leipzig 1847). It contained 36 cases from his (recently deceased) academic teacher Puchta and 100 cases compiled by Jhering himself. The collection went through numerous editions during and beyond his lifetime. Jhering's "Jurisprudenz des täglichen Lebens" was originally an appendix to that collection's second edition (Jena 1870) but was later published separately, also going through several editions (until 1927); for details, see *Hirsch*, Jhering als Reformator des Rechtsunterrichts (1970) 94. I have used the seventh edition (1889) because it is available in a modern reproduction. Thus, the work is cited as Jhering 1870/1889.

[430] Henry Goudy transl., Oxford 1904. Jhering also mentioned translations into Italian, Hungarian, Greek, and Portuguese (in part), *Jhering*, Die Jurisprudenz des täglichen Lebens (1870/1889) Vorwort (Preface).

[431] As *Hirsch*, Jhering als Reformator des Rechtsunterrichts (1970) 95, pointed out, the majority of scenarios of course reflected the life of the bourgois middle and upper middle class, not that of the working class or the poor.

[432] *Jhering*, Die Jurisprudenz des täglichen Lebens (8th ed. 1891) Vorwort (Preface).

[433] *Wolf*, Große Rechtsdenker (1963) 657; see also *Hirsch*, Jhering als Reformator des Rechtsunterrichts (1970) 100; for a more extensive discussion of Jhering as an academic teacher, see *Jäde*, Jhering als Rechtslehrer (2008) 13–16.

put a lot of effort into his teaching. He prepared, engaged his students, often tiring himself out. He also loved it.[434] He was a committed and enthusiastic teacher who could fire up his audience through his lively, provocative, and often humorous style which was devoid of all professorial stiffness. He was, however, not easy on his class. While he left aside the intricate doctrinal puzzles that so fascinated many of his colleagues, he was demanding and did not suffer fools gladly. Thus he appealed primarily to the stronger students while the weaker ones tended to fear him. He made little effort to lecture on what they could learn for themselves from Puchta's or Windscheid's treatises; instead he talked about what he found interesting, paying little attention to a systematic exposition of the material. Students who tried to keep notes during his classes often could not follow.[435] He cherished a healthy debate, appreciated a good argument, and was happy to recognize a good performance,[436] but he could also be dismissive of views he did not share.[437] Jhering was a feared examiner because he sometimes asked surprise questions when he was in the mood;[438] he even kept a list of particularly stupid answers.[439]

Despite the importance of teaching, or perhaps exactly because of it, Jhering was sometimes doubtful of his own abilities in the classroom. "My value as a teacher is dubious," he confessed to his close friend Gerber. "Hiring me is a game of chance."[440] As so often, he sought to assess himself realistically. He recognized "definite weaknesses" in his style, "for example, the complete lack of a beautiful form, a certain restlessness and insecurity of the presentation, big gaps in my knowledge." But he also saw his strengths, at least for those students who were committed and interested – "a certain liveliness and the juristic spirit which animates me and is imperceptibly conveyed to the listeners as well."[441]

Even though he did not, like many of his colleagues, present lectures as a form of art, Jhering's teaching was ultimately among the great success stories in his life. This became fully visible in Vienna. While enrollment in his classes in the smaller universities (Basel, Rostock, Kiel, Gießen, Göttingen) was necessarily modest,[442]

---

[434] See his letter to Bülow of June 22, 1873, Jhering in Briefen (1913) 290.

[435] *Kunze*, Rudolf von Jhering (1993) 17–18.

[436] *Mitteis*, Jhering (1905) 663. Jhering openly admitted that at times, he had recognized new ideas because a good student had pointed them out; *Jhering*, Scherz und Ernst (1884) 367.

[437] *Kunze*, Lieber in Gießen (2018) 20–21; *Hofmeister*, Jhering in Wien (1995) 12–13; see also *Dove*, Rudolf von Jhering und Bernhard Windscheid (1893) 151–52 ("The lively man, who frequently engaged in direct discussion, and in question and answer, and who occasionally did not lack sharp polemicism and crude mockery, was always engaging and interesting.").

[438] *Kunze*, Rudolf von Jhering (1993) 18.

[439] Cod.Ms. Jhering 23.

[440] Letter to Gerber of January 6, 1959, Jhering in Briefen (1913) 110 ("Wer mich beruft, spielt Lotterie.").

[441] Letter to Gerber of January 6, 1859, Jhering in Briefen (1913) 110.

[442] Jhering's classes in these venues would typically not exceed 20–30 students; see, e.g.,

in Vienna, he often lectured to large crowds. In one instance, he reported over 400 students in one class[443] – a staggering number by the standards of the time. Such success was not only a source of personal satisfaction[444] but also of considerable revenue since much of a professor's income came from the fees paid by the students in his classes (Hörergeld). Thus when Jhering went from Vienna to the smaller University of Göttingen in 1872, this income was much diminished – though his reputation among the students as an inspiring teacher was not.[445]

At first glance, it may seem odd that Jhering never had any academic disciples, i.e., students he trained to become law professors. Yet, he had not had a true academic mentor himself, and it seems that he did not care to become one. He also had his hands (or rather, his head) full with his own ideas which he could barely control and organize, so that there was little interest and no time to supervise graduate work by others. Still, several of his students eventually become prominent legal academics, whether inspired by Jhering or not.[446]

Teaching Doctrine, Preparing for Practice: Lectures and Practica. As a professor of Roman law, Jhering's main responsibility was to teach *Dogmatik*. While he occasionally offered classes on subjects like Roman legal history or general principles of Roman law, his bread and butter teaching concerned the doctrine of Roman jurisprudence. The introductory (first-year) course on the *Institutes* provided a more or less systematic overview before the advanced course on the *Pandekten* got into more detail, including debates among the Roman jurists on specific points. These, obligatory, courses were conceived, and usually held, as lectures (*Vorlesungen*) with the professor standing at the lectern and presenting the material to a passive audience. Jhering, however, tended to pace up and down the aisles, to ask questions, and to comment on the answers.[447] He was not much interested in intricate doctrinal puzzles because he considered them useless for pedagogical purposes,[448] but he insisted that students not only absorb the material but actually reflect upon it.

---

letter Gerber of December 2, 1854, Jhering in Briefen (1913) 47. In Gießen, he was worried about the generally declining number of law students, letter to Gerber of October 15, 1858, Jhering in Briefen (1913) 102.

[443] Letter to Windscheid of March 31, 1872, Jhering in Briefen (1913) 279.

[444] The Viennese law students wrote Jhering a – lavishly ornamented – farewell letter expressing their regret about his departure and their "unchanging love," reprinted in *Behrends* (ed.), Beiträge und Zeugnisse (1993) 73–75.

[445] *Behrends* (ed.), Beiträge und Zeugnisse (1993) 77.

[446] Among them were Victor Ehrenberg (1851–1929) who became Jhering's son-in-law, Rudolph Leonhard (1851–1921), Adolf Merkel (1836–1896), Gustav Rümelin 1848–1907), Max Rümelin (1861–1931), Karl Wieland (1864–936), and Ernst Zitelmann (1852–1923); see *Jäde*, Jhering als Rechtslehrer (2008) 20.

[447] *Kunze*, Lieber in Gießen (2018) 20. There were additional classes on specific areas of Roman law. Jhering, for example, sometime lectured on the law of succession; *Klippel*, Rudolf von Jhering an der juristischen Fakultät der Ludwigs-Universität Gießen (1993) 34.

[448] "On appropriate occasions, a good teacher must have the courage to be superficial. The instrument he hands to his student may be imperfect – if the student learns to play it better than a perfect one, the former is preferable for teaching purposes." *Jhering*, Scherz und Ernst (1884) 360.

Jhering was critical of the existing regime of legal education because it overemphasized theory and neglected practice. He considered a system where academic theoreticians trained future practitioners fundamentally problematic. Exams made matters worse. Since they were typically administered by professors who tended to focus on the content of their lectures, candidates crammed their heads full of theoretical knowledge – which then turned out to be utterly useless in practice.[449]

Yet, there was one type of course that ameliorated the situation: students who had passed the foundational courses could take a *Practicum*, i.e., a (smaller) class in which they learned to apply (Roman law) doctrine to real or hypothetical cases. These practical exercises first came up in the 1820s, and by mid-century, they had become a staple. Jhering himself had participated in one as a student in Göttingen in 1837. Pretty soon, professors began to publish collections of cases for use in such exercises,[450] and Jhering joined their ranks in 1847.[451] While teaching in that manner was thus not Jhering's original idea,[452] it is fair to say that he popularized it more than anyone else of his generation. As a result, he deserves substantial credit for its long-term establishment in the system of legal education in Germany[453] as well as in various other countries where Jhering's "Jurisprudenz des täglichen Lebens" was translated into the vernacular.[454]

From the very beginning of his academic career, these *Practica* were Jhering's pedagogical favorite,[455] and they eventually constituted the main reason for his fame as a teacher.[456] His "Jurisprudenz des täglichen Lebens" was written for use in these exercises. It became the most popular case collection (and his Pandektenpraktikum one of the most famous law classes offered) in nineteenth century Germany and beyond. In these advanced classes, Jhering was truly in his element. Here he could explore the limits of legal doctrine, its problems and inherent tensions, and the arguments hidden in the Roman sources. Here, he could engage the students, make them think, drive them to the limits of their understanding,

---

[449] *Jhering*, Scherz und Ernst (1884) 37–54.

[450] *Haferkamp*, Rechtsfälle in der juritischen Ausbildung der Pandektenwissenschaft (2021) 65–67; *Kuntze*, Der Wendepunkt der Rechtswissenschaft (1856) 12–14.

[451] *Jhering*, Civilrechtsfälle ohne Entscheidungen (1847).

[452] The claim made by *Hirsch*, Jhering als Reformator des Rechtsunterrichts (1970) 89, that this method was Jhering's invention, is proven wrong by *Haferkamp*, Rechtsfälle in der juristischen Ausbildung der Pandektenwissenschaft (2021) 65–67, as well as by *Kuntze*, Der Wendepunkt der Rechtswissenschaft (1856) 12–14. For a brief history of these kinds of classes, see *Jäde*, Jhering als Rechtslehrer (2008) 16–18; see also *Kierulff*, Theorie des Gemeinen Civilrechts (1839) xxvi–xxvii note. As far as I can see, Jhering never claimed any originality.

[453] See the account by *Rümelin*, Rudolf von Jhering (1922) 28.

[454] See *Hirsch*, Jhering als Reformator des Rechtsunterrichts (1970) 98–99.

[455] *Jhering*, Scherz und Ernst (1884) 366–367. For a more in-depth discussion of this side of Jhering's teaching, see *Jäde*, Jhering als Rechtslehrer (2008) 16–21; *Rempel*, Jherings juristisches Kabinett (2018).

[456] *Kunze*, Rudolf von Jhering (1993) 18.

and thereby expand it. Sometimes, he put one of the graduate students at the lectern and required him to present a particular doctrine while Jhering himself sat in the audience, instigated opposition, and was then greatly delighted when his victim had to capitulate.[457] Sometimes he handed out assignments to write papers that the students turned in or presented in class for discussion, and sometimes the give-and-take was just ad hoc and oral in the classroom, "a constant asking and responding"[458]

These *Practica* pursued, as their title indicated, eminently practical purposes. Jhering considered them essential for a proper understanding of the material because he was convinced that students could truly grasp abstract rules and principles only if they had to apply them to concrete problems. During the reign of Roman law as "gemeines Recht" (common law), learning to apply the Roman rules and principles to real problems was essential training for future practitioners. Jhering also wanted to focus his students' attention on the practical results generated by these rules and principles. "It is one thing to take responsibility for the logical correctness of a result," Jhering emphasized, "but quite another [to take it] for its practical appropriateness" ("Angemessenheit").[459] Thus, in Jhering's *Practicum*, future practitioners were supposed to learn how to reach outcomes that were not only doctrinally correct but also practically sensible. Of course, this required not only to apply existing Roman law but sometimes also to go "beyond" it. The salutory effect of the *Practica* was not limited to students but concerned their teachers as well; Jhering considered these classes "one of the most valuable correctives against unhealthy theoretical views."[460] For that reason as well, he recommended that every professor of Roman law be required to teach them.[461]

Preceding Harvard: "Socratic" Teaching and the Case Method. Thus, Jhering and his colleagues engaged in what in the United States came to be known as "Socratic" teaching, and they did so a full generation before Dean Christopher Columbus Langdell (1826–1906) introduced it at Harvard in the 1870s. Already in the 1840s, *Practica* in German speaking lands developed students' analytical and argumentative skills through a dialogue between teacher and learner, pushing the students to, and then beyond, their limits.[462] Jhering became that method's most famous and most vociferous advocate. "The teacher must not only tolerate, but actually provoke contestation of the claims he makes as well as the

[457] *Rümelin*, Rudolf von Jhering (1922) 30.

[458] Letter to Gerber of December 2, 1854, Jhering in Briefen (1913) 48 ("ein unausgesetztes Fragen und Antworten").

[459] *Jhering*, Scherz und Ernst (1884) 366.

[460] *Jhering*, Scherz und Ernst (1884) 339.

[461] *Jhering*, Scherz und Ernst (1884) 367–368.

[462] *Haferkamp*, Rechtsfälle in der juristischen Ausbildung der Pandektenwissenschaft (2021) 72–73. By way of illustration, Haferkamp provides a student's transcript from a *Practicum* taught by one of Jhering's contemporaries, id. 76–77.

attempt to falsify them," he demanded; "he must put himself on the same level with his listeners, as if he and they were colleagues on the bench – not the external authority of the teacher but the internal weight of the reasons provided must finally be decisive."[463]

Like Langdell, Jhering took guidance from the natural sciences, which had switched from learning by reading the writings of the ancients about the subject to learning by looking at facts and processes (e.g., in the laboratory). It was time for jurisprudence, Jhering wrote in 1852, to study law not (only) by reading the Roman jurists' writings but also by looking at law in the context of real life situations.[464] Still, there were substantial differences between Jhering's and Langdell's approaches. In Gießen, Vienna or Göttingen, Jhering presented his students with hypothetical cases without opinions and taught the students to apply the pertinent rules and principles to solve the problems; thus, the principles preceded the cases. At Harvard, it was the other way around: students were presented with actual opinions from which they had to tease out the underlying principles; thus the cases came first, the principles second. Both methods taught students "to think like a lawyer" but it was a civil lawyer reasoning, top-down, on one side of the Atlantic versus a common lawyer, thinking bottom-up, on the other.

Despite using hypothetical cases without opinions, the German approach was arguably more practice-oriented: Langdell taught his students merely *to understand* – namely how courts decided according to rules and principles. Jhering taught his students *to do* – i.e., to apply these rules and principles themselves.

6. Jhering and the Historical School: "Friedrich Karl von Savigny" (1861)

In 1861, Jhering published a lengthy eulogy for Friedrich Karl von Savigny in the "Jahrbücher für die Dogmatik des heutigen römischen Privatrechts." The twenty three-page essay was a reckoning not only with the great Savigny himself but also with the Historical School as the dominant version of jurisprudence in early to mid-nineteenth century Germany. Jhering pulled no punches: lavish (and honest) praise alternated with devastating (and at times tactless) criticism. Evincing an author who is highly ambivalent about the Historical School, the piece indicates that Jhering's position vis-a-vis its teachings was far from monolithic but complex.[465]

---

[463] *Jhering*, Scherz und Ernst (1884) 367. Of course, Jhering added, that means that a professor must reckon with questions he had not anticipated, id. It stands to reason that at least some of his colleagues were probably not very comfortable with that idea.

[464] Letter to Gerber of July 17, 1852, Jhering in Briefen (1913) 14.

[465] On the one hand, Jhering lamented the "Verlöschen" ("going out") of "the brightest star offered by German jurisprudence;" praised Savigny for a "revival of the spirit of Roman

Exploring Jhering's relationship with the Historical School puts the work of his earlier period into the larger context of German legal thought at the time. Of course, the topic has been much discussed, especially by German scholars, often with their characteristic thoroughness and love for intricate detail, in one instance filling an entire book.[466] The purpose of this subchapter is not to replicate all their findings, interpretations, and debates but rather to provide an account comprehensible to a reader who wants to understand the most important points.

Two Clarifications: which "Jhering"? And which "Historical School"? At the outset two clarifications are imperative in order to avoid confusion and misunderstanding: we have to be clear about which "Jhering" we will look at and what exactly we mean by the "Historical School."

As explained in the Introduction, Jhering was a multifaceted thinker whose views and interests shifted considerably over time. In line with the focus of this entire chapter, we will here consider mainly the "early" Jhering, i.e., the scholar of Roman law who, roughly during the first half of his academic life, was primarily interested in legal doctrine, method, and the construction of a new jurisprudence. This Jhering was inevitably engaged with the Historical School, if for no other reason because it dominated the academic environment in which he was trained and in which he emerged as a rookie scholar of Roman law. The later Jhering, who (especially after 1870) looked at law primarily from a sociological point of view, pursued a different agenda which bore scant relation to the Historical School and left it by and large behind.

Yet, even the early Jhering's relationship with the Historical School was neither stable nor entirely consistent. It was not stable because even during the first half of Jhering's career, it changed over time. Jhering expressed his views of the Historical School on several occasions: first very directly, in a series of essays he published in 1844 as a young lecturer;[467] then, more implicitly in various contexts

jurisprudence;" applauded the "plasticity, lucidity, and beauty" of his style; and he repeatedly ranked Savigny with Goethe (whom Jhering admired and sometimes quoted). On the other hand, he wrote that Savigny had for decades already belonged to "the great dead of science" – "a tree which had not borne fruit for years;" blamed him for unnecessarily intensifying the debate between the adherents and the opponents of the Historical School; pointed out that Savigny's works often did not deliver what their title promised; and stated that, contrary to common belief, Savigny was not much to write home about as an academic teacher; *Jhering*, Savigny (1861) 354–356, 358–360, 364–366, 371, 374–376.

[466] *Klemann*, Rudolf von Jhering und die Historische Rechtsschule (1989); for extensive analyses, see *Behrends*, Die Evolution des Rechts zwischen Historischer Rechtsschule und Moderne (1998) 102–170; *Mecke*, Der Begriffs des Rechts und die Methode des Rechtswissenschaft (2018); for a short summary, see *Luig*, Rudolf von Jhering und die historische Rechtsschule (1996) 255–259.

[467] *Jhering*, Die Historische Schule der Juristen (1844). The five, relatively brief, essays appeared in the "Literarische Zeitung," a general "literary journal" published in Berlin. They were published anonymously not because Jhering sought to hide his identity but simply because that was the rule in the "Literarische Zeitung" (though not revealing his identity may have been a welcome side-effect for a young scholar voicing considerable critique of the

in the first two volumes of "Geist" (published 1852–1858); partially in his essay "Unsere Aufgabe" (1857); and, again quite directly, in the eulogy "Friedrich Karl von Savigny" (1861), mentioned above. These publications illustrate a process of gradual liberation, marked by both continuity and change: originally subscribing to the Historical School's major tenets and praising its accomplishments (albeit neither entirely nor unconditionally),[468] Jhering became increasingly critical until he eventually turned against many (though not all) of its credos. The degree to which Jhering's views changed over time depended on the particular issue and ranged from minor variations to virtual *volte faces*. Exactly where Jhering stands in relation to the Historical School thus depends in part on what point in time one looks at.

In addition to changing over time, his position was also not entirely consistent because at least in its nuances, it sometimes depended, as in many other instances, on his momentary thinking, if not his mood. The problem is exacerbated by Jhering's frequently careless use of key terms. When Jhering used the same term as, for example, Savigny or Puchta (or, for that matter, Hegel) there was no guarantee that he meant the exact same thing;[469] and when he used the same term in different writings and contexts, there was no guarantee that it had the same meaning even for himself. Inevitably, therefore, Jhering sometimes left his readers guessing, and different readers have sometimes guessed different things.

We also need to be as clear as possible what we mean by the "Historical School." As mentioned,[470] the phenomenon can be conceived in a broader or narrower sense. Broadly understood, it was the execution of Savigny's program of a "historical legal science." Rejecting eighteenth century natural law thinking, despising law production through abstract reasoning, and abjuring philosophical

---

current mainstream). Jhering, still a lecturer at the University of Berlin, introduced himself not as a member of the School but expressly as a neutral, "non-involved third party" who wanted to present the Historical School to an educated lay audience without taking sides ("keine Partheischrift"); id. I, 197. This claim of entire neutrality is questionable. While it is often difficult to discern the line between simple presentation of the Historical School's ideas on the one hand, and Jhering's own views about these ideas on the other, Jhering occasionally voiced both agreement with, and criticism of, the Historical School very openly. On the whole, Jhering defended the Historical School more than he attacked it. Jhering's discussion is not especially profound (nor is it well organized). For a more detailed description and analysis of these early essays, see *Mecke*, Rudolf von Jhering. Anonym publizierte Frühschriften (2010) 109–143.

[468] Klemann's view that Jhering was originally entirely beholden to the Historical School, see *Klemann*, Rudolf von Jhering und die Historische Rechtsschule (1989) 75, 80, 97, is questionable in light of the may reservations and criticisms Jhering voiced in his early essays, i.e., *Jhering*, Die historische Schule der Juristen (1844). By contrast, *Haferkamp*, Die Historische Rechtsschule (2018) 316, opines that even in his younger years, Jhering was never really part of the Historical School.

[469] See *Mecke*, Begriff des Rechts und Methode des Rechtswissenschaft bei Rudolf von Jhering (2018) 21–22.

[470] Supra chapter I.1.

speculation, it postulated that Rechtswissenschaft be based purely on the positive sources of law. According to Savigny, such positive law had first to be explored through historical research and then to be organized into a logical system. In various iterations, this conception of the Historical School – as a science of positive law in its historical and systematic dimensions – constituted the mainstream of nineteenth century German jurisprudence.[471] At least until the 1860s (and in several ways beyond), Jhering was, like most of his academic colleagues, clearly a member of this, broadly conceived, Historical School: he rejected the eighteenth century "law of reason" ("Vernunftrecht"), focused on the positive sources of (in his case: Roman) law, believed in its historicity and thus explored its historical dimension (in "Geist" and various other writings), and called for its systematic organization (in his methodological discourses).[472] Recognizing Jhering's membership in this broadly conceived Historical School shows that until the 1860s, Jhering largely operated within the prevailing paradigms. In other words, he was a vociferous critic of many aspects of current jurisprudence but not yet the iconoclast he would become after the mid-1860s.[473]

More often, the Historical School is conceived more narrowly: as the jurisprudence initiated by Gustav Hugo, then openly founded by Savigny, and eventually further developed by his successor Puchta and various other contemporaries.[474] This conception is narrower in at least three ways: it sees the Historical School as dominant merely for (roughly) the first half of the nineteenth century;[475] it focuses on the scholarship dealing with Roman law (thus sometimes excluding the Germanist branch of nineteenth century German legal science); and it centers around a set of specific ideas about the origin, nature, and development of law that

[471] For a full exposition, see *Reimann*, Nineteenth Century German Legal Science (1990).

[472] Jhering doubted, however, that historical research could be joined with the development of present-day doctrine as easily as the Historical School's program provided. Instead, he emphasized early on that exploring legal history (especially of Roman law) and building a system of concepts were at least partially incompatible and thus better pursued separately; see, e.g., *Jhering*, Geist I (1852) 52–53, fn. 27; *Jhering*, Entwicklungsgeschichte des römischen Rechts (1894) 8–9. We will return to this issue in the context of Jhering's critique of contemporary historiography, infra chapter V.1., notes 20–24 and text.

[473] Infra chapter III.

[474] The most recent and thorough study is *Haferkamp*, Die Historische Rechtsschule (2018).

[475] Most commonly, the birth of the Historical School is dated to Savigny's main programmatic writings in 1814 and 1815, though in a sense, its beginning lie already in the earlier writings of Gustav Hugo and in Savigny's work at the century's beginning on legal methodology, *Savigny*, Juristische Methodenlehre (1802/3), and in his magisterial treatise on the law of possession, *Savigny*, Das Recht des Besitzes (1803). If one wishes to date the Historical School's end with any precision, 1846 as the year of Puchta's death is a possible, though questionably early, marker; perhaps the cessation of Savigny's productivity as a scholar around 1850 is more plausible. A tell-tale sign of its demise was the mid-century discussion about a re-orientation of legal science, see *Kuntze*, Der Wendepunkt der Rechtswissenschaft (1856).

largely fell out of fashion with the mainstream around mid-century. When Jhering embarked on his academic career in the 1840s, the Historical School, thus conceived, was already waning and his writings over the next two decades engaged with a jurisprudence whose heyday was over.[476] The following discussion deals with this narrower, and more common, conception of the Historical School.

Even in the narrower sense, however, the Historical School was not monolithic but rather comprised a considerable variety of views. Here, we will focus (even more narrowly) on the teachings of Savigny and Puchta as the School's most prominent representatives and leave all others aside. This is not so much to reduce complexity but mainly because Savigny and Puchta were the two figures on whose ideas Jhering himself focused time and again.[477] Yet even Jhering's relationship with their ideas requires a differentiated discussion because Jhering reacted quite differently to the various credos propagated by Savigny and Puchta. Thus we will have to take separate looks at his positions vis-a-vis their most important teachings: on the origin of law, on its defining sources, on the lasting value of Roman law, on the relationship between academic scholarship and legal practice, and on the general attitude of jurisprudence towards the past and present.

The Origin of Law: Versions of Volksgeist. The Historical School is famous for its credo that law originates in the *Volksgeist.* The idea is mainly associated with Savigny who originally spoke of the "common consciousness of the people" ("das gemeinsame Bewußtsein des Volkes")[478] and only later adopted the term *Volksgeist* from Puchta.[479] Yet, the term was neither Puchta's nor Savigny's invention. With roots in Montesquieu's "Esprit des loix" (1748), it was introduced in Germany by Johann Gottlieb Herder (1744–1803) with a linguistic turn (adopted by Savigny), animated Johann Gottlieb Fichte's (1762–1814) patriotic "Reden an die deutsche Nation" ("Speeches to the German Nation") (1808), and made an appearance Hegel's "Philosophie der Geschichte" ("Philosophie of History")[480]. As a result, in early to mid-nineteenth century Germany, it was a widely popular term with many shades of meaning.[481] Thus it is no surprise that Jhering often

---

[476] Already in 1844, Jhering declared the Historical School to be defunct, even though at that point, Puchta was still alive and active; *Jhering*, Die historische Schule der Juristen (1844) IV, 536; V, 566.

[477] The definitive work on Savigny is *Rückert*, Friedrich Carl von Savigny (forthcoming 2025); see also id., Idealismus, Jurisprudenz und Politik bei Friedrich Carl von Savigny (1984). The standard reference for Puchta is *Haferkamp*, Georg Friedrich Puchta und die Begriffsjurisprudenz (2004).

[478] *Savigny*, Vom Beruf unserer Zeit (1814) 8, 13.

[479] *Puchta*, Das Gewohnheitsrecht vol. I (1828) 144, 152; *Savigny*, System des heutigen römischen Rechts vol. I (1840) 13.

[480] In his Philosophy of Law, Hegel spoke of the "Nationalcharakter des Volkes" ("national character of the people"), *Hegel*, Grundlinien der Philosophie des Rechts (1821) 19 (sec. 3).

[481] Even Johann Paul Anselm Feuerbach (1775–1833), who was not an adherent of the

employed it as well, along with many similar expressions: "national spirit," "character of a people," "fundamental national views," "genius" or "individuality" or "mentality" of a people, etc.[482] It is not surprising either that his frequent invocations of the concept did not necessarily mean that Jhering adopted Savigny's or Puchta's version. In fact, Jhering subscribed to some of their ideas but differed from others.[483]

Jhering embraced Savigny's and Puchta's *Volksgeist* as an expression of the idea that law was not a reflection of timeless human nature nor a creature of abstract reason nor a product of legislative whim but rather, like language,[484] a historical and cultural phenomenon properly shaped by the character of a nation.[485] The whole project of "Geist" was based on the assumption that Roman law reflected an identifiable Roman "spirit" (with different versions prevailing in the three consecutive systems),[486] a claim Jhering asserted with particular emphasis for the second phase, i.e., the law of the late monarchy and early to mid-Republic.[487] Jhering stuck to this dimension of *Volksgeist* throughout his life,[488] even though he later explored it mainly from a sociological (rather than cultural-historical) point of view.

Jhering also embraced the Savignian idea that the law's rootedness in the spirit of the people entailed its organic wholeness[489] because it was ultimately all cut from the same cloth. This wholeness promised that despite an often apparent disparity, law could ultimately be understood and organized in a coherent and even systematic fashion. For Jhering, understanding law as an organic whole also had to inform legal historiography – that discipline had to transcend the mere aggregation of facts and look at them as expressions of a "higher unity – of the

---

Historical School, found it "cleary incontestable" ("ganz unbestreitbar") that law was born from the "spirit of the people;" quoted after *Klemann*, Friedrich Karl von Savigny und die Historische Rechtsschule (1989) 26.

[482] See e.g., *Jhering*, Geist I (1852) 13, 34, 37, 293–294.

[483] For a much more detailed analysis, see *Mecke*, Begriff des Rechts und Methode der Rechtswissenschaft bei Rudolf von Jhering (2018) 31–76.

[484] See, e.g., *Savigny*, Vom Beruf unser Zeit (1814) 9. Like Savigny, the early Jhering frequently compared law to language, see, e.g., *Jhering*, Geist I (1852) 16 fn. 3, 20 fn. 7, 22 fn. 10, 24 fn. 11, 63 fn. 30.

[485] For an early expression of this view, see *Jhering*, Die Historische Schule der Juristen (1844) V 566. He also agreed that at least at early stages of development, a people's characteristic features shaping its law were often unconscious, lingering in the "semi-darkness" of emotions and hunches; at this point, the "genius of a people" was still "dreaming"; *Jhering*, Geist I (1852) 37

[486] Supra 1., notes 72–77 and text; in a sense, then, there was not one, but at least a trias of "spirits," as noted by *Mecke*, Der Begriff des Rechts und die Methode der Rechtswissenschaft bei Rudolf von Jhering (2018) 25–26.

[487] Supra 1., note 76 and text.

[488] *Jhering*, Das Schuldmoment im römischen Privatrecht (1867) 2–3; *Jhering*, Entwicklungsgeschichte des römischen Rechts (1894) 29.

[489] *Savigny*, Vom Beruf unserer Zeit (1814) 8, 12.

individuality of the people."[490] Again, "Geist" was based on the very strategy to reveal within the diversity of ancient Roman law the features that demonstrated its internal coherence. And again, Jhering adhered to this (idealist) belief in the law's organic coherence virtually throughout his life, often expressing it through metaphors borrowed from the natural sciences, especially biology.

Yet, at least over time, Jhering's understanding of both *Volk* and *Geist* began to differ from that of Savigny and Puchta in important ways. Especially for Savigny, *Volk* was a rather romantic, cultural, and, one can even say, mystical, notion. Jhering soon rejected the romantic element and came to embrace a historical-empirical conception that was closer to Montesquieu's and even Hegel's ideas:[491] for Jhering, *Volk* was the actual people at a particular point in history – like the Romans in antiquity. Thus, as Jhering showed in Volume II of "Geist," attention must be paid not only to the respective people's mentality but also to the concrete social and economic circumstances of its existence – aspects largely and happily ignored by both Savigny and Puchta. And while Jhering originally agreed with Savigny that *Geist* was an innate cultural property of a people which had to be accepted as a given,[492] he later increasingly postulated that it was at least in part the product of a people's experiences and needs.[493] In short, Jhering eventually turned *Volksgeist* from a cultural and normative idea into a historical and descriptive concept.[494] By moving in a realist-empirical direction, Jhering's understanding of *Volksgeist* not only parted ways with the Historical School's orthodoxy, but it also foreshadowed his later turn to a decisively sociological approach.

An equally important difference concerned the role of *Volksgeist* in the actual production of law. For Savigny and Puchta, the spirit of the people was the ultimate foundation and source of law – from it, law originally developed quasi-automatically (and organically), just like language.[495] Originally inclined towards that position as well,[496] Jhering increasingly doubted and thus modified it, regarding the *Volksgeist* as just one law-influencing factor among others. The *Volksgeist* helped to shape law, but it was not the foundation of, nor did it produce, law. Instead, law was based on social needs and produced by human action.[497] Jhering

[490] *Jhering*, Die historische Schule der Juristen (1844) III, 423.

[491] On Montesquieu, see supra 1., notes 35–37 and text; Hegel sounded almost like Montesquieu when spoke of *Volksgeist* as the "common character ('Gepräge') of [its] religion, its political constitution, its ethics, its legal system, its customs, also its science, art, and technical skills," *Hegel*, Philosophie der Geschichte (1840/48) 118; see also id. 131.

[492] See *Jhering*, Geist II.2. (1858) 546.

[493] *Jhering*, Über die Entstehung des Rechtsgefühls (1884); see also infra chapter V.2., notes 85–91 and text.

[494] *Mecke*, Begriff des Rechts und Methode der Rechtswissenschaft bei Rudolf von Jhering (2018) 71.

[495] *Savigny*, Vom Beruf unserer Zeit (1814) 8–11.

[496] See *Jhering*, Die Historische Schule der Juristen (1844) I 199–200.

[497] See, e.g., *Jhering*, Geist I (1852) 219. In "Geist", Jhering was apparently still ambivalent

eventually turned Savigny and Puchta virtually upside down: he claimed that the law was created by human action and then shaped the people's (legal) mentality, rather than the other way around. As a result, *Volksgeist* was no longer the origin of historical development but rather its product.[498] As we shall see in a moment, Jhering's foregrounding of human action also determined his understanding of the various sources of law as well as his views on the orientation of jurisprudence towards the past, present, and future.

A final difference arose regarding the national character of law. The logical consequence of Savigny's and Puchta's view of law as growing from a particular people's spirit was an essentially nationalist conception. Jhering soon begged to differ. It is important to understand that the difference did not concern the tension between a national and a universalist conception of law; Savigny, Puchta, and Jhering were all scholars of Roman law and largely agreed on the Roman law's value as the material for a universally valid jurisprudence (a view that was difficult to reconcile with Savigny's and Puchta's, though not necessarily with Jhering's, notion of *Volksgeist*). Instead, the difference concerned what we may call the purity of law. For Savigny and Puchta, the law's rootedness in the spirit of a particular people meant that other nation's laws were alien elements which played no legitimate role and thus deserved scant or no attention in legal science. For Jhering, by contrast, the historically formed law and concomitant *Volksgeist* could be, and in fact often were, influenced by foreign imports. In Jhering's mind, that was not only descriptively true in many instances, it was also normatively desirable because one people could greatly benefit from another's ideas on how to solve social problems. As a result, Savigny and Puchta stood in antithesis to, while Jhering became an early advocate of, a comparative dimension in jurisprudence.[499]

The Sources of Law: Custom vs. Legislation.[500] To a large extent, the Historical School, as represented by Savigny and Puchta, was a theory of the sources of law. It foregrounded custom, marginalized legislation, and propagated the productive and thus leading role of legal science. Over time, Jhering came to differ in all three regards.[501]

---

in this regard because he also saw "the seat of the forces producing law in the individuality of the people" ("Sitz der rechtserzeugenden Kräefte in der Individualität des Volkes"), id., 34.

[498] See infra chapter V.2. notes 85–91 and text.

[499] Jhering lamented Savigny's narrow (nationalist) approach virtually from the beginning, see *Jhering*, Die historische Schule der Juristen (1844) II, 408. Jhering's role in the development of comparative law will be explored in chapter VII.4., notes 369–397 and text.

[500] For a much more detailed analysis, see *Mecke*, Begriff des Rechts und Methode der Rechtswissenschaft bei Rudolf von Jhering (2018) 173–242.

[501] Operating within the civil law tradition, neither Savigny and Puchta nor Jhering seriously considered judicial decisions proper sources of law. At the time and for scholars of Roman law, it went without saying that courts could not *make* law; especially since they were expressly forbidden to do so in the *Corpus Juris ("Non exemplis sed legibus iudicandum est,"* c. 7, 45, 13). In his later years, however, Jhering came to recognize that courts not only "apply"

Since Savigny and Puchta viewed law as developing quasi-automatically from the *Volksgeist*, they regarded custom as its definitive source.[502] To be sure, they did not focus on *popular* custom; since they agreed that at advanced stages of development, the people were represented by learned jurists, they saw the development of customary law largely in professional hands. Still, this development was envisaged as spontaneous, gradual, and collective. It is but a slight caricature to say that according to Savigny and Puchta, law was not consciously made but rather but just "became" – slowly, organically, and un- or semi-consciously.[503] Jhering rejected that proposition. He did give Savigny credit for emphasizing that law did not, as was widely believed in the eighteenth century, spring from sheer human reason or momentary legislative will but that it was rather a product of historical development and cultural evolution. Jhering also admitted that sometimes law indeed grew in a gradual, semi-conscious fashion resulting in custom (e.g., when it emerged from commercial usage).[504] Still, for Jhering, Savigny had badly overstated the case when he elevated custom to the definitive source of law. Custom played a decidedly minor role both in actual history and in modern law. Jhering's research in early Roman developments led him flatly to deny the Historical School's claim that law originally developed through custom – his historical studies found no evidence supporting that claim. Jhering thus blamed Savigny and Puchta for simply inventing the notion that law sprang from custom without even trying to marshal historical evidence.[505] That criticism struck at the heart of Savigny's and Puchta's jurisprudence because Jhering revealed that it was "historical" at best in a mystical, but not at all in an empirical, sense.[506] In modern law, Jhering considered custom an inferior source because it was often indeterminate. The problem was not only that its content could be difficult to ascertain, but that it was often unclear when custom actually rose from a merely social norm to a rule of law enforceable through the public power.[507]

---

but also "find" law, i.e., that they are participating in the process of law production; *Jhering*, Ist die Jurisprudenz eine Wissenschaft (1868) 89–90.

[502] *Savigny,* Vom Beruf unserer Zeit (1814) 8–14; *Puchta*, Das Gewohnheitsrecht (2 vols. 1828–1837). Roman law was (part of) customary law; *Savigny* id. 33.

[503] *Savigny*, Vom Beruf unserer Zeit (1814) 12 (law emerging "in an entirely organic mode, altogether without conscious will or intent;" "ganz auf organische Weise, ohne eigentliche Willkühr oder Absicht").

[504] *Jhering*, Kampf ums Recht (1872) 13.

[505] Jhering mocked that the Historical School had made custom "the pet ('Schoßkind') of modern jurisprudence [...] it seems as if it felt obligated to compensate it with blind love for the neglect it had suffered before," *Jhering*, Geist II.1. (1854) 25. In later years, he rejected likening the development of law to that of language, see, e.g., *Jhering*, Entwicklungsgeschichte des römischen Rechts (1894) 14.

[506] *Jhering*, Geist II.1. (1854) 36 (fn. 19), 38, 69; *Jhering*, Geist II.2. (1858) 20–25, 417; *Jhering*, Geist III (1865) 297–296. For a more detailed discussion, see *Mecke*, Begriff des Rechts und Methode der Rechtswissenschaft bei Rudolf von Jhering (2018) 184–190.

[507] See *Jhering*, Geist I (1852) 301; *Jhering*, Geist II.1. (1854) 24–26, 33. Neither Savigny nor Puchta had addressed this issue; for a fuller discussion, see *Mecke*, Begriff des Rechts und

Legislation was regarded mostly with skepticism by Savigny and Puchta. At least in private law, it was acceptable (but, in a sense, also unnecessary) when it either just enshrined already existing law – having grown through custom – or when it clarified technical issues.[508] But since it threatened to disturb or arrest the organic growth of law, it should be avoided as much as possible. For Jhering, the opposite was true: he came to regard legislation as the primary source of law. This was not only because he saw law mainly as a product of conscious human will rather than of unconscious and spontaneous growth – a view confirmed by his studies of early Roman developments. It was also for a theoretical and a practical reason. The theoretical reason was that for Jhering, the law came into its own only when it took the form of general and authoritatively posited rules, i.e., in a statute. Here, Jhering followed in the footsteps of Hegel.[509] It was through legislation that law cut loose from ad hoc decision making according to individual notions of justice, and that, as a set of abstract written rules, it could ensure equality of treatment and predictability of results.[510] The practical reason was that Jhering viewed legislation as the appropriate vehicle for the progressive development of law in modern society. In contrast to Savigny and Puchta, who considered statutory lawmaking tolerable as long as it did not entail significant change, Jhering welcomed legislation exactly to promote change and progress. While for Savigny and Puchta, society (represented by the learned jurists) took the lead which legislation could follow, for Jhering, legislation often had to charge ahead, with society then adjusting to its innovations. Of course, even according to Jhering, the legislator should not act capriciously and in disregard of the "conviction of the people," but that simply meant that legislation had to take actual public opinion into account,[511] not that it was bound to preserve existing custom, never mind to manifest a mythical *Volksgeist*.

It is no surprise therefore that Jhering disagreed with the most high-profile position of the Historical School: Savigny's staunch opposition to plans for a German private law codification. It was in part the call for such a codification by Anton Friedrich Justus Thibaut (1772–1840) in 1814[512] that had provoked Savigny to formulate the Historical School's fundamental credos in his most famous work, "Vom Beruf unserer Zeit für Gesetzgebung und Rechtswissenschaft" ("On the Vocation of Our Age for Legislation and Jurisprudence").[513] Jhering,

Methode der Rechtswissenschaft bei Rudolf von Jhering (2018) 177–184. Jhering would later tackle that problem in the context of his study of norms in society; *Jhering*, Zweck II (1883); see infra chapter VI.1.

[508] *Savigny*, Vom Beruf unserer Zeit (1814) 16–17. Michael Kunze aptly phrased this belief: "The legislator did not make the law but the law tasked the legislator with what he had to do." *Kunze*, Ein großer Jurist (2023) 13.

[509] *Hegel*, Grundlinien der Philosophie des Rechts (1821) 186 (sec. 211).

[510] *Jhering*, Geist II.1. (1854) 24–40.

[511] *Jhering*, Die Historische Schule der Juristen (1844) V 566.

[512] *Thibaut*, Über die Nothwendigkeit eines allgemeinen bürgerlichen Rechts für Deutschland (1814).

[513] *Savigny*, Vom Beruf unserer Zeit (1814); English translation by *Hayward*, On the Vocation of Our Age for Legislation and Jurisprudence (London 1831).

whose first academic teacher in Heidelberg had been none other than Thibaut, disagreed with Savigny and defended the idea of a private law codification – in the German vernacular and for all of Germany.[514] He found Savigny's arguments against it badly wanting, including the claim that jurisprudence was not ready to produce an appropriate code,[515] and essentially took sides with Thibaut. To be sure, Jhering did not fully engage in the debate for and against codification (which was somewhat stale by mid-century anyway), but he made it clear that continuing to work with the existing codification (or rather: compilation) of Roman law, i.e., Justinian's early sixth century *Corpus Juris Civilis* (written of course in Latin), was not sustainable.[516]

While the differences between the Historical School's and Jhering's views on the respective roles of custom and legislation are fairly obvious, the differences between their respective views on the role of legal science were more subtle. In that regard, there was much common ground. For both, the Historical School and Jhering, legal science mainly meant academic work on the doctrine of positive law. Both tasked *Rechtswissenschaft* with providing the received (private) Roman law with an appropriate conceptual apparatus and to organize it into a logically consistent system. Savigny, and to an even greater extent Puchta, had made important contributions to this enterprise – which Jhering recognized and praised. In this field, Jhering's own work was a continuation (and variation) of the Historical School's program, both in his methodological agenda and his doctrinal essays.[517]

It is thus easy to overlook that Jhering did not necessarily agree with Savigny and Puchta on the specific law-making function of legal science. For the leaders of the Historical School, the scientific work of scholars was a source of law in its own right for which Puchta coined the term "Juristenrecht" – "jurists' law."[518] Since (popular) custom had played a dominant role only in the early (long-gone) stages of a people's legal history, and since legislation was at best a necessary evil, the modern development of (private) law was mainly the job of legal science. In that fashion, Savigny and Puchta appointed themselves and their academic colleagues the proper leaders of present-day lawmaking. It was at this point that

---

[514] See *Mecke*, Rudolf von Jhering: Anonym publizierte Frühschriften (2010) 122 (with references to Jhering's earliest, anonymously published essays). Jhering also opined that codification did not have to be incompatible with the credos of the Historical School, *Jhering*, Die Historische Schule der Juristen (1844) I 201.

[515] Jhering rejected Savigny's argument that contemporary legal science was not advanced enough to produce a proper code in stinging language: "An age which puts its hands in its lap when it feels the need for a reorganization of its law or even just for a codification of law, because it does not consider itself advanced enough in its science, such an age does not suffer from too little science but from too much, such an age reveals not so much its scientific, but rather its moral, deficiency," *Jhering*, Savigny (1861) 363–364.

[516] *Jhering*, Geist I (1852) 3.

[517] Supra 2. and 3.

[518] *Puchta*, Das Gewohnheitsrecht I (1828) 161–167.

Jhering parted ways with the Historical School once again. He denied that legal science had the authority to make substantively new, or to change existing, law; that was reserved to the legislator.[519] It must be admitted that there is a tension between this position and Jhering's belief that "higher jurisprudence" was "productive:" that it could create "absolutely new material" through juristic construction; that the scientific system could be the source of new law; and that legal concepts could "mate and beget new ones."[520] Jhering did not resolve this tension with any clarity, and much ink has been spilt on exactly what he meant by (law) "production" in his methodological discourses.[521] Perhaps the best way to reconcile Jhering's rejection of scientific law-making authority on the one hand with his enthusiasm for juristic "production" on the other is to understand the work of legal science as limited to the confines of the existing sources:[522] if "construction" had to operate with the given (statutory or customary) material, then "construction" did not create entirely new substantive law; it merely extrapolated new concepts or rules from already-existing stuff. Jhering demonstrated that approach in his article on *Culpa in Contrahendo* when he painstakingly worked with the Roman sources but refused to go against them.[523] Thus understood, Jhering envisaged a division of labor between legislation and legal science: the legislator was in command of the law's content such that only he could add truly new substance, while the academic jurists were the masters of the law's form, i.e., of its conceptual apparatus and structure, from which they could derive hitherto undetected principles and rules.[524] Neither had any business of interfering with the other.[525] In short, for Jhering, legal scientists were not, as for Savigny and Puchta, the masters of the law's development but rather the legislator's partner.

The Value of Roman Law: Ending the "Cult of Mummies." The Historical School was primarily concerned with the classical Roman law as transmitted to the present in the form of Justinian's *Corpus Juris Civilis*[526] and, since its discovery

[519] See *Mecke*, Begriff des Rechts und Methode des Rechtswissenschaft bei Rudolf von Jhering (2018) 206–212 with further references, inter alia, to unpublished writings by Jhering.

[520] *Jhering*, Geist I (1852) 29; see supra 2., notes 244–245 and text.

[521] See especially *Mecke*, Begriff des Rechts und Methode der Rechtswissenschaft bei Rudolf von Jhering (2018) 217–242. As Mecke points out, once again, Jhering's position also underwent some changes between the 1840s and the 1860s.

[522] See *Mecke*, Begriff des Rechts und Methode der Rechtswissenschaft bei Rudolf von Jhering (2018) 245.

[523] Supra 3., notes 358–367 and text.

[524] See *Mecke*, Begriff des Rechts und Methode der Rechtswissenschaft bei Rudolf von Jhering (2018) 242–260. In footnote added in later editions of Geist II.2., Jhering, however, claimed that legal science could actually create new substance in case of complete legislative failure, *Jhering*, Geist II.2. (5th (unrevised) ed. 1898) 386–387, fn. 528.

[525] *Jhering*, Geist II.2. (1858) 399 fn. 515; further references in *Mecke*, Begriff des Rechts und Methode der Rechtswissenschaft bei Rudolf von Jhering (2018) 206–209.

[526] The name was not original to Justinian's sixth-century AD compilation but added in the late sixteenth century when printed editions became available; see *Dionysius Gothofredus*, Corpus Iuris Civilis Romani (Geneva 1583).

by Niebuhr and Savigny in 1816, also on the basis of Gaius' *Institutes* (ca. 160 A.D.). As a dyed-in-the-wool scholar of Roman law, the Jhering of the 1840s through the 1860s operated on the same terrain. In many important ways, his views on the Roman law thus went hand-in-glove with the convictions of Savigny and Puchta (as well as of most contemporary German legal academics). They all agreed on the crucial role of the Roman law as the current common (private) law of Germany (subject to regional codification and legislation).[527] They shared a deep appreciation of, and admiration for, the classical Roman law's intellectual sophistication. They all regarded it as the ideal training ground for the legal mind, i.e., as the proper drill for teaching students to think like a (civil) lawyer. Like Savigny and Puchta, Jhering taught almost nothing else, and as we have seen, he did so with great enthusiasm and success.[528]

There was also agreement in principle that the value of Roman law lay not so much in its particular positive rules but rather in those of its elements that early- and mid-nineteenth century scholars considered essentially timeless. This was particularly true for the Roman jurists' legal technique, i.e., the inherent logic and admirable precision which enabled them, as Savigny put it, "to perform calculus with their concepts."[529] Both the leaders of the Historical School and Jhering considered that technique not only exemplary but also universally applicable. In addition, they regarded many (though not all) substantive categories and doctrines of classical Roman law as expressions of enduring truths, such as the distinction between real (absolute) and obligatory (relative) rights, or the doctrines of contract formation and validity. And they were united in their belief that classical Roman law largely lacked a systematic organization that reflected its internal coherence. Savigny pushed in that direction in his "System des heutigen römischen Rechts" (1840–1849), which, however, was still a fairly loose organization of "legal institutions" and "legal relations;" Puchta constructed an

---

[527] As far as I can see, Jhering (as well as most of his Romanist colleagues) never questioned the *Corpus Juris Civilis'* force of law in mid-nineteenth century Germany. That force, however, was not beyond cavil. After all, Justinian's compilation had never been formally enacted in Germany; and even if its acceptance as (subsidiary) law in the Holy Roman Empire was de facto a *fait accompli*, that Empire had ended in 1806. It was far from obvious that the Justinian compilation should have any legislative force in the various individual member units of the German Federation. This was especially true, of course, in those Federation members that had enacted codifications, such as Bavaria and Prussia, as well as Austria where Jhering nonetheless taught Roman law from 1868 through 1872.

[528] Supra 5. Hans-Peter Haferkamp pointed out the importance of the Historical School's mission to improve the quality of German lawyers through rigorous training in the classical Roman law; *Haferkamp*, Die historische Rechtsschule (2018). See also *Mecke*, Rudolf von Jhering, Anonym publizierte Frühschriften (2010) 112. In this enterprise, Jhering was a convinced fellow-traveler of Savigny and Puchta.

[529] "[D]aß sie mit ihren Begriffen rechnen;" *Savigny*, Vom Beruf unserer Zeit (1814) 29; see also id., 29, 31, 35 (finding the most important value of Roman law in its method).

elaborate system along strictly logical lines;[530] and Jhering extolled the virtues and utility of such a system[531] though he never attempted to build one.

Yet, Jhering's attitude towards Roman law was significantly more detached and critical than Savigny's or Puchta's. This was true with regard to the Roman law's past, present, and future.

Jhering was more critical with respect to the Roman law as a heritage of the past because he had serious questions about the effects and the blessings of its "reception" in medieval and early-modern Germany. For Savigny and Puchta, that reception was performed by the learned jurists as the representatives of the German *Volk* on the field of jurisprudence; this had anchored classical Roman law firmly in the German legal culture. Jhering roundly rejected that view. In the opening pages of "Geist," he frankly stated what the Historical School had pasted over: the obvious contradiction between the claim that a people's law emanated from its own tradition on the one hand, and the reign of a "code that emerged more than a thousand years ago with an alien people" on the other.[532] For Jhering, Savigny and Puchta had completely misconstrued what the reception of Roman law was all about: it was not a matter of the innermost national character of the people[533] but simply the borrowing by one legal culture of the ideas, techniques, and institutions of another[534] – a phenomenon Jhering recognized as ubiquitous in legal history a century before modern comparative law presented it as a great discovery.[535] Jhering was also critical of Savigny's and Puchta's claim that through its reception, Roman law had become the proper law of Germany. Even though Jhering recognized its dominance in both private law theory and practice, he called it an "alien element of German law."[536] The exact meaning of that phrase is not clear, but its implications are: if Roman law was not an integral element of German law, it was not inexorably binding; instead, it was merely a mass of inherited material from which today's jurists should freely choose the suitable parts and then dispose of the rest. With regard to the broader effects of the reception as a historical process, Jhering saw both advantages and drawbacks. One the one hand, he did recognize important benefits: compared to the indigenous German (and largely regional or even local) law, Roman law was more rational, sophisticated, and uniform. Its method had fundamentally shaped modern legal thought[537] and its universal character made it a suitable basis for a general jurisprudence.[538] In these regards, the Roman law was "one of the most

---

[530] See supra 2., notes 188–192 and text.

[531] Supra 2., notes 240–243 and text.

[532] *Jhering*, Geist I (1852) 1.

[533] See *Jhering*, Geist I (2d ed. 1866) 8.

[534] *Jhering*, Geist I (2d ed. 1866) 5–9.

[535] See infra chapter VI.4., notes 383–387 and text.

[536] *Jhering*, Geist I (1852) 1.

[537] "Our legal thinking, our method, our way of looking at things, in short, our whole juristic education (Bildung) has become Roman," *Jhering*, Geist I (2d ed. 1866) 14.

[538] See supra 1., notes 53–61 and text.

precious gifts of antiquity to modern times"[539] – and its reception a blessing. On the other hand, Jhering acknowledged the costs of its adoption, i.e., the displacement and disruption of much indigenous and popular law. Here, Jhering echoed the Germanist scholars' critique of the Roman law's reception as a major blow to the indigenous legal culture, even though he stopped short of considering it, like some of his Germanist colleagues, a "national disaster."[540] At the end of the day, the reception of Roman law was what it was: "a fact that cannot be ignored by legal science"[541] and a phenomenon that should enrich, but it must not enslave, the present.

For the present, Jhering thus called for a much more liberal attitude towards the authority of the Roman sources. Roman law had to be critically examined with a view to its present-day utility; in particular, it had to be purified of all elements that were peculiarly Roman and thus of no value for a universal jurisprudence. It is important to note that in this instance, Jhering's campaign was not directed at the Historical School at large. As Jhering recognized, Savigny had already demanded that Roman law be de-cluttered in virtually the same sense, and Jhering praised the School's founder for his work in that regard.[542] The target of Jhering's ire were rather Savigny's successor Puchta and his generation. How much that had to do with the fact that Savigny was still alive and highly influential while Puchta was dead, is anyone's guess.[543] Be that as it may, Jhering's attack on Puchta was vehement even by Jhering's standards. While he greatly admired his former teacher's ability to extract general concepts from the Roman material and to organize them into a logical system, he now charged him with slavish adherence to the content of the Roman sources. Puchta and his followers had become victims of "blind fanaticism of literalism" ("blinder Buchstaben Fanatismus")[544] They had bent Roman law out of shape time and again in order to reach practically acceptable outcomes. Raging on for page after page and fully displaying his formidable dexterity in Roman law, Jhering provided a panoply of shocking examples of Roman rules and principles that had become dysfunctional under modern conditions but were still endorsed by Puchta & Co. Jhering created a veritable academic bloodbath. As usual, he minced no words. A "feeling of horror" ("Gefühl des Grauens")[545] overcame him, he wrote, when he looked at the nonsense that had been made of the Roman law since its reception. It was time

[539] Quoted after *Mecke*, Rudolf von Jhering (2010) 124.

[540] Thus the famous condemnation by *Beseler*, Volksrecht und Juristenrecht (1843) 42.

[541] *Jhering*, Geist I (2d ed. 1866) 5.

[542] See. e.g., Savigny, System I (1840) XV; *Jhering*, Unsere Aufgabe (1857) 39.

[543] At the time, Jhering was still stuck in the provincial university of Gießen and waiting for a professorship at a larger and more prestigious university so that offending Savigny would have been a dangerous business. Yet, Jhering was also quite fearless and often lashed out at scholars even at the risk of making himself unpopular among his contemporaries.

[544] *Jhering*, Unsere Aufgabe (1857) 38.

[545] *Jhering*, Unsere Aufgabe (1857) 38.

for jurists to approach the Roman sources in a spirit of "intellectual freedom" ("geistige Freiheit")[546] This required a "deconstruction" of the Roman law to first identify and then eliminate mere vestiges of the past.[547] In short, Puchta's "civilistic cult of mummies" ("civilistischer Mumien=Cultus") had to end.[548]

Jhering also differed from Savigny's and Puchta's views regarding the Roman law's future. For the Historical School's leaders, Roman law, as an integral part of the German legal system, was to remain its bedrock, albeit in modernized form. It is true that Savigny had already advocated a liberal use of the Roman law which, once fully mastered by the present, could then be left behind at some undefined point in the future,[549] and that Puchta's abstract concepts and systems were increasingly detached from the classical Roman source material as a historical phenomenon. Still, getting rid of Roman law altogether and replacing it with a new jurisprudence would have been anathema to Savigny and Puchta.[550] That, however, is what Jhering called for. As we have seen, his opening volley in the first volume of "Geist" both clearly predicted and unequivocally demanded that the Roman law, as such, be laid to rest. As a persistently alien element in German legal culture, it had to be "expelled" and then replaced with a modern jurisprudence, albeit one preserving of Roman law what had truly been absorbed.[551] In 1852, when Jhering expressed these views in his typically forceful fashion, the movement to free German law from the classical Roman sources as a regime of binding positive rules gathered momentum. It would eventually lead to the codification of private law in the BGB of 1900 which finally fulfilled Jhering's demand to end the centuries-long reign of Roman law in German lands.

The Relationship with Legal Practice: Law as a Problem-Solving Device. Jhering also distanced himself from Savigny and Puchta when he criticized them for

---

[546] *Jhering*, Unsere Aufgabe (1857) 39.

[547] *Jhering*, Unsere Aufgabe (1857) 30–31. The term "deconstruction" ("destruiren") was apparently Jhering's own creation and of course juxtaposed to the "construction" which was the hallmark of his own (higher) jurisprudence, see supra 2., notes 235 –239 and text.

[548] *Jhering*, Unsere Aufgabe (1857) 31.

[549] *Savigny*, Vom Beruf unserer Zeit (1814) 113, 125, 133.

[550] The extent to which this is true for Savigny depends in part on whether one looks at what he wrote in 1815 versus in 1840. In 1815, Savigny had unequivocally, and indeed categorically, claimed that the present is inevitably determined by the past (which for Savigny of course included most of all the Roman law adopted during the "reception"), and that it is of utmost importance to recognize and accept that. In fact, such a recognition was the very essence of the Historical School – which Savigny presented in openly (and indeed, aggressively) partisan terms, Savigny, Über den Zweck dieser Zeitschrift (1815). A quarter century later, Savigny suddenly spoke of the right of the present to determine its own fate and postulated the "equal recognition of the value and of the independence of every age," Savigny, System I (1840) XVI–XVII. Savigny denied that this evinced a change of view and (dubiously) claimed that he had never said otherwise; id. XIV. Even in 1840, however, Savigny demanded that we focus on the historical sources, i.e., the work of the classical Roman jurists; Savigny, System I (1840) IX–XII, XXVII.

[551] *Jhering*, Geist I (1852) 3.

neglecting the needs of legal practice. He bemoaned the "alienation between theory and practice" for which he blamed not only the Historical School as a whole "but therefore also, and in particular, Savigny."[552] That was somewhat unfair. After all, like Jhering, Savigny had long shared in the work of his law faculty in the process of *Aktenversendung*, i.e., in providing expertise to courts in pending litigation. Perhaps more importantly, Savigny had expressly called for closer cooperation between theory and practice; in fact, he almost sounded like Jhering when he demanded that theorists develop more practical sense; and like Jhering, Savigny had held up the classical Roman jurists as models in that regard.[553] In another sense, however, Jhering was right: in Savigny's scholarship practical considerations played at best a marginal role. In this regard, Puchta and his generation were an even more appropriate target. In the 1830s and 1840s, much mainstream Romanist scholarship had indeed remained highly, and at times almost absurdly, theoretical, and Jhering tore into it with gusto.[554] It is true that even Jhering sometimes got carried away with extolling the virtues as well as the beauty of purely theoretical constructs, especially in the context of his "natural-historical method."[555] Yet, as we have seen, he always kept one eye on firmly on the needs of legal practice – even in his methodology. And of course, in his work as a quasi-appellate judge, and certainly in his teaching,[556] he never ceased to admire and praise the practical sense of ancient Roman law.

Like Jhering, Savigny, and even Puchta and his followers, envisaged a division of labor between academic jurists and practitioners: the former developing law on the theoretical level, the latter handling real disputes. For Jhering, however, the two sides were not independent of each other; instead, legal science was an instrument in the service of legal practice. As we have seen, the early Jhering still saw academic theory as taking the lead from which practice got its guidance; the later Jhering saw it the other way around: practice was "acting and progressing, with theory following it and bringing its results into the proper form."[557]

For Jhering, the practical side of law was a much greater concern than for Savigny and Puchta not only as a matter of jurisprudential theory, and not even because he mingled more with practitioners.[558] Jhering was simply much more interested in how law actually operated. In the historical parts of "Geist", Jhering often kept his nose very close to the ground, and in many of his doctrinal writings,

---

[552] *Jhering*, Savigny (1861) 367.

[553] *Savigny*, System I (1840) Preface, xx–xxv.

[554] *Jhering*, Unsere Aufgabe (1857) 30–38. Jhering was neither the only, nor the first, legal scholar to critizice the Historical School for its lack of practical orientation; see *Kierulff*, Theorie des Gemeinen Civilrechts (1839) xix–xx.

[555] Supra 2., notes 305–307 and text.

[556] Supra 4. and 5.

[557] *Jhering*, Ist die Jurisprudenz eine Wissenschaft? (1868) 91. As Mecke has pointed out, this essentially amounted to the recognition of judicial decisions as a source of law, *Mecke*, Begriff des Rechts und Methode der Rechtswissenschaft bei Rudolf von Jhering (2018) 258.

[558] Supra 4., notes 423–428 and text.

he focused on very concrete practical problems. In these contexts, at least, Jhering was the civilian version of a case lawyer – not in the sense that he considered judicial decisions precedential, but that he grounded his legal analyses in practical issues found in real life. In the last instance, law was not an emanation of the *Volksgeist*, nor a creation of legal science, nor a logical system of abstract concepts, but a device to solve social problems.

On Looking Backward and Forward: Towards a Progressive Jurisprudence. Jhering's various critiques of the Historical School and its leaders were rooted in a fundamental disagreement about the proper orientation of legal science more generally. The Historical School's jurisprudence was essentially backward looking: Savigny and his followers, including Puchta, felt bound by the past, i.e., by the teachings of Roman law, albeit in modernized and de-cluttered form. Since the present could not escape the power of tradition and, as Savigny put it, ignored it at its peril,[559] jurists could not (and the legislator should not) significantly reform (private) law. This attitude ran entirely counter to Jhering's view of history as a heritage at the present's disposal, of the law as a device to solve current problems, and, last but not least, to his psychological predilection for action rather than contemplation.

Interestingly, Jhering originally attempted to reconcile the idea of the law's (organic) progress with the Historical School's credos; in fact, he extensively defended the Historical School against the charge of being implicitly anti-progressive.[560] This was not necessarily only out of respect for Savigny; it was probably also because in the early 1840s, Jhering was still under the spell of the Historical School and sought a way to square its tenets with his own progressive inclinations.

A few years later, Jhering sounded a very different note. He now openly chastised the Historical School for wanting to hang on to a long-gone past and, thus, denying the present its right to determine its own destiny: "The times of Ulpian and Paulus are gone and will not return despite all efforts. To wish them to return, one has to forget that each era should be an original, not a copy of another."[561] Jurisprudence had to focus on our own time, not on times long gone.[562]

Thus Jhering lamented the Historical School's "thoughtless reiteration of the doctrine of 'organic' development, of internal evolution," and its denial of the

---

[559] *Savigny*, Über den Zweck dieser Zeitschrift (1815) 4.

[560] *Jhering*, Die Historische Schule der Juristen (1844) I 201, V 567–569.

[561] *Jhering*, Unsere Aufgabe (1857) 42. This statement was a rejection of Savigny's call to "immerse ourselves in the writings of the old [scil. Roman] jurists," Savigny, System I (1840) XXVII, and to encounter the material bequeathed upon us in a "wholesome feeling of humility," id. XI.

[562] "The real interest of the present is more important to me than that of the historical exploration of the past" ("das reale Interesse der Gegenwart steht mir höher als das der historischen Erforschung der Vergangenheit"), *Jhering*, Scherz und Ernst (1884) 340.

"value and significance of human action, the role that free decision, reflection and intention have played in history."[563] Jhering re-defined the role of modern-day jurists: they were no longer curators of the past but architects of the present and future.[564]

Finally, there was a political side to Jhering's differences with Savigny and his followers. The Historical School's jurisprudential conservatism had important socio-political implications. In the beginning, they were not fully visible as Savigny and his followers supported the liberation of Germany from the Napoleonic yolk. Yet, these implications became more noticeable during the political oppression of liberal politics in the years after 1815 and then obvious in the context of the (failed) 1848/49 Revolution and beyond: insisting on continuity with the legal past implied support for the monarchy of the *ancien régime*, and rejecting active legal change implied opposition to liberal political reform.[565] A moderate liberal at heart, Jhering rebelled against these positions. The prime target of his attack was Savigny who – born from old nobility, belonging to the land-owning elite, and closely involved with the Prussian Crown – became the veritable symbol of the Historical School's political conservatism. Ignoring considerations of tact, Jhering used his eulogy for Savigny to voice his views in language worth quoting for its strength.

> "[R]omantic convervatism is an unfortunate product of the academic cloister. It is undeniable that the Historical School promotes the latter and thus indirectly also this conservatism. [... It acts] as if it were the task of mankind to put its hands in its lap and to wait until the genius of history offers what is necessary [...]. This reluctance towards the historical act suited the practical-political tendencies of the restauration period, aimed at the preservation of the status quo, very well, and the name of the Historical School found as much favor with the governments as it became unpopular with the mass of the people – a lack of popularity which had to impact the School's founder with particular force."[566]

No matter how much honest admiration Jhering had for some of Savigny's scholarship, with regard to politics, he could have hardly distanced himself from the Historical School' founder in starker terms.[567]

Selective Appropriation: Jhering's Independence. Jhering's relationship with the Historical School of Savigny and Puchta illustrates a general feature of his

[563] *Jhering*, Unsere Aufgabe (1857) 42; see also *Jhering*, Geist III (1865) 6.

[564] In later years, when Jhering had almost completely turned away from the Historical School, he condemned Savigny's theory in even stronger language, see *Jhering*, Kampf ums Recht (1872) 16–17 ("one of the most ill-fated wrong dogmas one can think of;" "eine der verhängnisvollsten Irrlehren, die sich denken lassen;" id. 17).

[565] For an original and intriguing discussion of the Roman law as a political program, see *Whitman*, The Legacy of Roman Law in the German Romantic Era (1990).

[566] *Jhering*, Savigny (1861) 368–369.

[567] Savignys and Jhering's different attitudes towards legal and political change were also the result of different mentalities. Savingy was old nobility, reserved, aloof, and afraid of change; Jhering was new bourgeoisie, extrovert, engaged, and believing in social progress.

thinking: independence. Even in his early years as a scholar, when he subscribed to many of the Historical School's then dominant teachings, Jhering did not view himself as a "member."[568] He never fully identified with this – nor with any other – "school" or ideology, and he found it unhelpful to think in terms of intellectual camps. Thus, he suggested early on to lay the conflict between the Historical School and its opponents to rest because he considered much of it trumped up (mainly by Savigny) and by now outdated.[569]

Rather than judging the Historical School as a whole, Jhering critically reflected on its various elements, selectively appropriated for his own purposes what he agreed with (modified as needed) and rejected what he deemed wrong. In addition, he reconsidered his position over time, gradually changing his views, and thus increasingly liberating himself from what he had been taught and originally accepted. As a result, in the 1840s and 1850s, Jhering sometimes sounded very much like Savigny and Puchta in some regards while he vociferously opposed them in other respects. Jhering never found it difficult to praise someone lavishly for ideas he agreed with while harshly criticizing the same person for views he considered erroneous. He saw much to admire in Savigny's and Puchta's work but also found much of it ill-conceived and misguided.

During the 1860s, Jhering then applied this very approach to himself: as his thinking evolved, he critically re-examined his own positions – maintaining some, modifying others, and in some instances loudly repudiating his erstwhile convictions. In the process, he finally left the Historical School behind for good. This was not because he had come to reject all of its elements but because now he pursued a new agenda for which the ideas of Savigny and Puchta were essentially irrelevant.

---

[568] See supra note 467.

[569] *Jhering*, Die Historische Schule der Juristen (1844) I, 200–201.

Chapter III

Jhering's "Conversion" – Abandoning "Conceptual Jurisprudence"?

In 1858, Jhering turned 40, the age at which, according to Oliver Wendell Holmes, a man must make his mark, if any.[1] Jhering had accomplished quite a lot: he was a well-paid professor of Roman law, had a respectable publication record, and was finally finishing the second volume of his "Geist des römischen Rechts." He had embarked upon a major project to create a new jurisprudence that pushed beyond the Historical School, and he had developed a sophisticated methodology designed for that purpose, building on, and modifying, Puchta's conceptualist approach. To be sure, much of his work was controversial among the academic establishment, which probably held up offers from more prestigious universities like Heidelberg, Berlin or Vienna, but Jhering also enjoyed a growing reputation as one of the most capable and interesting Romanist legal scholars of his generation. To put it colloquially, all in all, things were going pretty well.

The end of that year, however, changed Jhering's life as a scholar forever: it plunged him into an intellectual as well as personal crisis. In late 1858, Jhering had to write an opinion, as a member of the Gießen law faculty, in a case that presented a disconcerting dilemma: applying "general principles" led to an outcome that completely defied common sense and flatly contradicted his feeling of justice. The experience deeply shook Jhering's confidence in a strictly logical approach. (1.) In reaction, Jhering not only vehemently turned against such a method, he also made fun of it – in print. He ridiculed the mainstream of "conceptual jurisprudence" in a series of writings some of which eventually became world-famous for both their message and their style (2.). At first glance, it seemed as if Jhering had experienced his "Damascus" and turned radically away from all belief in a jurisprudence relying on abstract and systematic logic. Closer inspection reveals, however, that his *volte face* was less radical than his own rhetoric suggested, and that there was considerable continuity between his work before and after his life-changing experience (3.). Still, as we shall see in chapter IV, his perspective on law was permanently altered.

---

[1] *Novick*, Honorable Justice (1989) 157.

1. At the Limits of Legal Logic: "Gefahr beim Kaufcontract" (1859)

The Case of the Ship-Shares: Risk Distribution in Double-Sales. At first it looked like a fairly routine commercial case. An English trading company owned shares in the cargo (in this case coke) of several ships (*Schiffsparten*). While in Rostock (Germany), its sales representative sold one of these shares to a German merchant. Even though the trading company back home was notified of the transaction, it sold the share to an English customer.[2] The seller also immediately executed the (second) sale by delivering the pertinent documents to the English buyer. It assumed that the German buyer, with whom it had a longstanding and friendly business relationship, would understand and release it from the first contract. The German merchant refused to do so, however, because he had already sold the share to another party. Eventually, the cargo was destroyed because the ship sank. When both buyers thus refused to pay, the English seller sued the German purchaser in Germany. The court of first instance found for the seller, but the appellate court reversed. It then referred the case (by way of *Aktenversendung*[3]) to the law faculty of the University of Gießen for its opinion, and Jhering was tasked with writing it.[4]

The issue was, of course, whether the seller could still demand payment from the buyer after the seller's performance had become impossible. In order to understand the dispute, it is important to recognize that one element was entirely clear and undisputed: according to Roman law (which governed the case in the German courts), the seller had not lost its claim for payment simply because the object of sale had perished; instead, the risk of accidental loss was borne by the buyer (*periculum est emptoris*).[5] Another question, however, was hotly disputed: had the seller lost its claim because it had sold the object to a second buyer before it had perished? In other words, the core issue was who bore the risk of accidental loss in case of a double-sale (Doppelverkauf)? Jhering eventually published his analysis of the case in an article in his own (and Gerber's) "Jahrbücher."[6] A close

[2] The seller included it in a bundle of shares because its English customer wanted all or nothing.

[3] See supra chapter II.4., notes 411–417 and text.

[4] This is a considerably streamlined version of the facts based on the account Jhering provided in his article about the case, *Jhering*, Gefahr beim Kaufcontract (1859) 451–452. The full facts were considerably more complicated, see *Kroppenberg*, Die Plastik des Rechts (2015) 22–24. While the additional facts omitted here mattered for Jhering's opinion in the actual case (Jhering agreed with the appellate court that the German buyer could defeat the English seller's claim by invoking its bad faith under the *exceptio doli*), they are not relevant for our present purposes.

[5] There were various possible exceptions, e.g., if the seller was in delay (*mora*), but they played no role in this case. For an in-depth discussion of the Roman law principle, see *Bauer*, Periculum Emptoris (1998).

[6] *Jhering*, Gefahr beim Kaufcontract (1859). Two years later, Jhering published a second

look at Jhering's reasoning shows why the case was such a traumatic experience for him.

The Basic Dilemma: General Principles v. Sense of Justice. At the outset, Jhering was confronted with two issues that are often conflated in the literature commenting on Jhering's experience but must be kept strictly separate. The first issue was somewhat embarrassing but not all that thorny. As Jhering frankly conceded, in an article published fifteen years earlier, he had opined – more or less in passing – that the double sale had no impact on the enduring obligation of the buyer.[7] This view had been directly based on a reading of the Roman sources which was widely shared. Taking a harder look at the crucial text, Jhering now realized that he had been wrong: the text did not really address the present problem. Had that been all, the case would not have cost Jhering much sleep. Sometimes, the Roman sources were just not pertinent, and Jhering was, as usual, entirely candid about his error and even admitted that he had no good explanation for it.[8]

The second issue, however, was much more serious.[9] Since the Roman sources were of no direct help, Jhering turned to "general principles" to resolve the case. Perhaps surprisingly, however, these general principles rendered the double-sale irrelevant as well. Beyond doubt, both contracts were entirely valid; and beyond doubt, the seller thus had a claim to the purchase price (*actio venditi*) against each buyer. Of course, in principle each buyer had a (temporary) defense based on the seller's non-performance (*exceptio non adimpleti contractus*). But according to the firmly established rule about risk allocation, a buyer lost that defense when the seller's performance became impossible because the object of sale perished accidentally. This plainly applied to both buyers and there was no logical reason to treat them differently. As a result, each remained under an obligation to pay the purchase price. Of course, the seller could have fulfilled only one of the two contracts but that was now irrelevant because the loss of the object of sale had freed him from the obligation to perform either contract. Also, none of the buyers was really worse off on account of the double-sale because even without it, he would have borne the risk of accidental loss and remained liable for the purchase

---

part of the article which, however, dealt with an entirely different problem: when does the risk of accidental loss pass to the buyer in a sale of generic goods? Here, Jhering developed a new rule: the risk does not pass already when the seller has separated the goods destined for the buyer from the larger mass but only when the seller has done everything he is obligated to do, which may, for example, include shipping the goods; *Jhering*, Gefahr beim Kaufcontract, Teil 2 (1861). Jhering's new rule was adopted in § 243 sec. 2 of the German Civil Code (BGB) of 1900.

[7] *Jhering*, Abhandlungen aus dem römischen Recht (1844) 59, 71.

[8] *Jhering*, Gefahr beim Kaufcontract (1859) 453–454.

[9] The following analysis is somewhat simplified for the sake of readers who are not familiar with the intricacies of the classical Roman sources. For a closer look at them, and an explanation of the subtleties in their treatment of contracts of sale, see *Behrends*, Jhering heute! (2023) 208–212.

price. In summary, the *double*-sale had no impact on any of the two buyer's enduring liability for the purchase price.

Jhering considered it obvious that this result was irreconcilable with the most elementary requirements of the sense of justice. Why should the seller profit (by getting his money twice) from having entered into two contracts when he could never have fulfilled both? While Jhering did not spell this out, he also realized that such a rule made no economic sense. As Jhering explained, the rule created perverse incentives: especially in cases involving a significant risk of accidental loss (such as a ship at sea), the seller would be well-advised to sell the object to as many parties as possible; if the object then actually did get lost, he had multiple claims for the purchase price.[10] Jhering thus became convinced that such a result must be avoided; the question became how.

Roads not Taken: Possible Solutions and Their Rejection. There were several options. From today's standpoint, the most obvious would be simply to change the risk allocation rule, i.e., to put the risk of accidental loss on the seller and thus to deny his claim if the object of sale has perished. Jhering, however, did not even consider that option, and it seems pretty clear why not: it would have entailed a radical change of a fundamental and long established rule (of Roman law); and it would have had ramifications far beyond the present case. Entirely abandoning the traditional rule was simply above the paygrade of a jurist. The legislature could take such a step (and eventually did[11]), but Jhering would not.[12]

A more viable option was the reasoning of the appellate court: the seller had lost the claim against the – first – buyer because he had knowingly sold the object for a second time *and* actually delivered the documents to the second purchaser. These acts of the seller had already made performance of the first contract impossible; thus, the seller could not invoke the subsequent impossibility through accidental loss against the original buyer. This solution made considerable sense, but Jhering rejected it. In part, he found it doctrinally unconvincing. His reasoning demonstrates how important doctrinal arguments were to him. The seller's conclusion of the second contract in full knowledge of the first was surely intentional and thus perhaps amounted to *dolus*; that, however, had not caused the (first) buyer any harm – even in the absence of a second contract, the ship would have been lost so that the buyer would have remained liable for the purchase price. A *dolus* without harmful consequences, Jhering pointed out, was legally

[10] *Jhering*, Gefahr beim Kaufcontract (1859) 477.

[11] The German Civil Code of 1900 provided that in case of accidental impossibility of performance, the party owing performance is absolved from its obligation (§ 275 sec. 1 BGB), e.g., to deliver the goods, as is the other party to render the counter-performance (§ 323 sec. 1 BGB), e.g., to pay the price. According to *Kroppenberg*, Die Plastik des Rechts (2015) 28, this reversal of the Roman rule was at least in part due to Jhering's influence.

[12] Jhering also considered and rejected a solution suggested by Friedrich Mommsen (1818–1892), a fellow Romanist, because he considered it so unconvincing as to be "not worthy of its author," *Jhering*, Gefahr beim Kaufcontract (1859) 457.

irrelevant.[13] Of course, one could take a dim view of the seller's behavior, but the point of *dolus*-based remedies was not to punish wrongful conduct, it was to compensate for harm caused by it, and that was lacking.[14] Also, it was not true, Jhering argued, that by performing the second contract, a seller makes the performance of the first impossible. After all, the seller can re-purchase the object from the second buyer and then deliver it to the first.[15] In part, however, Jhering also rejected the appellate court's solution because it struck him as too narrow: it worked only if, as in the present case, the seller could be charged with both *dolus* and *traditio* (delivery – in this case, of the documents). It did not resolve cases of unintentional double-sale (e.g., where one salesperson sells an object to a customer without knowing that his colleague had already sold it to someone else[16]). Nor did it help in cases in which neither contract had yet been performed. Jhering was convinced that even in these cases, preserving the seller's claims against both buyers when performance vis-a-vis either had become impossible was so patently unfair that it needed to be avoided.[17] He thus sought a solution that covered all cases of double-sale.[18]

Jhering's Way Out: The Purpose of Risk Allocation. So far, Jhering's reasoning, sophisticated though it was, had stayed within conventional boundaries. He had applied generally recognized principles to the problem at hand and deduced the result in a logical fashion. At this point, however, his unwillingness to accept the result of that operation pushed him into new territory. Recognizing that the problem could only be solved by going to its root, he set out to re-think the basic rule of risk allocation. To decide how it should apply in cases of double-sale, Jhering went beyond the rule itself and explored its "meaning and purpose" ("Sinn und Zweck").[19]

Jhering thus asked why the law made the buyer bear the risk of accidental loss during the time between conclusion and (envisaged) performance of the contract.

---

[13] *Jhering*, Gefahr beim Kaufcontract (1859) 459.

[14] In the present case, it was also not clear that the seller's conduct was really reprehensible. After all, the seller had good reason to assume that the (first) buyer would release him from the contract. In fact, the buyer actually made an effort to do so, *Jhering*, Gefahr beim Kaufcontract (1859) 452.

[15] *Jhering*, Gefahr beim Kaufcontract (1859) 459–61. Of course, this may not work, but then the seller remains liable to the (first) buyer for performance damages.

[16] *Jhering*, Gefahr beim Kaufcontract (1859) 461 fn. 14.

[17] *Jhering*, Gefahr beim Kaufcontract (1859) 461. The unfairness of such a result in these cases is not as clear to me as it apparently was to Jhering. Even if the seller has sold the object twice without any fault, he is liable to both buyers for performance, and if the object does not perish will end up owing one of them performance damages, including lost profit. The seller is thus subject to a considerable risk of loss. It may thus not be altogether unfair to allow him to profit if things turn out in his favor because the object is accidentally lost. Note that the problem is not that any of the two buyers is worse off than in case of a single transaction, but merely that the seller is better off.

[18] *Jhering*, Gefahr beim Kaufcontract (1859) 459.

[19] *Jhering*, Gefahr beim Kaufcontract (1859) 461.

Rejecting some arguments made in the literature, Jhering saw the main reason as basic fairness between the parties: by entering into the contract, the seller bound himself, either to outright keep the object for the buyer or at least not to dispose of it otherwise. The seller then incurred a limitation of his freedom from which the buyer would normally benefit. It was thus only fair that the law protect the seller against the incidental risk during that holding period in case the object perished accidentally before it was delivered to the buyer. This revealed that the content of the seller's surviving claim was not really the purchase price as such anymore but rather compensation for a loss suffered.[20] "One could actually call the purchase price [a form of] insurance coverage."[21] Now we can also see exactly why our "sense of justice" rebels against giving the seller concurrent claims against both buyers in the case of the double-sale: it would amount not merely to compensation of the buyer but to his actual enrichment. The former is justified by good reasons, whereas the latter is not.[22]

That understanding of the claim was a game changer: if the purpose of the seller's claim was not to enrich the seller but merely to compensate him for harm suffered, it could survive the loss of the object only if it actually caused the seller harm. If, for example, the lost object did not even belong to the seller,[23] or if it was insured, there was no reason to preserve the seller's claim against the buyer because in the first case, he had not suffered any loss, in the second, he would be compensated by his insurance carrier.[24] The consequences in cases of double-sale were obvious. If the seller had already gotten paid by one of the buyers, or if at the time of accidental loss he had already conveyed title to one of them (performing the contract and thus becoming entitled to payment), the seller had no claim left against the other buyer. If things were completely open when the object of sale perished, the seller could choose which buyer to pursue for the purchase price.[25] He just could not go after both.

[20] *Jhering*, Gefahr beim Kaufcontract (1859) 465–468. Jhering proffered another explanation: basic fairness suggests to put the risk of accidental loss on the party who bore the responsibility for, or who had the primary interest in, the time gap between conclusion and performance of the contract. That could be either the seller or the buyer or both. Yet, making the outcome turn on that point would invite a lot of litigation because it will often be disputed, as well as hard to decide, who bore that responsibility. Thus the law might as well put the risk on the buyer – which the parties were free to change by agreement, of course; id. 464–465. This explanation was fairly crude, and Jhering did not pursue it further.

[21] *Jhering*, Gefahr beim Kaufcontract (1859) 473; again at 486.

[22] *Jhering*, Gefahr beim Kaufcontract (1859) 467.

[23] In Jhering's example, an artist displays a painting in a gallery and offers it to the owner for purchase. While the offer is pending, the owner sells the painting to a client. Before the client picks it up, the painting is accidentally destroyed. In that case, the loss is the artist's, not the gallery owner's; *Jhering*, Gefahr beim Kaufcontract (1859) 466–467.

[24] It is another question, subsequently discussed by Jhering, whether the buyer can claim the insurance proceeds in exchange for paying the purchase price, etc.; *Jhering*, Gefahr beim Kaufcontract (1859) 472–474.

[25] Jhering recognized of course that leaving the choice to the seller was somewhat unfortunate but could not think of a better solution; *Jhering*, Gefahr beim Kaufcontract (1859) 478.

Compatibility with Roman Law: "The Juristic Construction." It was only after all that was said and done that Jhering returned to Roman law on the last ten pages of the article.[26] This is noteworthy in two regards. On the one hand, Jhering spent only a quarter of his article on his solution's compatibility with Roman law, and the last quarter at that. This indicates in and of itself that arguments derived from Roman law were not crucial to his solution. Thus Jhering's claim that by finally turning to the Roman sources, he had reached "the truly crucial point" ("den eigentlich entscheidenden Punkt"),[27] was plainly untrue. On the other hand, he did indeed return to the Roman sources. This showed that he deemed it important to ensure that his solution was justifiable under Roman law, in part of course for the sake of his readership, but also, in part, probably also for his own mental (or rather, intellectual) peace.

Since he found no directly applicable rules in the Roman sources, Jhering's discourse here amounted to a mere compatibility check. He drew a plausible analogy to a rule concerning leases[28] but otherwise limited the discussion of his solution to showing "that the sources are at least not to the contrary."[29] He also invoked the common sense of the Roman jurists and their adherence to the principle of good faith (*bona fides*), claiming that they too would have made an exception from the general risk allocation rule in cases of double-sale – had they thought about it.[30]

It was only on the very last few pages that Jhering then turned to the "juristic construction" of his solution – i.e., the question of how it was to be understood from a doctrinal point of view. His answer was similar to the one he later gave to undergird a claim for *culpa in contrahendo*:[31] The contract of sale contains not only a primary obligation – to exchange the goods for money – but also a secondary obligation, herein of the buyer to insure the seller against loss if the goods accidentally perish between the making and the performance of the contract.[32]

Modes of Argumentation: From Principles to Purposes (to Roman Law). Thus, at the end of Jhering's article, all was well that ended well: Jhering found a solution that avoided the (in his view) absurd result of the traditional risk-allocation in contracts involving a double-sale. This solution followed from a re-interpretation (and restrictive application) of the rule; and it turned out to be compatible with the Roman sources. So, why was Jhering's article such an important turning point in his jurisprudential thinking?

---

[26] *Jhering*, Gefahr beim Kaufcontract (1859) 478–488.

[27] *Jhering*, Gefahr beim Kaufcontract (1859) 478.

[28] If the lessee cannot use the leased object for reasons lying in his own sphere of responsibility, he of course still owes the rent. Yet, he can subtract the amount the lessor has received by leasing the object to another. For Jhering, the analogy to his solution was obvious: the lessor cannot collect the full rent from both lessees; *Jhering*, Gefahr beim Kaufcontract (1859) 479.

[29] *Jhering*, Gefahr beim Kaufcontract (1859) 480.

[30] *Jhering*, Gefahr beim Kaufcontract (1859) 482–483.

[31] Supra chapter II.3., notes 344–346 and text.

[32] *Jhering*, Gefahr beim Kaufcontract (1859) 487.

It was because Jhering had reached the limits of legal logic in the pure form in which he had embraced it by driving Puchta's approach to extremes. He found himself unable to solve the problem with the tools he had first extolled in "Geist," and then again in his essay "Unsere Aufgabe" just two years earlier. After turning the matter this way and that, he had to admit that the logical application of established general principles inexorably led to results that not only violated his sense of justice but also had unacceptable economic implications. In addition, although Jhering did not mention it, the system of law he had so confidently pronounced gapless[33] sadly did not provide a solution for his problem, forcing Jhering to create one on his own. Contrary to what Jhering had confidently claimed before, even after centuries of doctrinal work, the law could indeed be "embarrassed by history."[34] In short, the method in which he had put so much trust had sent Jhering straight into a brick wall. He experienced the matter not from a detached, purely intellectual, perspective but, as he described it in a letter to his friend Gerber, as a real "nightmare." He found himself in an "utterly vexed position which [he had] never experienced to that degree" and which drove him "nearly to despair."[35] Ultimately, he had to push the once cherished mode of reasoning aside and to turn to the purpose of the rule. In other words, he had had to shift from logical to teleological reasoning. Only that shift had allowed him to develop a convincing solution. The "juristic construction," once the virtual centerpiece of his methodology, was now downgraded to an afterthought. Jhering had come to realize that, at least in this case, it was a "subordinate" issue and "devoid of all practical consequences" ("eine untergeordnete, praktisch, so viel ich sehe, völlig einflußlose Frage")[36]

2. Ridiculing the Mainstream: "Scherz und Ernst in der Jurisprudenz" (1861–66/1884)

Jhering could have laid his "higher jurisprudence" quietly to rest, but it was not his style to take such a defeat lying down. Instead, he did something that was highly unusual for any thinker and well-nigh unimaginable for a member of the sober and serious class of German law professors: Jhering not only turned openly against the very methodology he had so enthusiastically propagated, he publically ridiculed it – and with it, himself. Up to this point, Jhering had been a notable, up-and-coming, though somewhat eccentric, legal scholar; now, he outed himself as an iconoclast riding roughshod over established academic norms.

[33] Supra chapter II.2., note 273 and text.

[34] *Jhering*, Unsere Aufgabe (1857) 16.

[35] Letter to Gerber of January 6, 1859, Jhering in Briefen (1913) 108–109.

[36] *Jhering*, Gefahr beim Kaufcontract (1859) 485.

To be sure, Jhering's charge was directed only against the Romanist branch of German legal academia. He had no axe to grind with the Germanists' private and commercial law, nor with areas such as criminal, procedural, and public law.[37] Yet, since Romanist private law was the flagship and backbone of nineteenth century German legal academia, Jhering's attack was directed at its core.

His attack came in two waves. In the early 1860s, shortly after his upsetting experience in the "double-sale" case, Jhering published six "Vertrauliche Briefe über die heutige Jurisprudenz" ("Confidential Letters on Present-Day Jurisprudence") in which he subjected many methods and features of the Romanist establishment to biting criticism and painful derision. In 1884, i.e., more than two decades later, he came out with a small book entitled "Scherz und Ernst in der Jurisprudenz"[38] which included not only the "Letters" just mentioned but also two newly written critiques of what Jhering now called "Begriffsjurisprudenz" ("conceptual jurisprudence").[39] One of these critiques is among his most famous pieces: "Im juristischen Begriffshimmel" ("In the Juristic Heaven of Concepts") drove Jhering's mockery of contemporary scholarship to new heights. Both Jhering's "Letters" and his "Heaven of Concepts" merit some consideration, not because of any great intellectual content, but because they show Jhering engaged in something he greatly enjoyed – attacking and lampooning the academic profession of his time.

A Reckoning with the Romanist Mainstream: "Vertrauliche Briefe über die heutige Jurisprudenz" (1861–66). "These days, if someone has not mastered the 'civilistic construction'", Jhering wrote in 1861, "good riddance to him; as a lady does not want to appear without a crinoline today, so a modern private law scholar does not want to show up without a construction." One jurist, he continued, "has even created an elevated floor of jurisprudence for this purpose, which has thus been named 'higher jurisprudence.'" On this floor, "the civilistic artists shape the material and give it an artistic-civilistic form. Once they have found it, the liveless material turns into a living being; through some mysterious process it is infused, like the clay figure of Prometheus, with life and breath, and the civilistic homunculus, i.e., the concept, becomes productive and mates with others of his sort and creates offspring." In a footnote, Jhering cited the two key texts of his own methodology: the second volume of "Geist" and his article "Unsere Aufgabe."[40] Jhering now made fun of the very methodology he had so enthusiastically propounded just a few years earlier – and, by reference, of himself.[41]

---

[37] *Jhering*, Scherz und Ernst (1884) 358–359.

[38] *Jhering*, Scherz und Ernst in der Jurisprudenz (1884).

[39] Jhering first used the term in "Scherz und Ernst" (1884) 9–10 (fn. 1), 337, 345, etc. Apparently, however, his friend Windscheid had used it already in 1875, in a lecture on the *Pandects* in order to contrast it with Jhering's "Zweckjurisprudenz" ("jurisprudence of purpose"), see *Jansen and Reimann*, Begriff und Zweck in der Jurisprudenz (2018) 100 (fn. 71).

[40] *Jhering*, Scherz und Ernst (1884) 7.

[41] Jhering obliquely referred to his own work once again in the sixth (and last) letter.

Jhering's sarcastic discourse "On the Civilistic Construction" appeared in the first of his six "Confidential Letters." Jhering published them[42] between 1861 and 1866 in the law journal[43] of the newly established German Lawyers' Conference (Deutscher Juristentag) which he had helped to establish. As their subtitle "From an Unknown" ("Von einem Unbekannten") indicates, Jhering originally remained anonymous. He later wrote that he targeted himself in order to camouflage his authorship.[44] Yet, he could scarcely hope to remain anonymous in the long run, and perhaps part of him did not really want to.[45] After all, he had published unabashed attacks on colleagues and their work under his name before;[46] nor was he a stranger to making fun of himself in other contexts. In any event, his authorship was soon revealed.

In his six "Letters" (comprising more than 100 pages), Jhering attacked a broad variety of the Romanist mainstream's features.

As mentioned, he targeted the "juristic construction," though it remained unclear yet again what exactly he meant by that (and what was now so bad about it). He complained incessantly about scholarship that rose to great theoretical heights but lost sight of its practical utility, engaging in the "construction of a sophisticated clock which is not designed for actual operation."[47] He lamented bizarre conceptualizations – for example, when an old roof was considered a legal person holding rights,[48] or when notions of property were extended to the human body so that freedom of speech could be explained through ownership of one's

Scholars have tried to squeeze ever more ideas out of the tired old Roman law, Jhering wrote, like one might try to squeeze out ever more juice from grapes that have already been squeezed multiple times. Some have added water in the process. "One of them tried to add just *Spiritus*," which means alcohol in German and can also mean "Geist" in Latin; "unbeknownst to him, however, quite a bit of water is said to have run into his Geist," *Jhering*, Scherz und Ernst (1884) 110.

[42] As Jhering mentioned right at the beginning, "letters" were of course a popular literary genre (the perhaps most famous example being *Montesqieu's* Lettres Persannes (Cologne 1721): "Almost all sciences, arts, trades have been the object of letters, and we have chemical, botanical, zoological, musical letters, etc.. Just our poor jurisprudence, the Cinderella of science, stands empty-handed as usual;" *Jhering*, Scherz und Ernst (1884) 4. Jhering now ended that sorry state of affairs.

[43] Originally the Preußische Gerichtszeitung, in 1861 re-named Deutsche Gerichtszeitung.

[44] *Jhering*, Scherz und Ernst (1884) V (Vorrede).

[45] Already in the second letter, he intentionally provided some clues about his identity by telling the story of his legal education, including his early enthusiasm for Puchta; *Jhering*, Scherz und Ernst (1884) 17–19.

[46] See, e.g., supra chapter II.6., note 549 and text.

[47] *Jhering*, Scherz und Ernst (1884) 9.

[48] "See the old roof yonder from which the rain drips onto the neighbor's property? What do you think it is? An old roof. Sure, but don't you see the shine of the legal personality which illuminates it like an electric light? Let me tell you what it is: the old roof is a legal person, because it is the subject [holder] of a [real] right to let water run onto the neighbor's property (Traufgerechtigkeit);" *Jhering*, Scherz und Ernst (1884) 12 (citing a contemporary Romanist treatise).

vocal organs.[49] He lashed out with particular vigor against excessive *a priori* thinking that resulted when a scholar "rises, like the audacious aeronaut, into higher and higher regions of abstraction, regions where nothing reminds [us of] the intoxicated spirit of earth, and where it can bathe in pure, clear intellectual ether."[50] "Speculation begins," Jhering concluded in a well-known phrase, "where common sense ends; to commit to it, one must have either never had any sense or lost it."[51] He tore into elements of established doctrine, especially in the law of possession, highlighting how his pet peeve, Savigny's requirement of an *animus possidendi*, can create havoc in real cases.[52] He extensively criticized the current system of legal education where academics with their theoretical perspectives train future lawyers for their practical needs, so that students learn tons of abstract doctrine which turns out to be utterly useless on the bench and at the bar.[53] Simultaneously, he zeroed in on numerous colleagues whom he either ridiculed or subjected to devastating critiques or both[54] – all that within a fairly small circle of about three dozen Romanists then teaching at German-speaking universities.[55]

One of Jhering's attacks is particularly noteworthy since it transcends his own time and place and remains relevant in many academic environments up to the present: Jhering's lament of the deluge of scholarly publications without any real value. To be sure, Jhering's complaint focused especially on the custom of young scholars who, aiming at professorships, wrote ever more tracts about Roman law doctrine even though there was almost nothing left to say about it after centuries of squeezing all the juice out of the classical sources. "The Roman law has be-

---

[49] *Jhering*, Scherz und Ernst (1884) 15, quoting a late author writing about natural law. "Now," Jhering added sarcastically, "I know that I have a right to sweat, to digest, to scratch when I itch, etc., I merely exercise my property rights in my body;" id.

[50] *Jhering*, Scherz und Ernst (1884) 20–21. The second letter, which is devoted to this subject, reviews a number of books and extracts from them an impressive array of what can only be described as academic absurdities; id. 17–34.

[51] *Jhering*, Scherz und Ernst (1884) 34. In the following letter, published in the next year, however, Jhering had second thoughts, cautioning that he did not mean to attack all speculation per se but rather only its aberrations; id. 36.

[52] Jhering, Scherz und Ernst (1884) 63–69.

[53] *Jhering*, Scherz und Ernst (1884) 36–54.

[54] The starkest example is his critique of Savigny's disciple Adolf August Friedrich Rudorff (1803–1874), the perhaps most prominent representative of the Historical School at the time (i.e., in 1862 when Jhering published the respective (third) Letter). Jhering called Rudoff's "Römische Rechtsgeschichte" (1857–1859) "the worst mistreatment that Roman legal history has ever suffered, a complete disregard of all and every documentation (Nachweis) of the historical development of law – a heap of bricks (Bausteine] instead of a building," *Jhering*, Scherz und Ernst (1884) 56 fn. 1. Note that Rudorff was the very scholar who had brokered Jhering's admission as a graduate student at the University of Berlin in 1840. If Jhering felt any gratitude, it surely did not soften his attack.

[55] At the end of his last letter, Jhering provides a list in form of a (clumsy) poem; *Jhering*, Scherz und Ernst (1884) 177.

come senile ('altersschwach')," [56] Jhering contended, and just does not yield any new interesting insights.[57] Yet, Jhering's attack was not limited to that particular context. His critique applied more broadly to any system of academic recruitment under which "[t]he path to the chair leads through the printing press – "[o]hne Setzer, kein Professor" ("no typesetter, no professor.")[58] According to Jhering, such a system tended to reward the writing of big books even if they made little sense.

"Hence the curse and terror of our literature, the artificial and forced inflation of even the most pitiful content to the largest possible volume – one small, paltry, meager idea around which a book is built. And sometimes even that [idea] is lacking."[59]

But perhaps it doesn't really matter, Jhering suggested cynically:

"[W]hy deprive these folks of their harmless mental and physical exercises? Whether it is required, in order to climb on the academic chair, to turn somersaults or to write a book, may be entirely irrelevant. The books they write don't bite anyone, everybody can avoid them; and he who doesn't do that, i.e., who buys and reads them, has only himself to blame for the potential harm."[60]

Yet, Jhering explained, it is not that simple – because the bad books destroy the market for the good ones. If every Tom, Dick, and Harry[61] wrote ever more books about ever more abstract problems "from the sublime perspective of the 'pure scientific method,'" that would eventually make practitioners so gun-shy that they would turn away from the academic literature altogether.[62] So, what needs to be done? The most important task was "to render the *Privatdocenten* literature-wise innocuous."[63] Here, Jhering suggested a simple solution: keep them from

---

[56] *Jhering*, Scherz und Ernst (1884) 112.

[57] Jhering even invokes Emperor Justinian's prohibition to comment on his compilation of Roman law, see *Constitutio Tanta* (sec. 21) of 16 December 533 (the law introductory to the *Digest*). Jhering points out that the modern Romanists, who are otherwise so fond of strict adherence to the classical rules, suddenly don't feel bound anymore – "who likes to cut off his own fingers?" *Jhering*, Scherz und Ernst (1884) 105.

[58] *Jhering*, Scherz und Ernst (1884) 106. In German, "Setzer" (sort of) rhymes with "Professor."

[59] *Jhering*, Scherz und Ernst (1884) 106. In his typically colorful language, Jhering mocked the scholars' love for their own ideas even if they are entirely pointless: "Better [to hold] a pointless view for oneself than a reasonable one together with others. It is as with women – who would not prefer an ugly one for himself over a beauty together with others? Or as with children – who does not love his own more than someone else's, no matter how stupid the former are?" *Jhering*, Scherz und Ernst (1884) 111.

[60] *Jhering*, Scherz und Ernst (1884) 166–167.

[61] In the German original, Jhering played a word game he apparently found amusing: he used the common (last) name "Meier" and then ran it through the alphabet: "Ameier, Bmeier, Cmeier und die übrigen Meier durchs ganze Alphabet hindurch bis zum ZMeier", *Jhering*, Scherz und Ernst (1884) 107.

[62] *Jhering*, Scherz und Ernst (1884) 167.

[63] *Jhering*, Scherz und Ernst (1884) 113.

writing such pointless works[64] – or at least do not print their books but rather keep the manuscripts under lock and key for nine years (after which nobody will want to publish them anymore, least of all their authors!). Instead, hire faculty members primarily on account of their teaching abilities rather than their publication record.[65] The established professors, Jhering explained, were a lesser problem; they already had their chair and were thus less desperate to publish, and with all their other duties, they did not have that much time to write anyway; in addition, they had a broader perspective that made them more discriminating.[66] Even *their* zeal to publish should be reined in, however, in order to limit the deluge of legal publications.[67] Tongue-in-cheek, Jhering suggested a licensing regime modeled after the Roman *ius respondendi*:[68] only authors vetted for their quality may publish – perhaps at first on a probationary basis before they become permanently authorized.[69] All in all, eliminating the mass of pointless academic writing would, Jhering claimed, cause "a greater revolution than the *Zündnadelgewehr* (Dreyse needle-gun)."[70]

In the Logician's Paradise: Hair-splitting Machines and Hydraulic Interpretation Presses. When Jhering published "Scherz und Ernst in der Jurisprudenz"[71] in

---

[64] "If the police prohibits the sale of unripe fruit and spoiled beer, why not also the sale of immature books?" *Jhering*, Scherz und Ernst (1884) 115.

[65] *Jhering*, Scherz und Ernst (1884) 113.

[66] *Jhering*, Scherz und Ernst (884) 115–116.

[67] See also his letter to Bülow of February 3, 1872, Jhering in Briefen (1913) 275 ("One can no longer save oneself, our juristic literature amounts to a Red Sea, or rather a black one, in which one risks suffering the fate of the pharaoh – one perishes in all that water!") Jhering also complained that authors used far too many footnotes, which he considered a sign of not really being on top of the material; letter to Bülow of 24/25 December 1880, Jhering in Briefen (1913) 360. Modern authors, including this one, should keep that in mind.

[68] In the Roman Empire, a few or the most renowned jurists were vested with the *ius respondendi* which provided their opinions with imperial imprimatur; the details are disputed among Roman legal historians; for a brief summary, see *Nicholas*, An Introduction to Roman Law (1962) 31–32.

[69] *Jhering*, Scherz und Ernst (1884) 113–115.

[70] *Jhering*, Scherz und Ernst (1884) 115. The *Zündnadelgewehr* (literally: "firing pin rifle") was an early form of the breech-loading gun. It could be loaded, and thus fired, much more rapidly than the traditional muzzle-loader; in addition, it could easily be re-loaded while lying down (which was very difficult with a muzzle-loading rifle). It thus constituted a great advantage in the field. At the time, the *Zündnadelgewehr* was famous because the Prussian infantry's use of it was widely considered crucial in securing the Prussian victory over Austria in the battle of Königgrätz, fought on July 3, 1866, i.e., in the very year Jhering was writing the respective (sixth) Letter.

[71] A literal translation of the title is "Jest and Seriousness in Jurisprudence" but that does not reproduce the arresting brevity and rhythm of the German original. Munroe Smith translated it as "Jest and Earnest" which sounds a bit less clumsy; *Smith*, Four German Jurists II (1896) 307. Jhering's admirer, friend, and noted fellow Romanist Ernst Immanuel Bekker (1827–1916) later published a response, entitled "Ernst und Scherz über unsere Wissenschaft" ("Jest and Earnest about our Science") as a present to Jhering on the occasion of the 50th anniversary of obtaining his doctorate; *Bekker*, Ernst und Scherz (1892).

December of 1884, the book bore the subtitle "A Christmas Gift for the Juristic Readership" ("Eine Weihnachtsgabe für das juristische Publikum") as well as the motto "Ridendo dicere verum" ("while laughing, telling the truth"). Of the book's four parts, Jhering's persiflage "Im juristischen Begriffshimmel" ("In the Heaven of Concepts") is the most famous,[72] in part because of its catchy title which soon became common coinage among lawyers worldwide.[73]

It begins with an attention-getter: Jhering's death. "I had died. A luminous being met my soul when it left the body."[74] Jhering asked his guide where he was headed. He received a curious answer.

"Since you are a Romanist, you will go the heaven of concepts. There you will find all the juristic concepts that have kept you so busy on earth. Not, however, in their imperfect, disfigured form into which they have been put on earth by legislators and practitioners, but rather in their perfect, spotless purity and ideal beauty. Here, the theoretical jurists are being rewarded for the services which they have rendered these concepts on earth, there, they have seen them only in their veiled form, but here, they see them with complete clarity, they view them face-to-face and interact with them as equals. The questions for which they have vainly sought a solution on earth, here, these questions are being answered by the concepts themselves."[75]

Jhering describes his visit in the "heaven of concepts" as an introductory guided tour. He learns that the place is located far beyond the solar system and lies in complete darkness – there can be no sunshine because the sun is the source of all life, and the concepts need to exist completely separately from all life; for the same reason, all air is excluded.[76] The realm is accessible only to "theoreticians" –

[72] Three of the parts were variations on the common theme of attacking "conceptual jurisprudence." Of these, two were written in "jest" ("Scherz"): the reprinted "Confidential Letters" and the parody "In the Heaven of Concepts;" one was written in "earnest" ("Ernst"): an essay entitled "Wieder auf Erden. Wie soll es besser werden?" ("Back to Earth. How Can Things Be Improved?") in which Jhering developed various proposals to make legal education more practice-oriented. The remaining fourth part, however, had little to do with the theme common to the others: "Plaudereien eines Romanisten" ("Chats of a Romanist") was a series of "feuilleton essays," *Jhering*, Scherz und Ernst (1884) 122, on various aspects of Roman legal history. These essays were written for light after-dinner reading by practitioners. Thematically, these "chats" were thus a poor fit with the rest of the book. Subtitled "Bilder aus der römischen Rechtsgeschichte" ("Images from Roman Legal History"), they were written for, and originally published in, a Viennese journal for practitioners, the Juristische Blätter, in 1880. Jhering included them in the book because it was convenient to (re-)publish them together with the "Letters" and the other two pieces. He emphasized that these chats were not part of the academic literature and not meant "to be cited by German law professors;" *Jhering*, Scherz und Ernst (1884) 122. Instead, the reader should shut the door, stretch out on a sofa, light a good cigar ("not too heavy, not too light"), kick up his legs, enjoy the reading – and then forget everything if he wishes. "It is amazing," Jhering wrote, "what one can learn while smoking just one cigar!" id. 125.

[73] For a brief English summary, see *Seagle*, Rudolf von Jhering (1945) 89.

[74] *Jhering*, Scherz und Ernst (1884) 247.

[75] *Jhering*, Scherz und Ernst (1884) 247, 249–250.

[76] Jhering, Scherz und Ernst (1884) 250–253.

practitioners are barred and have their own heaven (see below) – and even the former qualify only if they are able to disregard all practical aspects of law. The first to arrive was Puchta († 1846), followed by various members of his school. Savigny († 1861) was a close call "because he did not yet fully know how to construct [concepts]," but he was finally admitted because of the conceptual work in his "Das Recht des Besitzes" ("Law of Possession")[77]. The majority of entrants are Romanists but some Germanists qualified as well.[78] Once here, all denizens are pure "spirits" and the world around them is all "spirit" as well.

Jhering first gets to visit the *Palästra*, a kind of gymnasium which is full of amazing devices: a hair-splitting machine (capable of splitting even thin hairs into 999,999 parts); a climbing pole with special problems at the top (so slippery that even a ray of sun would slip off); a dialectic-hydraulic interpretation press (capable of squeezing from each source whatever is needed); a dialectic drill (to drill down to the bottom of difficult issues); etc.[79]

There is also a palace which contains the "Hall of Concepts." Here Jhering gets to see (in their pure form) not only the *dolus, culpa lata, culpa levis,* and *mora* but "property," "obligation," and, of course, "possession" which constantly changes from fact to right to a combination of both.[80] To top it all, there is "quasi-possession" which constitutes a "juristic perpetuum mobile."[81] But there is also a cabinet of horrors showcasing concepts that have warped and turned into monstrosities by jurists concerned with practical consequences – not only by modern legislators and practitioners but sadly, sometimes even by the Roman jurists themselves.[82]

The entire time, Jhering is engaged in a discourse with his tour-guide, and he even manages to solve a few problems presented to him by this spirit. At some point, however, it is time for Jhering to take the extremely difficult entry-exam – and this is when he balks. He not only doubts that he can pass, he has also become disenchanted with the "Heaven of Concepts" – all its attractions notwithstanding, it strikes him as somewhat boring. His host agrees that Jhering is not a proper candidate – he has asked too many critical questions.

Fortunately, there are two alternative heavens. One is for legal philosophers and also requires an entry-exam. At first, Jhering is cocky because he believes that with some Hegelian fireworks, he should be able to pass it with flying colors. But then he finds out that he would also have to subscribe to the fundamental credos of the natural law school, and that he refuses to do.[83] This leaves, as a last resort, only the heaven for practitioners where admission is not a problem. This is where

[77] *Savigny*, Das Recht des Besitzes (1803).
[78] *Jhering*, Scherz und Ernst (1884) 253–255.
[79] *Jhering*, Scherz und Ernst (1884) 256–264.
[80] *Jhering*, Scherz und Ernst (1884) 278–284.
[81] *Jhering*, Scherz und Ernst (1884) 290–293.
[82] *Jhering*, Scherz und Ernst (1884) 296–309.
[83] *Jhering*, Scherz und Ernst (1884) 310–314.

Jhering is finally taken. And what a relief! The sun is shining in all its splendor; there is air to breathe; there are trees, woods, meadows, houses, and even bowling alleys! – there is life![84] Jhering knocks at the gate of the admissions office, and a voice says: "Come in!"

It was his own voice, though, responding to a knock on the door of his room by a messenger bringing a letter from a friend. Jhering rubs his eyes – he had fallen asleep while reading a new Romanist publication. The whole adventure had been a dream.[85]

Unrestraint Satire: The Artist Impetuous. "Scherz und Ernst" was widely read not only by lawyers but also in other educated circles. It went through five editions in the remaining eight years of Jhering's life and is available in several modern editions and reprints. Among the general public, the book made Jhering the best-known German jurist of both his time and among subsequent generations, eclipsing even Savigny in that regard.

Jhering's satires indeed have much to recommend them. To begin with, they are – at least to a large extent – entertaining reads. They are full of amusing aphorisms ("one must first lose all faith in theory before one can safely use it"[86]); witty metaphors ("attending lectures on the anatomy of the horse is poor preparation for riding one[87]); striking images (the personified "obligation" is always worried whether she will be fulfilled and is comforted only by the guaranty and the lien[88]) and some good stories[89]. Moreover, in many instances, Jhering provides, as an early American commentator put it, "not only good fooling – there is good sense to back it up."[90] The many absurdities he excerpted from contemporary writings were indeed a solemn warning that legal scholarship sometimes just

[84] *Jhering*, Scherz und Ernst (1884) 315.

[85] *Jhering*, Scherz und Ernst (1884) 315–316.

[86] *Jhering*, Scherz und Ernst (1884) 54 ("man [muß] erst den Glauben an die Theorie vollständig verloren haben..., um ohne Gefahr sich ihrer bedienen zu können").

[87] *Jhering*, Scherz und Ernst (1884) 57–58.

[88] *Jhering*, Scherz und Ernst (1884) 279.

[89] Jhering proffered the following tale: while the professor was on vacation, the chambermaid left the windows of his study open and a gust of wind turned the pile of manuscript pages for his new book into a whirling dance of sheets throughout the room. The chambermaid re-organized the pages as best she could. Upon his return, the professor began to teach according to their new order. By the time he noticed that something was not quite right, it was too late to go back to square one. Thus, he stuck to what he had, made his peace with the new arrangement and eventually turned it into a book. "Since I heard this story," Jhering commented, "a lightbulb went on in my head, as the saying goes, regarding many wondrous systematic arrangements in our legal literature. What happened in the case above, could it not have repeated itself in other instances?" This, he surmised, could even result in new insights. "The wind and chambermaids are unpredictable, and matters that are not recognized by the sense of the sensible may be effected by chance. Thus in my view, wind and chambermaids should always have free access to manuscripts and notebooks." *Jhering* , Scherz und Ernst (1884) 54–57.

[90] *Smith*, Four German Jurists I (1895) 691.

went off the rails. To be sure, these were the worst excesses Jhering could find, and they were scarcely representative of the larger mass of publications; still, a system is characterized, inter alia, by its extremes. There is something to be said for holding up a mirror to a culture, herein contemporary legal academia, especially if what the mirror reflects isn't pretty. Some commentators complained that Jhering thereby caused lasting damage to the public image of the legal profession[91] while others saw his satires as superficial antics that have harmlessly amused generations of jurists.[92] Be that as it may, critique ultimately is a service to those subjected to it.

Jhering's satires also have significant flaws. Of course, one must not judge them by academic standards; written as caricatures, they are entitled to considerable license.[93] Even as caricatures, however, they leave much to be desired. As several commentators pointed out, many of Jhering's tirades are one-sided, exaggerated, and plainly unfair. They are full of gross distortions, improper comparisons, and cheap shots. Many of Jhering's jokes are flat, several of his critiques are mean, and some of his comments smack of arrogance.[94] In addition, the discourse is often lengthy and at times outright tedious,[95] quite aside from the fact that parts of it are entirely unintelligible to readers not versed in the intricacies of Roman law doctrine. Jhering himself had mixed feelings about "Scherz und Ernst." "The sensation which my book has caused will cost me dearly," he wrote to his friend Windscheid. "I cannot deny the victims of my attacks that they will defend their skins and return the blows I have dealt them – that I must now quietly endure."[96]

In seeking to understand why Jhering went overboard, we need to distinguish between the early "Letters" and the later visit in the "Heaven of Concepts."

---

[91] *Wolf*, Große Rechtsdenker (1963) 656; Wolf provides no support for this claim, and it may simply reflect what he feared.

[92] *Wieacker,* Gründer und Bewahrer (1959) 206.

[93] At one point, however, Jhering rejected the idea that his rendition of current jurisprudence had essentially been a caricature. The picture he had given, he insisted, was accurate and should by no means be taken lightly. "I am deadly serious in the attack I have made against the conceptual jurisprudence, i.e., the scholasticism in today's Romanist science." *Jhering*, Scherz und Ernst (1884) 338.

[94] For particularly harsh reactions, see *Stintzing and Landsberg*, Geschichte der deutschen Rechtswissenschaft III.2. (1910) 810, 822; *Wolf*, Große Rechtsdenker (1963) 644, 656–657. *Wieacker*, Gründer und Bewahrer (1959) 206, reacted more forgivingly. Jhering's early biographer in the United States simply concluded that "Jhering's conception of humor may not be the taste of all," *MacDonnell*, Rudolf von Jhering (1914) 596. Landsberg sarcastically commented that "at least one cannot blame [Jhering] for having become weaker or milder with age," *Stintzing and Landsberg*, id. 822.

[95] In this regard, the fifth letter is the worst. Jhering droned on for 25 pages without much substance and even less to laugh about; *Jhering*, Scherz und Ernst (1884) 70–96. It is difficult to sustain parody for over a 100 pages (Letters) or even for 70 (Heaven). Less would have been more.

[96] Letter to Windscheid of December 31, 1884, Jherings Briefe an Windscheid (1988) 55.

Jhering's extremism in the "Letters" was largely a reaction against the frustration he had experienced in the double-sale case. Jhering-the-jurist had found himself at the limits of his approach; thus he turned into Jhering-the-artist to find relief in mockery. The strength of his mockery of abstract logic mirrored the strength of his erstwhile enthusiasm for it. For Jhering himself, this was probably a psychologically healthy reaction, even though it dragged many of his colleagues and their works into the mud. When Jhering penned the "Heaven of Concepts" twenty years later, this frustration lay far behind him. Now, he just wanted some breathing space from the hard work that otherwise occupied him. "With the book, I gave myself [the] relief through humor and satire [...] I had to get it off my chest! Now, I am at peace, and from now on my pen will be devoted to serious matters."[97] When he went to extremes now, he limited himself to attacks on abstract entities and left concrete individuals and their works by and large alone. The humor in "Heaven" is forced and lame at times, but it is not outright vicious.

It remains true, however, that in both instances, Jhering exercised little, if any, restraint. He enjoyed satirical writing so much that he let himself get carried away with it – at times with reckless abandon. On such occasions, Jhering-the-artist, perhaps assisted by a few glasses of his favorite wine, just could not keep himself from going over the top and probably did not even want to. Eventually, he sensed that he had driven his satires a bit too far and vowed to return to serious work.[98]

3. The Issue of Continuity: Jhering's "Damascus"[99]?

What does one make of a scholar who first propagates a jurisprudence of abstract concepts and systematic logic with great flamboyance and enthusiasm, then almost suddenly attacks and openly ridicules that very same jurisprudence with equal flamboyance and enthusiasm, and finally, as we shall see in the next chapter, embraces an entirely different jurisprudence that regards law as a means to the end of realizing social interests? It is tempting to interpret this development as a radical abandonment of *Begriffs-* and *Konstruktionjurisprudenz* and a concomitant radical turn towards a realistic and functional approach. Indeed, most of the older literature on Jhering saw it in these terms.[100] This interpretation is not only

[97] Letter to Windscheid of December 31, 1884; Jherings Briefe an Windscheid (1988) 51.

[98] Letter to Auguste von Littrow-Bischoff of December 30, 1884, Jhering in Briefen (1913) 382 ("I feel the need to compensate for 'jest' by some proper 'seriousness.'")

[99] *Wieacker*, Privatrechtsgeschichte (1967) 451.

[100] See *Stintzing and Landsberg*, Geschichte der deutschen Rechtswissenschaft III.2. (1910) 789, 807; *Kantorowicz*, Jherings Bekehrung (1914) 84; *Fuchs*, Jhering und die Freirechtsbewegung (1918/19) 16; *Heck*, Interessenjurisprudenz (1933) 12 ("Saulus to Paulus"); *Radbruch*, Vorschule der Rechtsphilosophie (1947) 16 ("Bekehrung"); *Wieacker*, Gründer und Bewahrer (1959) 203 ("epochemachende Wendung vom Konstruktionsjuristen zum Analytiker der sozialen Wirklichkeit"); *Wieacker*, Privatrechtsgeschichte (1967) 451 (but cf. *Wieacker*, Rudolf von Jhering (1969), infra note 103); *Wolf*, Große Rechtsdenker (1963) 643 ("innere Um-

supported by some of Jhering's own statements,[101] it also makes for a gripping story: a scholar naively falls in love with a misguided methodology, suddenly recognizes his error, sees the light, and pursues the righteous path. The image of Jhering's conversion from a Saulus, devoted to abstract logic, to a Paulus, looking at concrete social facts, is particularly appealing from the perspective of later generations because it is a tale of ostensible progress: Jhering becomes the hero who overcame the nefarious old ways and blazed the trail towards a brighter future.[102]

Such a view is not entirely wrong but is still far from entirely right. Today, it is widely recognized that in matters of methodology, Jhering's "conversion" was not a complete and radical change.[103] It is true that the early 1860s brought about an important reorientation in Jhering's thinking so that his jurisprudence can plausibly be divided into an earlier and a later period, and Jhering himself sometimes took that view.[104] Yet, Jhering neither entirely abandoned his original methodological convictions nor did he suddenly discover entirely new ideas. In-

wandlung," "grundsätzlicher Umbruch seines Rechtsdenkens"); *Larenz*, Rudolf von Jhering (1970) ("Bruch in seinem Denken"); *Larenz*, Methodenlehre der Rechtswissenschaft (1983) 24 ("tiefe Zäsur"); *Coing*, Rudolf von Jhering (1982) 9 ("vollständige Wandlung"); *Klenner*, Jhering's Kampf ums Recht (1982), opined that Jhering experienced not just one, but several "Damascus" events, stumbling "from one paradigm change to the next;" id. 438. *Kleinheyer and Schröder* (eds.) Deutsche und europäische Juristen (2017) 233–234, also still use the term "Bekehrung" ("conversion") but put it in quotation marks, indicating that this is simply a common view; they take no position on the issue of continuity in Jhering's *oeuvre*. See also *Bachmann*, Das Gäubahn-Gutachten (2023) 111 ("fundamental change on the basis of a momentous event").

[101] See infra notes 105–110 and text.

[102] This is essentially how American jurists eventually came to see him, prominently among the Roscoe Pound; see infra chapter VII.3., notes 208–214 and text.

[103] Wieacker, who had originally popularized the much-cited term of Jhering's "Damaskus," later modified his view, *Wieacker*, Rudolf von Jhering (1969) 22, 24; see also *Behrends*, Das "Rechtsgefühl" (1986) 89–95; *Behrends*, Der Durchbruch zum Zweck des Rechts (1987) 252–256; *Fikentscher*, Methoden des Rechts III (1976) 114, 202–203; *Klemann*, Rudolf von Jhering und die Historische Rechtsschule (1989) 191–193; *Klemann*, Jherings Wandlung (1991); *Kunze*, Rudolf von Jhering (1993) 17; *Rückert*, Der Geist des Rechts (2004) 136; *Jansen and Reimann*, Begriff und Zweck (2018) 105–106. Even Jhering's early American commentator Munroe Smith had doubted a radical change; *Smith*, Four German Jurists (1895) 688. For a more extensive discussion, see *Mecke*, Begriff des Rechts und Methode der Rechtswissenschaft bei Rudolf von Jhering (2018) 13–28. In some of his more recent work, Okko Behrends emphasized the fundamental nature of Jhering's reorientation, see *Behrends*, Jhering's "Umschwung" (2017); *Behrends*, Jhering heute! (2023) especially 219–226. Little attention has been paid to the early and fine-grained assessment by *Lange*, Die Wandlungen Jherings (1927) 135; unfortunately, the book is not easily available and thus widely unknown.

[104] *Kunze*, Rudolf von Jhering (1993) 17. Behrends labeled these two periods "pre-critical" and "critical;" *Behrends*, Der Durchbruch zum Zweck des Rechts (1987) 252, 255, etc. This is potentially misleading: the "early" Jhering was not generally uncritical, but it is true that he came to see the origin, meaning, and validity of fundamental legal concepts in a more "critical" light after his "conversion."

stead, between these two periods, there was considerable overlap and continuity, albeit more in some regards than in others.

Sorting out continuity and change in Jhering's development is crucial for our understanding of his work as a whole. It is, however, not free from difficulty. One problem is that what Jhering professed is neither fully consistent nor completely in line with what he did. Another difficulty is that Jhering's "conversion" was not a monolithic phenomenon but, rather, had several distinct dimensions. As a result, to assess the kind and degree of change in Jhering's attitude, one must distinguish between at least four elements: the basic question of operating with legal concepts and juristic constructions; the relationship between theory and practice; the corrective role of "justice;" and the difference between law as a system of rules and as a social instrument. In some of these regards, Jhering's change was more decisive than in others.

In His Own Words: Jhering's Many Voices. If we take Jhering at his own word, the change in his thinking indeed looks like a conversion from vice to virtue. Perhaps one could still ascribe the fun he made of his "higher jurisprudence" in the first "Letter" in 1861[105] to his usual playfulness. Four years later, however, he attacked the "craze" ("Irrwahn") of operating with abstract concepts – and openly accepted part of the blame for it – in complete seriousness. This is particularly remarkable because it occurred in the third volume of "Geist" – in the very same work in whose first and second volumes he had exalted the very "cult of logic" ("Cultus des Logischen") he now condemned.[106] (It must be pretty rare in the history of jurisprudence that an author builds up a theory in the earlier parts of a book only to tear it down in later chapters.) This was not just a matter of momentary frustration: almost two decades later, in the last part of "Scherz und Ernst," Jhering professed the error in his early ways for pages on end.[107] He portrayed his erstwhile self, not unjustly, as possibly worse than Puchta.[108] "Hardly anyone can have been as much a fanatic of the logical method as I once was," he wrote, referencing his homily in the programmatic essay "Unsere Aufgabe" (1857).[109] In particular, Jhering claimed that his own experience now supremely qualified him to show just how horribly misguided the current mainstream was. He understood, he wrote, "how seductive the craze" [of operating with abstract concepts] is, because "nobody has experienced its attraction more intensely than I myself."[110]

Yet, while Jhering ridiculed his own "higher jurisprudence," he simultaneously emphasized the "high value of the formal and technical side of law" and

[105] Supra note 41 and text.

[106] *Jhering*, Geist III (1865) 299–306, at 302 (incl. fn. 341).

[107] *Jhering*, Scherz und Ernst (1884) 337–347.

[108] *Jhering*, Scherz und Ernst (1884) 338.

[109] *Jhering*, Scherz und Ernst (1884) 338.

[110] *Jhering*, Scherz und Ernst (1884) 334. See also id. 340 ("One who was a slave himself knows the meaning of servitude.")

claimed that he had never had any interest in doctrinal work without practical utility.[111] While he stated that he was leaving "construction" more and more behind in 1864,[112] five years later, he left the methodological chapter exalting that exact "construction" largely unchanged, in a new edition of the second volume of Geist.[113] And although he spoke of his own (earlier) "reversal" ("Umschwung") in 1884[114], in 1889, he published a long treatise dealing with doctrinal questions.[115]

Some of these tensions will be resolved, or at least become more understandable, when we take a closer look at the various aspects of Jhering's "conversion" below. But some are just results of his penchant to say what was foremost on his mind at the moment, often without much regard to overall consistency. In fact, Jhering was quite aware of this tendency and not always proud of it.[116] Sometimes, Jhering – as the artist – just fell "in love" with an idea and completely immersed himself in it – whereupon he fell in love with the opposite side with equal passion.[117] In assessing Jhering's "conversion," it is important to keep this willingness to happily embrace different positions in mind, lest we vainly search for more consistency in his thought than there actually was.

Legal Concepts and Juristic Constructions: Abandoning Extremes. An important aspect of Jhering's change was that he abandoned the extreme devotion to logic that had driven his commitment to "higher jurisprudence" in the 1850s.[118] In this context, his principal new *bete noire* was Puchta.[119] Jhering now treated his former teacher and model (as well as himself!) as the incarnation of the misguided approach Jhering now derogatively termed "conceptual jurisprudence" – "Begriffsjurisprudenz."[120] Caring little for a fine-grained portrait, Jhering created an image of Puchta (and his followers) as an arch-formalist, stubborn believer in immutable truths, and reality-blind occupant of an academic ivory tower. In this

---

[111] Jhering, Scherz und Ernst (1884) 9.

[112] Letter to Windscheid of March 20, 1864; Jhering in Briefen (1913) 166.

[113] *Jhering*, Geist II.2. (2d ed. Leipzig 1869).

[114] *Jhering*, Scherz und Ernst (1884) 338; ditto already in his letter to Bernhard Windscheid of April 13, 1865, Jhering in Briefen (1913) 176 ("eine merkwürde Umwandlung meiner ganzen Anschauung").

[115] *Jhering*, Der Besitzwille (1889).

[116] See, e.g., his (apologetic) letter to Windscheid of July 29, 1854; Jhering in Briefen (1913) 67.

[117] *Jhering*, Scherz und Ernst (1884) 187.

[118] Klemann tentatively attributed this change to contemporary changes in the natural sciences, especially chemistry, in which Jhering had a lifelong interest, *Klemann*, Jherings Wandlung (1991) 146–49.

[119] In this context, Savigny was largely spared Jhering's ire – and with good reason: Savigny had never driven jurisprudence to extreme abstractness. Instead, he had emphasized that "law has no separate existence; its essence is rather human life itself viewed from a particular perspective" ("Das Recht hat nämlich kein Daseyn für sich, sein Wesen ist vielmehr das Leben der Menschen selbst, von einer besonderen Seite gesehen"), *Savigny*, Vom Beruf unserer Zeit (1814) 114–115.

[120] *Jhering*, Scherz und Ernst (1884) 337.

fashion, Jhering tainted the image of his erstwhile mentor for generations.[121] His portrait of Puchta is now widely recognized as simplistic and overblown.[122] Yet it was its very nature as a caricature that made it such a conveniently clear target for Jhering's attacks as well as for the contempt of future generations.[123]

Jhering's ostensive abandonment of a belief in strict legal logic had an emotional and an intellectual side. On the emotional side, the fervor of his former convictions gave way to a more sober attitude. He realized that he had treated Puchta's approach like a civil religion, and now he did penance. In a way, he just came to his senses. The jurist got the artist back under control.

On the intellectual side, Jhering turned mainly against the belief in absolutes. Sometimes he expressed this by accusing his colleagues of treating law like mathematics[124]. Sometimes, he identified the belief in absolutes with Hegelianism. Although quite a follower of Hegel in some other regards himself,[125] here he blamed Hegel's famous identification of reality with reason for providing "the positive" [meaning: law] with the aura of "logic."[126] As a result of this Hegelian influence, jurists (like Puchta) were "blinded by the glamour of logic" ("geblendet vom Glanz des Logischen")[127] If this connection between Hegelian philosophy and mainstream Romanist jurisprudence was a bit crude, it was because Jhering's understanding of Hegel's philosophy was quite superficial. When Jhering threw around terms like "dialectic" or "scholastic," they bore scant resemblance to concrete heuristic concepts. Instead, he employed them as popular and derogative expressions for something like "abstract logic of the undesirable kind."[128]

Jhering did have a point, though, and it became clearer when he focused more precisely on the prevailing understanding of (juristic) concepts as absolutes. In the wake of Puchta, many Romanist authors indeed treated such concepts as incarnations of ubiquitous and eternal certitudes.[129] Jhering now pointed out that

---

[121] See *Meder*, Rudolf von Jhering and the 'jurisprudence of concepts' (2023) 166–167.

[122] This is not to say that Jhering was all wrong, only that he painted with a very broad brush and disregarded many finer features of Puchta's jurisprudence. For example, Puchta had clearly emphasized the importance of economic considerations and needs for jurisprudence, see *Puchta*, Cursus der Institutionen (1841) 47 (sec. 19); the point was made by *Mecke*, Jherings Rechtsdenken im Kontext der zeitgenössischen Natur- und Sozialwissenschaften (2023) 285. For a detailed and subtle analysis, see *Haferkamp*, Georg Friedrich Puchta und die Begriffsjurisprudenz (2004) 443–460, 463–471.

[123] See *Haferkamp*, Georg Friedrich Puchta und die Begriffsjurisprudenz (2004) 27, 39, 463.

[124] E.g., *Jhering*, Geist III (1865) 302.

[125] See supra chapter I.1., notes 31–35 and text, and infra chapter V.3., notes 94–96 and text.

[126] *Jhering*, Geist III (1865) 299–300.

[127] *Jhering*, Geist III (1865) 300.

[128] See, e.g., *Jhering*, Geist III (1865) 337, 341.

[129] Note, however, that the modern literature tends to see the German Romanist legal science of the *Pandektenwissenschaft* in a more positive light; see *Haferkamp and Repgen* (eds.), Wie pandektistisch war die Pandektenwissenschaft? (2017); *Moriya*, Die Pandektenwissenschaft und ihre historischen Hintergründe (2019).

that legal concepts were not "logical categories" but "concentrated forms of substantive legal rules," i.e., not pre-existing absolutes but creations of the human mind. That was also true for the Roman concepts because even they were ultimately rooted "in psychological, ethical, and historical reasons."[130] Nor were they immutable – since the rules reflecting these reasons changed over time, so must the concepts.[131] Jhering now saw concepts not as truths to be believed but as tools to be adjusted according to circumstances and needs.[132] To put it differently: he downgraded legal concepts from masters of doctrinal work to its servants.[133] Jhering summarized his reformed view in pithy and often quoted language: "Life does not exist for the sake of concepts but concepts exist for the sake of life." ("Das Leben ist nicht der Begriffe, sondern die Begriffe sind des Lebens wegen da.")[134]

The vehemence of Jhering's reaction against Puchta, his former self, and *Begriffsjurisprudenz,* can easily lead the reader to overrate the actual change in Jhering's attitude. That change did not amount to a wholesale abandonment of concepts, juristic construction, and systematic logic.[135] To begin with, Jhering did not discard working with legal concepts – far from it. He considered them absolutely essential for proper legal reasoning. The expression "conceptual jurisprudence" was thus essentially a tautology, he admitted: "All jurisprudence operates with concepts; legal and conceptual thinking is identical, in that sense all jurisprudence is conceptual jurisprudence"[136] – and properly so as long as it was not driven to the extremes of a quasi-religion.[137] Nor did Jhering completely give up

[130] *Jhering,* Geist III (1865) 305.

[131] *Jhering*, Geist III (1865) 296.

[132] While Jhering claimed that the Roman jurists had by and large understood this, he conceded that they could fall prey to the same error as many of his contemporary colleagues. He expressly blamed the late-classical Roman jurist Paulus (first half of the third century AD) for being "completely caught up in the logic of the law," especially with regard to his concept of possession. "He reminds me mainly of Puchta – he is the Puchta of Roman antiquity... Both excellent minds, but violent, scientifically despotic, merciless doctrinaires." *Jhering*, Der Besitzwille (1889) 283–284.

[133] This is how *Behrends*, Der Durchbruch zum Zweck des Rechts (1987) 255, aptly put it.

[134] *Jhering,* Geist III (1865) 302–303. The phrase is pithy and memorable but it is also simplistic; see the critique by *Behrends*, Jhering heute! (2023) 214.

[135] This has, of course, been noted by others; see, e.g., *Wolf*, Große Rechtsdenker (1963) 660; *Behrends*, Der Durchbruch zum Zweck des Rechts (1987) 255–256; *Rückert*, Der Geist des Rechts (part 2) (2005) 139; *Rückert*, Das Methodenorakel Rudolf von Jhering (2019) 485–486; see also *Jansen and Reimann*, Begriff und Zweck in der Jurisprudenz (2018) 126–129.

[136] *Jhering*, Scherz und Ernst (1884) 347.

[137] Thus, Jhering continued to base his lectures on the Pandects on Puchta's treatise well beyond 1859, even though he commented on the work in an increasingly critical fashion vis-a-vis his students; *Jäde*, Jhering als Rechtslehrer (2008) 21–31. And thus Jhering emphasized as late as 1889 that he continued to appreciate everything he had learned from Puchta, but that he felt compelled openly to denounce "what is unhealthy in his approach" ("das Ungesunde in seiner Richtung"); *Jhering*, Der Besitzwille (1889) 293.

on "juristic construction." To be sure, after 1859, he no longer reveled in its sheer beauty, nor did he exalt it as the crucial operation of jurisprudence *tout court*. Construction simply became a tool like many others – though still a useful one. Jhering continued to employ it both to cast new norms and concepts into the appealing form of "simple rules" and to ensure that they fit into the existing framework of private law.[138] Finally, Jhering never lost faith in the importance of a systematic order of the law. Such an order, however, should not be determined by the strict logic of Puchta but rather be organized along functional lines and with regard to the needs of practice.[139] Jhering also no longer talked about its productive properties, i.e., as a source of new law constructed from within the system. Yet, he continued to stress the importance of an "internal systematic" ("innere Systematik") for understanding the overall coherence of law and for operating with its rules and concepts in an efficient manner. Just look at English law, he wrote, which lacks such an order, and you will see the advantage of continental (Roman law-based) jurisprudence. Continental jurists "achieve secure control over the whole of law by virtue of a relatively short course of university study, while the English jurists are specialists none of whom is capable of managing the whole law." Thus, the continental system with its systematic order "pays off in practical life."[140] It is tell-tale evidence of Jhering's continued belief in the importance of "juristic technique" that he kept the methodological discourse developed in the first edition of "Geist" throughout the later ones, beyond his reorientation and for the rest of his life.[141]

We must also be careful not to mistake Jhering's critique of *Begriffsjurisprudenz* as a wholesale turn against "formalism." The concept is ambiguous, and Jhering criticized one of its meanings while fully embracing another. "Formalism" can mean strictly logical reasoning from abstract principles followed by rule application without regard to substantive values or practical needs. As presented by Jhering, "conceptual jurisprudence" was formalist in that sense – and thus subject to his blistering attacks. "Formalism" can also mean, however, adherence to legally prescribed forms, e.g., in the making of agreements, the definition and limitation of rights or the requirements of procedure. Jhering discussed this kind of "formalism" mainly in the context of early Roman law, and he considered it a crucially important and highly beneficial element of law because it creates certainty and prevents caprice: "The form is the sworn enemy of arbitrariness, the twin sister of liberty."[142]

---

[138] See supra chapter II.3.

[139] See *Haferkamp*, Georg Friedrich Puchta und die Begriffsjurisprudenz (2004) 44.

[140] *Jhering*, Scherz und Ernst (1884) 352–353.

[141] Compare Jhering, Geist II.2. (1858) 359–414, with *Jhering* Geist II.2. (5th ed.) 1898 334–389. There were some revisions but they remained relatively slight. In a similar vein, the dedication of the first edition to Puchta was retained throughout all subsequent editions.

[142] *Jhering*, Geist II.2. (1858) 497 (§45). The point is also made by *Mede*r, Rudolf von Jhering and the 'jurisprudence of concepts' (2023) 170.

The Challenge of Practice: Jurisprudence and the Needs of "Life." A second notable feature of the "new" (post-1959) Jhering was his incessant critique that mainstream Romanist jurisprudence neglected the needs of real life. In this regard, the fault was not Hegel's (who was a philosopher, after all) but Savigny's. With his early treatise on Possession[143] Savigny had opened a new era of understanding of (classical) Roman law, and Jhering did not hesitate to recognize its brilliance in that regard. At the same time, he harshly criticized the book's "fundamental error," i.e., its "complete indifference towards the practical function of possession in life."[144] Savigny's bad example, soon to be topped by Puchta,[145] had entailed a Romanist jurisprudence which had increasingly behaved as if the law existed for theory's sake – "a grateful object for logical thinking, a circus for dialectic-acrobatic tricks."[146]Thus, the main problem with current jurisprudence was not its operation with concepts and systematic logic but its "nonchalance" towards "life."[147] To be sure, this was also somewhat of a caricature of mainstream Romanist legal science but it created an easy target for Jhering's attacks.

Jhering's emphasis on the needs of practice was not a real change of perspective. After all, he had already openly stated the importance of his discipline's practical utility in the second volume of "Geist" which had been published the year before his experience with the double-sale case. In another sense, however, that experience did cause a significant change in Jhering's work. In 1858, Jhering's statement that practice must predominate theory had essentially been a prelude to his elaborate methodological theory. Clear though it was, it had been overshadowed by his discourse on "higher jurisprudence" to the point that it could easily be overlooked – and often was. Beginning in the 1860s, however, Jhering embarked on an open, vigorous, and decades-long campaign against the overly theoretical nature of the Romanist mainstream. It began with his "Letters" (in 1861), continued in the third volume of "Geist" (1865), resurfaced in "Scherz und Ernst" (1884), and ended with his last great monograph, "Der Besitzwille" (1889) which was his final reckoning with the life-less dogmatism of Savigny and his followers. While it would be too strong to speak of a "conversion," there was a shift in emphasis: before 1859, Jhering made no big deal of his commitment to practical needs; after 1860, subjecting jurisprudence to their command became a major focus of his work.

Jhering now invoked "life" ("das Leben") at every turn. He never defined what exactly that meant to him and thus left his readers guessing.[148] Perhaps he saw no need because the term was familiar in contemporary jurisprudential discourse.[149] It also resonated, of course, with the imagery of the natural sciences so

---

[143] *Savigny*, Das Rechts des Besitzes (1803).
[144] *Jhering*, Scherz und Ernst (1884) 357.
[145] *Jhering*, Scherz und Ernst (1884) 357 fn. 1
[146] *Jhering*, Scherz und Ernst (1884) 357; in similar terms id., 347.
[147] *Jhering*, Scherz und Ernst (1884) 363.
[148] See, e.g., *Larenz*, Methodenlehre der Rechtswissenschaft (1983) 45.
[149] See, e.g., *Kuntze*, Der Wendepunkt der Rechtswissenschaft (1856) 47.

popular at the time. In Jhering's case, the meaning of "life" is perhaps best understood by distinguishing two dimensions. One was descriptive: "life" denoted the "real world," i.e., the totality of human interaction (which he often termed "Verkehr" – literally "traffic"), in the commercial as well as the personal context, to which the law must be applied. This application was the business of legal practice. The other dimension was normative: "life" was the lodestar to guide the content, shape, and development of law – it determined what law had to be and to do: "Not what logic, but what life, human interaction, the feeling of justice, postulate has to be done, whether it is logically required or impossible."[150]

Jhering insisted that there was no conflict between appreciating the formal and technical side of law on the one hand and due attention to its practical consequences on the other. He had always pursued both, he explained, and thus bore no responsibility for the neglect of "life" by mainstream Romanist jurisprudence. "Doctrinal work that does not generate any kind of useful practical results would not have the slightest attraction for me."[151] Nor, he implied, should it have such attraction for anyone else.

Jhering's extensive campaign was long on (often redundant) criticism but short on suggestions for remedies. Recognizing that weakness, he finally made three concrete proposals to ensure that law professors, at least, would become more attuned to practical concerns. First, every candidate for appointment to a professorship should be required to have passed not only the university and doctoral exams; he should also have to complete the practical training and pass the subsequent professional examination (*Assessorexamen*) required for appointment to the bench or admission to the bar (something Jhering himself had never done). This would force candidates to leave the academic ivory tower at least for a few years and thus ensure a minimum of familiarity with legal practice. Second, all professors should have to teach practical exercises (*Praktika*) in which rules and principles were applied to, and thus discussed in the context of, concrete cases.[152] This would not only generate great benefits for the students but also (hopefully) cure the professors of their obsession with logical games because they would soon realize how pointless many of the theoretical issues really are. Finally, university exams should focus much less on theoretical questions and much more on the rules' and concepts' practical implications. That would force professors to pay attention to these implications in their teaching – or be punished by a lack of students (and the loss of their fees).[153] It is not clear whether Jhering's proposals had any effect at the time, but it is perhaps worth mentioning that present-day legal education in Germany has by and large realized them all.[154]

---

[150] *Jhering*, Geist III (1865) 302–303.

[151] *Jhering*, Scherz und Ernst (1884) 9–10 (fn. 1).

[152] See supra chapter II.5., notes 450–461 and text.

[153] *Jhering*, Scherz und Ernst (1884) 365–379.

[154] While candidates for a chair are strictly speaking not required to have completed the post-university practical training period (Referendariat) and to have passed the Assessorex-

The Challenge of "Justice": From Mere Corrective to Ultimate Goal. A significant change in Jhering's thinking pertained the role of the "sense of justice" ("Rechtsgefühl"). In his earlier years, this subjective and emotional element was of little concern. His experience in the double-sale case, however, made Jhering painfully aware that applying traditional doctrine did not guarantee a just result – in fact, the former and latter could be at full loggerheads. The lesson he learned was that doctrinal reasoning must be checked by one's feeling of right and wrong.[155] Besides practical needs, he wrote in 1865, "the feeling of justice" was the crucial yardstick for the correctness of results; logic had to adjust as needed.[156]

This was a significant reorientation.[157] In his earlier works, especially in his 1857 essay "Unsere Aufgabe," Jhering's enthusiasm for jurisprudence had all been driven by the beauty of its logic; the realm of concepts, constructions, and systems was glorified as the jurist's paradise. After 1860, Jhering struck a very different note.

> "I have increasingly recognized that the gratification which jurisprudence provides for the mere intellect (Verstand) is not the supreme good (das höchste)... Above the formal element of juristic logic there is, as a higher and the highest [value] the substantive idea of justice and ethics, and immersing oneself in it, i.e., in how it is expressed and realized in the various institutions and rules of law is, in my view, the most beautiful and sublime task which [legal] science can set for itself."[158]

Now, Jhering saw law not only as subject for the human intellect but also for human emotion; thus, the "key" to its understanding was not only reason but also "the heart."[159]

As a result, "Rechtsgefühl" now became a central category in Jhering's thinking. Whence did it come, how did it develop, and how did it relate to positive law? Especially in the 1870s and 1880s, pursuing these questions became a major focus

---

amen (also known as the "Second State Exam,"), fulfilling these requirements is de facto obligatory, some rare exceptions nothwithstanding. As a result, virtually all full-time legal academics in Germany have had at least two years of exposure to legal practice as clerks to judges and prosecutors, practicing lawyers, and administrative officials. All professors are required to teach, and all students to pass, a series "exercises" (Übungen) in which rules are applied to real or (more often) hypothetical cases, though profound discussion of the outcomes' real world impact is often lacking. Final exams largely test the candidates' skills to apply rules to facts and thus to "solve" cases, with knowledge of general theoretical issues playing second fiddle, if any.

155 *Kunze*, Rudolf von Jhering (1995) 141, considers this the most significant change in Jhering's thought at the time.

156 *Jhering*, Geist III (1865) 302–303, 305. Jhering's concept of Rechtsgefühl was not, however, monolithic; instead, it had several dimensions, and its use as a control device and potential corrective for results produced by doctrinal analysis was only one of them; see infra chapter IV.3., notes 409–418 and text.

157 See *Behrends*, Jherings Umschwung (2017).

158 *Jhering*, Geist II.2. (4th ed. 1883) 361 fn. 506.

159 *Jhering*, Geist III (1865) 297.

of Jhering's work, as exemplified by his talk to the Wiener juristische Gesellschaft in 1884 "Über die Entstehung des Rechtsgefühls" ("On the Origin or the Sense of Justice").The evolution of Jhering's thinking about the "sense of justice" is a subject in its own right which we will explore in the next chapter.[160]

From Structure to Function: Turning towards Instrumentalism. The most momentous "conversion" has usually been found in Jhering's shift from a *Konstruktionsjurisprudenz* (jurisprudence of construction) to a *Zweckjurisprudenz* (jurisprudence of purpose). In Franz Wieacker's terms, Jhering turned from the law's structure to the law's function.[161]

There is much to be said for such a view. It is true that Jhering's principal concern in his earlier period was the methodological program outlined in the 1850s. It is also true that in his later work, Jhering focused on the social function of law, i.e., its utility as an instrument for the pursuit of interests and socio-economic goals. The signature work of his first period were the first two volumes of "Geist des römischen Rechts" (1852–1858), that of his second period, the two volumes of his "Zweck im Recht" ("Law a Means to an End") (1877/1883) to which we will turn in the next chapter.[162]

While this dichotomy indeed captures an essential shift, it must be qualified in two regards. First, Jhering's functional understanding of law was not a mid-career discovery but part and parcel of his thinking from early on. We must remember that in the first volume of "Geist" (i.e., as early as 1852), he had distinguished the "anatomical," or structural, perspective on law from the "physiological," or functional, viewpoint.[163] While the latter had received fairly short shrift, Jhering had already emphasized that the "true value" of law did not lie in its "intellectual content, its logical structure and unity" but rather "in its functions, i.e., in its practical utility."[164] Jurisprudence, he wrote already in 1858, was essentially a "theory of the *means* ...which the law provides for the purposes of life."[165] These were not empty programmatic statements; much of Jhering's early doctrinal work evinces virtually constant attention to the law's function and practical impact.[166] Second, while Jhering gradually lost interest in the methodological questions that had so fascinated him in the 1850s, he never lost interest in doctrinal work using concepts, construction, and systematic ordering. He con-

[160] Infra chapter IV.3.

[161] *Wieacker*, Gründer und Bewahrer (1959) 203; see also *Larenz*, Methodenlehre der Rechtswissenschaft (1983) 43–48.

[162] The third volume of *Geist* (1865) provides the bridge, so to speak from the former to the latter, see infra chapter IV. 2., notes 137–154 and text.

[163] *Jhering*, Geist I (1852) 12–39, 39–50.

[164] *Jhering*, Geist I (1852) 39–40.

[165] *Jhering*, Geist II.2. (1858) 392 (emphasis in the original).

[166] A good example is *Jhering*, Übertragung der Rei Vindicatio auf Nichteigentümer (1857). In Jhering's view, the idea of "Zweckmäßigkeit" ("utility") had triumphed already in Roman law, *Jhering*, Geist I (1852) 297. The Romans, Jhering argued, had just rarely emphasized it because they considered it a matter of course, *Jhering*, Geist II.2. (1858) 391, fn. 510.

tinued to publish doctrinal articles in the "Jahrbücher" well into the 1880s and concluded that branch of his work with the massive treatise "Der Besitzwille" in 1889.

The transition from the earlier "constructionist" to the later "instrumentalist" phase[167] was thus not a radical break either but rather a shift in emphasis. As such, however, it *was* significant: the early Jhering's interests were primarily doctrinal and methodological while the later Jhering's perspective was predominantly functional and sociological.[168] Once Jhering had left the extremism of his early conceptual jurisprudence behind, these perspectives were entirely compatible. Law can be a (conceptual, logical, systematic) structure as well as an instrument for the pursuit of social purposes. It is among Jhering's great accomplishments that he never lost sight of either perspective and that he worked hard throughout his life to bring them together.

---

[167] This is a slight modification of Wolfgang Fikentscher's labels "konstruktions-methodische" and "Zweck-Phase;" *Fikentscher*, Methoden des Rechts III (1976) 201.

[168] Wolfgang Fikentscher took a somewhat different view. For him, Jhering did not change perspective but continued to pursue his original goal. According to Fikentscher, Jhering just realized after 1859 that he could not reach that goal with the methods developed in the 1850s. He thus embarked on a methodological detour into the realm of interests and purposes; *Fikentscher*, Methoden des Rechts III (1976) 202. This is a plausible view in light of the fact that, as we shall see, Jhering never abandoned the plan to complete "Geist des römischen Rechts" but considered writing "Der Zweck im Recht" a necessary step towards that goal; see infra chapter IV, notes 137–161.

Chapter IV

Jhering's External Perspective – The Sociology of Law

The early- and mid-1860s were a time of intellectual crisis for Jhering. To be sure, he remained quite productive. Besides venting frustration with mainstream Romanist scholarship in his "Confidential Letters on Contemporary Jurisprudence,"[1] he wrote a variety of notable doctrinal studies (among them his famous article on the *Culpa in Contrahendo*[2]) as well as various smaller pieces. It is also tempting to count the publication of the third volume of "Geist" (1865) among the successes of this period. In a sense, however, it signaled failure: rather than completing the entire work, the volume ended abruptly when Jhering realized that he could not continue as planned; after struggling with it for two decades, Jhering found himself compelled to put "Geist" on hold.[3]

His intellectual crisis went hand-in-glove with considerable unhappiness. He often felt dissatisfied and tired, frustrated by being stuck in a second-rate university while he waited, year after year, for an offer from one of the great centers of German learning – Berlin, Heidelberg, Leipzig or Vienna (whence an offer finally came in 1868). At times, he cursed jurisprudence altogether and wished he had not devoted his life to it.[4]

Yet, it was also a time of transition. His interest shifted – not entirely but significantly – from looking at law from an internal perspective, i.e., as doctrine reflecting its structure, to considering law from an external point of view, i.e., as a sociological phenomenon. Jhering's legal theory began to focus increasingly on the law's instrumentalist dimension. Most of his efforts were now directed at exploring law as a means to accomplishing socio-economic ends. The resulting work became Jhering's most important contribution to the development of modern legal thought. It is the subject of this chapter.

Jhering's shift from a doctrinal and methodological to a sociological and instrumental perspective, from law as a world of concepts to law as a social reality, corresponded to broader trends in his intellectual and social environment. By 1860, philosophical idealism had lost much of its force in Germany; Kantian and Hegelian ideas still had an influence, but they no longer provided

[1] Supra chapter III.2., notes 41–70 and text.
[2] Supra chapter II.3.
[3] See infra 2., notes 137–161 and text.
[4] *Kunze*, Rudolf von Jhering (1995) 140.

the leading paradigms. In a similar vein, historicism, itself infused with a substantial dose of idealism, was receding into the background of the German mind.[5] Instead, scientific positivism of the Comtean sort was steeply on the rise. Under the influence of the natural sciences, the humanities now also focused increasingly on observable (social) data. Abstract "truth" ("Wahrheit") seemed less interesting than concrete "reality" ("Wirklichkeit"). Jhering's shift towards an instrumentalist as well as utilitarian conception of law was also in line with the mid-century rise of the capitalist economy, the increasing urgency of economic and welfare regulation, and the ascendancy of economics as a prominent academic discipline.[6] Jhering's later work must be understood in that overall context: it partook in the rise of positivism, social science, and economics – as well as in the concomitant decline of moral philosophy.

Much of that shift was already visible in Jhering's first open engagement with a sociological perspective, i.e., in his tract "Der Kampf ums Recht" ("The Struggle for Law," 1872) (infra 1). Subsequently, he elaborated on that perspective at hugely greater length in what may be called a second *magnum opus*, his two-volume monograph "Der Zweck im Recht" ("Law as a Means to an End," 1877/1883) (infra 2.). Finally, when he looked at "Die Entstehung des Rechtsgefühls" ("The Origin of the Sense of Justice," 1884), he fully recognized where his newly embraced positivism was taking him (infra 3.).

1. Social Facts and Moral Duties: "Der Kampf um's Recht" (1872)

In 1872, Jhering published "Der Kampf um's Recht," usually translated as "The Struggle for Law".[7] The book was a revised and expanded version of a talk Jhering delivered before the Wiener Juristische Gesellschaft (Viennese Law Society), an association of legal practitioners, shortly before his departure for Göttingen. Despite the books' brevity (it comprises merely 100 pages), it deserves more than passing attention because it is one of Jhering's most important works in at least four regards.[8]

First, in the context of Jhering's *oeuvre*, the book is a milestone. While its intellectual caliber is modest – the discourse is often passionate and colorful but

---

[5] *Wolf*, Große Rechtsdenker (1953) 627.

[6] See *Vesco*, Die Erfindung der ökonomischen Rechtswissenschaft (2021) 29–30.

[7] *Jhering*, The Struggle for Law (John Laylor transl., 2d ed. Chicago 1915).

[8] The book was the object of a symposium on the occasion of the 100th anniversary of Jhering's death, see *Luf and Ogris* (eds.), Der Kampf ums Recht (1995). See also *Ermacora* (ed.), Rudolf von Jhering, Der Kampf ums Recht (1992); the volume reprints the text of the original talk which was much shorter than the printed version and originally published in a local periodical (Wiener Juristische Blätter), id. 32–47. The volume also contains a multitude of contemporary accounts illuminating the surrounding circumstances, the reactions of the audience, and a report about the subsequent dinner with all its speeches.

rarely brilliant or profound[9] – , it is the first full-scale appearance of Jhering's revised (i.e., post-"conversion") understanding of law.[10] After struggling to find new jurisprudential grounding for several years, Jhering now showed where he had arrived: he no longer looked at law primarily as an abstract system of principles and rules but as a concrete social phenomenon and as a normative order the very essence of which lay in its enforcement. In a sense, the small volume is, at least in part, Jhering's first piece of legal sociology.[11]

Second, "Kampf" is easily Jhering's most widely read text. Published in numerous editions and translated more than 50 times into dozens of languages,[12] it may well be the most popular essay on law of all time.[13] In fact, in terms of global readership, it is probably unsurpassed. The tract's popular appeal has been due to a combination of factors that tend to ensure a large audience: a snappy (Darwinist) title gets the readers' attention; the book's brevity is an invitation to actually read it (it can easily be read in two hours); a largely one-sided argument skillfully displayed and marked by – at times wild – exaggerations appeals to the reader's emotions (more than to his or her intellect); and a lively style characterized by catchy phrases, memorable aphorisms, and an occasional colorful portrait keeps the reader entertained. Of course, the book's flamboyant style must be judged in light of Jhering's intent to address not only jurists but also an educated lay audience.[14] His discourse was not meant to be a careful and balanced scientific inquiry conducted by Jhering-the-jurist but (for the most part[15]) a piece of rousing rhetoric presented by Jhering-the-artist[16] – who once again was overwhelmed by sheer enthusiasm for his own ideas. Beyond Jhering's entertaining style, the book's psychological appeal has played a role as well. Jhering's claims and arguments resonate with many vague impressions and semi-conscious desires that are broadly shared among jurists and laypeople. By articulating these impressi-

[9] This was noted already by Jhering's early American biographer who concluded, in 1914, that the book "cannot be regarded as a scientific study of great value." *MacDonell,* Rudolf von Jhering (1914) 591.

[10] Some of the underlying ideas were already developed and expressed in the final part of the third volume of "Geist," published seven years earlier; *Jhering*, Geist III (1865) 302–306; see infra 2.

[11] As *Wolf*, Große Rechtsdenker (1963) 649, points out, it was one of the earliest such publications in Germany.

[12] Jhering was quite proud of the book's domestic popularity (there were at least 20 editions during his lifetime) and international success. In his preface to the 9th edition (1889) v–vii, he listed already 20 translations into 17 languages; see *Behrends* (ed.), Rudolf von Jhering (1993) 71–72.

[13] *Mecke*, Begriff des Rechts und Methode der Rechtswissenschaft (2017) 37, calls it "the most famous lecture ever given in the history of jurisprudence."

[14] *Jhering*, Kampf (1872) Vorrede, V. Jhering called his essay "a piece of the psychology of law" ("ein Stück Psychologie des Rechts"), id., perhaps because psychology was a new, up-and-coming discipline and thus a fashionable term at the time.

[15] At times, Jhering brings his skills as a jurist into play, see infra notes 117–119 and text.

[16] "It is a lay sermon addressed to the conscience of his readers." *Smith*, Four German Jurists II (1896) 301.

ons and desires, Jhering has made generations of readers feel vindicated in their own beliefs.[17] All in all, reading the book is good fun.

Third, the little book contains an amazing amount and variety of provocative, and in part original, ideas. It is a veritable firework of thoughts, views, beliefs, and opinions. Mostly presented in an overblown manner, often flippant, and sometimes inconsistent, they provide ample food for thought and discussion. It is true that (as has often been noted) the book's instant popularity was largely due to its expression of the Darwinist *Zeitgeist*, but it is also true that it has remained popular for generations thereafter – and for good reason: it captures some fundamental truths about (modern Western) legal culture and pushes the reader to re-think established positions. Many of its points are as pertinent today as they were 150 years ago or even more so.

Last, but not least, "Kampf" is also worth looking at because it shows, perhaps more than any other of Jhering's works, the unabashed eclecticism of Jhering's intellectual make-up. Darwinian ideas mix with Kantian precepts; individualism with collectivism; legal history with literature; positivism with idealism.[18] The upside of this eclecticism is that the book's dazzling display of facts, ideas, arguments, assertions, and stories makes it something of a page-turner. The downside is that, like many of Jhering's writings, it lacks consistent organization and analytical rigor. The book does consist of several distinct parts, and although Jhering did not assign them to discrete chapters, he clearly marked the transitions from one to the next. Yet, within and among these parts, his statements and arguments are all over the place, often popping up whenever they came to his mind, begun in one place and completed in another, sometimes redundant, and often fragmentary. Thus, presenting and summarizing the content of "Kampf" in an intelligible fashion requires considerable disentanglement and re-organization of Jhering's arguments.

"Kampf" has four fairly different parts. It begins by briefly presenting Jhering's new conception of law. It then proceeds to claim that all law is the result of struggle. Jhering next postulates that there is a moral duty to fight for the realization of one's rights. The book ends with a lengthy diatribe against the current legal system's lack of rigorous rights enforcement and its disregard for personal dignity.

A New Conception of Law: Driven by Purpose and Realized by Struggle. Jhering's very first sentence is remarkable: "The concept of law is notoriously (bekanntlich) a practical one, i.e., a concept of purpose (Zweckbegriff)."[19] What is

[17] At the time of its publication, it may also have resonated with German readers because of the very recent Franco-Prussian war (1870–1871) which could be perceived as a struggle between clashing claims of right (settled on the battlefield). Wolfgang Fikentscher speculated that Jhering's all-absorbing interest in the war had provided part of the motivation for the book; *Fikentscher*, Methoden des Rechts III. (1976) 125–126.

[18] See infra notes 124–127 and text.

[19] *Jhering*, Kampf (1872) 7.

remarkable is not that Jhering defined law through purpose – he had done that before[20] – but that he considered that definition "notorious." Of course, it was not. To be sure, by 1872, such an understanding had become of paramount importance to Jhering himself, and those who had read the third volume of "Geist" all the way to the end should have been aware of that. But for the (very large) rest of the world it was anything but obvious that purpose was the crucial element of law.

It is possible that Jhering truly believed in the notoriety he claimed, but it is unlikely – he could scarcely assume that his concept of law as purpose-driven had found universal acceptance.[21] It is also possible that he was just careless, as he often was when making broad claims. It is most likely, however, that he wanted to start his talk with a bang: in making this bold statement, Jhering announced to the world that from now on, a functional view of law was the ground zero of his jurisprudence.

Foregrounding the purpose ("Zweck") element in law also allowed Jhering to turn immediately to the means by which the law's purpose must be realized. That means was "Kampf," meaning struggle or fight. Fight, e.g., against injustice, Jhering claimed, was as much part of the concept of law as was purpose.[22] In the opening pages, Jhering thus put his new, essentially sociological, understanding of law squarely on the table: law had two dimensions – it was driven by "Zweck" and realized by "Kampf."

For now, Jhering focused only on the means-side of the law, on "Kampf." He left the element of "Zweck," for a later day. In that manner, "Der Kampf ums Recht" and "Der Zweck im Recht" would eventually complement each other.

Emphasizing the "Kampf" element in law was in and of itself a fairly original and important contribution to contemporary jurisprudence. As Jhering pointed out, that element had largely been overlooked. Legal philosophy as well as positive jurisprudence had understood law mostly as "an abstract order" and disregarded law as a "concept of power" ("Machtbegriff").[23] The principal object of Jhering's tract was to correct that one-sided view.

In the subsequent two parts of the book, Jhering explored "Kampf" in two different dimensions.[24] These dimensions correspond to the two different meanings of the two key words in the German title: "Recht" and "Kampf." "Recht" in the objective sense means "law," i.e., the existing legal order. Jhering postulated that this order was a result of "Kampf" in the sense of "struggle," i.e., between

[20] Chapter III.3., notes 163–165 and text.

[21] Had that been true, it would have made little sense subsequently to spend ten years of his life on a book explaining that point in a separate study, i.e., Der Zweck im Recht (1877/1883).

[22] *Jhering*, Kampf (1872) 8. Jhering pointed out that Law presented as a statue was endowed with both scales and sword. To be sure, "[t]he sword without the scales is naked force," he wrote, "but the scales without the sword is the impotence of law;" Jhering 1872, 9.

[23] *Jhering*, Kampf (1872) 11.

[24] *Jhering*, Kampf (1872) 11–12.

competing (social) forces. Thus, the book's second part deals with "Kampf ums Recht" in the sense of "struggle for law" (which raises the question whether Jhering was a "Darwinist"[25]). By contrast, "Recht" in the subjective sense means "right," i.e., a person's legal entitlement. Jhering argued that it must be enforced by "Kampf" in the sense of "fight" (which raises the question whether Jhering advocated unbridled litigiousness[26]). The book's third part thus discusses "Kampf ums Recht" in the sense of "fight for right."

The "Struggle for Law:" Kampf as the Origin of the Legal Order. "All law in the world has been fought for" ("Alles Recht in der Welt ist erstritten worden"), Jhering wrote in the opening pages the book[27]. Like many of Jhering's memorable phrases, it was an overstatement. Yet, it epitomized his postulate that law, in the sense of existing institutions and rules, was the result of "struggle" (or "battle") between competing social forces. Jhering presented this idea as if were new and revolutionary, and perhaps he believed that himself, but it was not. At the time, the view of contemporary society as a battlefield of opposing interests, and even of law as a product of their clashes, had already been expressed by others, though not as loudly, rhetorically brilliant and attention-getting as by Jhering.[28]

The reason why law resulted from struggle was simple: rights reflected interests, and the assertion of new interests required overcoming the inevitable resistance of existing ones. "To abolish a legal institution or rule means to declare war on all these interests, to tear loose a polyp that hangs on with a thousand tentacles."[29] In Jhering's view, the inevitable battles were not decided by the weight of the reasons supporting the respective interests but by the relative power of the opposing sides. The resulting law was not an ideal order but simply the prize of victory in a power struggle. Even though Jhering did not put it quite so bleakly, might made right.

Of course, that claim entailed a direct rejection of the Historical School's perhaps most fundamental credo: Savigny's (and Puchta's) *Volksgeist*-theory, according to which law emanated organically, peacefully, and silently from the spirit of the people. That theory, Jhering now claimed, was simply dead-wrong[30] (as was the historical jurists' likening of law and language[31]). Both the historical record and human psychology told us that law emerged from struggle.[32] Jhering

---

[25] Infra notes 39–57 and text.

[26] Infra notes 91–102 and text.

[27] *Jhering*, Kampf (1872) 8.

[28] See *Mecke*, Jherings Rechtsdenken im Kontext der zeitgenössischen Natur- und Geisteswissenschaften (2023) 288–290 (with further references).

[29] *Jhering*, Kampf (1872) 14.

[30] Jhering admitted that once upon a time, he had himself believed in it; *Jhering*, Kampf (1872) 12–13.

[31] *Jhering*, Kampf (1872) 16–17.

[32] As Christoph-Eric Mecke has pointed out, Savigny's and Jhering's contrary conceptions corresponded to the dichotomy between "community" and "society" as later developed by *Tönnies*, Gemeinschaft und Gesellschaft (1887). For Savigny, law evolved sil-

conceded that sometimes, law evolved in a more peaceful and gradual manner, e.g., in the customs of trade or in the doctrinal discoveries of legal scholarship.[33] Still, "[a]ll great accomplishments which the history of law records [...] had to be won by way of bitter, often centuries-long, struggle," Jhering postulated; and for drama, he added that "sometimes rivers of blood, and always trampled rights, mark the path taken by the law."[34]

Savigny's theory was not only wrong, it was also pernicious: "While man should act, and act in full, clear recognition of purpose and with all his might, it seduces him into believing that matters will take care of themselves, and that it is best to put one's hands in one's lap and trustingly await what gradually emerges from the original source of law, the national legal consciousness."[35] Jhering's protest against such passivity was fully in tune with the times. Two generations earlier, Savigny's conservative attitude was perhaps appealing as it catered to the romantic, backward-looking, mood of the early nineteenth century. When Jhering wrote "Kampf," rapid social and economic change made such a stance almost ludicrous, especially as law reform through legislation had become a powerful engine of change in the emerging industrialized and urbanized society.

Jhering contended that the law's origin in struggle was to be welcomed: having to win it through battle created a strong bond between man and law – like the bond between a mother and the child whom she brought into this world by painful labor. Again, Jhering found a gripping metaphor: "A law won without effort is on the same level with children brought by the stork; what the stork has delivered, the fox or vulture can take away. But it does not take it from the mother who has given birth to the child."[36] The battle required to win the law was "not a curse but a blessing."[37]

Jhering's thesis that law emerged from struggle applied not only to battles in the legislative arena but also to contests before the courts. This, of course, spoke directly to his audience which consisted not of fellow academics but of practitioners, i.e., attorneys and judges. Jhering essentially upgraded their work from mere

---

ently and organically from the *Volk* envisaged as an essentially harmonious community while for Jhering, it resulted from the conflicts within a society envisaged as a mass of individuals with conflicting interests; *Mecke*, Jherings Rechtsdenken im Kontext der zeitgenössischen Natur- und Sozialwissenschaften (2023) 287.

[33] *Jhering*, Kampf (1872) 13.

[34] *Jhering*, Kampf (1872) 15. Jhering's examples of such accomplishments were also dramatic: the abolition of slavery (the American civil war had ended just seven years earlier); the end of serfdom (in early nineteenth century Germany); freedom of religion (over which "rivers of blood" had indeed been shed in early modern Europe); and freedom of commerce (in Germany inter alia via the recent Gewerbeordnung (Regulation of Commerce) of 1869).

[35] Jhering, *Kampf* (1872) 17 (emphasis in the original). This protest against the passivity inherent in the Historical School's theory of law was not new; Jhering had voiced it already in the 1850s and 1860s, see supra chapter II.1. and 6.

[36] *Jhering*, Kampf (1872) 20.

[37] *Jhering*, Kampf (1872) 20.

law application to actual law production. One could even say that it elevated the practice of law above its academic study. No wonder, his listeners loudly cheered Jhering.[38]

Jhering's "Darwinism:" Influence, Similarity, and Kindredness. Jhering's claim that law is the result of struggle invites the question whether he was a "Darwinist."[39] The question is far too general. Before it can be meaningfully addressed at all, one must decide in what respect? Two ideas typically associated with Darwin's (slightly earlier) work are particularly relevant for our understanding of Jhering's thought. One is that outcomes are the result of a struggle between competing forces; this dimension is relevant in the present context, and we will turn to it in a moment.[40] The other is the concept of evolution as a process of natural selection leading towards higher forms of existence; that dimension is more relevant in, and thus better discussed later in the context of, Jhering's "Zweck im Recht."[41] Yet, even in looking only at the element of "struggle" here, we should distinguish at least three issues: influence, similarity of ideas, and mere kindredness in spirit.

Some have seen a strong Darwinian influence on Jhering.[42] It is fairly clear, however, that there was no direct influence in the sense that Jhering found ideas in Darwin's work and then adopted them in his own scholarship. It is true that Jhering could easily have read Darwin's "Origin of Species" (1859) in a German translation[43] but it is clear that he had not done that. To be sure, Jhering was familiar with Darwin's ideas in broad outline[44] – in the 1870s, that was hard to

---

[38] *Luf and Ogris* (eds.), Der Kampf ums Recht (1995) 127, 130.

[39] The most thorough discussion is *Wieacker*, Jhering und der Darwinismus (1973).

[40] Note that the third part of "Kampf," i.e., Jhering's discussion of the fight for (individual) rights and their enforcement, infra notes 58–102 and text, is an entirely different matter that has virtually nothing do with Darwinian ideas.

[41] Infra 2, notes 310–315 and text.

[42] See the references provided by *Wieacker*, Jhering und der Darwinismus (1973) 71. Wilhelm Dilthey (1833–1911) found Jhering's turn toward that paradigm deplorable: "yet another good brain [has] fallen into the murderous pit of Darwinism" ("wieder ein guter Kopf in die Mördergrube des Darwinismus gefallen"), quoted after *Behrends*, Der Durchbruch zum Zweck des Rechts (1987) 237.

[43] *Charles Darwin*, Über die Entstehung der Arten im Thier- und Pflanzenreich durch natürliche Züchtung (Heinrich Georg Bronn transl., Stuttgart 1860).

[44] *Wieacker*, Jhering und der Darwinismus (1973) 70. During the discussion following a lecture Jhering gave in Prague in 1877, Jhering remarked that he had noticed for some time that he was a Darwinist without ever having studied Darwin; id. 73. At the same time, he wrote in his Introduction to the first volume of "Zweck" that he did not want to judge the correctness of Darwin's theory, "even though the results, to which I have come for myself regarding the historical development of law, completely confirm it" [i.e., his theory], *Jhering*, Zweck I (1884) XIII. Jhering's son Hermann, who was a zoologist, reported that his father liked to listen to his explanations of Darwin's theories, *Hermann Jhering*, Erinnerungen (1913) 445, 463. This also indicates that Jhering's knowledge of Darwin's theories was entirely second-hand.

avoid because these ideas were "in the air," so to speak. Yet, it is virtually certain that if this familiarity helped to shape Jhering's idea of law as a result of struggle at all, Jhering was not fully aware of it.[45] Jhering was conscientious about giving credit where credit was due; he openly acknowledged the ideas of others even if that diminished his own originality.[46] If he did not mention Darwin in "Kampf," it was because in 1872, he did not have Darwin's ideas (consciously) in mind.[47] The title of his book, however, was a different matter – it was almost certainly inspired by Darwin's then widely known phrase "struggle for life." Jhering understood the importance of catchy titles and of implicit references to famous works (such as to Montequieu's "Esprit des loix" in his "Geist des römischen Rechts"[48]), and both the wording and the timing are too close to be coincidental.

Whatever the nature and degree of influence, there was an undeniable similarity between Jhering's and Darwin's ideas of "struggle" in some significant regards – though not in others.[49] Most importantly, in "Kampf," Jhering shared with Darwin the view that the order of things is not the reflection of timeless principles or ideals but the result of actual competition between opposite forces. That implied, of course, an important turn from idealism to positivism. Whether Jhering also endorsed Darwin's idea that struggle leads to higher forms of development is a more difficult question. On the one hand, Jhering did indicate his belief in progress in the history of law;[50] on the other hand, he did not associate victory in the struggle for law with the winner's superior adaptation to circumstances but simply with sheer superior power.[51] In other words, in "Kampf," Jhering shared Darwin's belief that struggle drove change but not necessarily Darwin's claim that it drove progress.[52] If Jhering saw a relationship between superior power and substantive advancement, he did not explain it here. This is an important point: in

---

[45] Behrends considers this confirmed also by Jhering's remark that "in nature, truth lies side-by-side (nebeneinander) while in history it follows in temporal order (hinteinander);" *Jhering*, Ist die Jurisprudenz eine Wissenschaft (1868) 71. In a footnote, Behrends sees this statement as an indication that Jhering's evolutionary thinking was not rooted in Darwinian ideas, id. fn. 80.

[46] See, e.g., supra chapter II.3. note 330; *Jhering*, Über die Entstehung des Rechtsgefühls (1884) 13–14 (admitting that John Locke had already taken Jhering's position almost 200 years earlier). Jhering added: "I considered this addendum necessary to avoid the impression of originality where I don't deserve it," id. 14.

[47] A few years later, in and after 1877, Jhering was more cognizant that Darwin's ideas resembled his own in many ways; see infra 2., note 312 and text.

[48] Supra chapter II.1., note 35 and text.

[49] For further perspectives, see *Behrends*, Das 'Rechtsgefühl' in der historisch-kritischen Rechtstheorie des späten Jhering (1986) 150–156.

[50] *Jhering*, Kampf (1872) 12 ("Fortschritt," "progress"); 15 ("grosse Errungenschaften", "great accomplishments"); see also 79 (earlier legal institutions badly contradicted a "healthy and strong sense of justice").

[51] *Jhering* 1872, 14 ("Machtverhältnisse der sich gegenüberstehenden Kräfte," "power of the opposing forces").

[52] Jhering expressed that belief, however, in his later writings, see infra 2, note 312 and text.

"Kampf," Jhering was not a "Darwinist" in the sense of legitimizing superior power because the resultant victory advanced mankind's ball.[53] Nor was Jhering a "social Darwinist:" Kampf does not envisage a "struggle for existence" in which only the "fittest" survive.[54] The losers in the struggle for law were not condemned to perish, just to suffer that someone else's interests prevailed over theirs.

Beyond this (partial) similarity of ideas, there was what one might call a kindredness in spirit, in particular in a spirit of harshness. Darwin's portrait of the natural world was that of a relentless struggle in which the strong prevailed, and in which morality played no role. Jhering's depiction of the world of law was animated by the same harshness. He spoke of "the instinct of self-preservation," of "violent exertion", of peoples "bleeding," and of "Saturn eating his own children."[55] This portrayed not a realm of justice or morality but a dog-eat-dog world, and Jhering reveled in its images. In that, vague and popular, sense Jhering was a "Darwinist" – or at least sounded like one. His instinct, if not his intellect, told him that such a tone appealed to an age of ever more powerful capitalism, competitive markets, and openly visible social conflict[56] The success of his book proved him right.[57]

The "Fight for Right:" Enforcement as a Moral Duty. The third (and much longer) part of the book turns to "Recht" in the subjective sense of "right" and to "Kampf" in the sense of "fight." Its theme is that individuals have an obligation

[53] It is true, however, that six years before publishing "Kampf," Jhering had, at least implicitly, legitimized victory as a motor of progress: "If a people proves itself incapable of making use of the soil which nature has entrusted to it, it must yield to another," he wrote in 1866. "The soil belongs to the hand that knows how to plant it [...];" Jhering, Geist I (2d ed. 1866) 7.

[54] *Behrends*, Rudolf von Jhering und die Evolutionstheorie des Rechts (1991) 88, expresses the same view. While the phrase "survival of the fittest" is often associated with Darwin, it was actually coined by Herbert Spencer, see *Spencer*, Principles of Biology (1864) 444. It is not clear whether by the time he wrote "Kampf," Jhering had already read Spencer or how familiar he was with his ideas, *Behrends*, id. 108. It is clear, however, that he knew of Spencer later when he worked on "Zweck," see infra 2., note 320 and text.

[55] *Jhering*, Kampf (1872) 14–20.

[56] While Jhering did not directly mention the struggle between interest groups and especially between capital and labor in late nineteenth century Germany (and Austria), Jhering's audience was surely conscious of living in a conflict-ridden society; see *Duxbury*. Jhering's Philosophy of Authority (2007) 44 (citing *Michael John*, Law and Politics in Late-Nineteenth Century Germany, Oxford 1989).

[57] In late nineteenth century Germany, "Kampf" was a fashionable literary theme, as in the hugely popular (historical) novel by *Felix Dahn*, Ein Kampf um Rom (2 vols. Leipzig 1876). See also the novel by *Karl Emil Franzos*, Ein Kampf um's Recht (Breslau 1882); the latter was mentioned and praised by Jhering in later editions of "Kampf;" see Jhering, Der Kampf um's Recht (13th ed. 1897) xi, 65 note. Whether these books were actually inspired by Jhering's work, as Neil Duxbury and Mario Losano have claimed, would have to be determined, see *Duxbury*, Jhering's Philosophy of Authority (2007) 44 fn. 118; *Losano*, Studien zu Jhering und Gerber (1984) 164.

to fight for their rights. Even in the relatively low-stakes environment of private law, Jhering presented that obligation as a moral duty. At this point, Jhering's discourse took a revolutionary turn as he pushed way past the traditional boundaries of jurisprudence in two significant respects. First, based on the postulate that law is not a concept of logic but of "power,"[58] he demanded focusing on its enforcement, i.e., he called for action. Second, he addressed not only jurists but all citizens, i.e., he made (enforcement of) the law everybody's business. "Kampf" took law out of the scholar's study and thrust it into what Jhering liked to call "life."[59]

If a person suffers injustice, he (today we would need to add "or she"[60]) might balance the importance of the matter against the burden (and risk) of a lawsuit. At first glance, Jhering admitted, that appears to be a perfectly rational reaction, and it seems that the calculus should be left to each individual himself. Yet, in many instances, Jhering noted, we see people pursuing their rights in court even though the trouble and costs clearly outweigh the value of the disputed object. This has traditionally been regarded as a sign of obsession with litigation ("Processsucht").[61] In many instances, however, lawsuits are brought in defense of the plaintiff "as a person himself" ("der Person selber") and of his feeling of justice. Such lawsuits are not motivated by material interests but by "the moral pain resulting from the injustice suffered."[62] Whether to fight for one's rights is thus not (just) a question of (material) interest but of character.[63] For Jhering, this turned it into a moral imperative.

> "Resistance against injustice is a duty, a duty the right-holder owes to himself – because it is a command of moral self-preservation – a duty owed to the community –because it must be a general one in order to succeed."[64]

In short, the duty to fight for one's rights had an individual and a collective dimension.

---

[58] *Jhering*, Kampf (1872) 9.

[59] It has variously been suggested that Jhering's call for general participation in the enforcement of rights was motivated at least in part by the atmosphere of the venue of his talk, i.e., the (at least widely assumed) Viennese lack of determination in that regard; see *Stintzing and Landsberg*, Geschichte der deutschen Rechswissenschaft III.2. (1910) 814; *Helfer*, Rudolf von Jhering als Rechtssoziologe (1968) 555 (with further references).

[60] The use of the male pronoun in summarizing Jhering's text is in accordance with Jhering's consistent reference to the male form. In part, Jhering, like most contemporaries, routinely thought in male terms (e.g., when he spoke of "manly resistance," "mannhafter Widerstand", against injustice, *Jhering*, Kampf (1872) 27). In part, this also reflected the reality that the enforcement of rights, especially in the courts, was predominantly a male domain; yet, as Jhering himself had painfully experienced, it was not an exclusively male prerogative; see supra chapter I. 4., note 210; infra note 110.

[61] *Jhering*, Kampf (1872) 24.

[62] *Jhering*, Kampf (1872) 25–26.

[63] *Jhering*, Kampf (1872) 26.

[64] *Jhering*, Kampf (1872) 27.

Jhering began with the individual aspect: "To fight for [his] right is a duty of the right-holder vis-a-vis himself."[65] The supreme law of creation is self-preservation. For a human being, this pertains not only to his physical, but also to his moral existence.[66] Entirely foregoing the defense of one's rights is "moral suicide."[67] Jhering presented a twenty-five-page explanation which was, however, seriously muddled. What follows is a re-organized and clarified rendition of his argument. Although he did not sufficiently distinguish them, Jhering supported his call for vigorous rights enforcement through a Kantian, an emotional-psychological, and a consequentialist argument.

The Kantian argument was that as a matter of personal dignity, nobody should let others trample on his rights.[68] This argument also served to distinguish the cases in which a moral duty calls for rigorous rights enforcement from the cases where it does not. For purposes of illustration, Jhering presented two hypothetical situations. The first involves a bona fide possessor who denies my property right because he believes the object to be his; the second involves a thief (or robber) who takes my property from me without any claim of right. Although Jhering fails to articulate them clearly, there are two differences between these situations. The first is that the bona fide possessor merely disputes my property right in an action that is not directed against me as a person; the thief, however, (knowingly) violates my property right which does imply an attack on an "essential condition of the existence of my person" ("wesentliche Existenzialbedingung meiner Person").[69] The second difference is that the act of the bona fide possessor does not deny property protection as such, in fact, he asserts it (for himself); the act of the thief, however, negates the notion of property rights because he disregards them. To show why this makes a crucial difference, Jhering invokes a simplified version of Kant's first categorical imperative: "Imagine the kind of conduct as a general maxim of law [...]"[70] (that property rights must be respected). We can now see the philosophical foundation of Jhering's position: fighting for one's rights – even property rights – can be morally required for two reasons: first, because violating these rights can be an attack on one's personhood, and second, because we cannot afford to tolerate such violations in civil society. At the same time, we can see the limits of the moral duty to fight for one's rights: the duty does not kick in if the violation does not imply an attack on the owner's

---

[65] *Jhering*, Kampf (1872) 27.

[66] *Jhering*, Kampf (1872) 27.

[67] *Jhering*, Kampf (1872) 28.

[68] While Jhering did not invoke Kant in text of "Kampf," he cited Kant for that proposition in the Preface of a later edition; *Jhering*, Kampf (13th ed. 1897, Vorrede, written 1891) VIII.

[69] *Jhering*, Kampf (1872) 29.

[70] *Jhering*, Kampf (1872) 29. Kant's first categorical imperative appears in a variety of versions. In his philosophy of law, it is phrased as follows: "handle nach einer Maxime, die zugleich als allgemeines Gesetz gelten kann." ("act according to a maxim which can simultaneously operate as a general law.") *Kant*, Metaphysik der Sitten (1797) 225.

personhood, and if it does not amount to a denial of rights as such. Thus, fighting back against the bona fide possessor is not a moral duty; it is merely a question of (economic) interest, and the owner may well settle or even forego his claim. Fighting back against the thief's act, however, is a moral duty because "tolerating it would constitute a single moment of lawlessness in my life, and that nobody is permitted to assist." ("Durch Duldung statuire ich einen einzelnen Moment der Rechtslosigkeit in meinem Leben, und dazu darf niemand die Hand bieten.")[71]

Jhering's second argument is emotional-psychological: fighting back may be required by one's Rechtsgefühl. Here we must remember that this concept had become a central element in Jhering's thinking after his frustrating experience with the double-sale case more than a decade earlier.[72] In "Kampf," Jhering now bluntly asserted that the ultimate root of the power of law was not the intellect but the feeling of justice.[73] A "healthy feeling of justice" is defined by two criteria: the sensitivity to the pain of injustice, and the courage and determination to fight back.[74] Whenever the pain of injustice is felt, the individual must defend his rights. For Jhering, this was a fundamental question of moral fiber: "an individual's or people's reaction to an injustice is the most reliable litmus test of its character."[75] It required willpower, resolve, and endurance – qualities Jhering saw, and admired, in ancient Rome[76] and now demanded of contemporary society. Jhering's overall message was loud and clear: "Let us thus reject it: this morality of convenience, which no people, no individual with a healthy sense of justice has ever embraced. It is the sign and the product of a sick, dumb, lame feeling of justice [...]."[77]

Finally, there was the – somewhat hidden – consequentialist argument: failure to fight back means failure to nip injustice in the bud and thus implicitly encourages more lawlessness. Thus, if a foreign power takes a square mile of land from a nation, that nation better defend its territory regardless of its size because the consequences of lumping the injury are dire. "If one can take a square mile from a people with impunity, one will also take the remaining ones, until nothing is left,

---

[71] *Jhering*, Kampf (1872) 29.

[72] See supra chapter II.3., note 10 and text.

[73] *Jhering*, Kampf (1872) 46.

[74] *Jhering*, Kampf (1872) 47. Jhering explained that the sensitivity to feel the pain of injustice is not absolute but determined by both culture and an individual's status. The English, for example, have a strong sense of justice, Jhering pointed out with admiration, and will fight for their rights regardless of cost; meanwhile the Austrians, he asserted with an apology to the audience of his talk (in Vienna!), will mostly prefer to avoid inconvenience, publicity, and the risk of misunderstanding – and thus take injustice lying down; id. 50–51. Also, look, Jhering argued, at how differently various professions will react: the farmer will be quick to fight for his property, the officer to defend his honor, the merchant to protect his credit, because these are the elements that matter most for them; id. 35–38.

[75] *Jhering*, Kampf (1872) 48.

[76] *Jhering*, Geist I (1852) 306–307.

[77] *Jhering*, Kampf (1872) 43.

and that people does not deserve a better fate"; and what is true for a people, Jhering asserted, may also be true for individuals.[78]

Jhering then turned to the collective dimension of the "fight for right": "This assertion of law is also a duty vis-a-vis the community."[79] It followed primarily from Jhering's very conception of law. In anticipation of legal realism, Jhering postulated that "the essence of law is practical realization."[80]

"A legal rule which has never experienced it, or which has lost it, has no claim to this name [of law], it is a worn-out spring that does not operate in the machinery of law, and that one can remove without causing the slightest change."[81]

Practical realization (in private law), however, is possible only if private individuals enforce their rights. Thus the "fight for right" is required by the very essence of law: if citizens fail to enforce their legal rights, there is in effect no (private) law – other than on paper. Yet, the collective duty to participate in the "fight for right" is also grounded, like the individual duty, in (Jhering's version of) Kant's first categorical imperative: as an individual act, cowardly giving up one's rights may not do great harm, Jhering points out, but "elevated to a general maxim of conduct," it would spell the "doom of law" ("Untergang des Rechts").[82] Enforcement is therefore "a great national task,"[83] and participating in it is a civic duty.

Jhering embellished the collective aspect of the duty for pages on end in language that is so passionate and dramatic that it strikes the – especially modern – reader as hopelessly overblown, even in a talk and certainly in print. He who shirks participation in the great national task, Jhering pronounced, commits "treason towards the common cause because he strengthens the power of the enemy by increasing his audacity and brazenness;"[84] he is like the defector who deserts his fellow soldiers on the battlefield;[85] those who fight for their proper rights and are abandoned by their fellow citizens, and then perish, are martyrs who die for the cause of justice;[86] etc. Almost inevitably, Jhering invoked Michael Kohlhaas, a symbolic and tragic figure in German folklore, who was well-known to Jhering's audience as a man who refused to tolerate the injustice suffered at the hands of a local lord, waged wild war against the authorities, and ended on the scaffold.[87] Yet, Jhering also nicely captured his call for participation in the en-

---

[78] *Jhering*, Kampf (1872) 25.
[79] *Jhering*, Kampf (1872) 51.
[80] *Jhering*, Kampf (1872) 52.
[81] *Jhering*, Kampf (1872) 52.
[82] *Jhering*, Kampf (1872) 42.
[83] *Jhering*, Kampf (1872) 57.
[84] *Jhering*, Kampf (1872) 54.
[85] *Jhering*, Kampf (1872) 53–54.
[86] *Jhering*, Kampf (1872) 53–54.
[87] *Jhering*, Kampf (1872) 66–69. The story is told in the well-known novella by *Heinrich von Kleist* (1777–1811) Michael Kohlhaas (Berlin 1810). It is based on real events occurring the 1530s in Brandenburg and Saxony. In German culture, the very name "Kohlhaas" has

forcement of private rights in one of his pithy and memorable phrases: "The first rule of law is: tolerate no injustice, the second: commit no injustice."[88] In other words, it is not enough to do no wrong oneself; it is even more important to fight against the wrongs committed by others.

At its core, Jhering's "Kampf" is a passionate argument for the rule of law – not just on paper, but in action. As Jhering pointed out, such a real rule of law is possible only if people fight for their rights. He concluded his tract by once again waxing poetic and by repeating the motto that adorned the title page: "The phrase 'By the sweat of your brow, you shall eat your food' is matched by another of equal truth: 'In fight you shall find your law.' At the moment when the law gives up its readiness to fight, it gives up itself."[89] In short: no fight, no rule of law.[90]

Jhering's "Litigiousness": Against "Moral Laxness." The reader could be forgiven for taking Jhering's call for vigorous pursuit of one's rights as an endorsement of unbridled, and perhaps excessive, litigiousness. Much in Jhering's discourse indeed creates that impression. If foregoing one's rights is "moral suicide"[91]; if "everyone is the guardian and executor of the law;"[92] and if, more dramatically, everyone is called upon and has the obligation "to smash the head of the hydra of arbitrariness and lawlessness where ever it dares to show itself,"[93] the immediate response to all violations of (private) law should be to file suit. Thus, Jhering's call to arms could be read as advocating a "zero tolerance" policy

come to stand for unyielding (and perhaps hopeless) resistance against injustice all the way to the (bitter) end.

[88] *Jhering*, Kampf (1872) 56.

[89] *Jhering* 1872, 100 ("Im Kampfe sollst Du Dein Recht finden.").

[90] Towards the end of his discourse, Jhering pushed his argument still further by exploring the implications of his position for the nation as a whole and in particular for its foreign affairs. He argued that a strong and healthy "feeling of justice" (which includes the resolve to enforce one's rights) was of utmost importance for the strength of the nation.

"The strength of a people is identical with the strength of its feeling of justice – caring for the national feeling of justice is caring for the health and strength of the state [...]

For a state that wants to be respected in its external relations [...] no good that it must guard and cultivate is more important than the national feeling of justice (das nationale Rechtsgefühl)." *Jhering*, Kampf (1872) 77, 75.

The implication was that those who fulfilled their duty to fight for right not only realized the law but at the same time strengthened the state – even as a player on the world stage. Jhering pointed to Switzerland as a positive example, and to China as a negative one, id. 74. A well-ordered legal system, Jhering claimed, gives the State more strength than "the highest increase of the military budget," id. 78. It is probably no accident that Jhering made these statements in the wake of the German victory over France in the Franco-Prussian war of 1870–1871 which Jhering greatly relished; see supra chapter I.4., notes 260–262 and text.

[91] *Jhering*, Kampf (1872) 28.

[92] *Jhering*, Kampf (1872) 54.

[93] *Jhering*, Kampf (1872) 57.

towards rights violations, or it could at least be used as cover for such an approach.[94] Yet, a closer reading of Kampf shows that matters are not so simple.

Regarding the extent of the moral obligation of rights enforcement (as well as in many other regards), Jhering sent potentially contradictory messages. On the one hand, he clearly did not advocate unrestrained litigiousness. He openly recognized the danger of "Processsucht" ("obsession with litigation") which can result, for example, from an exaggerated sense of property rights,[95] and he later complained that people had misunderstood his argument.[96] He clearly saw no obligation to sue the bona fide possessor who rejects one's property claim because he honestly considers himself the true owner.[97] On the other hand, however, Jhering postulated a moral duty to heed the call of one's "sense of justice" and to prove one's "character" by responding with vigorous legal action.[98] These positions can be difficult to reconcile because Jhering's various rationales for supporting the moral duty of rights enforcement can point in opposite directions. What if the bona fide possessor's rejection of my property claim outrages my feeling of justice? What if the thief steals a morsel of bread from my richly loaded table to feed his starving child so that my feeling of justice is not enraged? What if a bona fide claim leaves my feeling of justice cold but entails the risk of an avalanche of such claims and thus requires preventive action now? Jhering did not bother to tackle such questions.[99] He was keen to throw out a bundle of

[94] Wolf opined that Jhering "unwillingly supported the narrow-minded spirit of bourgeois cantankerousness (Rechthaberei) and antisocial egotism" and that he provided "dangerous justifications" that could be used to "camouflage one's petty motives." *Wolf*, Große Rechtsdenker (1963) 648. Wolf cites not support for these assertions; thus, they are no more than speculations. See also *Smith*, Four German Jurists II (1896) 301–302 ("the book impresses the reader as a *laus litium*, a pangyric upon quarrelsomeness," even though Jhering did not mean it that way). Jhering's near-contemporary Otto von Gierke (1841–1921) criticized Jhering by pointing out that sometimes, there may be a moral duty *not* to enforce one's rights, von *Gierke*, Deutsches Privatrecht vol. I (1895) 319 fn. 1.

[95] *Jhering*, Kampf (1872) 32.

[96] Jhering asserted that he had of course *not* advocated unbridled litigiousness; that reading "Kampf" in that manner was a misunderstanding; and that he bore no blame for the stupidity of his readers: "What good does objective clarity do if subjectively, there is darkness in the reader's head; if people dare to judge a work although they cannot read, who, when they have reached its end, don't know anymore what they have read at the beginning, and who blame the author of the work for falsities for which they should really blame their own sloppy reading and thinking?" *Jhering*, Zweck I (1884) 75 note; see also *Jhering*, Über die Enstehung des Rechtsgefühls (1884) 10; *Jhering*, Kampf (13th ed. 1897, Vorrede, written 1891) IX–X .

[97] Supra note 96 and text. The point is also emphasized by *Mecke*, Rudolf von Jherings "Struggle for Law" (2017) 43–44.

[98] *Jhering*, Kampf (1872) 43–51.

[99] Perhaps the most plausible reading is that Jhering's moral duty applied only to cases in which the offender's conduct was not just objectively unlawful but also subjectively unacceptable. When Jhering advocated a decisive legal response to injustice, he typically spoke of "bad intent," "arbitriness," "audacity" or "brazenness," ("schlechte Absicht," "Willkühr," "Dreistigkeit," "Keckheit"); *Jhering*, Kampf (1872) 31, 54, 57, 58, etc. This was not only in

appealing arguments but not interested in providing a coherent theory. What is clear, however, is that he saw taking legal action where appropriate as a matter of self-respect. Yielding to injustice because of cost, inconvenience or risk struck him as a sign of a lamentable lack of backbone.

Like so many things he wrote about, this position directly reflected Jhering's personal character and disposition. Perhaps because of his (quasi-)aristocratic background[100], Jhering had a strong sense of personal honor;[101] and perhaps because of his Frisian origins, he was feisty and at times even quarrelsome. In "Kampf," he shouted out his personal contempt for the "laxness of attitude" and the "politics of cowardice" ("Lauheit der Gesinnung," "Politik der Feigheit")[102] that he perceived in his environment. To be sure, Jhering could be blamed for occasional belligerence, but he did deserve credit for following his convictions. If he felt in the right, he did not shy away from conflict. He felt a moral obligation to stand by his beliefs, even at the cost of social or professional disadvantages. Thus for Jhering, "Kampf" was not just a tract on legal theory but also a personal credo.

The Weakness of the Legal Order: Against Softness and Materialism. "With that, I could conclude my lecture because my subject is exhausted," Jhering remarked at the end of the book's third part.[103] He could not, however, refrain from delving into an additional question "that is closely connected to the subject of my lecture": whether the current legal order was sufficiently geared towards protecting the feeling of justice.[104] This was indeed a very different matter because

line with his distinction between the bona fide possessor and the thief, it may also reflect the assumption that a "healthy" (as opposed to a distorted) sense of justice would be offended only by acts committed in bad faith. Three considerations support such a reading. One is that Jhering related the moral duty (of rights enforcement) vis-a-vis oneself to being injured not only in one's property rights but also (at least implicitly) in one's personhood; a good faith dispute would only pertain to the former, a bad faith act be an offense to the latter. The second consideration is that Jhering approvingly invoked the (classical) Roman law's distinction between (merely) objective and (also) subjective injustice; the former was sanctioned by mere liability for goods or damages, the latter by a variety of additional penalties; id. 83–85. Finally, such a reading is supported by Jhering's complaint in the closing pages of "Kampf" that the current legal order failed to pay sufficient attention to the sense of justice and thus to protect a person against insult in addition to injury – a point to which we will turn below.

[100] See supra chapter I.2., notes 57–58 and text.

[101] When the government awarded Jhering an honor he considered beneath his dignity (because people of, in his view, much lower rank also received it), he vowed to file a complaint, and if that bore no fruit, to resign from his post if need be. In a letter to a Viennese (woman) friend, he explained: "It is also a struggle for law that I have been fighting – not the law that is laid down in statutes, but for the law that everyone feels in his heart, the law of the personality that energetically refutes a lack of respect it has suffered." Letter to Auguste von Littrow-Bischoff "beginning of" 1877, Jhering in Briefen (1913) 319.

[102] *Jhering* , Kampf (1872) 41.

[103] *Jhering*, Kampf (1872) 79.

[104] *Jhering*, Kampf (1872) 80. "I hope," he said, "that you will permit me to claim your attention" for that question. His audience had no choice, of course, but it stands to reason

it pertained neither to the origin of law (in struggle) nor to moral duty of individuals (to fight for the law's realization) but rather to the objective state of affairs. Jhering felt very strongly that this state of affairs was badly wanting, and he needed to get that off his chest. While Jhering's discussion once again jumped from one point to another and sometimes went around in circles, he really had two major issues with modern private and procedural law; these issues were distinct but related.

One complaint was that modern law was far too soft on wrongdoers at the expense of right holders. For example, it tended to be lenient towards debtors to the detriment of creditors. Jhering saw this as a sad sign of decadence. "A vigorous era ensures, most of all, that creditors receive their due, even if the debtor perishes as a result."[105] In a similar vein, the law now so seriously curtailed the right to self-defense that it protected the attacker more than his victim. It required the victim to retreat rather than encouraging him to stand his ground. For Jhering this showed the "decay of the feeling for the personality, the unmanliness, and total degeneration and insensitivity of the plain, healthy feeling of justice." One felt "like being put into a society of castrates."[106]

Jhering's second, and more fundamental, gripe was that the modern legal order's standard was "the plain, desolate materialism: the merely financial interest."[107] The status quo was blind to the idealist side of law, i.e., to the fact that a violation of one's rights was "not only a matter of monetary value, but of satisfaction for the injured feeling of justice."[108] Jhering lamented that modern law was ready to compensate an injured party for its monetary loss but provided no remedy for the injury to personhood. It did not, for example, impose any additional sanctions if the wrongdoer had acted in bad faith; this virtually encouraged the reckless to try their luck at violating the law.[109] Jhering held up the contrary example of ancient Roman law that sanctioned bad faith denials of claims through additional penalties, deterring people from playing it fast and loose with other people's rights.[110]

---

that Jhering's subsequent critique of the current legal system probably met with hearty approval by the Viennese practitioners before whom he spoke.

[105] *Jhering*, Kampf (1872) 83; see also id., 94–95.

[106] *Jhering*, Kampf (1872) 95–96; see also id. 98–99.

[107] *Jhering*, Kampf (1872) 91.

[108] *Jhering*, Kampf (1872) 91.

[109] *Jhering*, Kampf (1872) 91.

[110] *Jhering*, Kampf (1872) 83–85. At least in part, Jhering's complaint about the current lack of respect for the feeling of justice reflected his own frustrating experience as a litigant to which he referred in the talk, though not in the printed version of "Kampf." Back in 1863 (when Jhering was still in Gießen), Jhering's maid had left her service without giving the requisite notice but still asked for her pay. When Jhering refused, she sued him and won; see *Hanewinkel and Linder*, "Ein Mann von kräftigem Rechtsgefühl" (2020). Jhering felt badly wronged by the court. The stenographic record of his talk shows that he told the story at some length, portraying himself as a victim of injustice: "Then I felt the sting of injustice; when one

The first part of Jhering's critique of the contemporary legal order expressed the social position and political inclinations of an upper middle class member at the time – which was a substantial part of the reason why it resonated with his audience. It was largely focused on the protection of property rights (rather than, e.g., labor or social rights), reflecting a mid- to late-nineteenth century version of "possessive individualism."[111] Yet, the author of "Kampf" was not just, and not even primarily, a representative of the contemporary *homo oeconomicus*.[112] As his second critique of the legal order showed, he was also, indeed most of all, an advocate of defending "personhood" ("Persönlichkeit"), i.e., the honor and dignity of the individual.[113] Of course, the kind of individual Jhering had foremost in mind was, again, the property owning member of the bourgeoisie[114] – but not only; as we will see in a moment, Jhering also considered others, like the Jew Shylock in Shakespeare's "The Merchant of Venice" (1600), as entitled to protection of their feeling of justice and their dignity. In "Kampf," Jhering never tired emphasizing that the ultimate touchstone of a legal order was its respect for personhood. At the height of the "Age of Capital,"[115] that lament reflected unease about the prevailing emphasis on wealth and financial power at the expense of more traditional, idealist, values.[116]

When the Legal Order Fails: Shylock's Pound of Flesh. Jhering's two complaints about the contemporary legal order – of insufficient protection of legal rights and insufficient attention to the feeling of justice and personal dignity – came together in his reaction to the case of Shakespeare's Shylock. Jhering thought that the Venetian court had cheated Shylock out of his right.[117] Unsurprisingly, this view has been highly controversial.[118] In order to form an opinion, however, one must understand exactly what Jhering did, and did not, argue.

---

is fully within one's right and the institutions of the state are such that one cannot enforce one's rights, not matter how one tries. And this is the charge I bring against the legal rules today, they are designed so that a man with a strong feeling of justice is basically forced today to commit an act of cowardice [...] and to abandon his good rights." Quoted after *Behrends* (ed.), Beiträge und Zeugnisse (1993) 69.

[111] *MacPherson*, The Political Theory of Possessive Individualism (1962).

[112] *Wieacker*, Rudolf von Jhering (1969) 26 ("Selbstverklärung der Vormacht und des Egoismus des besitzbürgerlichen homo oeconomicus").

[113] Jhering explored the rights following from personhood at much greater length and in much greater depth in a separate 200-page-essay, see *Jhering*, Rechtsschutz gegen injuriöse Rechtsverletzungen (1885); for a comment and interpretation, see *Fikentscher*, Methoden des Rechts III (1976) 178–180; for further discussion of Jhering's concept of Persönlichkeit, see *Pleister*, Persönlichkeit, Wille und Freiheit im Werke Jherings (1982) 31–46, 193–218.

[114] The hypotheticals Jhering collected in his "Jurisprudenz des täglichen Lebens," see supra chapter II.4., notes 439–432 and text, also reflected that world.

[115] *Hobsbawm*, The Age of Capital (1975).

[116] See *Fridell*, Kulturgeschiche der Neuzeit (1969/1927–31) 1293–1295.

[117] *Jhering*, Kampf (1872) 64 footnote.

[118] See *Kohler*, Shakespeare vor dem Forum der Jurisprudenz (1883) 3–6, 7–99 (esp. 83, 91–92). Jhering responded to Kohler's argument in the Preface (Vorrede) to a later edition of "Kampf," making fun of Kohler and refuting him resoundingly, *Jhering*, Kampf (13th ed. 1897, Vorrede, written 1891) XIV–XVII.

Jhering did not argue that the Venetian court should have enforced Shylock's contract with Antonio. In Jhering's view, the bargain was clearly null and void because of its immoral content. Jhering did argue, however, that since the court treated the deal as enforceable, it was wrong to make enforcement de facto impossible. Imposing the impossible condition that in cutting his pound of flesh, Shylock must not spill any blood (nor cut too much or too little) was a "miserable dogde, a pitiful trickster's wile" ("ein elender Winkelzug, ein kläglicher Rabulistenkniff")[119] It was bad enough that the court denied Shylock the protection of the law in a dishonest manner; it was worse that it also made a mockery of Shylock's feeling of justice and thus degraded him in a most despicable fashion.[120] It is not difficult to see that Jhering's interpretation was somewhat simplistic (after all, Shylock had been offered plenty of good reasons to forego the enforcement of his right), but in "Kampf" Jhering's purpose was rhetorical effect, not fine grained assessment.[121]

Jhering recognized that enforcement was denied "in the interest of humanity." Then, however, he asked his readers – and probably also himself – whether that meant that "injustice ceased to be injustice." The question was probably not purely rhetorical. Interestingly, Jhering left it open.[122]

Jhering also had a point in highlighting far-reaching and deeply troublesome implications: in disregarding Shylock's right, the court disregarded the law of Venice, "because his right and the law of Venice are one."[123] A legal order that lacked the resolve to enforce the rights it had recognized and that failed to adequately protect the litigants' feeling of justice against injury to his personhood was not worthy of respect.

Positivism and Idealism: Jhering's Dualism. As the foregoing discussion indicates, "Kampf" is shaped by a remarkable combination of positivism and idealism. On the one hand, the book describes the make-up of the existing legal order as a result of the struggle between opposing social forces asserting their interests, i.e., in quasi-Darwinian terms. In this context, Jhering forsook all the idealistic elements in vogue at the time: justice, liberty, personal autonomy, free will, etc. Instead, he took a purely positivist approach by providing an explanation based entirely on social and historical facts. The facts are what they are, and thus the

---

[119] *Jhering*, Kampf (1872) 65 note. Jhering pointed out that according to the ancient Roman law of the Twelve Tables (5th century A.D.), when the creditor was allowed to (physically) cut up the debtor, exactness was not required – a little more or less was declared acceptable; id.

[120] Jhering accused the court of treating Shylock "as a pariah of society, who vainly demands his right." It taught Shylock the lesson "that he is nothing but a medieval Jew who receives his right by being cheated out of it." ("daß er nichts ist als ein Jude des Mittelalters, dem man sein Recht gibt, indem man ihn darum betrügt"); *Jhering*, Kampf (1872) 65–66.

[121] For an entertaining but proper critique of Jhering's position, see *Pietscher*, Jurist und Dichter (1881).

[122] *Jhering*, Kampf (14 ed.1897, Vorwort, written 1891) XIII.

[123] *Jhering*, Kampf (1872) 64.

legal order is what it is; value questions are simply not raised. On the other hand, Jhering announced that persons have a moral duty – both vis-a-vis themselves and vis-a-vis society – to fight for the realization of law. This postulate is rooted largely (though not exclusively) in Kantian idealism.[124] And finally, Jhering demands that the legal order itself strictly enforce rights and, in particular, protect an individual's personhood. These demands are, again, essentially Kantian in spirit. In combining a positivist approach with idealist elements, "Kampf" shows the tension that characterized Jhering's thought after his "conversion" around 1860. Viewed from one perspective, law is the result of social competition and thus a "concept of power" ("Machtbegriff");[125] at the same time, "law is idealism" ("Recht ist Idealismus")[126] and its preservation is a moral duty.

In addition, there is the pervasive element of the feeling of justice. Rechtsgefühl appears to have both a positivist and an idealist dimension: in part, it is a social fact that the legal order must not disregard; in part it is a normative criterion that the legal order must aspire to vindicate. It seems that at this point, Jhering was still using the concept of Rechtsgefühl in a fairly indiscriminate fashion because he had not yet fully worked it out.[127]

2. A Sociological Theory of Law: "Der Zweck im Recht" (Volume One 1877/1884)

In the opening pages of "Der Kampf ums Recht" Jhering had identified two main elements shaping law: struggle and purpose. He had dealt with the former in "Kampf," leaving the latter for another day. That day arrived in 1877 when Jhering published the first volume of "Der Zweck im Recht" ("The Purpose in Law"[128]); the second, even heftier, volume would follow in 1883.

After "Geist des römischen Rechts," "Zweck" was Jhering's second *magnum opus* – the former was the fruit of his labor at mid-career, the latter the signature work of his old age. Despite fundamental differences in outlook and content, there are many parallels between these books: Jhering considered them the premier projects of his life; they were addressed not only to fellow jurists but also to an

---

[124] It does contain a positivist element, however, because Jhering's moral duty pertains to the enforcement of positive law, apparently *tout court*, i.e., without questioning its (moral) content.

[125] *Jhering*, Kampf (1872) 11.

[126] *Jhering*, Kampf (1872) 74.

[127] This was largely left for another day. Jhering focused on the feeling of justice again a dozen years later, i.e., *Jhering*, Über die Entstehung des Rechtsgefühls (1884), see infra 3.

[128] The English translation is entitled "Law as a Means to an End" (Isaac Husik transl., Boston 1913). Like the German title, it is far too narrow, see infra notes 176–177 and text, though it captures an essential, as well as the most famous, element of Jhering's theory of law, see infra notes 201–217 and text.

educated lay audience;[129] he struggled mightily with, but still lost control over, both; and he ultimately finished neither.

"Geist" and "Zweck" made their primary impression on different audiences. While "Geist" established Jhering's reputation (not entirely positive) mainly among his contemporaries and among scholars of Roman law, "Zweck" impressed future generations (often negatively[130]) and appealed to readers interested in legal theory. In the long run and on a global scale, "Zweck" became Jhering's most influential work. That is somewhat ironic because in several ways, it is also his worst.[131] Yet, it took an approach and launched ideas that helped to shape the twentieth century understanding of law like few other books – especially in the United States.[132]

"Zweck" can justly be called monumental – not only because of the sheer size of the two volumes (totaling more than 1200 pages) but also in terms of its ambition, breadth, and kaleidoscopic nature. If the brevity, fast-paced argument, and theatrical style of "Kampf" invited devouring it, the expanse, lengthy ruminations, and barely controlled complexity of "Zweck" have deterred all but the most determined readers. It is fair to assume that in the last hundred years, few people have read the book in its entirety, and everyone who has will hesitate to recommend it to others – even though reading "Zweck" selectively can be enormously rewarding.[133]

"Zweck" is marked by pervasive contradictions. It is fascinating and frustrating, deeply perceptive and highly simplistic, occasionally brilliant and often boring, right on target and wide off the mark – features to which we will return towards the end of this subchapter. As a result of these (and other) internal contradictions, of the book's daunting complexity, as well as of its strange organization, it is enormously difficult to come to grips with it. A full exploration of the work would require a full book in its own right, and this is not the occasion to write it.[134] This subchapter provides merely an overview, a discussion of its most important features, as well as a general assessment. Here, we will focus mainly on Volume One because that contains Jhering's mature theory or law and of the state; a closer look at Volume Two will be left to chapter VI because it is not a work of legal scholarship but rather part of Jhering's work beyond the law.

This subchapter begins by doing something that has rarely been done but that needs to be done if we want to understand the work: it tells the truth about what the book really is – which is quite different from what its title suggests, what most people think, and indeed what Jhering originally set out to write. We then focus

---

[129] *Jhering*, Geist I (1852) 4; Jhering, Zweck I (1884) X.

[130] Infra notes 370–376 and text.

[131] See infra notes 381–396 and text.

[132] Infra chapter VII.3.

[133] See infra notes 397–405 and text.

[134] For a succinct, but also very generous, overall interpretation of the work, see *Merkel*, Jhering (1893) 28–30.

on the (relatively small) part that deals with Jhering's theories of law and the state. To put these theories into a broader context, we will briefly relate them to four important contemporary ideas, i.e., Darwinism, utilitarianism, positivism, and Marxism. In conclusion, we will take a broader look at the work and explain why "Zweck" is a milestone of jurisprudence, a socio-political manifesto, a mess, and a treasure trove, all at the same time.

There were two editions of "Zweck" during Jhering's lifetime.[135] Recognizing serious problems with Volume One,[136] Jhering substantially reworked it for a second edition (1884). The revisions for the new edition of Volume Two (1886) were minor. The following discussion is based on the second, improved, edition.

The Truth about "Zweck:" How Norms Regulate Human Behavior. If a reader, who wants to get an idea of what to expect from the book, consults the two volumes' table of contents, he or she will be greatly puzzled. What on earth do chapters on "Reward" ("Der Lohn"), "Type of Profession" ("Der Erwerbszweig"), "Credit" ("Der Credit"), "Coercion" ("Der Zwang"), not to mention "Decency" ("Der Anstand") and "Courtesy" ("Die Höflichkeit") have to do with "purpose in law"? The answer is: anything ranging from very little to nothing. So, what is going on in this book?

To understand "Der Zweck im Recht" it is imperative to recognize that the book is not what it is often thought to be: it is neither mainly focused on "law" nor consistently about "purpose." Instead, it is essentially an – incomplete and rambling – treatise that explores how various norms regulate human conduct so that people can live together in society. Some of the norms are legal, most are not. This already indicates that there is a serious discrepancy between the book's title on the one hand, and the actual scope and object of the work on the other.

This discrepancy is the result of the work's evolution: it actually started out as project focused on "the purpose in law" but then developed into something much broader and quite different. Tracing this evolution shows why Jhering undertook the project (as well as its position and significance in his agenda writ large), how dramatically Jhering changed it while at work, and what "Zweck" ended up being. A reader who is not interested in grasping the work as a whole but wants to focus merely on Jhering's theory of law and state is invited to skip the next three sections (i.e., to proceed directly to p. 216).

From "Geist" to "Zweck": Abandoning "Will," Embracing "Interests." Jhering embarked on the project that was to become "Zweck" not because he really

---

[135] A third edition was edited by Jhering's son-in-law, Victor Ehrenberg, and published in 1898; leaving some stylistic changes aside, it was essentially identical to the second edition.

[136] "I have not been able to avoid the embarrassing confession that much in it is extraordinarily weak, some things are substantively wrong, exaggerated, others are complete failures in their form, exceedingly extensive, broad, sluggish." Letter to Windscheid, December 30, 1883; Jherings Briefe an Windscheid (1988) 50, 51. At one point, Jhering confessed outright that he failed to understand how he could have held some of his earlier beliefs; *Jhering*, Zweck I (1884) 77 note.

wanted to but because he felt he had no choice.[137] He thought that he must come to grips with the role and function of "purpose" in law if he wanted to fulfill his scholarly agenda. To understand why – and thus to grasp the function of "Zweck" in Jhering's *oeuvre* – we have to go back to "Geist des römischen Rechts."

We must remember that Jhering's ambition in "Geist" was not only to explore the definitive character of Roman law (its "spirit") in order to build a jurisprudence that could go "beyond" it; he also pursued a "general theory of the nature of law."[138] Originally considered a goal beyond "Geist" itself, that ambition gradually moved to center stage in the book as the work became ever more concerned with legal theory. As we have seen, in its first two volumes, Jhering developed a methodology and some theoretical foundations for a new, "higher," jurisprudence.[139] Yet, after publishing the second volume, he experienced his "conversion." He not only mocked and attacked his own former belief in "juristic construction," he also focused more strongly than before on practical concerns (the needs of "life"), the "feeling of justice," and, in the long run most importantly, the instrumental function of law.[140] By the time he was working on the third volume of "Geist" (mainly in the early 1860s), he no longer considered the methodological convictions expressed in the first two volumes solid enough to support a new general theory of law. As a result, he had a real problem on his hands: how could he complete "Geist," i.e., on what basis could he develop a new jurisprudence?

At the tail end of Volume Three (1865), Jhering took the bull by the horns. He reacted to the problem in two ways. First, he tore down the old edifice: he incorporated the attack on the logical approach first launched in his "Anonymous Letters" into the book.[141] Thus he again blasted the "cultus of logic,"[142] the operation with abstract concepts,[143] and the "blue smoke and mirrors of the juristic dialectic" ("das Blendwerk der juritischen Dialectic").[144] Second, he went back to square one: in the next section, he set out to develop a (new) "General Theory of Law" – from scratch.[145] Looking at the "The Concept of Law," he broadly asked: "What is the law?"[146] The answer, Jhering emphasized, was to look for the core of law, its essence (i.e., not just its form).[147]

At the time, the dominant,[148] largely Hegelian,[149] idea was that "the substance of the [private] law, both in the objective and the subjective sense" was founded

---

[137] *Jhering*, Zweck I (1884) VII.
[138] *Jhering*, Geist I (1852) 10 ("allgemeine Naturlehre des Rechts").
[139] Supra chapter II.1. and 2.
[140] Supra chapter III.3.
[141] This is the famous § 59 of the book, *Jhering*, Geist III (1865) 293–306.
[142] *Jhering*, Geist III (1865) 302.
[143] *Jhering*, Geist III (1865) 302–303.
[144] *Jhering*, Geist III (1865) 299.
[145] *Jhering*, Geist III (1865) 307–327 (§ 60).
[146] *Jhering*, Geist III (1865) 307.
[147] *Jhering*, Geist III (1865) 308.
[148] See *Jhering*, Geist III (1865) 310 footnote (citing Arnds, Sintenis, Windscheid, and most

on individual "will."[150] This approach saw the "final objective of all law in the [realization of the] will" (considering, e.g., an *animus possidendi* a crucial element of possession). It was one of Jhering's overstatements, but still caricatured the status quo quite aptly, when he wrote that the prevailing approach turned "all of private law into nothing but an arena for the will."[151] Even though one could find considerable support for the will-theory in the Roman jurists' frequent emphasis on *animus* and *voluntas*, Jhering now considered that approach completely wrongheaded – not only because of its hopelessly abstract nature, but also because it produced unacceptable consequences.[152] According to it, people lacking the capacity to have a will, like the incurably insane, should not be able to have any rights – but of course they did, for example, to hold property. Notably, these rights did nothing for the exercise of their will, but they did allow them to enjoy certain benefits. Jhering thus concluded that the true essence of subjective rights lies in the enjoyment (Genuß) they grant: rights exist not to realize the "legal will" but to serve the concrete interests, needs, and purposes of human interaction.[153] Here, Jhering coined one of his most memorable phrases: "rights are legally protected interests."[154]

These interests were not limited to the economic realm; "above that, there are higher goods of an ethical nature: personhood, liberty, honor, family relations."[155] In the last consequence, "every right in private law exists in order to grant a person some advantage, to satisfy his needs, to promote his interests and purposes."[156] In short, at its core, law was not about the private will of the indi-

---

of all, Puchta).

[149] *Hegel*, Grundlinien der Philosophie des Rechts (1821) 25–36 (sec. 4–15, in general); 54–72 (sec. 41–64, property rights); 79–87 (sec. 71–82, contracts). For Hegel, the centrality of (individual) "will" for the concept of law was intimately connected with the idea of law as the realm of "liberty," see, e.g., id. 44 (sec. 29). In this regard, Jhering's conception of law as developed in "Zweck" was the veritable opposite of Hegel's, see infra note 194–206 and text.

[150] See *Kuntze*, Der Wendepunkt der Rechtswissenschaft (1856) 32 fn. 2 ("The law is generally nothing more and nothing less than the organized will of the organic (historically given) associations, just like language is organized thought, art organized (aesthetic) feeling, religion organized faith.")

[151] *Jhering*, Geist III (1865) 310.

[152] *Jhering*, Geist III (1865) 310–316. Jhering explained his objection to an adherent of the will-theory, i.e., his close friend Benhard Windscheid: "The creation and the design of rights was not shaped by the idea of the power of the will but by the economic and ethical interest; *after* they had been created, the concept of will may well dress them in juristic garb, but it was not a product of the principle." Letter to Windscheid of April 18, 1865, Jhering in Briefen (1913) 178.

[153] *Jhering*, Geist III (1865) 316.

[154] *Jhering*, Geist III (1865) 317 ("Rechte sind rechtlich geschützte Interessen."). Jhering apparently did not notice the tautological element in his definition, i.e., that "rights" are what is "legally protected."

[155] *Jhering*, Geist III (1865) 317.

[156] *Jhering*, Geist III (1865) 317. Note that with regard to the *form* of the law, as well as to the reason for its force, Jhering found the Hegelian notion of "will" quite appropriate. The

vidual (nor about liberty or justice) but about the public power protecting interests and pursuing purposes.[157]

This was of course a view radically different from the pre-"conversion" Jhering's position that rights were personal entitlements: personal entitlements are held by the individual as a free member of society (and actor in the economy) while legally protected interests are essentially grants by the state.

It is important to note that for Jhering, this turn to a teleological view of law was not an abandonment of the Roman heritage – quite the contrary. True, the will theory derived by modern scholars from the Roman sources (or from Hegelian philosophy) had to go. Yet, as Jhering had emphasized as early as in the first volume of "Geist," at bottom the Romans themselves had "looked at everything from the perspective of purposefulness"[158] – and shaped their law accordingly. From Jhering's point of view, understanding law (*tout court*) as a creature, and instrument for the pursuit, of purposes was a veritable revival of the Roman tradition.

One can conceive of Jhering's turn to "interests" and "purposes" as a re-conceptualization of the "will:" it was no longer considered the constitutive core of (private) rights in the abstract but now aimed at realizing their objective, i.e., the enjoyment of their concrete benefits. Yet, precisely how "interests" and "purposes" related to each other, and what exact roles they played in the law was still a puzzle to Jhering. That puzzle, he decided, needed to be solved before he could proceed with "Geist." As he eventually explained to his readers on the very first page of "Zweck," "purpose in law" was "the Sphinx which blocked my way [and] whose riddle I had to solve if I wanted to regain my peace as a scholar."[159]

Jhering also decided that the problem could not be properly handled in another chapter or two of "Geist" itself; instead, it required a book in its own right.[160]

---

point of law, Jhering explained, was its "realization" ("Verwirklichung"), i.e., its application and enforcement; that required (state) power, and the instrument of that power was the will. Without that will (of the state) norms would just be "thoughts, ideas, views, like many others, but not legal rules." That, however, said nothing about the essence of the law's substance. *Jhering*, Geist III (1865) 308–309.

[157] In the respective chapter (§ 60) of Volume Three of "Geist," Jhering's turn to "purpose" appeared like a new discovery – but it was not. More than a decade earlier, in Volume One, Jhering had already discussed it at considerable length; *Jhering*, Geist I (1852) 297–302. This tied into his broader theoretical discourse of the first volume of "Geist." Its chapter on the "Physiological View of the Organism of Law" opened with the (essentially tautological) statement: "The purpose of the organs lies in their functions." Thus a proper understanding of the law's "anatomy" (i.e., systematic organization) required an understanding of its functional side, id. Geist I (1852) 39. At the time, however, these considerations had not yet taken center stage. Thirteen years later, in volume three, Jhering finally put a functional approach at the core of his agenda.

[158] *Jhering*, Geist I (1852) 295. According to Jhering, that was even true for Roman religion: the gods were "nothing but personified purposes." Id. 296.

[159] *Jhering*, Zweck I (1884) V–VI.

[160] *Jhering*, Zweck I (1884) V–VI.

Jhering thus took a time-out from Volume Three of "Geist" and began to write a monograph on "Der Zweck im Recht." After its completion, he planned to return to Geist and write what remained to be written. Thus, turning to "Zweck" did not signal the abandonment of "Geist" at all: the former was planned as a necessary building block for the latter.[161]

Jhering could (and should) have anticipated that "Zweck" would take on a life of its own. After all, the professed goal of the book was to uncover nothing less than the law's "overall context."[162] In other words, "Zweck" was originally meant to develop a general view of law based on the concept of purpose. That was clear enough, but then the project became a runaway train.

Expansion – and Failure to Complete: The "Mighty Torso." Jhering was aware of the organizational challenge presented by the project and thus carefully planned the flow of his discourse from general premises to concrete illustrations and final conclusions.[163] Unfortunately, as in "Geist," he did not stick to his original plan. As he candidly admitted in the respective prefaces, he repeatedly changed the book's design while writing it, especially by adding more and more material. As a result, the book's carefully planned original structure fell apart. It is worth observing that process because it illustrates how Jhering, once again, chose to follow his ideas as they arose to wherever they took him – with the result that he increasingly lost control over the project.

The problem manifested itself almost immediately. As Jhering was exploring the function of purpose in law, it occurred to him that he first needed to clarify what "purpose" really is and means in general. He therefore decided to devote the entire first volume to that endeavor.[164] Yet, while Volume One was thus originally meant as a kind of preface to the real project, it soon exploded in scope and size. Eventually, the first volume explored some human motivations for obeying certain norms – in the context of society and economy as well as in the context of law and the state.

In the meantime, however, Jhering had decided that he could not limit the discussion of purpose to law but must also include non-legal norms. Thus, Volume Two went beyond law and focused on what Jhering eventually called "Das Sittliche," which turned out to encompass both ethics and custom.[165] As a result, "Zweck" was now taking a turn that a reader looking for "purpose in law" had no reason to anticipate – because Jhering had not anticipated it himself. Jhering was completely aware of that and indeed somewhat apologetic.[166] After several exten-

---

[161] *Jhering*, Zweck I (1884) V–VI.

[162] *Jhering*, Zweck I (1884) X. Jhering's term "Gesammtzusammenhang" literally means "overall coherence," but since Jhering's ambition was to show how the law relates to its environment (i.e., to look it from an external perspective), "overall context" is a more appropriate translation.

[163] *Jhering*, Zweck I (1884) X–XI; *Jhering*, Zweck II (1886) XIX–XX.

[164] *Jhering*, Zweck I (1884) VI–VII.

[165] See infra chapter VI.1.

[166] "Rarely will a writer have miscalculated regarding the continuation of a work he has

sive discussions of various forms of social custom (especially "decency" and "courtesy"), Volume Two came to a sudden halt, and so did "Zweck" as a whole – far, far away from law, and essentially mid-course. Jhering intended to complete the book and thus kept working on a third volume but it was never finished.[167] After years of toiling like a "galley slave,"[168] he was nowhere near the completion of the work.

Adopting Franz Wieacker's metaphor, it has become common to call "Zweck" a "mighty torso."[169] That is fitting in the sense that it captures the incompleteness of the work. Beyond that, however, the metaphor may be too generous. In sculpturing, a torso is a statue with the body fully worked out; just the head and extremities are missing. In "Zweck," however, even the body was not fully worked out because Jhering had neither reached a coherent understanding of "purpose" (in law or otherwise) nor completed his discussion of (legal and other) norms.

"Zweck" Reconceived: "Das teleologische System der sittlichen Weltordnung." Then what does the final product of Jhering's labors really amount to? There is no easy answer to that question because the book ended up as a compilation of many diverse elements that are not fully integrated into a whole. We thus need to look at what the book ended up doing and covering. In substance, it consists of

---

begun as badly as I have with regard to the present volume," he admitted in the Preface to Volume Two with admirable candor. "Not only does it not bring the work to its conclusion, as I had planned and promised to the reader, its content is also completely different from what I had intended." *Jhering*, Zweck II (1886) IX.

[167] The planned third volume of "Zweck" never materialized; some fragments can be found in the collection of Jhering's manuscripts in the Niedersächsische Staats- und Universitätsbibliothek in Göttingen, COD MS Jhering 6:4, on Die Pflicht (Duty). In a sense, however, Jhering did eventually execute his plan to show that purpose (rather than will) was the foundation of (private) law, albeit only in a separate, narrow but prominent, context. In his treatise "Der Besitzwille" (1889), he deconstructed Savigny's will-based concept of possession and replaced it with a purpose-based approach. Thus, functionally, "Besitzwille" was something like a – limited and much belated – third volume of "Zweck." In fact, this was in accordance with Jhering's original plan to use the law of possession as a major example with "Zweck;" *Jhering*, Der Besitzwille (1889) X–XI. Thus, "Geist" led to, and was supplemented by, "Zweck" which in turn led to, and was supplemented by, "Besitzwille."

[168] Letter to Windscheid of December 30, 1883, Jherings Briefe an Windscheid (1988) 50, at 51; in a similar vein, letter to Auguste von Littrow-Bischoff of May 28, 1876, Jhering in Briefen (1913) 316; letter to Bülow of December 24, 1880, Jhering in Briefen (1913) 361–362. His lament is reminiscent of his remark that "Geist" had become his "Quälgeist" (literally: tormenting spirit), supra chapter II.1., note 19 and text.

[169] *Wieacker*, Privatrechtsgeschichte (1967) 452 ("machtvoller Torso"); *Wieacker*, Gründer und Bewahrer (1959) 206 ("monumentaler Werktorso"); *Wieacker*, Rudolf von Jhering (1969) 35 ("riesiger Torso"); see also *Kunze*, Rudolf von Jhering (1995) 137. The term was not, however, Wieacker's invention; it was used already by *Mitteis*, Jhering (1905) 685, as well as by *Stintzing and Landsberg*, Geschichte der deutschen Rechtswissenschaft III.2. (1910) 790, i.e., almost half a century earlier. *Behrends*, Jhering heute! (2023) 187, 231, also used the term for "Geist."

four main parts which are loosely connected. They do not cleanly match the division into its various chapters, and their rapidly increasing length is testimony to Jhering's failure to control the proliferation of the material: the first three parts are contained in Volume One; the fourth fills the entire Volume Two; further parts were planned but not completed.

The first part (chapters I–VI) is a general discourse on "purpose" as *the* driving force of human (and in part animal) behavior, both individually and in the social context. This part is something like a (biological-psychological) prolegomenon to the whole book. It claims that human nature is driven by self-interest, and that that drive is controlled (with a view to life in society) by four main, quasi-mechanical, forces.[170] Two operate on the "egoistical" level: "reward" ("Lohn") and "coercion" ("Zwang"); the other two work on the "ethical" level: the "sense of duty" ("Pflichtgefühl") and "love" ("Liebe").[171] This division provided the grand organizing scheme for the rest of the book as Jhering set out to show how these four forces function. We will return to this quadriga when we explore Jhering's explanation of how law secures "the conditions of life in society."[172]

The book's second and third parts explored the two "egoistical" motivations, respectively. Jhering first turned to "reward;" it mainly operates in the realm of what Jhering called "Verkehr" (literally "traffic" or "intercourse") by which he essentially meant commerce.[173] Jhering then explored the other egoistical force, i.e., "coercion." Only now do we finally enter the domain of law (and of the state). Thus, in chapter VIII, Jhering's leading theme is the use of law as the instrument of coercion necessary to regulate life in society.[174] As a result, this part includes Jhering's theory of law as well as his view of the state, and we shall consider it in more detail below.

Finally, the book's fourth part turns to what Jhering calls "Das Sittliche" which fills all of Volume Two. It essentially presents a socio-psychological study of non-legal norms; as mentioned, we shall explore it chapter VI.

As this overview shows, despite its title, most of "Zweck" is not about "Recht."[175] Only its third part, constituting one out of nine chapters and filling

---

[170] Jhering uses the mechanical term "Triebfedern." In the titles to chapters VII and VIII, he envisages them as quasi-mechanical forces, calling them "levers" ("Hebel") of the "social movement" ("der socialen Bewegung"); he also speaks of "social mechanism" ("sociale Mechanik"); *Jhering*, Zweck I (1884) XIX.

[171] *Jhering*, Zweck I (1884) 60–61.

[172] Infra notes 231–242 and text.

[173] Verkehr "is the organization [...] of the satisfaction of human needs;" *Jhering*, Geist I (1884) 97; very similar id., 99. As usual, Jhering provides various definitions without worrying about their compatibility; see, e.g., id. (Verkehr "is the perfected system of egoism, nothing else"); see also id. 226–230.

[174] See infra notes 194–205 and text.

[175] At least not in the sense of norms created and sanctioned by the state which were the only ones Jhering was willing to accept as law, see infra notes 201–204 and text.

around 340 out of about 1260 pages, contains something like a jurisprudential discourse. In other words, about three quarters of the book have almost nothing to do with law proper.

At the end of the day, the project had developed from the planned study of the "Zweck im Recht" into a work that Jhering himself later termed "das teleologische System der sittlichen Weltordnung."[176] It is tempting to translate that fictitious title as "The Teleological System of the Global Order of Ethics." That, however, would be misleading because Jhering's approach was considerably broader in two regards. First, as was common in German idealist philosophy, "sittlich" comprised all normative precepts that govern human behavior (as opposed to the laws governing the natural world). This was true, for example, in Kant's "Metaphysik der Sitten" (1797) which was of course familiar to Jhering, and which, like "Zweck" encompassed both ethics and law. Second, Jhering went beyond the philosophical concept of "sittlich" (ethical) and added the sociological concept of "Sitte," or (social) custom (mainly in Volume Two). Thus Jhering's retroactively proposed title indicated what "Zweck" had actually become: a study of the origin, function, and effect of all rules governing human behavior in society, i.e., of law, ethics, and custom – a "panorama of the world of norms."[177] Needless to say, that was a tall order. Thus it was no wonder that Jhering ultimately despaired when he, as Franz Wieacker put it, "faced the frightening vastness of the spaces that opened up before the aging and tired [scholar]."[178] In contrast to Jhering, we will make no attempt to explore these spaces here.

Yet, even though vastly outgrown by the eventual project, the original title, "Der Zweck im Recht," does retain considerable significance: after all, it is only the relatively small part about "Recht" that accounts for the work's fame and influence. In fact, the remaining three quarters of the book have by and large been forgotten. For the remainder of this subchapter, we will thus focus on Jhering's theory of law and his view of the state.

Understanding Jhering's mature theory of law is important because many of its elements had a strong influence on twentieth century legal thought (and beyond). Unfortunately, it is also not free from difficulty because in "Zweck," Jhering did not present a theory of law in any coherent form or fashion. Instead, he expressed various views on law in a highly disjointed and piecemeal manner. There is a reason for that: at bottom, Jhering's approach was not jurisprudential but psychological. As a result of the book's overall ambition to explain the motivations and goals underlying the norms governing human conduct in general, its chapter on law sought to explain the motivations and goals pertaining to legal norms in particular. Thus, the title of the respective chapter (VIII) was neither

---

[176] *Jhering*, Der Besitzwille (1889) X.

[177] *Rückert*, Der Geist des Rechts (2004) 125 ("Panorama der normativen Welt").

[178] *Wieacker*, Rudolf von Jhering (1969) 11 ("Unermeßlichkeit der Räume, die sich erschreckend vor dem Altersmüden auftaten").

"Law" nor "Jurisprudence" but "Coercion" ("Der Zwang").[179] Summarizing Jhering's theory of law requires pulling the relevant bits and pieces out of his discourse on "coercion" and then integrating them as best one can.[180] The result is neither fully consistent nor entirely coherent. After exploring the role of "purpose" undergirding Jhering's whole approach, we will look at five dimensions of Jhering's theory of law before considering his overarching view of the state.

A Theory of Law[181] *– Prelude: The Meaning and Role of "Purpose."* In approaching Jhering's theory of law, a threshold question is the meaning and role of "purpose." Again, it is easy to be confused because for the most part, "purpose" did not play the role Jhering so loudly proclaimed. To clarify the matter, we must once more disentangle strands of thought not clearly distinguished by Jhering himself. Looking at his discourse more closely, we can discern three perspectives on "purpose."

First, for Jhering, law was about "purpose" in the general sense that all human activity is driven by it. In an admittedly amateurish fashion,[182] Jhering asserted that while things in inanimate nature happen as a result of "causes," in animate nature (animals and humans), they happen because a creature's will is activated by a "purpose." Note that Jhering did not just claim that it makes more (heuristic) sense to look at human action from the perspective of "purpose" rather than "cause," but that the purpose-driven nature of human action is a "law" ("Zweckgesetz"[183]); there is "no will, or in the same vein, no action without purpose."[184] In fact, Jhering claimed, "to act and to act with a purpose is the same thing."[185] Although Jhering did not spell this out, it follows that law as a form of human

---

[179] In fact, since Jhering considered law merely the mechanism of "coercion," its treatment was, strictly speaking, incidental.

[180] Jhering's study of "coercion" as such is amateurish and of little interest today. It does, however, contain a smattering of interesting insights. For example, Jhering points out that once a power employs law to proclaim its commands, it tends to become bound by law itself. Thus, law tends to develop "from the Cinderella in the house of power to its governor" (Jhering use the Latin term Majordomus); *Jhering*, Zweck I (1884) 353.

[181] For a useful summary in English, see *Stone*, The Province and Function of Law (1946) 303–311. An admirably coherent rendition of Jhering's theory of law was presented in a widely, and unjustly, overlooked article by Iredell Jenkins more than half a century ago. The article, which evinces great analytical and synthetic power, should be read by everyone with a deeper interest in Jhering's legal theory. It has to be taken with a grain of salt, however. While Jenkins is far from blind to the vast problems in Jhering's writing and argumentation, he makes better sense of Jhering's ideas than Jhering himself; *Jenkins*, Rudolf von Jhering (1960). A helpful summary in German is provided by *Nörr*, Eher Hegel als Kant (1990) 37–42.

[182] Jhering, Zweck I (1884) IX–X.

[183] For an extensive and trenchant critique of Jhering's simplistic and confused construction of "purpose," see *Wieacker*, Jhering und der Darwinismus (1973) 77–83.

[184] *Jhering*, Zweck I (1884) 5. According to Jhering, this is true even if a person acts just habitually, i.e., without consciousness of a purpose, or under duress, id. 16–18, 20–21.

[185] *Jhering*, Zweck I (1884) 14.

action was invariably purpose-driven as well. In that – very general – sense, "purpose" was always "in law."[186] Of course, Jhering's "law of purpose" was no more than an extremely broad and entirely theoretical postulate but it tacitly underlay all that followed, including Jhering's discourse on law.[187]

Second, Jhering's take on "purpose" specifically for law was his claim that purpose is the origin of law. Jhering called this "the fundamental idea of the work"[188] and famously expressed it as its motto on the title page of Volume One: "Purpose is the Creator of All Law" ("Der Zweck ist der Schöpfer des ganzen Rechts").[189] As a result, the reader has every right to expect a demonstration of how law has been shaped to serve certain social, economic, political or other needs throughout history. Yet, such a demonstration is largely absent from the book.[190] To the extent Jhering sought to show the law's origin from purpose at all, he did so merely in a very general fashion – by alleging that law emerged to replace domination by violence with government by rules.[191]

This leads us to the third – and de facto dominant – perspective: for the most part, Jhering discussed how law *serves* certain purposes. In other words, his main focus was not on the law's origin but on its end.[192] Jhering went to great lengths to explain how law is employed as a mechanism in pursuit of certain goals, such as the functioning of the market (mainly through private law), the maintenance of social order (mainly through criminal law) or the operation of the state apparatus

---

[186] Thus, even in teaching law, Jhering now proclaimed it as the only relevant perspective; *Jhering*, Zweck I (1884) 360.

[187] Jhering distinguished between "organized" and "unorganized" purposes. He focused on the former because they pertained to life in society and the function of the state; *Jhering*, Zweck I (1884) 40–42. As he acknowledged, these ideas were heavily influenced by the work of (natural philosopher) Friedrich Adolf Trendelenburg (1802–1872), especially his "Logische Untersuchungen" (3d ed. Leipzig 1870); *Jhering*, Zweck I (1884) VII. For a discussion of Trendelenburg's influence on Jhering, see *Mecke,* Jhering's Rechtsdenken im Kontext der zeitgenössischen Natur- und Sozialwissenschaften (2023) 290–295

[188] *Jhering*, Zweck I (1884) VIII.

[189] As Larenz pointed out, "purpose" itself obviously cannot create law, only human actors can; *Larenz*, Methodenlehre der Rechtswissenschaft (1983) 46. Jhering of course meant that human actors always create law because of a purpose, rather than because of transcendental norms, first principles, or logical considerations.

[190] In fact, to the extent that "Zweck" is concerned with the historical origin of law at all, it focuses on force, not purpose; see infra notes 194–205 and text. At one point, Jhering offered something like an excuse for that lack of historical work: while all law was created by purpose, most this had occurred so long ago "that mankind has lost the memory of it." *Jhering*, Zweck I (1884) 442.

[191] Infra notes 194–200 and text.

[192] Note that he later termed "Zweck" "a teleological system," supra note 176 and text. In a similar vein, two of Jhering's English-speaking commentators translated Zweck as "telos", *MacDonnell*, Rudolf von Jhering (1914) 594; *Smith*, Four German Jurists II (1896) 290.

(mainly through the constitution and administrative rules). The English translation (of the first volume) captured that instrumental approach when it rendered the book's title as "Law as a Means to an End."[193] In a similar vein, the German title should really have been "Der Zweck des Rechts" ("The Purpose of Law").

Thus, Jhering's motto for, and Preface to, Volume One of "Zweck" are, once again, somewhat misleading by creating false expectations: the book is not about purpose as "the creator," but as the function of all law. To make matters worse, even a reader specifically interested in the purpose *of* law will often be disappointed. Much of Jhering's discussion has precious little do to with that notion – except as a background assumption.

A Theory of Law I: "The Organization of Coercion." In exploring Jhering's theory of law, we first need to look at his ideas about the law's origin. In and of themselves, these ideas are not all that interesting because they are neither very original nor particularly sophisticated. Still, they need to be clearly understood because they decisively shaped his instrumental conception of law.

Jhering explained the emergence of law not as an emanation from specific purposes but as a substitute for "Gewalt." That German term can mean "force" as well as "violence," and Jhering used it in both senses (without clearly distinguishing them). Sometimes, he talked about early (pre-law) societies as riddled with violence (and cruelty); sometimes, he talked about the force used by the strong to dominate the weak. According to Jhering, the force (and even the violence) prevailing in these earlier times was not per se an evil but rather an important means to teach human beings obedience to authority as a precondition for eventually living under law.[194] According to Jhering, at some point, the strong recognized that (more) raw force was less advantageous than order. Seeking to end violence and to establish peace for their own benefit, they began to establish rules that would later also bind the rulers themselves; these rules are the law.[195] Thus law did not originate in any kind of ethical considerations but was simply a

---

[193] *Rudolf von Jhering*, Law as a Means to an End (Isaac Husik transl., Modern Philosophy Series vol. 5, Boston 1913).

[194] Jhering once again indulged in tough talk: "The despots and inhumane [rulers] who chastised the peoples with iron and scorpios contributed as much to the education of mankind for law as the wise legislators who later erected the tables of law; the former had to precede so that the latter could follow. This is the mission of even the wildest, rawest, most inhumane force in the earliest periods of mankind – to get the will used to submitting to, and recognizing, a superior one above it." *Jhering*, Zweck I (1884) 254. Jhering also warned not to judge the cruelty of these earlier times according to our modern sensibilities, pointing out that the ancients considered compassion and mercy forms of despicable weakness; id. 255–256.

[195] *Jhering*, Zweck I (1884) 245–246 (Origin "of the law from force by virtue of self-restraint;" "Entstehungsweise des Rechts aus der Gewalt auf dem Wege der Selbstbeschränkung"); see also id. 378.

product of (the rulers') "egoism."[196] Ethical considerations appeared only later[197] – a point we need to discuss in greater detail below.[198]

When the state eventually arose, it began to exercise the coercion necessary to ensure peace and order. The mechanism it used for that purpose was the law. "The sphere of coercion is identical with that of law and the state."[199] Thus law is the "organization of coercion" ("die Organisation des Zwanges") by the public power.[200]

Since (legitimate) coercion is a monopoly of the state, law is limited to the norms enforceable by the state.[201] Here, Jhering's – formal – conception of law is highly similar to, though not quite identical with, John Austin's (1790–1859) somewhat earlier definition of law as a command of the sovereign.[202] For Austin, for norms to count as law, it was crucial that they were *created* by the state; for Jhering, that they were *enforced* by it. The consequences, however, were by and large the same. Like Austin, Jhering did not recognize non-state norms as law proper (which excluded Gewohnheitsrecht in the sense of customary law obeyed voluntarily[203]). Also like Austin, Jhering found it difficult to recognize international norms as full-fledged law.[204]

---

[196] *Jhering*, Zweck I (1884) 246–249. Jhering had discussed "egoism" ("Selbstsucht") already in volume one of "Geist," i.e., 25 years before he now elaborated on it in "Zweck;" *Jhering*, Geist I (1852) 298–300. Especially in later years, he considered it the most powerful driver of human activity, not only in commerce but also in law. Perhaps he had picked up the idea from Edward Gibbon, whose famous XXXIVth chapter (on Roman law) he had read; there, Gibbon stated that the "active, insatiate principle of self-love can alone supply the arts of life and the wager of industry;" *Gibbon*, The Decline and Fall of the Roman Empire vol. II, 241 (New York 1845, orig. 1781).

[197] "The beginning lies in naked egoism which yields to ethical ideas and an ethical mentality only over time." ("Der Beginn ist der nackte Egoismus, der erst im Laufe der Zeit der sittlichen Idee und der sittlichen Gesinnung Platz macht."); *Jhering*, Zweck I (1884) 246.

[198] Infra 3.

[199] *Jhering*, Zweck I (1884) 85.

[200] *Jhering*, Zweck I (1884) 291. On another occasion, Jhering defined law as "the epitome of the coercive norms prevailing in the state" ("der Inbegriff der in einem Staat geltenden Zwangsnormen"), id. 320. Jhering distinguished different types of coercion, in particular its use to prevent certain acts ("propulsiv") from its deployment to compel them ("compulsiv").

[201] *Jhering*, Zweck I (1884) 318–323. There is a tension between the notion of law that had animated "Geist," i.e., as a (at least in part) universal phenomenon exemplified by Roman law on the one hand, and the conception now announced in "Zweck" as a state-centered set of coercive rules on the other. Strictly speaking, these views were not incompatible because the former pertained to scope, the latter to enforcement: there can be universally valid concepts and rules which can, however, only be enforced by individual states. Still, the perspective was different, and the change perhaps reflected the change that was occurring in practice. When "Geist" was written, i.e. mainly in the 1840s and 1850s, German private law was still dominated by the universalist notion of Roman law as a *ius commune*. When "Zweck" was written, i.e., in the 1870s and 1880s, massive codification efforts were underway in the wake of German unification (1871), eventually casting most of German law into the form of national legislation.

[202] *Austin*, The Province of Jurisprudence Determined (1861) 1–2 (Lecture I).

[203] *Jhering*, Zweck I (1884) 321–323.

While Jhering's rendition of the origin, and his formal definition, of law were fairly unremarkable, their implications were anything but. As a substitute for coercion by pure force, law remained, in a sense, subsidiary to it. This is especially true since its efficacy depended on the continued availability of force. "If need be, force can exist without law [...]. By contrast, law without force is an empty name devoid of all reality, because only the force that realizes the norms of law makes law what it is and should be."[205] Thus, law was ultimately the "politics of force" ("Politik der Gewalt").[206] The law's secondary status vis-a-vis force becomes strikingly clear when we take a closer look at its function.

A Theory of Law II: "Merely a Means to an End." Just as unrestrained force was the instrument used to rule earlier societies, so law as the "organization of force" is the mechanism used to rule modern ones organized as states. Thus law is – in Jhering's most famous phrase – "a means to an end" ("Mittel zum Zweck").[207] That conception has far-reaching implications.

If we take the phrase as commonly stated, these implications are interesting, even eye-opening, but not necessarily dramatic.[208] If law is a "means to an end," we need to think about its impact and usefulness, i.e., consider it from a pragmatic and utilitarian point of view; as we shall see, future generations have mainly drawn that lesson. Yet, while these implications were very dear to Jhering's heart and repeatedly expressed in both his programmatic and doctrinal writings, they were not at the core of his argument at this point.

Instead, Jhering here embraced a much more striking idea: that law was "merely" a means to an end ("lediglich Mittel zum Zweck").[209] Jhering explicitly denied that law, in addition to being a means, could also be an end in itself.[210] Law was "not the highest [thing] in the world"[211] but always subservient to something else – in Jhering's view "the existence of society."[212] *That* conception *does* have truly dramatic implications, and Jhering was not shy to spell them out.

If the law's sole role was that of a means to guarantee the existence of society, its whole *raison d'être* vanished as soon as it could no longer play that part. In that case, the situation reverted to force.

---

[204] Since it is not directly enforceable by the state, international law cannot be "law" in the full sense of the term; *Jhering*, Zweck I (1884) 323–329. Jhering's discussion of international law is complex, obscure, and at least arguably, contradictory.

[205] *Jhering*, Zweck I (1884) 253.

[206] *Jhering*, Zweck I (1884) 249.

[207] *Jhering*, Zweck I (1884) 250.

[208] The idea was not entirely new either; see, e.g., *Kierulff*, Theorie des Gemeinen Civilrechts (1839) 2 ("Recht [...] als Mittel zum Zweck"). Kierulff's whole approach was much more Hegelian than Jhering's, however.

[209] *Jhering*, Zweck I (1884) 250.

[210] *Jhering*, Zweck I (1884) 250 ("nicht Selbstzweck").

[211] *Jhering*, Zweck I (1884) ("nicht das Höchste in der Welt").

[212] *Jhering*, Zweck I (1884) 250 ("das Bestehen der Gesellschaft").

"If it turns out that society cannot exist under the current state of law, and if law is not capable of remedying that situation, force intervenes and does what needs to be done [...]. In an emergency, law ends, as in the life of the individual, so in the life of the peoples and states."[213]

Especially in a situation where the choice becomes "law or life," "force sacrifices law and saves life."[214]

In part, this was merely a descriptive statement. It was another example of that fearless recognition of reality that often lent so much power to Jhering's writings. There was a point, Jhering acknowledged, at which a situation could no longer be governed by, nor judged according to, law.

"Thus we marked the point where law merges into politics and history, and where the judgment of the politician, the statesman, and the historian must supersede that of the jurist who only knows the standard of positive law."[215]

Law was designed to govern in the normal state of affairs but could just not handle true emergencies; here, the return of force was inevitable.

In part, however, Jhering also made a normative claim. He postulated that in such emergency situations, law not only did, but actually must, yield to force. "Law exists for the sake of society, not society for the sake of law." If either law or society must be given up, the state "is not just permitted, but obligated to sacrifice law and save society."[216] Cicero provided welcome support: "*Salus populi, summa lex esto.*"[217] Jhering's position was the veritable antithesis to Kant's famous postulate *"fiat justitia, pereat mundus"*[218] – *fiat societas, pereat justitia.*

Jhering, of course, fully recognized the inherent danger of abuse by "unscrupulous statesmen" but he stuck to his guns.[219] The state's power to sacrifice law, just like the ship captain's power to jettison cargo in a naval emergency, simply could not be denied. To be sure, Jhering argued that throwing the law overboard should be avoided as much as possible and was justified only in truly extreme situations;[220] he even supported codifying emergency powers in constitutional

[213] *Jhering*, Zweck I (1884) 250.

[214] *Jhering*, Zweck I (1884) 251. Jhering had taken that position, albeit in more truncated form, already 30 years before; see *Jhering*, Geist II.1. (1854) 75.

[215] *Jhering*, Zweck I (1884) 252. On Jhering's turn to history as the "world court" ("Weltgericht") in the Hegelian sense, see infra 3., notes 511–514 and text.

[216] *Jhering*, Zweck I (1884) 424.

[217] *Jhering*, Zweck I (1884) 424, citing *Cicero*, *De legibus* III 3 (between 58 and 43 B.C.).

[218] Kant, Zum ewigen Frieden (1795) (Anhang I). Kant's postulate was not as categorical as is often assumed, and, in fact, less categorical than Jhering's. Kant translated and explained it as "a proper legal principle that cuts off all devious ways designed by deceit and violence" ("ein wackerer, alle durch Arglist oder Gewalt vorgezeichnete krumme Wege abschneidender Rechtsgrundsatz"). Justice must be done, Kant wrote, even if all the "rogues" ("Schelme") perish; id. Thus Kant did not postulate that the whole world must be sacrificed for the sake of doing justice. Jhering, by contract, he was willing to sacrifice (all) law for the sake of saving society.

[219] *Jhering*, Zweck I (1884) 425.

[220] Thirty years earlier, Jhering had already warned of the cost in stirring terms: "Woe to an

form to spell out their conditions and limitations. But he also did not "shy away from arguing in favor of force and to thus disassociate [himself] from the traditional view in jurisprudence and legal philosophy."[221] At this point, Jhering's rejection of any idealist form of jurisprudence was categorical.

A Theory of Law III: The Standard of Law – not Truth, but Purpose. Jhering's conception of law as merely a means to an end determined the standard by which law was to be measured: law was not only shaped by its purpose, it was also legitimized by its pursuit of social ends. Thus, law had to be evaluated not according to some higher, ethical, values but purely according to how well it did its job.[222] Again, Jhering's position had several important consequences.

To begin with, since social needs and conditions of social life vary across time and space, law not only does, but must do so, as well. Jhering's conception of law made the differences in the laws found in the past and present not only acceptable but appropriate. Rejecting the notion of an overarching law of nature or reason, Jhering now openly embraced diversity[223] (arguably somewhat in tension with his earlier view of Roman law as a model for a generally valid jurisprudence[224]). As we shall see, Jhering thus became a strong advocate of comparative legal studies at a time when they were just beginning to gather steam.[225]

Another, perhaps even more important, consequence of Jhering's purely instrumental view was that law had to be regarded as appropriate whenever it effectively secured the respective society's conditions – whatever these conditions were. In other words, regarding law "merely as a means," excluded any substantive judgment about the particular ends it served – and thus about the law's substantive legitimacy – from the realm of jurisprudence.[226] Again, Jhering did not flinch. As an example of varying laws, he listed the different ways in which societies had regulated primary education – ranging from its prohibition for slaves in the antebellum American South to making it obligatory in modern day Western Europe. Which of these regulations, Jhering asked, was correct? The

---

era which does not adhere to law to the utmost [...]. Only the conviction of [the existence of] an insurmountable historical necessity can reconcile the moral feeling with the violence done to law; without it, every violation of the legal order amounts to a sacrilegious blow to the tree of law which violates and shocks its innermost core, i.e., the people's trust in the inviolability and sanctity of law." *Jhering*, Geist II.1. (1854) 75–76.

[221] *Jhering*, Zweck I (1884) 253. Jhering did not provide any references.

[222] Jhering, Zweck I (1884) 529 ("die Zweckmäßigkeit [ist] die einzige Aufgabe des Rechts" – "expediency is the only purpose of law.").

[223] Jhering, *Zweck* I (1884) 439–440.

[224] Supra chapter II.1, notes 53–61 and text.

[225] Infra chapter VII.4., notes 369–397 and text.

[226] Any such judgment thus belonged to the realm of politics, ethics, or personal convictions. At the same time, however, Jhering claimed that "justice" is the "life principle and supreme task" which society has to "to realize." *Jhering*, Zweck I (1884) 554. This created a tension (or even contradiction) between his purely positivist (and relativist) conception of law and an idealist notion of "justice;" see infra Conclusion, notes 55–83 and text.

answer was: all of them – because they all properly reflected the respective societies' conditions and needs. Thus, the prohibition to teach slaves literacy under penalty of death was perfectly justified at its time and in its place.[227] Conceiving law as a mere means to an end entailed unabashed relativism, especially since it was entirely up to each society to choose its goals:[228] "The standard of law is not the absolute one of truth but the relative one of purpose."[229] Like Hobbes, Jhering rejected *veritas* as the crucial criterion of law – though not in favor of *auctoritas* but of *finis* (Zweck).[230] Law as such had no inherent substantive content of its own.

A Theory of Law IV: Law as an Instrument of Social Control. When Jhering claimed that the purpose of law lay in "securing the conditions of life in society" ("die Lebensbedingungen der Gesellschaft")[231] that was as vague as it was trivial. For thinkers from antiquity through the natural law period and all the way to Kant, Hegel, and Savigny, obviously the purpose of law was to provide the rules that enable people to live together (hopefully in peace and prosperity). Jhering went beyond that triviality, however, by adding two (interrelated) elements: he proffered a broader view of the way, and particularly of the context, in which the law does its work; and he changed the focus from protecting individual interests to the collective welfare. The former aspect is noteworthy for its sociological nature, and we will consider it here; the latter is significant because of its long-term influence, and we will turn to it in the next section.

In the traditional liberal view, the law's function was to impose limits on individual freedom in order to make the freedom of one person compatible with the freedom of others; law was a system of boundaries.[232] For Jhering, the law's function was to reconcile the nature of the individual with the needs of society; thus law was an instrument of integration. Jhering's argument is complex and not always fully consistent. For present purposes, a much simplified (and heavily streamlined) version must suffice.

In order to understand Jhering's theory, we must go back to his overall approach in "Zweck."[233] His starting point was the tension between two basic human properties: self-interest (especially self-preservation) and the drive to live with others (in society).[234] The question then became how the former could be reconciled with the latter.[235] The particular challenge was how to harness human

---

[227] *Jhering*, Zweck I (1884) 446–447. Jhering's second example concerned the regulation of religious tolerance, id. 447–448.

[228] *Jhering*, Zweck I (1884) 450.

[229] *Jhering*, Zweck I (1884) 439.

[230] "Auctoritas, non veritas, facit legem;" Hobbes, Leviathan (1651/1668) 133 (book II, chapter 26).

[231] *Jhering*, Zweck I (1884) 511.

[232] *Kant*, Metaphysik der Sitten (1797) 230 (sec. B and C); *Savigny*, System des heutigen römischen Rechts I (1840) 331–332.

[233] Supra notes 194–205 and text.

[234] *Jhering*, Zweck I (1884) 87–88.

[235] *Jhering*, Zweck I (1884) 33, 92.

self-interest so that it aligned with the needs of social life. So far, that approach was nothing out of the ordinary, and Jhering himself was familiar with at least two earlier versions. One was of course Adam Smith's "Wealth of Nations" (1776), i.e., the idea that (economic) self-interest would, in the aggregate, promote collective wealth – quasi-automatically though an "invisible hand" and essentially without state intervention.[236] The other version was Hegel's conception of "Civil Society" ("Die bürgerliche Gesellschaft") in which "subjective egoism was transformed into a contribution to the satisfaction of the needs of all others,"[237] a point to which we shall return below.[238]

Jhering made an important original contribution, however, when he expounded the role of law in a much broader context of reconciling self-preference with life in society. As mentioned, Jhering envisaged four "social levers" to harness individual self-interest.[239] He labeled two levers "altruistic" (and "higher") because they aimed to benefit others by their very nature: love and the feeling of duty; these two he relegated to the realm or morality. The other two were labelled "egoistic" (and "lower") because they were external controls of self-interest: reward and coercion; these two were the concern of the market and of the state, respectively.[240] Even though Jhering never clearly spelled this out, from an overall point of view it is easy to see how he envisaged self-interest to be controlled through these four "levers" – and thus rendered compatible with life in society. Love can overcome egoism and lead to altruism; this can be expected to work particularly vis-a-vis those personally close to the actor. Next, a sense of duty can overpower selfish impulses and motivate socially useful conduct, for example, in the context of certain professions like the civil service or the military. Where these (higher) moral "levers" fail to work, the lower ones can kick in. Reward can often buy off self-interest through money or other economic benefits; this is mainly how commerce works.[241] Finally, if even that fails, coercion can be employed to control "egoism" through the threat of public sanctions; that is the realm of the state acting through law.[242]

---

[236] Jhering was familiar with that work; see., e.g., *Jhering*, Zweck I (1884) 201 note, 375. The idea that selfishness drives economic growth has older roots in Bernard Mandeville's satire "The Fable of the Bees" (Oxford 1714).

[237] *Hegel*, Grundlinien der Philosophie des Rechts (1821) 179 (sec. 199).

[238] See infra notes 297–307 and text. In addition, there are some remarkable similarities, but also some fundamental differences, between the ideas of Jhering and Schopenhauer (whom Jhering claimed to have read, see *Rümelin*, Rudolf von Jhering (1922) 17 note). Exploring their relationship would lead too far afield here; for an analysis; see *Pleister*, Persönlichkeit, Wille und Freiheit im Werke Jhering (1982) 21–23, 301–304.

[239] Supra notes 170–172 and text.

[240] *Jhering*, Zweck I (1884) 94–96.

[241] "Reward" may not be enough, however, and the feeling of duty may have to come to its assistance, e.g., to ensure that a worker performs as needed to produce a quality product; *Jhering*, Zweck II (1886) 5–7.

[242] A good example is the need to prevent excessive egoism leading to free-rider problems, *Jhering*, Zweck I (1884) 568–569.

By putting law into that (functional) overall context, Jhering showed it in a new light: not as a set of rules or institutions nor as a manifestation of normative precepts, but as an instrument of social control. Seeing law in the broader context of social control entails some important insights. To begin with, law is merely one instrument of social control among others; in one sense, it the least important because it is needed only when all others fail, i.e., as an *ultima ratio*;[243] in another sense, it is the most important because without its threat (of coercion), other forms may not work.[244] Furthermore, social control through law is necessary but not sufficient[245] because not all forms of conduct are susceptible to coercion. Finally, law is needed not only to limit individual action but also to facilitate collective interaction by providing a framework of stability and predictability; especially in the context of the market, self-interest can then operate in a socially beneficial manner.[246] In short, as amateurish, jumbled, disjointed, and obscure Jhering's discourse often was, it proffered not only an external, but a truly sociological, view of law – more than a generation before Ehrlich and Weber.[247]

A Theory of Law V: Jhering's Collectivism. Jhering's second deviation from the orthodox liberal view of law was his rejection of the individualism underlying early to mid-nineteenth century German moral and legal philosophy (as well as Bentham's version of utilitarianism[248]). According to thinkers like Kant and Savigny, the essence of law was that it delimited spheres inside of which individuals could exercise their freedom of will.[249] By contrast, Jhering embraced an unabashedly collective and almost socialist position: "All of our culture, our whole history rests on the utilization (Verwerthung) of the individual human existence for the purposes of the collective (Gesammtheit)."[250] As a result, the ultimate lodestar was not the welfare of the individual but of society.[251] It is true that Jhering also talked about "justice" and postulated that it required "equality" and perhaps even a "more just distribution of the worldly goods."[252] But even these

[243] This is particularly important in criminal law; *Jhering*, Zweck I (1884) 485–491.

[244] As Jhering of course recognized, the reward system of the market needs to be backed up by the coercive force of law, for example with regard to the enforcement of contractual promises; *Jhering*, Zweck I (1884) 72–73, 265–267.

[245] See *Jhering*, Zweck I (1884) 570.

[246] *Jhering*, Zweck I (1884) 264–70.

[247] On Jhering's influence on early sociology of law, see infra chapter VII.4., notes 337–368 and text.

[248] Infra notes 316–340 and text.

[249] With his emphasis on the (modern) state, Hegel was a more ambivalent case, but even in his legal philosophy, individualism played an important role in form of the centrality of the (individual) will; supra note 150 and text.

[250] *Jhering*, Zweck I (1884) 77–78.

[251] Creating one of the many contradictions within "Zweck," Jhering also envisaged "the human being, i.e., the individual," as "the true purpose;" *Jhering*, Zweck I (1884) 540; in a similar vein, id. 463. Once again, Jhering had two sides – one committed to a strictly collectivist view of the social order, the other embracing the ultimately Kantian ideal of individual dignity.

[252] *Jhering*, Zweck I (1884) 366–367, 533–534.

objectives served primarily social, rather than individual, interests: a certain minimum of (political and economic) equality was necessary because huge inequalities upset society's equilibrium and thus entailed a threat to, or even disturbance of, the social order.[253] Any benefits to the individual were merely derivative of benefits to society.

To be sure, like other thinkers, Jhering saw the welfare of both the individual and society as intimately connected: the individual could truly flourish only in society, and society benefitted from the success of the individual. Thus law had to be constructed in a way that reconciled the interests of both.[254] When push came to shove, however, Jhering left no doubt that the welfare of the collective had to prevail and that the interests of the individual had to be sacrificed on the altar of the common good.[255] In that regard, Jhering's mature concept of law was antithetical to the central tenet of nineteenth century liberalism: the principal purpose of law was not to protect the individual against others or the state but rather to coerce the individual as needed for social purposes.

Jhering's collectivist position motivated his campaign against what he saw as excessive economic individualism. He never tired of emphasizing that living in a community required substantial restrictions, even on private rights; people must accept limitations on the exercise of their economic freedom not only, as in classical liberalism, to the extent required by the equal rights of others[256] but also as required by the common weal: "All entitlements under private law [...] are influenced and bound by the concerns of society;" even private rights have a "*social* character."[257] This view was highly unusual for a representative of Romanist jurisprudence given its traditional emphasis on individualism[258]; in fact, Jhering sometimes sounded like his Germanist colleagues – for example, when he expressly embraced the "social theory of property,"[259] which entailed the legiti-

---

[253] *Jhering*, Zweck I (1884) 369–370. These thoughts almost surely reflected Jhering's experience in his own environment where the growing conflict between capital and labor was widely seen as a threat to social and political stability. Of course, Roman history provided plenty of examples as well.

[254] *Jhering*, Zweck I (1884) 77–89.

[255] See, e.g., *Jhering*, Zweck I (1884) 545.

[256] "Every man is free to do that which he wills, provided that he infringes not the equal freedom of any other man." *Spencer*, Principles of Ethics (1879) sec. 272.

[257] Jhering, Zweck I (1884) 532 *("Alle Rechte des Privatrechts [...] sind beeinflusst und gebunden durch die Rücksicht auf die Gesellschaft;"* Idee des "*gesellschaftlichen Charakters der Privatrechte")* (emphasis in the original).

[258] A widely noted foundation is the famous definition of private law in Justinian's *Institutes*: "ius...privatum [est] quod ad singulorum utilitatem pertinet," Inst. 1.1.4. ("private law is what pertains to the individuals' utility.") which in turn is based on a statement by Ulpian (D.1.1.1.2.).

[259] *Jhering*, Zweck I (1884) 526–527. The contemporary Germanist most famous for his critique of Romanist individualism and for his collectivist stance was *Gierke*, Das deutsche Genossenschaftsrecht (4 vols. 1868–1891). Similar opinions were voiced in France by Leon Duguit (1859–1928). For a discussion of Jhering's ideas in this broader context, see *Auer*, Der privatrechtliche Diskurs der Moderne (2014) 132–135.

macy of regulation[260] and even expropriation for the public good.[261] Jhering did not explain exactly how society benefitted from such restrictions on *laissez-faire* but he minced no words in attacking the unbridled egoism he observed all around him in the economic sphere.[262] Jhering still supported a free market economy driven by individual initiative, but he tasked the public power with reining it in as needed for the common good, in particular where competition failed to prevent the abuse of power.[263]

Jhering's collectivist position reflected the gradual turn of late nineteenth politics towards regulation especially of economic activity; in that regard, "Zweck" was even something of a harbinger of the regulatory state of the twentieth century. It was also destined to become highly influential a generation down the road on the other side of the Atlantic. Together with Jhering's instrumentalist conception of law, his collectivist stance was the most attractive feature of "Zweck" for the progressive jurists of Roscoe Pound's (1870–1964) generation; as we will see, they employed Jhering's ideas for their own battle against the (at least perceived) excessive individualism of the nineteenth century.[264]

Yet, while Jhering's collectivism mirrored the changing spirit of the times, foreshadowed the shape of things to come, and greatly impressed future generations, his credo that law must serve not individual interests but secure the conditions of life in society remained unsatisfactory. It said very little about what these needs really were, i.e., exactly what goals and values law had to promote and protect in order to ensure the functioning of society. It is not that Jhering failed to discuss any substantive values; at various points (especially in "Kampf" and "Zweck") he touched on equality, economic moderation, the dignity of the person, and even protection against the arbitrary exercise of state power. These values could not, however, plausibly claim universal and timeless validity. From Jhering's point of view, the determination of any absolutely valid social conditions was arguably impossible because societies varied vastly over time and space – and law simply had to serve each of them as needed.[265] Thus even in its collec-

---

[260] In the late nineteenth century, the need for regulation became a more prominent topic as the threat of industrial pollution became gradually recognized, as illustrated by Wilhelm Raabe's (1831–1910) novel "Pfister's Mühle" (1884).

[261] *Jhering*, Zweck I (1884) 523–534.

[262] Jhering, Zweck I (1884) 534–535; in a similar vein id. 137–138. For further discussion, see *Rümelin*, Rudolf von Jhering (1922) 77–78.

[263] *Jhering*, Zweck I (1884) 134–140. When Jhering acknowledged not only the crucial role of competition ("die Concurrenz ist die sociale Selbstregulierung des Egoismus," – "competition is the social regulation of egoism," id. 135) but also recognized the need for state intervention if competition does not work, he grasped the problem that modern economics calls "market failure."

[264] Infra chapter VII.3, notes 222–224 and text.

[265] Jhering actually tried to list "conditions" for life in society; *Jhering*, Zweck I (1884) 443–446. He even stated that they encompass not only material needs but immaterial goods as well; the latter included "honor, love, activity, education, religion, art, science" ("Ehre, Liebe,

tivist version, Jhering's conception of law remained essentially instrumental. Some authors have seen Jhering's failure to determine any universally valid conditions for life in society as a fatal flaw of his whole project.[266] It may indeed be possible to accept the change of societal conditions over time and space and still identify some absolutely necessary conditions for life in all societies – at least as far as law can ensure them. Jhering, however, never got that far.

Views of the State: Leviathan, the Rule of Law, and the Common Weal. Jhering developed nothing like a full-fledged theory of the state. He merely proffered various views on it in connection with his ideas about law. Also, whatever views of the state he propounded were neither particularly original nor very influential – nor always clear and coherent. They still deserve at least a brief look because they provide the broader context for his conception of law, and they show some of that conception's consequences for his understanding of state power. Jhering's views were marked by the tension between three different perspectives on the state: as a (slightly milder form of) Leviathan securing peace and order; as the realm of the rule of law; and as a more encompassing provider for the common weal.

Jhering did not allude to social contract theories[267] nor did he cite Hobbes, but his conception of the state is similar to the natural law tradition in important respects: the state is the organization of society that enables people to live in peace and order because the state has the power to guarantee these conditions. Instead of the brute force (or even violence) used to control earlier societies, the state employs law as the "machinery of coercion."[268] It can thus be defined as the "society that coerces"[269] Much like Hobbes' "Leviathan," Jhering's state has the "absolute monopoly" of the power of "external coercion."[270]

Jhering's conception of the state also had a Hobbesian flair in its rejection of inherent limitations on state power.[271] Jhering discussed three authors supporting

---

Thätigkeit, Bildung, Religion, Kunst, Wissenschaft"); id. 444–445. But on the very next page he re-stated that "the conditions of life vary, as with individuals so with society, what is dispensible here is necessary there, what is useful here is harmful there," id. 446. Again, Jhering sometimes talked in general terms, i.e., about law *tout court*, sometimes about his own environment in particular, i.e., about the law's here and now – usually without making that clear.

[266] See especially *Jenkins*, Rudolf von Jhering (1960); see also *Stone*, The Province and Function of Law (1946) 312; *Wolf*, Große Rechtsdenker (1963) 650.

[267] Jhering quoted from *Rouseau,* Du Contrat social (1762) – even in the original French – but in the slightly different context of the relationship between particular and collective interests; *Jhering*, Zweck I (1884) 567 note.

[268] *Jhering*, Zweck I (1884) 335.

[269] *Jhering*, Zweck I (1884) 309. Thus it is (partially) identical with society as "the keeper of the regulated and disciplined coercive power;" id. 308.

[270] Jhering, Zweck I (1884) 318. Today, the expression is usually associated with Max Weber's phrase about the "claim of the modern state to monopolize the use of force," *Weber*, Economy and Society vol. I (1978) 56 (orig. 1921–22).

[271] Even "the most unbearable form of existence in a state is better than a complete lack

such limitations. Immanuel Kant received short shrift because his idea that the state had to ensure the compatibility of the citizens' respective spheres of freedom[272] struck Jhering as hopelessly individualistic and thus misguided.[273] Wilhelm von Humboldt's (1767–1835) minimalist conception of the state[274] (often colloquially called the "night-watchman state" – "Nachwächterstaat") was dismissed because of its *a priori* character and for being an outdated product of eighteenth century natural law thinking.[275] Finally, Jhering rejected John Stuart Mill's (1806–1873) near-contemporary ideas[276] as self-contradictory and productive of absurd consequences.[277] Jhering's ultimate problem with these attempts to limit state power, however, was their fundamental misunderstanding of the whole enterprise. His response followed straight from his conception of law as means purely for social, not individual, ends.

"Securing the welfare of the individual is not an end in itself but merely a means to the end of securing the welfare of society; society is not concerned with preventing the primary negative effects on the subject, but with [preventing] the secondary ones on itself."[278]

Therefore the limits of state power had to be determined according to their impact on society as a whole. This turned the matter into a political question to which no generalized answer was possible.[279] Extending Jhering's instrumental view of law to the rules governing the limits of state power thus excluded the guarantee of pre-existing fundamental rights because how far the state could go ultimately depended on the "practical needs" of society.[280] Jhering's conception of the state was much closer to an essentially totalitarian model à la Hobbes than to a liberal one à la Mill.[281]

At the same time, however, Jhering envisaged the state as the realm of the rule of law. As mentioned, he described an evolution of legal norms from unilateral commands to bilaterally binding rules also recognized as obligatory by the state.

---

thereof" ("die unerträglichste Form des staatlichen Zustandes ist immer noch besser der gänzliche Mangel derselben."); *Jhering*, Zweck I (1884) 313.

[272] Supra note 232.

[273] *Jhering*, Zweck I (1884) 537–538.

[274] *Von Humboldt*, Ideen zu einem Versuch die Grenzen der Wirksamkeit des Staates zu bestimmen (1792).

[275] *Jhering*, Zweck I (1884) 538–542.

[276] *Mill*, On Liberty (1859). Jhering cited the German translation, i.e., *John Stuart Mill*, Über die Freiheit (E. Pickford transl., Frankfurt 1860); *Jhering* Zweck I (1884) 543.

[277] *Jhering*, Zweck I (1884) 543–550.

[278] *Jhering*, Zweck I (1884) 545.

[279] *Jhering*, Zweck I (1884) 551.

[280] *Jhering*, Zweck I (1884) 551.

[281] For a trenchant critique of Jhering's concept of the state with its totalitarian and nihilistic implications, see *Behrends*, Jhering heute! (2023) 242–244. As Behrends, id., also points out, Jhering's characterization of the early Roman Republic as more or less constantly in a state of war and thus pervasively shaped by the values of military discipline, was badly misleading.

The result was a "status of law" ("Rechtszustand"), a "legal order" ("Rechtsordnung"), and a "state of law" ("Rechtsstaat"). Jhering used these terms pretty much interchangeably to signify what in English is termed "the rule of law."[282] The hallmark of that state was the prevention of "Willkühr" (literally "arbitrariness)" which Jhering defined as the "injustice" committed under law.[283] The rule of law required two elements. The first was institutional and familiar: separation of the executive and judicial power, independence of the judiciary, and procedural guarantees, especially equality of the litigants (including the state) before the courts,[284] although Jhering did not require that these principles be enshrined in a constitution.[285] None of this was original – quite to the contrary: the "Rechtsstaat" and its basic features were a prominent topic in Germany at the time; in fact the two foundational works on the subject had just been published a few years before "Zweck" by Jhering's (almost exact) contemporaries Otto Bähr (1817–1895) and Rudolf von Gneist (1816–1895).[286] The other requirement, however, was more idiosyncratic but also particularly important to Jhering: a strong, broadly shared, and pervasive "sense of justice" ("Rechtsgefühl"). Without that, Jhering astutely observed, the rule of law cannot be guaranteed: "Ultimately, the security of law depends entirely on the moral power of the national feeling of justice."[287]

Jhering, never much concerned with the overall consistency of his thinking, did not make any attempt to reconcile his essentially totalitarian conception of the state with his support for the rule of law. Note that he both postulated the absolute power of the state and at the same time warned against, in fact: complained of, excessive state regulation.[288] Jhering was, again, wearing two hats. At times, he played the philosopher who expounded the inherent nature and de facto limits of state power (including in states of emergency). On other occasions, he played the citizen of late nineteenth century Germany whose political liberalism demanded that the state respect the rights of its subjects. The positions were actually not incompatible: as a philosopher, Jhering thought about the state in

[282] *Jhering*, Zweck I (1884) 357–358; Jhering also called it "die Herrschaft von Recht und Gesetz" ("the rule of law and legislation"); id. 357.

[283] *Jhering*, Zweck I (1884) 359–361.

[284] *Jhering*, Zweck I (1884) 387–405. Jhering had found many of these conditions in the "system of liberty" of the Roman Republic which he had portrayed in highly idealized form; *Jhering*, Geist II.1. (1854) 116–117, 160–161, 246; *Jhering*, Geist II.2. (1858) 134–303.

[285] *Behrends*, Jhering heute! (2023) 244.

[286] *Bähr*, Der Rechtsstaat (1864); *von Gneist*, Der Rechtsstaat und die Verwaltungsgerichte in Deutschland (1872).

[287] *Jhering*, Zweck I (1884) 381.

[288] See *Jhering*, Geist II.1. (1854) 130 ("If the state is allowed to turn into a statute everything that appears to it as good, moral or expedient, then the law is not subject to any limits."); Jhering, Geist I (1852) 117 (complaining about the "obsession that everything has to be done through the state"). Jhering also (approvingly) pointed to the "aversion to the interference by state officials" in republican Rome; *Jhering*, Geist II.2. (1854) 246.

general; as a citizen, he reacted to his own polity in particular. Still, that begged the question how to resolve a conflict between the Hobbesian and the rule-of-law state: What if the state decided to use its inherent sovereign power to run roughshod over the rule of law? Jhering essentially provided two answers. One was that vis-a-vis the state, the rule of law could be preserved only by the popular "Rechtsgefühl:" "The only thing that impresses [the state power] is the real force which backs up the law, a people, which has recognized law as a condition of its existence and which experiences its violation as a violation of itself."[289] The other answer was that the rule of law could, and should, prevail only as long as it could serve its purpose to secure the conditions of social life; when these conditions were threatened, for example, in a state of emergency, force returned and sent (the rule of) law packing.[290]

Jhering's state was not limited to securing peace and order through external and internal protection like its seventeenth century predecessor model.[291] In line with contemporary understandings, Jhering also tasked the state with securing the conditions of life in society in a proactive fashion. For example, it had to ensure that citizens act in the common interest if they lacked the maturity and understanding to do so on their own.[292] Jhering even likened the state to a father who guides his immature child so that he or she can learn to regard the state not as an enemy but as a friend and partner.[293] And like a father vis-a-vis his child, Jhering's state was under an ethical obligation not to abuse its power but to exercise it for the benefit of those under its protection.[294] Reflecting incipient notions of the welfare state, Jhering also pointed out that in return for the citizens' cooperation and obedience, the state provided them with considerable benefits, such as public institutions, ranging from universities and museums to research laboratories and even telegraphic communication.[295] Despite its essentially totalitarian foundations, Jhering's state was a benevolent protector of, and even provider for, the common weal.

Thus Jhering's views of the state and of law were not completely bleak. True, in Volume One of "Zweck," there is plenty of undeniable harshness. Jhering's mature theory of law and concept of the state entail a full-scale rejection of all idealist elements in favor of a purely positivist and instrumentalist position. Ultimately, however, this position must be viewed against the background of Jhering's personal idealism and especially of his unfailing trust in historical progress towards a more enlightened and humane society.[296]

[289] *Jhering*, Zweck I (1884) 381.
[290] Supra notes 213–218 and text.
[291] See *Jhering*, Zweck I (1884) 555–557.
[292] *Jhering*, Zweck I (1884) 561.
[293] *Jhering*, Zweck I (1884) 561–562.
[294] *Jhering*, Zweck I (1884) 363–364.
[295] *Jhering*, Zweck I (1884) 557–558.
[296] See infra chapter V.2.

Traces of Hegel: Conceptions of State and Society. There was, of course, a fundamental difference between Jhering's and Hegel's conceptions of the state: Jhering conceived of the state not only in quasi-Hobbesian terms, but also in a purely instrumental fashion – as a means for securing the conditions of life in society (by coercion through law); for Jhering, the state was a creature without inherent ethical qualities or a moral soul. By contrast, Hegel understood the state in idealist terms – as "the realization of the idea of morality,"[297] and, more specifically, as the "realization of concrete liberty."[298] As such, the state appeared as a manifestation of reason.[299].

This fundamental difference makes it easy to overlook that Hegel's and Jhering's conceptions of *civil society* were based on essentially the same idea: as a context in which individual interests (and the egoism driving their pursuit) are reconciled with the interests of the collective. Similar to Jhering, Hegel's discourse on "Die Bürgerliche Gesellschaft" construes it as a "system of needs" ("System der Bedürfnisse").[300] In that system, the pursuit of private interests by the citizens also satisfies the needs of all – and vice versa, so that the satisfaction of individual and collective needs is "mutually contingent" ("gegenseitig bedingt").[301] This idea was central to Jhering's conception of society as well, at least in the context of the market ("Verkehr").[302] In fact, Hegel's language in that regard could have been a quotation from Jhering's "Zweck": "In this dependency and mutuality of both labor and of the satisfaction of needs, the subjective egoism is transformed into the contribution to the satisfaction of the needs of all others."[303] To be sure, that conception of civil society was neither Hegel's nor Jhering's original insight but had been rather commonplace, as mentioned, at least since Adam Smith's "Wealth of Nations." It is still noteworthy that in this regard, Jhering and Hegel stood on similar ground.[304]

It is also noteworthy that Hegel had already looked at the state and civil society from the perspective of "Zweck." The concept is not nearly as central in Hegel's legal philosophy as it became in Jhering's work; still, Hegel invoked in on several occasions and in various contexts.[305] Remarkably, Hegel already used it to

[297] *Hegel*, Grundlinien der Philosophie des Rechts (1821) 214 (sec. 257) ("die Wirklichkeit der sittlichen Idee").

[298] *Hegel*, Grundlinien der Philosophie des Rechts (1821) 221 (sec. 260) ("die Wirklichkeit der konkreten Freiheit").

[299] *Hegel*, Grundlinien der Philosophie des Rechts (1821) 215 (sec. 257) ("das an und für sich Vernünftige").

[300] *Hegel*, Grundlinien der Philosophie des Rechts (1821) 174–180 (sec. 189–01).

[301] *Hegel*, Grundlinien der Philosophie des Rechts (1821) 176 (sec. 192).

[302] See supra note 240 and text.

[303] *Hegel*, Grundlinien der Philosophie des Rechts (1821) 179 (sec. 199) ("In dieser Abhängigkeit und Gegenseitigkeit der Arbeit und der Befriedigung der Bedürfnisse schlägt die subjective Selbstssucht in den Beitrag zur Befriedigung der Bedürfnisse aller andern um.")

[304] For a more extensive discussion, see *Pleister*, Persönlichkeit, Wille und Freiheit im Werke Jherings (1982) 324–328.

[305] See, e.g., *Hegel*, Grundlinien der Philosophie des Rechts (1821) 169 (sec. 183) 172, (sec. 187).

connect the individual and society: the former pursues its own purposes but it can fulfill them only in a relationship with others; through this relationship, the individual purpose attains the "form of generality."[306] In a manner reminiscent of Jhering, Hegel also saw the "ultimate purpose" of the individual in the collective.[307] This does not mean, of course, that Hegel's and Jhering's understandings and uses of the concept were identical, but it suggests that one of the inspirations for Jhering's engagement with "Zweck" may have been Hegel's legal philosophy, whether Jhering was aware of it or not.

"Zweck" in Context: Darwinism, Utilitarianism, Positivism, Marxism. "Zweck" as a whole, as well as Jhering's theory of law in general and his view of the state in particular, were developed in an environment shaped by a variety of broader intellectual currents. In the order of their importance for our present purposes, these were mainly Darwin's theory of the evolution of life, Bentham's and Mill's (and to some extent Spencer's) utilitarianism, Comte's sociological positivism, and Marx's views on the relationship between economic production and political power. Jhering's ideas in "Zweck" must be understood in that broader context.

This is not primarily a question of detecting influence. Direct and conscious influence of any of these approaches and currents was almost certainly negligible or non-existent. As we have noted before, Jhering conscientiously gave credit to others where it was due – and he gave little to any of these thinkers, even when he mentioned their work.[308] Indirect or unconscious influence was possible, of course, and in some respects even likely. "In order to avoid all semblance of arrogation," Jhering himself acknowledged that he owed "everything [he] was able to deliver [...] to the time in which [he] live[d]."[309] It is notoriously difficult, however, to trace such indirect influence, and speculating about it rarely yields useful results. Thus, the point of discussing the relationship between Jhering's ideas and those of others is mainly to situate the former in the intellectual climate created by the latter. Whether Jhering openly engaged with other thinkers or not, endorsed or rejected their ideas, his own writings were a voice in a larger concert. This is an important reason for the contemporary interest in, and subsequent influence of, the ideas Jhering presented in "Zweck."

Darwinism: The Evolution of Purposes. When Jhering published "Kampf" in 1872, the title certainly mimicked the "struggle for life," and some of the tract's core messages were strongly reminiscent of Darwin's writings.[310] Yet, as we have seen, Jhering did not attribute his own ideas to those of the Englishman; in fact,

---

[306] *Hegel*, Grundlinien der Philosophie des Rechts (1821) 169 (sec. 182 Zusatz) ("die Form der Allgemeinheit").

[307] Hegel, Grundlinien der Philosophie des Rechts (1821) 169 (sec. 184).

[308] An exception is Bentham, see *Jhering*, Zweck II (1886) 170–171; on Jhering's position vis-a-vis Bentham's utilitarianism, see infra notes 318–340 and text.

[309] Jhering, *Zweck* II (1886) 176.

[310] Supra notes 39–57 and text.

he never mentioned Darwin in the book. When Jhering published the first volume of "Zweck" five years later, he showed much greater familiarity with, as well as an interest in, Darwin's theory of evolution. The Darwinian element in the first volume of "Zweck" is limited but significant because it pertains to the nature of Jhering's project itself.[311]

Jhering brought up Darwin's ideas in the Preface of "Zweck" to explain their relationship to his own approach.

> "As for myself, I do not wish to judge the correctness of Darwin's theory, even though the results I myself have reached with regard to the historical evolution of law, confirm it completely [...].
>
> [T]he same necessity that, according to the Darwinian theory, makes one species evolve from another [also] makes one purpose of law generate another [...] each previous purpose generates its successor [...]."[312]

Jhering's discussion of Darwin at the outset of "Zweck" is important for three reasons. First, it calls the reader's attention to a major theme of the book that is easy to overlook: among other things, Jhering sought to demonstrate the inevitable evolution of purposes from earlier and lower to later and higher ones. Second, recognizing that theme helps to understand the seemingly odd sequence of the book's chapters: they actually follow the alleged progression of purposes from those of the animal to those of the individual to those of society to those of the state (which becomes, in an almost Hegelian manner, the climax of that development).[313] Finally, its affinity with Darwin's ideas made Jhering's theory look more plausible than it would otherwise have been: Jhering's evolution of the purposes of law appeared as the jurisprudential counterpart to Darwin's evolution of species; by associating his work with Darwin's, "Zweck" could gain prestige.

Jhering fully realized that compatibility with Darwinian ideas was important for the audience's acceptance of his book. Thus he took great pains to explain that, contrary to appearance, there was really no conflict between Darwin's ex-

---

[311] There are few other "Darwinian" elements in "Zweck" aside from occasional remarks, such as "[i]n all of creation, the stronger live at the expense of the weaker;" *Jhering*, Zweck I (1884) 239. Franz Wieacker found more pervasive elements of "Darwinism" in "Zweck," in part because he construed that term very broadly; *Wieacker*, Jhering und der Darwinismus (1973) 84–88. Elsewhere, Jhering also took a quasi-Darwinist view with regard to the competition between the peoples (or races) of the world: the Anglo-Saxon race pushing aside the indigenous population in (North) America was justified ("ein Recht") because the former made better use of the land than the latter. One must be careful though not to take this as moral approval; the process was justified only "from the perspective of world history" ("vom Standpunkt der Weltgeschichte"), *Jhering*, Geist I (2d ed. 1866, 7) which, as Jhering opined on another occasion, was the ultimate standard of right and wrong, see infra 3., notes 511–514 and text.

[312] *Jhering*, Zweck I (1884) XIII–XIV.

[313] "The organization of purpose reached its climax in the State;" *Jhering*, Zweck (1884) 43.

planation of the (natural) world through the "law of causation" ("Causalitätsgesetz") and his own explanation of human conduct through the "law of purpose" ("Zweckgesetz").[314] He and Darwin, Jhering assured his readers, were entirely on the same page.[315]

While the parallel between Jhering's and Darwin's evolutionary theories was important to Jhering himself at the time, it ultimately led him nowhere. It also contributed little to the lasting fame of "Zweck." Jhering's idea of an orderly and inevitable sequence of purposes (of law) still smacked of Hegel's Philosophy of History which was long past its prime when "Zweck" was published over half-a-century later. It is fair to assume that it sounded quite weird to most contemporary readers, to say nothing of later generations.

Utilitarianism: Law's Usefulness for Society.[316] Jhering has often been considered a utilitarian,[317] and it makes sense to think of him as such, at least as far as

---

[314] Jhering tried to reconcile these positions in a manner that was as curious as it was dubious: even if Darwin's idea that in natural processes, the sequence of forms was driven by the law of causation (and thus inevitable), was correct (a thesis on which Jhering refused to pass judgment), Jhering claimed that ultimately, everything was just an expression of the higher purposes determined by the Creator. In other words, the evolution of the world, even where governed by the "law of causation," inevitably pursued God's designs so that (his) purpose was the ultimate principle of all creation; *Jhering*, Zweck I (1884) XII–XIII. As Franz Wieacker noted, Jhering used the Creator to "save the teleology of the world;" *Wieacker*, Jhering und der Darwinismus (1973) 81.

[315] Jhering hastened to assure his readers that his theory was entirely compatible with a "divine conception of purpose" ("göttlichen Zweckgedanken") because God had foreseen [the evolution] of man; *Jhering*, Zweck I (1884) XIII. Perhaps Jhering saw a need to forestall charges of atheism.

[316] While Jhering addressed utilitarianism only in Volume Two of "Zweck," for our present purposes, his views on that topic are better discussed in the current context for two reasons. First, his theory of law in Volume One raises the issue of his utilitarianism with much greater urgency than his discourse on ethics and custom in Volume Two because the former has had a massive long-term influence (see infra chapter VII 2. and 3.) while the latter had almost none. Second, the present subchapter's objective to situate "Zweck" in the context of the various intellectual currents prevalent at the time would be woefully incomplete without considering nineteenth century utilitarianism.

That said, for Jhering, it made considerable sense to allocate issues of utilitarianism to Volume Two of "Zweck." That volume was concerned with ethics and thus (at least to some extent) with normative questions of right and wrong, and utilitarianism was primarily a theory of ethics dealing directly with these questions. By contrast, in Volume One, Jhering was concerned (inter alia) with law and in particular with the explanation of its historical origin and social function; but utilitarianism was not primarily a theory of law, and even when applied to law (especially by Bentham), it was mainly an instrument of critique, not an effort to explain whence law came and how it worked.

[317] See, e.g., *Drake*, Editorial Preface (1921) xvii–xxi; *Friedmann*, Legal Theory (1967) 322; *Geldart*, Introduction (1921) xlvi–lii; *Pound*, Jurisprudence vol. I (1959) 130–142; *Stone*, The Province and Function of Law (1946) 299–311; *Seagle*, Men of Law (1947) 71 ("Jhering has been called the German Bentham"); *Zweigert*, Jherings Bedeutung für die Entwicklung der rechtsvergleichenden Methode (1970) 242. While the title of an article by Helmut Coing

"Zweck" is concerned. He was clearly familiar with some of the pertinent English literature, perhaps because in Göttingen, where he had been a student and where he now wrote "Zweck," this literature was – for reasons of its political connection with England – more present than elsewhere in Germany.[318] Jhering cited and discussed Jeremy Bentham's (1748–1832) "Principles of Morals and Legislation" (1789) in a German translation,[319] and he also knew Herbert Spencer's (1820–1903) "Data of Ethics" (1879)[320] which combined utilitarian ideas with social evolutionism and progress just around the time when Jhering was working on "Zweck." There is no reference to John Stuart Mill's (1806–1873) "Utilitarianism" (1863),[321] although Jhering knew of Mill because he had read "On Liberty" (1859), also in a German translation.[322] Thus, Jhering understood English utilitarianism at least in rough outline.

Utilitarianism is a multi-faceted concept even if one limits it to the quasi-classical version developed mainly in the works of Bentham and Mill. Associating Jhering with their ideas thus requires considerable differentiation. A full-fledged comparison between "Zweck" and classic utilitarianism may be a worthwhile undertaking but it is neither feasible here nor is it necessary in order to situate Jhering's work in the intellectual climate of its time. Suffice it to show the most important similarities and differences and then to point to the broader affinities between the utilitarians' and Jhering's mode of thought and argumentation.[323]

The similarities resulted mainly from the fact that both English utilitarianism and Jhering's teleology were variations of consequentialism. Rejecting the transcendentalism dominant in late eighteenth- and early nineteenth-century continental philosophy, both shifted the focus from the compatibility of human action with abstract idealist precepts to its concrete effects on real life.[324] Both also

---

connects Jhering to Bentham, the essay itself touches on that connection only in passing and is mainly concerned with the origins of the German Jurisprudence of Interests (Interessenjurisprudenz); *Coing*, Rudolf von Jhering und Bentham (1982).

[318] Göttingen was the university of the Kingdom of Hanover which was ruled (first directly, then indirectly) by the English crown until 1866, when it became a Prussian province. The possible impact of this political connection on the intellectual climate in Göttingen is pointed out by *Stein*, Legal Evolution (1980) 53.

[319] *Jhering*, Zweck II (1886) 170–172 (citing and discussing *Jeremy Bentham*, Die Grundsätze der Civil- und Kriminalgesetzgebung, hrg. von Dumont, deutsche Ausgabe von F.E. Beneke (2 vols., Berlin 1830).

[320] *Jhering*, Zweck II (1886) 121 (citing and discussing *Spencer*, The Data of Ethics (1879) in the German edition by B. Vetter, i.e., Die Thatsachen der Ethik, Stuttgart 1879); the same work is referenced again id. 172.

[321] While a German translation was available in "John Stuart Mills Gesammelte Werke 1" (Theodor Gompertz ed., Adolf Wahrmund transl., Leipzig 1869), the lack of any reference to this work in Jhering's writings suggests that he never read it.

[322] See supra note 276 and text. Jhering also mentioned Mill in passing and without reference to any specific work in *Jhering*, Zweck II (1886) 378.

[323] For a longer discussion, see *Stone*, The Province and Function of Law (1946) 391–393.

[324] Jhering recognized and praised in Bentham in that regard; *Jhering*, Zweck II (1886) 170–171.

targeted jurists who had presented law as a system of abstract principles and rules – in Bentham's case Blackstone, in Jhering's Puchta.[325] Thus Jhering saw in Bentham an ally in his battle against the "enemies who stride along on speculative stilts and wave the Oriflame of idealism."[326] Jhering's applause for Bentham fit right into his general preference for the "real-practical" approach that he associated with the English mind over the "ideal-speculative" outlook he sadly saw in his fellow Germans.[327]

Regarding law in particular, the utilitarians and Jhering agreed that the crux of legislation was its impact on the human condition. For Bentham, that effect was a normative criterion: laws had to be designed, and judged, according to their effect on human happiness. For Jhering, it was primarily an explanatory device: the law's origin, evolution, and function were to be understood in light of its character as a means to an end.

None of this made Jhering a full-fledged follower of English-style utilitarianism which he disparagingly labeled "stale" and "desolate".[328] Jhering differed from Bentham's position in a crucial regard: Bentham was concerned with utility (of law, etc.) for the individual, while Jhering looked to society.[329] To be sure, that contrast was less pronounced in regard to Mill and Spencer who paid more attention than Bentham to society as a whole. Yet, for Jhering, the individual was simply not the crucial reference point at all; at least at a mature stage of development, law had to serve the "welfare and flourishing of the community," period.[330] That difference between an individualist and a societal orientation had two important consequences.

One was a different attitude towards state regulation. Bentham and especially Spencer were ardent supporters of *laissez faire* (Mill less so), while Jhering favored substantial limitations on the pursuit of individual interests in general and

---

[325] See *Drake*, Editorial Preface (1921) xix–xx.

[326] *Jhering*, Zweck II (1886) 170–171. Jhering apparently assumed that the meaning of "Oriflamme" was obvious to his readers, and right after the Franco-Prussian war of 1870/71, that may have been true: it was the traditional French battle standard, used in the Middle Ages.

[327] *Jhering*, Zweck II (1886) 170.

[328] *Jhering*, Zweck II (1886) XXI ("abgestanden", "öde"). Jhering was worried that his view might be identified with English utilitarianism; Jhering, Zweck II (1886) XXI. Theodor Viehweg's characterization of "Kampf" as "German Benthamism" is thus largely wrong; *Viehweg*, Rechtsdogmatik und Rechtszetetik bei Jhering (1970) 216.

[329] That – fairly obvious – difference has of course been noted by others; see, e.g., *Seagle*, Men of Law (1947) 71; *Zweigert*, Jherings Bedeutung für die Entwicklung der rechtsvergleichenden Methode (1970) 242.

[330] *Jhering*, Zweck I (1884) 374 ("das Wohl und Gedeihen des Gemeinwesens"). Jhering originally considered this – social – utilitarianism his own original idea. Yet, while working on the second edition of Volume Two of "Zweck," a review of the first edition brought it to his attention that the idea had already been expressed quite clearly some six centuries earlier by Thomas Aquinas (1225–1274). Jhering thus inserted a note and acknowledged the matter in his usual honesty; *Jhering*, Zweck II (1886) 161 note.

on the use of private property in particular.[331] The British utilitarians were trying to preserve the nineteenth-century status quo – and ultimately fighting a losing battle. Jhering was arguing for social and economic reform – and the modern regulatory state would eventually ratify his agenda in most of the Western world.

The other consequence was a disagreement about the exact object of utility. For Bentham, the judgment about a rule turned on whether it maximized "pleasure," i.e., a subjective sensation. Jhering rejected that approach as "eudaimonism" ("Eudämismus").[332] For him, utility was to be measured by the objective value for the well-being of society, regardless of subjective experience. Jhering provided a vivid illustration of his position in connection with the only reference to "the utilitarian point of view" in his jurisprudential discourse in Volume One of "Zweck". Here, Jhering argued that in enforcing its criminal law, the state must use executions and incarceration as sparingly as possible. That was not because of any considerations of anyone's subjective experience (e.g., the convict's pain or pleasure). It was purely in the objective ("well-considered") interest of society: executions and incarceration diminished society's workforce and thus impaired its wealth, Jhering argued, citing Adam Smith's "Wealth of Nations."[333]

Finally, the English thought about utility in timeless terms while Jhering saw it in historical perspective. Jhering's reference points were the conditions of social life, and these conditions invariably changed over time (and varied among peoples). Thus utility could not be determined once and for all but always remained relative.[334]

In summary, any classification of Jhering as a utilitarian must remain cognizant that in contrast to his counterparts from the Emerald Isle, his perspective was not individualistic, subjective, and absolute, but social, objective, and relative. The end of law was to secure not the greatest happiness of the greatest number but the social welfare of society under changing conditions.[335]

Regardless of these agreements and disagreements, Jhering's whole approach and argumentation were similar to that of the English utilitarians in important ways. As mentioned, both he and they were arguing in a consequentialist, rather than idealist, mode and thus concerned themselves, in one way or another, with the impact of norms on the reality of human experience. They all discussed norms

---

[331] Jhering, Zweck I (1886) 534–535. For Jhering, society was the only valid reference point even in the realm of ethics; *Jhering*, Zweck II (1886) 120.

[332] *Jhering*, Zweck II (1886) 171–172.

[333] *Jhering*, Zweck I (1884) 374–376; see also id. 486, 490. Jhering's argument was based on the dubious assumption that those convicted of crimes serious enough to receive the death penalty or prison sentences were likely contributors to the gross national product. Still, Jhering had good point: in designing and using its criminal justice system, a state should keep an eye on its social cost – which can be staggering as recent US-American mass incarceration has shown.

[334] *Jhering*, Zweck II (1886) 120–122.

[335] For a discussion of "social utilitarianism," see *Stone*, The Province and Function of Law (1946) 299–314.

in light of human psychology which became increasingly common at the time,[336] be it in terms of experiencing pain and pleasure, or be it from the perspective of individual and social purposes. Even though Jhering rejected the reduction of pain and the increase of pleasure as the proper end of norms, he considered them crucial means by which nature pushed human beings in a beneficial direction[337] – an idea readers could also find in Spencer's writings.[338] Both Jhering and the English utilitarians talked about egoism and altruism, seeking ways to harness the former for the benefit of the latter. And just like Jhering, the utilitarians in the days (and country) of Darwin increasingly came to think about society and its norms from the perspective of evolution,[339] thus sharing Jhering's fundamental belief in the progress of mankind.[340]

Positivism: Jurisprudence as Sociology. "Zweck" also needs to be considered in the context of nineteenth century sociological positivism. The purpose of that endeavor is not to resolve the much broader issue of whether Jhering was a "positivist." That is a complicated question on which much ink has been spilt, and it will require a nuanced analysis in its own right.[341] Here, the point is merely to elucidate the affinity between Jhering's approach in "Zweck" and the specific version of positivism much discussed at the time of its writing.

That version was developed by August Comte (1898–1857) in his "Cours de philosophie positif," published in six volumes 1830–1842. The two most widely-known elements of this work are also the two most relevant for our current purposes. The first was Comte's division of the development of human understanding into three stages: a religious (or theological) stage, at which mankind explains the phenomena of the world by reference to the (divine) will of a higher being; a metaphysical stage, at which these phenomena are understood by reference to abstract, transcendental concepts; and finally a positivist stage at which man focuses strictly on facts, turns his empirical observations into generalizations, and thereby discovers the laws that are inherent in, and thus govern, the phenomena. At the time, this three-stage model was a significant contribution to the history of science. The second principal element is Comte's organization of the major branches of science. At the top of all other sciences, Comte placed sociology. Conceived as the field that encompassed all others, sociology replaced philosophy as the discipline that reflected the sum total of human knowledge. The combination, so to speak, of these two elements was Comte's plea for a

---

[336] *Spencer*, Principles of Psychology (1855); for a broader assessment of psychological arguments in late nineteenth-century Germany, see *Schmoeckel* (ed.), Psychologie als Argument in der juristischen Literatur des Kaiserreichs (2009).

[337] *Jhering*, Zweck I (1884) 35 ("Through pleasure and pain, nature knows how to direct the course we should take, through both, it connects our interests with its purposes.")

[338] *Spencer*, Principles of Ethics II (1891).

[339] *Spencer*, Principles of Ethics II (1891).

[340] See infra chapter V.3.

[341] Infra 3.

strictly positive sociology that shuns all religious or metaphysical elements. Like the modern natural sciences, it had to limit itself to the study of facts and to the generalization of its observations into verifiable laws. Such an approach completed the agenda of positive philosophy. Here, Comte laid the foundations for sociology as a modern social science.

It does not take much to recognize the close affinity between Comte's program and Jhering's approach.[342] Comte would have loudly applauded Jhering's incessant campaign against metaphysical speculation and his concomitant demands to base jurisprudence on the reality of what Jhering liked to call "life" ("das Leben"). In Comte's terms, Jhering pushed for jurisprudence to advance from the second, metaphysical, to the third, i.e., positivist, stage of human knowledge. He would have heartily agreed with Jhering's efforts to look to the natural sciences (in "Zweck" mainly to biology) for guidance in understanding the nature and function of law. Comte would have found himself vindicated when Jhering approached law as a social phenomenon serving social purposes. And he would have hailed Jhering's agenda to trace the successive stages of human existence to show the progress of social development.

All in all, the similarities are so striking that they suggest a direct influence of Comte on Jhering. Yet, while Jhering was aware Comte,[343] there is no evidence that he ever actually read his work, perhaps simply because a German translation came too late.[344] Either Comte's sociological positivism was so much in the air in mid-nineteenth century Germany that it had an impact on Jhering even though he was not conscious of it, or Comte and Jhering both reacted to the situations in their respective fields in similar ways. Be that as it may, Jhering essentially ratified Comte's conception of sociology as the discipline overarching all others: in "Zweck," he pushed jurisprudence in the direction of legal sociology.[345]

Marxism: "Within a Hair's Breadth." In 1951, German legal philosopher Hans Welzel wrote that Jhering's positivism came "within a hair's breadth" of Marx' theory of law and state.[346] Jhering would probably have been horrified to read that. True, he had loudly denounced the excesses of contemporary capitalism,[347] and he had emphasized the social dimension of private law in general and

---

[342] See *Wieacker*, Privatrechtsgeschichte (1967) 452.

[343] Jhering cited Comte, though in a more specific context and more or less in passing, see *Jhering*, Zweck II (1886) 74.

[344] Apparently, the first German translation was Auguste Comte, Einleitung in die positive Philosophie (G.H. Schneider transl., Leipzig 1880). Perhaps Jhering could have read the French original, but given the size of the work, that would have been a major undertaking for which Jhering's busy schedule would not have left the necessary time.

[345] Supra notes 231–247 and text.

[346] *Welzel*, Naturrecht und materiale Gerechtigkeit (1964, orig. 1951) 191.

[347] *Jhering*, Zweck I (1884) 218 (corporations had turned into "organized institutions for robbery and fraud whose secret history contains more wickedness, infamy, and villainy than many a penitentiary, just that the thieves, robbers and fraudsters are sitting in gold instead of iron"); see also id. 530 ("insatiability and rapaciousness of egotism").

of property rights in particular.[348] But he had also openly disparaged communism,[349] defended private property (and inheritance) rights, and dismissed "socialist and communist ideas" directed at their abolition as "vain folly."[350]

Still, Welzel had a point. He did not refer to Jhering's socio-economic preferences – in that regard, Jhering was a free-marketeer who supported regulation as required for the common welfare – but to his view of the relationship between law and society. In that respect, Jhering did at times sound quite a bit like his contemporary Karl Marx (1818–1883[351]), even though he apparently never mentioned his name in writing. The strong will always try to rule weak, Jhering stated and explained:

"Applied to civil society, that means: its order will always correspond to the power relationships between the various social strata and classes of which it is composed [...and] the more powerful class will express the superiority of its power in the institutions of law.[352]

The similarity between Jhering's and Marx' views in this regard was no accident – it was based on something like a shared anti-Hegelianism: the conviction that law was not an expression of abstract principles but the product of concrete social conditions. Jhering could have easily agreed with Marx' famous statement that "[i]t is not the consciousness of men that determines their being but, conversely, their social existence that determines their consciousness."[353] In Jhering's case, this social existence was understood more broadly and included non-economic elements; with Marx, the focus was on the modes of economic production.[354] In both instances, however, law was essentially conceived as what Marx termed the "superstructure" ("Überbau") resting on the "base" ("Basis") of social reality.[355] It is interesting to note that in communist Russia, some legal scholars regarded the author of "Kampf" and "Zweck" as a kindred spirit and invoked him in support of socialist legal theory.[356]

Beyond that, Jhering shared with Marx the theme of social evolution and change (in Marx's case through the means of production, in Jhering's case largely

---

[348] Supra notes 257–263 and text.

[349] "Communisms flourishes only in the swamp in which the idea of property has gotten completely lost; at its source, [communism] is unknown;" *Jhering*, Kampf (1872) 41.

[350] *Jhering*, Zweck I (1884) 533.

[351] While they were born in the same year, Jhering outlived Marx by almost a decade.

[352] *Jhering*, Zweck I (1884) 553–554. Marx (and Engels) put it in very similar terms: "Since the state is the form in which the individuals of a ruling class assert their common interests" ("Da der Staat die Form ist, in welcher die Individuen einer herrschenden Klasse ihre gemeinsamen Interessen geltend machen"); *Marx and Engels*, Kritik der neuesten deutschen Philosophie (1845–46).

[353] "Es ist nicht das Bewußtsein der Menschen, das ihr Sein, sondern umgekehrt ihr gesellschaftliches Sein, dass ihr Bewußtsein bestimmt." *Marx*, Zur Kritik der politischen Ökonomie (1859) 9.

[354] *Marx*, Zur Kritik der politischen Ökonomie (1859) 9.

[355] *Marx*, Zur Kritik der politischen Ökonomie (1859) 8.

[356] *Rudokvas*, Jhering's Influence on Russian Legal thought (2023) 106–111.

through law); the orientation towards social forces and (group) interests; and a belief in the need for human agency to effect social change (in Jhering's case mainly in "Kampf") .[357]

Yet, "a hair's breadth" did remain between their views. Unlike the economist Marx[358], the jurist Jhering still clung to the notion of "justice" ("Gerechtigkeit") as the "life principle of society and thus the supreme mission it has to fulfill."[359] That, however, did not move Jhering very far away from Marx. For Jhering, even "justice" was determined in relation to existing social conditions[360] and conceived in utilitarian terms.[361] Also, as we shall see, even the "feeling of justice" (Rechtsgefühl), which played such a central role for Jhering, was ultimately conceived as a product not of some kind of general human conscience but of concrete social conditions and experiences.[362]

When we consider "Zweck" in the context of these various currents, we get a better sense of how it appeared to its readers at the time. Viewed in the narrow context of (especially German) jurisprudence, it was a distinctly weird and potentially revolutionary book. Yet, when seen in the broader intellectual environment shaped by Darwin, Bentham, Mill, Spencer, Comte, and Marx, it did not look all that outlandish and radical. It is true that "Zweck" with all its problems could scarcely match the work of these scholars,[363] but contemporary readers could easily regard Jhering's work as a valuable addition to that broader literature, i.e., as the voice of jurisprudence in that larger concert. Of all the German law books then on the market, "Zweck" discussed the questions most likely to interest a broader audience, even though it must have frustrated and exhausted many who read it – or at least tried.

From Nineteenth-Century Private Law to Twentieth-Century Law and Economics. Jhering's instrumentalism and social utilitarianism foregrounded the nature and role of law as an instrument for securing property rights and market transactions, thus connecting his discourse to the rising discipline of economics. Jhering's constant references to "Verkehr" (his term for human interaction in society, especially in the economic sense) throughout "Zweck,"[364] his emphasis on

---

[357] Supra 1.; *Schelsky*, Das Jhering Modell des sozialen Wandels durch Recht (1971) 52. On Jhering and Marx, see also *Rückert*, Der Geist des Rechts (2004) 136; *Viehweg*, Rechtsdogmatik und Rechtszetetik bei Jhering (1970) 211–212.

[358] It is often overlooked, that Marx was first a law student, however, before he turned to philosophy (Ph.D. from the University of Jena 1841) and eventually to economics.

[359] *Jhering*, Zweck I (1884) 554; see also infra 3. notes 490–496 and text.

[360] *Jhering*, Zweck I (1884) 554–555.

[361] Supra note 253 and text.

[362] Infra 3. Jhering's view of the interaction between the feeling of justice and the progress of law was also reminiscent of Marx, i.e., of his theory of dialectics between "Sein und Bewußtein" (existence and consciousness); see infra chapter V.2., notes 120–139 and text; *Helfer*, Rudolf von Jhering über das Rechtsgefühl (1968) 590.

[363] At least this was Ludwig Mitteis' – well informed – judgment; *Mitteis*, Jhering (1905) 658.

[364] More than a hundred pages of the first volume of "Zweck" are pure market theory,

legal certainty as a necessary condition for the functioning of the market,[365] and his repeated calls for curbing the excesses of private property (especially by entrepreneurs),[366] presented law as a means for economic regulation in the age of industrial capitalism. This foreshadowed the instrumental use of private law for the pursuit of efficiency by the twentieth-century law and economics approach as it has come to dominate jurisprudence the United States.[367]

Taken to its logical conclusion, Jhering's approach abandoned the traditional idea of "private law:" it was no longer an autonomous sphere of (economic and other) liberty defined by its independence from the state but a regulatory instrument in the hands of the state – and thus a form of public law.[368] The "will" it expressed was no longer the individual's but the state's.

Two Parting Views of Zweck: The Macro- and the Micro-Level.[369] After exploring the evolution of Jhering's project, his theory of law and his view of the state, as well as the book's relationship with contemporaneous intellectual currents, it is time to take a step back and view "Zweck" as a whole again.

Reactions to the book were mixed. In its own time and environment, it received disappointingly little attention and was not what one calls a success.[370] A detailed and profound critique was proffered by the prominent Germanist Felix Dahn (1834–1912) who admired Jhering but differed from him in fundamental regards.[371] Other critics were more summarily damning, like Jhering's nemesis Josef Kohler (1849–1919).[372] Jhering's close friend Windscheid probably spoke for many German legal academics when he dismissed Jhering's central idea, that all law was created and driven by purposes, as an old hat presented "with obtrusiveness."[373] That was perhaps a bit unfair; of course, the idea itself was not

---

dealing with the role and effect of (essentially economic) reward (Lohn) as a mechanism for the control of human conduct in society, in his case on the market; *Jhering*, Zweck I (1884) 93–233.

[365] Supra chapter II. 1., notes 263–269 and text.

[366] See especially *Jhering*, Zweck I (1884) 519–534

[367] The line from Jhering's instrumentalism and utilitarianism to modern law and economics is drawn by *Vesco*, Die Erfindung der ökonomischen Rechtswissenschaft (2021), especially 11–103.

[368] See *Nörr*, Eher Hegel als Kant (1990) 49–53.

[369] These terms are borrowed from comparative law where they describe the distinction between comparing the world's major "legal families" (such as the civil law and the common law) or whole legal systems as opposed to their individual features, institutions or rules; see *Zweigert und Kötz*, Einführung in die Rechtsvergleichung (3d ed. 1996) 4–5.

[370] *Eck*, B. Windscheid and R.v.Jhering (1893) 35–38 (with further references).

[371] *Dahn*, Die Vernunft im Recht (1879).

[372] Kohler considered Jhering "a wholly unphilosophical thinker" whose effort to come to grips with the concept of "Zweck" "never proceeded beyond the most pitiful stammer." In Kohler's view, "Jhering's whole attempt resulted in pathetic dilettantism;" *Kohler*, Lehrbuch der Rechtsphilosophie (1909) 16. He considered the whole work "built on sand"; *Kohler* Rechtsphilosophie und Universalgeschichte (1915) 12.

[373] "Aufdringlichkeit;" quoted by *Dove*, Rudolf von Jhering und Bernhard Windscheid (1893) 153.

entirely new, but Jhering still deserved credit for exploring it and making it a prominent topic of the jurisprudential discourse of the time. When the book became known in the United States in the late nineteenth and early twentieth centuries, reactions ranged from lavish praise to harsh criticism.[374] Later generations have likewise minced no words about the book's serious weaknesses, bemoaned the ultimate failure of Jhering's project, but also emphasized its great merits.[375] Jhering himself was ambivalent about his work; on the one hand, he was convinced that important elements were truly original; on the other hand, he emphasized that he had just put into words what was widely felt at the time.[376]

While much of this mixed reception simply reflects the varying views of various readers and reviewers, to a large extent, it is also the result of two distinct perspectives: "Zweck" looks very different depending on whether one views it on the macro-level, i.e., in the grand scheme of things, or on the micro-level, i.e., in and of itself.

In the grand scheme of things, "Zweck" is a "landmark in the history of jurisprudence."[377] It represents a paradigm shift by replacing the prevailing understanding of law as a creature of history and logic with a view of law as a psychological and social phenomenon. That shift had far-reaching implications. It reoriented jurisprudence from a study of the law's cultural tradition and systematic order to an inquiry into its social functions and practical, especially economic, effects. Instead of asking where law came from and how it was to be organized, it asked what law was good for and how it worked. It shifted the focus from abstract concepts to concrete effects, from speculation to observation, from the ideal to the real. That new agenda required new tools: the study of law had to transcend the traditional boundaries of jurisprudence proper and become broadly, and boldly, interdisciplinary; in particular, it needed to go beyond the text of the law and look at its interaction with the social conditions surrounding it.

---

[374] An early reviewer glorified "Zweck" as "undoubtedly the most profound and satisfactory contribution to the science of legal philosophy since the days of Austin and Bentham;" *Anon.*, Review of Jhering, Der Zweck im Recht (1880) 205. Unsurprisingly, the editors of, and commentators on, the English edition (1921) praised it as well, see *Drake*, Editorial Preface (1921); *Geldart*, Introduction (1921); *Lamm*, Introduction to this Volume (1921). By contrast, the review by Morris Cohen was devastating ("a work of [...] antiquated psychology and [...] mediocre philosophic power"); *Cohen*, Law as Means to an End (1914) 558; see also *Geldart*, Introduction (1921) xxxvii (criticizing Jhering for getting lost in detail at the expense of systematic coherence).

[375] Probably the harshest modern German critic was *Wolf*, Große Rechtsdenker (1963) 633, 640; see also *Pleister*, Persönlichkeit, Wille und Freiheit im Werke Jhering (1982) 341–346; *Helfer*, Ein Nachtrag Jherings zum "Zweck im Recht" (1970) 12. For an admirably balanced assessment, see *Jenkins*, Rudolf von Jhering (1960).

[376] *Jhering*, Zweck II (1886) 172–173.

[377] *Vinogradoff*, Outlines of Historical Jurisprudence I (1920) 142.

At the same time, "Zweck" departed radically from the tradition of the Historical School which had dominated jurisprudence in Germany and beyond since the early nineteenth century. "Zweck" challenged the Historical School's theory of the law's origin by not deriving law from *Volksgeist* and organic growth but from force and struggle. It rejected the will-theory (in both its Savignian and Hegelian versions) by centering the concept of law around interests and purposes. And it departed from the dominant individualism by putting the role and function of law for society at center stage.

With all that, Jhering's new approach brought jurisprudence up to date, so to speak. Much of mid-nineteenth century German legal thought had still lingered in the long shadow of Savigny's backward-looking and quietist program as well as that of Hegel's exaltation of the state as epitomized by the enlightened absolutism of early nineteenth century Prussia. By the 1870s, these positions were visibly outdated. The unified German *Reich* was a constitutional monarchy as well as a dynamic and fast-industrializing market society driven by rapid scientific and technological progress. That society needed law not as a heritage of the past but as an instrument to shape the future; not for the glory of the state but for the regulation of social and economic activity. "Zweck" pointed exactly in that direction. In addition, the book modernized jurisprudence by prying it loose from the disciplines prevailing in the past, i.e., philosophy and history, and by connecting it to the fields pointing to the future, i.e., the natural sciences, psychology, sociology, and economics. At the time of Darwin, Mill, Spencer, Comte, and Marx, historical jurisprudence seemed plainly irrelevant. Jhering's new paradigm, by contrast, related law to the ideas of all these thinkers in one way or another and fit right into the contemporary intellectual climate. Thus it helped to keep German jurisprudence at the forefront of legal thought on an international scale.[378]

Finally, Jhering's pervasive emphasis on the need for law to promote and protect social, rather than individual, interests also modernized jurisprudence in crucial ways. Urbanization, industrialization, and the emergence of capital markets made the need to limit the use of private property in the public interest too obvious to be ignored. This was no longer the world in which (private) law just needed to delimit the individual spheres of freedom propagated by Kant and Savigny, but an environment in which law had to protect the concerns of society as a whole. "Zweck" envisaged a world in which no one is an island;[379] it viewed human beings not as isolated individuals fending for themselves as best they could but as inevitably interdependent members of a society involved in the pursuit of the common good. This pointed the way from hard-core nineteenth century liberalism to the twentieth century social and regulatory state. In the words of Julius Stone, "Zweck" was a "bridge to twentieth century theories of justice."[380]

---

[378] See *Kuntze*, Rudolf von Jhering (1892) 617; *Mitteis*, Jhering 665.
[379] *Jhering*, Zweck I (1884) 79.

When we engage with the book on the micro-level, however, we see a very different picture. Viewed from close-up, "Zweck" is both a mess and a treasure trove. That suggests approaching it in an unconventional manner.

In many ways, "Zweck" is a hopeless mess.[381] It is, as Jhering's American biographer observed, Jhering's most ambitious work,[382] but it is also his most troublesome, even leaving aside that he lost control of the project and could not bring it to completion. The flaws of the book have been discussed by generations of (mostly German) scholars whose judgments have ranged from partially critical to virtually damning.[383] Let us focus on just the first volume here.

To begin with, the book's organization is difficult to grasp.[384] Following its own logic, which is driven by the peculiar (quasi-Darwinian) idea that lower purposes progressively generate higher ones, its order remains a source of confusion even to the reader who earnestly consults the table of contents – to which Jhering does not even completely adhere.[385] In fact, with the exception of the opening chapters, the whole text needs to be re-organized, cleaned-up, and re-written from beginning to end – though by someone with more talent for organization and clarity than Jhering possessed.[386]

Furthermore, the book's methodology is awfully weak. Jhering openly acknowledged that he was ill-equipped for the task he set for himself: it required a

---

[380] *Stone*, The Province and Function of Law (1946) 313.

[381] *Stintzing and Landsberg*, Geschichte der deutschen Rechtswissenschaft III.2. (1910) 816, called it "a monster which lacked all care for proportion."

[382] *MacDonell*, Rudolf von Jhering (1914) 591.

[383] See, e.g., *Eck*, B. Windscheid and R.v.Jhering (1893) ("embarrassing"); *Kuntze*, Rudolf von Jhering (1892) 613–614 ("trivial truths presented as novel and astounding and explained in the broad and smug manner typical for an amateur"); *Mitteis*, Jhering 658 ("weak," "somewhat embarrassing"); *Wolf*, Große Rechtsdenker (1963) 651 ("pompous" [aufgeblasen], "self-important" [wichtigtuerisch]; also referencing other scholars albeit without citations); *Helfer*, Rudolf von Jhering als Rechtssoziologe (1968) 566 ("lack of methodological precision, chaotic mix of interesting hypotheses and considerations..."). A more balanced (quasi-contemporary) assessment is *Merkel*, Jhering (1893) 30–38. On the other side of the Atlantic, Morris Cohen's review of the English translation also mercilessly laid open the book's many weaknesses; see *Cohen*, Law as a Means to an End (1914). The problems are summarized and characterized in an admirably clear and concise fashion by *Jenkins*, Rudolf von Jhering (1960) 175, 188–189.

[384] *Fikentscher*, Methoden des Rechts III (1976) 131, put it mildly when he spoke of the "infelicity of the arrangement."

[385] Often, the same or closely related topics are discussed in vastly different places and contexts, at times in a redundant or inconsistent fashion. Chapter headings sometimes confidently announce a topic but then the chapter deals with lots of things not covered by its title.

[386] With regard to Jhering's legal theory proper, such a re-writing is essentially performed by *Jenkins*, Rudolf von Jhering (1960). The problem of organization is exacerbated by the fact that even just Jhering's jurisprudential discourse is rife with digressions. Depending on the reader's inclination and patience, these digressions can be engaging or maddening, but they surely disrupt the flow of the discourse time and again, adding to the difficulty of reading the book.

thorough understanding of philosophical (and other) foundations which he had never acquired. This left him an admitted "dilettante" in many regards. He hoped that he could make up for that deficiency by supplying his expertise as a jurist so that the result would still be useful,[387] and in some regards, it is. Still, methodological deficiencies haunt the work at almost every turn.[388] In fact, Jhering had precious little control over his methodology altogether. Perspectives and approaches are constantly changing from nature to history to philosophy to economics to jurisprudence. The euphemistic term for such a potpourri is eclecticism; a less merciful moniker is disarray.

Many of Jhering's assumptions and claims are unbearably categorical: *all* human action is driven by purpose; *all* motivation is rooted in egoism; *all* law must serve (only) society as a whole; etc. These, and similar, assertions resulted in pithy phrases and have had a strong rhetorical appeal for generations of readers[389] but they did not reflect a careful and balanced inquiry into the subject matter of the discourse. The breadth of these assertions often forced Jhering to find proof for them by hook or crook, and at times, they simply replace the myth of *Volksgeist* with the myth of "purpose."[390]

To make matters worse, the methodological deficiencies are combined with Jhering's notoriously lackadaisical attitude towards terminological precision and consistency. Varying and potentially inconsistent definitions abound.[391] The problem with such definitions and statements was not that they could not be reconciled in one way or another, but that Jhering made no attempt to do so. Thus, he constantly created moving targets, inevitably confounding his reader. When Max Rümelin (1861–1931), a prominent legal scholar a generation after Jhering, commented that in "Zweck", "one obscurity was piled on top of another," he hit the nail on the head.[392]

[387] *Jhering*, Zweck I (1884) IX–X.

[388] For a fuller discussion, see *Wieacker*, Rudolf von Jhering (1969) 26–31

[389] *Rückert*, Methodenorakel (2019) 484.

[390] The point is made by *Helfer*, Rudolf von Jhering als Rechtssoziologe (1968) 562.

[391] As we have already seen, even the understanding of "purpose" announced at the beginning of Volume One is quite different from the actual use of the term in Jhering's legal theory; in addition, "purpose" sometimes refers to the individual, sometimes to society, and at one point it is even "the highest world-creating principle" ("höchstes weltbildendes Princip"); *Jhering*, Zweck I (1883) XIII.

[392] *Rümelin*, Rudolf von Jhering (1922) 67. Similar criticism came from several other scholars, including Jhering's American biographer *MacDonnell*, Rudolf von Jhering (1910) 594 ("great diffuseness"); see also *Fikentscher*, Methoden des Rechts III (1976) 113–114; *Helfer*, Jherings Gesellschaftsanalyse (1970) 87 (on Jhering's later work generally); *Merkel*, Jhering (1893) 35–38, and *Wolf*, Große Rechtsdenker (193) 651. By contrast, Helmut Schelsky opined that gratitude was in order for Jhering's "shaky intellectual structure" ("unsolides Denkgehäuse") because it facilitates prying his thought loose "from an often inappropriate and antiquated nomenclature;" *Schelsky*, Das Jhering-Modell des sozialen Wandels (1971) 48.

The roots of the confusion go much deeper, however. Jhering himself was often not entirely sure what the whole project was about. It was not only that its thrust and scope kept changing as he went along.[393] Even after completing the work, he was not really clear about its goal. At various points he claimed that "Zweck" was meant "to bring the practical conception of law to the fore, in contrast to the aprioristic-philosophical [view];" that "it aimed at disclosing the practical motives of legal institutions everywhere;"[394] that the book was dedicated to "justice" as the supreme value; etc.[395] and none of these statements were consistent with the claims made in the prefaces to the two volumes to begin with. As Yogi Berra (1925–2015) famously quipped: "You've got to be very careful if you don't know where you are going because you might not get there."[396]

The extent to which these rather glaring weaknesses are forgivable depends largely on the magnanimity of the reader. He or she needs to keep in mind that in his investigations, Jhering was driven by a genuine, and in fact burning, interest and curiosity to pursue a project for which he simply lacked the tools; that he essentially could not help himself in biting off more than he could methodologically chew; and that he honestly acknowledged the limits of his ability, even though he did not respect them.

All these problems notwithstanding, even on the micro-level, "Zweck" has redeeming value: it is a veritable treasure trove of ideas and insights. Though often half-baked, exaggerated, and eccentric, they are the products of an extraordinarily creative mind that constantly explored new angles, revealed interesting connections, and conjured up vivid images. Many had nothing to do with either Zweck or Recht. They could be just little asides, like the comparison between commercial credit and narcotic drugs which both entail the risk of overuse with deleterious consequences.[397] Some were excursions into the realms of economy or society that resulted in interesting essays in their own right, such as Jhering's observations about the workings of an already globalized economy with vast international supply networks.[398] Several of Jhering's insights into the law's economic foundations and effects fully anticipated what law and economics scholars in the United States have celebrated as their own path-breaking discoveries,[399]

---

[393] See supra notes 163–168 and text.

[394] *Jhering*, Zweck I (1884) 10 note.

[395] *Jhering*, Geist II.2. (5th ed. 1898) 261 fn. 506a. That was a bold statement in light of Jhering's view that law was "merely a means to an end," not an end in itself, supra note 209 and text.

[396] <https://performanceexcellencenetwork.org/>, September 15, 2015.

[397] *Jhering*, Zweck I (1884) 179–180. We need to remember at this point that as a connoisseur of wine, Jhering knew a thing or two about the effects of alcohol; see supra chapter I.4., notes 166–168 and text.

[398] *Jhering*, Zweck I (1884) 89–92.

[399] See, e.g., *Jhering*, Geist III (1865) 195. Jhering explained that a heavy burden of proof entails high costs of rights enforcement which diminish the ultimate value of the right itself; thus a legal system must pay careful attention not to make rights enforcement unnecessarily

and many of his observations about the law's actual effects foreshadowed the basic tenets of twentieth century legal realism.[400] Jhering explored the division of labor years before Durkheim's treatise made it a paradigm,[401] and he used the formula of the state's monopoly of the legitimate use of force decades before Weber followed suit.[402]

In addition, Jhering was constantly engaged with language. In footnotes throughout the book, he pointed out how etymology can help us understand social institutions and legal rules, even though his inferences were often highly adventurous. He played word games which, however, often work only in the original German. Along the way, he lampooned national habits,[403] made fun of philosophical arguments,[404] and coined memorable aphorisms.[405]

Last, but certainly not least, "Zweck" often grabs the reader's attention through Jhering's characteristic dauntlessness.[406] He intrepidly uncovered the inhumane sides of human nature, the unpopular implications of popular ideas, and the uncomfortable consequences of comfortable positions. Where others often feared to tread, he daringly advanced into delicate terrain, sometimes with the violence of the proverbial bull in the china shop.[407] One may disagree with Jhering's assertions or even be shocked by his conclusions, but as in Nietzsche's writings, one is in the presence of a refreshingly bold and independent spirit who often provokes, sometimes just tickles, but always engages the reader's mind.

---

difficult. This pointed to the importance of enforcement costs for the legal system, i.e., what Guido Calabresi, eventually came to term "tertiary costs" (of accidents), see *Calabresi*, The Cost of Accidents (1970) 28. As Jhering pointed out more than century earlier, "the most precious goods are worthless if the costs of their realization devour their value," *Jhering*, Geist III (1865) 195. See also *Jhering*, Zweck I (1884) 37–39; 68–69. On Jhering and modern law and economics, see *Vesco*, Die Erfindung der ökonomischen Rechtswissenschaft (2021) 27–103.

[400] See infra chapter VII.3., notes 253–260 and text.

[401] *Jhering*, Zweck I (1884) 149, 228; *Durkheim*, De la division du travail social (1893).

[402] See supra note 200–201 and text.

[403] *Jhering*, Zweck I (1884) 220 note, 303 note.

[404] Jhering, Zweck I (1884) 549 (ridiculing John Stuart Mill's idea of compulsory labor for the lazy – "All that on the terrain of liberty!")

[405] With regard to qualifications for judicial office: "Knowledge can be guaranteed, character cannot" ("Wissen läßt sich erzwingen, der Character nicht"); *Jhering*, Zweck I (1884) 398. "A man's ledger of expenses sometimes tells you more about his character than his diaries" ("das Ausgabenbuch eines Mannes sagt über seinen wahren Character unter Umständen mehr aus als seine Tagebücher."); id. 65.

[406] Franz Wieacker, perhaps Jhering's most astute, and certainly his most linguistically gifted, commentator termed this quality "intrepid sense of reality" ("unerschrockener Wirklichkeitssinn"), *Wieacker*, Rudolf von Jhering (1969) 33.

[407] One could, of course, sarcastically respond that Jhering should have heeded Alexander Pope's warning that "fools rush in where angels fear to tread," *Pope*, An Essay on Criticism (London 1711) 36.

Thus, actually reading the first volume of "Zweck" (rather than just contemplating its significance for modern legal thought) is best approached as an intellectual adventure. Like many jurisprudential classics, ploughing through Zweck requires plenty of forgiveness, equanimity, and patience.[408] But even if, in the end, the reader buys little of what Jhering offers, his or her eyes will have been opened to things not seen before.

3. Jhering's Positivism and the Challenge of Justice: "Die Enstehung des Rechtsgefühls" (1884)

In 1884, Jhering once again gave a talk to the Viennese Law Society. Twelve years earlier, he had said good-bye to the practitioners in the Habsburg metropolis with his rousing oration on "Der Kampf ums Recht." After his return to Germany, he had spent most of the next decade desperately wrestling with "Zweck." Now, after the completion of its second volume (1883), he was back in Vienna, this time to explore "Die Entstehung des Rechtsgefühls" ("The Emergence of the Feeling of Justice"). "Kampf," "Zweck," and "Rechtsgefühl" had an important common denominator: they were all manifestations of the socio-historical approach Jhering that had finally come to embrace after his "conversion." "Kampf" had claimed that law was born from social struggle; "Zweck" had explained law as a historically developed substitute for force, a mechanism to regulate social life, and an instrument to pursue social ends; now, "Rechtsgefühl" looked to historical development and social reality as the stuff from which the "sense of justice" emerged.

Neither in his talk nor elsewhere did Jhering provide a clear and uniform definition of *Rechtsgefühl;* in fact, Jhering used the expression in different contexts, for different purposes, and thus in different senses.[409] It is important, however, to be clear what he meant by the term in 1884 Vienna. In his talk he distinguished two forms.[410] One is subjective, individual, and ad hoc, so to speak: the "moral pain,"[411] which is aroused in a person in reaction to an injustice suffered

---

[408] One could say the same, for example, about *Montesquieu's* "Esprit des Loix" (1748). Those who focus not just on the few characterics and features for which the work is famous but actually look at, or even read, the work, will soon notice that it is every bit as disorganized, disjointed, and rambling as Jhering's "Zweck."

[409] Its dimensions have been carefully explored and perceptively explained by *Birr*, Der Schatten des Wanderers (2022), especially 160–189; see also the summary id. 220–224. As Birr shows, the concept was widely discussed at the time, id. 76–126, and has remained a topic in the present as well, id. 224–229.

[410] *Jhering*, Rechtsgefühl (1884) 9–10; see also *Jhering*, Zweck I (1st ed. 1877) 41; for reasons that are not clear the passage was omitted in the second edition; for a discussion, see *Birr*, Der Schatten des Wanderers (2022) 6.

[411] *Jhering*, Kampf (1872) 26 ("der moralische Schmerz").

and that provides (or should provide) the impulse to fight back. This is the *Rechtsgefühl* Jhering discussed in "Kampf."[412] It is linked to one's sense of personality, honor, and self-respect. Jhering did not further pursued this feeling of indignation, never analyzed it in any depth, and we will put it to one side here. The other version is objective and more enduring: *Rechtsgefühl* is the "critical" faculty by which legal outcomes are judged,[413] i.e., a yardstick for justice. Even though Jhering did not make any further distinctions in his talk, this version actually consists of two sub-types. The first is individual and professional: it is the seasoned jurist's sense of justice which he must apply to control, and if need be, correct, results reached via doctrinal analysis. This is the *Rechtsgefühl* Jhering experienced in the double-sale case and that he consistently invoked after his "conversion" around 1860.[414] In his talk, he did not directly focus on this type either. The second sub-type is collective and cultural: the feeling of justice of a given community, i.e., the socially shared moral judgments. This is the *Rechtsgefühl* Jhering set out to explore in his talk.[415] He thus used the term more or less interchangeably with "ethical truths" or "norms" or "principles"[416] or simply with "ethics".[417] In particular, he sought to determine "whence comes the substance of the supreme principles and truths that inform our sense of justice"[418] as a collective and cultural phenomenon.

Jhering spoke freely (for an hour-and-a-half), aided by few notes, and he apologized to his illustrious audience (which included members of the imperial family) for his rambling style.[419] While "lively agreement" by the listeners was reported in the press,[420] the long-term impact of "Rechtsgefühl" was negligible compared to the smashing public and global success of "Kampf." Jhering never published the talk, and other than in the contemporary papers, it was not available in print for the better part of a century.[421] While Jhering's Viennese rumi-

---

[412] *Jhering*, Kampf (1872) 1872, 20–51.

[413] *Jhering*, Kampf (1877) 42 ("das Gefühl der Urtheilskraft").

[414] See supra chapter III.1., note 10 and text.

[415] It is also the sense in which he used the term when he claimed that Rechtsgefühl can have a productive function, i.e., that it can drive the evolution of law towards new rules and standards, see infra note 479.

[416] *Jhering*, Rechtsgefühl (1884) 11, 19, 33.

[417] *Jhering*, Rechtsgefühl (1884) 13 ("das Sittliche"). Jhering also carelessly linked it to "conscience" ("Gewissen"), i.e., a subjective category, though the context suggests that this was simply a result of his usual terminological innocence; id. 42.

[418] *Jhering*, Rechtsgefühl (1884) 10.

[419] Since the text is based on the stenographic record created by a listener, it still has all the hallmarks of a talk. It thus illustrates, as Okko Behrends has pointed out, Jhering's strenghts as a presenter: a forceful, vivid, and clear language, and the effort to explain matters to the audience in a plain and unpretentious fashion. It also evinces, however, the wish to captivate the audience through both humor and gravitas; *Behrends*, Das 'Rechtsgefühl' in der historisch-kritischen Rechtstheorie des späten Jhering (1986) 66.

[420] Juristen Zeitung, Sunday, March 18, 1884, 1 note; reprinted in *Jhering*, Rechtsgefühl (1884) 5.

[421] It was eventually published as *Rudolf von Jhering*, Über die Entstehung des Rechtsge-

nations on the emergence and substance of society's *Rechtsgefühl* as a standard of justice have lingered on the margins of scholarship on Jhering, they are key for our understanding of a central feature of his thinking: his positivism – and its limits.[422] This is because his talk showed, in much more concentrated form than "Zweck," that Jhering had completed the gradual shift of emphasis from a "historical" to a "sociological" jurisprudence. As we shall see, *Rechtsgefühl* is a litmus test for the nature, strength, and limits of Jhering's positivism.

The issue of Jhering's "positivism" has been much debated, mainly by German academics,[423] sometimes in a less than lucid fashion.[424] The reason for the great interest in the question is not only that German scholars just love to debate theoretical issues, but also that in mid- and late twentieth century Germany, (legal) positivism was a hot topic with strong political implications. Many post-World War II German academics considered positivism – conceived as the rejection of higher values and a resultant blind obedience to rules – a major cause for the perversion of justice during the Nazi-regime.[425] As a result, the term became politically (and historically) loaded. In German jurisprudential discourse, "positivism" has often been not just a neutral expression for a particular approach to

---

fühls, in: Rudolf von Jhering, Der Kampf ums Recht. Ausgewählte Schriften mit einer Einleitung von G. Radbruch (Christian Rausche ed., Nürnberg 1965, 275–302). I have used the somewhat more recent version, edited, annotated, and published by Okko Behrends in 1986, i.e., *Jhering*, Rechtsgefühl (1884). Perhaps Jhering never published the talk because he planned to present its ideas later in a re-worked fashion. He did include the core argument about the origin and development of the sense of justice in the Introduction to his "Entwicklungsgeschichte des römischen Rechts," a project that was still in its early stages when Jhering passed away in 1892. The Introduction and the first chapter were posthumously published by his son-in-law, Victor Ehrenberg; *Jhering*, Enwickungsgeschichte (1894); in the Introduction, Jhering also provided a critique of contemporary historiography, see infra chapter V. 1.

[422] In conjunction with writings from the same period, "Rechtsgefühl" can also provide a basis for constructing a broader theory of law in society; see *Behrends*, Das 'Rechtsgefühl' in der kritisch-historischen Rechtstheorie des späten Jhering (1986); *Schelsky*, Das Jhering-Modell des sozialen Wandels durch Recht (1971); see infra notes 120–139 and text.

[423] For a summary of the debate, see *Pleister*, Persönlichkeit, Wille und Freiheit im Werke Jherings (1982) 1–12. The most probing analysis is provided by *Behrends*, War Jhering ein Rechtspositivist? (1996); inter alia, Behrends explores the implications of Jhering's positivism, as Behrends understands it, for the development of modern legal method, especially in the continental European context. Behrends also proffers an attractive reconciliation between what I will call Jhering's "sociological positivism" and Jhering's (clearly expressed) views on substantive justice, see infra notes 497–510 and text. See also *Dreier*, Jherings Rechtstheorie (1996); *Olivecrona*, Jherings Rechtspositivismus im Lichte der heutigen Wissenschaft (1970); *Wieacker*, Rudolf von Jhering (1959) 208–209.

[424] See *Wolf*, Große Rechtsdenker (1963) whose – in many regards admirable – essay on Jhering opens with a long and complex discourse on nineteenth century positivism as such, mingling various strands of thought with the author's personal predilections; id. 622–627. For Wolf, Jhering represented the "break-through of positivism as the fundamental credo ('Weltanschauung') in German jurisprudence," id. 627.

[425] See infra chapter VII.1., note 83 and text.

the production of knowledge but an implicit accusation, i.e., that lawyers all too often merely endorse and enforce the (positive) rules without scrutinizing them for their compatibility with the precepts of justice.[426] Thus, calling Jhering a "positivist" has potentially negative implications.[427]

The question of whether Jhering was a "positivist" is far too general to be answered with a simple yes or no. In nineteenth century Germany (and beyond), there were several widely prevalent versions of (legal) positivism, and they need to be sorted out in order to evaluate Jhering's jurisprudence in their respective contexts. We can then focus on the form Jhering finally arrived at and that I will call sociological positivism – which he eventually extended even to the "feeling of justice." This will still leave open the question of what role normative considerations, especially the idea of "justice," played in Jhering's thinking.

Positivism in Jurisprudence: Nineteenth Century Variations. On the most general level, positivism is an approach to knowledge production that focuses strictly on the data discernible by experience and declines to engage with standards lying beyond these data, such as *a priori* postulates or normative values. Greatly simplified, positivism focuses on the physical, historical or social *is* and leaves the metaphysical, timeless or ethical *ought* to one side. There were three broadly embraced versions of positivism in nineteenth–century (German and other) jurisprudence to which Jhering then added a fourth. They differed primarily with regard to the "data" on which they focused.[428]

The first may be called "historical positivism" because it found the relevant data in history. It lay at the heart of the modern legal science developed primarily by Savigny in the 1810s.[429] Savigny rejected the natural law tradition so widely embraced especially in the seventeenth and eighteenth centuries inter alia because (at least in his view) that tradition had failed to strictly observe the difference between what the law actually is from what it ought to be. Building on Kant's distinction between law, which dealt with externally enforceable norms, and ethics, which concerned norms subject to one's (internal) conscience,[430] Savigny (and Puchta) postulated a legal science that focused on the former and left the latter to the philosophers.[431] For Savigny and his followers, the positive concepts and norms of law were to be found in the existing legal culture, and they became tangible in the historical record (especially in the Roman law). In that sense,

---

[426] That (legal) "positivism" became "almost a dirty word" in US-American legal discourse after World War II as well, was due to different reasons; see *Lloyd*, Introduction to Jurisprudence (1960) XVI.

[427] This is clearly the message conveyed by Wolf in his essay on Jhering; Wolf, Große Rechtsdenker (1963), 622–668.

[428] For a critical discussion of the various forms of nineteenth century German legal positivism, see *Schröder*, Recht als Wissenschaft I (2020) 330–332.

[429] For a more thorough analysis, see *Reimann*, Nineteenth Century German Legal Science (1990).

[430] *Kant*, Metaphysik der Sitten (1797).

[431] See supra chapter I.1., notes 15–16 and text.

"historical legal science" ("geschichtliche Rechtswissenschaft") was essentially the same as a "positive legal science"[432] – a discipline concerned with the historical data, not with philosophical speculation about, or ethical evaluation of, law.

This, "historical," positivism explained and legitimized law on the basis of its evolution and, especially in Savigny's case, as an emanation of the culture's (intellectual) tradition, i.e., the *Volksgeist*. This indicates that Savigny's conception was not a stark version of positivism but that it contained considerable idealist elements. Also, for Savigny and his followers, historical, i.e., positive, jurisprudence was undergirded by philosophical idealism, such as the Kantian notion of individual autonomy or, later, the Hegelian notion of free will. Still, these ideas were not considered part of jurisprudence proper. Savigny's *Rechtswissenschaft* was a science of law, not of justice. The mainstream of nineteenth century jurisprudence followed this Savignian path: legal science had split off from philosophy (and ethics) and become a discipline of positive law.[433]

Regardless of his early proximity to, and later growing distance from, the Historical School, Jhering was a lifelong adherent of this "historical positivism." He fully shared the Savignian rejection of the natural law tradition, endorsed the separation of law and ethics (the whole structure of "Zweck" was built on it), and agreed that legal science was concerned with the positive law to be found in history (including its present stage). In fact, "Geist" was a project very much in the spirit of that "historical positivism:" its effort to show what was so special about Roman law (and how it could be overcome) was (at least supposed to be) based on a careful study of the Roman law as a historical record. Even though Jhering's attention was also focused on conceptual logic and only later fully turned to law as a social phenomenon, he never abandoned this "historical positivism" – his "Besitzwille" (1889) was still a study (and reinterpretation) of positive (Roman) law. In that sense, Jhering certainly *was* a positivist. That, however, only meant that in this regard, Jhering was part of mainstream nineteenth century German legal thought.

The second version may be termed "logical positivism."[434] It came to the fore in the 1830s and 1840s as the Historical School increasingly split into a properly historical branch that continued to explore the law's origin and development, and a systematic branch that pursued the law's logical conceptualization and organization. The latter's most prominent protagonist – and outright symbol – was

[432] Law is called "positive" when "as a given it already has a real existence" ("als ein gegebenes schon wirkliches Daseyn hat"), *Savigny*, System des heutigen römischen Rechts vol. I (1840) 14.

[433] To be sure, this did not mean unquestioned acceptance of history's record. Even mainstream nineteenth-century German jurists did critique, seek to improve, and to develop positive law, but their material were the norms of law, not the precepts of ethics.

[434] The discourse in German speaking lands mostly uses Wieacker's term "legal scientific positivism" ("rechtswissenschaftlicher Positivismus"); *Wieacker*, Privatrechtsgeschichte (1967) 430–439.

Savigny's successor Puchta with his elaborate endeavor to organize (private) law in the form a "pyramid of concepts."[435] The "data" still consisted of positive legal rules (mainly the Roman law as the *ius commune* in force before codification), although these rules were now largely pried loose from their historical origins and considered in a timeless fashion.[436]

"Logical positivism" explained, as well as legitimized, law by its consistency with ultimate principles accepted as generally valid as well as by its internal logical coherence – largely without consideration of external arguments or circumstances. Again, this "logical positivism" was not free from idealistic elements, especially since much of it ultimately rested on Hegelian philosophy. But again, these idealistic elements were *not* treated as parts of "legal science" itself; they informed it but lay beyond the sphere of the discipline proper. As Jhering's friend Windscheid famously put it: "Ethical, political or economic considerations are not the concern of the jurist as such."[437]

Needless to say, in the 1850s, Jhering was a card-carrying member of this "logical posivitism." With his "higher jurisprudence," his enthusiasm for "legal construction," and his belief that the system itself could produce new (positive) law, Jhering was the most vehement, vociferous, and visible proponent of this direction after Puchta.[438] It is true, of course, that he was not blindly obedient to the positive rules but often critical of them. In particular, he measured them against the needs of practice and modified them accordingly. In that sense, he was looking beyond the *is* and arguing for an *ought*. But he remained a positivist in that he did not measure the existing rules (nor the ones he sought to establish) against any a priori metaphysical principles or ethical values.

A third variant was what German scholars have often called "legislative positivism" ("Gesetzespositivismus")[439]: the relevant data are the positive rules created by the state. From a continental point of view, those were mainly statutes (Gesetze). Yet, to the extent that courts are authorized to create rules valid beyond the dispute before them, state-created norms would also include case "law."

In Germany, this "legislative positivism" was largely a phenomenon of the second half of the nineteenth century, and especially of its final third when, after 1871, the unified German *Reich's* legislature cranked out growing amounts of statutory law and codified the most important areas in a comprehensive fashion – a development that culminated in the German Civil Code (*BGB*) of 1900. It thus became increasingly plausible to take the position that the law is what codes and statutes (as interpreted by courts and scholars) say it is, and nothing else.

---

[435] See supra chapter II.2., note 190 and text.

[436] In the second half of the nineteenth century, this branch developed into the *Pandektenwissenschaft* of which Jhering's close friend Bernhard Windscheid was the most prominent member; see *Wieacker*, Privatrechtsgeschichte (1967) 443–447.

[437] "Ethische, politische, oder volkswirtschaftliche Erwägungen sind nicht Sache des Juristen als solchen." *Windscheid*, Die Aufgaben der Rechtswissenschaft (1904, orig. 1884) 101.

[438] Supra chapter II.2.

[439] *Wieacker*, Privatrechtsgeschichte (1967) 458–468.

As for John Austin on the other side of the Channel, law as the object of jurisprudence was now defined, as well as legitimized, through its origin in the sovereign power of the state.[440] In a constitutional system, the law's legitimacy also derived from its production in an ordered legislative process; and with the expansion of the franchise, legitimacy increasingly came from the will of the majority (at least of those entitled to vote) as well. In such an environment, compliance with "higher" values and *a priori* principles was a legislative, i.e., political question.

While Jhering developed his ideas largely before the heyday of German "legislative positivism," there is little doubt that he essentially subscribed to its basic tenets.[441] His approach was slightly different from the standard model, however. Although "Zweck" directly connected the validity of legal rules to the state, it focused not on their making but on their enforcement;[442] and although it considered the use of state power crucial, it looked not only to the legislature but also to the courts and the administrative apparatus. Thus, in Jhering's case, "statist positivism" is a more appropriate term.[443] Regardless of the label, it was not the vocation of legal science proper to evaluate rules created and enforced by state authority through resort to metaphysical concepts or ethical precepts. Jhering's "statist" positivism is subject to two important caveats, however. First, Jhering looked to state sanction merely in regard to the force of norms (as law); their origin lay in society and its needs.[444] Second, Jhering did not endorse, but rather vehemently opposed, blind adherence to state created norms. In Jhering's view, "[t]hat sort of positivism is the mortal enemy of jurisprudence because it degrades it to a mere trade," and he vowed to fight it as long as he could.[445] Thus, while jurisprudence had to focus on state enforced rules, the jurist was still tasked with reflecting upon, criticizing, and further developing them (largely through doctrinal work).

In summary, Jhering subscribed to all these versions of positivism, sometimes throughout his life, sometimes more temporarily, and with varying degrees of enthusiasm and emphasis. His "historical positivism" dominated his early years and lingered throughout his life, though after 1860 in a muted fashion; his "logical positivism" dominated his middle years but receded into the background after his "conversion;" and his "statist positivism" was clearly expressed only in his last two decades. Notably, these varieties of Jhering's positivism were nothing out of the ordinary because in each of them, he had plenty of fellow travelers. First

[440] *Austin*, The Province of Jurisprudence Determined (2d ed. 1861) 1–2.

[441] *Olivecrona*, Jherings Rechtspositivismus (1970) 174–175.

[442] Supra 2., notes 201–204 and text.

[443] I take this term from *Behrends*, War Jhering ein Rechtspositivist? (1996) 246 ("etatistischer Positivismus").

[444] See *Behrends*, Der Durchbruch zum Zweck des Rechts (1987) 267–268; *Behrends*, War Jhering ein Rechtspositivist? (1996) 244

[445] *Jhering*, Ist die Jurisprudenz eine Wissenschaft? (1868) 52, 55.

mainly in its "historical," then primarily in its "logical," finally in its "legislative" variant, legal positivism was prevalent throughout nineteenth century German jurisprudence, significant criticism (especially towards the century's end) notwithstanding.[446]

In Jhering's case, however, another variation, largely latent before his "conversion," eventually broke through, grew dominant, and finally became one of his most important contributions to the development of jurisprudence – his sociological version of positivism.

Jhering's "Sociological Positivism:" Law from Social Facts. As we have seen, at least since the 1870s, Jhering focused on law primarily as both a product of social needs and as an instrument of social control. As every reader of "Zweck" will immediately notice, however, this conception did not eliminate Jhering's view of law as a historical phenomenon nor did it conflict with his statist conception of law; instead, both these understandings were very much present in "Zweck." Yet, they were now subordinate to Jhering's sociological conception as the leading paradigm. The historical evolution and the state enforcement of law played contributing roles, so to speak, to the overarching concept of law as the means to the end of social welfare – the former put society in a historical perspective, the latter distinguished its legal norms from ethical or merely social ones.[447]

For Jhering, the crucial data for jurisprudence now came straight from social reality, and more specifically, from the conditions and needs of society in historical perspective.[448] There was, however, another kind of (alleged) facts that entered the mix in "Zweck:" the make-up of human nature and psychology, especially the innate natural drives (for survival, self-defense, association with others, etc.), the inevitably purpose-directed nature of human action, and the inherent motivations of egoism and altruism. Since Jhering's theory of law in "Zweck" also rested on these elements (as well as on observations about animal instincts[449]), German scholars have sometimes labeled his approach "naturalist,"[450] though

[446] The reader should not be left with the impression that in nineteenth century Germany, legal positivism went unchallenged. Especially during the codification phase, i.e., after ca. 1870, several prominent and influential scholars attacked it, prominently among them Otto von Gierke (1841–1921); for a summary, see *Wolf*, Große Rechtsdenker (1963) 675–676.

[447] By contrast, Jhering's "logical positivism" played virtually no role in this context. After Jhering's "conversion," it had receded into the background. Yet, as we have seen, supra chapter III.3., Jhering never completely abandoned it but merely modified it and scaled it back.

[448] As Theodor Viehweg observed, when Jhering used the term "historical" ("geschichtlich"), he often referred to the evolving conditions of society so that "sociological" may be a more appropriate term; *Viehweg*, Rechtsdogmatik und Rechtszetetik bei Jhering (1970) 49.

[449] *Jhering*, Rechtsgefühl (1884) 28–29.

[450] The term was particularly popular with Franz Wieacker, see, e.g., *Wieacker*, Gründer und Bewahrer (1959) 207; Wieacker, Privatrechtsgeschichte (1967) 450; *Wieacker*, Rudolf von Jhering (1969) 37; see also *Wolf*, Große Rechtsdenker (1963) 623–624. The view has been powerfully critisized by *Behrends*, Das 'Rechtsgefühl' in der historisch-kritischen Rechtstheorie des späten Jhering (1986) 44–156.

"anthropological-psychological" would be more precise. If we wanted to capture these elements as well, we would have to call Jhering's approach in "Zweck" "anthropological-psychological-sociological." The term is not only unwieldy, it is also misleading because it suggests that all these elements played co-equal roles. They did not. The anthropological-psychological elements in "Zweck" did not present free-standing explanations for the origin and role of law. Instead, the prolegomenon laying out Jhering's (fairly crude) anthropology (chapters I–VI) merely provided a basis for, and thus informed, Jhering's sociological theory of law. In other words, Jhering's theory of law in "Zweck" was sociological at its core but in part based on, and enriched by, anthropological-psychological elements.[451]

Thus, Jhering's approach in "Zweck" was surely "sociological" (in a broader sense); but was it also "positivist"? Some scholars have clearly taken that position[452] while others have doubted,[453] or at least modified it.[454] Perhaps oddly, both sides are right. This is because as so often, in "Zweck," two Jherings were at work at the same time. One Jhering was the hard-nosed and clear-eyed legal scientist; he took a tough look at the social (and anthropological-psychological) facts and developed a strictly instrumental concept of law (as a "mere means to an end"). The other Jhering was softer at heart and concerned about what seemed right; he could not make himself disregard notions of "justice" and thus engaged in a, non-positivist, discussion of various substantive issues in normative terms. These two Jherings constantly took turns (by and large randomly) such that "Zweck" oscillates between establishing a positivist theory of law and discussions of substantive values. Between these themes, there were some connections and overlaps. For the most part, however, the two discourses, like oil and water, did not really mix. For now, let us focus on the hard-nosed advocate of a sociological and instrumental approach, explore the significance of *Rechtsgefühl* in its context, and then return to Jhering's "justice."

Jhering's concept and theory of law, for which "Zweck" became famous, was clearly positivist because it defined the nature of legal norms, as well as their legitimacy, in strictly sociological terms: in form, law consisted of the norms enforced by the state; in substance, it reflected (and had to protect) the conditions of social life; and in function, it was a means to that end and thus a matter of sheer

[451] Jhering's conception of law as a creation of society and as a means to its ends could stand without the ("naturalist", i.e.) anthropological and psychological elements, even though it would be considerably narrower.

[452] See *Wolf*, Große Rechtsdenker (1963), especially 627. Wolf's assessment of Jhering as a positivist is far too general; for a critique, see *Pleister*, Persönlichkeit, Wille und Freiheit im Werke Jherings (1982) 2–3.; for a more guarded position, see *Wieacker*, Gründer und Bewahrer (1959) 197.

[453] *Dreier*, Jherings Rechtstheorie (1996) 233–234.

[454] *Behrends*, Der Durchbruch zum Zweck des Rechts (1987); *Behrends*, War Jhering ein Rechtspositivist? (1996).

expediency. If it fulfilled these criteria, it was normatively unassailable – simply because there was no room for any "higher" standards or values. In this regard, Jhering's refusal to consider such values was unequivocal. While his respective statements are not always entirely coherent, they all point in the same direction: law originates in egoism, not in ethics;[455] law is not "the highest [value] in the world, not an end in itself, but merely a means to an end which is the existence of society;"[456] it is the politics of force and the organization of coercion;[457] the whole law is nothing but a creature of purpose;[458] thus it must not be measured by any absolute standard of truth but by the relative standard of purpose.[459] If these statements leave any doubt about the positivist nature of this approach, Jhering himself put it to rest: "According to my theory the only mission of the law is expediency; what is held up against that as legitimacy (ratio juris) just contains, as the deepest and firmest layer deposited in law, what is expedient."[460] Jhering did not shy away from spelling out the consequences: even law that was oppressive and unjust was legitimate as long as it fulfilled the function of securing the conditions of life for society.[461] After all, law must correspond to the stage of a people's cultural development and the needs of the time.[462] In short, Jhering's concept and theory of law in "Zweck" strictly exclude considerations of substan-

---

[455] *Jhering*, Zweck I (1884) 249.

[456] *Jhering*, Zweck I (1884) 250.

[457] *Jhering*, Zweck I (1884) 249, 291.

[458] *Jhering*, Zweck I (1884) 442 ("Zweckschöpfung").

[459] *Jhering*, Zweck I (1884) 436–437, 439. With regard to criminal law, for example, "the ethical point of view is left completely to one side […];" id. 375. There are no absolute standards for punishment; instead, "the question for which cases the legislature should provide punishment, is one of social policy;" id. 486. In addition, law does not exist to protect the individual for its own sake, but only insofar as it is useful for society; id. 372. As a result, there are no absolute limits of state power; id. 546–551. More statements of that sort could be added.

[460] *Jhering*, Zweck I (1884) 529–530 ("Nach meiner Theorie bildet die Zweckmäßigkeit die einzige Aufgabe des Rechts; was man ihr als Rechtmäßigkeit (ratio juris) entgegenhält, enthält nur die tiefste und festeste Schicht des im Recht abgelagerten Zweckmäßigen." Id. 529–530). Jhering uses the term "Rechtmäßigkeit" which does not translate into Latin as *ratio juris*. It is thus not entirely clear what he means. Since he is talking about a value judgment that could arguably be posited against mere expediency, "legitimacy" seems to be most appropriate interpretion.

[461] It must be acknowledged, Jhering wrote, "that in the life of the peoples there can be situations in which social injustice can be, temporarily and relatively, just as legitimate and required as many other institutions which do not have a permanent legitimacy, e.g., slavery. Better to have slavery than to slaughter your enemy, better a society erected on the basis of inequality of law than naked force and lawlessness. In this society as well, law fulfills its assigned function of securing the conditions of social life." *Jhering*, Zweck I (1884) 554–555. Jhering's caveats "temporarily" and "relatively" evince his unease, but the logic of his argument renders them inapposite. If social injustice is the lesser evil (as compared to violence and lawlessness), there is no reason to tolerate it only "temporarily" or "relatively" (to what?).

[462] *Jhering*, Zweck I (1884) 440.

tive justice or other ethical values.[463] It is unabashedly, and indeed starkly, positivist.[464]

Consequently, the Jhering who propagated this instrumental, positivist, and at times harsh, concept of law pushed (non-instrumental) value judgments beyond the boundaries of jurisprudence and relegated them to the realm of ethics: in the last instance, standards of justice were not a matter of law but of *Sittlichkeit*. Exploring that perspective was planned for Volume Two of "Zweck". When that volume turned into something quite different, the envisaged chapters were pushed into Volume Three[465] – which was never published. As a result, in "Zweck," Jhering's starkly positivist theory of law remained without a corresponding theory of justice.[466]

Put into the wider context of the development of German, and more broadly: Western, legal thought, Jhering's sociological positivism completed the abandonment of idealist elements in jurisprudence. Before the age of enlightenment, the ideal in the law was derived mainly from religion, i.e., God's will and the precepts of Christian ethics. The Natural Law period turned more secular and found the normative element of law in a philosophy that looked to the qualities of human nature. At least in Germany, early nineteenth century jurisprudence then turned against that (philosophical) approach and based its understanding of law on historical evolution and cultural tradition (the *Volksgeist*) which still packed some normative punch. Jhering finally forsook even that idealist element and based his concept of law on actual social conditions and needs. Thus Jhering's jurisprudence left behind Christian religion, idealist philosophy, as well as history and culture in favor of pure (social) facts. Strictly speaking, that approach left no room for idealist elements at all because now, law was judged solely by its functionality, i.e., by how well it served any social conditions and needs whatsoever. In other words, Jhering's sociological approach was positivism in its ultimate form.

Jhering's Rechtsgefühl: The Opening of the "Abyss." If Jhering's instrumental conception and theory of law left no room for considerations of substantive justice, and if ethical standards (promised for a third volume of "Zweck") were never worked out, was there anything in Jhering's repertoire by which the "jus-

---

[463] Jhering expressly excluded considerations of "substantive justice" ("materielle Gerechtigkeit") from his theory ("they are not our concern here"). He did include, however, considerations of what he called "formal justice," by which he meant that the state must comply with the norms it has itself created; *Jhering*, Zweck I (1884) 367. As he acknowledged, even that is not strictly required under his instrumental approach. Jhering explained at length that the conditions of society may well permit, if not require, the state to break these self-imposed rules; id. 420–426.

[464] That does not mean that Jhering did not care about justice, but it means that his concept of law left no room for considerations of justice as an absolute value. Such considerations had to come from outside of law; *Jhering*, Ist die Jurisprudenz eine Wissenschaft? (1868) 77.

[465] *Jhering*, Zweck II (1886) XXI.

[466] But see infra notes 490–496 and text.

tice" of positive law could be challenged – other than personal preferences? Or must slavery, torture or infanticide be considered legitimate so long as they served the "needs of social life," as they arguably had for centuries in various societies?

For Jhering, normative guidance ultimately came from the *Rechtsgefühl* in the objective and general sense mentioned above, i.e., from "those final principles and truths that we consider the content of our feeling of justice."[467] Thus *Rechtsgefühl* was the source of (ultimately moral) judgments about right and wrong. So far, so good. Then, however, Jhering proceeded to deprive *Rechtsgefühl* itself of most of its normative force.

The main topic of the talk that Jhering gave in Vienna in 1884 was the question of whether the content of *Rechtsgefühl* was rooted in human nature or rather a product of history. Jhering termed the former view "nativist" and saw it as so dominant that it was hardly ever doubted. He admitted that he had once subscribed to it himself – without harboring any doubt: he had been firmly convinced "that every human being held within himself the guarantee of these truths."[468] Thus, the final arbiter of the law's substantive justice was the sense of right and wrong that was part of human nature. This was essentially a natural law position. Yet, further reflection, in particular comparison between societies, had shown Jhering that this view was wrong. Other societies had often embraced values vastly different from our own – for example, by giving high marks to mercilessness, cunning, and readiness to exact revenge, while ascribing "magnanimity, ethical conduct, and piousness" to fools.[469] These societies' "feeling of justice" was obviously quite different from our own, modern, notions. As a result, "ethical and legal truths cannot be innate."[470] Thus Jhering embraced the opposite, "historical," view according to which the norms of ethics were the fruits of experience. The human "feeling of justice" depended on the "real facts as they have manifested themselves in history."[471] It varied with the social circumstances and with the stages of cultural development – even "conscience" was a historical phenomenon.[472] In other words, just like law itself, *Rechtsgefühl* was a response to, and a reflection of, changing social needs and thus a matter of practical expediency.[473] Jhering now conceived of the "feeling of justice" not in terms of moral philosophy but of history and sociology.

---

[467] *Jhering*, Rechtsgefühl (1884) 10.

[468] *Jhering*, Rechtsgefühl (1884) 10–11. Jhering's position was not as straightforward as he now claimed. It is true that a decade earlier, he had indeed written that "the first and truly original source of law lies in every man's heart, the second, which was added later, is the need, the necessity of life and practical reason." *Jhering*, Ist die Jurisprudenz eine Wissenschaft (1868) 66; see also id. 41. Yet, 16 years before that, he had already claimed that need and expediency preceded legal principles as well as the "idea of justice" (in the context of the early Roman treatment of aliens and international commerce); *Jhering*, Geist I (1852) 229–230.

[469] "Edelmut, Sittlichkeit, Frömmigkeit;" *Jhering*, Rechtsgefühl (1884) 36.

[470] *Jhering*, Rechtsgefühl (1884) 11.

[471] *Jhering*, Rechtsgefühl (1884) 19. f

[472] *Jhering*, Rechtsgefühl (1884) 41.

[473] *Jhering*, Rechtsgefühl (1884) 19, 22. Jhering already developed these ideas in volume two of "Zweck," *Jhering*, Zweck II (1st ed. 1883) IX–XI.

Moreover, Jhering claimed that the feeling of justice was itself a product of law. As he had already stated in "Zweck": "It is not the feeling of justice that has generated the law but the law [that has generated] the feeling of justice."[474] Note that Jhering did not just assert an interdependence between *Recht* and *Rechtsgefühl*, i.e., that the former could help to shape the latter. He claimed (in his usual categorical fashion) that first social needs gave birth to law, which then determined the people's expectations of right and wrong, thus shaping the sense of justice.[475]

In summary, Jhering now treated the sense of justice just like law: as a product of history and society, a matter of expediency, a creature of purpose, and indeed of the law itself. This had a dramatically important consequence: the feeling of justice now inevitably mirrored the law's instrumentalism and relativism; thus it could no longer provide an independent, external, vantage point from which the law's moral correctness could be judged. Jhering fully understood that implication – and he shuddered. He felt like "the earth was wavering under [his] feet" and "as if an abyss had opened."[476] He realized that embracing the "historical" view ruled out even *Rechtsgefühl* as a source of absolute value judgments. With his usual, and in a sense admirable, intellectual fearlessness, Jhering had pursued his sociological positivism to its logical conclusion. This, of course raised the spectre of moral nihilism.[477]

Yet, Jhering was not ready to leave his audience staring into the abyss of a jurisprudence that denied the possibility of any substantive value judgments. He asked his listeners not to be scared,[478] implicitly acknowledging that after hearing him, they might have reason to be. It does not really matter, he asserted, whether our "sense of justice" is innate or a product of historical experience because even a historically developed *Rechtsgefühl* could, and indeed often did, help us recognize injustice in our own age.[479] That claim rested on two assumptions.

---

[474] *Jhering*, Zweck I (1884) XIV.

[475] For a hard-hitting critique, pointing out various logical weaknesses in Jhering's argument, see *Merkel*, Jhering (1893) 34–35.

[476] *Jhering*, Rechtsgefühl (1884) 11–12.

[477] This observation has, of course, been made by others as well, see, e.g., *Larenz*, Methodenlehre der Rechtswissenschaft (1983) 47–48.

[478] *Jhering*, Rechtsgefühl (1884) 41.

[479] One might think that this was logically impossible: if the feeling of justice was itself a product of law, it seems that the two would always have to go in tandem; as a result, the feeling of justice could not sit in judgment over the law. Jhering sought to refute that logic by asserting that the sense of justice could actually "get ahead of the law" ("Vorsprung vor dem Rechte"); *Jhering*, Rechtsgefühl (1884) 49. This is possible, Jhering explained, because we experience notions of justice in particular cases from which we then, by way of "abstraction," develop more general notions of right and wrong. These generalized notions can be applied to other instances, pushing the development of the law forward. *Jhering*, Rechtsgefühl (1884) 44–51. For a comment, see Helfer, Rudolf von Jhering über das Rechtsgefühl (1968).

One was Jhering's assumption of the historical progress of law and ethics (a topic that will require further exploration[480]): while other (earlier or primitive) societies lacked *Sittlichkeit*, modern (Western) societies had developed it – and with it an appropriate and evolving sense of justice which did allow substantive value judgments about the law.[481] To be sure, for a speaker and for listeners who viewed their society at the forefront of human progress, that was an attractive proposition.[482] It was also a comforting proposition because if that society did possess adequate ethical standards, and, on their basis, a developed sense of justice, it did not have to worry about falling into the "abyss." There was a problem, however: comfort was justified only as long as ethical progress (or at least its status quo) could be ensured.[483] After all, Jhering's *Rechtsgefühl* still remained contingent on social circumstances and needs, and if at some point, society and its law were to backslide for any reason, the sense of justice would promptly follow suit. For Jhering and his audience in 1884 Vienna, that may have been hard to imagine because belief in progress was almost unconditional. Still, Jhering acknowledged the possibility.[484] Note also that even in his own day, history proffered some disconcerting examples of societies that had reverted to barbarism, such as revolutionary France less than a century ago. Thus, history provided hope, but no guarantee, that the sense of justice protected against a bleaker legal future.

This is where Jhering's second assumption came into play. Jhering postulated that God revealed himself not only in nature but also in history[485] – in fact, particularly in history,[486] even though Jhering failed to explain why that was so. Thus, a historically evolving "sense of justice" was at least as much God's work as an innate feeling of right and wrong. It is not clear to what extent Jhering was speaking from true conviction or how much he just wanted to assuage his audience's concerns. On the one hand, Jhering's invocation of God as the "ultimate origin of all ethics"[487] must be taken seriously because it was consistent with

---

[480] See infra chapter V.3 and 4.

[481] Jhering, Rechtsgefühl (1884) 33–41. Jhering explained his theory about the relationship between law and the feeling of justice in greater detail in the Introduction to his very last (and also unfinished) work, *Jhering*, Entwicklungsgeschichte des römischen Rechts (1894) 26–27; see infra chapter V.2, notes 120–139 and text.

[482] Jhering repeatedly expressed optimism about the future of mankind, see, e.g., *Jhering*, Zweck II (1886) 133.

[483] In the conclusion of this talk, Jhering predicted a glorious future; Jhering, Rechtsgefühl (1884) 54.

[484] "In the long run, not even a healthy feeling of justice has a chance against bad law; it weakens, loses its edge, shrivels." *Jhering*, Kampf (1872) 78. See also *Jhering*, Zweck I (1884) 379; *Jhering*, Entwicklungsgeschichte des römischen Rechts (1894) 22.

[485] *Jhering*, Rechtsgefühl (1884) 12.

[486] "[E]rst recht in der Geschichte"; *Jhering*, Rechtsgefühl (1884) 12.

[487] "Ich betrachte Gott als den letzten Urgrund alles Sittlichen." *Jhering*, Rechtsgefühl (1884) 12.

references to divine providence in some of his other writings.[488] It expressed Jhering's belief that in creation (including history and nature) there is an inherent ethics that will gradually assert itself. On the other hand, the fact that he referred to God once again in the final volley of his talk also suggests an effort to assure his listeners that even though *Rechtsgefühl* was ultimately nothing but a creature of social circumstances, they had nothing to worry about.

Jhering's reliance on God can also be seen as an act of desperation. Having developed a purely instrumentalist concept of law, and having derived even the "feeling of justice" from "practical needs,"[489] Jhering had rendered notions of right and wrong entirely contingent on social facts and changing circumstances. As a result of this sociological positivism, nothing in human nature could reliably prevent law and ethics from going off the rails. Whether he was fully conscious of it or not, Jhering admitted that ultimately, it was all in God's hands.

Jhering's "Justice": the "Supreme Mission" of Society. While one Jhering thus remained true to his sociological positivism which denied the possibility of absolute (non-contingent) value judgments about law as well as ethics, there was another Jhering who was very much concerned with issues of justice and substantive outcomes.

In much of his work, including his jurisprudential discourse in "Zweck," that other Jhering kept talking about, invoking, and referring to "justice" in multiple contexts and ways. "Zweck," he claimed was dedicated to the "substantive idea of justice and ethics" as "the most beautiful and noble task which science can create for itself."[490] Even in the face of a starkly positivist notion of law, he called justice the "supreme mission" of society[491]; tasked the legislator with finding and realizing "the just" ("das Gerechte"), and claimed that substantive justice ranked above the written law and above merely formal justice.[492] And while he stated that his jurisprudential theory was not really the place to deal with substantive justice, he did engage in a lengthy discussion of one of its central principles – "equality" ("Gleichheit").[493] It is not easy to concoct from all these often enigmatic statements[494] anything like a consistent theory of justice; if Jhering seriously intended

---

[488] See especially *Jhering*, Zweck I (1884) XII–XIII. Jhering's belief in divine design in nature and history had deep roots in his early education, including his reading of *Gotthold Emphraim Lessing,* Erziehung des Menschengeschlechts (Berlin 1780), see *Kunze*, Ein großer Jurist (2023) 11.

[489] *Jhering*, Rechtsgefühl (1884) 19.

[490] *Jhering*, Geist II.2. (4th ed. Leipzig 1883) 361, fn. 506a.

[491] *Jhering*, Zweck I (1884) 554.

[492] *Jhering*, Zweck I (1884) 431. For Jhering, the prevalence of substantive justice could justify even the disregard of *nulla poena sine lege*, i.e., the punishment of misdeeds not defined as crimes by law, through an extraordinary court which stood above the law and could punish according to the needs of society; id. 429–341. The idea has been popular with many dictatorial regimes, of course, as the *Volksgerichtshof* (1934–1945) in Jhering's very own country eventually demonstrated with chilling clarity.

[493] *Jhering*, Zweck I (1884) 367–373.

[494] "Justice, plain and simple, is merely that which suits all, under which all can exist." *Jhering*, Zweck I (1884) 134.

to develop one, he never got around to it.[495] Still, Jhering's incessant references to "justice" in multiple contexts show that he was far from indifferent to it. However vaguely conceived or inconsistently defined, it remained a supreme value. The sword of law, symbolizing its force, always needed the scales.[496]

One can interpret the interplay between these two Jherings – the staunch positivist and the advocate of substantive justice – in several ways. One way is that Jhering's thinking was, once again, just not fully sorted out and that he gave in to whatever momentary impulse prevailed; the haphazardness of his discourse makes that, at least in part, a plausible explanation. Another way is to see Jhering acting in two different roles. The legal scientist developing a legal theory stuck to his observation of law as a means to an end and refused to admit anything else into the precincts of a strictly positivist jurisprudence – least of all precepts of justice. Meanwhile, the man and the citizen voiced his ideas about right and wrong, fully conscious that they applied only in his own time and environment (i.e., without claiming any absolute validity). These two approaches were actually compatible: the former explained the origin and function of law as a social phenomenon in a timeless fashion; the latter looked to its ideal content under present circumstances. Thus, when Jhering described and analyzed the origin, nature, and function of law, his (sociological) positivism was virtually undiluted; but when he reflected upon and opined on what society, the state, and the law should be (or least become), he thought in unabashedly normative terms that were for the most part enlightened, liberal, and humane. Finally, one can seek to integrate Jhering's ideas into a (more or less coherent) theory of law and justice. Okko Behrends, the most prolific Jhering expert of his generation, constructed such an integrated view from the various bits and pieces one can find in "Zweck," "Rechtsgefühl," and other writings. A full discussion of this view would require a long essay in its own right, but a brief summary is in order because it shows Jhering in a highly positive, as well as modern, light.

Behrends interpreted Jherings "purposes" not in a purely relativist way, i.e., as depending on the varying needs of whatever society, but as "teleological values" that pack normative punch: for Jhering, the development of law was progressive, and once the pursuit of purposes had hardened into law, it could create enduring normative standards.[497] Building on earlier work by German sociologist Helmut

---

[495] But see immediately infra note 497–510 and text.

[496] *Jhering*, Kampf (1872) 9. Beyond Jhering's haphazard musings about justice in the abstract, there are many discussions of concrete questions of law and social policy expressing his views on a variety of (mostly contemporary) issues: equality before the law, the limits of private rights and the necessity of social regulation, the features of the rule of law, the calibration of punishment, the protection of labor and the prohibition of strikes, etc. Add to that Jhering's apotheosis of individual honor (today we might say "dignity") in "Kampf," supra 1., notes 60–71 and text, and his references to personal autonomy in other writings, and one can discern, with some effort, the contours of Jhering's ideas of what was right and just.

[497] *Behrends*, Der Durchbruch zum Zweck des Rechts (1987) 232 note 6, 261.

Schelsky (1912–1984),[498] Behrends found a "formula of justice"[499] in Jhering's jurisprudence that was defined by "two poles": the free individual and human society (organized in states).[500] According to Behrends, Jhering thought that the state can impose limits on individual liberty as far as such limits are necessary to safeguard the social welfare – but no further because society thrives best when individuals enjoy a maximum of freedom and space to develop.[501] Thus, neither the individual nor society are absolute values; instead they must be regarded in their interrelatedness, and their interests need to be carefully balanced.[502] Behrends saw Jhering's legal theory as a project to reconcile free and self-assured human beings and citizens with the needs of social life and the existing legal order.[503] Jhering emerges as an advocate of a "socially responsible liberalism."[504]

Behrends' way of integrating Jhering's jurisprudential theory and his notions of justice is attractive and plausible – but it is also very generous. It is essentially a creative interpretation that makes the best sense possible of Jhering's positions.[505] In that endeavor, it lends a degree of coherence to Jhering's ideas even though it is viable only if one leaves many conflicting statements aside. Some of the elements in Behrends' rendition have a firm foundation in Jhering's writings,[506] for example the view that private property must both be preserved and reasonably regulated.[507] Some are more debatable, for example the claim that in Jhering's conception of justice, individual liberty was co-equal with the requirements of social coexistence.[508] And some derive features from Jhering's understanding of justice that look suspiciously like projections of twentieth century ideas, such as modern constitutionalism and human rights.[509] Still, in highlighting Jhering's liberalism

[498] *Schelsky*, Das Jhering-Modell des sozialen Wandels durch Recht (1971) esp. 55–57.

[499] *Behrends*, War Jhering ein Rechtspositivist? (1996) 239.

[500] *Behrends*, War Jhering ein Rechtspositivist? (1996) 239.

[501] *Behrends*, War Jhering ein Rechtspositivist? (1996) 239.

[502] *Behrends*, War Jhering ein Rechtspositivist? (1996) 242.

[503] *Behrends*, Der Durchbruch zum Zweck des Rechts (1987) 241–242.

[504] *Behrends*, Der Durchbruch zum Zweck des Rechts (1987) 257, note 96.

[505] In a similar vein, Helmut Schelsky extracted from Jhering's late writings, "Rechtsgefühl" prominently among them, a "theory of social change" (through law); *Schelsky*, Das Jhering-Modell des sozialen Wandels durch Recht (1971) 59–74. Schelsky openly acknowledged that this theory was more precise and better structured than Jhering's "mass of thoughts;" id. 59. Delving more deeply into Schelsky's theory would lead us too far afield here. One suspects that had Jhering been able to read Schelsky's interpretation of his ideas, he would have been pleasantly suprised by what an able theorist can extract from his work.

[506] The part of "Zweck" most relevant in this regard is its chapter VI which deals with "Life Through and for Others or the Society" ("Das Leben durch und für Andere oder die Gesellschaft"); *Jhering*, Zweck I (1884) 77–92.

[507] Some aspects of Behrends' interpretation are mainly supported by the totality of Jhering's writings (including his letters), e.g., Jhering's "universal humanism;" *Behrends*, Der Durchbruch zum Zweck des Rechts (1987) 267.

[508] *Behrends*, War Jhering ein Rechtspositivist? (1996) 254.

[509] *Behrends*, War Jhering ein Rechtsposivitist? (1996) 252; see also *Behrends*. Das

and his commitment to individual honor and self-determination, Behrends' portrait provides an important counterpoint to Jhering's sociological positivism with all its disconcerting implications and harsh consequences. In a felicitous phrase, Behrends ultimately calls Jhering a "critical positivist of classically liberal provenance."[510]

Beyond Human Justice: "Die Weltgeschichte ist das Weltgericht." Before we leave Jhering's struggle with the tension between a sociological (positivist) conception of law and the substantive (normative) demands for justice behind, we must take cognizance of an overarching point of view from which Jhering sometimes looked beyond the problem of human justice altogether. Jhering saw that problem as pertinent only in normal times and short term evaluations. It was rendered moot, so to speak, in times of emergency as well as from a long-term perspective.

To understand that perspective, we need to go back to Jhering's discussion of emergency situations in "Zweck." There he had argued that society and "life" were higher values than law so that if need be, the latter had to be sacrificed for the sake of the former: if society's preservation required that the law be cast aside, doing so was not merely the right but even the duty of state authority. Whether such a step was justified could thus no longer be judged according to law: "Here, we have reached the point, where law merges into politics and history, and where the judgment of the politician, statesman, and historian must supersede that of the jurist..."[511] In a similar vein, if the question was whether the peoples in the course of their histories had gone wrong, "the judgment will not be rendered according to a predetermined opinion but must be taken from history itself."[512] In short, the final decision about right and wrong was rendered by history. As Hegel had famously opined, and as Jhering now parroted with pathos: world history is the world court.[513]

But how does history tell us what is right or wrong? Jhering's answer was unabashedly consequential: "he who wants to look in history for what is good

---

'Rechtsgefühl' in der historisch-kritischen Rechtstheorie des späten Jhering (1986) 172, 182–183.

[510] *Behrends*, War Jhering ein Rechtsposivist? (1996) 251.

[511] *Jhering*, Zweck I (1884) 252.

[512] *Jhering*, Rechtsgefühl (1886) 75–76. ("wird sie das Urtheil nicht nach einer vorgefaßten Meinung fällen, sondern der Geschichte selber entnehmen."); see also *Jhering*, Zweck II (1886) 205.

[513] *Hegel*, Grundlinien der Philosophie des Rechts (1821) 294–295 (sec. 340); *Jhering*, Ist die Jurisprudenz eine Wissenschaft? (1868) 76 ("Denn die Geschichte selber ist, wie Hegel gesagt hat, das Weltgericht."). The orginal, and typically quoted, phrase ("Die Weltgeschichte ist das Weltgericht.") was neither Jhering's nor Hegel's but penned by Friedrich Schiller (1759–1803) in his poem "Resignation" (1786 or 1787). Obviously, for Hegel, and for Jhering, history itself was not just an empirical phenomenon (a series of events) but also a normative dimension (a realm of truth and reason); for further discussion, see *Rückert*, Der Geist des Rechts (2004) 137–139.

and evil will be able to recognize it [...] in the blessings of the good, and in the curse of the evil, deed."[514] One can justly blame Jhering for not telling us what counts as a "blessing" and what as a "curse," because that will all too often be a matter of perspective and opinion. And one can justly be upset about Jhering's claim that from history's point of view, the "the judgment about [human acts] lies in their success," because that gets awfully close to might makes right. Yet, notwithstanding his Hegelian jargon, his philosophical posturing, and his indeterminate standards, Jhering had a point: in the grand scheme of things, arguments about right or wrong are not settled by timeless notions of justice but by how the deeds of the past are judged by the present.[515]

[514] *Jhering*, Ist die Jurisprudenz eine Wissenschaft? (1868) 76 ("wer in der Geschichte suchen will, was gut und böse [sic], der wird es erkennen können an dem Segen, der auch hier auf der guten, und dem Fluch, der auf der bösen That ruht.").

[515] As Jacob Burckhardt put it: "Die Zeit wird sichten und richten." ("Time will review and judge.") *Burckhardt*, Die Kultur der Renaissance in Italien 220 (Köln 1956, orig. 1860).

Chapter V

Jhering's Historical Perspective – Historiography and the Development of Law

In 1905, Ludwig Mitteis (1851–1921), one of Jhering's first biographers, divided Jhering's *oeuvre* into the two categories we have considered so far: "juristic" (i.e., doctrinal and methodological) works and "philosophical" (i.e., theoretical) studies. "There are only these two categories," Mitteis opined. As the perhaps leading legal historian of his time, Mitteis added that from Jhering, "there are no historical works in the strict sense of the term."[1] One does not easily quarrel with an authority like Ludwig Mitteis, but his assessment is only partially correct.

Mitteis was right that Jhering did not write "historical works in the strict sense of the term," i.e., in the sense of delving into history purely for its own sake. As we have seen, Jhering warned that "Geist" should not be misunderstood as an "essentially historical work;"[2] instead, it purported to explore the "innermost spirit and ultimate grounds" of Roman law in pursuit of a "general theory of law."[3] In a similar vein, to the extent that Jhering traced the historical development of law in the first volume of "Zweck," he did so not to show or explain history but to construct a sociological theory of law as a product of purposes.[4]

Mitteis was wrong, however, that all of Jhering's work was either "juristic" or "philosophical."[5] In fact, Jhering did write legal history, even though it was produced for a specific, modern purpose. And he wrote a lot of it. By far the lion's share of "Geist" deals with Roman law as a historical phenomenon – for hundreds and hundreds of pages.[6] In addition, Jhering dabbled in legal history on various other occasions.[7] How much he viewed himself not only as a doctrinalist

---

[1] *Mitteis*, Jhering (1905) 655.

[2] *Jhering*, Geist I (2d ed. 1866, Vorrede, cited after the 6th ed. 1907) VII

[3] *Jhering*, Geist I (1852) 9–10.

[4] Supra chapter IV.2.

[5] See *Stintzing and Landsberg*, Geschichte der deutschen Rechtswissenschaft III.2. (1910) 693.

[6] This was true not only, as is often alleged, for Volumes One and Two but also for Volume Three, even though the discourse there became increasingly theoretical.

[7] As a very young scholar, Jhering had outlined, probably mainly for teaching purposes, a work on "Universalrechtsgeschichte" ("Universal Legal History") in an unpublished (and fragmentary) manuscript. It was an attempt to understand the development of law on a global scale with the – ultimately philosophical – goal to detect its most fundamental characteristics. Such an approach had strong Hegelian roots and was quite popular in early nineteenth century Germany; see *Kunze*, Jherings Universalrechtsgeschichte (1989–1990) 158–165. See

and legal theorist but also as a student of legal history became evident when he embarked on a major historiographical project towards the very end of his life: "Entwicklungsgeschichte des römischen Rechts" ("History of the Development of Roman Law")[8] which, however, never proceeded beyond an Introduction and a first chapter.

The most important result of Jhering's historical studies was the definition of the characteristic features, which for him constituted the "spirit" of early Roman law; these features have been summarized in chapter II above.[9] Beyond that, and along the way, so to speak, Jhering also dealt with an extensive list of more particular issues of early Roman law. They ranged from original forms of property acquisition and self-help to the structure of the family, the army, and the state; the relationship between law and religion; the position and power of the magistrates; the regulation of the public welfare; the role and function of the pontifices; legal transactions and procedures; the origin and importance of fictions; and others too numerous to mention. Some of what Jhering wrote in these contexts was fairly well known but some of his findings were original. His writing was vivid and engaging, and his lively imagination enabled him to elicit new perspectives and generate fresh insights. Yet, truth be told, the significance of Jhering's contribution to Roman legal history as such has been quite limited.[10] As we will see when we look at Jhering's influence, the impact of his historical work on later scholarship was minor.[11] Thus, the details of his work in early Roman law will not concern us here.

What does deserve closer attention is Jhering's work on legal historiography, i.e., on the methodological, theoretical, and one can even say philosophical, dimensions of writing legal history. Considering that work sheds light on significant features of Jhering's thinking in general. Jhering's writings on legal historiography had two main dimensions. The first is his critique of contemporary scholarship, in particular of its methods and results; Jhering ultimately advocated what we may call a social history of law. His critique and program were laid out mainly in his essay "Über Aufgabe und Methode der Rechtsgeschichtsschreibung" ("On the Objective and Method of Legal Historiography") (1894)

---

also *Jhering's* Plaudereien eines Romanisten (Chats of a Romanist), a series of essays originally published in a legal journal and eventually included in *Jhering*, Scherz und Ernst (1884) 121–243. As Franz Wieacker put it, these essays were "plain in form but flashing with insights;" *Wieacker*, Rudolf von Jhering (1969) 12.

[8] Jhering produced only a long Introduction, see infra 1., as well as a first chapter. In addition, also in his old age, Jhering wrote an extensive (though incomplete) history of the early Aryan peoples which was also published posthumously as "Vorgeschichte der Indoeuropäer" (1894). It was not a legal history, however, and we will consider it in chapter VI, in the context of Jhering's work beyond law.

[9] Chapter II.1., notes 79–156 and text.

[10] For a brief and informative assessment by one of the twentieth century's leading scholars of Roman legal history, see *Wieacker*, Rudolf von Jhering (1969) 12–17.

[11] Infra chapter VII.4., notes 321–336 and text.

(infra 1.). The second dimension is Jhering's explanation of historical development; once again, he proffered a positivist and an idealist version that were not easily reconciled. A key text in this regard is "Das Schuldmoment im römischen Privatrecht" ("The Element of Fault in Roman Private Law") (1867) (infra 2.). In conclusion, we will look at Jhering's evolutionary view of history in a broader context and in particular in comparison to two classic works of that genre, penned by Jhering's Anglo-American contemporaries Maine and Holmes (infra 3.).

1. A Critique of Historiography: "Aufgabe und Methode der Rechtsgeschichtsschreibung" (1894)

Jhering first tackled the method and function of legal historiography in the introduction to the first volume of "Geist" when he needed to distinguish his own approach from the contemporary literature.[12] A generation later, he discussed how and why to write legal history in greater depth in the forty-page-essay just mentioned, i.e., "Über die Aufgabe und Methode der Rechtsgeschichtsschreibung" ("On the Task and Method of Legal Historiography"). The essay constituted the Introduction to his incipient "Entwicklungsgeschichte des römischen Rechts" and was published posthumously.[13] There is something of a shift from the idealism that still pervaded the earlier discourse to a more positivist stance in the later essay – a shift that mirrored Jhering's intellectual development as a whole. Despite this shift in perspective, there was much overlap between these two discourses and little change in their major themes. On both occasions, Jhering trenchantly criticized the contemporary works on Roman legal history, explained their failure, and advocated a better approach.[14] Jhering's discussion is, once again, all over the place, but one can identify five main problems with the existing literature that Jhering wanted fixed: it indiscriminately amassed facts and failed to distinguish what is essential from what is not; it took a purely external view of law and failed to explore its internal coherence; in a similar vein, it stuck to an external chronology and thus obscured the defining features at various stages of development; it remained descriptive and failed to explore the reasons underlying historical evolution; and it focused almost exclusively on legal

[12] Jhering, Geist I (1852) 51–76.

[13] Jhering, Entwicklungsgeschichte des römischen Rechts (1894). For a summary in English, see *Smith*, Four German Jurists III (1897) 31–35. Almost exactly at the mid-point between these two discourses, Jhering also discussed the methods and goals of legal historiography in *Jhering*, Ist die Jurisprudenz eine Wissenschaft? (1868) 68–68, but that discussion remains fairly shallow and adds little to the other two discourses.

[14] Jhering nonetheless appreciated the important contributions that members of the Historical School had made to legal historiography, see *Jhering*, Die historische Schule der Juristen (1844) 535–536.

norms and neglected social reality, needs, and purposes. These critiques and arguments were closely interrelated and sometimes flipsides of the same coin but for clarity's sake, it is advisable to address them one-by-one. As Franz Wieacker pointed out, they are good food for thought even beyond their particular context and time.[15]

From Data Collection to Data Evaluation: Against a "Waschzettel" Approach. On the most basic level, Jhering lamented that the existing literature piled up sources and events in an indiscriminate fashion. Failing to distinguish what was important from what was not, it amounted to "a storage room" where material was amassed without rhyme or reason.[16] Jhering sarcastically compared the popular "Römische Rechtsgeschichte" of his senior colleague Adolf August Friedrich Rudorff (1803–1873)[17] to a "Waschzettel," i.e., "a laundry list: shirts, collars, handkerchiefs – leges, Senatus consulta, constitiones principum and so forth."[18] Lacking a "sense of what is essential"[19], this was merely an inventory of Roman law, not a true history.

Jhering saw the primary cause for this malaise in the unhappy combination of legal history with legal doctrine.[20] In nineteenth century Germany, Roman law had a dual nature: it was an object of historical inquiry as well as the current common (private) law. The effect was, Jhering complained, that scholars constantly regarded legal history as a handmaid of current legal doctrine – "a Cinderella in the house of the law which is tolerated only because it provides wood and water for the household."[21] Jhering recognized that the predominance of "practical interest" rendered "a clear pursuit of the historical perspective very difficult."[22] Thus, he was among the first scholars to postulate an unambiguous separation of (Roman) legal doctrine from (Roman) legal history – in both teaching and scholarship. The two disciplines were of a different nature, required different skills, and pursued different objectives. Legal history had to look at (ancient) Roman law not as a locus of abstract doctrine but as a concrete historical phenomenon which must be understood in its own time and environment.[23]

---

[15] *Wieacker*, Rudolf von Jhering (1969) 14–15.

[16] *Jhering*, Geist I (1852) 52 fn. 27.

[17] *Rudorff*, Römische Rechtschichte (1857/59). Rudorff was a disciple of Savigny, long-time professor, at, and at times Rector (president) of, the University of Berlin, privy counsellor, and member of the Royal Prussian Academy of Sciences. Rudorff's prominence notwithstanding, Jhering had nothing but scorn for him as a scholar of Roman legal history.

[18] *Jhering*, Entwicklungsgeschichte (1894) 7. To be sure, when Jhering wrote this, Rudorff was already dead and gone, but Jhering had not treated him more kindly during his lifetime either. In 1852, Jhering had already complained about "Roman legal history in several recent renditions" which was but a thinly veiled reference to Rudorff's work. See *Jhering*, Geist I (1852) 52 fn. 27.

[19] *Jhering*, Geist I (1852) 52.

[20] Jhering had already pointed this out decades ago, see Jhering, Die historische Schule der Juristen (1844) 409.

[21] *Jhering*, Entwicklungsgeschichte (1894) 9.

[22] *Jhering*, Geist I (1852) 53 fn. 27.

History ratified Jhering's agenda. When he first called for the liberation of legal history from the straitjacket of legal doctrine in 1852, the idea seemed somewhat eccentric and mostly fell on deaf ears. When he repeated it in 1894, it had become broadly accepted and widely realized.[24] A major reason was of course that, due to the project of private law codification (1874–1896) eventually resulting in the *BGB* of 1900, Roman law as a set of directly applicable rules was finally on its way out – just as Jhering had long foreseen.

From an External View to Internal Coherence: Exploring "das Innere der Uhr." By indiscriminately collecting material, the existing histories of Roman law could, at best, present an "external" point of view. The all-important goal, however, was to bring to light the "internal" essence and coherence of the law and its development.[25] Jhering, always happy to use metaphors, compared ancient Roman law to a clock: the current literature presented only its face and told us that the hands were moving; but what we really needed to understand was why and how the clock operated; for that we must examine its internal works ("das Innere der Uhr").[26]

Yet, exactly what Jhering was after was, once again, not entirely clear. In his 1852 discourse, he was echoing Savigny when he spoke vaguely of the "unity of development,"[27] "the internal relatedness and coherence,"[28] and the "harmonious whole"[29] of the law that awaited discovery. Thirty years later, he still sounded like Savigny when he mentioned "the contemplation of the historical development and growth of law."[30] Now, however, he also foregrounded "the driving forces which are alive in the interior of the world of law."[31] At the same time, he wanted

---

[23] Jhering, Entwicklungsgeschichte (1894) 8–13. The combination of the two disciplines was pernicious for doctrine as well because it could not be pursued independently from the historical record – just like legal history is under the spell of doctrine, so "doctrine is under the spell of legal history," id. 8. Jhering insisted, however, that even writing legal history be the domain of jurists (as opposed to mere historians) as only they could understand how the law really works; *Jhering*, Ist die Jurisprudenz eine Wissenschaft (1868) 77.

[24] See *Wieacker*, Privatrechtsgeschichte (1967) 416–430. A key text in this context is *Bekker*, Die Aktionen des römischen Privatrechts (2 vols. 1871–73); see especially vol. I, 2–3 ("Auseinanderdenken des Römischen und des heutigen Rechts;" "thinking apart of the Roman and the present law"). As a fledgling scholar, Ernst Immanuel Bekker (1827–1916) had befriended Jhering in Gießen where Jhering had hosted him beyond all expectations, conversing and drinking wine with him late into night, see *Bekker*, Meine erste Begegnung mit Jhering (1907).

[25] Jhering had voiced this concern decades earlier as well, *Jhering*, Die historische Schule der Juristen (1844) 422.

[26] *Jhering*, Entwicklungsgeschichte (1894) 7.

[27] *Jhering*, Geist I (1852) 53.

[28] *Jhering*, Geist I (1852) 53; he later also emphasized the need to recognize the connection between the succesive epochs, *Jhering*, Geist II.2. (1858) 72–73.

[29] *Jhering*, Geist I (1852) 54.

[30] *Jhering*, Entwicklungsgeschichte (1894) 5.

[31] *Jhering*, Entwicklungsgeschichte (1894) 4.

to "pursue the idea of causality in the history of Roman law," i.e., to demonstrate "the causal influence of one fact on another."[32] In other words, he blended Savignian organicism with the social psychology pursued in "Zweck" as well as with notions of causality borrowed from the natural sciences.

Perhaps all these elements could be integrated, but Jhering did not tell us how. Probably the best way to understand his agenda is simply to look at what he did in "Geist." There, he identified several fundamental institutions of early Roman legal culture, various "drives" (or "instincts," "Triebe") that shaped the development of law, as well as certain basic features of juristic "technique." For Jhering, these institutions, instincts, and features evinced the "spirit" of the Roman law that made it all coherent.[33]

From Mere Chronology to Meaningful Periodization: "Die Verkehrtheit, Zeiträume zu machen." Jhering was pretty clear, however, in his rejection of a strict chronology of law. Since he considered the "internal relationship and coherence of facts" much more important than "their external connection through time" (e.g., their simultaneousness), a chronology of events was at best unimportant.[34] Time, Jhering postulated, should be de-emphasized "because it is not the *vis movens* but merely the framework for the evolution of the system."[35] In fact, "external chronology"[36] could be harmful because it distracted from the internal connection between elements and developments. Thus Jhering refused – and in Geist indeed carefully avoided – to date events by year, inter alia because he considered the occurrence of events at specific points in time largely accidental.[37] Legal history was better written without reference to precise dates.

In a similar vein, Jhering rejected clearly demarcated periodizations. It was wrong "to create time periods" (Zeiträume zu machen"). They entailed a pernicious "dissection" of the material, a flaw Jhering found especially deplorable in Gustav Hugo's well-known "Lehrbuch der Geschichte des römischen Rechts" (1790/1832).[38] Instead, Jhering emphasized the "elasticity" of the various historical periods.[39] As he explained and demonstrated in "Geist," he conceived of these periods as defined by shifting emphases. They did not have a clear beginning and end date; instead, they overlapped, with the later ones often absorbing features of

[32] *Jhering*, Entwicklungsgeschichte (1894) 6.

[33] Jhering intended "Entwicklungsgeschichte" to become a continuation of, and "supplement" to, Geist, *Jhering*, Entwicklungsgeschichte (1894) 4–5.

[34] *Jhering*, Geist I (1852) 53.

[35] *Jhering*, Geist I (1852) 69.

[36] *Jhering*, Geist I (1852) 71.

[37] *Jhering*, Geist I (1852) 76.

[38] See *Jhering*, Geist I (1852) 56, fn. 28. Jhering's nearly vicious attack on Hugo ("Hugo'sche Willkühr," "Zerstückelungssystem") is remarkable in light of the fact that Jhering was still at an early point of his career while Hugo, though dead since 1844, continued to be revered as a founder of the Historical School and a towering figure in the study of Roman law and its history.

[39] *Jhering*, Geist I (1852) 67.

their predecessors.[40] Jhering's professed model in this regard, as well as in other respects, was the famous 44th chapter of Edward Gibbon's "History of the Decline and Fall of the Roman Empire" (1776–1788); in contrast to the dissected German renditions of Roman legal history, Gibbon presented "a short but coherent whole in a lively fashion."[41]

From Description to Explanation: Taking Away "das Faulkissen der Wissenschaft." The existing literature was also unsatisfactory, Jhering complained, because it merely described the course of Roman law and failed to search for explanations – it contained a lot of data, "but it provide[d] no information about the question of Why?" Mere recitation of data did not deserve the name of historiography.[42]

For Jhering, this lack of a search for explanations was the fault of the Historical School's mantra that all law originated in the *Volksgeist*.

"To all questions [the Historical School] everywhere has one, and always the same, answer: the soul of the people, the national feeling of justice [...] that's the end of it, it is the Fatum on the field of law – the historian need go no further."[43]

The Historical School's theory, Jhering charged, had become the "Faulkissen der Wissenschaft" – the "cushion of intellectual laziness."[44]

That "Faulkissen" "had to be pulled from underneath the head [of legal science] in order to wake it up and to make it open its eyes in order to recognize things as they really are and not as the mirage this theory makes us believe."[45] As Jhering had often said before, the whole theory of the Historical School was badly wrong because law did not just emanate from some mythical *Volksgeist* nor did it develop silently and imperceptibly through usage. Instead, it was made by people; even customary law had resulted from some purposeful human action, although exactly how may no longer be knowable.[46] In particular, law was made in response to social needs and circumstances, and legal history had to explain the origin and course of law in the light of these factors.

From Abstract Norms to Law in Life: Beyond "a History of Dogma." Finally, Jhering complained that most of the existing literature focused merely on legal norms and institutions. It thus proffered "nothing but a history of dogma"[47] "All we basically get are summaries of the *Institutes* or the *Pandects* in the various periods of Roman history."[48] The principal reason for this approach was, again,

---

[40] See supra chapter II.1., note 74.

[41] *Jhering*, Geist I (1852) 48, fn. 26.

[42] *Jhering*, Entwicklungsgeschichte (1894) 1.

[43] *Jhering*, Entwicklungsgeschichte (1894) 13.

[44] *Jhering*, Entwicklungsgeschichte (1894) 13. The term is hard to translate; it literally means "the lazy pillow" (herein of science). It is typically used in the sense of an accusation of doing nothing.

[45] *Jhering*, Entwicklungsgeschichte (1894) 13–14.

[46] *Jhering*, Entwicklungsgeschiche (1894) 15–16.

[47] *Jhering*, Geist I (1852) 47.

[48] *Jhering*, Entwicklungsgeschichte (1894) 11; see also *Jhering*, Geist I (1852) 49.

the dominance of modern doctrinal thinking. Authors had transferred this thinking to legal history[49] and produced "successive Dogmatik,"[50] i.e., descriptions of the successive development of legal doctrine.

What was needed, instead, was a showing of the "contingency of law on the historical conditions of the peoples and the times."[51]. Legal history had to go beyond "juristic abstractions" and focus on "the totality of [...] legal life."[52] It had to understand legal norms as responses to the respective factual circumstances and resulting social needs and thus in light of the purpose to which the norms ultimately owed their existence.[53] What such an approach looked like, Jhering pointed out, could be seen in his own work, i.e., in parts of "Geist" to which he referred the reader.[54]

Jhering essentially pushed for a reorientation from a doctrinal history to a social history of law. It is important to note, however, that the social element came into play mainly as an explanation for the law's origin, content, and form. Interestingly – and from a modern point of view somewhat disappointingly – the law's effects in and on society were not a major concern, even though Jhering occasionally noted and discussed them.[55]

We must not leave Jhering's critique of the methods and goals of legal history behind without noting a potentially important caveat. In the two texts considered here, Jhering wrote about the discipline in broad and general terms, implying that he meant to criticize and fundamentally reorient the writing about Roman legal history as a whole.[56] On another occasion, however, he backpedaled and proffered a more limited position. In the Preface to Volume Two (Part Two) of "Geist" (1858), he responded to the criticism that had been directed against his approach in the earlier volumes. He now presented his "new method" not as a replacement of, but as an addition to, the existing literature: it was not meant to be exclusive but merely supplemental. He went even further by stating that his method was not fit for introductory purposes: "If I had to teach Roman legal history, I would not consider my own method suitable, just like a course on the philosophy of history cannot be a substitute for a historical lecture."[57] It is unclear what motivated these remarks. Perhaps Jhering just wanted to admit that profiting from his

---

[49] *Jhering*, Entwicklungsgeschichte (1894) 9–10.

[50] *Jhering*, Entwicklungsgeschichte (1894) 11.

[51] *Jhering*, Entwicklunsgeschichte (1894) 16–17.

[52] *Jhering*, Geist I (1852) 48.

[53] *Jhering*, Entwicklungsgeschichte (1894) 19.

[54] *Jhering*, Entwicklungsgeschichte (1894) 10 fn. 1.

[55] See especially chapter XXXIV of the second volume of "Geist," discussing "Die Wohlfahrtsfrage und der Staat" ("The Question of Social Welfare and the State"), *Jhering*, Geist II.1. (1854) 239–267.

[56] See, e.g., *Jhering*, Entwicklungsgeschichte (1894) 37 ("Umschwung in der bisherigen Methode der Rechtsgeschichtsschreibung;" "reorientation of the established method of legal historiography").

[57] *Jhering*, Geist II.2. (1858) Preface, X.

(social and functional) approach required at least a basic familiarity with the sheer facts of Roman legal history. Perhaps he also wanted to assuage his numerous critics and soften his rebellion because in 1858, he was still stuck in Gießen and hoping for an offer from a more prestigious university. Be that as it may, there is no reason to doubt that he was serious. It remains an open question, however, to what extent he generally saw his own work as the true, or at least the best, form of Roman legal history or whether he really considered it a "philosophical" reflection supplementing the more orthodox works. It is entirely possible that he was not sure himself. In any event, Jhering's point is of enduring relevance: a social and interpretative history makes sense only on the basis of knowing the factual record.

2. Explaining History Through Social Conditions and the Force of Progress: "Das Schuldmoment im römischen Privatrecht" (1867)

Jhering looked at history not only as an object of academic study but also a manifestation of human progress. That perspective pervades all his theoretical work. It remained largely unaffected by his "conversion" around 1860 from a primarily logical to a predominantly sociological view of law: his views on history as progress changed amazingly little from his early to his later years. A key text in this regard is Jhering's 1867 essay "Das Schuldmoment im römischen Privatrecht."[58] On one level, the essay is mainly, as the title promises, a study showing the rise of "The Element of Fault in Roman Private Law." At the same time, however, it is a demonstration of Jhering's belief in the evolution of law from lower to higher stages of culture.

As an essay on a major shift in ancient Roman law, "Schuldmoment" is a doctrinal-historical study that stays close to the sources and often makes for hard reading. It seeks to show that in early Roman law (in the terms of "Geist" "the second system" encompassing the law based on the XII Tables and prevailing until the mid- to late republic), liability was strict, i.e., based on mere causation. In classical and post-classical Roman law (the "third system" envisaged in, but not covered by, "Geist"), liability became increasingly, and eventually almost entirely, fault-based. Jhering pointed out two dimensions of this development. First, since the early strictness of liability was largely due to the conception of sanctions as penalties (even for civil wrongs), the shift to a fault-based regime entailed the continuous decline of punishment[59] until it finally vanished altogether in private law and procedure.[60] Second, and in the long run more importantly,

---

[58] *Jhering*, Das Schuldmoment (1867). The essay was written as a "Festschrift" for, i.e., as an essay in honor of, one of his colleagues on the law faculty at Gießen.

[59] *Jhering*, Das Schuldmoment (1867) 4 ("Die Geschichte der Strafe ist ein fortwährendes Absterben derselben." – "The history of punishment is its continuing decline.").

[60] *Jhering*, Das Schuldmoment (1867) 58–67.

Jhering recognized and articulated a distinction that the Roman jurists themselves had used but not expressly stated: the difference between "objective" and "subjective" unlawfulness; the former means a mere violation of the objective legal order, the latter personal culpability (Schuld).[61] In cases of merely objective unlawfulness, liability could be imposed (without fault) but was limited to undoing the unlawful situation, for example, to returning an object to its legitimate owner or refunding unjust enrichment. In other cases, at least negligence was required, but then liability also encompassed the payment of damages.[62] In Jhering's view, this distinction between (mere) unlawfulness and fault eventually pervaded the whole system of Roman law.[63] Clear differentiation between the two categories was one of Jhering's lasting contributions to the doctrine of modern law, both on the civil and the criminal side.[64]

For Jhering, this development of Roman law was a vivid illustration of legal progress. Early Roman law's imposition of strict liability as a form of punishment had been a "pathological form of fighting civil wrongs," which served "more the desire for revenge than the idea of law."[65] Getting rid of revenge and punishment in private law demonstrated "the progress of mankind from wild, blind passion and vengeance to moderation, self-control, justice."[66] Thus, the rise of the fault principle and the decline of punishment showed that mankind "moves forward on its path."[67]

Jhering generally conceived of legal history as a progressive development leading from lower to higher "cultural stages of law" ("Culturstufen des Rechts")[68] – an understanding that had provided the architectural structure of "Geist." Jhe-

[61] In a footnote, Jhering pointed out that while jurists had so far overlooked this distinction, Hegel had already hinted at the idea of (merely) "objective wrongs" ("objectives Unrecht") in sec. 82 et seq. of his Philosophy of Law; *Jhering*, Das Schuldmoment 1867, 5 fn. 1. Hegel's language there is fairly cryptic, however, and the hint is quite weak.

[62] "It is not the damage, but fault, that makes liable," *Jhering*, Das Schuldmoment (1867) 40. As Jhering pointed out, the Romans also came to distinguish between *dolus* (roughly: bad intent) and *culpa* (roughly: negligence); liability for the former often went farther than for the latter; id. 51–53. As so often, however, Jhering repeatedly overstated his own case for additional drama, e.g., when he spoke of the "universality of the concept of fault," id. 25, or of fault as the "all-dominating ethical principle" in Roman law, id. 21. Jhering himself clearly saw, of course, that liability (e.g., to return property to the lawful owner) did not require fault – hence the very distinction between mere unlawfulness and fault. Jhering also admitted that even liability for damages had sometimes remained strict – "for reasons of public order" ("aus polizeilichen Gründen"); id. 45.

[63] *Jhering*, Das Schuldmoment (1867) 21.

[64] See *Fikentscher*, Methoden des Rechts III (1976) 171–173. In modern criminal law doctrine, the distinction between acts that are (merely) "rechtswidrig" (i.e., unlawful) and those that are also "schuldhaft" (culpable, i.e., intentional or negligent) is foundational.

[65] *Jhering*, Das Schuldmoment (1867) 61.

[66] *Jhering*, Das Schuldmoment (1867) 4.

[67] *Jhering*, Das Schuldmoment (1867) 67.

[68] *Jhering*, Das Schuldmoment (1867) 10, 16, 66; etc.

ring's belief in progress was not limited to law but also encompassed the development of ethics (Sittlichkeit).[69] In fact, it was just one aspect of his general belief in the constant advance of humankind[70] – which was widely shared among his contemporaries. At the same time, however, Jhering often cautioned against the tendency to evaluate the (less developed) past by the standards of the (more developed) present; instead every element of law had to be judged by the standards of its time.[71]

Jhering considered the evolution of law unstoppable and, thus, inevitable.[72] The rise of the fault paradigm in Roman law provided an example of "the persistence of an idea in pursuing its course, slowly but steadily, until it finally arrives at its goal."[73] To be sure, the final goal of legal development was unknown to the present, and indeed unknowable, just like we did and could not know what future species will develop. We can know, however, that evolution will keep going. The present is merely the "*provisionally* highest point of the development of law."[74]

Throughout his academic life, Jhering struggled with the question of what exactly drives the course of the law's progressive history. In a manner reminiscent of his dual stance on the issue of justice,[75] he took two different positions. At times, he adopted a decidedly positivist viewpoint and saw the driving force of legal history exclusively in human responses to changing conditions and needs. On other occasions, however, he saw history as an inherently progressive development driven by innate force and divine design. There was a palpable tension, if not an outright conflict, between the positivist and the idealist position that was difficult to resolve.

The Positivist Position: Social Conditions as Exclusive Causes. In the final third of his introductory essay "Aufgabe und Methode der Rechtsgeschichtsschreibung" ("The Task and Method of Legal Historiography"), Jhering proceeded from a critique of the current literature and an outline of a preferred approach to more fundamental claims about the factors that determine the development of law.[76] Rejecting the position of the Historical School, he saw these causes exclusively in factual conditions. In other words, he proclaimed a strictly positivist view of legal history. We have already encountered this attitude when looking at Jhering's earlier essay "Über die Entstehung des Rechtsgefühls" (1884); there, he had explored the origin of the "feeling of justice" and discussed

[69] Jhering, Über die Entstehung des Rechsgefühls (1884) 30–33.

[70] See, e.g., *Jhering*, Zweck II (1886) 133; *Jhering*, Über die Entstehung des Rechtsgefühls (1884) 54 ("ewiger Fortschritt"; "eternal progress").

[71] E.g., *Jhering*, Ist die Jurisprudenz eine Wissenschaft? (1868) 75; *Jhering*, Zweck I (1884) 246.

[72] See, e.g., *Jhering*, Zweck I (1884) 241–242.

[73] *Jhering*, Das Schuldmoment (1867) 62; see also *Jhering*, Zweck I (1884) 242–43.

[74] *Jhering*, Ist die Jurisprudenz eine Wissenschft? (1868) 79 (emphasis in the original).

[75] Supra chapter IV.3., notes 480–496 and text.

[76] *Jhering*, Entwicklungsgeschichte (1894) 29–41.

the origin of legal norms just incidentally.[77] Now, some years later, he focused directly on what drives the development of the law.

Jhering now put the "idea of causality"[78] at the core of legal historiography so that the discipline's principal goal became to show and explain "the dependence of law on the historical conditions of the peoples and the times."[79] He distinguished two types of factors that shape the law over time, calling them "external" and "internal impulses."[80] The former came from a people's environment, the latter lay in the character of the people. Both were the product of factual circumstances.

With regard to the environmental factors shaping the law, Jhering, in part, simply endorsed Montesquieu: the law was influenced, inter alia, by climate, geography, natural resources, and modes of subsistence, and, as Jhering emphasized in the case of Rome, by "the contact with other peoples."[81] Perhaps more directly, the law was also a result of the "economic, social, and political conditions" of the respective place and time.[82] "External impulses" especially determined the major "turning points" ("Wendepunkte") in the development of law.[83]

In part, Jhering also borrowed the idea that external factors cause "internal processes" from the contemporary natural sciences and from human medicine. These disciplines had come to understand that what happened inside of plants (e.g., decomposition) or bodies (e.g., illness) was not a matter of "internal spontaneity" but the result of external agents (such as bacteria). Jhering considered this "recognition of the dependence of internal processes on external causes" one of the most valuable general insights of his age and thus demanded that it be followed by legal historiography as well. Once again, the natural sciences became a model for legal science.[84]

The "internal impulses" lay in "the character of the people, the mental and intellectual properties of the people and of the state of its cultural development at the given time."[85] That sounded a lot like (Puchta's and) Savigny's *Volksgeist*, and in some sense it was: it regarded the law (in part) as a product of a particular mentality. There was a crucial difference, however: for Jhering, this mentality was not innate but the product of external factors as well. It was true, Jhering admitted, that Montesquieu had already linked the individuality of the peoples to

[77] See, e.g, *Jhering*, Über die Entstehung des Rechtsgefühls (1884) 11, 19.

[78] *Jhering*, Entwicklungsgeschichte (1894) 29.

[79] *Jhering*, Entwicklungsgeschichte (1894) 16–17.

[80] *Jhering*, Entwicklungsgeschichte (1894) 29.

[81] *Jhering*, Entwicklungsgeschichte (1894) 29.

[82] *Jhering*, Entwicklungsgeschichte (1894) 29.

[83] *Jhering*, Entwicklungsgeschichte (1894) 37. For Rome, Jhering listed five particular factors: the plebeians, the interaction with aliens, the geographic expansion of the state's territory, Greek law and learning, and the provinces; id. 28–32.

[84] *Jhering*, Entwicklungsgeschichte (1894) 37.

[85] *Jhering*, Entwicklungsgeschichte (1894) 29 ("des Volkscharakers, der Sinnes- und Denkweise des Volks und seiner Kulturstufe zu dieser gegebenen Zeit").

external influences, and that the Historical School had acknowledged his teachings. But Savigny and his followers had failed to put that insight to actual use. Thus, they had regarded the "various peoples as given entities which must be accepted as they come."[86] Jhering thought otherwise.

"I, for one, do not recognize anything *given* in history, everything has *become*, including the *peoples* [...]. The individuality of the peoples is not [...] a product of *nature* but of *history*. The character of a people contains all it has experienced in the course of its existence...[It is a result of] the conditions under which it exists, the soil, the climate, its kinds of subsistence and occupation, all important events of the people and even of exceptional persons."[87]

All that nature had provided to humans were the basic needs (especially of self-preservation) and the faculty of understanding (Verstand) how to satisfy them. Everything else had to be learned, and had been learned[88] – a process that eventually shaped a people's mental and intellectual make-up.

Jhering acknowledged that the learning processes that had shaped the various peoples' character lay largely in a past so distant that these processes were no longer visible today. Still, he warned, we must not mistake invisibility for non-existence – which was the cardinal error of the Historical School.[89] Also, some elements of that formative process, Jhering opined, were still accessible to the modern historian. After all, "certain facts concerning the living conditions and destinies of the peoples display the crucial influence they have exercised on the character of the people so openly that one must be blind not to recognize them."[90] In his very final years, Jhering acted on this belief and explored the emergence of the "type of the European" from that of the "Asian" during the pre-historic migration of the Indo-Germanic peoples, a work we will consider in chapter VI.

In the end, then, the origins and development of law had nothing to do with a people's innate character traits, and certainly not with any sort of abstract and general ideas of justice. It was all owed to confrontation with human needs and historical conditions. As Jhering had already explained in the first volume of "Zweck," when humans formed societies, they learned that they needed certain rules to live together, and when they eventually formed a state, some of these rules took the form of officially enforceable norms, i.e., law. Successive periods produced layers of this law which then piled up on top of each other. To the untrained eye and from a distance, the result might look like a product of human nature; in fact, however, it was nothing but the result of accumulated experience and expediency.[91]

[86] *Jhering*, Entwicklungsgeschichte (1894) 42.
[87] *Jhering*, Entwicklungsgeschichte (1894) 43.
[88] *Jhering*, Entwicklungsgeschichte (1894) 19.
[89] *Jhering*, Entwicklungsgeschichte (1894) 13–14.
[90] *Jhering*, Entwicklungsgeschichte (1894) 43.
[91] *Jhering*, Entwicklungsgeschichte (1894) 20; Jhering had used the term "layers" ("Schichten") of law as early as in the first volume of "Geist," *Jhering*, Geist I (1852) 76, and then further developed the idea in the first volume of "Zweck," *Jhering*, Zweck I (1884) 442, 529–530.

The Idealist Position: The Inherent Force of Progress. Yet, when we look at Jhering's discourse on what drives legal evolution, we see not only the positivist who focuses on actual conditions and social needs but also an idealist in the tradition of Kant, Schiller, and Hegel,[92] as well as Lessing[93] – a Jhering who waxes eloquent about a very different set of factors: history as a quasi-personified force, ideas unfolding in a quasi-autonomous fashion, and evolution driven by a quasi-divine design.

Jhering repeatedly characterized history – in a Hegelian fashion – as a quasi-personified actor in its own right. History was "at work;" it "assigned to the Roman people the mission to develop law;"[94] it had a will, pursued goals, and did not rest before it had fulfilled its purpose for all of mankind.[95] Within that history, there operated a Hegelian *Weltgeist*, which could sometimes be observed "in its workshop" where we might "perceive the secret of its operation.[96]

Driven by the *Zeitgeist's* "irresistible force,"[97] ideas unfolded quietly, imperceptibly, and in a more or less autonomous fashion. They stubbornly pursued their course for centuries or even millennia until "their work is done and the law is reshaped and rejuvenated."[98] This process, Jhering asserted – now in a Savignian fashion – was not one of haphazard change; instead "the ideas that unfold in history [...] join together to form a harmonious whole."[99] While their development may look random, we must not be misled by that appearance.[100] Instead, we need to recognize that in change there is truth. It is therefore the ultimate vocation of legal historiography to bring that truth to light.[101] The "poetry of the order and regularity of ideas" is especially observable in Roman law whose history is "an unsurpassed work of art."[102]

[92] *Kant*, Idee zu einer allgemeinen Geschichte in weltbürgerlicher Absicht (1784); *Kant*, Mutmaßlicher Anfang der Menschengeschichte (1786); *Schiller*, Was heist und zu welchem Ende studiert man Universalgeschichte (1789); *Hegel*, Philosophie der Geschichte (1840/1848). This is not to say, of course, that Jhering fully shared these philosophers' versions of (historical) idealism, but the fundamental idea of a progressive evolution of mankind towards higher and better stages of development was common ground.

[93] Infra notes 103–110 and text.

[94] *Jhering*, Geist I (1852) 64, 304.

[95] *Jhering*, Zweck I (1884) 84–85.

[96] *Jhering*, Geist I (1852) 85.

[97] *Jhering*, Das Schuldmoment (1867) 60.

[98] *Jhering*, Das Schuldmoment (1867) 67; see also id. 62.

[99] Jhering, Geist I (1852) 54. On one occasion, Jhering explained the existence of a "successive unity in the history of law" through the *longue durée* constancy of a people's "individuality" which shaped the law. Since the "individuality" of a people remained stable over long periods of time, so did the fundamental characteristics of its legal order; id. 61.

[100] *Jhering*, Geist I (1852) 57.

[101] *Jhering*, Ist die Jurisprudenz eine Wissenschaft? (1868) 71.

[102] *Jhering*, Geist I (1852) 55.

For Jhering, history was also "the revelation of God"[103] as the "ultimate source of all ethics."[104] Constituting a "free act of God,"[105] history evinced the "divine leadership in the course of the world." ("göttliche Weltleitung")[106] This belief betrayed the influence of one of the enlightenment's most important texts on the early Jhering,[107] i.e., Gotthold Ephraim Lessing's (1729–1781) "Die Erziehung des Menschengeschlechts" ("The Education of the Human Race") (1780). The short and somewhat enigmatic tract is difficult to understand outside of the context of the late eighteenth century debate about the relationship between religion and reason.[108] Suffice it to say that Lessing essentially attempted a reconciliation by presenting the development of mankind as a process of (moral) education according to a divine plan.[109] Spanning millennia, this development progressed through various stages, ultimately leading to moral maturity based on reason. In this manner, God's design and human reason were inextricably linked. Apparently, the essay instilled in Jhering a lifelong faith in the unity of divine will, evolution, and the human capacity for reason, as well as an unshakable faith in the progress of mankind.[110] Jhering, who was not a strongly religious person (he rarely attended church), did not necessarily refer to a strictly Christian notion of God. Instead, his "God" appears to be a more encompassing divine being transcending any particular religion.[111]

---

[103] *Jhering*, Das Schuldmoment (1867) 11.

[104] *Jhering*, Das Schuldmoment (1867) 12.

[105] *Jhering*, Geist I (1852) 54.

[106] *Jhering*, Geist I (1852) 55.

[107] When Jhering was still a student at the Gymnasium (i.e., the secondary school that prepared students for entry into the university) in his home town of Aurich, one of his teachers, Wilhelm Reuter, had a profound and lasting impact on Jhering's worldview, inter alia by introducing Jhering to Lessing; see *Kunze*, Ein großer Jurist (2023) 11; *Behrends*, Der Durchbruch zum Zweck des Rechts (1987) 267 fn. 135 (with further references).

[108] The most widely known text on the subject is *Kant*, Die Religion innerhalb der Grenzen der bloßen Vernunft (1793/94).

[109] Throughout the text, Lessing uses the term Offenbarung (revelation).

[110] Jhering was also impressed by Friedrich Julius Stahl (1802–1861) who, a generation after Lessing and during Jhering's formative years, called for a jurisprudence based on Christian faith and considered a belief in God an indispensable basis for legal philosophy; *Stahl*, Die Philosophie des Rechts nach geschichtlicher Ansicht (1830–1837); on Stahl's influence on Jhering's conception of "Persönlichkeit" (personality), see *Pleister*, Persönlichkeit, Wille und Freiheit im Werke Jherings (1982) 180–186.

[111] Jhering also saw in the ethical order resulting from divine design the same harmony as "that of the planetary system in the sky," *Jhering*, Geist I (1852) 55, – a notion suspiciously reminiscent of Kant's famous expression of admiration for both these elements at the beginning of the Conclusion of his Critique of Practical Reason: "Zwei Dinge erfüllen das Gemüt mit immer neuer und zunehmender Bewunderung und Ehrfurcht, je öfter und anhaltender sich das Nachdenken damit beschäftigt: Der bestirnte Himmel über mir, und das moralische Gesetz in mir." ("Two things fill the mind with forever new and growing admiration and awe, the more frequently and persistently one reflects upon them: the starry sky above me and the moral law within me."); *Kant*, Kritik der praktischen Vernunft (1869, orig. 1788) 300. Jhering

The Resultant Tension: Two Explanations of Historical Development. The dichotomy between the sociological and realist Jhering, whom we meet in much of his later work, and the idealist and theistic Jhering, whom we encounter when it comes to legal evolution and progress, cannot be explained away by allocating these two Jherings to different periods of his life. It is true that the idealist element was more pronounced in his younger years and that the realist tone become stronger as time went on. Yet, the former was never fully eclipsed by the latter – Jhering invoked history, ideas, and God as drivers of legal evolution far beyond his turn towards a predominantly sociological approach after 1860.

There are a few connecting points between these two sides. In one instance, Jhering claimed that evolution was "unstoppably" driven by the "law of purpose" ("Zweckgesetz"), indicating that the succession of practical needs ensured overall progress.[112] Jhering also alluded to "reason" ("Vernunft") as the factor promoting the appropriate development of law at each developmental stage; that could refer to an abstract, Kantian or Hegelian, concept of reason but also to the concrete human (and social) capacity to do the right thing under the circumstances, as indicated by the requirement that reason be "healthy."[113] In addition, Jhering sometimes brought human agency back into play: although he believed in progress, he cautioned that it was not ensured by simple reliance on the "spontaneous growth of the ethical spirit;" instead, it required that mankind "carefully take to heart and practically utilize the experiences, lessons, and warnings of history."[114] Still, these occasional cross-connections between a sociological and realist approach on the one hand, and an idealist and theistic view on the other, are far too rare, ad hoc, and superficial to integrate the two sides in a solid fashion.

At the end of the day, we must, once again, accept that Jhering held two kinds of views at the same time, here with regard to the progress of law – as a result of human responses to concrete circumstances and social needs on the one hand, and as a result of self-driving history, inevitable unfolding of ideas, and the power of divine will on the other. Jhering was not bothered by the tension between these views but rather quite happy to entertain them both because for him, they were actually not in conflict. Darwin's naturalist (positivist as well as secular) theory of evolution, Jhering claimed, was entirely compatible with his own "belief in the idea of divine purpose" ("Glauben an einen göttlichen Zweckgedanken");[115] and for Jhering, his conviction that all law was the result of human learning from experience was entirely reconcilable with the idea of history as following a divine design.[116] Probably as a result of Lessing's early influence, Jhering believed – or at

promptly compared the order in the ethical and natural world to the harmony of Roman law; Jhering, Geist I (1852) 55.

[112] *Jhering*, Zweck I (1884) XIII, 76.

[113] *Jhering*, Entwicklungsgeschichte (1894) 18.

[114] *Jhering*, Zweck II (1886) 133.

[115] *Jhering*, Zweck I (1884) XIII.

[116] *Jhering*, Geist I (1852) 54; *Jhering*, Über die Entstehung des Rechtsgefühls (1884) 12, 54.

least proclaimed to believe – that God's plan revealed itself in human activity. As John Fiske (1842–1901) allegedly put it, "[e]volution is God's way of doing things."[117]

Still, if Jhering held on to this belief of "God in history"[118], it was probably not only because he saw the positivist and the idealist positions as reconcilable. Perhaps he also needed both perspectives – for two possible reasons. One was his own peace of mind. His keen power of observation and sharp intellect told him that law was a human creation, which, determined by external conditions and subject to human choice, could develop in all sorts of unpredictable directions. But his mind was perhaps not able, or at least not willing, to face the consequence that there might be neither a reliable order nor a higher purpose in the development of law – and thus no convincing reason to believe in inherent progress. Embracing both a realist and an idealist view of legal history allowed him to have his cake and eat it too – to focus on sheer facts and yet believe in deeper meaning. The other reason may have been his audience, or rather audiences. On the one hand, Jhering catered to the adherents of modern positivist science whose assent had to be won by reliance on hard (historical) facts and causal connections between social conditions and social norms. On the other hand, he operated in a society that was still steeped in philosophical idealism and devoted to Christian (and in many instances Jewish) faith. If Jhering wanted to please both these constituencies,[119] he had to talk out of both sides of his mouth.

Legal Progress through "the Auto-Critique of Law:" The Hiker and His Shadow. There is, however, an element in Jhering's idealist view on history as progress that sits more comfortably with his positivist conception of law as a human creation and a social phenomenon: his theory of the interplay between positive law and the sense of justice. Jhering first presented a version of it in his 1884 talk "Über die Entstehung des Rechtsgefühls"[120] and then developed it more fully in the Introduction to his "Entwicklungsgeschichte des römischen Rechts."[121] This theory has often been overlooked[122] even though it is one of Jhering's most creative constructs.

---

[117] The phrase is attributed to John Fiske by *Abbott*, The Theology of an Evolutionist (1897) 3.

[118] *Jhering*, Über die Entstehung des Rechtsgefühls (1884) 54.

[119] Individuals could of course be members of both audiences at the same time, i.e., spend their weekdays in a chemical laboratory and attend religious services on the weekend.

[120] *Jhering*, Über die Enstehung des Rechtsgefühls (1884) 44–51; see supra chapter IV.3.

[121] There is some indication that Jhering had already been working on that Introduction when he gave the earlier talk, see *Jhering*, Über die Entstehung des Rechtsgefühls (1884) 49–50, fn. 24 by *Behrends*.

[122] But cf. *Schelsky*, Das Jhering-Modell des sozialen Wandels (1972), duly noted by *Behrends*, Das 'Rechtsgefühl' in der historisch-kritischen Rechtslehre des späten Jhering (1986) 58–60. For a detailed analysis and discussion, see the more recent study by *Birr*, Der Schatten des Wanderers (2022).

As we have seen, in "Die Entstehung des Rechtsgefühls," Jhering had claimed that the sense of justice was not at all innate (a matter of "nature") but purely a result of experience (acquired in "history"). He had also claimed that the sense of justice did not precede (and thus determine) the law but that it was the other way around: law was made first (in response to the needs of life in society) and then shaped the sense of justice. This had created a bit of a quandary: if law determined the sense of justice, it is difficult to see how the latter could provide a normative check on the former. Jhering had sought to defuse this dilemma by making three arguments. The first two were apodictic: ethical standards were advancing from lower to higher states; and history was in God's hands;[123] for these two claims, Jhering provided virtually no explanation, and they need not concern us in the present context. The third argument was much more interesting: surprisingly, the sense of justice actually could sometimes "be ahead [...] of the legal norms" (and thus guide their further development).[124] In "Rechtsgefühl," Jhering's explanation for this phenomenon remained sketchy,[125] but in the Introduction to "Entwicklungsgeschichte," he provided a fuller account: in a manner reminiscent of Marx's dialectics between existence and consciousness (Sein und Bewußtsein), law and the sense of justice interact, and their interaction could push the law forward.

Jhering, himself an avid hiker, compared the relationship between law and the sense of justice to the relationship between a man and his shadow while the man walks all day from West to East: in the morning, the shadow was behind him, at noon next to him, and in the evening ahead of him. Originally, the feeling of justice was shaped by the law and thus followed it; over time, the people became so used to the prevailing norms that their feeling of justice (largely) corresponded to them; finally, the feeling of justice went ahead of the law – though only sometimes.[126]

Yet, how could the feeling of justice be shaped by the law on the one hand, and still get ahead of the law on the other? Once again, Jhering's explanation is poorly organized and not entirely consistent. A somewhat streamlined version is this: Jhering envisaged three scenarios – one driven by a small intellectual elite, one by the people, and one by legal science. In the first scenario, "outstanding intellects who first abandon the traditional views, get public opinion on their side, and force legislation to take the course they charted."[127] This may take some time, possibly centuries. Jhering did not provide concrete examples, but his mention of "enlightened spirits" indicates that he had, inter alia, the great thinkers of the

[123] Supra chapter IV.3., notes 485–489 and text.

[124] *Jhering*, Über die Entstehung des Rechtsgefühls (1884) 48.

[125] Supra chapter IV.3., fn. 479.

[126] *Jhering*, Entwicklungsgeschichte (1894) 27. In that sense, Jhering's metaphor was a poor choice because the shadow inevitably gets ahead of the hiker while the feeling of justice gets ahead of the law only on some occasions.

[127] *Jhering*, Entwicklungsgeschichte (1894) 23.

enlightenment in mind. In other instances, the people themselves push for legal progress. If (and only if) they suffer severely enough from the current state of the law, they may begin to reflect upon it, raise their voice, and demand reform. As an example, Jhering mentioned the contemporary "claims of the working class for an improvement of their lot."[128] Finally, legal science could come up with new ideas that eventually found acceptance and thus contributed to legal progress. Here, Jhering pointed to the emergence of modern copyright and patent protection.[129]

As an empirical matter, these claims were entirely plausible. Sometimes, the ideas of enlightened minds had indeed provided the crucial impetus for legal reform.[130] Sometimes, popular pressure had advanced the legal ball (Jhering may well have had the repeated uprisings of the plebeians in the early Roman republic in mind); and sometimes, the law was forced ahead by a combination of both, enlightened ideas and popular pressure, as in the French revolution. Also, sometimes, legal scholarship had generated new ideas that found acceptance in courts and legislatures, such as the Roman jurists' typology of contracts, or, eventually, Jhering' very own *culpa in contrahendo*.[131] Still, none of this answered the vexing question of exactly how the feeling of justice could be both dependent on existing law and yet get ahead of it.

With the regard to the "great thinker" scenario, Jhering simply did not tell us anything; he did not point to any link between these "spirits'" progressive ideas, historical experience, and existing law.[132] With regard to the processes driven by the people or by legal science, however, Jhering's provided an answer that was both complicated and intriguing. The people – and apparently legal scientists as well – did not really come up with entirely new ideas but rather always built on existing law. Finding certain law already in place, they resorted to established principles, or extrapolated new ones from the existing material,[133] and then demanded that these principles be applied to novel situations. For example, farmers

[128] *Jhering*, Entwicklungsgschichte (1894) 25.

[129] *Jhering*, Entwicklungsgeschichte (1894) 26.

[130] A nearly perfect example would be *Beccaria*, Dei delitti e delle pene (1764), a work Jhering was familiar with; see *Jhering*, Zweck I (1884) 375. Beccaria (1738–1794) propagated enlightened principles for criminal law and procedure (*nullum crimen sine lege*, proportionality of crime and punishment, public nature of criminal trials, etc.). These principles were revolutionary in the 1760s but largely implemented in Jhering's time a century later.

[131] Supra chapter II.3.

[132] Jhering merely wrote that "[a]t all times, they have been the path finders and trailblazers ('Pfadfinder und Bahnbrecher')" who have "discovered the right way and open up a new path;" *Jhering*, Entwicklungsgeschichte (1894) 24. That explained nothing, of course.

[133] Again, Jhering's article on *culpa in contrahendo* provides a nearly perfect example, see supra chapter II.3. While Jhering did not mention the piece in this context, he may very well have had it – more or less consciously – in mind. Jhering did not limit this capacity to recognize general principles to jurists, however; instead he ascribed the capacity to generalize to the human mind as such, see *Jhering*, Über die Entstehung des Rechtsgefühls (1884) 45–50.

pushed to expand the general protection of land ownership to include specific protection against the damage inflicted by the roaming wildlife owned by the nobility.[134] In a similar vein, legal scholars (like Jhering himself) had pushed to extend the protection of the ownership of tangible goods to also cover intellectual creations like scientific inventions or works of art.[135] Reformers thus demanded to take already existing principles to their logical conclusions – "to turn half-truths into full ones" ("aus halben Wahrheiten ganze machen").[136] Jhering called this a "critique of law through law itself."[137] This process kept pushing the law forward and would eventually be capable of "progress in the law which we can currently not even dream of."[138] In short, the auto-critique of law drove its improvement. Jhering envisaged law as an instrument of perpetual social progress.[139]

3. Evolutionary Histories: Jhering, Maine, and Holmes

At the time, Jhering's claim that societies and their laws evolved in a progressive direction was nothing out of the ordinary. Instead, it was one voice in a much larger chorus that involved scholars from various countries, lasted for over a century-and-a-half, reached its peak exactly in Jhering's lifetime, and then gradually petered out. Thus, his ideas in this regard are noteworthy not because they were altogether novel or particularly brilliant but because of how they fit into a specific tradition of legal thought. After taking a summary look at this tradition, we will focus on two contemporary protagonists from the common law world whose work proved to be particularly influential – Henry Sumner Maine and Oliver Wendell Holmes.

Variants of (Legal) Evolutionism: A Tale of Two Centuries. In 1748, Montesquieu's "Esprit des loix" had pointed to the differences among the various peo-

[134] *Jhering*, Entwicklungsgeschichte (1894) 24–25.

[135] See *Jhering*, Rechtsschutz gegen injuriöse Rechtsverletzungen (1885) 375–396.

[136] *Jhering*, Entwicklungsgeschichte (1894) 26. Jhering compared the people pushing for a recognition of fuller rights to "a child taking her mother by her word. What you have taught me, it says to the law, now bring to full effect, [because] you are lagging behind the principles which you have established yourself." *Jhering*, Entwicklungsgeschichte (1894) 25. This illustration may be related to a personal experience: as a boy, Jhering obtained a book on the principles of pedagogy – and gave it to his mother demanding that she abide by them; *Kunze*, Rudolf von Jhering (1993) 11.

[137] *Jhering*, Entwicklungsgeschichte (1894) 26.

[138] *Jhering*, Entwicklungsgeschichte (1894) 26. The obvious problem with this theory is that the law is apparently always stuck with the existing principles, be they already known or yet awaiting discovery. Jhering did not discuss whether truly new principles could ever arise, and if so, whence they came.

[139] For a more extensive discussion in the context of modern sociological theory, see *Schelsky*, Das Jhering-Modell des sozialen Wandels (1972) 59–68.

ple's laws and to their contingency on environmental conditions, but his comparative perspective did not have a significant historical dimension. A decade later, French, and then mainly Scottish, authors began to emphasize variation not only across space but also across time: societies and their laws had developed through successive stages and in the general direction from primitive (barbaric) to civilized (modern) states.[140] A particularly prominent member of this group was Adam Smith (1723–1790) of "Wealth of Nations" fame, who in his "Theory of Moral Sentiments" (1759) envisaged the progression of different ages and periods of society. Smith was not a jurist by training and thus not primarily concerned with law, but as an educated Scotsman, he had some basic familiarity with Roman law.[141]

During Jhering's formative period, i.e., the early- to mid-nineteenth century, ideas of (legal) evolution became prominent in Germany as well. They appeared in two main forms. One was of course the Historical School's romantic and sometimes mystical idea of law emanating silently from the depths of the *Volksgeist* as organically developing custom. As we have seen, Jhering viewed this position with skepticism and at later stages of his career fought it with all his might.[142] Savigny's view of evolution also differed from Jhering's in that it was not based on the idea of eternal progress; it was rather cyclical, envisaging improvement and decline[143] – a view probably informed by the Roman law's development from the early republic to late antiquity. The other form of evolutionism influential in early- and mid-nineteenth century Germany took a decidedly philosophical stance and stood in declared opposition to the Historical School: the Hegelian belief in the progress of the *Weltgeist* towards its gradual perfection. The most famous manifestation on the field of jurisprudence was *Eduard Gans*, "Das Erbrecht in weltgeschichtlicher Entwickelung" (1824–1835). The work was well-known to Jhering, and it shared some characteristics with "Geist," especially the conception of historical development as a progressive succession of distinct "stages" ("Stufen").[144]

At the same time, the idea of evolution and progress gripped disciplines beyond the law and in other countries as well. A relatively early manifestation is Auguste Comte's "Cours de philosophie positive" (1830–1842) with its idea of

---

[140] For an overview of the literature, see *Stein*, Legal Evolution (1980) 19–50.

[141] On Smith, see *Stein*, Legal Evolution (1980) 29–45.

[142] Supra chapter II.6, notes 495–498, 502–507 and text; chapter IV.1., notes 28–38 and text.

[143] *Savigny*, Über den Zweck dieser Zeitschrift (1815) 11.

[144] *Gans*, Das Erbrecht I (1824) XIII. There were further similiarities between Gans' "Erbrecht" and Jhering's "Geist": Gans' work was also centered around (though not limited to) Roman Law (its alternative title was "Das römische Erbrecht in seiner Stellung zu vor- und nach-römischem", i.e., "The Roman Law of Succession in Its Relation to the pre- and post-Roman"); it was also plagued by internal tensions because like Jhering, Gans had changed his game plan several times; and it also remained incomplete. (Gans had planned six volumes but published only four.)

the progressive development from a theological to a philosophical and finally a positivist explanation of the world.[145] One also thinks of Marx' and Engel's mid- and late-nineteenth century theory of social and economic evolution through successive stages of production and political (super-)structures. Of course, with the publication of Darwin's "Origin of Species" in 1859, evolutionism soon became all the rage in biology and the natural sciences more broadly, with spillover effects on social studies and in part also on jurisprudence.[146] In the 1870s, early works in cultural anthropology were added to the mix.[147] Thus, when Jhering wrote about the Roman law "at the various stages of its development," propagated the idea that law evolved over time, and alleged its historical progress, he reiterated a well-known theme.

The love affair of jurisprudence with the idea of evolution and progress did not end with Jhering. Savigny's influence in the realm of the common law, which extended throughout the nineteenth century,[148] helped to spawn a specific Anglo-American Historical School in its closing decades.[149] And even in the early twentieth century, Paul Vinogradoff (1854–1921), professor at Oxford and one of the great Roman law scholars of his time, outlined six successive stages of legal development.[150]

The idea of legal evolution was at its most popular exactly when Jhering embraced it, roughly from the 1850s through the 1880s. Of the pertinent works written in that period, two deserve to be compared to Jhering's approach because they became classics in their own right: Henry Sumner Maine's "Ancient Law" and Oliver Wendell Holmes' "The Common Law."[151]

"Ancient Law" (1861)[152]*: "From Status to Contract."* Henry Sumner Maine (1822–1888) was almost exactly Jhering's contemporary and had much in common with him. Like Jhering, Maine was (among other things) a scholar, and for a

---

[145] See supra chapter IV.2., note 342 and text.

[146] See infra notes 189–197 and text.

[147] *Tyler*, Primitive Culture (1871); *Morgan*, Ancient Society (1878). Even *Durkheim's* "Division de la travail social" (1893) still belonged to this evolutionary genre because Durkheim portrayed the progressive development from early to modern forms of economic organization (from "mechanical solidarity" to "organic solidarity").

[148] See *Stein*, Legal Evolution (1980) 72–86.

[149] *Rabban*, Law's History (2013); *Reimann*, Historische Schule und Common Law (1993).

[150] *Vinogradoff*, Outlines of Historical Jurisprudence I (1920) 146, 157–160.

[151] When Jhering was writing "Geist," two other works were published which also attained the status of classics, one Swiss, the other French: *Bachofen*, Das Mutterrecht (1861), and *Fustel de Coulanges*, La cité antique (1864). While both toyed with ideas of evolution and progress (from matriarchy to patriarchy, and from a religious to a secular public order, respectively), this was not their primary theme. Instead, they were mainly works describing social orders in antiquity; for a comparison of Jhering's "Geist" with these works, see *Reimann*, Jhering's "Geist des römischen Rechts" as a Study of Ancient Social Order (2022).

[152] Citations are to the Everyman's Library edition (London 1917, reprinted numerous times). The literature on Maine and "Ancient Law" is extensive; for a succinct essay, see *Stein*, Legal Evolution (1980) 86–89.

time also a professor, of Roman law.[153] He was, however, originally trained in the classics, and it is fair to say that he could not match Jhering's deep knowledge of, and certainly not his doctrinal dexterity in, Roman law. Still, Maine shared Jhering's enthusiasm for Roman law as the most influential legal system in history and as, at least in some ways, a model for modern jurisprudence. In a manner typical for the empirically inclined British mind, Maine also rejected eighteenth century rationalism, philosophical *a priori* assumptions, and metaphysical approaches to law more generally. Also, like Jhering, Maine was interested in the history of Roman (and other) law not so much for its own sake but in pursuit of a broader jurisprudential agenda.

Despite considerable similarities in their work, especially between Jhering's "Geist" and Maine's "Ancient Law" (to which we will turn in a moment), there is no reliable indication of influence in either direction.[154] When Maine worked on "Ancient Law" in the 1850s, he had no reason to be aware of "Geist,"[155] and his only direct citation to German Romanist scholarship was to Savigny's work on possession.[156] Conversely, when Jhering worked on "Geist," especially on the historical parts (i.e., Volumes One and Two), Maine's work had not yet been published. Later influence is highly unlikely as well. As Jhering confessed to Frederick Pollock, he read English with difficulty,[157] there was no German translation of Maine's work, and there are no citations to it in Jhering's writings either. The similarities between the works of these two scholars are largely the results of operating in the same intellectual atmosphere shaped by a broad interest in the connections between ancient Roman law, modern jurisprudence, and legal evolution. In addition, both drew on notions of the natural sciences – Jhering mainly

[153] Maine was Regius Professor of Civil Law at Cambridge 1847–1854.

[154] An influence by Jhering on Maine was suggested by *C.K. Allen* in his introduction to the Worlds Classics edition of "Ancient Law" (Oxford 1954) XIII; the argument was rejected by *Stein*, Legal Evolution (1980) 89 fn. 25, as well as by *Frederick Pollock*, Introduction and Notes to Sir Henry Maine's "Ancient Law" (London 1908) X. It is widely assumed that Maine was influenced by Savigny, see, e.g., *Stein*, Legal Evolution (1980) 89–90; *Vinogradoff*, Outlines of Historical Jurisprudence I (1920) 139. While there is little direct evidence, the assumption is plausible. Like Savigny, Maine saw the origins of (early) law in custom, and his belief in the "inherited qualities of the race" echoed Savigny's *Volksgeist*, though on an anthropological level. For what it is worth, Maine also spoke of Savigny as "the great German jurist" and as a "genius," *Maine*, Ancient Law (1861) 150, 171. There is also some indication that Maine was influenced by Barthold Georg Niebuhr (1776–1831), see *Stein*, Legal Evolution (1980) 90–91.

[155] There is no indication that Maine read German, and the only translation of "Geist" available at the time was in Italian, "Lo spirito del diritto romano nei diversi gradi del suo sviluppo" (Bellavite transl., Milano 1855).

[156] *Maine*, Ancient Law (1861) 170–171. Maine most likely read Savigny's treatise in an English translation, i.e., Von Savigny's Treatise on Possession (Erskine Perry transl., London 1848).

[157] *Pollock*, Introduction and Notes to Sir Henry Maine's Ancient Law (London 1908) X–XI.

on biology and chemistry, which were flourishing in Germany at the time, and Maine primarily on geology, which was highly popular in mid-nineteenth century England. Interestingly, neither Jhering nor Maine were directly influenced by Darwin although both expressed agreement with the key aspects of his theory once they learned of it.[158]

"Geist" and "Ancient Law" are contemporary works that both deal (mainly) with the ancient Roman legal order as it relates to modern jurisprudence. Beyond that, however, they are rather different books. The differences are immediately obvious with regard to their appearance, style, and method. One is a three-volume, 1400-page, *magnum opus* in the literary sense of the word; the other is a relatively slender book, less than a quarter of the former's size. The books also differ greatly in terms of elegance and user-friendliness. As we have seen, "Geist" is often longwinded and poorly organized, full of digressions, contradictions, and redundancies, and it remained unfinished.[159] As a result, reading "Geist" requires an uncommon degree of determination, perseverance, forgiveness – and time; profitably absorbing "Geist" is a demanding full-time job for at least a week or two. "Ancient Law," by contrast, consists of ten fairly succinct chapters arranged in a plausible order. It is written in the conversational and elegant style reflecting its origins in a series of lectures; as a result, it can be read on the side over a weekend. Yet, when judged by standards of academic scholarship, "Geist" is the more impressive book. Jhering tried to stay close to the available sources, provided many concrete examples and illustrations, and took care to point out when speculation came into play. To be sure, one could argue with many of Jhering's views and conclusions, but there was no lack of effort to provide evidence and to go into detail. By contrast, Maine presented one assertion after another without showing much concern for the original material. He essentially asked the reader to have faith in his knowledge and judgment – the book contains virtually no footnotes or other references. Thus, with Maine, there is always the suspicion, as Frederick William Maitland (1850–1906) famously put it, "that he trusted much to a memory that played him tricks and rarely looked back at a book that he had once read."[160] In short, "Geist" was a serious scholarly effort that squarely faced the difficulty of the subject; "Ancient Law" was a series of essays presenting grand ideas with an air of "apparent simplicity."[161]

In terms of substance, "Geist" and "Ancient Law" had quite a lot in common, at least on the surface: both looked at Roman law in antiquity; both agreed on some of its fundamental features, such as its early emphasis on the family and the

---

[158] For Jhering, see supra chapter IV.1., notes 39–57 and text; chapter IV.2., notes 310–315 and text; for Maine, see *Stein*, Legal Evolution (1980) 88, fn. 24.

[159] Supra chapter II.1., notes 10–17 and text.

[160] Letter to Frederick Pollock of January 21, 1901, The Letters of F.W. Maitland, (C.H.S. Fifoot ed., London 1965) 222 (letter no. 279).

[161] Review of Ancient Law in the Law Magazine N.S. XI, 124, quoted after *Stein*, Legal Evolution (1980) 97.

clan; and both trumpeted its universality and thus its significance for our understanding of law in general.[162] Yet, beneath that surface, there were significant differences. Jhering and Maine pursued different agendas because they reacted against different jurisprudential situations in their respective countries.

In Jhering's mid-nineteenth century Germany, the mainstream understanding of law was largely historical: a relic from a distant past (Roman private law) still reigned in practice, and the Historical School provided support for it by defining law as a heritage of history. Jhering wanted to overcome both these elements. He sought to help end the reign of Roman law as a set of positive rules; and he wanted to replace the Historical School with a forward looking jurisprudence based on social needs and legislative choice.

By contrast, in Maine's mid-nineteenth century England, jurisprudence was mainly "analytical": in the wake of Jeremy Bentham (1748–1832) and John Austin (1790–1859), scholars widely conceived of law as the command of a sovereign and as a logical system of principles. Maine wanted to overcome that theoretical approach by showing that many modern legal institutions were neither creatures of sovereign will nor products of abstract logic but rather results of specific historical developments.[163] Thus Maine searched for "some of the earliest ideas of mankind, as they are reflected in Ancient Law, and [sought] to point out the relation of these ideas to modern thought."[164] In this search, Roman law was not, as for Jhering, the only relevant system but rather one among others in the ancient world.[165] It is true that in "Ancient Law," Roman jurisprudence received the lion's share of attention[166] because Maine (questionably) considered it "typical" and because it provided particularly rich material.[167] Still, Maine also looked at various other legal orders, such as Hindu, Hellenic, Celtic, and even "Mahom-

---

[162] There were other similarities as well. Both authors largely eschewed working with precise dates and clearly demarcated time periods, often leaving the reader guessing exactly what time or period they were talking about. Both saw Rome (and its law) as rooted in the Aryan culture and were thus interested in linguistic clues and connections; see *Stein*, Legal Evolution (1980) 91–92. They emphasized the origins of Roman property rights in the taking of bounty in war; see *Jhering*, Geist I (1852) 103–115; *Maine*, Ancient Law (1861) 144–148; and they shared an interest in the Roman jurists' use of fictions; *Jhering*, Geist III (1865) 260–292; *Maine*, Ancient Law (1861) 13–25; etc.

[163] *Maine*, Ancient Law (1861) 4–5, 69–70. The perhaps best demonstration of this approach is chapter VIII, dealing with "The Early History of Property," id., 144–178.

[164] *Maine*, Ancient Law (1861) XV (Preface).

[165] At least in part, the two scholars' different perspectives on Roman law was probably also due to different frames of reference. Jhering operated in a more or less national context in which Roman law had played the central role for centuries and still dominated the practice of private law. Maine thought about jurisprudence in the context of a common law-centered global empire in which Roman law was one of many legal systems and just one, rather limited, ingredient of the present regime.

[166] Many parts are pure Roman law, e.g., chapter IX (Contracts); *Maine*, Ancient Law (1861) 179–200.

[167] *Maine*, Ancient Law (1861) XV (Preface).

etan" law.[168] As a result, his work contained a comparative dimension that was largely lacking in Jhering's writings.[169]

In summary, by reacting against the almost opposite jurisprudential situations in their respective countries, Jhering and Maine pulled in almost opposite directions. Jhering's agenda in "Geist" was essentially anti-historical: he wanted to free the law of the present from the clutches of tradition; Maine's approach in "Ancient Law" was essentially historical: he wanted to demonstrate how much of present law had deep roots in the past.[170] Much of Jhering's significance lay in overcoming the Historical School in Germany where it had dominated legal thought in the first half of the nineteenth century; Maine's principal contribution lay in initializing an Historical School in the Anglo-American orbit where it would shape legal thought in the century's closing decades.[171]

Despite these differences, Jhering and Maine did share a view of legal history as a process of evolution and progress. While Jhering asserted this view in a general fashion, Maine opined that only some societies were capable of progress whereas most remained stationary.[172] For Maine, ancient Rome was the prime example of a progressive order[173] which made it particularly worth studying.[174] Thus both scholars focused on ancient Roman law as an evolving system. Both also saw its progress in terms of successive stages, even though they conceived of these stages differently. For Jhering, the progress of Roman law lay mainly in the development from the formalism, verbalism, and symbolism of the "second system" (the *ius strictum* of the pre-classical era) to the more refined, equity-oriented, and universalist law of the "third system" (roughly the classical and post classical periods);[175] it was progress in the whole conception, texture, and appli-

[168] See, e.g., *Maine*, Ancient Law (1861) 142–143.

[169] Ancient law beyond Rome, and thus the comparative perspective, played an increasingly important role in Maine's later writings, see *Maine*, Village Communities in the East and West (London 1871); id., Lectures on the History of Institutions ((New York 1875); id., Early Law and Custom (London 1883). That work was part of the emerging field of legal anthropology rather than of more traditional legal history. Maine developed a particular interest in Hindu law when he learned about it as a legal member of the council of India from 1863 to 1869. After his return to England, Maine held the chair of comparative and historical jurisprudence at the University of Oxford (1869–1877).

[170] In this regard, Maine was a true follower of Savigny, especially of his "strictly historical method" to trace modern law all the way back to its historical origins; *Savigny*, Vom Beruf unserer Zeit (1814) 117–118.

[171] See *Rabban*, Law's History (2013); for a brief summary, see *Reimann*, Historical Jurisprudence (2018) 400–403.

[172] *Maine*, Ancient Law (1861) 13–15. The idea was not altogether original; it had already been voiced by George Long in 1847, see *Stein*, Legal Evolution (1980) 79.

[173] "From its commencement to its close, it was progressively modified for the better." *Maine*, Ancient Law (1861) 14–15.

[174] *Maine*, Ancient Law (1861) 14–15.

[175] See, e.g., *Jhering*, Geist I (1852) 78–82. While Jhering of course never reached the "third system" in "Geist," he subsequently provided an example of this progressive development in "Das Schuldmoment" (1867); see supra 2.

cation of law. Maine characterized its progress in more technical terms by a succession of predominant "instrumentalities": fictions, equity, and legislation – a succession that evinced the maturation of law from primitive to modern forms.[176]

Beyond all this, there was another, more substantive, view of progress. The difference between Maine's and Jhering's views in this respect was subtle, but it is important to recognize it because it related to their divergent positions on the proper form of mid- to late-nineteenth century liberalism in their respective countries.

For Maine, the most significant substantive progress of Roman law was its development from a legal order based on group membership to one based on the individual. Early Roman law was centered around the household whose members were subject to the *patria potestas* of the oldest male. In this environment, the rights of individuals were defined by their status within the family. Over time, the *patria potestas* became weaker, and an individual's position within the household became less important.[177] Eventually, rights arose mainly from (individual) agreements.[178] Thus, as Maine put it in his most famous phrase, progress consisted of "a movement *from Status to Contract*."[179] Since Maine considered this development characteristic of all progressive societies, he presented the rise of private autonomy (including the will-theory as its doctrinal manifestation[180]) as a sign of progress in general. History vindicated the diminishment of group obligations and the maximization of self-determination. Maine's view of legal progress thus provided perfect support for the ideology of *laissez faire* popular in nineteenth-century Britain.

Jhering did not subscribe to this view of progress. To be sure, he also emphasized that in early Roman law, group membership played a powerful, and in many ways a defining, role – not only with regard to the family and household, but also the *gens*, the military, and eventually the state.[181] Nor did he deny that over time, status became gradually less significant while the creation of private

---

[176] *Maine*, Ancient Law (1861) 15.

[177] In a similar vein, Maine claimed a development from communal to individual forms of ownership, *Maine*, Ancient Law (1861) 144–178. This was a fairly common position at the time – from which Jhering partially deviated by claiming that in Roman law, individual ownership developed already at an early stage, *Jhering*, Geist I (1952) 183–185.

[178] *Maine*, Ancient Law (1861) 99–100.

[179] *Maine*, Ancient law (1861) 100 (emphasis in the original).

[180] This is pointed out by *Stein*, Legal Evolution (1980) 114.

[181] See especially *Jhering*, Geist I (1852) 161–255. This was not incompatible with Jhering's emphasis on the central role of the individual will and individual power in the establishment of private rights, nor with his celebration of individual liberty in early Rome, see supra II.1. notes 104–110 and text. These attributes pertained only to the Roman citizen of full legal capacity, i.e., at least in the early stages of development, only the *paterfamilias*. The other members of the household (mainly women, children, slaves) obviously did not enjoy such self-determination.

rights and obligations by agreement came more and more to the fore.[182] But Jhering never presented this development as the hallmark of the Roman law's progress. This was not only for lack of opportunity, i.e., because "Geist" never reached the "third system" in which Roman contract law became such a prominent topic. More importantly, Jhering saw the strength of Roman law not in a move from group obligations to individual autonomy but rather in its perfect reconciliation of these two aspects (already in the "second system"). As in Maine's case, Jhering's view had direct implications for his position on the contemporary legal order.[183] Considering Roman law a model, Jhering advocated a balance between individual autonomy and collective duties.[184] Jhering envisaged a social order in which the individual was not only a free agent in his private sphere but also a community member subject to multiple duties vis-a-vis society and state.[185] In later years, Jhering portrayed the course of history in a manner almost opposite to Maine: as leading from individual egoism to collective responsibility and thus from unbridled self-determination to increasing social obligations.[186] Here Jhering's ideas corresponded to, and thus supported, the gradual rise of the modern administrative and social state in Germany and on the European continent more generally.

In this manner, both Maine and Jhering saw in the history of Roman law what they preferred to see given their socio-political preferences and environments: the former an ideal progression from group membership to personal autonomy, the latter an ideal combination of individual rights and collective duties.

"The Common Law" (1881): Progress towards "External Standards."[187] Two decades later, Oliver Wendell Holmes (1841–1935) published "The Common Law." It was his only book and became the most famous work in the history of American jurisprudence. While every American lawyer knows of it, it is, like Jhering's "Geist" and Maine's "Ancient Law," rarely read today except perhaps for the very few parts that have become classic pronouncements on the law in general.

Holmes was almost a generation younger than Jhering and Maine (he also outlived both by almost half-a-century) and in many ways a very different kind of jurist: he was a dyed-in-the-wool common lawyer with a limited knowledge of Roman law; when he wrote "The Common Law" he was not a legal academic but

---

[182] *Jhering*, Geist I (1852) 333–334.

[183] Jhering did not hide his intention of using the Roman law as a lesson for the present, see, e.g., Jhering, *Geist* II.1. (1854) 128, fn. 145.

[184] See, e.g., *Jhering*, Geist II.1. (1854) 131–132.

[185] See, e.g., *Jhering*. Geist I (1852) 128–134; *Jhering*, Zweck I (1884) 532; see supra chapter IV.2., notes 248–263 and text.

[186] *Jhering*, Zweck I (1884) 77–93. "Life in society is the supreme cultural law of history," id. XIX.

[187] *Holmes*, The Common Law (1881) 88. Citations are to the standard modern edition, Boston 1963 (with an Introduction by Mark DeWolfe Howe).

a part-time (one can almost say: hobby) scholar in his thirties, practicing law at the bar; he then spent the remaining fifty years of his life on the bench.[188] Still, as a young man, Holmes intensely studied the history of law, and, like Jhering and Maine, he did so for broader jurisprudential reasons: he wanted to construe a general theory of the common law from its historical record.[189]

As a result, "The Common Law" was, like Jhering's "Geist" and Maine's "Ancient Law," a book with a dual nature: a study in the law's development and a project in legal theory.[190] In the present chapter, we will consider only the former side, leaving its jurisprudential aspects for later.[191]

As a study in legal development, "The Common Law" was heavily influenced by Maine's "Ancient Law," and there were many similarities.[192] In a sense Holmes was now trying to do in his own environment what Maine had done in England: in reaction against the rise of analytical jurisprudence and against a (at least perceived) trend to think about law in purely logical terms, Holmes sought to demonstrate that, as he famously put it, "[the] life of the law has not been logic; it has been experience."[193] Understanding the law of the present required understanding its historical genesis. Thus, like Maine, Holmes sought to trace legal rules and institutions back to their origins.[194] Jhering's work, by contrast, had at best a minimal influence on "The Common Law" as a historical study. It is true that Holmes cited Jhering in several contexts, but he did so mainly to refute his

---

[188] Holmes held a professorship at Harvard Law School for merely a couple of weeks and then resigned when he was nominated to the Massachusetts Supreme Judicial Court on which he served 1882–1902. Subsequently, as a justice on the United States Supreme Court for thirty years (1902–1932), Holmes became the most iconic judicial figure in American history and popular culture.

[189] He made this clear in the first very sentence of the work: "The object of this book is to present a general view of the Common Law," *Holmes*, The Common Law (1881) 5.

[190] For a masterful explanation of the book's major dimensions, see *DeWolfe Howe*, Introduction (1963) XI–XXVII.

[191] See infra chapter VII.3., notes 152–195 and text.

[192] The topics of the individual chapters in "The Common Law" are highly similar to those in "Ancient Law." Like Maine, Holmes also drew on a variety of (old) legal systems though for him, Roman law played a distinctly smaller role. Unlike Maine, Holmes provided abundant references to a broad range of both original sources and secondary literature. As has been noted, in many instances Holmes cherry-picked the evidence in order to support his claims, see, e.g., *DeWolfe Howe*, Introduction (1963) XX.

[193] *Holmes*, The Common Law (1881) 5.

[194] See supra notes 163–164, 170 and text. Yet, Holmes parted ways with Maine in an important regard. Maine sought to demonstrate the Roman roots or modern law, including much of the common law, and he considered the Roman law a model for the present. Holmes, by contrast, endeavored to show that the common law's origins were not Roman but rather "teutonic," i.e. that they lay in the Germanic laws and institutions of the middle ages, and that the Roman law influence was to be avoided. Here, Holmes' agenda tied into a broader late-nineteennth century ideological battle about the origins of Anglo-American law, see *Reimann*, "In Such Forests Liberty was Nurtured" – vom germanischen Ursprung der angloamerikanischen Freiheit (1997).

ideas.[195] Jhering's influence on "The Common Law" in its jurisprudential dimension is a different matter that will require a more elaborate discussion.[196]

All three authors – Jhering, Maine, and Holmes – had something very significant in common: they shared the belief in the law's historical evolution and progress. While Holmes did not think in terms of successive "stages," he was as convinced as were Jhering and Maine that "the law has grown, without a break, from barbarism to civilization."[197] Moreover, like Jhering's view of development from strict and formalist law to equitable and flexible justice, and like Maine's idea of evolution "from status to contract," Holmes propagated a specific form of progress: he postulated that over time, the common law had increasingly employed "external" standards of conduct.[198] The law, Holmes wrote, often talked about liability in moral terms, e.g., about fault, negligence, malice, etc. In reality, however, such terms had simply come to mean that an individual had fallen below an objective standard of conduct, i.e., below what was expected of "the ideal average prudent man."[199] As a general rule, the law thus no longer really cared whether an individual was morally blameworthy; instead, before the law, a man "acts at his peril always and wholly irrespective of the state of his consciousness upon the matter."[200]

This view of the common law's evolution was almost the exact opposite of Jhering's claim that the Roman law had moved from a regime of strict liability (originally for penalties) to a fault-based system.[201] To be sure, the two positions were not necessarily irreconcilable: the law can forego strict liability in favor of "fault" but then measure it objectively, by external standards. Still, Jhering's view of Roman jurisprudence clearly differed from Holmes' portrait of the common law: Jhering postulated that Roman law had arrived at an "individualized han-

[195] See, e.g., *Holmes*, The Common Law (1881) 15 note 33, 165, 166 note 11, 258 note. 25. As an exception, Holmes gave Jhering credit for showing that the origins of certain forms of early Roman law lay in the "warlike capture" of property, id. 276 note 34.

[196] Infra chapter VII.3., notes 152–196 and text.

[197] *Holmes*, The Common Law (1881) 8. Holmes added an interesting observation to this evolutionary credo: he noted (mainly in the development of the common law) that often, old forms were retained over long periods of time but were eventually justified on novel grounds that reflected changing social circumstances and needs. In this fashion, the law's growth often consisted in filling traditional rules or formulas with new content, id.

[198] *Holmes*, The Common Law (1881) 242.

[199] *Holmes*, The Common Law (1881) 89.

[200] *Holmes*, The Common Law (1881) 65. The same was true, *mutatis mutandis*, for contractual liability: "The law has nothing do to with the actual state of the parties' minds. In contract, as elsewhere, it must go by externals and judge parties by their conduct;" *Holmes*, The Common Law (1881) 242. This was, of course, a blow against the will-theory of contract which prevailed on both sides of the Atlantic at the time – and which Jhering had also come to attack in the third volume of "Geist", albeit on the different ground that rights were not manifestations of (individual) will but of legally protected interests, *Jhering*, Geist III (1865) 307–316; see supra chapter IV.2., notes 149–154 and text.

[201] Supra 2., notes 58–62 and text.

dling of the concept of fault" and that the Roman jurists resolved the question of fault "always in a concrete and individualized fashion."[202] At least in this regard, Jhering's and Holmes' notions of progress pointed in virtually opposite directions. One can see these opposite views simply as descriptions of two different legal systems. Yet, by presenting the respective developments as progress, Holmes and Jhering also indicated that they regarded them as normatively desirable. Holmes clearly considered the rise of external standards justified by social need: individualized justice was properly sacrificed on the altar of the common good.[203] Jhering did not embrace such a position. At least in "Geist" and implicitly also in "Schuldmoment," Jhering saw the Roman law's crucial progress in its transition from the "second system's" formalistic and unforgiving *ius strictum* to the "third system's" more flexible and equity-oriented *ius honorarium*. In summary, for Jhering, legal progress meant more equity in the individual case, for Holmes, it meant less.

Thus, while Jhering, Maine, and Holmes all agreed that the law's development was progressive, they disagreed about its direction: for Jhering, it led to increasing social responsibility, for Maine to every greater individual autonomy; for Jhering, progress brought more individualized justice, for Holmes, more standardized treatment. What counted as progress in the development of the law was in the eye of the beholder.

[202] *Jhering*, Das Schuldmoment (1867) 48–49.

[203] "[W]hen men live in society, a certain average of conduct, a sacrifice of individual peculiarities going beyond a certain point, is necessary to the general welfare. If, for instance, a man is born hasty and awkward, is always having accidents and hurting himself and his neighbors, no doubt his congenital defects will be allowed for in the courts of Heaven, but his slips are no less troublesome to his neighbors than if they sprang from guilt or neglect." *Holmes*, The Common Law (1881) 86. Exceptions would apply for "well-known categories, such as infancy or madness," id. 43, a point on which Jhering agreed, *Jhering*, Das Schuldmoment (1867) 42.

Chapter VI

Jhering's Perspectives Beyond Law – Ethics, Custom, and Cultural History

For most of his life, Jhering focused on law, looking at it from a wide range of perspectives – its doctrine and method, social contingency and purpose, historical foundations and evolution. This is the work he is known for because these are the areas to which he made lasting contributions. Over time, however, Jhering increasingly ventured beyond law. The non-legal part of his *oeuvre* has received little attention by posterity – and justly so because it has had fairly little impact; today, even jurists who are otherwise familiar with Jhering are mostly not aware of it.

Jhering's work beyond law is still worth looking at for three reasons. To begin with, it was increasingly important to himself, occupied him for much of his old age, and eventually became a significant element of what defined him as a scholar. Second, it vividly illustrates an important feature of his personality, i.e., his constant hunger for, and pursuit of, new perspectives as well as his obsession with going to the very roots of the phenomena he observed, at almost any cost. Finally, it highlights a feature pervading some of his work more generally: his willingness to engage with difficult material without adequate professional training and thus to engage in a form of academic risk-taking that he both recognized and accepted.

Some of Jhering's non-legal work is still loosely related to law in the sense that it deals with norms regulating social behavior: in the second volume of "Zweck" (and in his delightful essay "Das Trinkgeld"), Jhering set out to explore non-legal norms governing conduct in society. Towards the very end of his life, Jhering then turned away from norms altogether and pursued a cultural study: seeking to understand the very roots of the ancient Mediterranean civilizations, he delved into the pre-history of the Aryan peoples. In both contexts, he was a fearless amateur oscillating between stunning perceptiveness and worrisome speculation.

1. Social Norms Beyond Law: "Der Zweck im Recht" (Volume Two 1883/1886)[1]

Six years after the first volume of "Zweck," Jhering published the second.[2] It is a massive tome of over 700 pages that spun even more out of control than Volume One, and it remained incomplete as well. Its general strengths and weaknesses are also quite similar to those of Volume One:[3] on the one hand, there is a plethora of fascinating insights and brilliant ideas, a freshness and fearlessness of thought, and a vivid style that keeps the reader's attention; on the other hand, there is an idiosyncratic original structure which is then not entirely followed; a lack of terminological precision and uniformity; and an overall weakness of intellectual discipline resulting in multiple and lengthy digressions, annoying redundancies, and irritating obscurities that tax the reader's forgiveness.

In order to come to grips with the book, we first need to get a sense of what it undertakes and covers: it is not a jurisprudential work but an exploration of the forms and functions of non-legal normativity.[4] Only then can we consider its two constituent parts: Jhering's "realist theory" of ethics and his extensive foray into the sociology of custom and related phenomena.

The Topic and the Game Plan: Exploring "Das Sittliche." The subtitle in the table of contents tells us that the object of Volume Two is "Das Sittliche."[5] That term would most commonly be translated as "The Ethical." Yet, at least to the modern reader, that suggests something considerably narrower than the term's eventual meaning for Jhering – as well as something quite different from the lion's share of the book. Explaining what Jhering meant by "Das Sittliche" takes some effort, but understanding it is crucial to grasp what the second volume of "Zweck" is, or, rather, was supposed to be, about. The matter is best approached in two steps: first by looking at the role and position of "Das Sittliche" in Jhering's overall approach, and second by looking at Jhering's game plan in dealing with its two component parts.

To understand the role of "Das Sittliche" in Jhering's overall approach we have to go back to Volume One of "Zweck." There, Jhering had distinguished three basic kinds of norms that govern human conduct in society: law, ethics, and custom.[6] The first, i.e. law, was enforced by the state through a form of coercion

---

[1] Consistent with the discussion of Volume One (supra chapter IV.2.), citations are to the second edition (1886). While Jhering heavily revised the text of Volume One for the second edition, the revisions for the second edition of Volume Two were relatively minor.

[2] In contrast to Volume One, there is no English translation of Volume Two.

[3] See supra chapter IV.2. notes 381–396.

[4] There are a few references to law but they serve only to illustrate certain particular points and occasionally to compare legal to non-legal norms, see, e.g., *Jhering*, Zweck II (1886) 400–401.

[5] *Jhering*, Zweck II (1886) XXIX.

[6] Repeated in the Preface to Volume Two, *Jhering*, Zweck II (1886) X.

(Zwang) that Jhering called "mechanical" (one could also say "external"); this was covered in Volume One. Since, as Jhering acknowledged, law alone is insufficient to ensure appropriate social conduct (as not all forms of human behavior can be regulated through state coercion), it must be supplemented by the other two kinds of norms, i.e., ethics and custom; they are enforced by a form of coercion that Jhering termed "psychological". Jhering grouped these two together under the heading of "Das Sittliche;" they became the object of Volume Two. Thus, Volume Two deals with the (two types of) norms governing human conduct in society that are not enforced by the state. The reason why Jhering could group norms as different as ethics and (social) custom together under one term is an idiosyncrasy of the German language: "Sittlichkeit" means "ethics," and "Sitte" means (social) "custom" – thus, "Das Sittliche" could serve as an umbrella concept for both. To Jhering, the linguistic similarity indicated the relatedness of "Sittlichkeit" and "Sitte."[7]

Jhering astutely observed the respective strengths and weaknesses of strictly legal rules (enforced by the state through "mechanical" coercion) versus social norms (enforced by society through "psychological" coercion). Even though some of Jhering's statements may strike a modern reader as too simplistic, in a key passage, he puts his finger on some crucial differences.

> "Both kinds of coercion are imperfect, both have their advantages and flaws. The advantage of mechanical coercion exercised by state power is the certainty of its effect – where it is proper (angemessen), it reaches its intended goal. But it is not proper everywhere, and therein lies its imperfection. It is too slow-moving and clumsy to enforce all norms which society recognizes as necessary. [...] The advantage of psychological coercion in society is that it does not have to exclude any social relations, [but] like air, it reaches all spheres, the interior of the house just like the steps of the throne, places where mechanical coercion would be entirely ineffective. Its weakness is the uncertainty of its effect – one can defy the judgment of society and public opinion but one cannot resist the arm of the law."[8]

Jhering thus acknowledged the (rather narrow) limits of regulation through law. Like few jurists of his generation, he explained why vast areas of social relationships lie beyond the law's reach; and like no jurist of his generation, he set out to explore these areas.[9]

This brings us to Jhering's original game plan for the second volume of "Zweck." That plan was to explore "Das Sittliche" in the sense of "ethics".[10] Up to this point, Jhering's endeavor to complement his discourse on law (in Volume One) with a discourse on ethics (in Volume Two) was very much in line with German idealist philosophy which had often seen law and ethics as complemen-

---

[7] *Jhering*, Zweck II (1886) 20–21.

[8] *Jhering*. Zweck II (1886) 182–183.

[9] *Jhering*, Zweck II (1886) 11–14. Up to this point, Jhering thus contrasts Recht and Sittlichkeit in a quasi-Kantian fashion, id. 182.

[10] Volume One ends with a reference to Volume Two, pointing, at its very end, to a discussion of "die Sittlichkeit," *Jhering*, Zweck I (1884) 570.

tary sets of norms.[11] In his actual approach to the subject of ethics, however, Jhering departed radically from that tradition: he wanted to replace the "idealist" theory (or theories) with a "realist" approach[12] because he was convinced that, just like law, ethics was not rooted in moral (*a priori*) absolutes but was, instead, the product of social conditions and historical experience. As we have seen, he had previously made that claim already in his lecture on the origins of the feeling of justice (Rechtsgefühl);[13] now he wanted to prove and demonstrate it in detail. So far, it was still all about ethics. Yet, to demonstrate the origins of ethics in social experience and reality, Jhering pursued a bottom-up approach: he first wanted to understand the social reality of non-legal norms and then explore how they resulted in certain ethical rules.[14] Jhering saw this social reality in the usages and customs de facto prevailing in society, i.e., in "Sitte." As a result, Jhering's ultimate game plan encompassed exploring both dimensions of "Das Sittliche": first, as a preliminary topic, "Sitte" (custom) as the factual basis; then, as the primary objective, "Sittlichkeit" (ethics) as the resulting moral norms. In light of Jhering's overall approach, that made good sense. Unfortunately, as it so often happened, the preliminary topic, i.e., the exploration of "Sitte," took on a life of its own, filled hundreds of pages, exhausted its author, and eventually crowded out the original primary objective, the exploration of ethics.

The structure and content of Volume Two is the result of this game plan. Even though the table of contents does not properly reflect it, beyond the introductory matter, the book consists of two main parts.[15] The first part is a discourse on "Das Sittliche" in general; it fills the first third of the volume and lays out Jhering's "realist" approach to ethics.[16] The second part then focuses on "Sitte," i.e., the social phenomena in particular (custom and related norms and habits); it fills the remaining two thirds of the work and is, essentially, a sociological study.[17] The book ends before that second part is completed, in mid-air, so to speak. As a result, the originally envisaged systematic exploration of "Sittlichkeit" in the sense of ethics is still missing. Jhering promised with great fanfare to address

---

[11] See *Kant*, Metaphysik der Sitten (1797); the separateness of legal and moral norms was, however, not Kant's invention but had earlier, English, roots in the work of Francis Hutcheson (1694–1746) and Bernard de Mandeville (1670–1733).

[12] *Jhering*, Zweck II (1886) 587.

[13] Supra chapter IV.3.

[14] *Jhering*, Zweck II (1886) IX–XII.

[15] While Jhering explained at length how he had paid meticulous attention to the structure of the book and the sequence of the argument, *Jhering*, Zweck II (1886) XVIII–XX, neither is easily grasped by, nor very helpful to, the reader. Especially in the second half of the book, Jhering once again comes up with ever new topics and ideas which he then pursues at length even though that leads the discourse ever farther from his main line of argument – until that argument vanishes entirely from sight.

[16] *Jhering*, Zweck II (1886) 14–241.

[17] *Jhering*, Zweck II (1886) 241–723.

"ethical idealism" in a third volume which, however, he barely began and never published.[18]

A "Realist" Approach to Ethics: *"die Allgewalt des Zwecks."* Jhering's general discussion of "Das Sittliche" in the first third of Volume Two is prolix and complex, and it would make little sense to attempt a summary of its substance here. For our purposes, its most important feature is Jhering's "realist" approach to ethics.[19] It is largely identical to Jhering's approach to law,[20] and it largely amounts to an amplification of his position in "Rechtsfühl."[21] It consists of three major elements. They are closely interrelated, and Jhering does not clearly distinguish them. They are the (non-legal) norms' origin, essence, and objective.

Jhering's baseline belief was that the origin of all social norms lies exclusively in social conditions and historical experience. Thus, the norms comprised by "Das Sittliche" are neither *a priori* nor innate but rather constitute responses to the changing needs of society. After he had come to that conclusion on his own, Jhering was astounded to learn that almost two hundred years earlier, John Locke had made essentially the same claim.[22] Jhering not only gave Locke credit, he also praised his insight as "one of the greatest acts of the human mind in the course of the world's history."[23] Unfortunately, Jhering lamented, "later ethics and legal philosophy" (in particular German idealism) had entirely disregarded Locke's insight. Also, while Locke had demolished the belief in innate morality, he had not yet shown, "how and whence humankind came into possession of its ethical principles."[24] Jhering now wanted to complete Locke's work by developing an "empirical understanding of ethics, as it originates and grows and operates in the life of society."[25] Such an undertaking – Jhering (over)claimed in a manner reminiscent of Comte[26] – would be of immense practical value and fit to become "the queen of social sciences."[27]

Since social norms originated in social conditions and needs, their essence lay in their "purpose" ("Zweck") to respond to these conditions and needs. The

[18] A brief draft on "tact" was published posthumously, *Jhering*, Der Takt (1968). A planned addendum was found in the form of handwritten notes and published in print by *Helfer*, Nachtrag zu Jherings Zweck im Recht (1970).

[19] That approach is not clearly formulated in a single place. Several of its essential elements are dispersed throughout Jhering's discourse, often in a highly redundant fashion.

[20] Supra chapter VI.2.

[21] Supra chapter VI.3.

[22] Jhering cited Locke's "well-known work on human understanding," *Jhering*, Zweck II (1886) 109, i.e., *Locke*, An Essay Concerning Human Understanding (1790). Jhering had most likely read the work in the translation of J.H. v. Kirchmann, i.e., Locke's Versuch über den menschlichen Verstand (2 vols., Berlin 1872–73).

[23] *Jhering*, Zweck II (1886) 109.

[24] *Jhering*, Zweck II (1886) 111.

[25] *Jhering*, Zweck II (1886) 134.

[26] See supra chapter IV.3., note 342 and text.

[27] *Jhering*, Zweck II (1886) 133–134.

claim (at the heart of Volume One) that "purpose is the creator of all law" was now expanded to cover all social norms: purpose "is the creator of the whole *sittliche* order – of all its constituent parts, custom, morality, law."[28] Thus the make-up of the entire social order was subject to the "omnipotence of purpose" ("Allgewalt des Zwecks").[29]

Since the essence of all social norms lay in their purpose to respond to social needs, their function was distinctly societal. Jhering never tired emphasizing that the norms' purpose is not the welfare of the individual but that of society – and only society.[30] Like law, non-legal norms were means to secure "the conditions of life in society".[31] "Society did not exist for the sake of ethics, but ethics exists for the sake of society."[32] In contrast to Kant's or Bentham's "Individualethik," Jhering postulated a "Socialethik."[33] In one of his careless overstatements, Jhering even claimed that the terms "sittlich" and "gesellschaftlich" mean the same thing.[34]

Because social norms were meant to serve a purpose, the standard by which they had to be judged was, as for law, how well they performed that task, i.e., their utility. In that sense, Jhering's approach was expressly utilitarian. Yet, as we have seen,[35] Jhering took great pains to distinguish his utilitarianism from its English version: Bentham's (and Spencer's) utility was that of the individual, Jhering's that of society (only). Jhering also cautioned that utility must be gauged by reference to society as a whole as well as in the long run; catering to particular, or short term, interests was not appropriate.[36]

Like his theory of law, Jhering's approach to non-legal norms thus entailed unabashed relativism.[37] As he repeatedly emphasized, the origin of all norms in the conditions of the respective societies, as well as their purpose to fulfill the respective societies' needs, meant not only that the content of these norms necessarily depended on, and thus varied with, the social conditions at their respective points in history.[38] It also meant that the only valid standard for judging these norms was whether they adequately responded to the various social conditions and needs. In other words, the proper ethical yardstick was not "truth" ("Wahr-

[28] *Jhering*, Zweck II (1886) 214.

[29] *Jhering*, Zweck II (1886) XVII.

[30] *Jhering*, Zweck II (1886) 104.

[31] *Jhering*, Zweck II (1886) 156, 192, 194, 506.

[32] *Jhering*, Zweck II (1886) 586. The phrase of course paralleled Jhering's (more) famous jurisprudential statement that "life does not exist for the sake of concepts, but concepts exist for the sake of life." *Jhering*, Geist III (1865) 302–303.

[33] *Jhering*, Zweck II (1886) 160–172.

[34] *Jhering*, Zweck II (1886) 104.

[35] Supra chapter IV.2., notes 328–335 and text.

[36] *Jhering*, Zweck II (1886) 210–12.

[37] Expressly *Jhering*, Zweck II (1886) 121 ("beruht auf der Anerkennung der *Relativität* des Sittlichen;" emphasis in the original).

[38] *Jhering*, Zweck II (1886) 105, 120–121. 147.

heit") but "rightness" ("Richtigkeit"), which Jhering defined as "what is appropriate to the practical purposes of life."[39]

To be sure, none of this was surprising to those familiar with Jhering's theory of law (in Volume One). Still, Jhering now drove his relativism and consequentialism to new extremes. He went on a rampage against core elements of an idealist conception of ethics. Justice (as an ethical precept), he claimed, is not a value in and of itself "as an unhealthy, idealistic view ... wants to make us believe;" it is valuable only "because, and insofar as, it is a condition for the welfare of society."[40] Lying is not an evil in and of itself but may well be allowed or even required, depending on the needs of society and on the particular situation,[41] especially since truth is not absolute either but rather depends on social circumstances and conditions[42]. Even fundamental ethical categories like "good" and "evil" are not absolutes but rather results of social experience.[43] For idealists who

[39] *Jhering*, Zweck II (1886) 121. This is also why earlier stages of cultural development must be judged on their own terms rather than by modern standards, id.

[40] *Jhering*, Zweck II (1886) 229.

[41] Jhering's forty-two-page discourse on truthfulness and lying is an essay in its own right, *Jhering*, Zweck II (1886) 581–623. In a truly consequentialist fashion, he considered the argument that lying implies "self-contradiction" ("Selbstwiderspruch") ethically irrelevant, id. 586 note. Beyond that, his discussion of truth and lying contains contradictory statements. On the one hand, truthfulness (Wahrhaftigkeit) is an indispensible prequisite for a functioning society because people have to be able to rely on each other's word, id. 604, 614. Since lying thus corrodes one of society's foundations, "the ethical reprehensibility of the lie is beyond reasonable doubt," id. 604. On the other hand, whether lying is allowed depends on the underlying purpose. Thus, lying is not only permitted when it avoids unnecessary distress to others ("schonende Lüge"), it is even required when it saves others from harm ("rettende Lüge"), though mere good intent is insufficient, id. 620–622. Of course, one can resolve the contradiction by distinguishing principle from individual case: in principle, life in society requires truthfulness, but it allows for exceptions under particular circumstances. Yet, permitting exceptions for the benefit of individuals is difficult to reconcile with Jhering's otherwise strictly social construction of utility. Jhering fails to explain how permitting lies where they save individuals from harm benefits society as a whole.

[42] Jhering challenged the notion of objective truth (Wahrheit) in a strikingly postmodern fashion. He pointed out that most of what we consider true depends not on our own experience but on what we learn from others (and that with increasing availability of information, such second hand knowledge becomes an ever greater part of our overall knowledge). In that sense "truth" is mostly (and increasingly) just "belief" ("Glaube"). How strongly we believe certain information to be true depends largely on how many people subscribe to it. Yet, even if millions do, the resulting truth is not really objective but ultimately still subjective, *Jhering*, Zweck II (1886) 599–600. Thus, it is wrong to assume that we measure subjective by objective truth; instead, what we call objective truth is determined by subjective truth ("die objective Wahrheit bildet nicht den Maßstab der subjectiven, sondern die subjective den der objectiven."), id. 599. At bottom, even "truth" is not absolute but rather socially constructed; it ultimately depends on the purpose it serves in society; id. 593.

[43] "[G]ood in the social, or ethical sense means what experience has shown to be socially advantageous, bad or evil, by contrast, what has turned out to be disadvantageous or detrimental." *Jhering*, Zweck II (1886) 216; Jhering provided a variety of illustrations, id. 217–219.

propagated "virtue" regardless of its consequences for others, Jhering had nothing but contempt, which he expressed in scathing terms: he blasted "the egotism of the narrow-minded fanatic of virtue who sacrifices the world in order to prevail, a hyena of virtue bathing in blood to quench its thirst for virtue – may the world go up in flames if only the wretched ego can preserve its virtue."[44] Sometimes one cannot but wonder what possessed him.

While the parallelisms between Jhering's theory of law and his approach to ethics render the latter largely redundant, they do not render it irrelevant. It is one thing to subscribe to a strictly relativist and consequentialist conception of law but quite another to abjure all absolute standards of ethics by which law can be judged. If law and ethics – and, as we have seen, even the "feeling of justice"[45] – are all conceived in relativist and consequentialist terms, then there really is no fixed vantage point whatsoever for judgments about right or wrong. What the state commands, conscience requires, and the heart feels all depend on the conditions and needs of the respective society and thus vary across time and space.

Jhering could – and perhaps should – have left it at that. Yet, it seems that he could not quite stomach his own positivism and relativism. Part of him still wanted to reach firmer ethical ground. Thus, in the Introduction to the second volume of "Zweck," he promised his readers a third volume that would deal with "ethical idealism." It would show that "nobody has ever planted the banner of ideal ethics on ground as solid as I."[46] Whether Jhering was capable of that feat is open to doubt, but we will never know because, as mentioned, a third volume was never written – for better or worse.

Jhering's Sociology: "Die Theorie der Umfangsformen." The second, and much longer, part of "Zweck's" second volume is an entirely different ballgame: it takes the reader on an expedition into the realm of custom and other norms (and forms) of social life.[47] Originally planned as merely the real-life basis for a theory of ethics, it soon developed into a project of its own. Since Jhering once again allowed himself to follow his interests from one thing to the next, the enterprise took on such gargantuan proportions that even the 500 pages he devoted to it did not suffice to complete his "theory of forms of social interaction" ("Theorie der Umgangsformen").[48]

As both contemporary and later critics have pointed out, Jhering's discourse surely has its weaknesses.[49] It is (admittedly) amateurish, poorly organized, often

---

[44] *Jhering*, Zweck II (1886) 585.

[45] Supra chapter IV.3.

[46] *Jhering*, Zweck II (1886) XXI.

[47] Peter Stein suggested that Jhering's foray into these subjects may have been inspired by Montesquieu's discussion of custom and similar phenomena; *Stein*, Legal Evolution (1980) 16. This is a plausible idea in light of chapter XIX of "De'l esprit des loix." Note that Jhering's recognition of the importance of social custom dated back at least to the mid-1850s; see, e.g., *Jhering*, Geist II.2. (1854) 207.

[48] *Jhering*, Zweck II (1886) XXXIII, 351.

[49] See, e.g., *Helfer*, Nachtrag zu Jherings "Zweck im Recht" (1970) 12.

endlessly rambling, and full of unfortunate exaggerations and simplifications. While it strives for an integrated whole, Jhering does not derive from all his observations anything like a general and consistent theory of social norms. Instead, what we get is an assortment of essays and fragments on a variety of more or less loosely related social phenomena.[50]

Yet, Jhering's discourse has its redeeming values, both as a work of early sociology and as an enlightening read for a lay audience.

As a study of social life it preceded the rise of sociology as a fully developed discipline in the subsequent decades. It was a serious attempt by a determined scholar to understand and define the basic forms and norms of social interaction, to provide a typology, and to explain their functions in society. That was a pioneering effort because Jhering explored terrain that had, as he emphasized, hitherto been neglected.[51] Abandoning the lofty heights of theory, Jhering ventured into "the lowest regions of daily life."[52] He kept his nose close to the ground and paid careful attention to social reality – a perspective highly unusual for a jurist at the time.[53] His crisp definitions of key terms, which evince Jhering's training in conceptual jurisprudence, are eye-opening: we learn, often from Jhering's observations of language,[54] about "usage" ("Gewohnheit," not binding) and "custom" ("Sitte," binding);[55] about "good" and "bad" habits and customs;[56] about "fashion" ("Mode") and norms concerning traditional garb ("Tracht");[57] about various forms of social obligations and social coercion,[58] and lots more. Long chapters explore the nature, normative force, and social implications of "decency" ("Anstand") and "courtesy" ("Höflichkeit") as well as the relationship between these clusters of social norms.[59] These chapters contain a systematic ordering of the various manifestations of decency and courtesy as well as explanations of their connections with concepts like respect, benevolence, and gratitude.[60] At the same time, Jhering concocted a multifaceted portrait of life in the bourgeois society of his time. In all that, Jhering ranged so broadly and went

[50] Franz Wieacker called it "Fragmente einer Elementarsoziologie mitmenschlichen Verhaltens, die sich nicht mehr kontingent interpretieren lassen" ("fragments of an elementary sociology of human interaction which can no longer be interpreted consistently"), *Wieacker*, Rudolf von Jhering (1969) 31.

[51] *Jhering*, Zweck II (1886) 332–335.

[52] *Jhering*, Zweck II (1886) XII. This corresponded to his interest as a jurist in "Law in Daily Life," supra chapter II.5.

[53] *Helfer*, Rudolf von Jhering als Rechtssoziologe (1968) 563.

[54] A long chapter is entirely devoted to what can be learned from language about non-legal norms ("Die Aussagen der Sprache über das Sittliche"); *Jhering*, Zweck II (1886) 15–93.

[55] *Jhering*, Zweck II (1886) 24.

[56] *Jhering*, Zweck II (1886) 78–84, 253–254.

[57] *Jhering*, Zweck II (1886) 230–241.

[58] *Jhering*, Zweck II (1886) 281–351.

[59] *Jhering*, Zweck II (1886) 384–480; 480–723.

[60] *Jhering*, Zweck II (1886) 495–541; 541–558; 558–559.

into so much detail that he himself wondered whether it was all "too much of a good thing."[61] It is a pity that Jhering's work was largely ignored by subsequent generations of sociologists, some notable exceptions notwithstanding.[62]

For a non-specialist audience, much of Jhering's discourse makes for enlightening and often outright fascinating reading. It bristles with astute observations, original insights, and intrepid confrontations with sometimes uncomfortable truths. Along the way, we encounter a potpourri of mini-essays on topics as diverse as the aesthetics of eating and drinking (much informed by Jhering's own experience, of course),[63] the symbolic meanings of body language,[64] and the social implications of "phraseology," names and titles, and even syntax.[65] Readers with an interest in such matters will find much of the volume a page-turner and come away with a much better understanding of how people interact socially (at least in Western societies) – even today.

2. A Critique of Social Norms: "Das Trinkgeld" (1882)

Around the time that Jhering published the massive second volume of "Zweck," in which he dealt with a broad variety of "Sitten," he also put out a slim, sixty-four-page, pamphlet in which he focused on one particular custom: the tip (Trinkgeld)[66] received by waiters, bell-boys, chambermaids, coach drivers, and domestic servants. Even though "Das Trinkgeld" is largely forgotten today,[67] it deserves at least brief attention for three reasons.

Most importantly, more than any other work, it shows several of the Jherings we have encountered in joint action. The sociological Jhering, the author of the study of custom in Volume Two of "Zweck," presented a detailed "scientific"

[61] *Jhering*, Zweck II (1886) XIII. He concluded that no, it was not, because all the detail was necessary to lay the necessary foundations for an empirically grounded theory of ethics, id. XIV.

[62] See infra chapter VII.4., note 342 and text. A rare modern reader to take the second volume of "Zweck" seriously is *Rückert*, Der Geist des Rechts (2004) 129–132.

[63] *Jhering*, Zweck II (1886) 427–442. The topic was probably particularly dear to Jhering's heart because he loved an elaborate meal and good wine, supra chapter I.4. notes 166–168 and text.

[64] *Jhering*, Zweck II (1886) 644–661.

[65] *Jhering*, Zweck II (1886) 661–723.

[66] Literally translated, the term means "drinking money," as in the French "pourboire."

[67] In the modern literature on Jhering "Das Trinkgeld" has received scant attention. An exception is the essay by Michael Martinek which provides much interesting context, *Martinek*, Rudolf von Jherings Kampf gegen das Trinkgeld (1993); for a short assessment, see also *Helfer*, Jhering als Rechtssoziologe (1968) 564. More than a century ago, the Law Quarterly Review published an English summary of Jhering's main argument, *Kenny*, Jhering on Trinkgeld and Tips (1916). The piece is accurate, informative, and enriched by various references to developments at the time, including decisions by courts in England and elsewhere. Yet, it just cannot do justice to Jhering's passion and verve.

investigation of a common social phenomenon[68] that, he claimed, had not received any scholarly treatment.[69] In the course of this endeavor, the juristic Jhering, the author of the methodological discourses in "Geist des römischen Rechts," proffered a crisp definition and useful typology of the social phenomenon, proving that his analytical skills as an erstwhile conceptual jurist had not atrophied. Finally, the combative Jhering, the author of "Der Kampf ums Recht," launched a forceful campaign against what he considered a social ill and suggested various means for getting rid of it.[70] In addition, towards the end of the tract, another Jhering made a brief appearance: the advocate of the welfare of the working class.[71]

Second, "Das Trinkgeld" easily became Jhering's most widely-known work among the general population in German-speaking lands.[72] After it had first appeared in a monthly journal,[73] it was picked up by a publisher and turned into a little book, which eventually went through five editions.[74] It introduced Jhering to the general public and turned him into the kind of celebrity that today would be invited to talk shows. The success of the pamphlet was owed to a combination of features: the topic was much discussed at the time, and Jhering's argument fanned the flames;[75] Jhering's complaints about the custom of Trinkgeld resonated with many similarly angry contemporaries; and his discourse helped people who dimly felt frustration to understand more clearly why.

Last, but not least, "Das Trinkgeld" is just an enlightening, entertaining, and often outright amusing read. Once again, Jhering was in his element. His observations of social reality are acute and eye-opening, his style is lively and humorous, and his argument is passionate and engaging. To be sure, his diatribe at times

---

[68] As Jhering pointed out, his essay was an off-shoot of "Zweck" and turned into a free-standing publication; *Jhering*, Das Trinkgeld (1882) V, 7–8.

[69] This was not quite true. The year before, Franz v. Holtzendorff had published a tract on the topic in a journal, see *Martinek*, Rudolf von Jhering's Kampf gegen das Trinkgeld (1993) 885–886 (with further references). Apparently, Jhering became aware of that publication only after he had (originally) published his essay in a journal. When "Das Trinkgeld" appeared as a book, Jhering, always conscientiously giving credit to others where it was due, acknowledged Holtzendorff's work in laudatory terms and stated that he "was happy to make reference to points on which we agree in the following discourse." *Jhering*, Das Trinkgeld (1882) 8 note.

[70] Infra notes 106–112 and text.

[71] Infra notes 109–11 and text.

[72] In contrast to "Der Kampfs ums Recht," "Das Trinkgeld" was largely unknown abroad, however, because while the former had been translated into many language, the latter had not.

[73] Westermanns Monatshefte, April 1882.

[74] Three editions appeared during Jhering's lifetime (1882, 1885, and 1889), two additional ones were published after his death (1902 and 1903).

[75] See *Jhering*, Das Trinkgeld (1882) V–VI; for more background, see *Martinek*, Rudolf von Jherings Kampf gegen das Trinkgeld (1993) 886–887.

displays, as a commentator put it, traits of "professorial-pedantic doctrinalism."[76] Still, once picked up, the little book is hard to put down.[77]

A Definition and Typology of Tipping:"Zwischen Lohn und Geschenk." Although he aimed at a sociological and economic analysis of tipping, Jhering initially approached the topic with the intellectual tools of a jurist trained in Romanist jurisprudence. This was not spur of the moment: Jhering had long used tipping as practice turf for the students in his law classes, forcing them to define the concept by distinguishing it from related ones.[78] Now, in a similar vein, he first proffered a crisp definition of tipping and then a typology of its principal manifestations. It is interesting to watch how Jhering's jurisprudential skills helped him to clarify what tipping is and in what forms it occurs.

Jhering defined tipping as a "non-legally actionable reward for a service."[79] If the reward is the result of a binding agreement, it is wages (Lohn); and if it is merely a gesture of benevolence, it is a gift (Geschenk). Thus, a tip lies "in between wages and a gift" ("zwischen Lohn und Geschenk"), sharing with the former its relatedness to a service rendered, and with the latter the lack of an underlying legal obligation. Once again, Jhering saw the driving force behind the phenomenon in egoism (thus disregarding other possible motives, such as sheer kindness or simple generosity[80]). Originally it was the egoism of the tipper: he wished to receive additional or above-average service. Pretty soon, however, the tippee's egoism came into play (and quickly took over): he or she essentially demanded the tip as a form of remuneration for the service rendered.[81] Jhering was not interested in any potential legal implications of his definition[82] but rather used it as the basis for his social, psychological, and economic analysis and critique.

Jhering distinguished three basic types of tipping, each shaped by its social context. The first is the context of daily life, in which people (usually strangers)

[76] *Stinzing and Landsberg*, Geschichte der deutschen Rechtswissenschaft III (1910) 821.

[77] Jhering had also been working on a "Philosophie der gemischten Getränke" ("Philosophy of Mixed Drinks") in which he reflected – both humorously and seriously – on the art of making a good punch, a matter that was very dear to his heart. The work never progressed beyond the stage of various draft fragments. They were compiled and published by *Helfer*, Prolegomena zur Philosophie der gemischten Getränke (1968).

[78] *Jhering*, Das Trinkgeld (1882) 7.

[79] *Jhering*, Das Trinkgeld (1882) 11.

[80] In some cases, Jhering astutely observed, the tipper was motivated not by the wish for improved service but by his desire to show off his status or wealth vis-a-vis those socially below him. For those individuals, Jhering expressed his scorn with biting sarcasm, *Jhering*, Das Trinkgeld (1882) 25–26.

[81] *Jhering*, Das Trinkgeld (1882) 22–28.

[82] Even though tipping is not legally obligatory, it can have legal consequences, e.g., for employment law or for the calculation of income for tax purposes, support obligations or welfare benefits. Modern German jurists also have debated a variety of private law issues, see *Martinek*. Rudolf von Jherings Kampf gegen das Trinkgeld (1993) 896–902.

sometimes render others small ad hoc favors – such as showing the way to the train station or picking up a dropped item. Jhering found such a "courtesy tip" ("Gefälligkeitstrinkgeld") "harmless" and unobjectionable.[83] Yet, his social and psychological perceptiveness made him suggest caution in offering a tip for minor courtesies because it could be demeaning: it may suggest that the recipient acted not as a good Samaritan but "out of a lowly motive," i.e., in the expectation of a financial reward.[84]

The second context is commercial: it involves services rendered by individuals who are already getting paid by a third party, i.e. those working in hotels, restaurants or the transportation sector.[85] In this context, tipping is an entirely different matter for two reasons. First, in most instances, it is a reward in addition to pay already received from the tippee's employer (as wages); it adds to the tippee's legal claim against his master a social claim against the client so that the person rendering the service is paid twice. Second, in contrast to the "courtesy tip," the commercial tip is not truly voluntary but socially obligatory: it can be (and usually is) enforced by social sanctions, ranging from mere expressions of displeasure to rudeness or even denial of further services. This type of tip aroused Jhering's indignation because he considered it a social nuisance, economically objectionable, and demeaning for the recipients.[86]

The third context is social, i.e., that of invitations to private homes; it involves services rendered to the master's social guests by his domestic servants, such as butlers and maids (Domestikentrinkgeld[87]). A tip given in this context is similar to one in the commercial setting in that those rendering the services are already paid for them; it is different in that the guest is not the paying client of a commercial enterprise but the beneficiary of (otherwise gratuitous) hospitality.[88] Jhering considered this form of tipping the "greatest aberration" of all and called for its complete abolition.[89]

All that is Wrong with Tipping: "Eine wahre Plage des gesellschaftlichen Lebens." In classifying different kinds of tipping, Jhering spoke essentially as an observer who, as in Volume Two of "Zweck," analyzed a custom from a sociologist's point of view. For the remainder of the pamphlet, however, he took a normative stance and took up the position of a social reformer. There are, he pointed out, good customs and bad customs, and tipping was a prime example the latter (Jhering's other examples were the funeral feast (Leichenschmaus) and

[83] *Jhering*, Das Trinkgeld (1882) 13–15.

[84] Jhering thus suggested to offer a "courtesy tip" only if the recipient is obviously needy or if the courtesy clearly goes beyond routine favors and was rendered in the expectation of a reward, *Jhering*, Das Trinkgeld (1886) 14.

[85] *Jhering*, Das Trinkgeld (1882) 17–19.

[86] Infra note 111 and text.

[87] *Jhering*, Das Trinkgeld (1882) 61.

[88] *Jhering*, Das Trinkgeld (1882) 40–44.

[89] Infra note 101 and text.

the duel[90]). Thus tipping was what Germans call an "Unsitte."[91] In more dramatic terms: it was "a true nuisance of social life."[92] Jhering spoke largely from his own experience, apparently especially in Austria where the "Unsitte" had grown to particularly obnoxious proportions.[93] Disregarding any positive aspects of tipping (such as wealth transfer from the rich to the poor[94]), Jhering presented a long list of complaints.[95]

To begin with, tipping was arbitrary. Why did the waiter receive a tip but not the cook? The messenger who delivered the page proofs but not the printer who had created them? It was only because the former came face-to-face with the recipient of the service while the latter did not. That, however, was an irrational criterion. Not only did it randomly privilege some people over others, it also disregarded the value of the services rendered: those of the cook or the printer were more valuable than those of the waiter or the messenger but not rewarded by a tip. In short, rather than being based on any rational principle, tipping was "capricious."[96]

Next, having to tip people was a constant nuisance, especially when traveling. Since the customary tip varied regionally, as well as often over time, a traveler always had to inform himself about what was expected. He constantly risked getting it wrong – to over-tip (and throw away his money) or to under-tip (and suffer social sanctions).[97] Thus the "tipping question" was a traveler's constant companion. "I can imagine more pleasant company," Jhering quipped.[98]

Jhering's most extensive critique was directed against tipping in the economic context: it had continuously proliferated in two respects. First, it was demanded by more and more people. At a hotel, for instance, one often had to tip not only the waiter but also the headwaiter, the bellboy, the chambermaid, the coachman,

[90] *Jhering*, Das Trinkgeld (1882) 7. He discussed both these examples in Zweck II (1886) 247–249, 253–254.

[91] *Jhering*, Das Trinkgeld (1882) 7, 36, etc. The prefix "Un" typically indicates the negativ version of a phenomenon, similar to the English "in," as in Untreue (infidelity) or Ungenauigkeit (inaccuracy). Jhering provided a more extensive discussion of the concept in Zweck II (1886) 252–256.

[92] *Jhering*, Das Trinkgeld (1882) 10.

[93] See *Kuntze*, Rudolf von Jhering (1892) 611. It has been reported that Jhering gave up his chair in Vienna after only a few years there in no small part because he was extremely annoyed by the excesses of tipping in the Habsburg capital; *Kenny*, Jhering on Trinkgeld and Tips (1916) 306–307.

[94] See *Kuntze*, Rudolf von Jhering (1892) 611.

[95] Even though Jhering did not make that sufficiently clear, some of these complaints pertained to both its commercial and its domestic form, others only (or primarily) to one or the other.

[96] *Jhering*, Das Trinkgeld (1882) 22.

[97] *Jhering*, Das Trinkgeld (1882) 21, 36–38.

[98] *Jhering*, Das Trinkgeld (1882) 37. Since the German word for "question" (of how to tip) has a female gender ("die Frage"), Jhering likewise couched "company" in female terms, suggesting a woman companion ("Reisebegleiterin").

and possibly even the hotel gardener. As a result, a guest was forced "to run the economic gauntlet."[99] Second, the guests often ended up paying multiple times for the same service. This was because once the servant's master recognized tips as a valuable source of income, he increasingly absorbed them: at first, he subtracted them from the servant's regular pay – while adding a tip to the bill; in some instances, he then stopped paying his servants altogether because they could earn enough just through tips; or he even leased the job to the employee who then paid the master for the opportunity to receive tips from the clients. Now, the guest paid the regular bill (which should include the service), often a surcharge for service, and on top of it a tip to the servant. And he paid all that without even receiving any benefit in form of above average service – for which yet another tip would be required. Things had clearly spun out of control.[100]

Tipping in the context of social invitations was even worse. De facto forcing invitees to tip the house servants, either in general or to receive particular services (such as the use of playing cards) was incompatible with the very principle of hospitality: being invited meant that the host covered the expenses, not that the guest had to pay for the incidental services. Burdening social invitations with financial obligations was undignified and offensive, especially since the amounts customarily expected were often seriously burdensome.[101]

So far, Jhering had complained about the negative impact of the "Unsitte" on the tipper. His last two grievances, however, focused on the impact on the tippee. One was a form of well-intended paternalism: sometimes, tipping generated excessive income (he cited some examples); the members of the servant class then came into the possession of means that they could not responsibly handle; that, in turn, could lead to moral depravation.[102] The other complaint expressed concern for the tippee's dignity: making the servants' income dependent on money to which they had no legal claim to was demeaning. Tipping was essentially "a custom-based form of begging"[103] which induced "feigned friendliness."[104] That was fundamentally wrong: "A man who is conscious of his worth does not beg."[105]

For all these reasons, Jhering called for a "fight" against tipping.[106] He asked innkeepers and social hosts to abolish it; for travel guides to mark establishments that had done so (with two crossed swords as a symbol of the fight[107]) which

[99] *Jhering*, Das Trinkgeld (1882) 35.

[100] *Jhering*, Das Trinkgeld (1882) 24–36.

[101] *Jhering*, Das Trinkgeld (1882) 40–44. It stands to reason that paying maidservants for their services could easily entail sexual harassment or even prostitution; see *Kenny*, Jhering on Trinkgeld and Tips (1916) 319.

[102] *Jhering*, Das Trinkgeld (1882) 43–50.

[103] *Jhering*, Das Trinkgeld (1882) 50.

[104] *Jhering*, Das Trinkgeld (1882) 52.

[105] *Jhering*, Das Trinkgeld (1882) 51. "Man" did not mean "males" (only) but was the then usual term for person. Here, it clearly included women who – as chambermaids or maidservants – also received (and often depended on) tips.

[106] *Jhering*, Das Trinkgeld (1882) 52.

[107] *Jhering*, Das Trinkgeld (1882) 58–59.

would give them a competitive advantage; and, more generally, for "organized resistance" against the pernicious practice.[108]

Protecting the Servant Class: "Vergütung in Form des Lohns." Jhering's call to abolish tipping was not intended to deprive the servant class of its livelihood, quite to the contrary. It would be "a grave injustice," he emphasized, to take away a source of income which they needed without providing compensation for it.[109] This compensation should consist of a legal claim against their employer. The servant class deserved "what is due to all social classes engaged in work and income-earning: remuneration for the services rendered in the form of wages."[110] They should not have to hold out their hand, "in part begging, in part demanding," demeaning themselves in the process. In other words, the wages had to be sufficient to end the recipient's dependency on tips. "The worker deserves what he has earned."[111]

Regarding domestic servants in particular, Jhering suggested, again showing his social conscience, that tips be replaced by a system of social protection. He outlined the statutes of an association the members of which promised not to give any tips but, instead, to contribute to a fund for domestic servants in need. This would show that the members were not skimping at the expense of others but rather supported the servant class in a sensible manner.[112]

It has been argued that Jhering's campaign against "Das Trinkgeld" was a failure because tipping has survived.[113] Jhering himself was skeptical whether his arguments would succeed. He also emphasized, however, that if they did not, those lacking the courage to fight the "Unsitte" had only themselves to blame.[114] It is true that tipping is still with us in many countries. Yet, at least in Jhering's part of the world, its most lamentable excesses have largely disappeared. Note that this is mainly because the call to provide the servant class with a legal claim for regular wages has carried the day. At least in German speaking lands, and indeed in much of Europe, twentieth century unionization, employment legislation, and social insurance systems have improved the lot of waiters, hotel employees, and other service providers to the point where their economic survival no longer depends on the generosity of their clients.[115] If Jhering traveled through Germany, Austria, Switzerland, and Italy today, he would justly feel vindicated.

---

[108] *Jhering*, Das Trinkgeld (1882) 53.
[109] *Jhering*, Das Trinkgeld (1882) 63–64 note.
[110] *Jhering*, Das Trinkgeld (1882) 55 note.
[111] *Jhering*, Das Trinkgeld (1882) 55 note.
[112] *Jhering*, Das Trinkgeld (1882) 62–63.
[113] *Martinek*, Rudolf von Jherings Kampf gegen das Trinkgeld (1993) 887–896.
[114] *Jhering*, Das Trinkgeld (1882) VI, 64.
[115] That is not true, of course, where, as in the United States, waiters in particular are not (fully) protected by minimum wage legislation and thus remain dependent on tips.

3. Toying with Pre-History: "Vorgeschichte der Indo-Europäer" (1894)

Towards the very end of his life, Jhering finally admitted to himself that neither of his two principal works, i.e., "Geist" and "Zweck," would ever be completed. Induced by a request to contribute to a prestigious "Handbook,"[116] he turned once more to legal history: he began to work on a "Entwicklungsgeschichte des römischen Rechts" ("Evolutionary History of Roman Law"). Yet, again, and now for the last time, the combination of his obsession with getting to the bottom of things and his inability to limit the scope of his inquiry made him take on a task beyond his (remaining) powers. The planned book's first chapter was supposed to explore how the Romans' fundamental character had been shaped by their pre-historic experience; this led Jhering to look into the origins of the Aryan peoples of Europe more broadly; and that endeavor grew into another book project of its own, which then occupied him for most of his final two years: "Vorgeschichte der Indo-Europäer" (literally: "Pre-History of the Indo-Europeans"). This time, it was death that kept Jhering from completing the work. He had, however, written more than half of the planned chapters, and his son in law Viktor Ehrenberg published them posthumously.[117] By contrast, the underlying "Entwicklungsgeschichte" never proceeded beyond the very beginnings.[118]

In terms of its substance, Jhering's last book has been his least important in the long run. It is true that it was translated into several languages[119] but whatever contribution it made to the contemporary debate about the origins and migrations of the Indo-Germanic peoples has long lost its relevance. It is fair to say that "Vorgeschichte" (in which law plays a very minor role[120]) is not part Jhering's lasting legacy. Yet, it would be wrong to omit it entirely from our survey of his works. This is not only because Jhering himself was passionate about it,[121] and not even only because it is a substantial work of nearly 500 pages which proffers an intriguing thesis. "Vorgeschichte" deserves our attention for three other re-

---

[116] *Karl Binding and Friedrich Oetker*, Systematisches Handbuch der deutschen Rechtswissenschaft (München and Leipzig 1883 et seq.).

[117] Jhering wrote four of the planned seven chapters; for the rest, we only have some sketches and fragments. The manuscript required massive amounts of work by both Jhering's last wife and his son in law before it could be published; *Ehrenberg*, Vorwort des Herausgebers (1894) VII.

[118] *Jhering* did produce an introduction, however, in which he outlined his views on proper legal historiography; see supra chapter V.1.

[119] *Rudolf von Jhering*, Les Indo-Européens avant l'histoire (de Meulenaere transl., Paris 1895); id., Evolution of the Aryan (A. Drucker transl., London 1897, New York 1898); id., Prehistoria de los Indoeuropeos (Adolfo Posada transl., Madrid 1896).

[120] Jhering discussed the law of the original Aryans at some length, only to conclude that it stood at a very low level of development; *Jhering*, Vorgeschichte (1894) 43–86. The rest of the book contains almost no references to law.

[121] *Ehrenberg*, Vorwort des Herausgebers (1894) X.

asons: it is the most pronounced expression of Jhering's fundamental credo of the historical contingency of all cultural character traits; it illustrates his belief in historical progress of successive civilizations; and it evinces one of his most fundamental features as a scholar, i.e., his willingness to skate on very thin ice in order to bring the past to life.

The Historical Contingency of the Peoples' Character: How the Aryans Became Europeans. As a scholar, the later Jhering's perhaps most fundamental idea was that of "external causality" ("äußere Kausalität").[122] Loosely inspired by Montesquieu,[123] Jhering was deeply convinced that, like the feeling of justice and the norms of ethics,[124] a people's character was not innate but purely the result of factual conditions and historical experience.[125] His rejection of a nativist position in favor of a historical approach was unequivocal: a people's "character is nothing but the result of its history."[126] This conviction drove the entire project of "Vorgeschichte."[127] Trying to understand the fundamental character traits of the Romans as a people (in order to better explain the fundamental features of their law), Jhering now turned to their experience as part of the Aryan people that had settled Europe in pre-historic times.[128]

The starting point and context of Jhering's investigation was a theory that was much in vogue at the time: that there once had been an Aryan "mother people" ("Muttervolk") in Asia;[129] that parts of it had migrated to Europe millennia ago; and that this part had then split up into the major European peoples and cultures, notably the Greeks, Italics, Celts, Germans, and Slavs. As Jhering noted, that theory was largely based on the recent discovery of an Indo-Germanic language group.[130]

---

[122] *Jhering*, Entwicklungsgeschichte (1894) 44, 45; Jhering, Vorgeschichte (1894) 96.

[123] *Jhering*, Entwicklungsgeschichte (1894) 42.

[124] Supra chapters IV.3. and VI.1.

[125] See supra chapter II.6., notes 491–498 and text.

[126] *Jhering*, Entwicklungsgeschichte (1894) 48.

[127] The book's objective and thesis are summarized both in its introduction, *Jhering*, Vorgeschichte (1894) 1–9 and in the Introduction written for the planned history of the development of Roman law, *Jhering*, Entwicklungsgeschichte (1894) 42–45.

[128] Acknowledging that the time of the migration is unknown, *Jhering*, Vorgeschichte (1894) 5, Jhering did not provide an exact time frame but it fair to assume that he envisaged roughly the fourth to second millenium B.C.

[129] See *Heinrich Zimmer*, Altindisches Leben (1879). Jhering's description of the "Aryan Mother People" ("das arische Muttervolk") apparently relied heavily on this work; *Jhering*, Vorgeschichte (1894) 26 n. 15.

[130] *Jhering*, Vorgeschichte (1894) 2–3. These studies had discovered that the Sanskrit of prehistoric times was related to various European languages, see *Franz Bopp*, Über das Konjugationssystem der Sanskritsprache in Vergleichung mit jenem der griechischen, lateinischen, persischen und germanischen Sprache (Frankfurt 1816). This suggested the existence of a language once common to a "Muttervolk" with subsequent differentiation into the various Indo-Germanic languages; *Jhering*, Vorgeschichte (1894) 2–3, The theory of an Aryan mother language had its roots in the work of Friedrich Schlegel (1772–1829) and was

Jhering had long subscribed to this view.[131] Now, however, he vigorously challenged the popular conclusion that the fundamental traits of the European "mentality" and "character"[132] were largely a heritage of its Asian past. At the same time, he also rejected the view that the most fundamental features of European-ness were the result of the environmental conditions of the continent. Instead, Jhering presented his own thesis: the particular character of the "European" was the result of the Aryan emigrants' experience during their long migration from Asia to Europe.[133]

Jhering ultimately claimed that the character of the European peoples had been formed in two stages. The first stage was the migration: the part of the Aryan people that had left its old home and that over centuries or even millennia had traveled to central and Western Europe had been shaped by the trials and tribulations of its journey. In fact, along the way, there were several successive migrations, and every time, those who had left had become tougher and smarter than the ones who had stayed behind. This quasi-Darwinian selection process had continuously improved the character of those travelling on.[134] As a result, the people who eventually arrived in Europe were fundamentally different from those who had stayed in their original home: the former were "Europeans", the latter "Asians." The second stage occurred after the Aryans-turned-Europeans had arrived in Europe. The group now broke up into several branches that settled in different regions. Only now did the respective environmental conditions (in the manner suggested by Montesquieu) shape the specific character traits of the major European peoples we have known since antiquity. As a result of the first stage, these peoples were all still "Indo-Europeans" with common fundamental characteristics; as a result of the second stage, they all had their particular character and culture on top of that.[135] "Vorgeschichte" was the endeavor to substantiate these claims.[136]

---

further developed by Jhering's contemporary Max Müller (1823–1900). For a detailed overview of the "Aryan Controversy", see *Taylor*, The Origin of the Aryans (4th ed. New York 1914) 1–53.

[131] He had alluded to it already more than a generation before, see *Jhering* , Geist I (1852) 314.

[132] "Sinnesart," "Charakter"; *Jhering*, Vorgeschichte (1894) 6. On other occasions, Jhering also used the term "Volksart," see especially id., 283–286. Jhering never explained exactly what he meant by these rather diffuse terms.

[133] Thus, according to Jhering, the Roman law had scarcely been influenced by the character of Aryan mother people; instead, many of the early Roman culture's characteristic features were traceable to the migration period – ranging from military organization and discipline to the competences of the pontifices and the family structure (including monogamy and the position of women), *Jhering*, Entwicklungsgeschichte (1894) 45.

[134] *Jhering*, Vorgeschichte (1894) 462–463. Jhering explicitly likened this process to Darwin's theory. It is not clear, however, whether he considered the continuous improvement merely one of character or whether he assumed that it would ultimateley become genetic as well.

[135] *Jhering*, Vorgeschichte (1894) 93–101, 469–470.

[136] Jhering thus proceeded from a description of the Aryan "Muttervolk" in Book (chap-

A Tale of Progress and Superiority: Aryans, Asians, and Semites. "Vorgeschichte" is not only an attempt to lay bare the deep roots of the European character and culture, it is also, at least implicitly, a tale of historical progress from lower to higher forms of civilization. That was much in line both with Jhering's fundamental view of history and with a broader literature popular at the time, including the writings of Maine, Fustel de Coulanges, and Bachofen.[137] In this context, Jhering's tale contains some assertions that must raise a modern reader's eyebrows and may even send shivers down his or her spine. We must take heed, however, not to misunderstand Jhering.

Jhering clearly considered the modern Europeans descending from the Aryans superior to the other peoples in his narrative[138] – inter alia by virtue of the Europeans' "pronounced sense of personality" ("Persönlichkeit") and justice ("Rechtsgefühl"), their penchant for independence ("Unabhängigkeitssinn") and drive for liberty ("Freiheitstrieb") but also because of their work-ethic.[139] In

ter) One to the exodus of the Aryans from their original home in Book Three and on to a discussion of their migration in Book Four. Further Books about the migrants' new home, the origin of the (different) European peoples, and their ultimate diversity were never written. Book Two does not easily fit into this sequence because it contains somewhat of a deviation from the main course. Entitled "Aryans and Semites," it is essentially a comparative study of these peoples' respective character traits and civilizations with a particular focus on the Babylonian culture. This comparative study is by far the longest part of the work (at over 200 pp., it is more than twice as long as any other Book). The question that connects it to the main argument is why the leadership in history passed from the Semites, who were the superior civilization in Babylonian times, to the Aryans who succeeded them as the dominant culture for the coming centuries. Jhering claimed that at some point, after having contributed what they could to world history, the Semites had eventually grown exhausted and weak with age; they were then pushed aside by the still young and vigorous Aryans. Thus neither was innately superior to the other; they only had leadership roles at different points in history. The cultural accomplishments of the Semites were (at least in part) transferred to the Aryans who thus became the beneficiaries of the Semites' endeavors, *Jhering*, Vorgeschichte (1892) 286–287. Jhering also sought to refute the theory that the critical difference between the two peoples was rooted in the difference between polytheism and monotheism, id. 288–305. For a good English summary of Jhering's main argument in "Vorgeschichte," see *Smith*, Four German Jurists III (1897) 35–39.

[137] *Maine*, Ancient Law (1861); *Fustel de Coulanges*, La Cité Antique (1864); *Bachofen*, Das Mutterrecht (1861). Jhering critically discussed some of Fustel de Coulanges' views, *Jhering*, Vorgeschichte (1894) 62–71; he also discussed the (then popular) topic of a "Mutterrecht," oddly, however, without citing Bachofen; *Jhering*, Vorgeschichte (1894) 61–62. On Jhering and Maine, see supra chapter V.3., notes 152–185 and text; see also *Smith*, Four German Jurists III (1897) 23–27.

[138] Among the European peoples, Jhering also considered the Slavs inferior to the others. They descended from a part of the Aryans which had stopped its migration in Eastern Europe and there mingled with a local population whose inferior moral quality had dragged them down, so to speak. This had made the Slavs submissive, resigned, and passive; *Jhering*, Vorgeschichte (1894) 484–486.

[139] *Jhering*, Vorgeschichte (1894) 485. Jhering only sketched, but died before he could fully elaborate on, the most important European qualities allegedly created by the migration; they

this context, Jhering pointed to the "type of the European in contrast to that of the Asian."[140] Again, that contrast was the result of the migration: the emigrating part of the original Aryans had been forced by the challenges of their journey to develop a tougher character, while the part that had stayed at home had remained complacent and thus failed to make much progress. In short, the migration "turned the soft[141] Asian into the defiant, steely European." Jhering also considered the European descendants of the Aryans morally (though not intellectually[142]) superior to the Semites, i.e., the peoples of the Middle East, who had lost their position as the once leading civilization of the world millennia ago. European superiority was of course what Jhering's contemporaries saw when they looked at the then comparatively low level of economic and technological development of the Middle East and most of Asia – which had consequently been subdued by the military might of the colonial European powers.

From today's, post-colonial, point of view, and especially after the genocidal antisemitism of the Nazi period, these views will strike many modern observers as troublesome. We must be careful, however, not give them meanings that Jhering did not intend. First, at the time, the term "Aryan" did not have the horrifying connotation it acquired in the twentieth century; instead, it was widely employed in ethno-cultural and linguistic studies to designate Proto Indo-Europeans, and Jhering used it (roughly) in that sense. More importantly, for Jhering, superiority of character or culture was decidedly not a matter of race.[143] As he emphasized ad nauseam, it was the very objective of his whole enterprise to show that the properties of a society were determined not by nature but by history.[144] That race had nothing do with these properties is also evinced by the fact that Jhering rated the original Aryan mother people's level of development as very low.[145] In fact, he argued that Aryans and Semites were exchangeable: if the latter had been in the position of the former (i.e., of a migrating people), then they would have become

included "military discipline," "a higher level of education for obedience," monogamy, and "the respect of the man for the woman," id. 465. He did explain, however, how the migration led to some these features in the chapter entitled "Die Wanderschaft" ("The Migration"); id. 377–465.

[140] *Jhering*, Vorgeschichte (1894) 6. When Jhering spoke of "the Asian," he really meant Indian or, more specifically, Hindu as the descendants of the Aryans who had stayed behind, see, e.g., id. 88–90. "Asian" thus did not include China or other parts of the Far East, simply because they had nothing to do with the Aryan origins of the Indo-Europeans.

[141] *Jhering*, Vorgeschichte (1894) 463. The German word used by Jhering, i.e., "weichlich," is a clearly negative term which implies weakness.

[142] *Jhering*, Vorgeschichte (1894) 301.

[143] Jhering hardly ever used the term and never in a genetic sense but merely as a synonym for "people," see *Jhering*, Vorgeschichte (1894) 280, 282.

[144] *Jhering*, Vorgeschichte (1894) 94–99, 188–189, 269–270, 284, etc.

[145] *Jhering*, Vorgeschichte (1894) 13–90 (summary id. 87–90). The modern Hindu, Jhering claimed, had essentially remained on that low level of development, id. 90. Jhering considered contemporary attempts to glorify the original Aryans as "an effort to provide us with particularly worthy ancestors," id. 3, a strategy he labeled "scientific chauvinism," id. 24.

superior.[146] Thus, Jhering's view contrasted sharply with emerging theories of Aryan racial superiority,[147] a fact that would eventually render his work useless for Nazi propaganda.[148] Moreover, superiority was not timeless but rather depended on the period under consideration. There had been a time when the Semites, notably in Babylon, had reached a level of civilization that had put the contemporary Aryans to shame.[149] As a result, the latter had much to learn from the former. It was only once the Aryans had absorbed the cultural accomplishments of the Babylonians and then further developed them, that the Aryans could gradually become superior.[150] Finally, the fact that the Aryans, or rather their European descendants, eventually became the world's leading civilization and culture, did not mean that they would keep that leadership forever. Although Jhering entertained a quasi-Hegelian view of history as a force of progress, he did not consider his own time as the point where history had finally fulfilled its mission. Instead, he conceived of historical progress as an open-ended process the future course of which was impossible to predict. For now, it was the Europeans' turn in the driver's seat of history but whether, or rather for how long, they would remain in that position, nobody knew. Thus, even though Jhering occasionally sounded jingoistic (as at times he surely did) he was quite explicit that Aryan-European superiority was neither racially programmed nor historically constant and hardly eternal.

Skating on Thin Ice: A Rich Story Based on Poor Evidence. Jhering's explanation of the origins of Aryan-European superiority made for a good story. Even more than his account of early Roman law in "Geist,"[151] it showed his "genius [...] for importing life and character into the remote past," as an early American reviewer put it.[152] Jhering's vivid style, palpable enthusiasm for his subject, and lively imagination keeps the reader engaged.

Yet, Jhering's story suffered from several serious weaknesses. To begin with, it was based on extremely scant evidence. To be clear, Jhering did not just make things up. He drew on historical sources from antiquity (Herodotus, Strabo, Tacitus, Caesar) as well as contemporary literature. He constantly invoked linguistic evidence, drawing inferences from connections between Sanskrit and later languages; sometimes he consulted respectable linguistic studies; often, however, he drew his own conclusions even though he lacked the requisite training. He

---

[146] *Jhering*, Vorgeschichte (1892) 98.

[147] Their best-known source was *Joseph Arthur de Gobineau*, Essai sur l'inegalité des races humaines (2 vols. Paris 1853–1855).

[148] See infra chapter VII.1., notes 96–100 and text.

[149] *Jhering*, Vorgeschichte (1894) 103–104. At the time when Babylonic culture was at its peak, the "old Aryans" were still a people without a "state," id. 202.

[150] "Culture has its origins in Babylon," *Jhering*, Vorgeschichte (1894) 271; it was transferred to the Aryans through trade, conquest and emigration with the Phoenicians playing a key role; id. 271–288. Thus, the Aryans became the (cultural) "heirs of the Semites," id. 286.

[151] Supra chapter II.1.

[152] *Cohen*, Evolution of the Aryan (review, 1899) 87.

looked to features of early Roman and Germanic culture and extrapolated preceding practices and their origins. All this evidence, however, was at best circumstantial. It was not that his hypotheses were demonstrably false; far too little was known about the Aryan migration to prove him wrong; but nor were they demonstrably right. As a result, Jhering "failed to establish anything that is safe in laying hold of and adopting as established."[153] Moreover, Jhering tended to argue in a one-sided manner. He "perceive[d] quickly what supports his theory but [did] not always see what has been or what may be added against it."[154] In addition, there was the problem that he did not always properly understand and implement the research results of the contemporary literature, especially in the history of Germanic law. For that, Ludwig Mitteis tore into him without mercy,[155] and even Jhering's son in law, i.e., the very editor of the work, admitted that much in his preface.[156] Finally, as an account of historical fact, Jhering's whole story was pretty implausible.[157] His idea that the Aryan migrants stayed by and large together as a group for centuries, if not millennia, of travel; that they took a centuries-long break from their trip in the Southern regions of modern Russia where they encountered and conquered a people from which they learned agriculture;[158] that they then took that skill with them as they journeyed on to Europe; that as a collective they established an organized army and learned military discipline – all that, and lots more, was not impossible but it seriously pushed a critical reader's credulity. On the whole, Jhering's story was largely the result of speculation, if not imagination.[159] Yet, since he had convinced himself, he felt that the reader must be convinced as well.[160]

There are several arguments in Jhering's defense. First, despite its weaknesses, Jhering's work was not without merit. Some of his speculations were actually quite plausible and some were, as an expert reviewer acknowledged, even "brilliant."[161] Time and again, Jhering also proffered original and reasonable expla-

---

[153] *Cohen*, Evolution of the Aryan (review, 1899) 91; in a similar vein, *Smith*, Four German Jurists III (1897) 39.

[154] *Müller*, Prehistoric Antiquities of the Indo-Europeans (1896) 637.

[155] *Mitteis*, Jhering (1905) 662.

[156] *Ehrenberg*, Vorwort des Herausgebers (1894) VIII–IX.

[157] *Cohen*, Evolution of the Aryan (review, 1899) 87.

[158] *Jhering*, Vorgeschichte (1894) 7.

[159] See, e.g., Jhering's discourse on the significance of the traditional Aryan loin cloth ("Schurzfell"); *Jhering*, Vorgeschichte (1894) 14–18, resulting in its characterization as "the certification of the origins of the Indo-European," id. 18. Or consider his claim that the Europeans' passion for gambling still reflected their descent from the "old Aryans," id. 107.

[160] "I believe that I have succeeded in throwing some unusual light on a piece of pre-history [that was] hitherto completely in the dark [...] I have made findings that I count among the most important things that I have done in my life [...and I am convinced] "that I have chosen the right path." Letter to Binding of May 3, 1891, Jhering in Briefen (1913) 425–426; see also *Cohen*, Evolution of the Aryan (review, 1899) 87.

[161] *Müller*, Prehistoric Antiquities of the Indo-Europeans (1896) 639. The extensive review, while critical in several respects, was not entirely negative and gave "Vorgeschichte" the

nations for hitherto unexplained cultural practices in antiquity.[162] Second, Jhering openly admitted that "some of what I intend to present may be extremely problematic." He was convinced, however, to produce enough reliable results "to make the journey, which I have undertaken into hitherto almost untrodden terrain, worthwhile."[163] In other words, he considered himself a pioneer who had to take risks in order to break new ground. Others more expert in the matter were welcome to correct him – if they could.[164] Third, drawing dicey conclusions from dubious, scant, or even nonexistent hard evidence was not uncommon at the time. In Germany, legal historians constructed elaborate portraits of the Germanic legal order based largely on an uncritical reading of Tacitus' "Germania;"[165] in the United States, Henry Baxter Adams (1850–1901) and others waxed eloquent about democracy and liberty in the Anglo-Saxon forests;[166] and in England, Maine described early (communal) property regimes in various regions of the world, all without providing much hard evidence either.[167] Of course, the common nature of a practice does not necessarily excuse it, and Jhering drove his flights of fancy particularly far. Still, the age was more tolerant of speculation than the present, even though many more careful and circumspect scholars thought poorly of it already then. Finally, we must not forget that the version of "Vorgeschichte" that was posthumously published was still a rough draft. We do not know what revisions Jhering would have made before calling it final. On the one hand, one would suspect that given Jhering's general penchant for speculation, it is unlikely that he would have retreated to safer ground. On the other hand, that is what he had done in several instances when revising the first volume of "Zweck" for its second edition.[168] Since this time around, death left him no chance to do so again, he deserves the benefit of the doubt. *De mortuis nil nisi bonum.*

Judging "Vorgeschichte:" Academic Standards v. the Elderly Artist. In judging Jhering's last work, it is easy to emphasize its flaws. Even though the book had its merits, there is no gainsaying that much of it was highly problematic. As men-

overall rating "valuable and suggestive," id. 643. This assessment was backed by massive authority: the author, Jhering's contemporary Max Müller, was Professor of Comparative Philology at Oxford University and widely recognized as the era's preeminent expert in questions of Aryan language and culture.

[162] *Müller*, Prehistoric Antiquities of the Indo-Europeans (1896) 631; *Smith*, Four German Jurists III (1897) 40.

[163] *Jhering*, Vorgeschichte (1892) 8; see also id. 453 (leaving open whether his conclusion was correct).

[164] See, e.g., *Jhering*, Vorgeschichte (1894) 378. A German reviewer agreed that this was a laudable undertaking; *Streitberg*, Vorgeschichte der Indo-Europäer (undated).

[165] See *Kroeschell*, Die Germania in der deutschen Rechtsgeschichte (1996); see also id., Germanisches Recht als Forschungsproblem (1996).

[166] See *Reimann*, "In Such Forests Liberty was Nurtured" (1997).

[167] Maine, Ancient Law (1861) 152–161.

[168] Supra chapter IV.2, note 136 and text.

tioned, there was an awful lack of reliable evidence, an awful lot of wild speculation, and there was excessive confidence in its conclusions. Yet, there are other ways to look at the work as well.

One was proffered by Jhering's best American commentator more than a century ago. After properly pointing out the flaws of "Vorgeschichte," Munroe Smith (1854–1926)[169] paid tribute to Jhering's courage and effort, in words worth quoting at some length.

"Whatever opinion will be held of the value of Jhering's *Indo-Europeans*, no one will deny that it is an extraordinary work for a septuagenarian to conceive and so nearly to execute. That a man of so advanced an age should have attacked such problems, that he should have brought to their solution such quickness and fecundity of imagination, that, at the very last, he should have thrown himself with such energy into a field of investigation so remote from all his previous studies as Assyriology – all this bears witness to an exceptional intellectual vitality. Jhering was one of those whom the gods love, for, though full of years, he yet died young."[170]

Still another way of looking at the work is to shift from Jhering-the-jurist, or more broadly: the academic, to Jhering-the-artist. In his review, Albert Hermann Post (1839–1895), a leading representative of the legal ethnography then much in vogue, wondered whether the book was "still scholarship or already fiction."[171] If we look at "Vorgeschichte" as the latter, i.e., not as the work of academic research but of literature, it appears in a much more positive light. To be sure, Jhering's intent was not to write some kind of historical novel like Felix Dahn's immensely popular" Ein Kampf um Rom" (1876), and yet, in part that is what he ended up doing. Jhering's repeated emphasis on a scientific and realist approach notwithstanding, "Vorgeschichte" is a romantic tale of sorts: forced by overcrowding, part of an ancient people leaves its ancestral home in Asia; centuries of migration and warfare toughen and improve its character and culture; thus it arrives in Europe and becomes destined to take the lead in the course of world history. If we regard "Vorgeschichte" as such a tale, the paucity of factual proof and the inherent questionability of its plot become secondary, while its fascinating setting, vivid imagination, and tempting conclusions move into the foreground. In short, as the work of an artist trying to bring a distant past to life even at the expense of historical reliability, "Vorgeschichte" is a pretty good read. As they say in Italy: "se non e vero, e ben trovato."[172]

[169] Smith was a professor of Roman law and comparative jurisprudence at Columbia Law School. He had obtained his doctorate (*juris utriusque doctor*) at the University of Göttingen in 1880, i.e., when Jhering taught there; he thus knew Jhering personally and well.

[170] *Smith*, Four German Jurists III (1897) 40. Smith's affection for Jhering is palpable.

[171] *Post*, Review of Vorgeschichte der Indo-Europäer (undated).

[172] "If it is not true, it is nicely invented." Müller also used that phrase in his review of Jhering's "Vorgeschichte," *Müller*, Prehistoric Antiquities of the Indo-Europeans (1896) 639.

4. The Overconfident Amateur: The Benefits and Perils of Imagination

When Jhering wrote about legal doctrine, theory, and history, he worked in the field he was trained in, as a professional. When he wrote about social custom, ethics, and even ethno-cultural history, he worked in areas in which he lacked formal training, as an amateur. There is something like a trajectory from an early focus almost completely on law to his later period which was increasingly occupied with subjects ever more distant from jurisprudence. Jhering always explained that he needed to explore these subjects to complete his jurisprudential agenda, and in a sense that was true. It also seems, however, that later in life, non-legal subjects simply came to interest him more.[173] Be that as it may, over time, the professional jurist was increasingly eclipsed by the amateur sociologist, linguist, and cultural historian.

Jhering often clearly announced that he was about to venture beyond his area of expertise and asked the specialists in the respective fields to forgive him for trespassing and possibly blundering.[174] He knew that leaving his professional comfort zone was particularly demanding and inevitably risky; and indeed, the critics were often harsh.[175] Still, Jhering accepted working as an amateur because it was the price to pay for pursuing his interests beyond the law. He refused to stop at the boundaries of his own discipline, just as he often wrote not only for fellow jurists but also for a broader audience.[176]

Jhering ventured into amateur territory at a time when that was much more acceptable than it is in today's academic world of ubiquitous specialization, demanding professional standards, and merciless peer review. Despite the rise of modern science, in the nineteenth century, the long and venerable tradition of

[173] On October 28, 1871, Jhering wrote to Oskar Bülow that during a vacation in the Austrian mountains, he had read legal as well as economic studies, and that he had enjoyed the former very little and the latter very much. He added: "Between us: I find jurisprudence increasingly boring," Jhering in Briefen (1913) 268. Towards the end of this life – when he was working on "Vorgeschichte" – he stated that he was "done with doctrinal work for good," letter to Windscheid of May 3, 1891, id 429.

[174] See, e.g., *Jhering*, Geist I (1852) 291 note 224 (asking forgiveness from professional philosophers for "tackling a problem of the philosophy of history for which my powers are insufficient."); *Jhering*, Zweck I (1884) IX–X (admitting to insufficient philosophical training).

[175] See, e.g., *Kuntze*, Rudolf von Jhering (1892) 613–614, who criticized the first volume of "Zweck" for proffering "trivial truths presented as novel and astounding and explanations in the smug manner typical for an amateur." See also *Mitteis*, Jhering (1905) 662; *Kohler*, Rechtsphilosophie und Universalgeschichte (1915) 12.

[176] With regard to "Geist," this was still largely a side-effect as well as a forlorn cause, see supra chapter II.1., note 14. Much of his later work, however, was not primarily addressed to his professional colleagues but rather, such as the second volume of "Zweck" and the "Vorgeschichte," to a broader audience or, like his tract "Das Trinkgeld," to the general public.

thinking broadly and writing confidently about matters without formal training was still alive. For example, scholars (Jhering prominently among them) continued to draw on Montesquieu who, though also a jurist by training and trade, had happily discussed matters far beyond his legal and administrative expertise – such as military organization, slavery and polygamy in distant regions, not to mention Chinese customs.[177] In the early nineteenth century, Goethe (1749–1832), a jurist by training as well, published his famous theory of colors (Farbenlehre).[178] At the same time, Friedrich Schleiermacher (1768–1834), a theologian by profession, laid the foundations for modern hermeneutics.[179] It is true, of course, that the rise of the German universities during Jhering's lifetime raised the bar and made it ever more difficult to produce respectable results without specialized academic education. Still, even in the late nineteenth century, amateur scholarship was far from unheard of. While the aging Jhering pushed beyond jurisprudence, another former student of law (and philosophy) developed a path-breaking economic theory;[180] a businessman who had never studied archeology made sensational discoveries at pre-historic sites;[181] and a priest actually wrote a much discussed book also on "The Origin of the Aryan."[182] When Jhering dived headfirst into areas beyond his professional training, he was in pretty good company.[183]

At the time, scholars still recognized that amateurs trespassing on expert territory could have an important salutary effect on an established field. As the review of Jhering's "Vorgeschichte" by a leading scholar of the "Aryan debate" put it,

"in an age of ever increasing specialization the best thing that can happen is that a scholar eminent in his own department, and who knows what sound learning means, should for once step boldly out of his own domain, and take an independent survey of the preserves of his neighbours. There is, no doubt, considerable risk to the bold adventurer. He is sure to be called an interloper, an ignoramus, a mere dilettante; but, whatever accidents may meet with himself, the subject itself is sure to be benefited. [...]

---

[177] See *Montesquieu*, De'l esprit des loix (1748) books IX, XVI, XIX, XIV (chapters 13, 17–20)

[178] *Johann Wolfgang von Goethe*, Zur Farbenlehre (Tübingen 1810).

[179] *Friedrich Schleiermacher*, Hermeneutik und Kritik mit besonderer Beziehung auf das Neue Testament (posthum Berlin 1838).

[180] *Marx*, Das Kapital (3 vols. 1864–1894)

[181] Heinrich Schliemann's (1822–1890) discovery of the ruins of Troy and his excavations at Mycene in the 1870s and 1880s were milestones in the history of archeology.

[182] *Taylor*, Origin of the Aryan (1890). The book was apparently not known to Jhering.

[183] The line between professional legal research and amateur pursuits could also be a fine one. Towards the end of the nineteenth century, Jhering's (near)contemporaries Josef Kohler (1849–1919) and Albert Hermann Post (1839–1895) published books about legal cultures of which they had no first-hand knowledge whatsoever, see, e.g., *Kohler*, Das chinesische Strafrecht (Würzburg 1895); id., Altindisches Prozeßrecht (Stuttgart 1891); *Albert Hermann Post*, Afrikanische "Jurisprudenz" (Oldenburg and Leipzig 1887).

[An outsider] should in surveying a new field see things which, from being too familiar, have failed to rouse the attention of the ordinary student."[184]

Jhering's "Vorgeschichte," the reviewer continued, was a case in point.[185]

"What [...] is most valuable in his book are his own new and original ideas, his ingenious combinations and his bold guesses. These will offer the most useful materials for students of language whether on other points they agree with or differ from his conclusions."[186]

In short, while the book had its flaws, it was also a fresh breath of air that stimulated further discussion and, thus, promoted the development of knowledge in the field.[187]

The fundamental problem with Jhering's work outside the law was not that it was written by an amateur nor that it failed to make any valuable contributions. Nor was it, for that matter, that Jhering cared too little for established knowledge[188] or that he did not work hard enough – in fact, he worked as hard, or harder, as he did in his legal scholarship.[189] Instead, it was that he almost invariably overrepresented his own results. Jhering all too often presented interesting speculation as indisputable truth. When the reviewer of "Vorgeschichte" wrote that "Professor Jhering does not always distinguish between what is plausible and what is absolutely certain," that was a British understatement as well as a polite way of saying that Jhering regularly took the former for the latter.[190] Jhering's premier American commentator was more explicit: "It may have been so; it must have been so; it was so – is a sequence that fairly represents his mental process."[191] Jhering often claimed that his conclusions were too solid to be doubted and, thus, eventually became completely convinced himself. That was unfortunate. Presenting plausible speculation as scientific certainty did not make his results more convincing; instead, it made it easier for experts to discount or even to disregard them.

---

[184] *Müller*, Prehistoric Antiquities of the Indo-Europeans (1896) 620–621.

[185] *Müller*, Prehistoric Antiquities of the Indo-Europeans (1896) 621.

[186] *Müller*, Prehistoric Antiquities of the Indo-Europeans (1896) 637. Jacob Burckhardt agreed, see *Burckhardt*, Die Kultur der Renaissance in Italien (Köln 1956, orig. 1860) 256–257.

[187] Another reviewer agreed, also pointing to the importance of broad perspectives that transcend the nitty-gritty and open new perspectives.

"Ultimately, what advances science is not the collection of factual details but the imagination that strives to combine the scattered building blocks into a systematic whole. Even though the immediately tangible utility may be small, the impulse and the inspiration [...] will never be lost." *Streitberg*, Review of Jhering, Vorgeschichte der Indo-Europäer (undated) 352–353.

[188] Jhering consulted much, though at times not enough, of the existing literature, often sought the advice of experts, and sometimes expressly thanked them for helping him out, see e.g., *Jhering*, Zweck II (1886) notes at 219–221, 230, 236, 333–334, 490.

[189] *Kunze*, Ein großer Jurist (2023) 9.

[190] *Müller*, Prehistoric Antiquities of the Indo-Europeans (1896) 627.

[191] *Smith*, Four German Jurists III (1897) 39.

Even though Jhering's amateur work had its regrettable sides, it should not be regretted. It has been suggested that rather than dabble in matters beyond his competence, Jhering should have focused on his jurisprudential work and finished "Geist."[192] To be sure, that would almost certainly have enriched our understanding of Roman law. It is not clear, however, that overall, it would have left either Jhering or posterity better off. As far as Jhering himself is concerned, we must not forget that an *amateur* is someone who pursues an activity out of love or, one might say, passion. This was precisely the case for Jhering in his forays beyond the law. As he entered old age, it was this passion that gave him the joy and the energy to keep thinking, working, and publishing. As Goethe wrote, "[i]t is such a pleasant sensation to engage with a matter one can but half master that nobody should scold the dilettante."[193] As far as posterity is concerned, much would be lost if Jhering had always stayed within the four corners of his discipline. Of course, he still would have been a brilliant jurist with a rich doctrinal and methodological *oeuvre*, but there was also no shortage of such jurists in nineteenth century Germany. What made Jhering stand out was his adventurous spirit, his bold imagination, and his exceptional courage to push beyond the boundaries of mainstream jurisprudence even at the risk of going astray.

[192] *Kuntze*, Rudolf von Jhering (1892) 614.

[193] *Johann Wolfgang von Goethe*, Die Wahlverwandtschaften (Stuttgart 1956) 264 (Part Two. Chapter Three) (orig. Tübingen 1809).

Chapter VII

Jhering's Influence – Shaping Twentieth Century Legal Thought

Jhering ranks among the most influential jurists of all time.[1] In fact, for the period since the beginning of modern jurisprudence in the nineteenth century, those who could beat him in that regard are few and far between. Among his German colleagues, Savigny of course comes to mind, but even he was more famous in his own age than influential in the long run. At least today, the most notorious elements of Savigny's legacy, especially his historical theory of law, his *Volksgeist* idea, and his anti-codification stance, play minor roles on the global stage. Meanwhile, Jhering's sociological approach to, and in particular his instrumental conception of, law have become a staple of contemporary jurisprudence in many parts of the world. It was Jhering, more than perhaps anyone else, who "opened the door to a modern understanding of legal method."[2]

A comprehensive study of Jhering's influence on a global scale would be a massive and enormously complex undertaking. As we have seen, there are many Jherings – the doctrinalist, the scholar of legal method, the legal theorist, the historian, the humorist, the sociologist – who appealed to, or at commanded the attention of, a broad spectrum of readers with a large variety of interests and orientations. As the various chapters in this book have shown, each of these Jherings had his strength and weaknesses, the former attracting admirers, the latter critics. At the same time, there are dozens of potentially influenced jurisdictions – in Europe, the Americas, and Asia, in the civil and the common law orbit and various hybrids, operating in numerous languages. Needless to say, a comprehensive account of the resulting multitude of facets is impossible here. It would require a broad and international collaborative effort and a very substantial book in its own right.

It is possible, however, to address several particularly significant aspects of that influence. We will begin by looking at Jhering's home front and assess his impact on twentieth century developments in German legal thought (infra 1.).

---

[1] In the German literature, Jhering's international influence has long been recognized, see, e.g., *Wolf*, Große Rechtsdenker (1963) 659; *Wieacker and Wollschläger* (eds.), Jherings Erbe (1970); *Fikentscher*, Methoden des Rechts III (1976) 268–271; *Meder and Mecke* (eds.), Jhering Global (2023). For an assessment from an American perspective, see *Jenkins*, Rudolf von Jhering (1960) 170.

[2] *Fikentscher*, Methoden des Rechts III (1976) 282.

Expanding our view, we will take note of Jhering's influence on a global level, even though the existing evidence is patchy and fragmentary (infra 2.). We will then take a much closer look at the discussion of Jhering's ideas in America and explain why his impact in United States as "the father of sociological jurisprudence" was especially significant (infra 3.). Finally, we need to explore Jhering's influence on the development of three particular sub-disciplines that are closely related to his work: Roman law, the sociology of law, and comparative law (infra 4.).

What is missing from this picture is an assessment of Jhering's influence on a field that occupied him much of his time and absorbed much his energy: private law doctrine. The main reason for this omission is that Jhering's doctrinal work was highly context-specific: though rooted in the classical Roman sources, it was geared specifically towards nineteenth-century private law in Jhering's own environment. With the possible exceptions of the *culpa in contrahendo* and his (anti-Savignian) theory of possession, its long-term spillover effects into other jurisdictions were very limited. Thus, most of Jhering's doctrinal studies are of little interest for an international readership today.[3] Their content and impact would also be very difficult to understand for anyone not trained in Roman law.

"Influence" is an amorphous and multifaceted term, of course. It can mean anything from direct and certain to indirect and speculative impact. In this chapter, the use of the term will be reserved for demonstrable connections that cause at least a highly likely effect. Beyond that, however, we will also point to more attenuated connections between Jhering's work and subsequent developments as well as to mere affinities between his ideas and those of others to situate his views in various broader contexts.

1. At the Home Front: Jhering in Twentieth-Century Germany

In Germany, there was a fundamental difference between the fate of Jhering's earlier scholarship and the reception of his later work. His writings in the field of private law doctrine and logical legal method (i.e., in his articles in the "Jahrbücher" and in "Geist") had a significant impact in his own time. This earlier work essentially operated within the existing the paradigms, and though it often pushed their limits, it established Jhering's reputation as both a leading scholar of private law doctrine[4] and the foremost scholar of legal methodology of his generation. Yet, this part of his *oeuvre* became largely moot with the codification of private law in the Civil Code of 1900; while the Code incorporated some of

[3] But cf. supra chapter III.3., notes 375–387 and text.

[4] An assessment of Jherings influence on (mainly German) legal doctrine is provided by *Diederichsen*, Jherings Rechtsinstitute im deutschen Privatrecht der Gegenwart (1993); *Fikentscher*, Methoden des Rechts III (1976) 163–186; *Fikentscher and Himmelmann*, Rudolph von Jherings Einfluß auf Dogmatik und Methode des Privatrecht (1995) 96–105.

Jhering's ideas, it ended the reign of Roman law in Germany and with it the *Pandektenwissenschaft* (Pandectist legal science) of which Jhering's doctrinal and methodological scholarship had been an integral part. For Jhering's later work, i.e., his development of an instrumental conception of law and a sociological approach to jurisprudence (beginning in "Geist," then becoming dominant in "Kampf" and "Zweck"), it was just the other way around. This work frontally challenged contemporary paradigms and met with more criticism than success during Jhering's lifetime.[5] After the turn of the century, it received diminishing attention outside of a small circle legal theorists.[6] Over time, however, Jhering's post-"conversion" approach did become highly influential in twentieth-century private law methodology.[7] It also influenced, albeit in a more limited fashion and almost as a side-effect, fundamental conceptions of criminal law.[8]

---

[5] See supra chapter IV.2., notes 370–373 and text. See also *Eck*, B. Windscheid and R.v.Jhering (1893) 35–38; *Stintzing and Landsberg*, Geschichte der deutschen Rechtswissenschaft III.2 (1910) 793–794. Their criticism notwithstanding, Stintzing and Landsberg fully recognized Jhering's significance for the reorientation of jurisprudence from abstract reasoning to the needs of modern life, id. 819–820.

[6] But cf. *Lange*, Die Wandlungen Jherings in seiner Auffassung vom Recht (1927). Lange provided a balanced discussion and sought to rehabilitate Jhering as a scholar. For an informative summary of the early twentieth century German literature on Jhering, see id. 1–3.

[7] For a reflection on Jhering's overall significance for modern German legal thought, and in particular, legal method, see *Fikentscher*, Methoden des Rechts III (1976) 279–282; *Fikentscher and Himmelmann*, Rudolph von Iherings Einfluß auf Dogmatik und Methode des Privatrechts (1995) 114–115; see also *Lange*, Die Wandlungen Jherings in seiner Auffassung vom Recht (1927) 134.

[8] Jhering's distinction between objective and subjective wrong in his essay on the role of fault in Roman private law (Das Schuldmoment im römischen Vertragsrecht, 1867; see supra chapter V.2., notes 61–64 and text) became foundational for the distinction between "Rechtswidrigkeit" (illegality) and "Schuld" (fault) in modern criminal law; for a brief analysis see *Fikentscher and Himmelmann*, Rudolph von Iherings Einfluß auf die Dogmatik und Methode des Privatrechts (1995) 98–99. Jhering's conception of law as a means to an end had a significant impact on the work of Franz von Liszt (1851–1919) who had been Jhering's student in Vienna. Von Liszt openly built on Jhering in his foundational essay, i.e., *von Liszt,* Der Zweckgedanke im Strafrecht (The Idea of Pupose in Criminal Law) (1883) 4, 10–11, 16–18, 22, etc. Subsequently, von Liszt became one of the most influential criminal law scholars of the twentieth century. Jhering's impact manifested itself in three principal regards. First, von Liszt overcame the then prevalent understanding of crime as a moral wrong by adopting Jhering's conception of crime as "the endangerment of the conditions of life in society that can only be averted by punishment;" *Jhering*, Zweck I (1884) 490–91; *von Liszt*, id. 6–8; in other words, von Liszt followed Jhering in replacing a moral conception of crime with a sociological approach. Like Jhering, von Liszt considered metaphysics "unscientific" ("Die Wissenschaft hört auf, wo die Metaphysik beginnt," id. 8). Second, von Liszt rejected the traditional understanding of punishment primarily as retribution (i.e., a form of social revenge) by following Jhering's view that punishment was an instrument serving social goals; id. 16–18, 21. Thus von Liszt argued that the state should not just blindly mete out punishment for its own sake but rather create a more fine-tuned system of measures purposefully designed to prevent crime. In particular, criminal law should not only deter those capable of being

To say that Jhering's later work became highly influential does not mean that it was universally accepted. In fact, while the path-breaking nature and beneficial effect of Jhering's instrumental and sociological approach in general eventually became widely recognized, many particular aspects remained extremely controversial.[9]

---

deterred, and to render those persistently dangerous innocuous by incarceration; it should also seek to rehabilitate those capable of rehabilitation; id. 35–43. Third, von Liszt was influenced by Jhering's view that punishment is justified only as an *ultima ratio*, i.e., if other means of securing the conditions of life in society are insufficient ("Punishment [only] wherever society cannot do without it"), *Jhering*, Zweck I (1884) 490; see also id. 488). Von Liszt thus stated that "*the correct, i.e., the just punishment is the necessary punishment.* Justice in criminal law is observing the measure of punishment required by the idea of purpose." *von Liszt* id., 31 (emphasis in the original); thus the state should use criminal punishment as sparingly as possible, id. 32. This, in turn, led von Liszt to his most famous statement, i.e., that "the penal code is the criminal's Magna Charta" ("das Strafgesetzbuch ist die *magna charta* des Verbrechers."); *von Liszt*, Die deterministischen Gegner der Zweckstrafe (1893) 357. Here, von Liszt probably drew on Jhering who had written that "the organization of criminal law is just as much a benefit to the criminal as it is to society," *Jhering*, Zweck I (1884) 461. In all these regards, von Liszt paved the way to a modern understanding of criminal law in Germany and beyond. For a more detailed analysis, see *Hurwicz*, Rudolf von Jhering und die deutsche Rechtswissenschaft: mit besonderer Berücksichtigung des Strafrechts (1911) 105–128; see also the (often lamentably opaque) discussion by *Baratta*, Über Jherings Bedeutung für die Strafrechtswissenschaft (1970).

[9] It is fair to say that the reaction of German scholars to many aspects of Jhering's later work, and in particular to "Zweck," was largely negative for most of the twentieth-century. Many critics noted the lack of solid philosophical foundations which resulted in much superficiality and several misunderstandings. Jhering's most vicious opponent, Josef Kohler (1848–1919), who apparently just hated everything about Jhering, openly mocked him when he wrote that "Jhering's metaphysics are roughly on the level of the metaphysics of a pastor from the Frisian countryside" (Jhering's home region), *Kohler*, Rechtsphilosophie und Universalgeschichte (1915) 12; Kohler's Jhering bashing sparked an extensive controversy, see *Hurwicz*, Rudolf von Jhering und die deutsche Rechtswissenschaft (1911) VIII n. 1, with further references). Scholars also justly lamented Jhering's lack of conceptual clarity and consistency, the confusing organization of his work, his frequent platitudes, digressions, excessive lengths, and unfounded claims; see supra chapter IV.2., notes 384–396 and text. Justly or not, they variously decried Jhering's utilitarianism, Darwinism, socialism, relativism, and amateurism; his concept of law as being devoid of ethical foundations; and his disregard of fundamental human values. For an overview of the early criticism, see *Rümelin*, Rudolf von Jhering (1922) 2–4, 65–69; a more detailed summary is provided by *Behrends*, Rudolf von Jhering (1818–1892), Der Durchbruch zum Zweck des Rechts (1987) 230–238 (with further references). Beginning in the 1960 and 1970s, several scholars proffered more positive assessments, finding greater merit in Jhering's later work than had previously been recognized; see especially *Helfer*, Rudolf von Jhering als Rechtssoziologe (1968); *Wieacker*, Rudolf von Jhering (1969); *Larenz*, Rudolf von Jhering und die heutige Lage der deutschen Rechtswissenschaft (1970); *Schelsky*, Das Jhering-Modell des sozialen Wandels durch Recht (1972); *Fikentscher*, Methoden des Rechts III (1976) 273–282; see also *Pleister*, Perönlichkeit, Wille und Freiheit im Werke Jherings (1982); *Mecke*, Begriff des Rechts und Methode der Rechtswissenschaft bei Rudolf von Jhering (2018). A particularly interesting attempt at an "open rehabilitation and restoration of honor" is *Behrends*, Rudolf von Jhering (1818–1892).

The twentieth-century German debate about Jhering's later work has been so broad and diversified that it cannot be fully explored here.[10] Nor are its many ramifications and details of sufficient interest to an international audience. This is all the more true since the German controversies about Jhering have sometimes become, like the deluge of US-American scholarship on Holmes, a matter of academic debate for its own sake – a field on which larger battles about divergent jurisprudential positions have been waged. The current subchapter thus focuses only on the generally recognized influence Jhering has had on modern German legal methodology.

Jhering's later work influenced in particular how twentieth century German jurisprudence reacted to the new situation of living under a private law codification, i.e., an allegedly comprehensive system of legislative rules. One initial reaction was the early twentieth-century "school of free law" ("Freirechtsschule"), which drew on Jhering's work when it protested against the view of law as a closed and logical system of concepts and rules. Another, somewhat later, response was the emergence of a "jurisprudence of interests" ("Interessenjurisprudenz") which built on Jhering's view of law as an expression of conflicting social forces. The latter movement, especially, eventually entailed the absorption of Jhering's ideas into the mainstream of German jurisprudence where they have since operated all the way up to the present. A final, and rather self-contained, topic is the somewhat surprising fate of Jhering's writings during the Nazi period.

The "School of Free Law": Building on Jhering's "Conversion." In 1906, Hermann Kantorowicz (1877–1940), a brilliant young scholar with an iconoclastic temperament, used the pseudonym "Gnaeus Flavius" to publish a short tract entitled "Der Kampf um die Rechtswissenschaft" ("The Struggle for Legal Science"). The title obviously drew not only on Darwin's "struggle for life" but also, and more immediately, on Jhering's "Kampf ums Recht," published a generation before. While Jhering was mentioned just in passing, the tract clearly reflected his work. Kantorowicz argued that the abstract logic of nineteenth century jurisprudence (i.e., the approach of the "early" Jhering) must be abandoned in favor of a

---

Der Durchbruch zum Zweck des Rechts (1987); Behrends undertakes a sophisticated reconciliation of Jhering's stark positivism on the one hand, and his irrepressible idealism on the other. See also *Behrends*, Jherings Rechtsdenken (1996).

[10] Since the end of World War II, German legal historians and especially legal theorists have maintained a fairly steady interest in Jhering. This interest was rekindled by various anniversaries. The 150th anniversary of his birth (1968), the 100th anniversary of the publication of "Der Kampf ums Recht" (1972), the 100th anniversary of his death (1992), and the 200th anniversary of his birth (2018) occasioned symposia and a host of individual publications. For a while, interest in Jhering's work was cultivated mainly by a small number of scholars such as Franz Wieacker (1908–1994) and (in Italy as well as in Germany) Mario Losano, and then, more recently, Okko Behrends and Michael Kunze. Several others, such as Josefa Birr, Eric-Christoph Mecke, and Wolfgang Pleister, published monographs on particular aspects of Jhering's work. As a result, the German literature on Jhering is extensive and likely to keep growing.

sociological method (i.e., the approach of the post-"conversion" Jhering). Kantorowicz recognized Jhering as an early fighter for that cause; unfortunately, however, Jhering had not prevailed: "Like a passing meteor," he had made "a deep impression," but had not had "a lasting impact."[11]

Kantorowicz' essay became the most widely read manifesto of the largely German-Austrian[12] phenomenon known as the "school of free law" ("Freirechtsschule"). With roots in the late nineteenth century,[13] it came into its own in the years after 1900. It was not an integrated "school" in the orthodox sense but rather a fairly loose movement consisting of a group of scholars – next to Kantorowicz most prominently Ernst Fuchs (1859–1929) and Eugen Ehrlich (1862–1929).[14] The various members did not always agree in all regards but they did pursue a common cause and embrace a common underlying creed.

Their common cause was an attack on the fundamental assumptions of contemporary mainstream jurisprudence as the iconoclasts understood (and in part, caricatured) it. These assumptions were that law consisted of a closed system of abstract rules; that their diligent application allowed judges to decide all cases before them in an unequivocal and predictable fashion; that if there are no clearly applicable norms, judges could extrapolate rules of decision from the existing ones; and that judges were thus strictly bound by legislative rules which left little or no room either for creative lawmaking nor for considerations of justice in individual cases. Orthodoxy also (allegedly) assumed that the new Civil Code of 1900 now enshrined the relevant rules and was thus pretty much all judges needed for private law adjudication. The "free law" scholars undertook a deconstruction of these assumptions. They argued that all systems of law (including the Civil Code) inevitably had gaps; that these gaps were much bigger than commonly assumed; that judges should fill them not by contorted "constructions" but rather in a free and creative fashion; that even directly applicable rules were often so indeterminate that judges could easily reach different results under the same written norm; and, lastly, that judges should interpret existing rules and fill gaps by looking at social needs and justice in the individual case. In all these regards, the "free law" movement was primarily a theory of adjudication which – incidentally – massively influenced the American legal realism that emerged two decades later.[15]

---

[11] *Kantorowicz*, Der Kampf um die Rechtswissenschaft (1906) 7.

[12] Most of its leaders were German but one (Eugen Ehrlich) was an Austrian academic. On the parallel French development, see infra notes 43–48 and text.

[13] See *Bülow*, Gesetz und Richteramt (1885); *Rümelin*, Werturteile und Willensentscheidungen im Civilrecht (1891).

[14] Some of the movement's key texts appeared in a volume of English translations that also included related writings from various German, French, and American authors: Science of Legal Method (Ernest Bruncken and Layton Register transl., 1917).

[15] *Herget and Wallace*, The German Free Law Movement as the Source of American Legal Realism (1987). See also *Curran*, Rethinking Hermann Kantorowicz (2001).

The "free law"-adherents' common creed was that law was not limited to official, i.e., typically legislative, rules. Next to these rules, there was a regime of "free law." This regime consisted of norms not created (and perhaps not even recognized) by the legislature but rather emanated directly from the changing needs of society, often in the form of custom.[16] If there was no clear legislative command – as would frequently be the case – this "free law" took over, so to speak. Both scholars and judges were tasked with its recognition and development. In this respect, the "free law" movement was a theory about the sources of law. As should be obvious, this creed implied a diminished role of the legislator and a much enhanced function of the judge, who might even be allowed to disregard existing rules if justice so required.

Jhering's impact on the "free law" movement was as unmistakable as it was limited.[17] As far as direct acknowledgement is concerned, the record is mixed. Kantorowicz openly claimed Jhering as a major influence.[18] Ehrlich gave him little express credit but alluded to him in various ways.[19] Fuchs wrote an entire article about "Jhering and the Free Law Movement," although the piece not only evinced the debt the movement owed to Jhering, it also criticized and even disparaged him.[20] A fellow traveler of the movement, Josef Kohler, was openly contemptuous of Jhering.[21] In order to understand Jhering's significance for the

---

[16] See, e.g., *Kantorowicz*, Aus der Vorgeschichte der Freirechtslehre (1925) 10.

[17] *Fikentscher*, Methoden des Rechts III (1976) 366, termed the members of the movement Jhering's "disciples" which, however, is true, only in the most general terms. In a similarly general fashion, William Seagle recognized Jhering's influence on the "free law" movement the United States; *Seagle*, Rudolf von Jhering (1947) 86. Also in the United States, Edwin Patterson considered Jhering "the founder of the 'free law' movement," because Jhering "had developed the idea of the purpose of law;" "introduced [...] the idea of interest;" had shown the fallacy of "the logical deduction of decisions from fixed premises;" and had attacked the "over-emphasis of historical thinking;" Patterson proffered this assessment in the footnotes he provided to a text by Kantorowicz, i.e., *Kantorowicz and Patterson*, Legal Science – a Summary of Its Methodology (1928) 700 fn. 63.

[18] Kantowicz saw Jhering as having turned "more and more towards a free law perspective," *Kantorowicz*, Aus der Vorgeschichte der Freirechtslehre (1925) 38, and concluded that "everything that has been done in the spirit of the free law theory in Germany as well as abroad is subject to Jhering's dominant influence," id. 39.

[19] *Ehrlich's* now classical work "Freie Rechtsfindung und freie Rechtswissenschaft" (1903) directly mentions Jhering only in passing but openly alludes to Jhering's satire about the heaven of concepts, id. 33 (referring to a "hair splitting machine" and a "hydraulic press"). Ehrlich then echoes what Jhering had famously demanded for modern jurisprudence of Roman law, supra chapter II.1., note 31 and text, i.e., to proceed, in Ehrlich's terms "through the law and beyond positive law." Id. 29.

[20] *Fuchs*, Jhering und die Freirechtsbewegung (1918/19). Fuchs endorsed a number of ideas that are clearly owed to Jhering (Zweck, Interesse, Verkehrsbedürfnisse, Rechtsgefühl). His argument that there is nothing wrong with using legal concepts – as long as one does not overrate them, is pure Jhering, see supra chapter III.3. notes 135–138 and text. Then, however, Fuchs attacked Jhering for his "crypto-sociology" which he called half-baked and wrong-headed, resulting in "pure utilitarianism," id. 16–17.

[21] *Kohler*, Lehrbuch der Rechtsphilosophie (1923) ("Zweck" a work of "philosophy with-

"free law" campaign it is best to distinguish four of its aspects: its critique of nineteenth century orthodoxy; its basic understanding of law; its view of the proper role of the judge; and its belief in a "free law" beyond state-created norms. Jhering provided significant support for the first and second aspects and arguably some for the third, but virtually none for the fourth.

At its core, the "free law" movement was an attack on the orthodoxy of nineteenth century conceptual jurisprudence and Pandectist legal science, which some of the movement' adherents now saw enshrined in the BGB[22]. It was also, more broadly, a revolt against the dictates of logic,[23] and in particular, against the "constructive jurisprudence" that still prevailed in practice.[24] In this regard, Jhering was of course the most important predecessor. The devastating critique he had leveled in the 1860s and beyond against the reign of juristic logic provided crucial support and inspiration. Here, the "free law" movement built on Jhering's "conversion." It was no accident that Kantorowicz was the first writer who used that very term.[25]

It is fairly obvious that the "free law" movement also adopted the later Jhering's understanding of law as a result of social struggle, a means to social ends, and thus a sociological, rather than logical, business. "Law," Ehrlich wrote, "is just not a fixed dogma but a living force,"[26] which must reflect social reality, i.e., "conditions of life" ("Lebensverhältnisse").[27] In a similar vein, Fuchs emphasized the "legal facts from which law originates." Norms "must be supplemented and interpreted according to their true purposes and the conditions of life."[28] In all these regards, the "free law" advocates stood on the shoulders of Jhering.[29]

---

out philosophy"), 45 (charging Jhering with "dilettante platitudes"). Kohler, who was arguably the most widely known jurist in Wilhelmine Germany, apparently hated Jhering as a result of their dispute about Jhering's comment on the fate of Shylock in Shakespeare's "The Merchant of Venice," supra chapter IV.2., note 118 and text. Jhering considered Kohler brilliant as a scholar but unbearably arrogant as a person, letter to Julius Glaser of May 24, 1881; Jhering in Briefen (1913) 366.

[22] *Fuchs*, Jhering und die Freirechtsbewegung (1918/19) 10–12, 17. See also *Fuchs*, Die Gemeinschädlichkeit der konstruktiven Jurisprudenz (1909).

[23] See *Ehrlich*, Die juristische Logik (1918).

[24] *Fuchs*, Die Gemeinschädlichkeit der konstruktiven Jurisprudenz (1909).

[25] *Kantorowicz*, Jherings Bekehrung (1914); Kantorowicz saw Jhering's "conversion" as a turn towards "freie Rechtsfindung" ("free law-finding"), id. 87. In this context, "finding" did not just mean "discovering" but rather "creating." id. See also *Kantorowicz*, Aus der Vorgeschichte der Freirechtslehre (1925) 23–35. As Okko Behrends has shown, this was largely a misinterpretation because Jhering never completely broke with the tradition of Pandectist legal doctrine, *Behrends*, Das 'Rechtsgefühl' in der historisch-kritischen Rechtstheorie des späten Jhering (1986) 95, 180–181.

[26] *Ehrlich*, Freie Rechtsfindung und freie Rechtswissenschaft (1903) 27, 32.

[27] *Ehrlich*, Freie Rechtsfindung und freie Rechtswissenschaft (1903) 34, 36.

[28] *Fuchs*, Jhering und die Freirechtsbewegung (1918/1919) 22.

[29] See supra chapter IV.1. and 2.

Gauging Jhering's influence on the "free law" scholars' vision of a less-restrained and more powerful judge requires more differentiation. On the one hand, there was considerable affinity. On at least one occasion, Jhering outlined a model of adjudication that anticipated the "free law" scholars' ideas in important regards. In his 1868 talk on whether jurisprudence is a "science,[30] Jhering postulated that legal decisions must be made not by abstract rules but by "personalities" ("Persönlichkeiten"); that the judge is not just "a piece of the machinery of justice" but a human being with a feeling of justice that he should not suppress;[31] and that the judge ought to be creative and participate in the development of the law.[32] Beyond these generalities, Jhering distinguished two situations. In the first, the judge is working with an existing norm of positive law. In that case, he should "subject the law, before he applies it, to the critique of the feeling of justice."[33] In case of a conflict between what the norm commands and what the feeling of justice suggests, the judge should reconsider and dig more deeply – whereupon he will probably find that there is a way to apply the norm in harmony with his "Rechtsgefühl."[34] The second situation is a gap ("Lücke") in the law, i.e., an absence of a norm. In that case, the judge should fill the gap by deciding – like the legislator – according "to the idea of justice, expediency ("Zweckmäßigkeit") or, where there is a hint in existing law, extrapolate the result from it" ("aus der Consequenz").[35] To all this, the "free law" scholars would have gladly agreed. On the other hand, Jhering never went as far as the more radical members of the movement: he never suggested that judges could disregard established rules for the sake of justice in individual cases. For Jhering, the judge was not an independent master of the law who could decide freely according to social interests and needs; instead, he remained bound by legislation and doctrine and was obligated to respect the systematic structure of law.[36] To be sure, judges could – and if need be should – tweak rules but they could not push them entirely aside.[37]

---

[30] See supra chapter II.4.

[31] *Jhering*, Ist die Jurisprudenz eine Wissenschaft? (1868) 88–89.

[32] *Jhering*, Ist die Jurisprudenz eine Wissenschaft (1868) 87–89.

[33] *Jhering*, Ist die Jurisprudenz eine Wissenschaft (1868) 88.

[34] *Jhering*, Ist die Jurisprudenz eine Wissenschaft (1868) 88; Jhering alluded to his own experience, see supra chapter III.1. He did not say what to do if the norm and the feeling of justice could not be reconciled.

[35] *Jhering*, Ist die Jurisprudenz eine Wissenschaft (1868) 89.

[36] For further discussion, see *Behrends*, Das 'Rechtsgefühl in der historisch-kritischen Rechstheorie des späten Jhering (1986) 93–95, 180–181.

[37] In addition to drawing inspiration from Jhering, the "free law" adherents' vision of the judge was influenced by what they observed (not entirely correctly) in ancient Rome and modern England, see, e.g., *Ehrlich*, Freie Rechtsfindung und freie Rechtswissenschaft (1903). They also looked to famous Art. 1 of the recent Swiss Civil Code of 1907/12 (Zivilgesetzbuch, ZGB), which envisaged a much more flexible mode of judging than the prevalent German approach. Art. 1 ZGB provides:

1. The statute applies to all legal issues for which it provides a norm according to its wording or its interpretation.

Finally, Jhering's work provided scant support for the core concept of a "free law" that exists alongside the law of the state and that judges should follow in all cases not clearly covered by existing legislation. For Jhering, law was decidedly a matter of state power – the totality of norms that were enforced through coercion by official authority.[38] One could argue, of course, that the "free law" envisaged by Ehrlich and others *was* ultimately enforced by the courts as state institutions – and thus proper "law" even in Jhering's sense. Still, for Jhering, law really came into its own only when it took the form of legislation. Statutes (and codes) were what counted; of course, norms developed by courts and scholars also played a role;[39] but Jhering did not envisage a "free law" beyond the authority of the state.

It is interesting to note that although both Jhering and the adherents of the "free law" movement never tired of proclaiming the ultimate goal of "justice," neither defined exactly what justice is or requires.[40] Jhering had rejected all absolute standards as products of idealist illusions and, instead, embraced a historical relativism, under which justice was a matter of "feeling" that completely depended on changing social conditions, just like law itself.[41] Ehrlich followed in his footsteps: "There is no justice which is determined once and for all, each justice is the result of historical development, just like the law itself."[42] It is not clear whether this position was a result of Jhering's influence or rather of Ehrlich's own reflections. Be that as it may, Ehrlich did no better than Jhering in coming to grips with the very concept that was the ultimate reference point of his whole project.

In addition to his direct impact on the German "free law" school, Jhering also had an indirect, but nonetheless significant, influence on the movement by way of a detour through France. There, Francois Gény (1861–1959) developed his own methodological agenda that slightly preceded, and was significantly related to, the German side. Gény also reacted against the contemporary orthodoxy in his own country where the interpretation of the *Code civil* of 1804 dominated legal theory and practice and where judges were supposed strictly to follow the letter of the law. Like his German "free law" colleagues, Gény refused to regard law,

---

2. If a norm cannot be found in the statute, the court shall decide according to custom and, if that is lacking as well, according to the rule which it would enact as a legislator.

3. It [i.e., the court] follows established doctrine and tradition.

At the very beginning of the twentieth century, the "free law" scholars referred mainly to the draft; the ZGB was finally adopted in 1907 and entered into force in 1912. For a comment, see *Rümelin*, Das neue schweizerische Zivilgesetzbuch (1908).

[38] Supra chapter IV.2. notes 199–201 and text.

[39] In support of his demand that legal scholarship develop the "free law," Ehrlich cited Jhering's essay "Unsere Aufgabe" (1857), *Ehrlich*, Freie Rechtsfindung und freie Rechtswissenschaft (1903) 38. This is somewhat odd because that essay was still written by the "early" Jhering and exudes his enthusiasm for his "natural-historical method" as an advanced form of conceptual jurisprudence, see supra chapter II.2.

[40] See, e.g., *Kantorowicz*, Aus der Vorgeschichte der Freirechtslehre (1925) 46–47.

[41] Supra chapter IV.3.

[42] *Ehrlich*, Freie Rechtsfindung und freie Rechtswissenschaft (1903) 28.

including the *Code civil*, as a closed system; he also argued for a more creative and independent role of the judge and a strong role for "justice;" and he developed his own program of a "libre recherche juridique" ("free legal research").[43] While Gény referred to Jhering in his published work only sporadically,[44] he expressly recognized Jhering's ideas as a primary source of inspiration,[45] although he ended up deviating from Jhering's approach in significant regards.[46] In turn, Gény was recognized by the German "free law" scholars as an important comrade-in-arms.[47] Gény had a tremendous influence on twentieth-century legal thought not only in his homeland but in other countries as well. Thus, he was instrumental in spreading Jhering's pragmatic and sociological approach to many parts of the world, including the United States.[48]

The "free law" movement flourished in the first decade of the twentieth century but waned around the time of World War I. Eventually, its postulates that found support in Jhering's work have become part of mainstream legal thought in most Western legal systems: the rejection of logical formalism nineteenth-century German style, the turn towards a pragmatic and instrumental conception of law, and the emergence of a creative role for judges. By contrast, the positions not supported by Jhering's jurisprudence have not carried the day on a broad scale: the judges' freedom to disregard binding rules in favor of individual justice, and the concept of a "free law" beyond the state (the twenty-first century revival of a transnational *lex mercatoria* notwithstanding).[49]

The "Jurisprudence of Interests:" Applying Statutes in the Spirit of Jhering. Jhering's most lasting impact on twentieth-century jurisprudence was his formative influence on an approach to adjudication that rose to prominence just as the "free law" movement waned: the "jurisprudence of interests." While this was not

---

[43] *Gény*, Méthode et sources en droit privé positif (1899).

[44] See, e.g., *Gény*, Méthode et sources en droit privé positif (2d ed.1919) 3–4.

[45] Hermann Kantorowicz reported that in 1911, Gény had written to him that "the most important influence of which I am conscious is primarily that of von Ihering;" other French and German jurists were of secondary importance, *Kantorowicz*, Aus der Vorgeschichte der Freirechtslehre (1925) 39.

[46] *Whitman*, Jhering parmi les Français (1997) 160–162, considers the difference between Jhering and Gény "radical" with regard to their conceptions of justice – socially and historically contingent for Jhering, moral and religious for Gény. One must also consider that Jhering and Gény wrote under different conditions: the former dealt with the Roman law as the common law of German speaking lands before the BGB, the latter with a system dominated by a (quasi-natural law) codification, i.e., the French *Code civil* (1804); see *Fikentscher*, Methoden des Rechts I (1975) 484–487.

[47] See, e.g., *Ehrlich*, Freie Rechtsfindung und freie Rechtswissenschaft (1903) IV; *Kantorowicz*, Aus der Vorgeschichte der Freirechtslehre (1925).

[48] Substantial parts of *Gény's* magnum opus, i.e., Méthode d'interprétation et sources en droit privé positif (1899), were translated and published in the United States, see The Science of Legal Method (Bruncken and Register transl. 1917) 2–26, 498–557.

[49] See *Zimmermann*, Juristische Methodenlehre in Deutschland (2019) 283 (with further references).

just a German, but rather an international, phenomenon, for now, we are looking only at its German version, i.e., the "Interessenjurisprudenz." It was developed mainly by Philipp Heck (1858–1943)[50] roughly between 1912 and 1933,[51] but it was also associated with Max Rümelin (1861–1931), Heinrich Stoll (1891–1937), Rudolf Müller-Erzbach (1874–1959), and others.[52] Similar to the "free law" movement, "Interessenjurisprudenz" reacted against the lingering tradition of conceptual jurisprudence. It also looked at law, and especially at statutory rules, as the results of the struggle between conflicting social interests and as instruments for the realization of social purposes.

Jhering's influence was obvious, straightforward, and openly acknowledged. The very first law book Philipp Heck ever read was Jhering's "Geist," and it was this book that motivated Heck to switch from studying mathematics to pursuing a career in legal academia.[53] Thus, Heck later called Jhering not only the "precursor" but "the founder of the teleological direction and with it, of the jurisprudence of interests."[54] It is easy to see why: the conception of law embraced by Heck and his colleagues was directly adopted from Jhering.[55]

---

[50] Heck was arguably the most influential scholar in twentieth century German jurisprudence on the field of private law and adjudication. The reason why he is not in the frontline of the most famous German jurists is not the lesser quality of his work – quite to the contrary: Heck was a perceptive, creative, and thorough scholar. It is rather that he was too careful and circumspect to trumpet provocative generalizations in the fashion of Savigny, Jhering or Kantorowicz.

[51] Convenient, though not indisputable, markers are the most important works by its most prominent representative, i.e., Philipp Heck. In the first two, Heck laid the foundations, i.e., *Heck*, Das Problem der Rechtsgewinning (1912); *Heck*, Gesetzesauslegung und Interessenjurisprudenz (1914); in the second and third, he presented the mature theory, see *Heck*, Begriffsbildung und Interessenjurisprudenz (1932); *Heck*, Interessenjurisprudenz (1933). The effects were long-lasting, see infra notes 60–65 and text. For summaries of *Interessenjurisprudenz*, see *Fikentscher*, Methoden des Rechts III (1976) 373–384; *Schröder*, Recht als Wissenschaft II (2020) 346–347; *Wieacker*, Privatrechtsgeschichte (1967) 574–578; *Reimann*, Jurisprudence of Interests (2007).

[52] Several of the key texts penned by Heck, Rümelin, Stoll, and others were translated into English: The Jurisprudence of Interests (Magdalena Schoch transl., 1948; 20th Century Legal Philosophy Series vol. II).

[53] *Kleinheyer and Schröder*, Deutsche und europäische Juristen (2017) 194–195.

[54] *Heck*, Interessenjurisprudenz (1933) 12; *Heck,* Gesetzesauslegung und Interessenjurisprudenz (1914) 308. Helmut Coing saw the roots of Heck's *Interessenjurisprudenz* ultimately in English utilitarianism which Jhering had imported into German legal thought; *Coing*, Rudolf von Jhering und Bentham (1982) 9. It is true that Heck had probably read Bentham, Mill, and Spencer as well, and that that there were significant similarities between English utilitarianism and Heck's approach, id., 12–14. None of this, however, changes the fact that according to Heck himself, the influence of Jhering was dominant. Iredell Jenkins claimed that German interest jurisprudence misunderstood Jhering by construing his ideas far too narrowly. In particular, Jhering's conception of "interest" was objective while interest jurisprudence construed it as subjective; *Jenkins*, Rudolf von Jhering (1960) 172–174, 184–185.

[55] Okko Behrends has argued that claiming Jhering as a predecessor of interest jurisprudence is dubious. That is because Heck's approach was state-centered in the sense that it saw

Strictly speaking, however, German "Interessenjurisprudenz" was not a general theory of law but a specific approach to adjudication in the age of statutes. Heck and his colleagues recognized that statutes were often unclear and that they left considerable gaps. A true disciple of the later Jhering, Heck rejected the approach pursued by orthodox German jurisprudence, i.e., the idea of deriving solutions from the logic of abstract concepts.[56] He also rejected the approach by Kantorowicz and his colleagues of letting the judge resort to "free law" or to a subjective sense of justice. Instead, a judge should understand existing norms as means to the end of resolving social conflicts. Thus, he should extrapolate results by way of a multi-step interest analysis: first, he should identify the conflicting (social, economic, religious, ethical, etc.) interests at stake; next, he needed to recognize how the legislator had resolved that or similar conflicts (i.e., which interests had prevailed and why); at the same time, the judge had to understand the value judgment underlying that resolution; finally, he should replicate that resolution and realize this value judgment as best he could. In short, the judge should decide the case before him according to the hypothetical will of the legislator with a view to the social interests involved. The judge should continue to obey the legislator; he should just not do so blindly but rather in what Heck famously called "thoughtful obedience" ("denkender Gehorsam").[57] This implied that the judge should inquire into, and calibrate his decision to, the realities of "social life."[58]

In this manner, "Interessenjurisprudenz" transmitted Jhering's ideas to the twentieth century[59] while also going beyond him. Jhering, who had focused on the Roman law in pre-codification Germany, had never much occupied himself with issues of statutory construction. A generation after Jhering's death, Heck took Jhering's perception of the law – as an instrument for the resolution of social conflicts – and fashioned from it a pragmatic approach to judging. In other

(positive) law as a product of modern legislation, while Jhering, dealing with the Roman law in pre-codification times, saw it as a centuries-old (and in that sense pre-state) tradition; see *Behrends*, Rudolf von Jhering (1818–1892). Der Durchbruch zum Zweck des Rechts (1987) 268.

[56] More precisely, the process of first distilling more and more general legal concepts from existing norms and then deriving new norms from these concepts in order to interpret statutes and to fill gaps. Heck famously called this process "Inversionsmethode" and saw it at work in Jhering's *Konruktionsjurisprudenz* (see supra chapter II.2.), *Heck*, Das Problem der Rechtsgewinnung (1912) 13–18; *Heck*, Begriffsbildung und Interessenjurisprudenz (1932) 92–94, 166.

[57] *Heck*, Gesetzesauslegung und Interessenjurisprudenz (1914) 51. In a sense, Heck combined Jhering's sociological approach with "legislative positivism" ("Gesetzespositivismus," see supra chapter IV.3. notes 439–445 and text), see *Wieacker*, Privatrechtsgeschichte (1967) 576.

[58] *Heck*, Interessenjurisprudenz (1933) 29.

[59] As Wolfgang Fikentscher observed, without interest jurisprudence, Jhering's pragmatic and sociological approach may have become a matter of history, *Fikentscher*, Methoden des Rechts III (1976) 374.

words, Heck turned Jhering's general observations into a concrete legal methodology of adjudication.

Jhering's Lasting Legacy for Contemporary German Jurisprudence: Absorption into the Mainstream and Modern Modification. In German speaking lands,[60] the influence of interest jurisprudence – and thus of Jhering's ideas – has been overwhelming and enduring throughout the twentieth century and beyond. Especially in private law, which was both Jhering's and Heck's primary focus, a teleological approach and a consideration of the competing interests have become virtually *de rigeur*[61]. This is true not only in academic discourse but also, and more importantly, in the courts.[62] To be sure, statutory language and established doctrine provide both crucial guidance and important limits for judicial decisions, but within those limits judges routinely proceed in an "interest-jurisprudence mode."[63] Results derived from statutory texts and doctrinal analysis have to be tested against the standards of legislative purpose, a consideration of underlying interests, and practical sense.[64] As Wolfgang Fikentscher put it, the substantive (private) law used by today's jurists bears the mark of Windscheid, but the method they employ is that of Jhering.[65] In this manner, Jhering's ideas have become part of mainstream legal methodology, although most German-speaking jurists are no longer aware of its origin in his work.

The utility of "Interessenjurisprudenz" had its limits, however, that in turn reflected the limits of Jhering's interest-oriented and instrumental view of law. These limits became visible in two particular contexts. One was the traditional question of statutory interpretation ("Gesetzesauslegung"). Here, Heck (and Jhering) required the consideration of conflicting interests, but they provided scant help in deciding which of these interests should prevail. Jhering's general reference to the "conditions of life in society,"[66] and his relativist position that purposes completely depended on the respective society,[67] had considerable explanatory power but packed no normative punch – it said precious little about what these conditions required or how these purposes were determined. In a similar vein, interest jurisprudence offered little assistance to the courts in developing the law ("Rechtsfortbildung") when legislation provided no clue or was

[60] The following description applies, *cum grano salis*, also to Austria and Switzerland, where legal methodology has developed largely along the same lines as in Germany; *Zimmermann*, Juristische Methodenlehre (2019) 245.

[61] In other areas, such as criminal, constitutional, and administrative law, this influence has been more limited, see *Fikentscher*, Methoden des Rechts III (1976) 379.

[62] *Larenz*, Rudolf von Jhering und die Lage der deutschen Rechtswissenschaft (1970) 136–137; *Fikentscher*, Methoden des Rechts III (1976) 380–381; *Wieacker*, Privatrechtsgeschichte (1967) 577; *Zimmermann*, Juristische Methodenlehre (2019) 261, 265.

[63] *Fikentscher*, Methoden des Rechts III (1976) 380 ("interessen-juristisch").

[64] *Jansen and Reimann*, Begriff und Zweck in der Jurisprudenz (2018) 115.

[65] *Fikentscher*, Methoden des Rechts III (1976) 282, 375.

[66] Supra chapter IV.2., notes 232–242 and text.

[67] Supra chapter IV.2., notes 226–229 and text.

simply absent. In such cases, how were judges to decide who should win and who should lose and on what grounds?[68] For Jhering and his age these normative questions were perhaps less crucial because of the prevalent consensus about liberal (and Christian) values and because of the widely shared belief in human and social progress. Yet, once these beliefs were shaken (or shattered) after the cataclysms of the first half of the twentieth century, fundamental normative questions were starkly raised and could no longer be ducked. In search for answers for both "Gesetzesauslegung" and "Rechtsfortbildung," mid- and late twentieth century German jurisprudence increasingly modified the consideration of interests by a consideration of (potentially competing) values. These values have often been derived from the constitutional order, especially the rule of law and the catalog of basic rights, but also from broadly accepted precepts of justice, such as equality before the law, protection of weaker parties, the validation of legitimate expectations, and the principle of proportionality.[69] In this fashion, "Interessenjurisprudenz" has morphed into the "Wertungsjurisprudenz" ("jurisprudence of values"), which continues to dominate the theory and practice of adjudication in Jhering's home country.[70]

Jhering 1933–1945: The Lack of Nazi Endorsement. Much of what Jhering wrote can be quite troubling to a modern reader: law is a "concept of power;" "[y]ou shall find your rights in battle," because who prevails in law turns on power, not merit. Half-heartedness ("Lauheit") is despicable, manliness is laudable, and there should be no duty to retreat from an attack on one's rights.[71] In times of emergency, the law must yield to force because the protection of society is more important than the rule of law.[72] All this is true not only for individuals but also for peoples:[73] a people must be ready to defend its territory and its honor with full force against the slightest incursion.[74] The earth belongs to those who make the best use of its resources, and if a people fails properly to exploit the land it inhabits, it deserves to be pushed aside by another.[75] Ultimately, law is "*merely*

---

[68] To be sure, the Civil Code's general clauses have implicitly authorized judges to decide questions not covered by specific norms, but these clauses are necessarily phrased in terms too vague to provide concrete guidance to the courts.

[69] *Larenz*, Rudolf von Jhering und die Lage der deutschen Rechtswissenschaft (1970) 137; *Zimmermann*, Juristische Methodenlehre (2019) 272, 286. An striking example is the decision of the German Constitutional Court (*Bundesverfassungsgericht*) of February 2, 1973, BvR 112/65, BVerfGE 34, 269 (Soraya case).

[70] See *Fikentscher*, Methoden des Rechts III (1976) 382–387; *Zimmermann*, Juristische Methodenlehre (2019) 254. For an in-depth discussion and analysis, see *Peterse*n, Von der Interessenjurisprudenz zur Wertungsjurisprudenz (2001); for a shorter account, see *Fiken*tscher, Methoden des Rechts III (1976) 405–429;

[71] *Jhering*, Kampf (1872) 9, 11, 25, 41, 43, 48, 95–96, 98, 100.

[72] *Jhering*, Zweck I (1884) 251–254.

[73] *Jhering*, Kampf (1872) 25, 73.

[74] *Jhering*, Kampf (1872) 25.

[75] *Jhering*, Geist I (2d ed. 1866) 7.

a means to an end;"[76] it must serve *whatever* the goals of a certain society are;[77] all standards of justice depend *entirely* on historical experience and are thus relative.[78] And so it goes. In summary, there was a very harsh, on occasion outright brutal, side to Jhering who time and again appeared as an advocate of naked power, the primacy of force over law, might makes right, unbounded instrumentalism, moral relativism, and Western intervention in developing countries.[79] At least from today's point of view, it is not a pretty picture.

It is also a picture that Nazism should have loved. Jhering's various utterances could provide cover for running roughshod over traditional notions of justice, for the glorification of raw power, for using law as an instrument for establishing the Nazi regime, and for the expansion of the Nazi empire. Here was a German jurist who emphasized and welcomed the legitimacy of force; who had a fondness for the term "rücksichtslos" ("ruthless")[80] also favored by Nazi orators; who argued that the principle *nulla poena sine lege* was not absolute and that particular crimes could be tried before a special court (perhaps a "Volksgerichtshof"?);[81] and whose purpose-driven concept of law was at most one step away from the Nazi motto "Recht ist, was dem Volke nützt" – "law is (whatever) serves the people."[82] Small wonder, then, that Jhering has been blamed for paving the way towards twentieth century totalitarianism (and sometimes also racism).[83]

---

[76] *Jhering*, Zweck I (1884) 250 (emphasis added); see also id. 529 (the only function of law is to serve its purpose).

[77] See, e.g., *Jhering*, Zweck I (1884) 446–448.

[78] *Jhering*, Über die Entstehung des Rechtsgefühls (1884); see supra chapter IV.3, notes 471–473 and text.

[79] Jhering approved of the European powers' forcible opening of China and Japan to international trade. This was based on his belief that the peoples of the world have a duty to cooperate (i.e., to exchange goods), just like individuals in a society. Thus, a country's attempt to isolate itself from the rest of the world was "a mortal sin against the [other] peoples." ("eine Todsünde gegen die Völker"). This did not mean that the European powers had a right to subjugate these countries as colonies; it did mean, however, that if a people staunchly refused to participate in global interchange, it forfeited its right to exist; *Jhering*, Geist I (2d ed. 1866) 7.

[80] Sometimes, Jhering used it just descriptively, e.g., *Jhering*, Geist I (1852) 303; on other occasions, he expressed admiration for "the ruthless tyranny of consequence," id., 307.

[81] *Jhering*, Zweck I (1884) 429–431.

[82] This is pointed out by *Helfer*, Rudolf von Jhering als Rechtssoziologe (1968) 559.

[83] *Wieacker*, Gründer und Bewahrer (1959) 209–210; *Wieacker*, Privatrechtsgeschichte (1967) 453, 585–586; *Wolf*, Große Rechtsdenker (1963) 650, 654; in a similar vein, *Larenz*, Methodenlehre (1983) 48. Wieacker and Wolf recognized that personally, Jhering could not be blamed for a lack of commitment to ethical values, even though he did not manage clearly to define them, see *Wieacker*, Rudolf von Jhering (1969) 10; *Wolf*, Große Rechtsdenker (1963) 663. It is interesting to note that Wieacker, Wolf, and particularly Larenz, were, at one time or another, closely involved with the Nazi-regime. Erik Wolf (1902–1977) was initially an ardent supporter of the Nazi's rise to power and became a member of the NSDAP, though his enthusiasm cooled markedly in the late 1930s. Franz Wieacker (1908–1994) obtained his first academic post in 1933 at the University of Kiel whose law faculty was designated as the center

The treatment of Jhering during the Nazi-period has not been systematically researched. It appears, however, that Nazi propaganda made virtually no use of Jhering;[84] there seems to be no evidence that Nazi politicians invoked his ideas. To be sure, that is not all that surprising because Nazi orators generally paid scant attention to legal scholarship. What is potentially surprising, however, is that Nazi-friendly *jurists* did not instrumentalize Jhering either. The most notorious of Nazi jurists, Carl Schmitt (1888–1985), apparently had no particular interest in Jhering and failed to invoke him even when the occasion invited a reference.[85] The

---

of Nazi jurisprudence; Wieacker later worked with the Nazi regime in several contexts and became a member of the *Akademie für deutsches Recht*, a legal research institute founded by, and beholden to, the Nazi government. Karl Larenz (1903–1993) likewise joined the law faculty at the University of Kiel (1933), became a member of the Nazi party (1937), and justified Nazi racist ideology in several of his publications; as a result, he was forbidden to teach after World War II until 1949. Regardless of their past, all three men became highly prominent and greatly revered legal scholars in post-World War II Germany. From an academic point of view, this was fully deserved because each was brilliant in his own way. Yet, by looking back at Jhering, they also looked back at themselves and their own problems with upholding ethical values during the Nazi-period. To be sure, that makes their concerns about Jhering's at times stark positivism neither unfounded nor illegitimate. But their post-war critiques smack of self-righteousness, and it is time to put them to rest; see *Rückert*, Der Geist des Rechts (2004) 127–28. Hans Hattenhauer's (1931–2015) (implicit) accusation of Jhering as a precursor of Nazism is based on Jhering's (alleged) social Darwinism; *Hattenhauer*, Die geistesgeschichtlichen Grundlagen des deutschen Rechts (1996) 211. Hattenhauer's diatribe is both sensationalist and unfounded, especially in light of Jhering's well-documented commitment to equal treatment for Jews, supra chapter I.4., note 283–285 and text. For a summary of the pertinent literature, see *Rückert*, Der Geist des Rechts (2005) 127–129; *Rückert*, Methodenorakel (2019) 462. Rückert himself justly rejects the view of Jhering as jurisprudential precursor of Nazism, id.Wieacker eventually reacted much the same way even though he (correctly) pointed out Jhering's occasional infatuation with sheer political power; *Wieacker*, Rudolf von Jhering (1969) 9–10.

[84] This was asserted, though merely in a general fashion, already by Helfer, Rudolf von Jhering als Rechtssoziologe (1968) 555.

[85] Schmitt was, of course, familiar with Jhering's principal works (as well as with much of the jurisprudential literature of nineteenth century Germany); see, for example, the references in *Schmitt*, Gesetz und Urteil (1912) 23, 34. 37. 46, 91, 123. Whether Schmitt was in any way influenced by Jhering has, to my knowledge, not been investigated, but it is highly unlikely. Schmitt's authoritarian and anti-liberal stance, which he had already developed way before 1933, had its (historical) origins mainly in much earlier political theorists like Hobbes and Bodin. Two of Schmitt's post-1933 writings presented obvious opportunities to invoke Jhering. In 1934, Schmitt (in)famously sought to legitimize Hitler's liquidation of the SA leadership in the summer of 1934 as a necessary act of supreme power in times of state emergency; Schmitt, Der Führer schützt das Recht (1934). Schmitt could have invoked Jhering's discourse on the primacy of political power over (positive) law where the existence of state and society are at stake, supra chapter III, notes 213–215 and text, but Schmitt did not mention Jhering at all. Another premier opportunity to engage with Jhering's thought was Schmitt's famous tract "Über die drei Arten des rechtswissenschaftlichen Denkens" ("On the three Modes of Reasoning in Legal Science") (1934). Here, Schmitt could have relied on Jhering's repeated statements that law consists not of norms in the abstract but rather requires that

two legal scholars who wrote about Jhering at some length during the Nazi period – Erik Wolf and Franz Wieacker – did not enlist him for the Nazi cause, even though they both were significantly affiliated with the regime.[86] Nor did Ernst Forsthoff – also an early supporter of Nazism – instrumentalize Jhering in an article about him published in the quasi-official journal of Nazi jurisprudence, the "Zeitschrift der Akademie für deutsches Recht," in 1937.[87] And when Philipp Heck sought to ingratiate himself to the Nazi leadership by showing that his "jurisprudence of interests" was ideally suited for the current "renewal of law," Jhering remained barely visible in the background.[88]

Yet, the lack of Nazi enthusiasm for Jhering is not hard to explain. The interest of legal scholars like Wieacker, Wolf, and Forsthoff in Jhering was not political, but rather (almost purely) jurisprudential; they happened to write about him during the Nazi-period, but they still treated him as a legal theorist, not as a political forebear.[89] More importantly for our current purpose, Jhering was not really a good candidate for a pro-Nazi jurist. To begin with, Jhering was an ardent admirer of Roman law which was anathema to Nazi propaganda because it was seen as alien, individualistic, and formalist; Nazi ideology much preferred the Germanic legal tradition and thus looked to the scholars exalting its indigenous, communal, and anti-formalist character. In addition, Jhering's thinking was too full of contradictions. While many of his pronouncements could have

these norms be actually enforced; see *Jhering*, Geist I (1852) 41; id. 52, 305; *Jhering*, Geist II .2. (1858) 334; *Jhering*, Kampf (1872) 52; *Jhering*, Zweck I (1884) 318. Yet, again, Schmitt's work contains no references to Jhering.

[86] Wolf's long chapter on Jhering, first published in 1939, made no reference to Nazi ideology; *Wolf*, Große Rechtsdenker 491–540 (1939). Wieacker's essay on Jhering, published in 1942, proffers an interpretation that is original and brilliant but not tainted by Nazi ideology. Only its concluding pages contain something like a nod to the new era; even here, it is not clear whether Wieacker spoke with conviction or simply wanted to avoid censorship, *Wieacker*, Rudolf von Jhering (1942).

[87] *Forsthoff*, Vom Zweck im Recht (1937). Forsthoff's book "Der totale Staat" (Berlin 1933) legitimized an authoritarian state under the *Führerprinzip*. In a similar vein, the dissertation by Rudolf Walder on Jhering and Adam Smith, published in 1943, shows no signs of Nazi-influence, even though it was supervised by Karl Larenz, who was involved with the Nazi-regime, see supra note 83; *Walder*, Das Wesen der Gesellschaft bei Adam Smith und Rudolf von Jhering (1943).

[88] *Heck*, Die Interessenjurisprudenz und ihre neuen Gegner (1936); *Heck*, Rechtsphilosophie und Interessenjurisprudenz (1937).

[89] An exception of sorts is a book by one Friedrich Hueber which outlined a "political jurisprudence" for the Nazi state; it was published in 1939 and is largely unknown today. Hueber listed Jhering's teleological approach as a precursor among others for a political jurisprudence in general but found his approach too positivistic and thus wanting. Thus, he did not enlist Jhering for the Nazi cause in particular either; *Hueber*, Grundlegung der politischen Rechtslehre (1939) 22–23, 55–56. Contrary to the (at least implicit) assertion by *Helfer*, Rudolf von Jhering als Rechtssoziologe (1968) 567 (endnote 22), *Schober*, Politische Jurisprudenz. Eine Würdigung ihres Wegbereiters Jhering (1933) is not a work of Nazi jurisprudence, even though Schober became a supporter of the regime.

served the Nazi cause well, many others were completely antithetical to it. Law was not only power, it was also "idealism" and expressed "ideal value."[90] It was not only a matter of force but also of justice – it needed both the sword and the scales.[91] The instrumental character of law notwithstanding, justice remained "the ultimate objective" and "principle" of society.[92] In addition to the Hobbesian Jhering who defended the sovereign's right to resort to naked force in times of emergency, there was the liberal Jhering who (like his friend Otto Bähr[93]) championed the rule of law; who tirelessly advocated for limitations on state power, the independence of the judiciary, as well as justice through equality;[94] who supported the constitutional order of Wilhelmine Germany; and who extensively railed against despotism.[95] Last, but certainly not least, Jhering's views were not compatible with Nazi anti-Semitism: Jhering praised the Semitic peoples' early cultural achievements,[96] lamented the treatment of Shakespeare's Shylock by the Venetian court,[97] supported the establishment of an organization against anti-Semitism,[98] and was proud of his Jewish son-in-law.[99] All this rendered Jhering largely useless for the Nazi cause.[100]

Jhering apparently did not find much favor in the other totalitarian regime in twentieth century Germany, i.e., the former German Democratic Republic (1949–1990), either.[101] Still, looking at Jhering from a socialist point of view sheds an interesting light on him. For example, it brings into sharp relief that Jhering was truly a jurist for the bourgeoisie at the height of industrial capitalism – witness, for example, his almost obsessive emphasis on the central role of egoism as the driving force of human conduct.[102] A socialist perspective also shows how

---

[90] *Jhering*, Kampf (1872) 45, 74.

[91] *Jhering*, Kampf (1872) 9.

[92] *Jhering*, Zweck I (1884) 554.

[93] *Bähr*, Der Rechtsstaat (1864).

[94] *Jhering*, Zweck I (1884) 365–372.

[95] *Jhering*, Kampf (1872) 78; Jhering, Zweck I (1884) 355–361, 391–393, 403–408.

[96] *Jhering*, Vorgeschichte der Indoeuropäer (1894) 93–305.

[97] *Jhering*, Kampf (1872) 63–65; see supra chapter IV.1., notes 117–121 and text.

[98] *Dove*, Rudolf von Jhering und Bernhard Windscheid (1893)149.

[99] See supra chapter I.4., footnote 284 and text.

[100] The extent to which Jhering's ideas had an indirect influence on Nazi jurisprudence via the school of "free law" is a different question. On that school's connection with Nazi ideology, see *Behrends*, Von der Freirechtsbewegung zum konkreten Ordnungs- und Gestaltungsdenken (1989). Note, that many of that school's leaders, such as Hermann Kantorowicz, Eugen Ehrlich, and Ernst Fuchs, were Jewish.

[101] In 1982, Hermann Klenner, perhaps the internationally most highly respected legal theorist hailing from the German Democratic Republic, published an article on Jhering's "Kampf." Klenner does not claim Jhering as a political supporter of socialism; Klenner, Jherings Kampf ums Recht (1982).

[102] Supra chapter IV.2., note 224 and text. Hermann Klenner called "Kampf" a "juristic vindication of bourgeois society" ("Juristenapologie der bürgerlichen Gesellschaft"); *Klenner*, Jherings Kampf ums Recht (1982) 440.

his definition of law as the regime of coercive rules securing the conditions of social life implies that the ruling class employs law to discipline and police the lower classes – as Jhering actually recognized.[103] And it highlights Jhering's support for the expansionist politics of a rising imperial power.[104] Thus looking at Jhering through a socialist lens reveals that many of his central ideas are appealing only against the backdrop of nineteenth-century Western liberalism and capitalism.

2. A Global Perspective: Evidence of Worldwide Influence

As mentioned, Jhering's global influence has not been comprehensively explored. There is ample evidence, however, that his ideas were noted, discussed, and often adopted in many jurisdictions around the world. This evidence is of two kinds: the diffusion of his work through translations, and a variety of studies of his impact in particular countries and contexts.

Global Diffusion: Jhering Translations. The global diffusion of Jhering's works is impressive: since the middle of the nineteenth century, they have been translated about 150 times[105] which may even beat Savigny's works.[106] Translations appeared in at least twenty (mostly European) languages[107] and were published in dozens of countries on several continents. Many works were translated multiple times over, sometimes without Jhering's authorization. "Kampf," which appeared in about twenty translations, clearly leads the pack and is probably the most frequently translated work of any German jurist ever. It is followed by "Geist" and "Zweck" which were of course much longer so that translating them required much greater effort. Most of Jhering's non-doctrinal writings and even several of his doctrinal essays, are available in one foreign language or another. Translations began to appear as early as 1855 (an Italian version of the first volume of "Geist"), were published by the dozens even during Jhering's lifetime,

---

[103] Supra chapter IV.1., notes 352–355 and text.

[104] *Sellnow*, Gesellschaft – Staat – Recht (1963) 228–250. Another commentator from the former GDR was more circumspect and skeptical towards broad political judgments about Jhering, *Klemann*, Rudolf von Jhering und die Historische Rechtsschule (1989) 109 fn. 150.

[105] The most up-to-date list of translations is *Kunze*, Lieber in Gießen (2018) 55–62, listing 157 titles. It supersedes the earlier bibliography by *Losano*, Bibliographie Rudolf von Jherings (1970) 281–294, which lists 111 titles. Kunze does not claim that his list is complete, and since its compilation, more translations may have been published.

[106] A bibliography of Savigny translations compiled in 2015 has 103 entries but is limited to seven languages (Chinese, English, French, Italian, Japanese, Portuguese, and Spanish), *Duve and Rückert* (eds.), Savigny International (2015) 456–474. A global count would result in a higher number.

[107] Chinese, Croatian, Czech, Bulgarian, Danish, Dutch, English, Finnish, French, Greek, Italian, Japanese, Latvian, Polish, Portuguese, Romanian, Russian, Slovak, Swedish, and Turkish; *Kunze*, Lieber in Gießen (2018) 55–62.

and have continued being published well into the twenty-first century. The frequency of Jhering translations was in part due to the extraordinary breadth of his *oeuvre* that thus appealed to a multitude of audiences. Reading Jhering was also popular all across the globe because of his often catchy titles, lively style, bold assertions, and memorable phrases. Jhering the jurist-artist strove to captivate his readership, and he succeeded.

Today one would assume the lion's share of translations to consist of English versions, but at merely five, their number is much lower than that of translations into other major languages including French, Italian, Spanish, and Russian. One reason was probably that many of Jhering's writings were of no or low interest to common lawyers; his doctrinal studies were so geared towards Roman law and nineteenth century German jurisprudence that few Anglo-American jurists had much use for them. Also, many highly educated scholars in nineteenth-century England and the United States could read Jhering in German which was the premier (foreign) language of legal learning at the time.

Translations do not prove influence, but they do suggest it. If someone invested the time and effort to translate Jhering's work, he was not only himself highly interested in Jhering's ideas, he also had reason to believe that many others were as well. It also stands to reason that if Jhering was available in translation, he was actually read in the respective country or region. However, how widely he was read, and to what extent that reading had an impact on legal thought or practice, we often do not know.

Country Studies: A Potpourri of Perspectives. There is a considerable assortment of studies on Jhering's influence in a variety of countries around the world. Some are easily accessible because they are collected in edited volumes and written in major Western languages, but they cover only a small number of jurisdictions.[108] Some of the standard literature on Jhering also briefly addresses his impact in a few major countries.[109] In addition, there are many studies published

---

[108] The respective contributions to *Wieacker and Wollschläger* (eds.), Jherings Erbe (1970) deal with Spain (Gibert), Skandinavia in general (Jorgensen), and Sweden in particular (Schmidt). The essays collected in *Meder and Mecke* (eds.), Jhering Global (2023) address only the Netherlands (Heutger), Hungary (Földi), Russia (Rudokvas), Brasil (Maliska, Herzog), and the United States (Rabban). Jhering's reception France is throroughly discussed and explained by *Whitman*, Jhering parmi les Francais (1997); Whitman points out the importance of the late-nineteenth century French translations and discussions for the dissemination of Jhering's ideas to other countries where scholars could read French but not the original German, id. 151; see also *Fikentscher*, Methoden des Rechts III (1976) 269. On Italy, see *Bonazzi*, La Fortuna di Jhering in Italia (1977) (a bibliographical essay collecting the translations of, and writing about, Jhering in Italy); *Vano*, Itinerari italiani di Rudolf von Jhering (1993). On the substantial literature on Jhering's reception in the United States, see the notes to infra 3.

[109] See *Losano*, Studien zu Jhering und Gerber (1984) 165–171 (Russia, Italy, Serbia, Romania, Hungary, Spain, Latin America with Brazil in particular, Denmark, Norway, Sweden, United States); *Fikentscher*, Methoden des Rechts III (1976) 269–271; *Wolf*, Große Rechtsdenker (1963) 659, 662 (France, Russia, Spain, United States); *Wieacker*, Privatrechtsgeschichte (1967) 578 (France).

in venues and languages more difficult to access for those from outside of the respective legal cultures.[110]

These studies are so diverse and, for the most part, detail-oriented that is impossible to summarize them in a meaningful way, nor would it make sense to reproduce their contents here. Some focus on Jhering's doctrinal work, others on his methodology; some look at him as an early sociologist, others as a legal and cultural historian; some discuss his significance for modern legal thought, others his impact on politics; and some cover most, or all, of these aspects for a particular country. In the aggregate they show that Jhering's global influence was, to put it colloquially, all over the place.

Still, looking through the fog of endless detail, one can perceive some common themes:[111] the frequent dissemination of Jhering's thought through scholars who had studied with him, returned to their home countries, and then propagated his ideas;[112] the controversial manner in which his teachings were often discussed abroad – praised and propagated by some, criticized and repudiated by others, but always providing ample for thought and debate;[113] the gradual absorption of some of his ideas into the respective legal discourse where they linger even though their author is no longer read and, often, forgotten;[114] and overall, the repeated recognition of Jhering (sometimes even by his adversaries) as perhaps the most influential jurist of the mid- and late nineteenth century.[115]

In addition, there are three more specific themes that are not universally shared but recurrent and noteworthy for the light they shed on Jhering's long term significance. First, in many countries, Jhering was (justly) regarded as the jurist who overcame the outdated Historical School with its focus on the past, and who established a legal theory oriented towards the future.[116] In these coun-

[110] For a list of works on Jhering by authors from countries around the world, see *Kunze*, Lieber in Gießen (2018) 63–85. The list is extensive but scarcely complete.

[111] The following observations can also be made, *mutatis mutandis*, with regard to Jhering's influence in the United States, see below 3.

[112] The perhaps most notable example is Gusztáv Szászy-Schwartz (1858–1920) who has been called "the Hungarian Jhering;" *Földi*, Aspekte der Jhering-Rezeption in Ungarn (2023) 75; see also id 75–83; *Rudokvas*, Jhering's Influence on Russian Legal Thought (2023)103–106.

[113] The reaction to Jhering was particularly mixed in France where earlier enthusiasm to his historical work soon gave way to a more critical attitude, *Whitman*, Jhering parmi les Francais (1997) 156–169, and where significant differences remained between Jhering's and Gény's jurisprudence, id. 160–162; on Jhering and Gény, see supra 1., notes 43–48 and text. In several countries, critics attacked especially Jhering's repeated exaltation of power and force; see *Wieacker*, Rudolf von Jhering (1969) 10 (with further references).

[114] *Gibert*, Jhering in España (1970) 67.

[115] *Földi*, Aspekte der Jhering-Rezeption in Ungarn (2023) 95; *Rudokvas*, Jhering's Influence on Russian Legal Thought (2023). Jhering's influence and fame in Tsarist Russia was probably unparalleled in any other foreign county; he received three honorary doctorates from Russian universities, id. 97. See also *Gibert*, Jhering in España 67; *Vano*, Itinerari italiani di Rudolf von Jhering (1993) 125.

[116] *Rudokvas*, Jhering's Influence on Russian Legal Thought (2023) 101; *Gibert*, Jhering in

tries, he revitalized legal theory, initiated jurisprudential engagement with the conditions of modern, industrializing society, and laid the foundations for a sociology of law.[117] Second, Jhering's conception of law – as a result of the struggle between competing social interests – fascinated scholars in many countries[118] but it was far from universally welcomed. Instead, his utilitarianism and positivism also met with critique and rejection; the dangers inherent in a theory of law built on social facts, rather than moral values, did not escape his readers in foreign lands.[119] Last, but not least, in some countries, Jhering's call to fight for law was embraced and instrumentalized by progressive scholars pushing for political reform, if not revolution. While "Kampf" was hardly meant to instigate political upheaval, the idea that one must fight for law and justice, and that law is an instrument for social ends, was invoked both against the quietism and conservatism of the existing order and for political and social progress.[120] The claim that as the author of "Kampf," Jhering even "became a spiritual grandfather of the Russian Revolution, no less than Karl Marx or Friedrich Engels"[121] may be exaggerated but it points to the political potential of his jurisprudence. It is fair to assume that Jhering would have been horrified by the idea that he contributed to the radical and bloody overthrow of an entire regime but such is the law of unintended consequences.

3. Jhering's Reception in the United States: The Triumph of Instrumentalism

Jhering's work had its greatest foreign resonance in the United States.[122] His turn from a logical to a sociological conception of law, from a focus on the will to a

---

España (1970) 41, 54. Jhering received praise for pushing jurisprudence towards modernity even from Ortega y Gasset (1883–1955), see id. 63–64.

[117] *Rudokvas*, Jhering's Influence on Russian Legal Thought (2023) 104–106; *Hamza*, Wege der Entwicklung des Privatrechts in Europa (2008) 200; see also *Jorgensen*, Die Bedeutung Jherings für die neuere skandinavische Rechtslehre (1970) 126.

[118] *Maliska*, Die Rezeption Jherings in Brasilien (2023) 118.

[119] *Gibert*, Jhering in España (1970) 50–52.

[120] For Russia, *Rudokvas*, Jhering's Influence on Russian Legal Thought (2023) 102–103, 108–109. Even after 1917, some legal scholars drew on Jhering's ideas for socialist legal theory, id. 106–110. This is somewhat surprising given that Jhering was clearly a representative, and wrote in the spirit of, the bourgeois society of his time; see, e.g., supra chapter IV.1., notes 111, 114 and text. For Spain, *Gibert*, Jhering in España (1970) 46–49; *Losano*, Studien zu Jhering und Gerber (1984) 167.

[121] *Rudokvas*, Jhering's Influence on Russian Legal Thought (2023) 103, 109.

[122] Considerable amounts of ink have been spilt on Jhering's influence in the United States. Pride of place among this literature belongs to *Rabban*, Jhering's Influence on American Legal Thought (2023); according to Rabban id., 147–148, Jhering was cited a total of 1326 times in US law journals – which, over a ca. 130 year period, amounts to about ten times a year. Jhering was easily bested by Savigny, however, who was cited 3,478 times. Yet, even if

focus on interests, and from an individualist to a social approach played a key role the development of American jurisprudence from the late nineteenth to the mid-twentieth century. We will first take account of the general American engagement with his ideas over the last century-and-a-half and then turn to the more particular question of actual influence in three specific contexts: the ideas of Oliver Wendell Holmes, the emergence of "sociological jurisprudence," and the legal realism movement. We will conclude this subchapter by looking at the long-term impact of Jhering's concept of law as "merely a means to an end."

As in this chapter generally, we will not analyze Jhering's impact on the doctrine of American law – mainly because that impact has been fairly negligible. It is true that in the 1930s and 1940s, some leading private law scholars in the United States referred to Jhering's work, especially on the "negative interest" in contract damages and on *culpa in contrahendo.*[123] These references have been repeatedly discussed (and even celebrated) in the literature.[124] Yet, such instances were very few and far between. Also, while Jhering's ideas inspired the respective authors, his ideas were not the only, and in most cases not even the principal, foundations of the respective articles. The primary meaning of referencing Jhering's writings was to inspire, and then to lend support to, arguments largely derived from American sources; to put it differently: Jhering essentially played the role of a fellow-traveler.[125] The reasons why Jhering doctrinal work did not have a broader impact in the United States are not difficult to fathom. Jhering's doctrinal ana-

---

Savigny was the more widely noted German scholar, he was not nearly as influential as Jhering on modern American legal thought. See also *Jansen and Reimann*, Begriff und Zweck in der Jurisprudenz (2018) 118–126.

[123] *Fuller and Purdue*, The Reliance Interest in Contract Damages (1937); see also *Full*er, Consideration and Form (1941) 800 (fn. 4), 801 (fn. 5); *Kessler and Fine*, *Culpa in Contrahendo* (1964).

[124] See, e.g., *Summers*, Rudolf von Jhering's Influence on American Legal Theory (1996), 70–74; *Rabban*, Jhering's Influence on American Legal Thought (2023) 163–165; *Behrends*, Jhering heute! (2023) 233.

[125] The most celebrated of the articles engaging with Jhering's ideas is *Fuller and Purdue*, The Reliance Interest in Contract Damages (1937). Yet, even here, Jhering's influence is quite limited. To be sure, the opening paragraph is almost pure Jhering in its call to make and construct legal rules with a clear view of their purpose, id 52. The doctrinal substance of the article, however, is overwhelmingly based on American sources. Jhering is discussed and cited on but a few occasions, and his arguments are invoked to lend additional support to the authors' theses and conclusions or to explain particular points, see id. 86–87 (fn. 54–55), 361 (fn. 101); 411–412 (fn. 208); 416 (fn. 219), etc. While it is true that the article itself was highly influential on the development of the American law of damages, see *Behrends,* Jhering heute! (2023) 233 (n. 114), that does not mean Jhering's arguments in particular were crucial in that regard. In fact, the article could have been written quite easily without any references to Jhering. Note that the authors also drew on other German scholars and sources, including the Civil Code (BGB). The same is true for *Fuller*, Consideration and Form (1941) where references to Jhering play a distinctly minor role, especially when compared to the numerous other German sources cited.

lyses were closely tied to Roman law in which few twentieth-century American scholars had any expertise or interest. Scholarship based on classical Roman law could also be considered obsolete once it was superseded even in Germany by the Civil Code (BGB) of 1900. In addition, after World War I, and even more so after 1933, American scholars often viewed German legal ideas with great skepticism because they were associated with a nation whose political image was heavily tarnished.[126]

Engaging with Jhering: A Century-and-a-Half of Discussion. "Even in North America, my writings have enjoyed a wide audience's attention," Jhering proudly wrote to his colleague Oskar von Bülow in 1881, "[A] review of my *Zweck* in an American journal is the most splendid that has ever been published about any of my works."[127] Indeed, some of Jhering's writings were read –and often praised – in the United States in his lifetime. Yet, it was mainly during the generation immediately after his death in 1892 that his ideas were being imported into the United States on a broader scale.

One would expect the major means of transatlantic transmission to be English translations, but these actually played a secondary role. To be sure, "Kampf" appeared in a first English version as early as 1879;[128] a year later, part of the introduction to the second edition of "Geist" as well as some other passages from this work followed suit;[129] and over the next several decades other works were translated into English as well,[130] most importantly, the first volume of "Zweck" (in 1913).[131] Yet, most American scholars who discussed Jhering's ideas had read

---

[126] See infra note 249 and text.

[127] Letter to Bülow of November 11, 1881, Jhering in Briefen (1913) 366, 369. The review appeared in The National Quarterly Review vol. XL of the First Series (which equals vol. VI of the Second Series) (1880) 203–205. The anonymous author first praised "Geist" as a "masterly production," id. 203, then summarized Volume One of "Zweck" in some (confusing) detail, and concluded that it "is undoubtedly the most profound and satisfactory contribution to the science of legal philosophy since the days of Austin and Bentham," id. 205. See also *U.M. Rose*, Controversies of Modern Continental Jurists (part IV, 1876).

[128] *Rudolf von Jhering*, The Struggle for Law (transl. of the 5th ed. by John Lalor, Chicago 1879, 2d ed. Chicago 1915). A second translation followed four years later in England, *Rudolf von Jhering*, The Battle for Right (Philip Arthur Ashworth transl., London 1883).

[129] *B.T.C[rump],* The Value of the Roman Law to the Modern World, Virginia Law Journal 4 (1880) 453–464; *William Hammond*, Note F. The Interpretatio of the Roman Jurists, in *Francis Lieber*, Legal and Political Hermeneutics (W. Hammond ed., St. Louis 1880) 262–275 (condensed translation of Geist II.2., 427, 455).

[130] "Vorgeschichte der Indoeuropäer" (1894) was translated as "The Evolution of the Aryan" (Adolphus Drucker transl., London 1897); and a translation of "Die Jurisprudenz des täglichen Lebens" (1870) was published as "Law in Daily Life" in England (Henry Goudy transl., Oxford 1904). None of these translations had a major impact in the Anglo-American world, however. A latecomer was the (partial) translation of Jhering's sojourn "Im juristischen Begriffshimmel" (1884) by Morris Cohen and Felix Cohen which further popularized the term "heaven of concepts," *Cohen and Cohen* (eds.), Readings on Jurisprudence and Legal Philosophy (1951) 678–689.

[131] *Rudolf von Jhering*, Law as Means to an End (I. Husik transl., Boston 1913). There is no

him either in a French translation (like Holmes) or in the original (like Pound), a knowledge of German being almost *de rigeur* among the elite of American legal scholars in the late nineteenth and early twentieth centuries. Some of these scholars had actually attended German universities, as was quite common at the time. Among them were Munroe Smith (1854–1926) and Christopher Tiedemann (1857–1903) who had both studied with Jhering in Göttingen. Smith, a member of the Columbia Law School faculty, presented Jhering's ideas to a broad American audience in a long, multi-part, essay published 1895–1897; his discussion remains among the best writings about Jhering in English.[132] Tiedemann built on Jhering's ideas in his highly influential treatise on US constitutional law.[133] In addition, there were scholars who had never been to Germany but who also read Jhering in the original; the most important of these jurists was Roscoe Pound (1870–1964), who became the primary importer of Jhering's ideas in the United States.[134] As a result, Jhering and his works were widely known and cited in the United States in the late nineteenth and early twentieth centuries: several of his books were reviewed (sometimes very negatively);[135] his death in 1892 was duly noted;[136] and in 1914, he was included a volume on the "Great Jurists of the World" published in Boston.[137] As a result, by World War I, Jhering's ideas were common currency in American jurisprudence[138] with spillover effects into political science, especially in the work of Arthur F. Bentley (1870–1957).[139]

English translation of "Geist," however, so that it had to be read either in the original German or one of the available French (or other language) translations.

[132] *Smith*, Four German Jurists (1895–1897); for a succinct summary, see *Rabban*, Jhering's Influence on American Legal Thought (2023) 149–151; see also *Smith*, Review of Rudolph von Jhering, Law as a Means to an End (1915).

[133] *Tiedemann*, The Unwritten Constitution of the United States (1890); see infra notes 196–197 and text.

[134] See infra notes 199–224 and text.

[135] *Anon*, Review of Jhering, Der Zweck im Recht (1880); *Cohen*, Evolution of the Aryan (review, 1899); *Cohen*, Law as a Means to an End (review, 1914). Both of Cohen's reviews were highly critical.

[136] See the eulogy by *Rivier*, Rudolph von Jhering and Bernhard Windscheid (1893). The author noted that he "had the privilege in the month of June of last year [1992] to pass with him at Göttingen three days, which I shall never forget," id. 7.

[137] *MacDonnell and Manson* (eds.), Great Jurists of the World (1914) 588–599. The book lists a total of 26 jurists since antiquity. The only other German included is Savigny.

[138] American readers could also resort to articles published in England, see, e.g., *J.M.*, Rudolf von Jhering (1908) (likening Jhering to Montesquieu); *Kenny*, Jhering on Trinkgeld and Tips (1916).

[139] In a widely noted book, Bentley presented a thorough and thoughtful discussion and critique of the social and political theory Jhering had developed in "Zweck;" *Bentley*, The Process of Government (1908) 56–91. Bentley expressed great admiration for Jhering as a "master", id. 57, considered him superior to Spencer, id. 56, and found much to praise in Jhering's ideas, id., 83. In the main, however, he levelled a lethal epistemological critique at Jhering's work. He analyzed Jhering's use of the concepts "Zweck" and "Interesse" in painstaking detail and concluded that "his theory of 'Zweck' is merely a mess of words." It is,

Around the time of the Great War and in the 1920s, Jhering was still much admired in the United States,[140] but the focus shifted from discussing his ideas in and of themselves to using them as arguments in the general jurisprudential debates of the times.[141] In the interwar period, prominent scholars continued to refer to Jhering in a variety of contexts and for a variety of purposes[142] but rarely focused directly on him and his work.[143] Thus, Jhering remained on the American jurisprudential radar screen even though his ideas were no longer a novelty and no longer an object of outright fascination.

In second half of the twentieth century, Jhering's fame in America waned. To be sure, his ideas were included in the standards works on jurisprudence[144] and sometimes referred to in particular contexts,[145] but they were no longer discussed on a broader scale. A noteworthy exception is an article by philosopher Iredell Jenkins, published in 1960, that provides an extraordinarily thorough and per-

---

Bentley continued, "merely one great elaborate pun upon the word 'Zweck', and as a theory entitled to no more scientific respect than any other pun," id. 83. The deeper reason was not a lack of acumen or insight, Bentley opined; instead, Jhering had "set himself a fictitious and hence insoluble problem," id. 90. As a result, Jhering had asked questions that could not be meaningfully answered. On Bentley, see *Herget*, American Jurisprudence (1990) 160–162.

[140] Praise came also from English jurists published in the United States, see *Lamm*, Introduction (1921) xxvi ("If he is not a god, he is at least a half-god (and a very good one at that) in philosophy"); *Geldart*, Introduction (1921) xxxvi ("Jhering is a legal philosopher of the first rank, the greatest thinker on law whom Germany has produced since Savigny.").

[141] An early example is *Gray*, The Nature and Sources of Law (1909) which cited Jhering numerous times in specific contexts (and not always with approval), see id. 18, 30–37, 61–64, 171, 297–298, 318. John Chipman Gray, who was widely read in nineteenth century German legal scholarship, referenced Jhering along with more than a dozen other German jurists, including Gierke, Savigny, Thibaut, and Windscheid. See also *Cohen*, The Place of Logic in the Law (1916) 622, 633, 636 (repeatedly referencing Jhering in the context of defending the need for (deductive) logic in legal reasoning).

[142] See, e.g., *Pound*, The Spirit of the Common Law (1921) 203–205; *Cohen*, Transcendental Nonsense and the Functional Approach (1935) 809–810; *Fuller and Purdue*, The Reliance Interest in Contract Damages (1937) (see supra note 125); *Radin*, Law as Logic and Experience (1940) 92, 142–144.

[143] An exception was the article by *Seagle*, Rudolf von Jhering, or Law as a Means to an End (1945). The article provides an overview of Jhering's life, major works, and principal ideas, but it is entirely unoriginal, mostly superficial, and replete with inaccuracies.

[144] *Pound*, Jurisprudence I (1959) 130–142; *Friedman*, Legal Theory (1967) 321–325; *Sinha*, Jurisprudence (1993) 221–223.

[145] See e.g., *Frank*, Civil Law Influence on the Common Law (1956) 891–93; *Summers*, Instrumentalism and American Legal Theory (1892) 28, 176, 268; *Alschuler*, Law Without Values (2000) 92, 144. Remarkably, Duncan Kennedy, the most prominent leader of the Critical Legal Studies movement, professed to Jhering's influence on him as a young scholar; Kennedy had read Jhering in the same French translation used by Holmes a century earlier; see *Kennedy*, The Rise and Fall of Classical Legal Theory (2006/1975) IX. In a later article, Kennedy called Jhering "unutterly brilliant" and his discussion of the issue at stake much superior to Kennedy's erstwhile hero Lon Fuller; *Kennedy*, From the Will Theory to the Principles of Party Autonomy (2000) 104 fn. 29.

ceptive analysis of Jhering's theory of law in "Zweck" and that is still worth reading today.[146] More recently, there have been some writings about Jhering but they did not seek – and have not interested – a broad audience.[147] It is fair to say that today, most American legal scholars would not recognize Jhering's name, and even among legal philosophers and theorists, few have more than a passing familiarity with his ideas.[148]

The reason why Jhering is no longer a household name in contemporary American jurisprudence is not, however, that his ideas have become irrelevant. It is rather that as a result of their early influence, they have been absorbed into the mainstream of American legal thought.[149] That influence has been long and widely noted, but it has rarely been explored in depth.[150]

Between ca. 1880 and 1940, American legal thought underwent a fundamental reorientation: it abandoned the combination of natural law precepts with analytical jurisprudence and instead embraced what Robert Summers aptly termed "pragmatic instrumentalism."[151] This process can be divided into three phases:

---

[146] *Jenkins*, Rudolf von Jhering (1960).

[147] Mc*Laughlin*, The Unification of Germany: What Would Jhering Say? (1994); *Angle*, Should We All be More English? (2000); see also, on the English side, *Hart*, Jhering's Heaven of Concepts and Modern Analytical Jurisprudence (1970); *Duxbury*, Jhering's Philosophy of Authority (2007); *Cotterrell*, The Struggle for Law (2009) 380.

[148] There are exceptions, of course, prominently among them Robert Gordon (Yale), Duncan Kennedy (Harvard), David Rabban (University of Texas), Brian Tamanaha (Washington University), and James Whitman (Yale). Many more recent works on the history of American law and legal thought do not deal with Jhering, see, e.g., *Lawrence Friedman*, A History of American Law (New York 1973, 4th ed. 2019); *Lawrence Friedman*, American Law in the Twentieth Century (New Haven 2002); *William LaPiana*, Logic and Experience. The Origins of Modern American Legal Education (New York 1994).

[149] See infra notes 275–399 and text.

[150] In the German literature, Jhering's influence on American legal thought was noted in passing already in 1956 by *Josef Esser*, Grundsatz und Norm in der richterlichen Rechtsfortbilding (1956) 48 fn. 159. Since then, it was explored in somewhat greater detail by *Zweigert*, Jherings Bedeutung für die Entwicklung der rechtsvergleichenden Methode (1970); *Fikentscher*, Methoden des Rechts I (1975) 483–490; II (1975) 170–171, 279; III (1976) 268, 483–490; *Behrends*, Rudolf von Jhering (1818–1892). Der Durchbruch zum Zweck des Rechts (1987) 229; *Behrends*, Jherings Rechtsdenken (1996) 296, 319. For a more extensive discussion, see *Jansen and Reimann*, Begriff und Zweck in der Jurisprudenz (2018) 118–126. There are many acknowledgements of Jhering's influence on US legal thought in the American literature as well, see, e.g., *Frank*, A Conflict of Oblivion (1954) 443 (note 87); *Friedman*, Legal Theory (1967) 324–325; *Kelley*, A Critical Analysis of Holmes's Theory of Contract (2000) 1690 n. 26; *Seagle*, Men of Law (1947) 328–329; Summers, Instrumentalism and American Legal Theory (1982) 28; *Tamanaha*, Law a Means to an End (2006) 3–4, 61–62. A more detailed account is *Summers*, Rudolf von Jhering's Influence on American Legal Theory (1996). As mentioned, to date the most comprehensive analysis is *Rabban*, Jhering's Influence on American Legal Thought (2023). The following discussion builds on some of these earlier works even though it pursues largely its own course.

[151] *Summers*, Pragmatic Instrumentalism in Twentieth Century American Legal Thought (1980–81); see also *Alschuler*, Law Without Values (2000) 2 ("utilitarian pragmatism"). A

the initial departure from established paradigms in the late nineteenth century which was triggered by the work of Oliver Wendell Holmes; the establishment of a new, "sociological," jurisprudence mainly by both Roscoe Pound and Benjamin Cardozo in the early twentieth century; and the emergence of legal realism in the interwar period of which Karl Llewellyn was the most notorious representative. In all three phases, Jhering's ideas played important, albeit varying, roles.

The Late-Nineteenth Century Departure: Jhering and Holmes. In a sense, modern American legal thought was born on March 3, 1881 – the day when Oliver Wendell Holmes's (1841–1935) "The Common Law" was published.[152] The book was not only Holmes's *magnum opus*, it was also one of the most influential works of American jurisprudence. To appreciate its (and its author's) significance, as well as Jhering's role in this context, one has to understand the status of American legal thought at the time.

In late-nineteenth century America, there were essentially three schools of jurisprudence. The first and oldest was the natural law approach. It was the heritage of the founding days of the Republic when continental natural law thinkers had profoundly shaped political and constitutional thought and also, in conjunction with Lockean ideas, the understanding of private law, in particular of property rights. Though past its peak, this natural law thinking still lingered in Holmes's day. The most prominent legal methodology at the time, however, was analytical jurisprudence which had its roots in England, especially in the work of John Austin (1790–1859). As an import, it became the most powerful methodological paradigm in the post-bellum period. Connected to German Pandectist legal science through Austin,[153] it shared many crucial features with mid- and late-nineteenth century German "Begriffsjurisprudenz," such as a belief in the power of abstract and general legal concepts, in logical reasoning, and in systematic ordering of (mainly private) law.[154] The third, and most recent, approach was the Anglo-American version of the Historical School. It had its direct roots in the ideas of Jhering's English contemporary Henry Sumner Maine (1822–1888)[155] but also took much guidance from its German variety. In the United States, it came into its own in the closing decades of the nineteenth century.[156]

---

sophisticated German study of two of the main components, i.e., sociological jurisprudence and legal realism, is *Reich*, Soziologische Rechtstheorie und legal realism im Rechtsdenken Amerikas (1967).

[152] *DeWolf Howe*, Justice Oliver Wendell Holmes I (1957) 135.

[153] *Schwartz*, John Austin and the German Jurisprudence of His Time (1934); *Vogenauer*, An Empire of Light (2005).

[154] This does not mean that (Anglo-American) analytical jurisprudence and (German) *Begriffsjurisprudenz* were identical in all regards; for an analysis of their differences, see *Hart*, Jhering's Heaven of Concepts and Modern Analytical Jurisprudence (1970) 73–78.

[155] On Jhering and Maine, see chapter V.4., notes 152–186 and text.

[156] The definitive study is *Rabban*, Law's History (2013). For a short account, see *Reimann*, Historical Jurisprudence (2018) 402–403.

For present purposes, we can leave aside Holmes's position vis-a-vis the third approach; it is true that Holmes was one the founders of (Anglo-American) historical jurisprudence[157] but that role was scarcely linked to Jhering's ideas[158], and the Historical School ultimately had but a minor influence on twentieth century American legal thought.[159] What does connect Holmes to Jhering, and what did hugely influence twentieth-century legal thought in the United States, was Holmes's position vis-a-vis the first and second schools of thought – as well as his advocacy for an alternative: Holmes categorically rejected the natural law approach with its lack of separation between ethics and law, and he staunchly opposed a jurisprudence that was based on abstract concepts, endorsed strictly logical reasoning, and pursued a perfect systematic order. Like Jhering's depiction of Puchta as the icon of "conceptual jurisprudence," Holmes's portrait of contemporary American legal thought was somewhat of a caricature; and like Jhering's diatribes against "Begriffsjurisprudenz," Holmes's attack on "logic" served the purpose of presenting himself as the savior from pernicious beliefs and methods.[160] Thus, Holmes advocated a new jurisprudence that was conscious of the realities and needs of social life, recognized law as the result of social struggle, and was oriented towards social interests.[161] In summary, Holmes took essentially the same positions towards contemporary American legal thought that Jhering took in the context of German jurisprudence (after around 1860): both Jhering and Holmes were vigorous critics of natural law and of abstract legal logic as well as equally vigorous advocates for an interest-oriented and realist jurisprudence. In these respects, Holmes was essentially the American Jhering.

[157] In fact, by far most of the "The Common Law" is concerned with legal history, in particular with tracing the roots of fundamental modern doctrines to their origins in the past.

[158] To be sure, Holmes shared with Jhering a focus on legal history as well as the conviction that modern law had to be understood against the backdrop of its past; they both also believed that understanding the law's historical roots could liberate the present from the shackles of the past and thus foster modern law-making according to present-day social needs. Yet, for Jhering, these ideas were a reaction against the German Historical School in early- and mid-nineteenth century Germany, see supra chapter II.6., while Holmes was particularly inspired by Maine's "Ancient Law" (1861). Jhering and Holmes also worked in different contexts. Jhering built on the heritage of the Roman law for the civil law tradition. Holmes' agenda, especially in "The Common Law," was to demonstrate that the Anglo-American law had Germanic, not Roman, roots.

[159] The issue of the common law's historical origins was a major bone of contention among jurists in the common law orbit in the closing decades of the nineteenth century, see *Graziadei*, Changing Images of the Law in XIX Century English Legal Thought (1993) 116–163; yet, the issue went quickly out of fashion in the early twentieth century; today, it is merely of historical interest.

[160] *Hoyos*, Beyond Classical Legal Thought (2013) 89–90; *Tamanaha*, A Realistic Theory of Law (2017) 27–43. On the debate about "legal formalism" in the United States, see also *Meder*, Rudolf von Jhering and the "jurisprudence of concepts' (2023) 174–176.

[161] For an illustrative example, see *Holmes*, The Common Law (1881) 263–264.

It is easy to see why the question whether Holmes was influenced by Jhering is important for our understanding of modern American legal thought: if Holmes was a truly original thinker, then he deserves almost all the credit for the propositions that first put American jurisprudence on its modern track towards "pragmatic instrumentalism."[162] Such has been the long-standing assumption on the American side.[163] If, however, Holmes took his most important credos from Jhering, then credit for the ideas that initialized modern American jurisprudence goes largely to the latter; in that case, Holmes's contribution is mainly that of an importer and popularizer of foreign views. Small wonder, then, that whether, or to what extent, Holmes was influenced by Jhering has been debated by legal scholars on both sides of the Atlantic for many decades.[164] The question is difficult and the answer is not clear beyond cavil.

At the outset we need to be clear that the issue is not whether Holmes knew of Jhering's ideas – he clearly did. In 1879 – exactly when Holmes was working on "The Common Law" – he read both Jhering's "Geist des römischen Rechts" in a French translation and "Kampf um's Recht" in its first English translation.[165] To be sure, Holmes apparently did not read "Der Zweck im Recht" (the first volume of which had appeared only in 1877) so that he was not exposed to the full-blown version of Jhering's instrumentalist approach. Still, from reading "Geist" and "Kampf," Holmes was (or at least should have been) familiar with Jhering's critique of a purely logical method, with his conception of law as the result of struggle between social forces, and with his dramatic switch from a view of (private) law as an emanation of the individual will to a conception of law as an instrument for the protection of social interests.

Of course, the fact that Holmes knew of Jhering's ideas does not mean that he copied them. He could have conceived of them before reading "Geist" and "Kampf" or found them somewhere else. A closer look at the matter shows that the evidence for influence by Jhering on Holmes is conflicting: on the one hand, several observations suggest that Holmes did adopt some of Jhering's most fundamental insights. On the other hand, there are various other sources on which Holmes drew or at least could have drawn.

---

[162] *Summers*, Instrumentalism and American Legal Theory (1982) 20–26.

[163] See, e.g., *DeWolfe Howe*, Introduction (1963) XIX.

[164] See, e.g., *Behrends*, note 96 to Jhering, Ist die Jurisprudenz eine Wissenschaft (1868/1998) 81–82; *Behrends*, Jhering heute! (2023) 239–240; *Fikentscher*, Methoden des Rechts II (1975) 170–172; id. III (1976) 268; *Hart*, Jhering's Heavon of Concepts (1970) 69; *Howe*, Justice Oliver Wendell Holmes II (1963) 152; *Rabban*, Jhering's Influence on American Legal thought (2023) 153–157, *Reimann*, Holmes' '*Common Law*' and German Legal Science (1992) 101–103; *Stein,* Logic and Experience (1979) 437*;* *Summers*, Rudolf von Jhering's Influence on American Legal Theory (1996); *Zweigert and Siehr*, Jhering's Influence on the Development of Comparative Legal Method (1971) 225–226. On the significance of Jhering and Holmes in the development of legal thought, see also *Tamanaha*, A Realistic Theory of Law (2017) 19–21.

[165] Holmes kept a list of the books he read; see *Little*, The Early Readings of Justice Oliver Wendell Holmes (1954) 2, 200, 202.

The evidence suggesting a direct influence consists mainly of the striking similarity not only of fundamental ideas but also, in several instances, of how they were expressed. As has been pointed out by various other observers,[166] this is true, for example, for Holmes' most famous statement in "The Common Law."

"The life of the law has not been logic; it has been experience. The felt necessities of the time, the prevalent moral and political theories, institutions of public policy, avowed or unconscious, even the prejudices that judges share with their fellow-men, have a good deal more to do than the syllogisms in determining the rules by which men should be governed."[167]

Sixteen years before Holmes, Jhering had put the essentially the same idea in similar terms in Volume Three of "Geist" – which Holmes had just read:

"What must be realized is not what logic commands but what life, commerce, and the feeling of justice postulate, whether it logically necessary or impossible."[168]

Note that Holmes did not postulate that logic had no place in the law whatsoever, he just considered it a "fallacy" to believe "that the only force at work in the development of law is logic;"[169] instead, "others tools are [also] needed."[170] This was essentially Jhering's post-"conversion" conviction as well. He was in full agreement with Holmes that "[it] is something to show that the consistency of a system requires a particular result, but it is not all."[171]

Further similarities abound. Consider Holmes's call to refer every legal rule "articulately and definitely to an end which it subserves"[172] and Jhering's conception of law as means to an end. Compare Holmes' critique of the "notion that a given system [...] cannot be worked out like mathematics"[173] with Jhering's rejection of the "cult of logic that seeks to elevate jurisprudence to a mathematics of law."[174] Like Jhering, Holmes saw the main driving force of human conduct in "justifiable self-preference;"[175] like Jhering, Holmes recognized that "[m]any things which we take for granted have had to be laboriously fought out or thought out in past times;"[176] like Jhering, Holmes, opined that "[l]aw, being a practical thing, must found itself of actual forces;"[177] and like Jhering, Holmes

[166] See, e.g., *Summers*, Rudolf von Jhering's Influence on American Legal Thought (1996) 63.

[167] *Holmes*, The Common Law (1881) 5.

[168] *Jhering*, Geist III (1865) 302–303.

[169] *Holmes*, The Path of the Law (1897) 465.

[170] *Holmes*, The Common Law (1881) 5.

[171] *Holmes*, The Common Law (1881) 5. The similarity between Jhering's and Holmes's attitude towards logic in the law was already duly noted by *Cohen*, The Place of Logic in the Law (1916) 622.

[172] *Holmes*, The Path of the Law (1897) 186.

[173] *Holmes*, The Path of the Law (1897) 465.

[174] *Jhering*, Geist III (1865) 302.

[175] *Holmes*, The Common Law (1881) 38.

[176] *Holmes*, The Common Law (1881) 6.

[177] *Holmes*, The Common Law (1881) 168.

considered legal rules that cannot be enforced "empty words."[178] In addition, there are reasons to believe that Holmes adopted several more specific ideas that he had encountered in Jhering's "Geist."[179]

In light of these similarities, it is tempting to conclude that the case for Jhering's influence on Holmes is open and shut. Yet, closer inspection reveals that the matter is considerably more complicated because there are several arguments pointing the other way.

The weakest of these arguments is that Holmes's failure to mention Jhering in connection with his call for an instrumentalist and realist jurisprudence indicates that Holmes was not aware of Jhering's ideas.[180] The argument is exceedingly dubious. Holmes was generally notorious for his reluctance to acknowledge intellectual debts.[181] Perhaps more importantly, in the particular context of "The Common Law," there is good reason to belief that Holmes was guilty of willful silence. This requires some explanation. A major goal of Holmes's campaign against the purely logical method was to save his beloved common law from the detrimental influence of German idealist philosophy (especially of Kant and Hegel) and of the conceptualist Roman law scholarship that built on it.[182] Holmes thus openly attacked German Pandectist doctrine as the most prominent manifestation of a speculative and abstractly logical jurisprudence.[183] Notably, he presented Jhering, along with Bruns, Puchta, Windscheid, and others, as a representative of that pernicious approach.[184] This was, of course, quite proper with

---

[178] *Holmes*, The Path of the Law (1897) 460.

[179] Holmes's famous theory that the law often grows by filling old forms with new content closely resembles Jhering's like observations about ancient Roman law, see *Reimann*, Historische Schule und Common Law (1993) 102–103. In a similar vein, there are striking similarities between Holmes' claim that common law judges are usually guided by (often unarticulated) social needs and policies and Jhering's discourse on the Roman lawyers' preference for practically sensible results over literal application of rules; see *Frank*, Civil Law Influence on the Common Law (1956) 891–893; *Frank*, A Conflict of Oblivion (1954) 443 fn. 87. Borrowing is also suggested by a comparison between Holmes's texts at different stages of their development: when Holmes turned earlier essays into chapters of "The Common Law" after having read "Geist," he added elements that are virtually identical to Jhering's ideas; see *Kelley*, A Critical Analysis of Holmes's' Theory of Contract (2000) 1690 fn. 26.

[180] *Fikentscher*, Methoden des Rechts II (1975) 170–171. In a similar vein, Holmes' biographer Mark DeWolfe Howe argued that "there is no indication that [Holmes] ever recognized" how much of an ally Jhering was to him; *DeWolfe Howe*, Justice Oliver Wendell Holmes II (1963) 152.

[181] *DeWolfe Howe*, Justice Oliver Wendell Holmes II (1963) 71–72, 84–85. For example, Holmes basically refused to acknowledge the debt he owed, especially in "The Common Law," to Maine's "Ancient Law"; see *DeWolfe Howe*, Introduction (1963) XIV; see also *White*, Justice Oliver Wendell Holmes (1995) 115, 146, 194.

[182] His more important, and somewhat hidden, target, however, was the contemporary jurisprudence of (Harvard dean) Christopher Columbus Langdell and his cohort; see *Reimann*, Holmes's 'Common Law' and German Legal Science (1992).

[183] See *Holmes*, The Common Law (1881), Lecture IV. Possession, especially 163–173.

[184] *Holmes*, The Common Law (1881) 163. The passage concerns Holmes' discussion of the

regard to the early Jhering. Interestingly, however, Holmes never mentioned that the later Jhering (i.e., the author of the third volume of "Geist" and of "Kampf") had been fighting against the German Romanists' love affair with Hegelian logic every bit as hard as Holmes now did himself. In other words, while Holmes mentioned the Jhering in the enemy camp, he made no mention of the Jhering who was actually his (almost perfect) ally.[185] Of course, people sometimes encounter ideas in the work of others, then forget their source, and come to assume that these ideas are their own creation. In Holmes's case, this is extremely unlikely. For one thing, Holmes read "Kampf" and "Geist" precisely when he was working on "The Common Law."[186] For another, Holmes actually did cite Jhering's "Geist" on several occasions (at times with approval) – though only with regard to some points of early Roman law or specific doctrinal issues.[187] Thus, Holmes was fully aware of what he had read in Jhering's works, often all the way down to minute detail. All this suggests that Holmes's failure to cite Jhering for other, more fundamental, propositions was intentional.[188] Remaining silent about Jhering's ideas allowed Holmes to present his own jurisprudential credos as entirely original.

Still, there are three other, much more plausible, arguments against Holmes being influenced by Jhering.

First, and perhaps most importantly, there is evidence that Holmes had conceived of his social and instrumentalist view of law to some extent before he read Jhering. In a short note published in 1873, Holmes already expressed skepticism vis-a-vis "logical deductions from axioms;" opined that "self-preference" is at the root of all human action; referred to conflicts between "interests" of "different parts of a community;" presented "the struggle for life" as "the law of human existence;" and saw legislation as the expression of "the more powerful interests."[189] At that time, these ideas were just briefly mentioned and still inchoate, but they were already at least vaguely on Holmes's mind.

---

issue of Possession. Holmes refers to "the speculative jurists of Germany, from Savigny to Ihering" who "have been at once professors of Roman law, and profoundly influenced, if not controlled by some form of Kantian or post-Kantian philosophy. Thus everything has combined to give a special bent to German speculation." Id. The claim that Jhering was "controlled by some form of Kantian or post-Kantian philosophy" was at minimum careless and dubious; see chapter I.1., notes 27–30 and text.

[185] When Holmes called Jhering "a man of genius," he did so in the context of discussing a particular point of the law of possession, not with regard to Jhering's jurisprudential ideas; *Holmes*, The Common Law (1881) 165.

[186] The same point is made is by *Behrends*, Das 'Rechtsgefühl' in der historisch-kritischen Rechtstheorie des späten Jhering (1996) 81–82 fn. 96.

[187] *Holmes*, The Common Law (1881) 15 fn. 33; 165–166; 258 fn. 25; 276 fn. 34.

[188] This conclusion is shared by *Rabban*, Jhering's Influence on American Legal Thought (2023) 153.

[189] *Holmes*, Summary of Events: The Gas Stokers' Strike (1873).

Second, when Holmes wrote "The Common Law," there were three broader intellectual trends from which he could, and did, derive inspiration. To begin with, Darwinism, much in vogue after the publication of "The Origin of Species" (1859), proffered the concept of struggle between competing interests and of evolution more broadly not only to Jhering but also to Holmes, inter alia through Herbert Spencer (to whom Holmes repeatedly referred). Furthermore, English utilitarianism, especially the work of Bentham and Mill, engaged not only Jhering's thought but also, and probably even more strongly, Holmes's approach to jurisprudence, pushing them both towards a consequentialist view of law.[190] Finally, Holmes's thought was strongly shaped by the philosophy of pragmatism, which had emerged in his most immediate environment.[191] Pragmatism was perhaps the most powerful philosophical source of Holmes's skepticism vis-a-vis abstract (Kantian and Hegelian) logic and of his commitment to an instrumentalist conception of law.[192]

Third, there was the common law's traditional and deeply-rooted skepticism towards lofty theorizing, speculative reasoning, abstract concepts, and logical systems. As a dyed-in-the-wool common lawyer, Holmes shared this skepticism and articulated it in particularly poignant and memorable form. In this regard, Holmes did not really break new ground but rather re-validated what he considered traditional notions of (common law) reasoning and, in particular, judging.

Considering these counterarguments, it is tempting to conclude that Jhering's ideas probably did not have much impact on Holmes at all. Apparently, reading Jhering's writings just confirmed what Holmes had known and thought and felt all along as a Darwinian, utilitarian, pragmatist, and common lawyer. To put it differently: contrary to what was said above, Holmes's reading of Jhering did not really matter.

In short, we have weighty arguments both for and against the proposition that Holmes' fundamental ideas were influenced by Jhering.[193] These two positions are easily reconciled, however, if we fine-tune the concept of influence. On the one hand, it is fair to say that Holmes was not influenced by Jhering in the sense that he simply took his fundamental jurisprudential credos from "Kampf" and "Geist." At least in rough outline, these credos predated his reading of these works, and they were rooted in the general intellectual climate of the times as well

---

[190] See *Pohlman*, Justice Oliver Wendell Holmes and Utilitarian Jurisprudence (1984). Interestingly, however, both Jhering and Holmes embraced a "social," rather than "individual" version of utilitarianism.

[191] Holmes was closely acquainted with Charles Saunders Peirce (1839–1914), William James (1842–1910), and others who laid the foundations for pragmatism in the 1870s and 1880s; see *DeWolfe Howe*, Introduction (1963) XIII.

[192] See *DeWolfe Howe,* Justice Oliver Wendell Holmes I (1953) 151.

[193] David Rabban concluded that such influence was "more a probability than a possibility;" *Rabban*, Jhering's Influence on American Legal Thought (2023) 157; in a similar vein id. 156.

as in Holmes' common law predilections. On the other hand, it is also fair to conclude that Holmes was influenced by Jhering in the sense that finding these credos in Jhering's work was very helpful for Holmes's own agenda.[194] It not only confirmed Holmes' commitment to them, Jhering's formulations could also help Holmes further to develop and then more clearly to articulate his conception of an instrumentalist and pragmatist jurisprudence. In short, Jhering was Holmes jurisprudential forerunner, aide, and fellow-traveler. Holmes must have recognized that, and it is not to his credit that he failed to disclose it to his readers.

Jhering's significance for the late-nineteenth century departure of American legal thought to new horizons was not limited to his influence *on* Holmes, however; it also manifested itself in his impact *together with* Holmes: Holmes's impetus for a reorientation of legal thought towards an instrumentalist and pragmatist jurisprudence was fortified and legitimized by Jhering's similar demand. One could of course argue that Holmes's ideas would have prevailed even without any help from Jhering, and that may well be true. That help was still significant for two reasons. First, at the time, Jhering carried more prestige. It is easy to forget that in 1881, Holmes was not yet a major player in the theatre of American law. At that time, he was a (moderately successful) practicing lawyer and occasional author who gave a series of lectures in Boston – prestigious and well-attended lectures to be sure, but not the work of the legal giant Holmes was to become decades later (after his ascent to the US Supreme Court in 1902). Jhering, by contrast, was one of the most prominent representatives of the universally admired and globally leading German legal science, whose works had already been translated into several languages (including English). In colloquial terms: in 1881, Holmes still played in the minor leagues of jurisprudence while Jhering was on the world-team of legal science. Second, Holmes's "The Common Law" contained nothing like a coherent jurisprudential theory; it was largely an historical discourse designed to prove that the common law's roots were Germanic rather than Roman. It is true that its jurisprudential statements became its most important legacy, but in the book, they are actually few and far between and scattered almost randomly throughout the text. By contrast, Jhering's work, especially the eventually much noted first volume of "Zweck," contained a full-blown (albeit somewhat chaotic) instrumentalist theory of law that was superior to Holmes's work in depth and detail. In short, while Holmes merely touched on certain fundamental ideas, Jhering expounded upon them in an entire book.[195]

---

[194] As Robert Summers pointed out, "influence [...] may also take the form of reinforcing an idea already held or the form of articulating an idea better so that it stands more of a chance of survival," *Summers*, Rudolf von Jhering's Influence on American Legal Theory (1996) 62 fn. 2.

[195] It is interesting to speculate how Holmes's "The Common Law" and Jhering's "Der Zweck im Recht" would have fared in the United States had Jhering's book been available in an English translation already in 1881 (rather than three decades later). It is quite possible that Jhering's work would have become the dominant jurisprudential reference for an instru-

In addition, Holmes's conception of law, as the reflection of the struggle between opposing social interests, received indirect support from Jhering via Christopher Tiedemann (1837–1903). As mentioned, Tiedemann had studied in Göttingen in 1877, inter alia, with Jhering,[196] and subsequently became one of the most prominent constitutional law scholars in late nineteenth century America. Especially in "The Unwritten Constitution" of the United States (1890), Tiedemann cited Jhering and propounded his idea that law reflects "the prevalent sense of right" and that it is settled through "a vigorous contest between opposing social forces."[197] Jhering's influence on American legal thought through Tiedemann should not be underrated. While Tiedemann is largely forgotten today, his constitutional law textbooks were hugely successful in his day and far more widely read (especially by law students) in the United States than any of Jhering's own writings, and, for that matter, than Holmes's much more esoteric book.

Thus, Jhering lent significant assistance to the late-nineteenth century departure of American legal thought towards new horizons. The prize for first expounding the fundamental ideas that would shape future legal thought in the United States belongs to Jhering rather than to Holmes. It is simply not true that, as even his biographer Mark DeWolfe Howe stated, Holmes offered "an interpretation of law which no one before him had attempted"[198] – Jhering had beaten Holmes, though just barely. Holmes, in turn, deserves most of the credit for actually initiating the turn of American legal thought towards an instrumentalist and pragmatist conception of law.

The ideas propounded by Holmes in the late nineteenth century eventually developed into the two major (and related) forms of jurisprudence that came to shape twentieth-century American legal thought. Holmes's conception of law – as the result of a struggle between, and as a means for the effectuation of, social interests – became an important foundation of the "sociological jurisprudence" formulated and promoted mainly by Roscoe Pound and Benjamin Cardozo in the first quarter of the new century. Holmes's call for a jurisprudence that was

---

mentalist and realist approach, overshadowing Holmes's book. A major obstacle, however, would have been Jhering's often chaotic, rambling, and thus tiring discourse; see supra chapter IV.2.

[196] See *Tiedemann*, Methods of Legal Education (1891) 151.

[197] *Tiedemann*, The Unwritten Constitution of the United States (1890) 9, 12. In a footnote, Tiedemann provided a quote from "Kampf" which he had translated into English; id. 12, note 1. Tiedemann also propounded various other ideas he had adopted from Jhering, such as the crucial role of the "sense of right" ("Rechtsgefühl"); its development through the avantgarde of "ethical teachers;" the notion that the same social forces shape both moral and legal rules; and the observation that at early stages of legal development the construction of rules tends to be stricter than at later stages; see *Tiedemann*, The Unwritten Constitution of the United States (1890) 7, 9–11, 15, 145 (fn. 1). On Jhering and Tiedemann, see also *Rabban*, Jhering's Influence on American Legal Thought (2023) 152–153.

[198] *DeWolfe Howe*, Introduction (1963) XIX.

empirical – grounded in social facts and oriented towards the actual enforcement of rules – grew into the legal realism associated, inter alia, with Karl Llewellyn, Jerome Frank, and Felix Cohen, that came to dominate avant-garde American legal thought in the 1920s through the 1940s. In both these contexts, Jhering's work remained highly relevant.

The Early Twentieth Century Birth of Sociological Jurisprudence: Pound and Cardozo. Nobody imported Jhering's ideas into the United States more broadly than Roscoe Pound (1870–1954); and nothing incorporated Jhering's ideas more clearly than Pound's "sociological jurisprudence."[199]

As a scholar of vast erudition, a prolific writer, and as the long-time dean of the Harvard Law School (1916–1937), Pound was not just a towering figure in American law for over half a century, he was arguably the most influential legal theorist in American history because his "sociological jurisprudence" shaped modern American legal thought perhaps more than any other paradigm.[200] Pound developed his approach in a series of articles published in the early 1900s.[201] His new position was a reaction not only against the prevailing analytical jurisprudence's operation with abstract concepts and strictly logical reasoning, which Holmes had attacked so severely; Pound also fought against the courts', and especially the US Supreme Court's, practice to strike down progressive social legislation by invoking abstract principles like freedom of contract – most (in)famously in the *Lochner* decision of 1905.[202] For Pound, these decisions were the unfortunate results of a "mechanical jurisprudence" that failed to consider the social and economic problems at stake and sabotaged the reforms necessary in modern industrialized society.[203] In reaction, Pound demanded a shift from viewing law "from within" to studying it "from without"[204], instead of regarding law mainly as a set of principles, doctrines, and rules, it should be understood primarily "as a social institution to satisfy social wants – the claims and demands involved in the existence of civilized society."[205]

It is generally acknowledged that Jhering's influence on Pound's "sociological jurisprudence" was direct and pervasive.[206] Pound was thoroughly familiar with

---

[199] For a lucid summary and analysis of this approach (in German), see *Reich*, Soziologische Rechtstheorie und legal realism (1967) 44–81.

[200] See *Summers*, Rudolf von Jhering's Influence on American Legal Theory (1996) 61.

[201] *Pound*, The Need for a Sociological Jurisprudence (1907); *Pound*, The Scope and Purpose of Sociological Jurisprudence (3 parts, 1911–12).

[202] Lochner v. New York, 184 U.S. 45 (1905) (striking down a New York statute limiting the working hours of bakers (to 10 a day) as a violation of freedom of contract under the fourteenth amendment to the US Constitution.

[203] *Pound*, 'Mechanical Jurisprudence' (1908).

[204] *Pound*, The Spirit of the Common Law (1921) 212.

[205] *Pound*, The Spirit of the Common Law (1921) 99.

[206] *Rabban*, Jhering's Influence on American Legal Thought (2023) 157–160. Jhering has even been called "the father of sociological jurisprudence," *Friedman*, Legal Theory (1967) 325, as well as its "fountain-head," *Kantorowicz*, Some Rationalism about Realism (1934) 1241.

the German philosophical and legal scholarship from Kant to Hegel and from Savigny to Kantorowicz. He had read most of it in the original German[207] – including Jhering's "Zweck." In contrast to Holmes, Pound openly admitted how indebted he was to Jhering as "the pioneer in the work of superseding [the] jurisprudence of conceptions (Begriffsjurisprudenz)."[208] In the second installment of his foundational article in the Harvard Law Review 1911–12, Pound extensively discussed Jhering's "Zweck" and praised its "enduring value for sociological jurisprudence."[209] To be sure, Jhering was not the only source of Pound's new approach. Pound also drew heavily on the German "free law" movement, especially Eugen Ehrlich, Ernst Fuchs, and Hermann Kantorowicz, as well as on Josef Kohler.[210] Like Holmes's ideas, Pound's thinking was also strongly shaped by philosophical pragmatism as the increasingly dominant mode of thought in early twentieth-century America.[211] Still, it is fair to say that with regard to "sociological jurisprudence" proper, Jhering was Pound's primary source of inspiration. His influence is visible in many of Pound's statements and phrases, for example that "the sociological jurisprudence pursues a comparative study of legal systems, legal doctrines, and legal institutions as social phenomena;" that its representatives "look more to the working of the law than to its abstract content;" and that "they regard law as a social institution," laying "stress upon the social purpose which law subserves rather than upon sanction."[212] Pound's postulate that in law we should "be thinking not of an abstract harmonizing of human wills but of a concrete securing and realizing of human interests"[213] is sheer Jhering, as is, by Pound's own admission, his statement that "rights are means conferred by law for securing the interests which it recognizes."[214]

In reading Pound, it becomes quickly obvious, however, that his engagement with Jhering's ideas was not particularly thorough. Pound just adopted Jhe-

[207] Pound had acquired a near native mastery of German as a child.

[208] *Pound*, 'Mechanical Jurisprudence' (1908) 610 (citing both "Zweck" and "Scherz und Ernst" in fn. 19).

[209] *Pound*, The Scope and Purpose of Sociological Jurisprudence (1911) 591; id., (1912) 146. Almost half a century later, Pound again broadly reflected on Jhering's jurisprudence and on the importance of his contribution to the development of modern law, see *Pound*, Jurisprudence I (1959) 130–142.

[210] See *Pound*, The Scope and Purpose of Sociological Jurisprudence (1912) 489–516 (511 fn. 88, 512 fn. 95, 515 fn. 101, 516 fn. 102).

[211] Pound linked his own ideas expressly to pragmatism; see *Pound*, The Scope and Purpose of Sociological Jurisprudence (1912) 516, and he repeatedly cited William James' now classic work, i.e., "Pragmatism" (1907); see *Pound*, 'Mechanical Jurisprudence' (1908) 607 fn. 10, 608 fn. 12, 621 fn. 64.

[212] *Pound*, The Scope and Purpose of Sociological Jurisprudence (1912) 516.

[213] *Pound*, The Spirit of the Common Law (1921) 195–196; see *Jhering*, Geist III (1865) 307–317.

[214] *Pound*, The Spirit of the Common Law (1921) 203–204; see *Jhering*, Geist III (1865) 317.

ring's sociological conception of law – the notion that law serves the protection of social interests, the overall instrumentalism pervading "Zweck" as well as few other ideas. He showed no interest in the intricacies of Jhering's theory of law, society, or the state. In other words, he dealt with "Zweck" on the wholesale, rather than retail, level.[215]

Pound's "sociological jurisprudence" shared five particularly characteristic features with Jhering's thinking. These features are important to note because they cast very long shadows on American legal thought in the twentieth century and beyond.[216] To begin with, Pound shared Jhering's "conception of law as a means to social ends."[217] Like Jhering in "Zweck" – and in fact even more unequivocally – Pound's "sociological jurisprudence" thus focused on law as a tool for purposes beyond itself, not as a realm of substantive justice unto itself. Second, Pound followed Jhering in pointing out that what legal rules say is not necessarily identical to how they work in practice; if we want a true picture of the law, we must constantly subject its concepts and rules to a reality check.[218] Pound cast that insight into the now proverbial distinction between "law on the books and law in action."[219] Third, Pound followed Jhering in viewing law as a result of the struggle between, and an instrument for the realization of, interests; in that sense, Pound's approach was, like Jhering's, a version of a jurisprudence of interests. Fourth, like Jhering, Pound focused not on individual, but rather on social, interests. This preference for society's needs over its various members' concerns was also fully in line with Holmes, who had stated that "justice to the individual is rightly outweighed by the larger interests on the other side of the scale."[220] Both Pound and Holmes thus shared the "social utilitarianism" expounded by Jhering in "Zweck."[221] Finally, Pound endorsed Jhering's idea that this shift from an individualist conception of law to its increasing "socialization"

---

[215] See chapter IV.2., footnotes 377–380 and text. Pound thus had no reason to address the glaring weaknesses of "Zweck" – which did not escape other American readers; see *Bentley*, The Process of Government (1908), supra note 139; *Cohen*, Law as a Means to an End (review, 1914); *Seagle*, Rudolf vom Jhering (1947) 85. Pound did point out some of the weaknesses of Jhering's approach half a century later, see *Pound*, Jurisprudence I (1959) 138–141.

[216] See infra notes 275–300 and text.

[217] *Pound*, The Spirit of the Common Law (1921) 205.

[218] Jhering had explained early-on that "there is no complete congruence between the objective law as it actually lives and works and its manifestation in the form of legal rules (we could also call them the theory of law)," so that we must not "identify the law at any given time with the legal rules"; see *Jhering*, Geist I (1852) 20, 22.

[219] *Pound*, Law in Books and Law in Action (1910).

[220] *Holmes*, The Common Law (1881) 41. Reflecting his own experience in the Civil War, Holmes put this credo into stark terms: "No society has ever admitted that it could not sacrifice individual welfare to its own existence. If conscripts are necessary for its army, it seizes them, and marches them, with bajonets in their rear, to death." Id.

[221] Supra chapter IV.2., notes 316–349 and text.

was the hallmark of progress,[222] a conviction also shared by Holmes.[223] Thus, Pound considered it Jhering's great contribution to legal science that he had overcome the individualism of earlier forms of jurisprudence and developed a "social theory of law" fit for the modern age.[224] In short, in large part as a result of Jhering's influence, Pound's sociological jurisprudence embodied a conception of law that was instrumentalist, reality-oriented, interest-focused, collectivist, and trusting in social progress.

Three early twentieth-century American judges have long been associated with putting Pound's (and thus Jhering's) sociological conception of law to work in practice: Holmes, Brandeis, and Cardozo. Oliver Wendell Holmes and Louis Dembitz Brandeis (1856–1941) were among the most celebrated justices on the US Supreme Court where they often worked in tandem against the conceptualism, abstractly logical reasoning, and the resulting social conservatism still common in the early-twentieth century judiciary.[225] Important as they were for the development of American law, we can leave Holmes and Brandeis to one side here since as justices, neither paid any attention to Jhering. Cardozo, however, is a different story because he did.

Benjamin Nathan Cardozo (1870–1938) was one of the giants on the American bench in the first third of the twentieth century. His fame rests not so much on his fairly short term on the US Supreme Court (as Holmes's successor, 1932–1938); instead, it is primarily due to his decisions as a judge on the Court of Appeals of New York (1914–1932), the highest court of the then most important American jurisdiction. In this capacity, Cardozo rendered several path-breaking common law decisions in which he openly embraced a sociological approach to law and unabashedly shaped rules according to the needs of contemporary society.[226] Yet, Cardozo's most significant contribution to the development of American legal theory is his book "The Nature of the Judicial Process." The slim volume was a fruit of the prestigious Storr's Lectures which Cardozo gave at Yale University in 1921. It soon became a classic of American jurisprudence and thus deserves a closer look.[227]

---

[222] *Pound*, The Spirit of the Common Law (1921) 195; for Jhering, see chapter V.3., notes 181–186 and text.

[223] See *DeWolfe Howe*, Introduction (1963) XXVI.

[224] *Pound*, The Spirit of the Common Law (1921) 204–205.

[225] Holmes and Brandeis overlapped on the Supreme Court 1916–1932. Holmes's most well-known pronouncements in that regard are found in his dissent in the *Lochner* case, where he opined that "[g]eneral propositions do not decide concrete cases," and where he emphasized the "right of a majority to embody their opinion in law," 195 U.S. 75–76. Brandeis has been celebrated mainly for his reliance on social science and social facts rather than legal doctrine, initially in writing briefs as a practicing lawyer ("Brandeis brief"), most famously in the Supreme Court case Muller v. Oregon, 208 US 412 (1908).

[226] The most well-known example is MacPherson v. Buick Motor Co., 111 N.E. 1050, 217 N.Y. 382 (1916) which laid the foundations for modern product liability law.

[227] *Cardozo*, The Nature of the Judicial Process (1921). The book is still available in mod-

While Jhering, Pound, and Holmes (as the author of "The Common Law") were more broadly concerned with the history and theory of law, Cardozo focused – as the title of his lectures indicates – primarily on judicial decisionmaking. His central thesis was that courts not only find and then apply the law, as had been the traditional myth in the Anglo-American tradition, but that they actually make and develop it. According to Cardozo, this was not only inevitable but also desirable because the common law had to keep pace with changing social realities and fulfill newly arising needs. Thus the most prominent common law judge of the time openly presented the courts as progressive lawmaking institutions.[228] Moreover, Cardozo admitted that in adjudication, the judge's subjective sense of justice as well as various other, perhaps even unconscious, factors played an important role.[229] From the perspective of the mainstream of common lawyers, this was heresy.

The obvious similarities with the "free law" movement are no accident. Cardozo drew heavily – and openly – on the writings of its members, not only on the German, but also on the French, side.[230] In a sense, Cardozo used the ideas of these continental authors as building blocks for an American version of the school.[231] Here, Jhering's thought merely lurked in the background.[232]

However, Cardozo called on judges not only to be creative lawmakers, he also demanded that they overcome their doctrinal and formalistic reasoning in favor of a pragmatic and sociological approach – in Holmes's terms: that they rely less on logic and more on experience. In this regard, Cardozo was a faithful follower of Pound and, thus, indirectly of Jhering. In addition, he relied on Jhering directly: advocating the "method of sociology," Cardozo mentioned especially the concept of law as a means to an end which was "Jhering's great contribution to the theory of jurisprudence."[233]

---

ern editions. Some of the book's leading ideas, especially regarding the creative function of the judge, were already touched on decade earlier by *Gray*, The Nature and Sources of Law (1909).

[228] See, e.g., *Cardozo*, The Nature of the Judicial Process (1921) 115

[229] See, e.g., *Cardozo*, The Nature of the Judicial Process (1921) 11–12, 117.

[230] Especially in Lecture III. The Method of Sociology. The Judge as a Legislator. On the German side, Cardozo cited mainly "Flavius" (i.e., Kantorowicz), (Johann Georg) Gmelin, and (Lorenz) Bruett, as well as, with regard to contemporary legal philosophy more broadly, (Fritz) Berolzheimer, (Josef) Kohler, and (Rudolf) Stammler; on the French side, he relied primarily on (Francois) Gény and (Raymond) Saleilles. Similar citations appear in *Cardozo*, The Paradoxes of Legal Science (1928). Excerpts from the writing of these and other European authors had been made available in English translations in The Science of Legal Method (1917).

[231] Cardozo of course addressed a tradition mainly of case law, not of statutes, and certainly not of codification. With regard to legislation, he was careful enough to adopt only the more moderate claims of the "free law" adherents. He asked judges to fill gaps in statutes but objected to deciding *contra legem*, *Cardozo*, The Nature of the Judicial Process (1921) 129.

[232] See supra 1., notes 36–37 and text.

[233] *Cardozo*, The Nature of the Judicial Process (1921) 102 fn. 9 (citing "Der Zweck im Recht"). There is also a long quotation from "Zweck;" id. 115–116. (fn. 23).

Thus, Cardozo's ideal method of judging breathed the spirit of Holmes, Pound, and Jhering: the courts should understand law in light of the purposes it has to serve;[234] they need to address the conflicting interests underlying the disputes before them; and they must employ it as a means to the end of the "welfare of society."[235] Cardozo's request to his contemporaries, and especially his judicial colleagues, essentially summarized Jhering's basic postulate: "[I]t is not of logical deduction, it is rather of social needs, that we are to ask the solution."[236]

Cardozo's familiarity with, and high regard for, Jhering is also illustrated by a reference in one of his judicial opinions. Hotel personnel had accused a guest of making repeated and unwarranted complaints; since this accusation took place in front of other patrons, the guest sued the hotel for injuring his reputation. In response to the lawsuit, the hotel argued, inter alia, that the defendant had suffered at most trivial harm so that it was wrong for him to sue. Cardozo disagreed:

> "To enforce one's rights when they are violated is never a legal wrong, and may often be a moral duty [...] the law, which creates a right, can certainly not concede that insistence upon its enforcement is evidence of a wrong. A great jurist, Rudolf von Jhering, in his "Struggle for Law,"[...] maintains the thesis that the individual owes the duty to himself and to society never to permit a legal right wantonly to be infringed. [...] The plaintiff chose to resist a wrong which, if it may seem trivial to some, must have seemed substantial to him [...]."[237]

Cardozo thus found for the plaintiff – in part on the authority of Jhering.

The Rise of Legal Realism in the 1930s: Karl Llewellyn (et al.). The second major branch of twentieth-century American jurisprudence that grew out of (inter alia) Holmes's late-nineteenth century ideas was legal realism. Arising in the late 1920s, peaking in the 1930s, and then partially absorbed into the mainstream of American legal thought in and beyond the 1940s, legal realism was not a clearly defined, uniform, and monolithic theory but rather a cluster of more or less interrelated ideas. These ideas were shared by a loosely affiliated group of legal scholars who developed them in various directions and whose positions on a multitude of issues ranged from moderate to iconoclastic.[238] The movement was so broad and diverse that any general statements about it inevitably entail simplification.[239]

---

[234] *Cardozo*, The Nature of the Judicial Process (1921) 102–103 (invoking both Salleiles and Jhering, fn. 12).

[235] *Cardozo*, The Nature of the Judicial Process (1921) 66, 112–113.

[236] *Cardozo*, The Nature of the Judicial Process (1921) 123.

[237] Morningstar v. LaFayette Hotel, 105 N.E. 656, 657 (NY 1914). The case was brought to my attention by *McLaughlin*, The Unification of Germany (1994) 277–278.

[238] See *Llewellyn*, Some Realism about Realism (1931). Llewellyn expressly rejected the idea that "legal realism" is anything like a "school," id. 1222, 1233.

[239] Many of the most important texts are collected (in part in excerpts) and introduced in *Fisher III, Horwitz, and Reed* (eds.), American Legal Realism (1993). A rendition and analysis of the defining features of legal realism still worth reading (for those who can do so in German) is *Reich*, Soziologische Rechtstheorie und legal realism (1967) 82–120; an informa-

Various scholars have claimed, or at least suggested, that Jhering had a considerable influence on legal realism as well.[240] Felix Cohen (1907–1953), a prominent and knowledgeable fellow-traveler of the movement, opined that "[s]urely, Jhering's critique of the jurisprudence of conceptual jurisprudence gave a worthy start to the labors of Holmes, Oliphant, Llewellyn, and even Jerome Frank,"[241] and Hermann Kantorowicz saw Jhering's work as one of the origins of the movement as well.[242] Yet, realism was too multifaceted, amorphous, and at times internally contradictory for any general claims about such an influence to illuminate the matter. We will thus take a narrower approach and focus on the hard core of realism, represented mainly by the movement's most prominent protagonist, Karl Llewellyn (1893–1962). Taking Llewellyn as our principal guide makes sense for three reasons. First, Llewellyn was more representative of the movement than anyone else[243] because he authored the scholarship that defined legal realism more than any other writings;[244] as a result, any influence Jhering may have had on Llewellyn could fairly count as influence on the core of legal realism itself. Second, of all the realists' critiques, claims, and demands, those propagated by Llewellyn were the most influential in the long run. Finally, Llewellyn was the most likely realist to be influenced by Jhering because he had far more extensive ties to Germany than any of his American colleagues,[245] and because he was more familiar than most with late-nineteenth and early-twentieth century German le-

---

tive introduction to the ideas of some of the most prominent realists is *Rea-Frauchinger*, Der amerikanische Rechtsrealismus: Karl N. Llewellyn, Jerome Frank, Underhill More (2006).

[240] Albert Kocourek (1875–1952) called Jhering "a founder of modern legal realism" already in 1915, i.e., way before a movement under that name established itself; *Kocourek*, Introduction (to The Struggle for Law) (1915) xxvii; *Pound*, Fifty Years of Jurisprudence (1938) 796 (legal realism "anticipated" by Jhering – and Kantorowicz); *Pound*, Jurisprudence I (1959) 132; *Wolf*, Große Rechtsdenker (1963) 659; *Zweigert and Siehr*, Jhering's Influence on Comparative Legal Method (1971) 227–228; *Rabban*, Jhering's Influence on American Legal Thought (2023) 161–163; for a more critical and ultimately contrary view, see *Duxbury*, Jhering's Philosophy of Authority (2007) 29–30; *Rückert*, Das Methodenorakel (2019) 482.

[241] *Cohen*, Law and Language (1960) 113.

[242] *Kantorowicz*, Some Rationalism about Realism (1934) 1241.

[243] The authoritative work on this topic is *Twining*, Karl Llewellyn and the Realist Movement (1973).

[244] Three of his publications laid out the core positions, critiques, and demands: *Llewellyn*, The Bramble Bush (1930); *id.*, A Realistic Jurisprudence – the Next Step (1930); *id.*, Some Realism about Realism (1931). Today, they are widely considered classic texts on legal realism.

[245] As a result of spending several years at a high school (*Gymnasium*) in Germany, Llewellyn was fluent in German (he had also fought for the *Kaiserreich,* i.e., on the German side, in World War I). He twice taught in Germany as a visiting professor (at the University of Leipzig 1928–29 and 1931) and was acquainted with many leading German jurists of the time as well as thoroughly familiar with the German jurisprudential literature; see *Twining*, Karl Llewellyn and the Realist Movement (1973) 89–91, 106–109.

gal scholarship. (The extent to which he was actually influenced by German ideas is of course another matter.[246])

Even if we focus, *pars pro toto*, on Llewellyn and his version of realism, gauging Jhering's influence is not a simple task.[247] Unlike in Pound's work, direct citations provide little help. Like most realists, Llewellyn rarely referenced Jhering openly, and when he did, it was mainly in passing and in a general fashion. That does not mean that Llewellyn or his cohort were not apprised of Jhering's ideas. Both Llewellyn himself and several other leading realists had clearly read their share of Jhering. In fact, in one of the signature articles of legal realism, Felix Cohen used Jhering's mockery of conceptual jurisprudence in "The Heaven of Concepts" as a launching pad for a trenchant critique of the "transcendental nonsense" in current legal reasoning.[248] Yet, such overt references were more the exception than the rule. That Jhering was infrequently cited by Llewellyn or other realists is not all that surprising, however. By the time of the movement's heyday, Jhering had been dead for more than a generation and his ideas were more than half-a-century old. More importantly, they had largely been absorbed into the American jurisprudential discourse by Holmes, Pound, Cardozo, and others. Thus, in order to engage with these ideas, there was no need to go all the way back to "Geist," "Kampf" or "Zweck." In addition, in the 1920s and 1930s, American scholars were less enthusiastic about invoking German jurisprudence than they had been around the turn of the century. As mentioned, after the Great War, Germany became politically unpopular in many quarters as a (former) enemy nation; and after 1933, the rise of Nazism tainted the image of all things German even further. In fact, Llewellyn apparently avoided mentioning German ideas for

---

[246] For a careful and cautious assessment, see *Twining*, Karl Llewellyn and the Realist Movement (1973) 108–109.

[247] More than a decade ago, a team of three scholars looked at the issue: *Grisé, Gelter and Whitman*, Rudolf von Jhering's Influence on Karl Llewellyn (2012). The result is disappointing. To begin with, the authors spend 18 pages on preparatory matters and turn to their proper topic only on the last two pages of their article. They then conclude that Rudolf von Jhering's influence on Karl Llewellyn and the American legal realist movement was "substantial and meaningful" and that "Jhering [...] undoubtedly helped to shape and motivate what is known today as American Legal Realism," id. 116. Unfortunately, however, the authors provide no direct support for that assertion at all. Instead, they rely on claims made in the secondary literature, mainly by *Herman*, Llewellyn the Civilian: Speculations on the Contribution of Continental Experience on the Uniform Commercial Code (1982). Yet, Herman himself provides no evidence for the authors' conclusion either; in fact, he expressly cautions that "[d]emonstrating Jhering influence on legal realism is beyond the scope of this paper," id. 1163.

[248] *Cohen*, Transcendental Nonsense (1935).The reference to Jhering in the opening parts of the article is not proof of Jhering's substantive influence on Cohen's argument. As Cohen notes, "[V]on Jhering's dream has been retold, in recent years, in the chapels of sociological, functional, institutional, scientific, experimental, realistic, and non-realistic jurisprudence." Id. 809. In short, it was a broadly shared satire invoked for in all sorts of contexts and for all sorts of purposes.

that very reason.[249] In short, the paucity of direct references to Jhering does not mean that his ideas were not at work among the realists, just that any influence was now much more indirect, diffuse, and unacknowledged than before.

In gauging Jhering's impact on Llewellyn and American legal realism, it is helpful to distinguish two clusters of ideas. The first cluster consisted of the credos Llewellyn and his fellow realists had adopted from, and thus now shared with, Pound's sociological jurisprudence.[250] Like Pound (and before him Holmes), they rejected the formal logic and abstract conceptualism of both Anglo-American analytical jurisprudence and German Pandectism. They understood law to be based not on general principles but on concrete and often conflicting interests. They emphasized the interests not of individuals but of society. They focused not on the law's past development but on its potential for future progress. And they regarded law not as a realm of idealist justice but, ostensibly in the wake of Jhering, as a means to social ends.[251] These ideas were not much foregrounded by the realists because they accepted them, by and large, as a matter of course. Since in all these regards, Llewellyn and his cohort were the heirs of Pound (and in some regards, of Holmes and Cardozo), they were also – though for the most part indirectly – the heirs of Jhering.

The second cluster of fundamental credos consisted of those that Llewellyn and others added to the mix, taking Pound's approach in new directions and giving legal realism its own distinctive – and more radical – profile.[252] Let us look at the three postulates that set the movement apart from Pound's version of sociological jurisprudence and consider Jhering's influence *vel non* on each of them.

The most fundamental of these postulates was the one that also gave the movement its name: Llewellyn and his fellow realists saw the essence of law not in its apparatus of norms but in its realization on the ground. The classic statement of this idea was Holmes's famous "prophecy" paradigm: "The prophecies of what the courts will do in fact, and nothing more pretentious, are what I mean by the law."[253] A generation later, Llewellyn adopted and broadened this approach by defining law as what "officials do about disputes."[254] Note that this position went far beyond Pound's distinction between "law on the books and law in

[249] Stefan Riesenfeld famously reported that Llewellyn avoided references to the German origin of certain legal ideas because mentioning it would have been "a kiss of death;" *Riesenfeld*, The Impact of German Legal Ideas and Institutions on Legal Thought and Institutions in the United States (1993) 89, 96.

[250] Supra note 206–224 and text.

[251] "[T]he conception of law as a means to social ends and not as an end in itself;" *Llewellyn*, Some Realism about Realism (1931) 1236.

[252] *Kantorowicz*, Some Rationalism about Realism (1934) aptly portrayed legal realism as a combination of the ideas of the school of "free law" and of sociological jurisprudence which were subsequently exaggerated.

[253] *Holmes*, The Path of the Law (1897) 460–461.

[254] *Llewellyn*, The Bramble Bush (1930) 3.

action."[255] For Pound, the law still consisted of principles and rules, though not necessarily in the form in which they appeared on paper. As we have seen, Pound's position could draw direct support from Jhering's ideas.[256] For Llewellyn-the-realist, however, the law was ultimately defined by the actual results of official rule application, i.e., essentially by facts.[257] Did Jhering's ideas also lurk beneath Llewellyn's more radical re-conception of law as what was enforced "in fact"? The answer is not clear for two reasons. First, as so often, Jhering's own statements in this context varied substantially. At times, he just warned (like Pound after him) that in studying law, we must not overlook that theory and practice often diverge.[258] Yet, on many occasions, he almost sounded like Holmes and Llewellyn, defining law through its realization: "What is not realized, is not law, and what serves the function [of law] is law even if it not recognized as such."[259] Second, we cannot be sure whether first Holmes and later Llewellyn actually took their views (at least in part) from such statements by Jhering. We do know that Holmes had read the works in which Jhering made the respective claims,[260] and we can safely assume that Llewellyn was cognizant of these works as well. This makes it possible that Jhering's reality-based definition of law had inspired Holmes's and Llewellyn's like positions, whether they were fully cognizant of it or not. If that is true, then the most defining tenet of legal realism has at least some of its origins in Jhering's work.

From this factual conception of law followed the second defining feature of realism that set it apart from Pound's approach – a different conception of legal science. For Pound's sociological jurisprudence, legal science was still heavily concerned with concepts and rules, even though they had to be treated as means to accommodate and realize interests as well as understood by how they worked out in practice. Thus, at its core, Pound's legal science remained a discipline of norms. For Llewellyn-the-realist, legal science was primarily concerned with what judges and other officials actually did. At its core, then, Llewellyn's legal science, as a discipline dealing with facts, was essentially an empirical endeavor.[261] This feature of legal realism bore scant relation to Jhering's ideas. For Jhering, jurisprudence was a normative enterprise, albeit one that must be aware of how

---

[255] Supra note 219.

[256] Supra note 206 and text.

[257] This may seem like an overstatement in light of Llewellyn's extensive engagement with the making, meaning, construction, and application of rules; still, for the realist agenda, the main importance of rules was their function as "generalized predictions of what courts will do;" *Llewellyn*, Some Realism about Realism (1931) 1237. For a trenchant critique of this view, see *Kantorowicz*, Some Rationalism about Realism (1934) 1242–1247.

[258] See, e,g., *Jhering*, Geist I (1852) 20, 22.

[259] *Jhering*, Geist I (1852) 41; see also id. 52, 305;; *Jhering*, Geist II.2. (1858) 334; *Jhering*, Kampf (1872) 52*;* *Jhering*, Zweck I (1884) 318.

[260] See supra note 165 and text.

[261] The epistemological confusions underlying this approach to jurisprudence are mercilessly laid bare by *Kantorowicz*, Some Rationalism about Realism (1934) 1247–1252.

norms worked out in reality; it was not, at its core, an empirical discipline, in which concepts and norms played mere contributory roles. Thus when (and to the extent) the legal realists embraced fact-based conception of jurisprudence, they did not follow the lead of Jhering (nor of Pound[262]) but sought to turn their discipline into a form of empirical social science.[263]

The third defining characteristic of legal realism was its skepticism vis-a-vis, if not denial of, the determinacy and uniformity of legal outcomes. True to the Anglo-American tradition, the realists' focus was almost entirely on judicial decisionmaking. Many, if not most, rejected the prevailing understanding that judges produce foreseeable and uniform decisions by faithfully applying legal principles and rules to a given set of facts. The realists challenged this orthodoxy on two principal grounds. Positive law was often incapable of producing clear outcomes because it was riddled with gaps, its principles were vague, and its rules were subject to vastly different interpretations so that in cases worth litigating courts were vested with much wiggle room. In addition, positive rules were only one outcome-determinative element among many others – and not even "*the* heavily operative factor in producing court decisions."[264] How judges actually used their wiggle room was strongly influenced by their socio-economic background, personal preferences, and psychological conditioning.[265] Thus, at least in close cases, decisions depended mainly on how these and other elements played out in the individual dispute. As a result, certainty of outcomes was "in good measure an illusion"[266] The connection of this perception to Jhering's ideas was weak. To be sure, the realists' attack on the dogma of certainty and predictability of judicial decisions was significantly inspired by the German-Austrian school of "free law"[267], and the "free law" adherents, in turn, were indebted to Jhering in some important regards.[268] Yet, the "free law" movement's iconoclastic views –

[262] With regard to the turn away from rules and logical reasoning, Pound parted ways with the realists, *Pound*, The Call for a Realist Jurisprudence (1931). An early warning against disparaging logic in legal reasoning was sounded by *Cohen*, The Place of Logic in the Law (1916).

[263] See *Schlegel*, American Legal Realism and Empirical Social Science (1995).

[264] *Llewellyn*, Some Realism about Realism (1931) 1237.

[265] The perhaps most extreme version of this attitude was Jerome Frank's belief that judicial decisions were primarily determined by the judge's (usually unconscious) psychological predispositions, if not hang-ups, rather than by legal principles, rules or precedents. Frank's psychoanalytical approach resulted in the even broader claim that the jurists' belief in, or hope for, certainty in the law was driven by a childish dependence on the authority of a father; *Frank*, Law and the Modern Mind (1930). Frank actually paraded not only Pound but also Jhering as examples of this phenomenon, id. 202–216, 217–221. Llewellyn considered Frank his comrade-in-arms, see *Llewellyn*, Some Realism about Realism (1931) 1222, *note. Yet, even though Llewellyn endorsed inquiries in the psychology of judges, id., 1243, he did not go to Frank's psychoanalytical extremes.

[266] *Llewellyn*, Some Realism about Realism (1931) 1242.

[267] *Herget and Wallace*, The German Free Law Movement as the source of American Legal Realism (1987).

[268] Supra notes 27–35 and text.

specifically on adjudication – were but loosely related to Jhering's position.[269] Of course, Jhering was well aware of the limited power of concepts and rules and would hardly have denied that judicial outcomes are neither completely predictable nor entirely uniform. Still, Jhering would scarcely have agreed with the realists that judicial decisions were mainly driven by extra-legal factors and thus inherently, not to mention incurably, indeterminate.

Yet, despite all the undeniable differences between Jhering's and Llewellyn's jurisprudence, in a very fundamental sense they looked at law the same way: "Before rules were facts; in the beginning was not a Word but a Doing," Llewellyn wrote in 1931.[270] The author of "Kampf" and "Zweck" would have agreed.

In addition, there is a specific element that connects Jhering's thought with the realists' perception of adjudication, i.e., the idea of "Rechtsgefühl." The "feeling of justice" played an important role for Jhering;[271] subsequently, it was foregrounded by some of the "free law" advocates as a guide for the judge;[272] America legal realists, in turn, emphasized the "hunch" of the judge, i.e., the intuitive feeling of the proper result that often ultimately determines how a case is being decided.[273] This feature of American legal realism was not necessarily the result of any direct influence by Jhering;[274] nor did this intuitive element play exactly the same role in all these contexts. For Jhering, the jurists' "Rechtsgefühl" was mainly a necessary control device for decisions normally reached through the process of (interest-conscious) rule application; it had to supplement, and perhaps check, rules, not replace them; for the "free law" adherents and for the more radical realists, it was a factor in its own right that could – and in appropriate cases even should – sideline rules. Still, the affinity of the respective views is noteworthy: for Jhering as well as for the "free law" advocates and the legal realists, the intuitive sense or right and wrong was a crucial element in making legal decisions; they all pointed out that it had been overlooked by formalist jurisprudence; and they all demanded that it be not only acknowledged but also recognized as legitimate.

Jhering's Long Term Significance: Five Fundamental Features of Modern American Legal Thought. Looking back on more than half-a-century, in 1959, Roscoe Pound concluded that "Jhering has had a far-reaching influence upon the law in all directions."[275] Nowhere was this more obvious than in Pound's own

---

[269] Supra notes 36–37 and text.

[270] Llewellyn, Some Realism about Realism (1931) 1222.

[271] Supra chapter IV.3., notes 467–496 and text.

[272] Supra note 14–16 and text.

[273] A frequently cited text, often credited with creating the label of the (judicial) "hunch," is *Hutcheson*, Judgment Intuitive. The function of the Hunch in Judicial Decision, Cornell Law Review 14 (1929) 274–288. A later variation on this theme is Karl Llewellyn's concept of the judge's "situation sense," Llewellyn, The Common Law Tradition (1960) 121–126.

[274] Hutcheson, Judgment Intuitive (1929), for example, shows no sign of Jhering's direct influence, but the essay does invoke Cardozo's "Nature of the Judicial Process" (1921), id. 285 note 27, which, in turn, referenced Jhering, see supra note 230 and text.

[275] *Pound*, Jurisprudence vol. I (1959) 132.

country. In evaluating Jhering's overall, long-term, significance for modern American law let us look at five elements of his jurisprudence that contributed to the rise of the "pragmatic instrumentalism"[276] prevailing in twentieth-century American legal thought and beyond. These five elements were influential inter alia because they all resonated, and thus worked in conjunction, with broader intellectual and political trends in the United States at the time.

To begin with, Jhering's vehement attack on "conceptual jurisprudence" inspired and supported Holmes's and Pound's turn away from, and even the realists' vilification of, the reliance on *a priori* principles and strictly deductive reasoning which had been widespread in late nineteenth and early twentieth century American jurisprudence.[277] Here, Jhering's critique fit perfectly into the broad "revolt against formalism" in American philosophy, economics, politics, history, and law at the time.[278] The resultant skepticism vis-a-vis first principles, abstract concepts, and "logic" has been a defining feature of American legal thought for the last century. Even today, Holmes's statement that "[t]he life of the law has not been logic; it has been experience"[279] is an American article of faith; part of its origins lies in Jhering's work.

Second, Jhering's "insistence upon the interests which the legal system secures rather than upon the formal legal rights by which it secures them"[280] provided crucial assistance to shifting the jurisprudential focus from general principles and abstract rules to concrete social realities – a shift which Holmes had initiated, Pound (following Jhering) then deepened, and the realists eventually foregrounded. This shift coincided, and received support from, the establishment of sociology as a field in its own right which had begun in Jhering's age and was completed in Pound's. At the same time, Jhering's concomitant insight – that the law results from the struggle between conflicting interests – resonated with Darwinist conceptions of society (shared, e.g., by Holmes as well as by Spencer in England), was expounded in the United States by Arthur Bentley,[281] and simply made sense at a time of intensifying class conflict. Ever since, the view of law as a reflection of interests, and of rights as the prize for winning the battle between them, has been

---

[276] *Summers*, Instrumentalism and American Legal Theory (1982) 20–26.

[277] Contemporary observers sometimes emphasized the similarities between the German conceptual jurisprudence and the formalism of American legal reasoning; see, e.g., *Drake*, Editorial Preface (1921) xxiii ("[...] we find many a Puchta among our American jurists, both on and off the bench, who apply the principles that have been worked out in the development of our Common Law as if they were "a priori" mathematical axioms and not "a posterior" working formulae, which have to be constantly reshaped to adapt them to the ever changing requirements of a developing society. American juristic thinking at the present time needs a von Ihering."); see also id., xxxiv ("The days of 'laissez faire' in legal matters have gone by in America as well as in Germany.")

[278] *White*, Social Thought in America. The Revolt against Formalism (1949).

[279] *Holmes*, The Common Law (1881) 5.

[280] *Pound*, Jurisprudence vol. I (1959) 133.

[281] Supra note 139 and text.

front and center in the American legal consciousness. Every law student is thoroughly exposed to this view in his or her first year, and most American lawyers today consider it a matter of course.

Third, Jhering made a perhaps even more important contribution to the formation of modern American legal thought with his preference for social over individual interests.[282] His vigorous rejection of the traditional "individual" utilitarianism, that prevailed in nineteenth-century England, in favor of a "social" variety[283] was matched by Holmes's like orientation towards collective concerns.[284] Together, they shaped Pound's conviction that social interests trump individual ones. The realists, largely on the left side of the political spectrum, by and large adopted that view as well. As a result, modern American legal thought has been infused with a much heavier dose of collectivism than foreign observers typically expect. To be sure, American legal culture has a reputation (both at home and abroad) for being individualistic, and in many regards it is (most notably in the constitutional context with its emphasis on individual rights). Yet, in part as a result of Holmes's and Pound's, and thus also of Jhering's, influence, there is an amazingly strong and pervasive collectivist counter current. It manifests itself, inter alia, in the ongoing debate about racial or gender discrimination (which is concerned with groups rather than individuals), the vexed issue of affirmative action (which centers on the best social policy rather than just desserts in the individual case), and the dominant theory of punishment (which looks to collective security concerns much more than to personalized justice). The most pervasive and influential manifestation of this collectivist orientation is the economic analysis of law, as it has come to dominate American legal thought since the 1970s. To be sure, in this regard, there are no signs of any direct influence by Jhering. Yet, his conception of law as "merely a means" for securing the "conditions of life in society"[285] (by which Jhering often meant the market conditions) is a noteworthy precursor to the law and economics school's use of law (only) for the pursuit of social welfare. Note how decisively both Jhering and modern law and economics have sidelined the more traditional idea of law as an expression of, and an instrument for, the realization individual justice.[286]

Fourth, Jhering's understanding of law as tied to social evolution and progress resonated not only with evolutionary thinking in American jurisprudence,[287]

---

[282] See *Pound*, Jurisprudence I (1959) 138. As mentioned, Pound saw this turn to social interests as Jhering most important bequest to contemporary American jurisprudence; supra notes 222–224 and text.

[283] Supra chapter IV.2., notes 316–340 and text.

[284] See, e.g., *Holmes*, The Common Law (1881) 37; *DeWolfe Howe*, Introduction (1963) XXIV, XXXVI.

[285] *Jhering*, Zweck I (1884) 250, 443.

[286] For an in-depth and thought-provoking analysis of the connection between Jhering's approach and twentieth-century economic analysis of law (exemplified by Friedrich Hayek and Richard Posner), see *Vesco*, Die Erfindung der ökonomischen Rechtswissenschaft (2021).

[287] See *Herget*, American Jurisprudence (1990) 117–146.

it also lent significant support to the political reform agenda underlying Pound's "sociological jurisprudence." In particular, Jhering's call for reining in the excesses of capitalism[288] aligned with Pound's campaign against the *laissez faire* ideology of the conservative judiciary in the *Lochner* era.[289] Both Jhering's and Pound's agenda fit into the "progressive era" in American history, i.e., the period from the 1890s through World War I, which was marked by government-led law reform in response to industrialization, urbanization, massive immigration, and political corruption.[290] In the 1930s, many leading realists adopted this reformist position as well; it undergirded the New Deal during the Roosevelt administration when many members of the realist camp occupied key functions in the federal bureaucracy. In all these contexts, Jhering's emphasis on the importance of legislation as the primary motor of legal progress[291] provided support for reform through statutory and administrative (rather than judicial) law-making in the emerging regulatory state in America.[292] Ever since, American society in general, and its lawyers in particular, have associated law not only with order and stability but at least as much with social change and general progress. Of course, people disagree on exactly what counts as progress (or how much of it is desirable), but there is a broad consensus that social improvement through law is a perennial need and that lawmakers owe society virtually constant upgrades.[293]

Last, but certainly not least, Jhering's conception of law as a means to an end has had a profound long-term impact on American legal thought.[294] Pound directly adopted Jhering's instrumental view as early as 1907,[295] Llewellyn followed

---

[288] *Jhering*, Zweck I (1884) 250, 443.

[289] In Pound's view, the arch conceptualists and logicians populating Jhering's fictitious heaven of concepts had "their counterpart in American judges of the end of the last century who insisted upon a legal theory of equality of rights and liberty of contract in the face of notorious social and economic facts." *Pound*, The Spirit of the Common Law (1921) 205; see also *Pound*, Jurisprudence I (1959) 141–142.

[290] Key developments include the passing of antitrust legislation, first in the Sherman Act of 1890 (15 U.S.C. 1–7), then in the Clayton Act of 1914 (15 U.S.C. 127), and legislation requiring compensation of employees suffering work accidents, e.g., the Federal Employers Liability Act of 1908, 45 U.S.C. 51 et seq., and in various Workers Compensation Acts on the state level.

[291] See supra chapter II.6., notes 509–511 and text.

[292] See *Pound* , Jurisprudence (1959) 134–136.

[293] This systemic bias in favor of change and progress also has deeper historical roots in the activism marking the early decades of the republic. At the time, lawmakers, and in particular courts, adapted the inherited common law to the conditions prevailing on the new continent and created new legal institutions and rules catering to the needs of a dynamic and expanding society and economy; see *Horwitz*, The Transformation of American Law 1780–1860 (1977).

[294] In a sense, it is what connects the previously mentioned elements: it underlies the shift from an internal and doctrinal to an external and social view of law; it drives the protection of interests; it makes law the tool by which social policies are realized; and it proffers law as the instrument used for the promotion of progress.

[295] *Pound*, The Need for a Sociological Jurisprudence (1907).

suit in 1931,[296] and in 1936, Lon Fuller stated that "[t]he notion that law exists as a means to an end has been commonplace for at least half-a-century.[297] Ever since, that view has been at the very core of modern American legal thought – from the progressive era to the New Deal and from the civil rights movement to law and economics. To be sure, an instrumental (and thus ultimately political) understanding and use of law is by no means an American idiosyncrasy, but it is more broadly accepted, consistently embraced, and more unabashedly practiced than in comparable jurisdictions. In modern American legal consciousness, the purpose and politics of law are not just background considerations but consistently at center stage.

In virtually all these regards, Jhering's instrumentalism dovetailed with wider intellectual currents. It directly corresponded to the utilitarian approach (whether "individual" or "social"), which had been present in American legal thought since the nineteenth century. Just as importantly, it closely matched the credos of pragmatism as the most prominent epistemology and philosophy in late-nineteenth and early twentieth-century America: like pragmatism, Jhering's instrumentalism understood phenomena and judged acts not according to any intrinsic essence or absolute value but according to their function in, and their effects on, the real world.[298] In a sense, Jhering's instrumentalism combined utilitarian and pragmatist ideas and cast their overlapping features into a form of jurisprudence. No wonder this jurisprudence resonated deeply with the early twentieth-century understanding of those in the camp of Holmes and Pound. In 1915, Munroe Smith – Jhering's erstwhile student and later most important American commentator – wrote in a review of the English translation of "Zweck" that although the book was very important in Germany, "it is not needed by us in anything like the same degree" because it expressed "[v]iews largely held among us." Smith added that "it is still welcome" because it presented these views "from a new angle."[299] In other to words, "Kampf" and "Zweck" helped progressive American legal thinkers better to understand and to articulate what they thought, or at least dimly felt, anyway.[300]

---

[296] *Llewellyn*, Some Realism about Realism (1931) 1236.

[297] *Fuller and Purdue*, The Reliance Interest in Contract Damages (1936) 52.

[298] See, e.g., *Jhering*, Zweck I (1884) 374. In the words of Henry Steele Commager, "[t]he sociological movement in jurisprudence [was] a movement for pragmatism in the law;" *Commager*, The America Mind (1950) 378. For a lucid summary of the fundamental features of American pragmatism, see *Reich*, Soziologische Rechtstheorie und legal realism (1967) 37–42.

[299] *Smith*, Rudolph von Jhering, Law as a Means to an End (review, 1915) 472. In a similar vein, Munroe Smith reported a conversation with an American fellow-student in Göttingen in the late 1870s. Referring to the first volume of "Zweck," the student asked Smith: "Is it not odd that Jhering should be writing a big book to prove what no English or American lawyer would dispute?" Smith basically agreed: "what is self-evident to an Anglo-Saxon is not necessarily self-evident to a German." *Smith*, Four German Jurists II (1896) 306.

[300] In addition, Jhering could also appeal to American common lawyers in several other

Thus, to the – very large – extent that modern American legal thought is anti-formalist, interest-oriented, collectivist, progress-seeking, and instrumentalist, it is in no small part indebted to Jhering. Today, most American lawyers would, if they cared to read Jhering's jurisprudential writings, find his basic approach entirely congenial – and perhaps even obvious.

Beyond Jhering: American Variations and Expansions. The fact that modern American law thus bears many marks of Jhering's direct or indirect influence does not mean that it is a perfect realization of Jhering's jurisprudential agenda. In several regards it has pushed this agenda well-beyond Jhering's original intentions. In doing so, it has often disregarded limitations and countervailing considerations that were important to him.

This is most obvious with regard to the rejection of a "logical" or "conceptual" approach to law. While Jhering had of course come to chastise Puchta-style "conceptual jurisprudence," he had never doubted, but rather consistently emphasized, the importance of legal concepts and of a sound doctrinal structure of law paying due respect to logical consistency.[301] In fact, he had considered such a logical doctrinal structure essential for the rationalization, simplification, efficient handling, and equal administration of law;[302] he had even used English common law to show how poorly a regime fared without an "internal systematic order."[303] In early twentieth-century American legal discourse, there was no lack of voices (including Cardozo's[304]) agreeing with Jhering's position, and some scholars, like Morris Cohen, invoked Jhering in that context.[305] Others, however, like the radical realists, departed from that traditional stance: they openly and vigorously disparaged reliance on concepts, doctrine, and logical reasoning altogether.[306] Whether or not as a result of the realists' iconoclasm, traditional doctrinal work subsequently suffered a gradual but steady decline in twentieth-cen-

---

ways. His emphasis on conflicting interests and his view of law as a struggle matched their adversarial mentality. His insistence on the needs of practice resonated with the common lawyers' practical mind. His theory of self-interest as the basic driver of all human endeavor, especially in the economic realm, rang true in the particularly merciless market societies of England and America at the time. Also, the incorporation of sociological, psychological, and economic (market) elements in Jhering's jurisprudence was congenial to the American turn towards an interdisciplinary approach in the wake of legal realism.

[301] Supra chapter III.3.

[302] See especially *Jhering*, Geist II.2. (1858) 341–346.

[303] *Jhering*, Scherz und Ernst (1884) 352–353. Continental European (private) law had been systematically organized, Jhering argued, which made it possible to master its basics within a relatively short course of university study and greatly facilitated its practical application; by contrast, English law had not achieved a systematic structure which made it impossible for English lawyers "to master the whole of the law;" id.

[304] *Cardozo,* The Nature of the Judicial Process (1922) 62.

[305] *Cohen*, The Place of Logic in the Law (1916) 622.

[306] See, e,g., *Frank*, Law and the Modern Mind (1930); *Cook*, The Logical and Legal Bases of the Conflict of Laws (1942); *Robinson*, Law and the Lawyers (1935); see also *Arnold*, The Symbols of Government (1935); *Cohen*, Transcendental Nonsense (1935).

tury America. It is not that there is no respectable scholarship of that sort at all but at least by comparison to most civil law jurisdictions, doctrinal work has become so poorly developed and so little respected in the United States that if Jhering were to look at the current state of American legal doctrine, he would find it deplorable. He would wonder how a law so weakly conceptualized, poorly structured, and disorganized can be intellectually mastered and consistently applied with reasonable effort – which, of course, it cannot.[307]

In a similar vein, the collectivist element in modern American law has developed in a direction not intended by Jhering. Jhering's collectivism was (much like Pound's) mainly an antidote to *laissez-faire* ideology. It rested on the conviction that when push comes to shove, social interests must prevail over individual ones because only thus can the necessary conditions for life in society be guaranteed. The ultimate bearer of rights, however, was still the individual as such – not only as a property-owner or head of household but also, and perhaps more importantly, as a person endowed with dignity and honor.[308] Modern American law has gone far beyond mere limitation of individual rights in the social interest. It has increasingly conceived of rights themselves in collective terms. American law routinely operates not only with individual entitlements, but also with group rights – i.e., those of racial minorities (freedom from discrimination), women (equal rights), homosexual and transgender people (sexual self-determination), the disabled (accommodation of needs), etc. In a similar fashion, "justice" is often conceived in group terms; in fact, claims to "justice" have much greater traction in contemporary America if they are couched in terms of race, gender or other collective categories than in terms of fairness to an individual simply as a human being.

American legal discourse has pushed even the instrumental conception of law beyond Jhering's original idea. In "Zweck," Jhering looked at law as a means to an end primarily to understand the law's origins, growth, and function; his perspective was essentially historical and causal: purpose, he claimed, was "the *creator* of all law."[309] Pound's "sociological jurisprudence," however, focused mainly on the potential of law; his perspective was essentially forward-looking and political: law is an instrument to be employed for "social engineering."[310] In other words, Jhering provided a theory that explained law as a means to an end; Pound called for a practice that demanded its use as such. To be sure, the differ-

[307] Jhering's warning against lack of organization and clarification reads almost like a critique of modern American law: "The more the law hinders those who have to apply and thus learn it to maintain an overview because of its prolixity and to understand it correctly because of its obscurity and lack of precision, the more imperfect [...] its application will become." *Jhering*, Geist II.2. (1858) 341.

[308] *Jhering*, Kampf (1872) 28–51; generally *Pleister,* Persönlichkeit, Wille und Freiheit im Werke Jherings (1982).

[309] *Jhering*, Zweck I (1884) VIII (emphasis added).

[310] *Pound*, The Nature of the Common Law (1921) 195–196.

ence is largely one of emphasis but it has significant implications. While an explanation of existing law as a descriptive enterprise does not need to pass value judgments on the law's substance, a programmatic conception of law is a normative approach that owes guidance to its proper content. Pound, however, provided scant guidance beyond generalities.[311] In a similar vein, for Jhering, the instrumental nature of law did not necessarily ensure its legitimacy; note that Jhering considered the use of law as a means to an end legitimate only if it served the interests of society as a whole, not just of particular groups.[312] In modern America, however, the use of law as an instrument is widely regarded as legitimate per se, i.e., even if law serves only the current interests of particular segments of society.[313] Thus law is treated as a per se legitimate weapon in the hands of minorities and women, corporate managers and shareholders, advocates for or against affirmative action, promoters or opponents of free abortion, friends and foes of gun rights, etc.

The effect of a strictly instrumental use of law is worrisome: the law is nothing but a weapon employed in the fight for particular interests and does not itself provide any standards of justice.[314] Guidance about right and wrong must thus be found outside the law. Of course, such guidance may come from a viable consensus about basic moral or social values – which Jhering apparently took for granted. Yet, in a society marked by widespread value skepticism and deep disagreement about moral and social issues, such a consensus is widely lacking. At that point, value questions must be settled in the political arena, where the winners often take all, especially in a two-party system. In other words, combining the use of law purely as a means with a lack of consensus about its ends leaves the content of law almost entirely at the mercy of political power.

How far modern American law has traveled down that road is a thorny issue beyond the scope of this book. Today, an instrumental use of law is clearly

---

[311] As Pound's contemporaries noted already, the idea that law must decide between conflicting interests (or "balance" them) tells us next to nothing how this is to be done and which interests deserve to win; see *Patterson*, Roscoe Pound, The Spirit of the Common Law (review, 1922) 813.

[312] *Jhering*, Zweck II (1886) 211. Privileges for particular groups could be justified, however, if they benefitted society as a whole, id. While that claim is, of course, often made by the respective groups in contemporary America, it is by no means necessary to legitimize the pursuit of special interests through law.

[313] See *Tamanaha*, Law as a Means to an End (2006) 6–7.

[314] Demands for "justice" are ubiquitous of course but they are mostly just claims to presumed entitlements by particular groups or individuals. Note that inherently *legal* conceptions of justice are perfectly conceivable. Perhaps the most obvious Anglo-American example is the notion of due process. Due process is so definitive a value of law itself that most Anglo-American lawyers would hesitate to recognize a system not providing due process as a system of law at all. For a list of inherently legal values recognized in German jurisprudence, see *Larenz*, Rudolf von Jhering und die heutige Lage der deutschen Rechtswissenschaft (1970) 137.

dominant in the United States, and critics have pointed out its negative impact on the rule of law itself.[315] It is also fair to say that value skepticism is a pervasive feature of American legal thought,[316] and it has even been asserted that American society has arrived at a "law without values."[317] While that is an exaggeration,[318] it can fairly be argued that the combination of instrumentalism with moral skepticism has had a severely negative impact on the commitment of modern American law to fundamental precepts of justice, the notable exceptions of equal protection and due process notwithstanding. Be that as it may, the extreme dependence of modern American law on shifting political majorities (and thus on the power of lobbies) illustrates the perils inherent in Jhering's approach. It is true that Jhering never *advocated* a purely instrumental use of law regardless of any notions of justice, but it is also true that much of "Zweck" could be read in such a fashion.[319]

---

[315] *Tamanaha*, Law as a Means to an End (2006) 215–245.

[316] See *Alschuler*, Law without Values (2000) 1–13.

[317] *Alshuler*, Law without Values (2000). Alshuler attributes that development largely to the pernicious influence of Holmes' moral nihilism. It is important to note that that nihilism was not a result of Jhering's influence but rather due to Holmes' experience in the Civil War and to his early involvement with philosophical pragmatism. To be sure, Jhering and Holmes shared the rejection of absolute moral values, at least in the realm of jurisprudence. Yet, as Wolfgang Fikentscher pointed out, Holmes's position was more radical than Jhering's, *Fikentscher*, Methoden des Rechts II (1975) 171–172. Holmes rejected the validity of *all* moral values in law, see *Alshuler*, Law Without Values (2000) 1; Jhering merely rejected their absolute nature, considering them dependent on the development and current state of each society. Thus Holmes can fairly be considered a moral nihilist while Jhering was merely a moral relativist.

[318] Modern American law is clearly not "without values." Notably the US Constitution contains several of them. Some are the heritage of the natural law tradition, i.e., the protection of life, liberty, and property, and the equal administration of the law guaranteed by the Fourteenth Amendment. Others are freedoms deemed essential to a liberal order, i.e., the rights to free speech, the press, religion, and assembly, and arguably even the right to keep and bear arms, enshrined in the First and Second Amendments. It is true, of course, that especially the latter group of rights also has an instrumental character: they are meant to serve the end of democratic government. Yet, they also contain intrinsic substantive values. For example, the right freely to express one's views contains the notion of liberty of opinion as a basic feature of humanity. Even the right to keep and bear arms can be said to reflect a substantive ideal, i.e., that of the self-reliant individual who even as a citizen of a state retains the power to use armed force, though such a view is highly contested. Substantive values are also inherent in much of private law, of course, viz. the principle of fair compensation for harm caused by another in the law of torts, of being bound by one's promise under the law of contracts, and the moral values undergirding much of family law, e.g. that decisions involving children must be made in their best interest.

[319] Supra chapter IV 2. and 3.

4. Specific Areas: Roman Law, Sociology of Law, and Comparative Law

Beyond Jhering's influence on twentieth century legal thought in general, his impact on three sub-disciplines deserves a somewhat closer look. The most obvious case is the study of ancient Roman law pursued mainly in "Geist," which, however, had surprisingly weak long-term resonance. An almost equally plausible candidate is the sociology of law, for which Jhering's "Zweck" was a forerunner, albeit on an amateur level. More surprisingly, Jhering has also been claimed as a force in the establishment of modern comparative law, especially by virtue of the universalist elements of his jurisprudence.

The Study of Ancient Roman Law: A Surprisingly Weak Impact. Jhering wrote hundreds of pages on ancient Roman law, not only in search of its "spirit" but also touching on many more particular topics,[320] and "Geist des römischen Rechts" became one of his signature works on a global level, as evinced by numerous translations into several foreign languages.[321] Thus one would expect that Jhering had a major influence on the future study of the substance and history of ancient Roman law. Yet, at least in his home environment, the resonance of his work in this area was ambivalent and, on the whole, surprisingly weak. That is true both among his contemporaries and in the twentieth century.

Many of Jhering's contemporaries met his endeavor to view Roman law not under a "magnifying glass" but rather through a "telescope" and "from a distance" ("aus der Ferne")[322] with distrust and skepticism, if not with outright rejection. More interested in meticulous detail than in any kind of "spirit," they remained understandably wary of Jhering's broad assertions and flowery rhetoric.[323] To be sure, Jhering knew, and openly admitted, that he often flirted with speculation, and he accepted the inherent risks as a price for breaking new ground; here as elsewhere, he was ready to forego solid proof in the interest of developing thought-provoking hypotheses.[324] Yet, for many of his contemporaries, the dose of creative interpretation (and outright conjecture) was a tad high.[325] Nor did it escape them that Jhering often failed to consult all the existing

---

[320] See, e.g., supra chapter II.1., notes 130, 137, 148 and text.

[321] *Kunze*, Lieber in Gießen (2018) 55–62.

[322] *Jhering*, Geist I (1852) 9–10; see supra chapter II.1., note 52.

[323] *Wieacker*, Rudolf von Jhering (1969) 13–14.

[324] See *Jhering*, Entwicklungsgeschichte des römischen Rechts (1892) 34–35; see also *Jhering*, Geist I (1852) 88, where he admitted that many conclusions about the earliest Roman law are (inevitably) "more or less plausible guesses. Distrust is certainly more appropriate than credulity." On this occasion, Jhering was still confident that he could generate valuable findings based, inter alia, on etymological observations. The conclusions Jhering drew from these observations were often pushing, and sometimes exceeding, the limits of plausibility, see, e.g., *Jhering*, Geist I (1852) 136.

[325] See *Kuntze*, Rudof von Jhering (1892) 612–613; *Rümelin*, Rudolf von Jhering (1922) 18.

literature, and that by writing for a purpose, he tended to present the evidence in a skewed manner.[326] In addition, it probably did not endear Jhering to his colleagues that he blasted and actually ridiculed the work of prominent scholars in the field like Gustav Hugo (1764–1844) and Savigny's erstwhile student Adolf August Friedrich Rudorff (1803–1873).[327]

When the enactment of the German Civil Code (*BGB*) in 1900 ended the reign of Roman law as the common private law of Germany, studying the ancient sources became a decidedly historical enterprise. Under the leadership of scholars like Ludwig Mitteis (1859–1921), Otto Lenel (1849–1935), and Ernst Levy (1881–1968), Roman legal historiography took a new direction and became dedicated to the meticulous investigation of its classical and post-classical texts. Jhering's jurisprudential agenda, his search for the Roman law's "spirit," and his rather broad ("philosophical") generalities were scarcely relevant in this new context.

For the remainder of the twentieth century, the picture is mixed. Mainstream Roman legal historiography paid no more than occasional attention to Jhering's historical work.[328] It is true that he (sometimes) received credit for various specific discoveries and ideas,[329] but unlike his contemporary Theodor Mommsen (1817–1903) or, a generation later Lenel and Mitteis, Jhering has not been considered a major figure in the study of ancient Roman law.[330] As Franz Wieacker noted, Jhering's historical work was wedged uneasily between the earlier discov-

---

[326] *Mitteis*, Jhering (1905) 655–656. Mitteis thus recommended to regard Jhering's historical discourses from a philosophical perspective, i.e., not as a claim to historical accuracy but as a broader argument for a particular position.

[327] See, e.g., Jhering, Geist II.2. (1858) XIII–XVIII; see also supra chapter V.1., notes 16–19 and text.

[328] See *Kaser*, Das altrömische Jus (1949); id., Römische Rechtsgeschichte (1950); id., Das römische Privatrecht (Erster Abschnitt: Das Altrömische, klassische und vorklassische Recht) (2d ed. 1971); *Kunkel*, Römische Rechtsgeschichte (1948) 254–290. In the study of the Roman legal process under the Twelve Tables by Okko Behrends, soon to become the most prominent expert on Jhering in our day, Jhering's work on early Roman law played almost no role either; *Behrends*, Der Zwölftafelprozeß (1974). Jhering enjoys more attention in *Wieacker*, Römische Rechtsgeschichte (1988). The situation is similar in the English speaking literature; see, e.g., *Radin*, Handbook of Roman Law (1927); *Jolowicz*, Historical Introduction to the Study of Roman Law (1939). Notably, *Watson*, Rome of the Twelve Tables (1975), makes no reference to Jhering despite the fact that much of Jhering's work on early Roman law was directly pertinent in this context. Shorter accounts of Roman law mention Jhering's work either not at all or at best in passing. Whether Jhering's historical work on Roman law had a greater impact in any other areas of the world would have to be examined.

[329] Summary in *Wieacker*, Rudolf von Jhering (1969) 15–16.

[330] The strongest praise came from Franz Wieacker who acknowledged various lasting contributions and concluded that the legal historian Jhering provided "continuing impulses" for the discipline, *Wieacker*, Römische Rechtsgeschichte, esp. 322–334 (incl. footnotes). Still, Wieacker's chapter on the Entdeckung der Rechtsgeschichte (The Discovery of Legal History) in the mid- and late nineteenth century does not mention Jhering at all, *Wieacker*, Privatrechtsgeschichte (1967) 416–430.

eries of the Historical School and the meticulous inquiries of modern Roman legal historiography.[331] Jhering's dangerously broad assertions, at times daring conclusions, and occasional outright errors are major problems under modern standards of scholarship.[332]

Part of the reason for Jhering's marginal relevance was that among twentieth-century Romanists, interest in a broad perspective on Roman law was more the exception than the rule. Yet, even where scholars embraced such a perspective, they did not necessarily reference Jhering's work. To be sure, some built on "Geist", like Fritz Schulz (1879–1957),[333] or at least gave Jhering credit for his characterization of early Roman law, like Franz Wieacker (1908–1994).[334] Others however, like Max Kaser (1906–1997) and Paul Koschaker (1879–1951), paid scant attention to Jhering, even where their portraits of Roman law essentially mirrored the one Jhering had drawn a century earlier.[335]

---

[331] *Wieacker*, Rudolf von Jhering (1969) 16. Thus, as a work of legal history, "the justly immortal 'Spirit of the Roman Law' is, if we are honest, the cause of considerable perplexity," id. 1.

[332] In personal correspondence with me, noted contemporary Romanist Detlev Liebs attributed to Jhering a "gift for performances" ("Gabe für Inszenierungen") which also does not go over well with modern-day Roman law scholars.

[333] Fritz Schulz presents the strongest case of a German twentieth century Roman legal historian drawing on Jhering's work in "Geist." This is true in three regards. First, in his "Prinzipien des römischen Rechts," Schulz sought to identify the Roman law's characteristic features in a manner strongly reminiscent of Jhering's quest for its "spirit." Second, many of the features identified by Schulz are closely similar to, if not roughly identical with, those foregrounded by Jhering, in particular the Roman law's "isolation," "abstractness," "simplicity" (and economy), commitment to "tradition," and "liberty." Finally, in all these regards, Schulz explicitly built on Jhering's work which he duly cited on numerous occasions and for which he voiced great admiration, occasional critique notwithstanding; *Schulz*, Prinzipien des römischen Rechts (1934/1957); see the citations in the footnotes on pp. 13–15, 22, 47, 57, 96, 162. Schulz' work was translated and became a standard text in the English speaking world; *Schulz*, Principles of Roman Law (1936).

[334] Franz Wieacker expressed his appreciation for Jhering's broad characterizations, even comparing the respective parts of "Geist" to Montesquieu and Gibbon, *Wieacker*, Rudolf von Jhering (1969) 15.

[335] Max Kaser repeatedly announced an agenda closely resembling Jhering's quest for the characteristic features of (early) Roman law. In fact, Kaser often sounded quite similar to Jhering, see, e.g., *Kaser*, Das altrömische Jus (1949) 8 (trying to grasp "den erschließbaren Geist der altrömischen Ordnung"); id., Römische Rechtsgeschichte (1950) 15 ("Wesen und Eigenart des römischen Rechts [...] sind im Keim schon in altrömischer Zeit vorhanden"); id., Das römische Privatrecht (1971) v ("die geistige Struktur jeder dieser drei Perioden in ihrer geistigen Eigenart erfassen"). Yet, Kaser rarely referenced Jhering's highly similar ideas, some exceptions notwithstanding, see, e.g., Kaser, id. 10. *Koschaker*, Europa und das römische Recht (1966, orig. 1947), also essentially ignored Jhering's work; this is true even though Jhering's perception of the universality of Roman law and its concomitant significance for the development of European law since the Middle Ages (supra chapter II.1., notes 53–67 and text) is virtually identical to Koschaker's "fundamental idea" of Roman law as a central element of European legal culture, id. IX. It is difficult to imagine that Koschaker was not

All in all, it is not much of exaggeration to say that if Jhering had never written "Geist" or any other of his historical studies, the majority of present-day Roman law scholars – at least in the German language orbit – would barely notice.[336]

The Sociology of Law: The Amateur as a Forerunner. Since the object of sociology is the study of society, and since Jhering spent most of his later years on that endeavor, he was not only a jurist but also a sociologist.[337] More precisely: he gradually turned from the former to a hybrid and then, increasingly, into the latter: his earliest work (in the 1840s) was purely that of a jurist; in "Geist" (1852–1865), he already began to look at law in relation to society; in "Kampf" (1872) as well as in the first volume of "Zweck" (1877), he then approached law from a decidedly sociological perspective; finally, in the second volume of "Zweck" (1883) as well as in "Das Trinkgeld" (1882), he went beyond law and dealt with purely social norms. In essence, he proceeded from law to sociology of law and eventually to sociological studies proper.[338] Since he was trained in law but not in sociology, this trajectory entailed a turn from professionalism to amateurism[339] – and also, in the eyes of many contemporaries and successors, a deplorable loss of academic quality.[340]

To understand the significance of Jhering's sociological work we need to position it in the development of sociology as a discipline. The modern foundations were laid by Auguste Comte in the 1830s. Jhering's sociological writings followed a generation later, in the 1870s and 1880s, running roughly parallel with the work of his contemporary Herbert Spencer (1820–1902) in England. Another generation later, sociology finally came into its own with Emile Durkheim (1858–1917) in France and Ferdinand Tönnies (1855–1936), Georg Simmel (1858–1918), and of course Max Weber (1864–1920) in Germany. At the same time, legal sociology

---

aware of that. A similar disregard is shown in *Watson,* The Spirit of the Roman Law (1995), where Jhering is mentioned just in passing despite massive similarities between Jhering's and Watson's characterizations of early Roman law; see supra chapter II.1., note 71.

[336] The impact of Jhering's eventual turn towards an anti-formalist, instrumental, and state-centered jurisprudence on the broader understanding and image of Roman law is a different issue. Okko Behrends has argued that especially Jhering's vociferous attacks on a conceptual approach at the end of the third volume of "Geist" and his failure to deal with the "third system," i.e., the classical period in which Roman jurisprudence reached its pinnacle, have skewed his successors' understanding of Roman law in pernicious ways. According to Behrends, these elements have led important parts of the literature to (at least partially) denigrate the classical Roman jurists' accomplishments. This, in turn, has severely damaged the traditional understanding of private law *tout court* as a liberal order rooted in republican principles – by replacing it with a concept centered around interests protected by the state; *Behrends*, Jhering heute! (2023) 230–238 (with further references).

[337] See *Helfer*, Jhering als Rechtssoziologe (1968).

[338] *Helfer*, Nachtrag zu Jherings Zweck im Recht (1970) 12, seems to count these studies as a form of sociology of law – which they are not. They can of course still be of interest to legal sociology because they border on the study of legal rules in society.

[339] See supra chapter VI.4.

[340] See supra chapter IV.2. notes 370–375 and text.

was established as a special branch mainly by Eugen Ehrlich (1858–1922) in Austria. As a result, Jhering's sociological studies were wedged between the subject's modern beginnings and its establishment as an academic discipline. To put it differently, when Jhering wrote "Zweck," sociology was already a recognized agenda but not yet a fully recognized field with a defined methodology.[341] Thus, Jhering was an amateur forerunner of professional sociology.

Whatever influence Jhering-the-amateur-sociologist may have had on the development of sociology in general is beyond the scope of this chapter.[342] His contribution to the emergence of the sociology of law in particular is widely acknowledged. Since Jhering lacked a defined sociological methodology (as well as methodological self-reflection), it is perhaps too strong to call Jhering "the founder" of legal sociology.[343] Yet, he certainly provided a crucial impulse by replacing the philosophical and idealist orientation of jurisprudence with a focus on the connections between law and society. After all, the two principal ideas permeating the first volume of "Zweck" lie at the core of a sociology of law: that law depends on social conditions and that it serves social purposes. Moreover, Jhering's discussion of law in the broader context of all norms governing life in society (ethics, custom, conventions, etc.) presented law as but one means of social control among others.[344]

Jhering's influence is quite obvious in the foundational work of Eugen Ehrlich. The basic message Ehrlich formulated in 1913 in the preface to his "Grundlegung der Soziologie des Rechts" ("Fundamental Principles of the Sociology of Law"[345]) was also the late Jhering's most fundamental credo: "the center of gravity of legal development lies not in legislation, nor in juristic science, nor in judicial decisions, but in society itself."[346] To be sure, Ehrlich did not openly name

[341] Such a canon was supplied three years after Jhering's death by *Durkheim*, Les règles de la méthode sociologique (1895).

[342] For an example of modern sociology making use of Jhering's ideas, see *Schelsky*, Das Jhering-Modell des sozialen Wandels durch Recht (1972). Schelsky saw the principal merit of Jhering's work in his analysis of law as a crucial element in the process of social change. *Helfer*, Jhering als Rechtssoziologe (1968) 565, also finds much in Jhering's studies of social norms (in the second volume of "Zweck") that is useful for sociology generally – as, by the way, did Max Weber, infra notes 348–349 and text; see also *Helfer*, Nachtrag zu Jherings Zweck im Recht (1970).

[343] *Fikentscher*, Methoden des Rechts III (1976) 387; ditto *Helfer*, Jherings Gesellschaftsanalyse im Lichte der heutigen Sozialwissenschaften (1970) 78 ("founding father"); Helfer's term "precursor" ("Vorläufer") is more appropriate; *Helfer*, Jhering als Rechtssoziologe (1968) 553.

[344] See supra chapter IV.2., notes 231–247 and text. *Ross*, Social Control (1932) contains several, and in part very substantial, references to Jhering, see esp. 94, fn. 1; see also 62 (fn. 2), 70 (fn. 1), 123 (fn. 1), 193 (fn. 2).

[345] *Ehrlich*, Fundamental Principles of the Sociology of Law (1936).

[346] *Ehrlich*, Fundamental Principles of the Sociology of Law (1936) Foreword. Note that the statement concerns what drives the *development* of law; its *nature* is a different issue; see subsequent note and text.

Jhering as a predecessor; he also embraced a much broader concept of law which was not, like Jhering's, limited to the coercive rules created by the state.[347] Yet, Ehrlich's conception of legal sociology as the science that explores the social facts and analyzes the social forces driving the development of law was a continuation of Jhering's agenda.

Jhering's influence on Weber is harder to assess and a thorough analysis would require its own study. Weber, who had completed his legal studies and had then become a legal academic still during Jhering's lifetime, not only knew Jhering's "Zweck," he also cited the work and recommended it to his readers.[348] Weber's overt reference, however, does not concern Jhering's sociology of law but rather his studies of purely social norms in Volume Two of "Zweck," to which Weber's own ideas bore a strong resemblance.[349] By contrast, Weber's sociology of law contains no citations to Jhering's sociological approach; if Weber was in any way impressed by Jhering's discourse on law and society in the first volume of "Zweck," he did not show it.[350]

Yet, there is a significant connection between these two scholars' approaches in another regard: both understood the development of law as a process of rationalization.[351] Here, Jhering not only preceded Weber by more than a generation, he probably also inspired him. Jhering demonstrated the process of rationalization in his account of early Roman law in "Geist."[352] Weber was familiar with that

---

[347] For Ehrlich, "law" included norms operating purely in society if they were sufficiently clear and habitually observed, essentially as a form of custom; *Ehrlich*, Die Tatsachen des Gewohnheitsrechts (1907) 7–8; for Jhering, only state-sanctioned norms counted as law, *Jhering*, Zweck I (1884) 320.

[348] *Weber*, Economy and Society I (1978/1922) 29.

[349] Weber's reference appears in chapter I which deals with "Fundamental Concepts of Sociology" ("Soziologische Grundbegriffe") and concerns Jhering's discourse on usage and custom. Weber's recommendation is shared by at least one modern sociologist, see *Helfer*, Nachtrag zu Jherings Zweck im Recht (1970) 12. Like Jhering (see supra chapter VI.1.), Weber distinguishes various kinds of social norms according to their enforceability. He differs from Jhering mainly in his terminology, calling non-binding norms "Sitte" instead of "Gewohnheit" (Jhering) and binding norms "Konvention" instead of "Sitte" (Jhering); *Weber*, Economy and Society I (1978/1922) 29.

[350] It is interesting to note, however, that Jhering already postulated that "the right to coerce is the *absolute monopoly* of the state" ("das Zwangsrecht bildet das *absolute Monopol* des Staats"); *Jhering*, Zweck I (1884) 318 (emphasis in the original), a notion famously expounded by *Weber* a generation later in "Politik als Beruf" (1919); see also *Weber*, Economy and Society I (1978/1922) 56. Of course, this was not Jhering's original idea but had much earlier roots in the work of Jean Bodin (1530–1596) and Thomas Hobbes (1588–1679) on sovereignty.

[351] See *Gromitsaris*, Theorie der Rechtsnormen bei Rudolf von Jhering (1989) 7, 63. Jhering described the process of rationalization in the introduction to the second volume of "Geist," *Jhering*, Geist II.1. (1854) 24–26, and then linked it to early Roman law, id. 36–40. Weber connected the rationalization of law to the emergence of professional jurists; *Weber*, Economy and Society II (1978/1922) 775–776.

[352] See *Gromitsaris*, Theorie der Rechtsnormen bei Rudolf von Jhering (1989) 76–78.

work[353] and illustrated the rationalization of law by the very same Roman developments that Jhering had described. As a result, Weber's famous concept of (formal) "logical rationality"[354] closely fits the law and legal process Jhering considered characteristic for the Roman law's "second system."[355] In fact, Weber's illustrations remind the reader of Jhering's account at almost every turn.[356] This close resemblance between Weber's and Jhering's discourses strongly suggests that at least in this respect, Weber's concept of (formal) "logical rationality" was based on Jhering's work in "Geist."[357]

Echoes of Jhering can clearly be heard in Arthur Nussbaum's (1877–1964) path-breaking book on "Rechtstatsachenforschung" ("legal fact research"). "One has become tired of empty doctrine," Nussbaum wrote in 1914, "everything is pushing for [consideration of] living nature from which the sources of law spring."[358] In fact, his program followed straight from Jhering's approach: "That jurisprudence has to consider 'the purpose in law' is commonplace today, and that already opens the path towards the consideration of the factual circumstances [...], because often only they allow us to recognize the purpose of a norm."[359] Nussbaum's postulate that "the facts that must be considered in understanding the law are in the main of a purely political, social, and psychological nature" could have been taken straight from Jhering's "Zweck."[360]

Jhering has also been considered influential on the French side, including on Emile Durkheim.[361] In Durkheim's now classic work "De la division du travail social" (1893), law is a sufficiently crucial factor to consider the book part of early legal sociology. Jhering's influence on Durkheim is difficult to pin down. On the one hand, Jhering had talked about the division of labor in society years before Durkheim,[362] and there are also considerable affinities between the two scholars'

---

[353] Jhering's work on early Roman law was directly relevant for Weber's postdoctoral research, see *Weber*, Die römische Agrargeschichte und ihre Bedeutung für das Staats- und Privatrecht (Stuttgart 1891).

[354] Weber developed his typology of forms of law, and explained his concept of (formal) "logical rationality," in his Sociology of Law: *Weber*, Economy and Society II (1978/1922) 656–657. Weber also directly associated the concept of "logical rationality" with the German Pandectist legal science of the late nineteenth century, id. 657–658, i.e., the jurisprudence of which Jhering was first a leading representative, then an outspoken critic, as Weber surely knew.

[355] Supra chapter II.1., notes 91–98 and text.

[356] *Weber*, Economy and Society II (1978/1922) 792–802.

[357] *Gromitsaris*, Theorie der Rechtsnormen bei Rudolf von Jhering (1989) 7 (claiming that Weber "adopted and further developed" Jhering's approach in all important respects). Gromitsaris analyzed Jhering's theory of legal norms through the lens of Weber's (as well as Theodor Geiger's and Helmut Schelsky's) sociology of law. Although the study is illuminating, engaging it more thoroughly would lead us too far afield here.

[358] *Nussbaum*, Rechtstatsachenforschung (1914) 1

[359] *Nussbaum*, Rechtstatsachenforschung (1914) 8.

[360] *Nussbaum*, Rechtstatsachenforschung (1914) 7

[361] *Fikentscher*, Methoden des Rechts III (1976) 269.

[362] *Jhering*, Zweck I (1884) 149–150, 228.

approaches.[363] In a sense, Durkheim's work was, like Ehrlich's, a validation of Jhering's idea that law serves to "guarantee the conditions of life in society"[364] so that we must explore it in the context of the realities of life and commerce.[365] On the other hand, Durkheim cited Jhering only once and almost in passing,[366] although he otherwise copiously referenced German sources (as well his main antagonist, Herbert Spencer). Some of Durkheim's views also differed significantly from Jhering's.[367] Thoroughly to evaluate the relationship between Jhering and Durkheim would require a study in its own right. By contrast, Jhering's influence on Francois Gény is clearly recognized;[368] Gény's work focused on legal methodology, however, and was but loosely related to legal sociology.

Modern Comparative Law: Weak Influence, Strong Affinity. In 1971, Konrad Zweigert (1911–1996) published an article entitled "Jhering's Influence on the Development of Comparative Legal Method."[369] At first glance, it was astounding to see one of the leading comparative law scholars of his time[370] claim that Jhering had an influence on the discipline. After all, Jhering has not normally been thought of as a comparatist – neither in his own day nor by mainstream comparative law scholars in the twentieth century.[371] Yet, Zweigert had a point, at least in the sense that Jhering's work was related to modern comparative law in several important regards.[372]

To begin with, Jhering thought about law in universalist terms. Sharply rejecting the Historical School's "theory of the national character of the laws," he saw the greatest significance of Roman law for the modern world in its eventual universalism.[373] He looked back with nostalgia at the erstwhile unity of the *ius*

[363] For example, like Jhering, Durkheim approached his topic in a decidedly functional manner; drew on biology for illustration; and he focused on the purpose of the phenomenon under investigation (including law). Yet, it may be difficult to determine whether these ideas were in any way derived from Jhering's work.

[364] *Jhering,* Zweck I (1884) 443.

[365] See supra chapter IV.2., notes 365–367 and text.

[366] The only reference to Jhering is in a footnote pertaining to theories of social utilitarianism, *Durkheim*, De la division du travail social (1893) 11, fn. 3.

[367] See *Whitman*, Jhering parmi le francais (1997) 158–159.

[368] See supra 1., notes 44–45 and text.

[369] While the English version of the article was co-authored by Kurt Siehr, it was mainly Zweigert's work. It was largely based on an article Zweigert had written in German shortly before for a symposium on Jhering, see *Zweigert*, Jherings Bedeutung für die rechtsvergleichende Methode (1971).

[370] Konrad Zweigert was the Director of the Max Planck Institute for Comparative and International Private Law in Hamburg 1963–1979 and the co-author of the treatise on comparative law that defined the discipline from the 1970s well into the twenty-first century, see infra notes 396–397.

[371] For a history of the field, see *Reimann*, Comparative Law (2020) 28–78 (with further references).

[372] Max Rümelin had already noted this relationship half a century before Zweigert; *Rümelin*, Rudolf von Jhering (1922) 76.

[373] *Jhering*, Geist I (2d ed. 1866) 1–9.

commune and lamented its destruction by modern national codifications which had also resulted in the fragmentation of legal science.[374] As a result, (legal) "science has been degraded to a national jurisprudence, the boundaries of legal science coincide with the political ones. A humiliating, undignified form of science!"[375] Jhering thus propagated a jurisprudence that transcends the boundaries between legal systems.

Jhering also pointed to the means by which such a jurisprudence could be established – a comparative approach: "It depends on [legal science] itself to cross these boundaries and secure the universal character it so long possessed for all times in a new form as comparative jurisprudence."[376] Such a comparative jurisprudence would entail crucial benefits: "Its method changes, its perspective becomes wider, its judgment more mature, its treatment of the material more liberal, [...thus] it will rise to a higher level of scientific work."[377] Jhering noted that such a development was already underway in some fields which did not, however, include private law.

A comparative perspective was very much in line with Jhering's own mindset. Jhering considered himself "addicted" to comparing everything – both in his personal life and in his professional work; from this habit, he quipped, "nothing is safe."[378] It is true that he never engaged in any sustained and explicit comparative studies with regard to contemporary legal systems.[379] Yet, as he himself noted, comparison was inherent in much of his historical work which contrasted early with later Roman law and both areas with present conditions,[380] often implicitly, sometimes explicitly. Whatever legal system or element or feature thereof he looked at, comparing it to others was always at least in the back of his mind.

---

[374] *Jhering*, Geist I (2d ed. 1866) 14–15; see also id. 10.

[375] "[D]ie Wissenschaft ist zur Landesjurisprudenz degradiert, die wissenschaftlichen Grenzen fallen in der Jurisprudenz mit den politischen zuammen. Eine demüthigende, unwürdige Form für eine Wissenschaft!" *Jhering*, Geist I (2d ed. 1866) 16. Jhering's universalist stance, as well as his dislike of "a purely territorial or national development of law," was noted already by Jhering's early American biographer, see *MacDonell*, Rudolf von Jhering (1914) 598. Jhering's position was not unique. Around the same time, similar sentiments were expressed, and a similar call for comparative law made, for example, by one of the most prominent American jurists, i.e., David Dudley Field (1805–1892), see *Clark*, American Comparative Law 2022) 144.

[376] *Jhering*, Geist I (2d ed. 1866) 15.

[377] *Jhering*, Geist I (2d ed. 1866,) 15.

[378] *Jhering*, Scherz und Ernst (1884) 127–128.

[379] In "Geist", there are occasional references to jurisdictions other than the Roman law of his own day, mainly to English law, see the references in *Zweigert and Siehr*, Jhering's Influence on Comparative Legal Method (1971) 229 fn. 77, but they were few and far between and not essential to Jhering's discussion. Off and on Jhering did, however, compare the customs and mentalities of different legal cultures, e.g., those of England, France, and Germany, see, e.g., *Jhering*, Zweck I (1886) 377–380.

[380] *Jhering*, Scherz und Ernst (1884) 128.

As Zweigert pointed out, Jhering's overall approach to law was also very much in line with the approach that became prevalent in modern comparative legal studies. Jhering's conception of law as an instrument for the pursuit of particular purposes corresponds to the "functional method" embraced by most comparatists since the middle of the twentieth century: rules and institutions must be compared not on the basis of their written manifestations but according to the function they serve; the crucial reference point (*tertium comparationis*) is the social or economic problem the rules are meant to solve.[381] In a similar vein, Jhering's approach was "critical, undogmatic, and realistic" and, thus, congenial to modern comparative law methodology.[382]

In addition to the ideas mentioned, or at least hinted at, by Zweigert, Jhering is connected to modern comparative law in ways not mentioned in the article. Jhering proffered several insights that are common currency among comparatists today. Credit for them mostly went to others, however, who presented them as new and original ideas decades after Jhering had first developed them. The most important of these insights was that there is a constant exchange of ideas between legal systems that Jhering not only observed but also welcomed, once again sharply rejecting the nationalistic outlook of the Historical School. Jhering's starting point was of course the notorious reception of Roman law in medieval and early modern (mainly Western) Europe. For Jhering, this was not a unique historical event but just one instance of a pervasive phenomenon. He observed that "[t]he life of the peoples is not an isolated existence next to each other [...] but a system of mutual contact and influence, peaceful or hostile, a giving and taking, borrowing and communicating."[383] The underlying rationale was utility.

> "The question of the reception of foreign legal institutions is not a question of nationality but simply a question of utility, of need. Nobody will fetch from afar what he can find just as well or better at home, but only a fool will reject quinine because it is not home-grown."[384]

Half-a-century after Jhering's death, comparatists began to focus on "receptions" and "transfers" and to discuss them in greater depth. In 1974, in Alan Watson (1933–2018) published a slim book on "Legal Transplants"[385] which became a classic and made its author – like Jhering a scholar of Roman law – famous among comparatists.[386] Today, the study of receptions and transplants is a major

---

[381] See *Michaels*, The Functional Method of Comparative Law (2019).

[382] *Zweigert and Siehr*, Jhering's Influence on Comparative Legal Method (1971) 220–222.

[383] *Jhering*, Geist I (2d ed. 1866) 5. Jhering's discourse was not entirely benign. He argued that the peoples of the world had a duty to cooperate and to contribute to the common good of mankind; those who refused to do so by isolating themselves (like the Japanese until the middle of the nineteenth century) could be forced out of their isolation.

[384] *Jhering*, Geist I (2d ed. 1866) 8–9. Jhering used the term "Chinarinde", i.e., the common name of the plant from which quinine, then used as a treatment for malaria and other diseases, is made.

[385] *Watson*, Legal Transplants (1974).

[386] *Reimann*, Comparative Law (2020) 201–203.

subfield of the discipline.[387] Jhering also noticed early on that entirely different legal systems often agreed on essential points, and that they seemed to converge with the advance of the various peoples' cultural development. Looking for an explanation, he suggested that it was the pursuit of identical purposes that eventually entailed identical solutions.[388] Modern comparative law has often embraced the idea of a "convergence" between legal systems,[389] and the leading treatise popularized the thesis that legal systems typically reach the same solutions when they are faced with the same social or economic problems.[390] Another example is Jhering's almost casual observation that in addition to the legal norms that are expressly stated, there are also latent ones which may not even be consciously recognized but can still play an important role in a legal system.[391] Today, this discovery is attributed to Italian comparatist Rodolfo Sacco (1923–2022) who spoke of the latent norms as "cryptotypes."[392] In all these instances, modern authors did not give Jhering credit for his observations, perhaps because they were not aware of them. By contrast, Konrad Zweigert did point out the connection between Jhering's view "that every legal order possesses its particular, individual 'spirit'" and Zweigert's own perception that the great legal families in the world are largely defined and distinguished by their particular "style"[393] – an idea that has become yet another staple in modern comparative law.[394]

While all these observations evince ample connections between Jhering's work and modern comparative law, they do not establish any direct "influence." There is no evidence that during the formative stage of their discipline, comparatists relied on Jhering's work. Indeed, a close look at Zweigert's article shows that he was cautious enough not to claim any direct influence either, his essay's title notwithstanding. Zweigert merely asserted that "the ways in which we compare laws today is infused more than a little with Jhering's spirit" and that Jhering "exercised a powerful influence on modern comparative law through his teaching of living reality and his teleological method."[395] In other words, Jhering's outlook and methodology helped to shape the discipline indirectly, and there are strong affinities between Jhering's approach and the theory and practice of current mainstream comparative law. Thus, even if Jhering was not among the fathers of the modern discipline, he was an important kindred spirit and methodological fellow traveler.

---

[387] *Graziadei*, Comparative Law (2019) 442–473.

[388] *Jhering*, Zweck II (1886) 400–401.

[389] *Reimann*, Comparative Law (2020) 186–190.

[390] *Zweigert and Kötz*, Einführung in die Rechtsvergleichung auf dem Gebiete des Privatrechts I (1971) 35–36.

[391] *Jhering*, Geist I (1852) 18.

[392] *Sacco*, Legal Formants (1991).

[393] *Zweigert and Siehr*, Jherings Influence on Comparative Legal Method (1971) 222.

[394] *Zweigert and Kötz*, Einführung in die Rechtsvergleichung vol. I (1971) 72–80.

[395] *Zweigert and Siehr*, Jherings Influence on Comparative Legal Method (1971) 215, 218 (referencing Gustav Radbruch, Vorschule der Rechtsphilosophie, 1947).

There is one instance, however, in which Jhering did have a direct influence on the twentieth century understanding of comparative law, and it was a result of Konrad Zweigert's own work. In 1969–1971 (i.e., just when he wrote his article), Zweigert and his co-author Hein Kötz published a two volume-treatise on comparative law.[396] In its introductory section, the authors referred to Jhering and quoted his language on the need for, and the benefits of, the comparative method at some length.[397] Their book soon became a canonical text. Going through three editions and translated into numerous languages, it has been one of the most widely read works in the field. As such, it has brought Jhering's remarks on comparative law to the attention of many thousands of readers all over the world, thus employing his ideas to shape the modern understanding of the discipline.

---

[396] *Zweigert and Kötz*, Einführung in die Rechtsvergleichung (2 vols. 1969–1971, 3d. ed. 1996).

[397] *Zweigert and Kötz*, Einführung in die Rechtsvergleichung vol. I (1971) 16, 46,

In Conclusion: Modes of Legal Thought

Rudolf von Jhering left an *oeuvre* of extraordinary breadth, diversity, and richness – ranging from doctrinal scholarship on modern Roman law, methodological writings, and historical studies to theories of the law's origin, nature, and function, research on social custom, and even a book on the pre-historical roots of European civilization. Some of this work became highly influential, especially his critique (and mockery) of a purely logical jurisprudence and his exposition of the law as a result of social struggle as well as a means to social ends. Other elements, like his reflections upon the origins of the feeling of justice, his critique of historiography, and his views on legal evolution, are known only to a small circle of specialists, even though they also contain many insights of enduring value.

In a Conclusion, it is tempting to undertake an integration of all these elements into some kind of overarching whole in order to discover the one true Jhering and the ultimate essence of his thought, and various scholars have claimed to have identified this or that theme that ties Jhering's work together.[1] Yet, as mentioned in the Introduction, it seems wiser not to embark on such an adventure. This is not only because it presents a fearsome challenge, and not even because the prospects of failure are formidable. It is also, and perhaps most importantly, because it would not be in Jhering's very own spirit. Jhering relished exploring his topics in multiple dimensions and usually remained unconcerned by the resulting tensions and contradictions.

Still, we can gain some general perspectives on Jhering's work as a whole by taking stock of the several modes through which Jhering thought about law in its historical and social context. These modes can be grouped in five clusters, each marked by tensions between different, and at times opposite, vantage points. They pertain to kinds of jurisprudence (internal vs. external views of law); orientations of law (individualist vs. social); frames of mind (as a jurist vs. artist, professional vs. amateur, etc.); methods of cognition (positivist science v. philosophical idealism); and, finally, understandings of justice (realist v. idealist).

Modes of Jurisprudence: The Internal and the External View of Law. The most easily recognized duality in Jhering's thinking was the result of his two basic perspectives on law. On the one hand, there was the "internal perspective" of looking at law as a world of principles, concepts, and rules. As we have seen in

---

[1] See Introduction, note 14 and text.

chapter II, this was the main focus of his work during the first half of his academic career, in the 1840s and 1850s. On the other hand, there was his "external perspective" of looking at law as a social and psychological phenomenon (often in its historical dimension), in particular as a creature of human "purpose" ("Zweck") and as an instrument of social control (ensuring the "conditions of life in society"). As chapter IV explained, this point of view dominated the second half of his academic life, during the 1870s and 1880s. In between, roughly in the 1860s, there was a period of transition from the former to the latter perspective which was explored in chapter III.

In pursuing the "internal perspective," Jhering played the traditional role of a legal scholar as defined by the civil law tradition since the high Middle Ages: that of an expert on legal principles, concepts, and rules, and on the methods of maintaining and developing them. It was precisely the role for which he had been trained. Thus, in his doctrinal and methodological work, his knowledge and understanding were broad and deep; he was in full control of the material and sure-footed in his analyses. Still, the most lasting contribution he made in this role was neither the dozen or so first-rate doctrinal pieces nor his development of a special ("natural-historical") method but rather his reshaping of the relationship between legal theory and practice. During the preceding generation (i.e., under Savigny and his successors, led by Puchta) academic theory had increasingly taken on a life of its own and had come to deal with law as a regime of abstract and timeless logic that could be organized in a perfect system; the needs of practice were often disregarded. Jhering eventually protested against this kind of abstract and theoretical scholarship. He not only brought the needs of practice back into the picture but actually insisted that they become the dominant concern even of legal academics. He thus downgraded principles and concepts from self-sufficient entities, developed and refined for their own sake, to mere working tools used for the solution of real-world problems. Thus he re-shuffled the priorities: the ultimate touchstone of law was no longer logical purity but practical sense. As Jhering later provocatively put it, jurisprudence needed to come from the "heaven of concepts" back down to earth.[2] Jhering's reorientation of jurisprudence towards practical needs was not a paradigm shift; in a sense, it was merely the correction of a temporary aberration in German jurisprudence. Jhering reminded his academic colleagues – whose civilian tendency for abstract reasoning and enthusiasm for systematic ordering had run a little amok – that the law's foremost goal is not logical perfection but practical utility; that reminder has by and large stuck.

In pursuing the "external perspective," Jhering thought and wrote about the origin, nature, and function of law as a whole. Here, he operated not as a jurist in the traditional, civilian, sense, but as a theorist reflecting upon law from a broad point of view. At the time, such broad reflection was often termed "philosophy"

[2] *Jhering*, Scherz und Ernst (1884) 335; see supra chapter III.2.

(by both Jhering and others); today, we would say that Jhering constructed a (social) theory of law. This was a project for which Jhering was *not* specifically trained. His philosophical knowledge was narrow and superficial,[3] and training in social theory was not available beyond reading the great thinkers like Montesquieu, Bentham or Mill. As a result, Jhering was now venturing onto terrain on which he was anything but sure-footed. His typically self-confident style of argumentation notwithstanding, he was skating on – at times terribly – thin ice. That had its upsides and downsides. The main upside was that his thinking was not much constrained by background knowledge; as a result, his own imagination and creativity had fairly free reign; this, in turn, produced a discourse that was much more adventurous and provocative – as well as much more interesting to a broader audience – than his work as a traditional jurist. The downsides were that Jhering's writings often became muddled, and that he lacked full control over the material; in fact, the material overwhelmed him time and again, and his major work in this area, "Der Zweck im Recht," was doomed to remain unfinished. As a result, Jhering's most important contribution in this context was not a solid, well-rounded, and consistent theory of law but rather a collection of provocative ideas and gripping theses about what law really is and does. Even though these ideas and theses were often half-baked, unsupported by meaningful evidence, and inconsistent, they decisively advanced modern jurisprudence: Jhering's social, psychological, and instrumentalist explanations and claims helped to free jurisprudence from the spell of idealist philosophy, the domination of the Historical School, and the grip of abstract conceptualism. They connected jurisprudence to the discourses in the upcoming natural and social sciences; and they updated legal thought in a manner needed in a fast industrializing and urbanizing environment. Jhering's shift from the established (internal) view of law as a set of principles, doctrines, and rules to an (external) understanding of law as purpose-based and instrumentalist *was* a paradigm change. Jhering propagated the social dimension of law and especially its utility as an instrument of social policy so unequivocally and loudly that his message eventually got through to future generations, most visibly in the United States.[4] As some of his contemporaries already noted, Jhering was ringing in a new era.[5]

Jhering never much connected his internal and external perspectives on law. To be sure, there was, strictly speaking, no need to reconcile them because they could easily co-exist: regarded from the inside, law can be a regime of principles, concepts, and rules; looked at from the outside, it can be a product of purpose

---

[3] See supra chapter I.1., notes 22–26 and text; see also infra notes 47 and text.

[4] Supra chapter VII.3.

[5] *Kuntze*, Rudolf von Jhering (1892) 616; see also *Stintzing and Landsberg*, Geschichte der deutschen Rechtswissenschaft III.2. (1910) 819. Kuntze also noted that, at the same time, Jhering's dear friend Bernhard Windscheid closed the era of *Pandektenwissenschaft* by casting its results into their final and authoritative form in his masterful treatise; *Kuntze* id. On Jhering and Windscheid, see supra chapter I.2., notes 133–155 and text.

and an instrument for the realization of social goals. Nor is the methodological perspective in his earlier work irreconcilable with the "philosophical" approach prevailing in his later work; both entail different questions calling for different answers and thus operate on different levels.[6] Still, Jhering made no sustained effort to explain exactly how the two sides connected – how the purpose-based nature and instrumental utility of law informed its content, structure and method as a system of principles and rules.[7] At the end of the day, the internal and external perspectives stood largely side-by-side without being integrated into an all-encompassing whole.

It must be emphasized that Jhering never considered one perspective a substitute for the other; instead they must both be employed, as he demonstrated in his doctrinal essays as well as in his teaching.[8] Even after he had turned his attention primarily to law as a social phenomenon and instrument, he continued to insist on the importance of a clearly defined conceptual apparatus and a logically organized system of rules.[9] Looking at law's purposes and uses, accounting for its historical and psychological origins, and considering the role of the "feeling of justice" ("Rechtsgefühl") did not render legal doctrine and technique superfluous. They still had to organize, streamline, and thus simplify the law, rendering it comprehensible, user-friendly, and effective.[10] Without a sound conceptual framework, Jhering warned, legal science will be "pushed to the ground under the weight of the growing mass of material and become a victim of its own richness;"[11] and, as in any other science, without a sound systematic ordering, the internal relationship between the various elements will not be truly understood – which will lead to massive confusion and fundamental error.[12] In short, while a realist and instrumental jurisprudence is utterly desirable, without a proper conceptual toolbox, sufficiently developed doctrine, and rational organizational structure, it will be a costly mess. It is fair to say that, by and large, jurists in charge of the legal

[6] See *Fikentscher*, Methoden des Rechts III (1976) 202.

[7] It is true that on some occasions, he demonstrated a connection in particular contexts, e.g, in his essay on the distribution of risk in contracts of sale; see supra chapter III.1, but he never developed a theoretical framework nor any general guidance for that purpose.

[8] Jhering employed both, however, in his doctrinal essays, see supra chapter II.3. and chapter III.1., as well as in his teaching, supra chapter II.5.

[9] Supra chapter III.3., notes 135–141 and text.

[10] See especially *Jhering*, Geist II.2. (1858) 341–346.

[11] *Jhering*, Geist II.2. (1858) 342. In a similar vein, Jhering emphasized the importance of a precise terminology, id. 344.

[12] "Thus, mistakes regarding the system are not harmless and innocent errors but are among the most dangerous of all, and the care which theory exercises in systematic questions is of utmost importance [...]. Every systematic error is the product, as well as the source, of a deficient understanding of the subject matter [...], and as long as science has not identified the proper systematic place for its object, it has not properly understood it either because understanding means not only to grasp the object in and of itself but also its connection with others." *Jhering*, Geist II.2. (1858) 344 note 480.

systems in the civil law tradition have continued to heed that admonition while those in charge of twentieth century US-American law (as well as of the law of the European Union) have not.

Thus, Jhering's understanding of law from an external perspective – as a result of social struggle and "merely" as a means to social ends – did not entail that law was nothing but politics. To be sure, for Jhering it was not, and should not be, an entirely autonomous field. Yet, it remained a professional discipline and practice in its own right with its own functions and benefits. Its doctrinal system not only rationalized, streamlined, and organized the law, it also stabilized it by working against erratic and hasty change and by helping to ensure the equal administration of the law. In the context of praising the "autonomy" of early Roman law (vis-a-vis religion, morality, and politics) in "Geist", Jhering warned against demands that "law keep constant pace with the movements of the times, that it meet all its requirements, [and] legalize all its ideas." To do so would result in a law "devoid of all indigenous stability, without will or character;" such a law would "soon deteriorate into a cheap tool of the current [political] power."[13] Law as a professional practice should certainly not prevent change, but it should slow it down and carefully control it because "the more easily, quickly, and frequently law is produced in a state, the weaker its moral force."[14] In other words, the stability provided by the law's doctrinal and systematic order is a precious commodity that should not be sacrificed lightly on the altar of momentary political moods or fashions. Thus, law is not only an indispensable instrument of politics but also an important counterweight to it.

Orientations of Law: The Individual and Society. Jhering also envisaged two orientations of law – one towards the individual, the other towards the collective: at times, the individual personality and its rights took center stage; on other occasions, society and its interests became the dominant concern. This dovetailed with the tension between the two prevalent political forces in Jhering's environment: the individualist credo of classical liberalism and the rising socialist tendencies that responded to industrialization and urbanization. At the same time, it reflected the duality of Jhering's self: he was both a strong-willed individual who jealously guarded his independence and his honor, as well as an eager member of various collectives, ranging from his family and law faculties to the German Lawyers Association and the Prussian State, each of which he served with a strong sense of duty towards the community.

The individualist side showed itself in several contexts. To begin with, there was Jhering's original conception of private law. He saw its historical origin in the individuals' forceful taking of property as bounty – which established rights entirely independently from the state.[15] Thus (private) law "originated not in the

---

[13] *Jhering*, Geist II.1. (1854) 22.

[14] *Jhering*, Geist I (1852) 63. "Witness that also in individuals," Jhering added, "[a great] production of good intentions is a sign of a weak character," id. note 31.

[15] Supra chapter II.1., notes 101–103 and text.

state but in the individual".[16] In addition, at times Jhering's conception of law was centered around the individual as a personality endowed with honor and dignity.[17] This was most pronounced in "Der Kampf ums Recht," where Jhering demanded that the law protect these attributes and that the individual stand up for his rights as matter of self-respect.[18] The ideal behind this view of the individual was the free and manly Roman citizen who took nothing lying down. Finally, the author of "Geist" extolled a "system of liberty" which bore the features of classical liberalism.[19] This was the Jhering who spoke out against the "crazy idea that everything has to be done by the state"[20] and who reminded his readers of the (alleged) Roman "aversion against interference by state officials."[21]

Yet, it was the collectivist element that eventually came to shape Jhering's theory of law as developed in the first volume of "Zweck." Here, the dominant player was no longer the individual but society itself that Jhering now conceived of almost like a person, especially when organized as a state. Here, the primary concerns were no longer the rights of the individual but the interests of society. As a consequence, Jhering never tired emphasizing that private (property and other) rights were not untouchable at all but rather subject to limitation as needed in the collective interest.[22] As a consequence, Jhering rejected the individualist (British) version of utilitarianism in favor of a "social" variety: the ultimate question was not what was good for individual happiness but what was best served the needs of society and the state.[23]

In this case, Jhering did try to integrate the two sides of his thinking into an overall theory. It was the theory of bounded liberty, i.e., of individual freedom as duly limited by the needs of social life. Here, Jhering, who so often took radical positions, avoided extremes: he rejected both *laissez faire* liberalism and fundamentalist socialism, instead advocating a harmonization of individual and collective interests.[24] Jhering once again paraded early Roman society as the model. In Jhering's idealized rendition, the Romans had managed to create a "system of liberty" which both guaranteed individual freedom and subordinated individual interests to those of the state whenever necessary. They had been able to pull that off because the Roman citizens had understood that it was in their own best interest to exercise their liberty with moderation.[25] Jhering thus propagated a

---

[16] *Jhering*, Geist I (1852) 146; see also id. 205.

[17] For a detailed discussion and analysis of Jhering's conceptions of Persönlichkeit (personality), see *Pleister*, Persönlichkeit, Wille und Freiheit im Werke Jherings (1982) 193–218.

[18] Supra chapter IV.1., notes 65–67 and text.

[19] *Jhering*, Geist II.2. (1858) 123–134.

[20] *Jhering*, Geist I (1852) 117.

[21] *Jhering*, Geist II.2. (1858) 246.

[22] Supra chapter IV.2., notes 257–263 and text.

[23] Supra chapter IV.2., notes 316–340 and text.

[24] At the time, this was not an unusual idea; it was also propagated by the historian Heinrich von Treitschke (1834–1896) – whom Jhering admired – in his essay "Die Freiheit" ("Liberty") (1861).

[25] *Jhering*, Geist I (1852) 310–311; *Jhering*, Geist II.1. (1854) 124–134, 146–149, 222–225, 319–320, etc.

view of the citizen as, at the same time, an individual who was endowed with rights, honor, and dignity, and a socially conscious group member who willingly accepted that his interests may have to be subordinated to those of society and the state, because their well-being was crucial for his own.

But what if citizens were not as perceptive, socially minded, and loyal to their state as in ancient Rome? For Jhering, the primary instrument to ensure the adjustment of individual and collective interests was the state's power of coercion through law. Law had to constrain the innate egoism of the individual as required by life in society, and it had to establish a system of rules and institutions which harnessed this egoism in a way that benefited the collective. In short, law was the means that enabled naturally egoistical human beings to live in society and form a state.[26]

Exactly how this was to be accomplished, Jhering did not say. He was of course aware of the problem that at some point a line had to be drawn between individual rights and social interests. Yet, he also understood that for this problem, there was no universally valid solution. Instead, how to balance personal liberty and societal concerns depended on the varying historical and social circumstances and was for each age and society itself to decide. Jhering did, however, believe that mankind was gradually overcoming egoism and thus progressing towards reconciliation of individual and collective interests.[27] This was a happy prospect, of course, and it found great favor with the jurists of the progressive era in early twentieth century America.[28]

Frames of Mind: The Jurist and His Alter Egos. Jhering is generally known as a jurist but as the foregoing chapters have shown, he transcended that role in several ways and directions: he was also a legal historian, a student of social norms, and a writer of cultural history. In addition, he approached many of his topics not only with an academic intellect but also with the mentality of an artist, and not only with professional expertise but also with the sheer curiosity of an amateur. Depending on the respective frame of mind, Jhering thought and wrote in remarkably diverse fashions and voices, displaying a variety of strengths and weaknesses.[29]

"As a jurist, he has few equals," Ludwig Mitteis wrote in 1905.[30] Such praise was well-deserved when Jhering operated on the field of legal doctrine. Here, he displayed superb analytical skills, great dexterity in handling the sources, and a remarkable intuition for sensible solutions. His argumentation was precise and careful without getting lost in minutiae; circumspect and sober without becoming

---

[26] See supra chapter IV.2., notes 194–200 and text.

[27] Supra chapter IV.3., notes 480–481 and text; chapter V.3., notes 68–69, 92, 111–484 and text.

[28] Supra chapter VII.3., notes 220–224 and text; see also id. notes 287–293 and text.

[29] Rückert describes Jhering's many faces as a variety of "talents;" *Rückert*, Der Geist des Rechts (2004) 129.

[30] *Mitteis*, Jhering (1905) 658.

labored; courageous and creative without losing its grounding; in addition, his doctrinal essays were informed by common sense and the needs of practice.[31] In short, here he produced first-rate legal scholarship. His work on the field of legal method was a more mixed bag. Jhering deserves credit for formulating a sophisticated methodology for the Romanist jurisprudence of his time; he not only described and analyzed its various steps but explained their *raison d'etre* and their benefits in an original fashion.[32] Yet, he also extolled the virtues of this method with quasi-religious fervor – which he later came to regret.[33]

When Jhering left the traditional jurist's role behind and sought to construct a social theory of law, especially in the first volume of "Zweck," we suddenly encounter a very different, and much more problematic, thinker. To be sure, it was here that Jhering truly broke new ground and where his insights into the origin, nature, and function of law were most penetrating, provocative, and influential in the long run. At the same time, however, Jhering's discourse now lacked almost all the qualities that marked his doctrinal and methodological work. It suffered from irritating terminological confusion; it became rambling, redundant, and at times incoherent; and its overall structure was not only bewildering but also repeatedly ignored by Jhering himself and subject to change without notice.[34] In fact, Jhering's terminological carelessness and organizational confusion are unforgivable for a civilian, let alone a nineteenth century German, jurist. It seems that Jhering was extremely capable at analyzing and solving discrete problems in a masterful manner but also surprisingly incapable of handling broad theoretical challenges in a controlled and conclusive fashion. The primary reason for this fatal weakness was not his lack of philosophical training but his intellectual predisposition: he generated too many ideas, could not resist following too many leads, changed his views too quickly and frequently, and he began publishing work piecemeal way before he was sure where it would ultimately take him. As a result, "Geist" remained incomplete and "Zweck" collapsed under its own weight.

The same is true, *mutatis mutandis*, for Jhering as a student of social norms. As long as he focused on concrete phenomena, such as fashion, usage, and custom, his mind operated largely as it did on the field of legal doctrine, i.e., in an exploratory, analytical, and disciplined fashion. Especially in the second volume of "Zweck," he carefully distinguished and defined individual types of social norms (mainly according to their degree of bindingness), diligently laid out their origin and function, and patiently elucidated their relationship to one another.[35] Occasionally, he also proffered critiques and suggestions for reform, as in his tract

[31] See supra chapter II.3.

[32] Supra chapter II.2.

[33] Supra chapter II.2., notes 248–250 and text; chapter III.2., notes 39–51 and text, notes 105–110 and text.

[34] Supra chapter IV.2., notes 381–396 and text.

[35] See supra chapter VI.1.

"Das Trinkgeld."[36] All this work was grounded in astute first-hand observations of social circumstances and practices which was highly unusual before the rise of sociology as an established discipline. As a result, Jhering's exploration of the patterns of social norms created not only a portrait of contemporary bourgeois society, along the way it also generated insights that are eye-opening even to a modern reader. Yet, as soon as Jhering turned to broad theorizing in pursuit of "a teleological system of the universal ethical order,"[37] things went awry: his structure disintegrated, he lost control over the material, and eventually abandoned the quest. Once again, he lacked the organizational skill, as well as the intellectual discipline, to keep his inquiry on track and to bring it to conclusion. Once again, the reader was left with a ragbag of fascinating observations and a firework of ideas but no coherent theory or overall result.

As a legal historian, Jhering worked in a very different mode. His subject – mainly early Roman law – presented challenges that diverged radically from those of doctrinal, methodological or theoretical work. As Jhering understood and openly acknowledged, the main difficulty with early Roman law was the scarcity of original sources. To make matters worse, most of these sources, like the writings of Cicero (106–43 A.D.) or Livy (59 A.D.–17 B.C.), dated from later centuries and thus had to be approached with caution. On the whole, reliable knowledge about early Rome and its law was extremely limited. To most modern historians, this suggests limiting its description accordingly, i.e., to a fairly sketchy account. That, however, Jhering was not ready to do. Instead, he supplemented the existing knowledge by two, interconnected, means each of which reflected a side of his personality. One evinced his commitment to serious academic research: Jhering carefully and doggedly mined additional material for information; in particular, he looked for linguistic clues and extrapolated from later (well-known) Roman law, reasoning backwards, so to speak. The other means reflected his lively imagination: Jhering interpreted the clues he found in a creative and speculative fashion that sometimes pushed the boundaries of plausibility. Overall, Jhering's approach demonstrated both his worrisome willingness to proceed on the basis of scant evidence and his great talent for bringing history to life.

When Jhering, at the end of his life, ventured into cultural history in his "Vorgeschichte der Indoeuropäer" ("Prehistory of the Indo-Europeans") (1894), he displayed the same strategies – only in a more extreme form. Here, original sources or other reliable evidence were well-nigh non-existent. Thus Jhering had to rely almost entirely on the often shaky conclusions he drew from linguistic (especially Sanskrit) studies and other secondary evidence as well as on his imagination. Now, however, imagination was no longer one ingredient among others but the predominant element in Jhering's account. While the available data could

[36] See supra chapter VI.2.

[37] Supra chapter IV.2., note 176–177 and text.

not support the writing of a verifiable history, Jhering's imagination still enabled him to present an intriguing and marginally plausible account, thus taunting others to prove him wrong.[38]

The diversity of these frames of mind and the tensions between them, were rooted in, or at least fueled by, two dichotomies that marked Jhering's personality.

One was his dual character as both a scholar and an artist; a man who became a law professor but who had originally wanted to become a writer; who loved (and played) classical music; and who sought (and found) beauty even in law.[39] As a scholar, Jhering was committed to working with the existing sources and evidence, arguing in a precise and consistent fashion, and drawing conclusions that were supported by the material. He exercised intellectual discipline, respected the limits of his understanding, and wrote in a sober and unspectacular style. As an artist, he refused to be constrained by academic conventions and pushed beyond established boundaries. His thinking was bold and creative, but it could also be heedless and disorganized. He was happy to take intellectual risks and followed his imagination wherever it took him even though that was often far away from his original topic. His rhetoric was flamboyant, full of wit, and irony, but it could also deteriorate into triviality and bad taste. On some occasions, the scholar was dominant, as in his doctrinal work and his studies of social norms.[40] Sometimes, the artist took over, most visibly in his "Heaven of Concepts."[41] Often, the scholar and the artist operated in tandem, creating a mixture of serious academic work and flights of imagination, as in his writings on legal and cultural history and in parts of his methodological discourse.[42] The respective weight of the academic and the artistic elements varied with the occasion.

The other, related, dichotomy was that of the professional and the amateur. Jhering's academic training and qualifications were strong but narrow: he had studied, and was primarily a scholar of, ancient and modern Roman law. On that terrain, he worked with the ethos of a highly qualified professional. He adhered to the standards of his guild, sought recognition by his peers, and eagerly participated in the academic give-and-take. As time went on, however, he found that terrain too narrow. When he first ventured beyond it in order to theorize more broadly about the law, he was still dealing with a thoroughly familiar subject, but he was no longer working with familiar tools – on the fields of "philosophy" and social theory, he was, as he openly admitted, a "dilettante".[43] And when he later he turned away from law altogether and towards social custom and cultural history, he was an amateur with regard to both his subject and his method. As an

[38] Supra chapter VI.3.

[39] See supra chapter I.4., notes 220–223 and text; chapter II.2., notes 306–307 and text.

[40] Supra chapters II.3. and VI.1.

[41] Supra chapter III.2.

[42] Supra chapters II.1., VI.3., and II.2.

[43] *Jhering*, Zweck I (1884) IX; see also *Jhering*, *Zweck* II (1886) XIV–XV.

amateur, Jhering eventually granted himself much (some would say excessive) license. He no longer wrote primarily for his fellow-jurists but for a broader audience as well as, increasingly, just for himself. He cared less and less for satisfying professional standards and became more and more interested in exploring unchartered territory and generating new insights. It is interesting to observe that Jhering made his most lasting and influential contributions on that middle-ground between fully professional academic scholarship (in legal doctrine and methodology) and fully amateurish work (in social custom and cultural history). On that middle ground, i.e., in the construction of his legal theory (primarily in the first volume of "Zweck"), he knew enough about the subject (i.e., law and its history) to deal with it authoritatively but not enough about philosophical theory to tie him to established paradigms. Thus, he could make short order of Kantian, Hegelian, English utilitarian, and other ideas and then promptly proffer his own historical and social theory of law. In other words, Jhering produced his most interesting ideas when the professional and the amateur complemented one another.

Methods of Cognition: The Scientist and the Philosopher. During Jhering's lifetime, the older metaphysics of German idealist philosophy, most prominently represented by Kant and Hegel, gradually lost its grip on the minds of intellectuals in favor of the positivism advocated by Comte and underlying the rise of both the natural and social sciences. Simply put, the focus shifted from speculation about abstract ideas to the observation of concrete facts. Jhering's own thinking evinced that shift by avidly embracing the newer paradigm while still clinging to the older one. On the one hand, Jhering saw himself as a scientist who looks at real-world data and draws conclusions from his findings. He employed the terminology of the natural sciences in his methodological discourses; he insisted that jurisprudence focus on the realities of life ("das Leben"); and on at least some occasions, he wanted to recognize as law only that which is actually being enforced on the ground. In his legal history, he often checked the stated rules against (presumed) actual practices, and in constructing his legal theory, he foregrounded social conditions and needs. He also based his analyses of social customs in the second volume of "Zweck" on first-hand, real-world observations. Here, his mindset resembled that of Comte, Darwin, and the coming generation of professional sociologists. One the other hand, Jhering saw himself as an (amateur) philosopher[44] and thus viewed law (and other phenomena) from a somewhat dated idealist perspective. Unable – or unwilling – to content himself with the mere observation of the real world, he sought to understand how it all made (philosophical) sense. Thus, he looked beyond his factual observations and searched for higher meanings, strove to establish a system of ethics,[45] and appealed to the ideal element in law.[46]

---

[44] See, e.g., *Jhering*, Zweck I (1884) IX–X.

[45] Supra chapter VI.1., notes 10–18 and text.

[46] Supra chapter IV.1., notes 124–126 and text.

Both these modes of thinking were problematic because Jhering did not possess sufficient competence for either. He was not a trained scientist and showed no signs of being versed in the basic scientific methods of controlled data collection and systematic testing of hypotheses. Thus, his observations were largely random and his conclusions mostly ad hoc. Still, while they were, strictly speaking, not scientifically solid, these observations and conclusions were usually interesting, often perceptive, and occasionally brilliant. Nor was Jhering thoroughly trained or versed in philosophy.[47] He referred to, and quoted from, Kant and Hegel from (often apparently vague) memory and as it suited his current purposes, and many of his references were no more than window-dressing. Thus it is no surprise that Jhering's philosophical musings yielded meager results. They embellished his talks and writings and probably catered to his audiences' desires, but they generated no eye-opening insights, and, truth be told, posterity would be no worse off without them.

Jhering also failed to demonstrate how the scientific-positivist and philosophical-idealist perspectives could be integrated. To be sure, he clearly saw them as intimately connected. In this regard a true Hegelian, Jhering believed that in reality there was truth;[48] that the study of history could (and should) reveal that truth;[49] and that the ultimate court in which good and evil were judged was history itself.[50] Yet, these were just Hegelian generalities, which Jhering uncritically adopted to express vaguely held convictions.[51] They provided no explanations of any kind, did not add up to any sort of theory, and had no analytical traction. Here, Jhering essentially subscribed to the kind of metaphysical postulates he otherwise so strongly condemned. Unable, and perhaps even unwilling, to think about their relationship more deeply, Jhering mostly oscillated between the scientist's and the philosopher's perspectives more or less at random. Which of them predominated at any given moment apparently depended on what the occasion called for or what was currently stronger: the positivist's determination to stick to reality and its observable facts or the idealist's longing for some higher meaning.[52] If, at the end of the day, Jhering could reconcile the positivist's commitment to the recognition of the facts of life with the idealist's faith in the existence of reliable ethical precepts at all, it was only through the idea – apparently taken from Lessing – that the development of mankind was guided by

---

[47] See supra chapter I.4., notes 22–26 and text.

[48] "Truth does not lie beyond the world, it lies in the world." ("Die Wahrheit liegt nicht außerhalb der Welt, sie liegt in der Welt.") *Jhering*, Über die Entstehung des Rechtsgefühls (1868) 68.

[49] "The true task of historiography is to find, in change, the truth." ("Die wahre Aufgabe der Geschichtsschreibung ist, im Wechsel die Wahrheit zu finden.") *Jhering*, Über die Entstehung des Rechtsfühls (1868) 71.

[50] Supra chapter IV.3., notes 511–514 and text.

[51] *Rückert*, Der Geist des Rechts (2004) 136–139.

[52] On Jhering's "historical-metaphysical perception of the fundamental unity of fact and norm," see *Rückert*, Der Geist des Rechts (2004) 137–138.

God's design which guaranteed progression towards moral perfection.[53] Yet, that argument was not substantiated; it was merely presented as an article of faith.

Still, by importing conceptions and methods from biology, chemistry, and sometimes human medicine into jurisprudence (however crudely and imperfectly), Jhering linked his own discipline to the hard sciences and thus updated it (so to speak) in crucial ways. At a time when the tenets of philosophical idealism and the credos of the Historical School looked hopelessly old-fashioned if not plainly irrelevant, Jhering pointed to a new form of legal science that could be regarded as a worthy counterpart to the meteorically rising natural sciences. As Ludwig Mitteis observed, it was Jhering more than anyone else at the time who ensured the continuing prestige and popularity of jurisprudence.[54]

Modes of Justice: The Positivist and the Idealist. Last, but certainly not least, Jhering took two fundamentally different positions vis-a-vis the law's core postulate, i.e., the notion of justice. These two positions were related to his two modes of cognition: taking the position of the scientist, he subscribed to a strictly positivist view; thinking in philosophical and idealist terms, he sought to grasp a notion of justice based on fundamental values. The tension between these views was palpable.[55]

In the (social) theory of law he proffered in the first volume of "Zweck," Jhering took a categorically positivist position that, as we have seen, combined instrumentalism with relativism.[56] Law was "merely" a means used by the state to the end of securing "the conditions of life in society."[57] From this purely instrumental point of view, law was judged not according to any substantive values but only by how well it did its job – whatever that job might be. To put it differently, since law was merely a means to an end, the end ultimately justified the means – a position which Jhering was, at least at times, perfectly ready to take.[58] The ends, in turn, were relative because the respective social conditions to be secured varied greatly over time and space; thus, the law's requisite content was necessarily "infinitely various."[59] Jhering's combination of instrumentalism and relativism implied rejection of a universally valid normative position from which law could

---

[53] See supra chapter IV.3., note 104–110 and text. Note that a century earlier, Goethe was not so sure: in his poem "Das Göttliche" ("The Divine"), written in 1783, Goethe portrayed nature as indifferent to good or evil, put responsibility for ethics squarely on man (der Mensch), and treated the gods essentially as reflections of human qualities.

[54] *Mitteis*, Jhering (1905) 682–683.

[55] The interplay was recognized already by the early commentators on Jhering and his work, see, e.g., *Stintzing and Landsberg*, Geschichte der deutschen Rechtswissenschaft III.2 (1910) 821.

[56] Supra chapter IV.2., notes 207–230 and text.

[57] *Jhering*, Zweck I (1884) 443.

[58] Letter to Windscheid of August 19, 1866, Jhering in Briefen (1913) 206–207. Jhering approved of Bismarck's political machinations, which Jhering had previously considered morally despicable, as "indispensible means to an end" – not grudgingly but enthusiastically.

[59] *Jhering*, Zweck I (1884) 439.

be judged: "The standard of law is not the absolute one of truth, but the relative one of purpose."[60]

The disconcerting consequences of Jhering's positivism are obvious and have been extensively discussed in the literature. If law is reduced to an instrument serving any purpose whatsoever, then there are no absolute constraints on what its creators are allowed to do. The logical result is that jurisprudence is indifferent even to the abuse of law by tyrants, dictators, and other rogue regimes. Thus, some commentators assigned to Jhering part of the responsibility for the perversion of law by the totalitarian regimes of the twentieth century – not because he envisaged or intended this perversion but because his positivism eroded the trust in fundamental ethical values that might have prevented or at least limited civilization's descent into barbarism.[61]

Various German scholars tried to come to Jhering's defense but they did so in ways that do not always hold up to much scrutiny. In his methodological study, Wolfgang Fikentscher argued that Jhering always implicitly assumed that all "purposes" of law must be "just."[62] This argument is not only unsupported by any evidence, it also contradicts Jhering's express acceptance of laws that he recognized as clearly unacceptable according to the values of his own time and environment.[63] Others reckoned that Jhering did not really grasp the implications of his positivism.[64] That would be difficult to reconcile with Jhering's sharp and fearless intellect, and it is also hard to square with indications that he did, indeed, understand the inherent dangers of law entirely reduced to politics.[65] Legal philosopher Erik Wolf, generally a harsh critic of the nineteenth-century turn from idealism to positivism,[66] interpreted Jhering's failure to embrace absolute values of justice as a sign of prudent self-limitation, philosophical modesty, and even "intellectual shyness." Yet, it is not true that "Jhering persisted in remaining silent about any deeper or higher justification of law;"[67] instead, he struggled long and hard with this deeper or higher meaning. At the end of the day, we have to accept that when Jhering took a strictly positivist, and thus potentially bleak, view of law, he meant it.

There are three considerations that put Jhering's positivist conception of justice into perspective and moderate its inherent dangers. First, Jhering's refusal to recognize any absolute values must be understood in the context of an environ-

---

[60] *Jhering*, Zweck I (1884) 439.

[61] Supra chapter VII.1., notes 424, 427.

[62] *Fikentscher*, Methoden des Rechts III (1976) 276.

[63] *Jhering*, Zweck I (1884) 446–447, see supra chapter VI.2., notes 222–229 and text.

[64] *Wolf*, Große Rechtsdenker (1963) 650; *Larenz*, Methodenlehre der Rechtswissenschaft (1983) 48 (fn. 27); *Wieacker*, Privatrechtsgeschichte (1967) 463, is more cautious ("lack of a clear understanding of the consequences").

[65] *Jhering*, Geist II.1. (1854) 22–23, 75–76; see also supra chapter IV.4., notes 219–221 and text.

[66] *Wolf*, Große Rechtsdenker (1963) 622–627, 654, etc.

[67] *Wolf*, Große Rechtsdenker (1963) 663.

ment which Austrian writer Stefan Zweig (1881–1942) termed, and vividly described as, "the world of security."[68] The late nineteenth century was an era when people in Jhering's world had enormous confidence in the stability of the social, political, and economic order. The bourgeoisie of Jhering's generation neither could nor wanted to imagine the total collapse of the rule of law, the rise of brutal dictatorships, and the decline into the unspeakable savagery which would mark much of Europe after 1914. Thus, for Jhering and his contemporaries, not embracing absolute values of justice did not raise the specter of barbarism as it does for us today. Second, most contemporaries – Jhering himself prominently among them – also had enormous faith in the progress of civilization.[69] "I live in the firm belief," Jhering wrote in the second volume of "Zweck," "that mankind becomes steadily better, rather than worse"[70] – a process ultimately driven by divine design.[71] In particular, for Jhering, history promised constantly to improve the lot of the weak vis-a-vis the strong and thus to move towards a more equal and just society.[72] Such a firm belief in social progress, again, largely obviated an urgent need to commit to absolute values. Finally, Jhering's denial of timeless notions of justice was based on the unspoken assumption that the law's doctrinal and systematic apparatus provided a fair amount of stability and thereby insurance against extreme abuses of justice. At least the private law of the time was predicated on the autonomy of the person and the equality of rights. These foundations must have seemed unshakable to Jhering, his professional colleagues, and the majority of his contemporaries. In short, for people who trusted that civilization will not go off the rails but rather continue on the path of progress, the ethical risks inherent in Jhering's sociological positivism would have appeared small.[73]

In contrast to Jhering-the-positivist who refused to embrace the notion of substantive justice as a value in and of itself, there was Jhering-the-idealist who frequently proclaimed the importance of justice as such a value, almost desperately tried to come to grips with it, and actually proffered some ideas of its substantive content.

This idealist Jhering emerged mainly during the second part of his professional life when substantive justice became a recurrent theme in his work. At first, he

---

[68] *Zweig*, Die Welt der Sicherheit (2013, orig. 1942).

[69] See, e.g., *Jhering*, Geist II.2. (1858) 97 ("the gigantic progress of history"); see supra chapter V.3. and 4.

[70] *Jhering*, Zweck II (1886) 133; Jhering added, however, that this would not happen automatically but rather required sustained effort, in particular learning form historical experience, id.

[71] See supra chapter V.2., notes 103–110 and text.

[72] *Jhering*, Zweck I (1884) 243.

[73] The virtually unconditional belief in progress largely collapsed in the wake of World War I and the social upheaval it triggered in many parts of Europe; witness the entirely different perspective of *Spengler*, Der Untergang des Abendlandes (The Decline of the West) (1918–1922).

invoked it against the purely technical (doctrinal and methodological) approach to law that he had embraced his earlier writings. He now reminded his readers – as much as himself – that "above the merely formal juristic logic, there is the higher and supreme [value] of the substantive idea of justice and ethics." Immersing oneself in "how it realizes itself in the individual legal institutions and rules is [...] the most beautiful and sublime task [legal] science can set for itself."[74] Later, when Jhering called on his audience to fight for the realization of law in "Kampf," he envisaged not only the enforcement of positive rules but also the satisfaction of the demands of justice.[75] Perhaps most importantly, in the very context of developing his positivist theory of law in the first volume of "Zweck," Jhering not only touched on the idea of justice time and again,[76] he also presented it as "the life principle of society" and, thus, its "supreme goal."[77] In this manner, "Gerechtigkeit" constituted an increasingly important counterpoint to Jhering's otherwise technical and positivist approach.

Remarkably, Jhering did not leave it at periodic reminders that justice mattered but repeatedly struggled to come to grips with its substantive content – though ultimately without much success. One attempt was to locate its standards in "the feeling of justice" ("Rechtsfühl"). Yet, Jhering's initial faith in an innate and thus absolute human sense of right and wrong soon crumbled. Instead, Jhering became convinced that the sense of justice was just as much a product of historical circumstances and experiences as was law itself – and, thus, just as relative.[78] Another attempt was Jhering's investigation of ethics as a possible source of absolute standards by which law could be judged. Yet, again, the principles and rules of ethics also turned out be historically and culturally contingent and thus as varying as the laws themselves.[79] In short, both attempts to identify fixed reference points from which law could be evaluated ended in failure. Accordingly, Jhering found himself relegated to finding "the idea of higher justice in world history."[80] Like the standards for the welfare of society, the question of

[74] *Jhering*, Geist II.2. (5th ed. 1898, unrevised) 361 note 506a. Jhering's articles on the double-sale and on the *culpa in contrahendo* demonstrated that Jhering put his money where his mouth was: in both these (as well as in various other) instances, he went beyond the technical and doctrinal level to find solutions that satisfied his sense of justice, see supra chapter II.2. and chapter III.1.

[75] Note Jhering's frequent references to the feeling of justice (Rechtsgefühl) in "Kampf," *Jhering*, Kampf (1872). That justice was part of his concern is perhaps most obvious in his discourse on Michael Kohlhaas' struggle against the wrong he had suffered, id. 66–69.

[76] *Jhering*, Zweck I (1884) 139–140, 184, 230–231, 365–369, 372, etc.

[77] "Das Lebensprinzip der Gesellschaft;" "höchste Aufgabe"; *Jhering*, Zweck I (1884) 554; see also *Jhering*, Kampf (1872) 74.

[78] Supra chapter IV.3.

[79] Supra chapter VI.1., notes 23–45 and text.

[80] "[I]n der Weltgeschichte;" *Jhering*, Entwicklungsgeschichte des römischen Rechts (1894) 6. On Jhering's idealist search for absolute principles of law in history, see *Kunze*, Lieber in Gießen als irgendwo anders (2018) 36–37.

justice could be answered only by history – "by unfolding one page after another of its book."[81] In the end, the substantive content of justice remained elusive.

Like his internal and external perspectives on law, and like his scientific and philosophical quests for understanding the world, Jhering did not integrate his positivist and idealist approaches to the problem of justice into an overarching theory. As discussed before, there are several ways to envisage their relationship.[82] One is simply to let these approaches exist side-by-side and recognize the inherent tension between them – i.e., simply to accept what we actually see in Jhering's work. Another way is to regard these two views as manifestations of two different projects. Jhering's project as a scientist and positivist was to recognize and state what is; this resulted in the portrayal of justice as an historically and culturally contingent construct devoid of absolute content. By contrast, Jhering's project as a philosopher and idealist was to determine what ought to be and thus to identify the substantive requirements of justice. These two projects were compatible, of course. It is just that pursuing the former was largely successful while engagement with latter ended largely in failure: Jhering constructed a plausible positivist theory of law, by which its development and function could be *explained*, but he did not manage to define a system of (ethical) precepts, by which law could be *evaluated*. A third way to relate his two positions rests on the distinction between an absolute and a relative conception of justice: while the diversity of societies throughout history made it impossible to define justice in absolute and eternal terms, it was still possible to define it in relative and temporary terms, i.e., for a given society and stage of development. Jhering's calls for substantive justice, as well as his occasional attempts to define it (e.g., as rooted in equality), would then be implicitly limited to his own civilization and age. Although Jhering never explicitly proffered such a squaring of his positivist and idealist positions, it is perhaps the most plausible way to reconcile them.

Contradictions and Extremes. The modes of thought discussed in this Conclusion have two common features: Jhering reflected upon the law (and other matters) in an almost habitually diverse and often contradictory fashion, and he often embraced extreme positions that ultimately defied reconciliation.

Jhering was well aware, and apparently outright proud, of his habit of looking at the subjects of his inquiries from opposite perspectives. After he had presented a particular view (on Roman law) in an essay, he turned directly to the reader.

"You ask whether I am serious about it? To be honest: No! When it is crucial to do justice to the different sides of one and the same institution, it is my habit to immerse my thoughts in the side I am currently discussing, in a consciously and intentionally one-sided manner, to fall in love with it, so to speak, as if it were the only one worth considering. I proceed likewise with the next [side] to be considered; the previous one is then completely forgotten

[81] *Jhering*, Zweck II (1886) 205.
[82] Supra chapter IV.3., notes 496–510 and text.

– as is also often true when falling in love! – I can then be sure that none [of the two sides] gets the short end of the stick."[83]

It is true that Jhering also had a tendency to announce monolithic truths, such as the character of law as solely a creature of purpose[84] or the feeling of justice as merely the result of evolving social conditions.[85] At bottom, however, Jhering was a dialectical thinker who acknowledged the *sic et non.* For him, to let contradictory positions develop and battle each other freely was a "privilege of true strength," just as enduring the contradictions inherent in human nature are a touchstone of character.[86]

Jhering was not only convinced that looking at phenomena from different perspectives was the best path to their understanding, he also believed that taking extreme positions advanced that cause. "Every new and fundamental truth," he asserted, "has a right to one-sidedness when it is first presented."[87] Jhering recognized the inherent risk of error – and gladly accepted it. "Try who may whether he can remain free from [error]," he challenged his colleagues, and added "I feel strong enough to provoke judgment on me, and I waive the right to lenient treatment."[88] To be sure, he also tended to get carried away by his own enthusiasm for a position – a tendency he was fully aware of and acknowledged as a weakness.[89] Still, at the end of the day, he believed that we often learn more from being boldly wrong than from being timidly right.

In short, Jhering tended to think and argue in both dialectical and provocative terms. As Karl Larenz put it, "the patient accommodation of extremes was not his cup of tea."[90] Jhering's great strength lay in challenging established wisdom, opening new perspectives, and promoting intellectual progress by triggering strong reactions from both friend and foe. His great weakness was that he mostly left it at that – that he by and large failed to integrate, or at least to reconcile, his various positions. In Hegelian terms, Jhering proffered a lot of theses and many

---

[83] *Jhering*, Scherz und Ernst (1884) 187.

[84] Supra chapter VI.2., notes 209–210 and text.

[85] Supra chapter IV.3., notes 471–477 and text.

[86] *Jhering*, Geist I (1852) 310; for Jhering, the early Romans exemplified this strength, id. 311.

[87] *Jhering*, Geist II.1. (5th ed. 1891) 26.

[88] *Jhering*, Geist II.2. (1858) VI.

[89] "If I have ensconced myself in a certain set of ideas for some time, I become a fanatic, the "spirit" overcomes me, and it may happen then that, in addition to the good results produced by such an agitated mood, I also cause trouble, e.g., get ahead of myself ("Wenn ich mich längere Zeit in einen gewissen Ideenkreis hineingesponnen habe, so werde ich Fanatiker, der 'Geist' kommt über mich, und da passiert es mir dann wohl, daß ich neben dem Guten, das ich einer solchen gehobenen Stimmung verdanke, auch Unheil anrichte, mich, wie man so sagt, vergallopiere.") […]; letter to Windscheid of July 29, 1856, Jhering in Briefen (1913) 67

[90] *Larenz*, Rudolf von Jhering und die heutige Lage der Rechtswissenschaft (1970) 141. Jhering left that to his friend Bernhard Windscheid who mastered the art of accommodation and reconciliation of the various positions on a given issue.

antitheses, but little success at synthesis. As a result, it seems best to accept Jhering's *oeuvre* as what it is: a largesse of ideas that provide vast amounts of food for thought not despite, but often exactly because of, their perennial diversity, frequent extremism, and inevitable contradictions.

In his last work, published posthumously, Jhering stated his perhaps most fundamental credo:

> "Failed hypotheses and daring combinations have often proven to be the first step towards the discovery of the truth; they already contained the presentiment of what is true. They are flares, thrown into the dark, which the quest of science cannot do without; even if only some of them have illuminated matters not recognized before, then the remaining ones, though thrown uselessly, have paid off."[91]

---

[91] "Verfehlte Hypothesen und gewagte Kombinationen haben sich vielfach als der erste Schritt zur Entdeckung der Wahrheit herausgestellt, es war bereits die Ahnung des Richtungen, die sich in ihnen kundgab, es sind Leuchtkugeln, geworfen ins Dunkle, welche die suchende Wissenschaft einmal nicht entbehren kann; haben auch nur einige von ihnen Dinge ins Licht gesetzt, die man bisher nicht wahrgenommen hat, so haben sich die übrigen, die nutzlos geworfen sind, bezahlt gemacht." *Jhering*, Entwicklungsgeschichte des römischen Rechts (1894) 34.

Bibliography

A. Unprinted Sources

A collection of Jhering's handwritten notes and drafts are kept by the Niedersächsische Staats- und Universitätbibliothek in Göttingen, Germany, in 24 boxes under Cod.Ms.Jhering (1–25). The institution's website provides links to a list of these materials as well as to the digitized version.

A list of unprinted sources is provided by *Christoph-Eric Mecke*, Rudolf von Jhering. Anonym publizierte Frühschriften und unveröffentlichte Handschriften (Göttingen 2010) 259–260.

B. Works by Jhering

The following list contains only the works referenced in the text and is organized in chronological order. There are several more complete bibliographies of Jhering's works. The most important collections are *Michael Kunze*, "Lieber in Gießen als irgendwo anders…" (Baden-Baden 2018) 42–53; *Mario Losano*, Bibliographie Rudolf von Jherings, in: Franz Wieacker and Christian Wollschläger, Jherings Erbe (Göttingen 1970) 255–280; *Christoph-Erich Mecke*, Rudolf von Jhering. Anonym publizierte Frühschriften und unveröffentlichte Handschriften aus seinem Nachlass (Göttingen 2010) 254–258.

De Hereditate Possidente (Berlin 1842, reprinted in *Rudolf von Jhering*, Vermischte Schriften juristischen Inhalts, Leipzig 1879) 1–46.

Anonym publizierte Frühschriften und unveröffentlichte Handschriften aus seinem Nachlass (Christoph-Eric Mecke ed., Göttingen 2010)

Die Historische Schule der Juristen, Literarische Zeitung (Berlin) 1844, 5 parts, columns 197–201, 405–410, 421–425, 533–536, 565–569.

Abhandlungen aus dem römischen Recht (Leipzig 1844, reprint Aalen 1968)

Civilrechtsfälle ohne Entscheidungen (Leipzig 1847)

Geist des römischen Rechts auf den verschiedenen Stufen seiner Entwicklung
- Erster Theil (Leipzig 1852)
- Zweiter Theil. Erste Abtheilung (Leipzig 1854)
- Zweiter Theil. Zweite Abtheilung (Leipzig 1858)
- Dritter Theil. Erster Abtheilung (Leipzig 1865)
- (There were several new editions of the various volumes which are cited where relevant.)

Unsere Aufgabe, Jahrbücher für die Dogmatik des heutigen römischen und deutschen Privatrechts 1 (1857) 1–52

Übertragung der Reivindicatio auf Nichteigenthümer, Jahrbücher für die Dogmatik des heutigen römischen und deutschen Privatrechts 1 (1857) 101–188

Pandektenvorlesung nach Puchta. Ein Kollegheft aus dem Wintersemester 1859/60 (Christian Jäde ed., Göttingen 2008)
Beiträge zur Lehre von der Gefahr beim Kaufcontract, Jahrbücher für die Dogmatik des heutigen römischen und deutschen Privatrechts 3 (1859) 449–488 (part I); 4 (1861) 366–483 (part II)
Culpa in Contrahendo oder Schadensersatz bei nichtigen oder nicht zur Perfection gelangten Verträgen, Jahrbücher für die Dogmatik des heutigen römischen und deutschen Privatrechts 4 (1861) 1–112
Friedrich Karl von Savigny, Jahrbücher für die Dogmatik des heutigen römischen und deutschen Privatrechts 5 (1861) 354–377
Zur Lehre von den Beschränkungen des Grundeigentümers im Interesse des Nachbarn, Jahrbücher für die Dogmatik des heutigen römischen und deutschen Privatrechts 6 (1863) 81–130
Der Lucca=Pistoia-Eisenbahnstreit, Archiv für praktische Rechtswissenschaft, Neue Folge, 4 (1867) 225–344
Das Schuldmoment im römischen Privatrecht (Giessen 1867, reprinted in Vermischte Schriften Juristischen Inhalts Leipzig 1879, reprinted Aalen 1968) 156–240
Ist die Jurisprudenz eine Wissenschaft? (Okko Behrends ed. Göttingen 1998, 2d ed. 2009, orig. 1868)
Über den Grund des Besitzschutzes (Jena 1869)
Die Jurisprudenz des täglichen Lebens (Jena 1870)
Der Kampf um's Recht (Wien 1872)
Der Kampf ums Recht. Vortrag des Hofrates Professor Jhering. Gehalten in der Wiener Juristischen Gesellschaft am 11. März 1872, in Hermann Klenner (ed.), Der Kamf ums Recht (Freiburg und Berlin 1992) 113.
Der Zweck im Recht (2 vols. Leipzig 1877/1883, 2d ed. 1884/1886)
Vermischte Schriften juristischen Inhalts (Leipzig 1879, reprint Aalen 1968)
Ein Rechtsgutachten, betreffend die Gäubahn, Jahrbücher für die Dogmatik des heutigen römischen und deutschen Privatrechts 18 (1880) 1–128.
Gesammelte Aufsätze aus den Jahrbüchern des heutigen römischen und deutschen Privatrechts (3 vols. Jena 1881–1886)
Das Trinkgeld (Braunschweig 1882)
Scherz und Ernst in der Jurisprudenz: Eine Weihnachtsgabe für das juristische Publikum (Leipzig 1884)
Über die Entstehung des Rechtsgefühls, in Okko Behrends (ed.), Über die Entstehung des Rechtsgefühls (Napoli 1986) 7–54 (orig. 1884)
Rechtsschutz gegen injuriöse Rechtsverletzungen, Jahrbücher für die Dogmatik des heutigen römischen und deutschen Privatrechts 23 (1885) 155–338
Der Besitzwille. Zugleich eine Kritik der herrschenden juristischen Methode (Jena 1889)
Der Besitz, Jahrbücher für die Dogmatik des heutigen römischen und deutschen Privatrechts 32 (1893) 41–98
Vorgeschichte der Indoeuropäer (Viktor Ehrenberg ed., Leipzig 1894)
Entwicklungsgeschichte des römischen Rechts (Viktor Ehrenberg ed., Leipzig 1894)
Der Takt (draft) (Christian Helfer ed., Göttingen 1968)
Nachgelassene Aphorismen Rudolf von Jherings (Christian Helfer ed.), Archiv für Kulturgeschichte 48 (1966) 148–151

C. Editions of Jhering's Letters

Okko Behrends (ed.), Briefe von und an Jhering, in: Okko Behrends, Rudolph von Jhering (1818–1892). Der Durchbruch zum Zweck des Rechts, Studien zum römischen Recht in Europa 1 (1992) 58, 99–119
– Briefe von und an Jhering, in Rudolf von Jhering. Beiträge und Zeugnisse (2d ed. Göttingen 1993) 99–119, 134–143
Johannes Biermann (ed.), Rudolf von Jhering, Briefe und Erinnerungen (Berlin 1907)
Albert Bruckner (ed.), Unbekannte Briefe Rudolf von Jherings aus seiner Frühzeit, Zeitschrift für schweizerisches Recht, neue Folge 53 (1934) 34–71
Helene Ehrenberg (ed.), Rudolf von Jhering in Briefen an seine Freunde (Leipzig 1913, reprint Aalen 1971)
Karl Kroeschell (ed.), Jherings Briefe an Windscheid 1870–1891 (Göttingen 1988)
Mario Losano (ed.), Carteggio Jhering-Gerber 1849–1872 (Milano 1977)
– Der Briefwechsel zwischen Jhering und Gerber (Ebelsbach 1984)
– Der Briefwechsel Jherings mit Unger und Glaser (Ebelsbach 1996)
Heinrich von Poschinger (ed.), Otto Fürst von Bismarck und Rudolf Jhering. Aufzeichnungen und Briefe (Berlin 1908)
Christian Wollschläger (ed.), Briefe der Göttinger Zeit in Auszügen, in: Georgia Augusta. Nachrichten aus der Universität Göttingen 10 (Göttingen 1968)

Additional published letters are listed in *Christoph-Eric Mecke*, Rudolf von Jhering. Anonym publizierte Frühschriften und unveröffentlichte Handschriften aus seinem Nachlaß (Göttingen 2010) 260–261.

D. Secondary Literature

The following list is limited to the titles referenced in this book. The literature on Jhering is vast. A fairly up-to-date, but far from complete, bibliography is *Michael Kunze*, "Lieber in Giessen als irgendwo anders…" (2018) 63–84.

Abbott, Lyman, The Theory of an Evolutionist (Boston and New York 1897)
Alschuler, Albert, Law Without Values. The Life, Work, and Legacy of Justice Holmes (Chicago 2000)
Angle, Stephen, Should We All Be More English? Liang Qichao, Rudolf von Jhering, and Rights, Journal of the History of Ideas 61 (2000) 241–261
Anon., Review of Jhering, Der Zweck im Recht, The National Quarterly Review XI (1880) 202–205
Arnold, Thurman, The Symbols of Government (New Haven 1935)
Auer, Marietta, Der privatrechtliche Diskurs der Moderne (Tübingen 2014)
Austin, John, The Province of Jurisprudence Determined (2d ed. London 1861)
Bachmann, Benedikt, Das Gäubahn-Gutachten. Der Einzelfall als Katalysator und Korrektiv in Rudolf von Jherings Rechtsdenken (Berlin 2023)
Bachofen, Johann Jakob, Das Muterrecht (Stuttgart 1861)
Bähr, Otto, Der Rechsstaat (Cassel und Göttingen 1864)
Baratta, Alessandro, Über Jherings Bedeutung für die Strafrechtswissenschaft, in: Franz Wieacker and Christian Wollschläger (eds.), Jhering's Erbe (Göttingen 1970) 17–26.

Bauer, Martin, Periculum emptoris. Eine dogmatische Untersuchung zur Gefahrtragung beim Kauf (Berlin 1998)
Beccaria, Cesare, Dei delitti e delle pene (Harlem 1864)
Behrends, Okko, Die Evolution des Rechts zwischen Historischer Rechtsschule und Moderne, in: id., Rudolf von Jhering, Ist die Jurisprudenz eine Wissenschaft? (Göttingen 1998) 92–202
– Jhering heute! Seine Wirkung als Jurist, Rechtsdenker und Rechshistoriker der Historischen Rechtsschule, in: Stephan Meder and Christoph-Eric Mecke (eds.), Jhering Global (Göttingen 2023) 185–255
– (ed.), Jherings Rechtsdenken (Göttingen 1996)
– Jherings "Umschwung," Zeitschrift der Savigny Stiftung für Rechtsgeschichte, rom. Abt. 134 (2017) 539–557
– Privatrecht heute und Jhering evolutionäres Rechtsdenken (Köln 1993)
– Das 'Rechtsgefühl' in der historisch-kritischen Rechtstheorie des späten Jhering, in: Okko Behrends (ed.), Rudolf von Jhering, Über die Entstehung des Rechsgefühls (Napoli 1986) 55–184
– Rudolf von Jhering. Beiträge und Zeugnisse (2d ed. Göttingen 1993).
– Rudolf von Jhering (1818–1892). Der Durchbruch zum Zweck des Rechts., in: F. Loos (ed.), Rechtswissenschaft in Göttingen (Göttingen 1987) 229–269
– Rudolf von Jhering und die Evolutionstheorie des Rechts, in: Der Evolutionsgedanke in den Wissenschaften (Günter Patzig ed., Göttingen 1991) 80–110
– Rudolf von Jhering, der Rechtsdenker der offenen Gesellschaft, in: Rudolf von Jhering, Beiträge und Zeugnisse (2d ed. 1993) 8–10
– Von der Freirechtsbewegung zum konkreten Ordnungs- und Gestaltungsdenken, in: Ralf Dreier and Wolfgang Sellert (eds.), Recht und Justiz im "Dritten Reich" (Frankfurt 1989) 34–79.
– War Jhering ein Rechtspositivist? Eine Antwort auf Ralf Dreiers Frage, in: Okko Behrends (ed.), Jherings Rechtsdenken (Göttingen 1996) 235–254
– Der Zwölftafelprozeß (Göttingen 1974)
Bekker, Ernst Immanuel, Die Aktionen des römischen Privatrechts (2 vols., Berlin 1871–1873)
– Meine erste Begegnung mit Jhering, in: Rudolf von Jhering. Briefe und Erinnerungen (Johannes Biermann ed., Berlin 1907) 101–106
– Ernst und Scherz über unsere Wissenschaft, Festgabe an Rudolf von Jhering zum Doctorjubiläum (Leipzig 1892)
Bentham, Jeremy, Principles of Morals and Legislation (London 1789)
Benedict, Jörg, Culpa in Contrahendo I: Historisch-kritischer Teil (Tübingen 2018)
Bentley, Arthur, The Process of Government (Chicago 1908)
Beseler, Georg, Volksrecht und Juristenrecht (Leipzig 1843)
Birr, Josefa, Jhering's Concept of Rechtsgefühl and its Role in the The Struggle for Law, in: Transformacje Prawa Prywatnego 4 (2017) 5–16
– Der Schatten des Wanderers. Einzelfall, Rechtswandel und Fortschritt in Rudolf von Jherings Lehre vom Rechtsgefühl (Berlin 2022)
Blumenthal, W. Michael, The Invisible Wall. Germans and Jews (Washington D.C. 1998)
Bohnert, Joachim, Über die Rechtslehre Georg Friedrich Puchtas (Karlsruhe 1975)
Bonazzi, Ermanno, La Fortuna di Jhering in Italia, in: Mario Losano (ed.) Carteggio Jhering-Gerber (1849–1872) (Milano 1977) 629–694
Bülow, Oskar (von), Gesetz und Richteramt (Berlin 1885)

Bumke, Christian, Rechtsdomatik. Eine Disziplin und ihre Arbeitsweise (Tübingen 2017)
Calabresi, Guido, The Cost of Accidents (New Haven 1970)
Cardozo, Benjamin, The Nature of the Judicial Process (New Haven and London 1921)
– The Paradoxes of Legal Science (New York 1928)
Choe, Byoung, Culpa in Contrahendo bei Rudolf von Jhering (Göttingen 1988)
Clark, David, American Comparative Law. A History (Oxford and New York 2022)
Cohen, Felix, Law and Language, in id., The Legal Consciousness (Yale University Press 1960) 111–120
– Transcendental Nonsense and the Functional Approach, Columbia Law Review 35 (1935) 810–849
Cohen, Morris, Evolution of the Aryan (book review), The Annals of the American Academy of Political and Social Science 13 (1899) 87–91
– Law as a Means to an End (book review), The Philosophical Review 23 (1914) 557–561
– The Place of Logic in the Law, Harvard Law Review 29 (1916) 622–639
Cohen, Morris and Felix Cohen (eds.), Readings in Jurisprudence and Legal Philosophy (NewYork 1951)
Coing, Helmut, Der juristische Systembegriff bei Rudolf von Jhering, in: Jürgen Blühdorn and Joachim Ritter (eds.), Philosophie und Rechtswissenschaft. Zum Problem ihrer Beziehung im 19. Jahrhundert (Frankfurt/M. 1969) 95–115
– Rudolf von Jhering und Bentham, in: 375 Jahre Rechtswissenschaft in Gießen (Günter Weick ed., Gießen 1982) 1–14
Commager, Henry Steele, The American Mind (New Haven 1950)
Comte, Auguste, Cours de Philosophie Positif (6 vols. Paris 1830–1842)
Cook, Walter Wheeler, The Logical and Legal Basis of the Conflict of Laws (Cambridge, Mass. 1942)
Cotterrell, Roger, The Struggle for Law: Some Dilemmas of Cultural Legality, International Journal of Law in Context 4 (2009) 373–384
Curran, Vivian, Rethinking Hermann Kantorowicz and the Legacy of Anti-Formalism, in: Annelise Riles (ed.), Rethinking the Masters of Comparative Law (Oxford 2001) 66–91
Dahn, Felix, Die Vernunft im Recht (Berlin 1879)
Darwin, Charles, On the Origin of Species (London 1859)
Dawson, John, The Oracles of the Law (Ann Arbor 1968)
DeWolfe Howe, Mark, Introduction, in: id. (ed.), Oliver Wendell Holmes, The Common Law (Boston and Toronto 1963 (orig. 1881)) XI–XXVII
– Justice Oliver Wendell Holmes 2 vols. (Cambridge, Mass. 1957–1963)
DeStaël, Germaine, On Germany, in: Morroe Berger (ed. and transl.), Madame de Staël on Politics, Literature, and National Character (Garden City 1965, orig. 1813) 249–313
Diederichsen, Uwe, Jherings Rechtsinstitute im deutschen Privatrecht der Gegenwart, in: Okko Behrends (ed.), Privatrecht heute und Jherings evolutionäeres Rechtsdenken (Köln 1993) 37–76
Dove (Landrichter), Rudolf von Jhering und Bernhard Windscheid, Berichte des Freien Deutschen Hochstifts zu Frankfurt (Frankfurt 1893) 138–154
Drake, Joseph, Editorial Preface to this Volume, in: Rudolf von Ihering, Law as a Means to an End (Isaac Husik transl., New York 1921) xv–xxiv.
Dreier, Ralf, Jherings Rechtstheorie – eine Theorie evolutionärer Rechtsvernunft, in: Okko Behrends (ed.), Jherings Rechtsdenken (Göttingen 1996) 222–234
Durkheim, Emile, De la division du travail social (Paris 1893)
– Les règles de la méthode sociologique (Paris 1895)

Duve, Thomas and Rückert, Joachim (eds.), Savigny International? (Frankfurt 2015)

Duxbury, Neil, Jhering's Philosophy of Authority, Oxford Journal of Legal Studies 27 (2007) 23–47

Eck, Ernst, B. Windscheid und R.v.Jhering (Berlin 1893)

Ehrenberg, Viktor, Vorwort des Herausgebers, in: Rudolf von Jhering, Vorgeschichte der Indoeuropäer (Leipzig 1894) v–x.

Ehrlich, Eugen, Freie Rechtsfindung und freie Rechtwissenschaft (Leipzig 1903); transl. as Judicial Freedom of Decision: The Principles and Objects (Ernest Bruncken transl.) (Modern Legal Philosophy Series IX. Science of Legal Method, Boston 1917) 47–84

– Fundamental Principles of the Sociology of Law (Walter Moll transl., Cambridge, Mass. 1936)

– Grundlegung der Soziologie des Rechts (München and Leipzig 1913)

– Die juristische Logik (Tübingen 1918)

– Die Tatsachen des Gewohnheitsrechts (Czernowitz 1907)

Ermacora, Felix, Rudolf von Jherings Brücke zum öffentlichen Recht, in: Gerhard Luf and Walter Ogris (eds.), Kampf ums Recht (Berlin 1995) 117–123

– Vorrede, in: id. (ed.), Rudolf von Jhering, Der Kampf ums Recht. Zum hundertsten Todestag des Autors (Wien 1992) 9–57

Esser, Josef, Grundsatz und Norm in der richterlichen Rechtsfortbildung (Tübingen 1956)

Falk, Ulrich, Ein Gelehrter wie Windscheid (Frankfurt 1989)

Fikentscher, Wolfgang, Methoden des Rechts (4 vols., Tübingen 1975–1977)

Fikentscher, Wolfgang and Himmelmann, Ulrich, Rudolph von Iherings Einfluß auf Dogmatik und Methode des Privatrechts, in: Gerhard Luf and Werner Ogris (eds.), Kampfs ums Recht (1995) 95–115

Fisher III, William, Horwitz, Morton and Reed, Thomas (eds.), American Legal Realism (New York 1993)

Földi, Andras, Aspekte der Jhering-Rezeption in Ungarn, in: Stephan Meder and Christoph-Eric Mecke (eds.), Jhering Global (Göttingen 2023) 71–95

Forsthoff, Ernst, Vom Zweck im Recht, Zeitschrift der Akademie für deutsches Recht 4 (1937) 174

Frank, Jerome, Civil Law Influence on the Common Law, Pennsylvania Law Review 104 (1956) 887–926

– A Conflict of Oblivion: Some Observations on the Founders of Legal Pragmatism, Rutgers Law Review 9 (1954) 425–463

– Law and the Modern Mind (New York 1930)

Fridell, Egon, Kulturgeschichte der Neuzeit (München 1969, orig. 3 vols. München 1927–31)

Friedman, Wolfgang, Legal Theory (5th ed. London 1967)

Frier, Bruce, Autonomy of Law and Origins of the Legal Profession, Cardozo Law Review 11 (1989) 259–297

– A Casebook on the Roman Law of Contracts (New York 2021)

– The Rise of the Roman Jurists (Princeton 1985)

Fuchs, Ernst, Die Gemeinschädlichkeit der konstruktiven Jurisprudenz (Karlsruhe 1909)

– Jhering und die Freirechtsbewegung, Archiv für Rechts- und Wirtschaftsphilosophie 12 (1918/1919) 10–24

Fuller, Lon, Consideration and Form, Columbia Law Review 41 (1941) 799–824

– The Law in Quest of Itself (Chicago 1940)

Fuller, Lon and William Purdue, The Reliance Interest in Contract Damages, Yale Law Journal 46 (1936) 52–96; 373–420

Fustel de Coulanges, Numas, La Cité Antique (Paris 1864)
Gans, Eduard, Das Erbrecht in weltgeschichtlicher Entwickelung. Eine Abhandlung der Universalgeschichte (4 vols., Berlin 1824–1835)
Geib, Gustav, Die Reform des deutschen Rechtslebens (Leipzig 1848)
Geldart, W.M., Introduction, in: Rudolf von Ihering, Law as Means to an End (Isaac Husik transl., New York 1921) xxxv–lii
Gény, Francois, Méthode et sources en droit privé positif (Paris 1899, 2d. ed. 1919)
Gerber, Carl Friedrich von, Grundzüge eines Systems des deutschen Staatsrechts (Leipzig 1865)
– System des deutschen Privatrechts (2 parts, Jena 1848–1849)
– Das wissenschaftliche Prinzip des gemeinen deutschen Privatrechts (Jena 1846)
Giaro, Tomasz, Jhering and Politics, in: Stephan Meder and Christoph-Eric Mecke (eds.), Jhering Global (Göttingen 2023) 57–69
Gibbon, Edward, The Decline and Fall of the Roman Empire (6 vols., London 1776–1788)
Gibert, Rafael, Jhering in España, in: Franz Wieacker and Christian Wollschläger eds., Jherings Erbe (Göttingen 1970) 40–67
Gierke, Otto von, Das deutsche Genossenschaftsrecht (4 vols. Berlin 1868–1891)
– Deutsches Privatrecht I (Leipzig 1895)
Gneist, Rudolf von, Der Rechtsstaat und die Verwaltungsgerichte in Deutschland (Berlin 1872)
Goff, Robert, In Search for Principle (British Academy, London 1984)
Gossman, Lionel, Basel in the Age of Burckhardt (Chicago and London 2000)
Granitsaris, Athanasios, Theorie der Rechtsnormen bei Rudolf von Jhering. Eine Untersuchung der Grundlagen des deutschen Rechtsrealismus (Berlin 1989)
Gray, John Chipman, The Nature and Sources of Law (New York 1909)
Graziadei, Michele, Changing Images of Law in XIXth Century English Legal Thought, in: Mathias Reimann (ed.), The Reception of Continental Ideas in the Common Law World 1820–1920 (Berlin 1993) 115–163
– Comparative Law, Transplants and Receptions, in: Mathias Reimann and Reinhard Zimmermann (eds.), The Oxford Handbook of Comparative Law (2d ed. 2019) 442–473
Grisé, Julie, Gelter, Martin, and Whitman, Robert, Rudolf von Jhering's Influence on Karl Llewellyn, Tulsa Law Review 48 (2012) 93–116
Haferkamp, Hans-Peter, Georg Friedrich Puchta und die Begriffsjurisprudenz (Frankfurt 2004)
– Die Historische Rechtsschule (Frankfurt 2018)
– Rechtsfälle in der juristischen Ausbildung der Pandektenwissenschaft, Zeitschrift der Savigny Stiftung für Rechtsgeschichte (germ. Abt.) 138 (2021) 283–294
Haferkamp, Hans-Peter und Repgen, Tilman (eds.), Wie pandektistisch war die Pandektistik (Tübingen 2017)
Hamza, Gabor, Wege der Entwicklung des Privatrechts in Europa (Passau 2008)
Handwörterbuch zur deutschen Rechtsgeschichte (Albrecht Cordes et al. eds, 2d ed. Berlin 2004)
Hanewinkel, Inge, and Linder, Nikolaus, "Ein Mann von kräftigem Rechtsgefühl:" Rudolf von Jherings Prozeß gegen seine Hausangestellte und der *Kampf um's Recht*, Zeitschrift für Neuere Rechtsgeschichte 42 (2020) 61–76.
Hart, H.L.A., Jhering's Heaven of Concepts and Modern Analytical Jurisprudence, in: Franz Wieacker and Christian Wollschläger (eds.) Jherings Erbe (Göttingen 1970) 68–78

Hattenhauer, Hans, Die geistesgeschichtlichen Grundlagen des deutschen Rechts (4th ed. Heidelberg 1996)
Heck, Philipp, Gesetzesauslegung und Interessenjurisprudenz, Archiv für die civilistische Praxis 112 (1914) 1–318
– Begriffsbildung und Interessenjurisprudenz (Tübingen 1932)
– Interessenjurisprudenz (Tübingen 1933)
– Die Interessenjurisprudenz und ihre neuen Gegner, Archiv für die civilistische Praxis 142 (1936) 129–202, 297–332.
– Das Problem der Rechtsgewinnung (Tübingen 1912)
– Rechtsphilosophie und Interessenjurisprudenz, Archiv für die civilistische Praxis 143 (1937) 129–196
Hegel, Georg Friedrich Wilhelm, Grundlinien der Philosophie des Rechts (Frankfurt 1972, orig. 1821)
– Vorlesungen über die Philosophie der Geschichte (Stuttgart 1961, based on the 2d/3d ed., Karl Hegel ed., posthum Frankfurt 1840/48)
Helfer, Christian, Jherings Gesellschaftsanalyse im Lichte der heutigen Sozialwissenschaft, in: Franz Wieacker and Christian Wollschläger (eds.), Jherings Erbe (Göttingen 1970) 79–88
– Nachtrag zu Jhering's Zweck im Recht, Juristenzeitung 1970, 12–14
– Prolegomena zur Philosophie der gemischten Getränke, Georgia Augusta. Nachrichten aus der Universität Göttingen 10 (1968) 43–56 (Manuscript by Rudolf von Jhering)
– Rudolf von Jhering als Rechtssoziologe, Kölner Zeitschrift für Soziologie und Sozialpsychologie 1968, 553–571
– Rudolf von Jhering über das Rechtsgefühl, Österreichische Juristenzeitung 23 (1968) 589–590
Herberger, Maximilian, Dogmatik. Zur Geschichte von Begriff und Methode in Medizin und Jurisprudenz (Frankfurt 1981)
Herget, James, American Jurisprudence 1870–1970 (Houston 1990)
Herget, James, and Wallace, Stephen, The German Free Law Movement as the Source of American Legal Realism, Virginia Law Review 73 (1987) 399–455
Herman, Shael, Llewellyn the Civilian, Tulane Law Review 56 (1986) 1125–1170
Herzog, Benjamin, Rudolf von Jherings Wirkungen auf die Anwendungs- und Auslegungslehre in Brasilien, in: Stephan Meder and Christoph-Eric Mecke (eds.), Jhering Global (Göttingen 2023) 127–145
Heusler, Andreas, Die Gewere (Weimar 1872)
Heutger, Viola, Rudolf von Jhering, Deventer Honigkuchen und Schiedammer Jenever. Zeitzeugnisse aus den Niederlanden, in: Stephan Meder and Christoph-Eric Mecke (eds.), Jhering Global (Göttingen 2023) 25–55
Hirsch, Ernst, Jhering als Reformator des Rechtsunterrichts, in: Franz Wieacker and Christian Wollschläger (eds.), Jherings Erbe (Göttingen 1970) 90–100
Hobbes, Thomas, Leviathan (revised Latin edition 1668, orig. London 1651)
Hobsbawm, Eric, The Age of Capitalism (London 1975)
Hofmeister, Herbert, Jhering in Wien, in: Der Kampfs ums Recht (1995) 9–30; reprinted in Okko Behrends (ed.), Rudolf von Jhering. Beiträge und Zeugnisse (Göttingen 1993) 38–48
Holmes, Oliver Wendell, The Common Law (Mark deWolfe Howe ed., Cambridge, Mass. 1963, orig. Boston 1881)
– The Path of the Law, Harvard Law Review 10 (1897) 457–478

– Summary of Events: The Gas Stokers' Strike, American Law Review 7 (1873) 583–585; reprinted in Harvard Law Review 44 (1941) 795–796
Hommes, Hendrik Jan, Der Begriff der "Juristischen Konstruktion," in: Werner Krawietz (ed.), Theorie und Technik der Begriffsjurisprudenz (Darmstadt 1976) 327–357
Hondius, Ewoud, Pre-contracutal Liability, General Reports, International Academy of Comparative Law, XIIIth International Congress (Montreal 1996) 1–28
Horwitz, Morton, The Transformation of American Law 1780–1860 (Cambridge, Mass. 1977)
Hoyos, Roman, Beyond Classical legal Thought: Law and Governance in Postbellum America, 1865–1920, in: Sally Hadden and Alfred Brophy (eds.), A Companion to American Legal History (Oxford 2013) 86–104
Hueber, Friedrich, Grundlegung der politischen Rechtslehre (Graz 1939)
Hugo, Gustav, Lehrbuch der Geschichte des römischen Rechts (11th ed. Berlin 1832, orig. 1790)
Humboldt, Wilhelm von, Ideen zu einem Versuch, die Grenzen der Wirksamkeit des Staates zu bestimmen (posthum Breslau 1852, orig. 1792)
Hurwicz, Elias, Rudolf von Ihering und die deutsche Rechtswissenschaft: mit besonderer Berücksichtigung des Strafrechts (Berlin 1911)
Hutcheson, Joseph, Judgment Intuitive. The Function of Hunch in Judicial Decisions, Cornell Law Review 14 (1929) 274–288
Jäde, Christian, Jhering als Rechtslehrer, in id. (ed.), Rudolf von Jhering, Pandektenvorlesung nach Puchta (Göttingen 2008) 13–21
Jansen, Nils, and Reimann, Mathias, Begriff und Zweck in der Jurisprudenz – Ein Geburtstagblatt für Rudolf von Jhering, Zeitschrift für europäisches Privatrecht 2018, 89–129
Jansen, Nils, and Zimmermann, Reinhard (eds.), Commentaries on European Contract Laws (Oxford 2018)
Jelowik, Lieselotte, Gerber, Carl Friedrich von, Handwörterbuch zur Deutschen Rechtsgeschichte II (2d ed., Albrecht Cordes et al. eds., Berlin 2012) 117–118
Jenkins, Iredell, Rudolf von Jhering, Vanderbilt Law Review 14 (1960) 169–190
Jhering Global (Stephan Meder and Christoph-Eric Mecke, eds., Göttingen 2023)
Jhering, Friedrich von, Zur Gießener Wirksamkeit Rudolf von Jherings, in: Johannes Biermann (ed.), Rudolf von Jhering. Briefe und Erinnerungen (Leipzig 1907) 78–90
Jhering, Hermann von, Erinnerungen an Rudolf von Jhering, in: Helene Ehrenberg (ed.), Rudolf von Jhering in Briefen an seine Freunde (Leipzig 1913) 445–471
Jolowicz, Herbert F., Historical Introduction to the Study of Roman Law (Cambridge 1932)
Jorgensen, Stig, Die Bedeutung Jherings für die neuere skandinavische Rechtslehre, in: Franz Wieacker and Christian Wollschläger (eds.), Jherings Erbe (Göttingen 1970) 116–126
The Jurisprudence of Interests (Magdalena Schoch transl. and ed., Cambridge Mass 1948)
Kant, Immanuel, Einleitung zur Metaphysik der Sitten (Hamburg 1865) (orig. 1785)
– Idee zu einer allgemeinen Geschichte in weltbürgerlicher Absicht, in Kants Werke VIII (Akademie Textausgabe, Berlin 1912/23) 15–32 (orig. 1784)
– Kritik der praktischen Vernunft, Immanuel Kant, Werke in 12 Bänden, vol. II (Wilhelm Weischedel ed., Frankfurt 1869, orig. Riga 1788)
– Metaphysik der Sitten, Kant Werke VI (Akademie Textausgabe, Berlin 1907/1914, orig. 1797)
– Mutmaßlicher Anfang der Menschheitsgeschichte, in Kants Werke VIII (Akademie Textausgabe, Berlin 1912/23) 107–124

– Die Religion innerhalb der Grenzen der bloßen Vernunft (Königsberg 1793)
Kantorowicz, Hermann, Aus der Vorgeschichte der Freirechtslehre (Mannheim, Berlin, Leipzig 1925)
– Jherings Bekehrung, Deutsche Richterzeitung 6 (1914) 84–87
– *(Gnaeus Flavius)*, Der Kampf um die Rechtswissenschaft (Heidelberg 1906)
– Die Epochen der Rechtswissenschaft, in: id., Rechtshistorische Schriften (Karlsruhe 1970) 346–361 (orig. 1914)
– Some Rationalism about Realism, Yale Law Journal 43 (1934) 1240–1253
Kantorowicz, Hermann, and Patterson, Edwin, Legal Science – a Summary of Its Methodology, Columbia Law Review 28 (1928) 679–707.
Kaser, Max, Das altrömische Jus (Göttingen 1949)
– Das römische Privatrecht (2 vols., 2d ed. München 1971/1975).
– Über Verbotsgesetze und verbotswidrige Geschäfte im Römischen Recht (Wien 1977)
Kelley, Patrick, A Critical Analysis of Holmes's Theory of Contract, Notre Dame Law Review 75 (2000) 1681–1773
Kennedy, Duncan, From the Will Theory to the Principle of Private Autonomy, Columbia Law Review 100 (2000) 94–175
– The Rise and Fall of Classical Legal Theory (Washington D.C. 2006, orig. manuscript 1975)
Kenny, Courtney, Jhering on Trinkgeld and Tips, Law Quarterly Review 32 (1916) 306–321
Kessler, Friedrich, and Fine, Edith, *Culpa in Contrahendo*, Bargaining in Good Faith, and Freedom of Contract, Harvard Law Review 77 (1964) 401–449
Kierulff, Johann Friedrich Martin, Theorie des Gemeinen Civilrechts (Altona 1839)
Kirchmann, Julius von, Die Werthlosigkeit der Jurisprudenz als Wissenschaft (Berlin 1848)
Kleinheyer, Gerhard, and Schröder, Jan, Deutsche und Europäische Juristen aus Neun Jahrhunderten (6th ed. Heidelberg 2017)
Klemann, Bernd, Jherings Wandlung, in: Heinz Mohnhaupt (ed.), Rechtsgeschichte in den beiden deutschen Staaten (1988–90) (Frankfurt/M. 1991) 130–150
– Rudolf von Jhering und die Historische Rechtsschule (Frankfurt/M., New York 1989)
Klenner, Hermann, Jherings Kampf ums Recht, Demokratie und Recht 1982, 437–445
Klippel, Diethelm, Rudolf von Jhering an der Juristischen Fakultät der Ludwigs-Universität Gießen (1852–1867), in: Okko Behrends (ed.), Rudolf von Jhering. Beiträge und Zeugnisse (2d ed. Göttingen 1993) 31–37
– Juristischer Begriffshimmel und Funktionale Rechtswelt. Rudolf von Jhering als Wegbereiter der modernen Rechtswissenschaft, in: Diethelm Klippel, Hans Jürgen Becker and Reinhard Zimmermann (eds.), Colloquia für Dieter Schwab zum 60. Geburtstag (Bielefeld 2000) 116–135
Kocourek, Albert, Introduction to The Struggle for Law (John Laylor transl., 2d ed., Chicago 1915)
Kohler, Josef, Lehrbuch der Rechtsphilosophie (Berlin und Leipzig 1909)
– Rechtsphilosophie und Universalgeschichte, in: Franz v. Holtzendorff and Josef Kohler (eds.), Enzyklopädie der Rechtswissenschaft vol. I (7th ed., München und Berlin 1915) 3–62
– Shakespeare vor den Toren der Jurisprudenz (Würzburg 1883)
Koschaker, Paul, Europa und das römische Recht (München 1947)
Kraft, Fr., Erinnerungen eines alten Schülers an Professor Dr. Rudolf von Jhering, in: Johannes Biermann (ed.), Rudolf von Jhering. Briefe und Erinnerungen (Berlin 1907) 91–100

Kroeschell, Karl, Die Germania in der deutschen Rechtsgeschichte, in: id., Studien zum frühen und mittelalterlichen deutschen Recht (Berlin 1996) 89–110
– Germanisches Recht als Forschungsproblem, in: id. Studien zum frühen und mittelalterlichen deutschen Recht (Berlin 1996) 65–88
– Zwei unbekannte Briefe Jherings, in: Festschrift für Franz Wieacker zum 70. Geburtstag (Göttingen 1978) 274–280
Kroppenberg, Inge, Die Plastik des Rechts. Sammlung und System bei Rudolf von Jhering (Berlin 2015)
Kunkel, Wolfgang, Römische Rechtsgeschichte (Heidelberg 1948)
Kuntze, Johannes Emil, Rudolf von Jhering, Sächsisches Archiv für Bürgerliches Recht und Prozess 2 (1892) 609–618
– Der Wendepunkt der Rechtswissenschaft (Leipzig 1856)
Kunze, Michael, Ein großer Jurist. Eine Persönlichkeit. Jhering biografisch skizziert, in: Stephan Meder and Christoph-Eric Mecke (eds.), Jhering Global (Göttingen 2023) 9–23
– Jherings Jubliläum, in: Michael Stolleis et al. (eds.), Die Bedeutung der Wörter, Festschrift für Sten Gagnér (München 1991) 1–13
– Jherings Universalrechtsgeschichte. Zu einer unveröffentlichten Handschrift des Privatdozenten Dr. Rudolf Jhering, in: Heinz Mohnhaupt (ed.), Rechtsgeschichte in den beiden deutschen Staaten (1988–1990) (Frankfurt/M. 1991) 151–186
– "Lieber in Gießen als irgendwo anders…" (Baden-Baden 2018)
– Rudolf von Jhering. Ein Forschungsbericht, in: Gerhard Luf and Werner Ogris (eds.), Der Kampf ums Recht (Berlin 1995) 125–148
– Rudolf von Jhering. Ein Lebensbild, in Okko Behrends (ed.), Rudolf von Jhering. Beiträge und Zeugnisse (2d ed. Göttingen 1993) 11–28
– Das unsichtbare Recht (forthcoming, Göttingen 2025)
Lamm, Henry, Introduction to this Volume, in Rudolf von Ihering, Law as a Means to an End (Isaac Husik transl., New York 1921) xxv–xxxiii.
Lange, Harry, Die Wandlungen Jherings in seiner Auffassung von Recht (Berlin-Grunewald 1927)
Larenz, Karl, Methodenlehre der Rechtswissenschaft (5th ed. München 1983)
– Rudolf von Jhering und die heutige Lage der deutschen Rechtswissenschaft, in: Franz Wieacker and Christian Wollschläger (eds.), Jherings Erbe (Göttingen 1970) 135–141
Larenz, Karl and Canaris, Claus-Wilhelm, Methodenlehre der Rechtswissenschaft (6th ed. München 1995)
Lehmann, Matthias, Die Zukunft der CIC im europäischen Vertragsrecht, Zeitschrift für europäisches Privatrecht 2009, 893–915
Lessing, Gotthold Emphraim, Die Erziehung des Menschengeschlechte (Berlin 1780) engl.: The Education of the Human Race (London 1858)
Link, Mathias, Possession, Possessio und das Schicksal des Common Law (Frankfurt etc. 2002)
Liszt, Franz von, Die deterministischen Gegner der Zweckstrafe, Zeitschrift für die gesamte Strafrechtswissenschaft 13 (1893) 325–370
– Der Zweckgedanke im Strafrecht, Zeitschrift für die gesamte Strafrechtswissenschaft 13 (1893) 1–47
Little, Eleanor, The Early Reading of Justice Oliver Wendell Holmes, Harvard Library Bulletin 8 (1954)
Llewellyn, Karl, The Bramble Bush (New York 1930)

– The Common Law Tradition. Deciding Appeals (Boston and Toronto 1960)
– A Realistic Jurisprudence – the Next Step, Columbia Law Review 30 (1930) 431–465
– Some Realism about Realism –Responding to Dean Pound, Harvard Law Review 44 (1931) 1222–1264.

Lloyd, Dennis, Introduction to Jurisprudence (New York 1959)

Locke, John, An Essay on Human Understanding (London 1790)

Losano, Mario, Bibliographie Rudolf von Jherings, in: Franz Wieacker und Christian Wollschläger (eds.), Jherings Erbe (Göttingen 1970) 252–294
– Der Briefwechsel Jherings mit Unger und Glaser (Ebelsbach 1996)
– Der Briefwechsel zwischen Jhering und Gerber (Ebelsbach 1984)
– Carteggio Jhering-Gerber 1849–1891 (Milano 1977)
– Dichtung und Wahrheit in Jherings Konstruktionslehre, in Franz Wieacker and Christian Wollschläger (eds.), Jherings Erbe (Göttingen 1970) 142–154
– Studien zu Jhering und Gerber (Ebelsbach 1984)

Luf, Gerhard, and Ogris, Werner (eds.), Der Kampf ums Recht. Forschungsband aus Anlaß des 100. Todestages von Rudolf von Jhering (Berlin 1995)

Luig, Klaus, Zur Bedeutung der Psychologie in Jherings Lehre vom Rechtsgefühl, in: Mathias Schmoeckel (ed.), Psychologie als Argument in der juristischen Literatur des Kaiserreiches (Baden-Baden 2009) 209–213
– Rudolf von Jhering und die historische Rechtsschule, in: Okko Behrends (ed.), Jherings Rechtsdenken (Göttingen 1996) 235–268

M., J., Rudolf von Jhering, Journal of the Society of Comparative Legislation 9 (1908) 9–10

MacDonnell, John, Rudolf von Ihering, in: John MacDonnell and Edward Manson (eds.), Great Jurists of the World (Continental Legal History Series, vol. 2, Boston 1914) 588–599

MacPherson, C.B. , The Political Theory of Possessive Individualism (Oxford 1962)

*Maine, Henry Sumne*r, Ancient Law (London 1861)

Maliska, Marcos Augusto, Die Rezeption Jherings in Brasilien. Tobias Barreto und die "Recife Schule", in: Stephan Meder and Christoph-Eric Mecke (eds.), Jhering Global (Göttingen 2023) 113–125

Martinek, Michael, Rudolf v. Jherings Kampf gegen das Trinkgeld, in Hermann Lange et al. (eds.), Festschrift für Joachim Gernhuber (Tübingen 1993) 879–903

Marx, Karl, Das Kapital (3 vols., Hamburg 1867–1894)
– Zur Kritik der politischen Ökonomie (1859), in: Karl Marx und Friedrich Engels, Werke VIII (Berlin 1961) 71.

Marx, Karl, and Engels, Friedrich, Manifest der kommunistischen Partei (London 1848)
– Kritik der neuesten deutschen Philosophie in ihren Repräsentanten Feuerbach, B. Bauer und Stirner und des deutschen Sozialismus in seinen verschiedenen Propheten (1845–46), in: Karl Marx und Friedrich Engels, Werke I (Berlin 1959) 13–77.

McLaughlin, Joseph, The Unification of Germany: What Would Jhering Say? Fordham International L.J. 17 (1994) 277–293

Mecke, Christoph-Eric, Begriff des Rechts und Methode der Rechtswissenschaft bei Rudolf von Jhering (Göttingen 2018)

Mecke, Christoph-Eric, Jherings Rechtsdenken im Kontext der zeitgenössischen Natur- und Sozialwissenschaften, in: Stefan Meder and Christoph-Eric Mecke (eds.), Jhering Global (Göttingen 2023) 258–301
– Rudolf von Jhering: Anonym publizierte Frühschriften und unveröffentlichte Handschriften aus seinem Nachlaß (Göttingen 2010)

– Rudolf von Jherings "Struggle for Law" – The Rejection of Alternative Forms of Dispute Resolution, in Transformacje Prawa Prywatnego 4 (2017) 37–50
Meder, Stephan, Rudolf von Jhering and the 'jurisprudence of concepts': was Jhering wrong to bring his predecessors' teachings into disrepute?, in: Stephan Meder and Christoph-Eric Mecke (eds.), Jhering Global (Göttingen 2023) 167–184
Meder, Stephan, and Mecke, Christoph-Eric (eds.), Jhering Global. Internationales Symposium zum 200. Geburtstag Rudolf von Jherings (1818–1892) (Göttingen 2023)
Menger, Anton, Das bürgerliche Recht und die besitzlosen Volksklassen (Tübingen 1890)
Merkel, Adolf, Jhering, Jherings Jahrbücher für die Dogmatik des heutigen römischen und deutschen Privatrechts, Neue Folge, 20 (1893) 6–40
Michaels, Ralf, The Functional Method in Comparative Law, in: Mathias Reimann and Reinhard Zimmermann (eds.), The Oxford Handbook of Comparative Law (2d ed. Oxford 2019) 345–389
Mill, John Stuart, On Liberty (London 1859)
– Utilitarianism (London 1865)
Mitteis, Ludwig, Jhering, Allgemeine Deutsche Biographie 50 (Leipzig 1905) 652–664
Möller, Cosima, Die juristische Konstruktion im Werk Rudolf von Jherings – vom universellen Rechtsalphabet bis zur juristischen Schönheit, Juristenzeitung 2017, 770–777
Mommsen, Friedrich, Beiträge zum Obligationenrecht (3 vols., Braunschweig 1853–55)
Montesquieu, Charles Louis de Secondat, De l'esprit des loix (Genéve 1748), The Spirit of the Laws (unnamed transl., New York York 1900)
Morgan, Lewis, Ancient Society (New York 1877)
Moriya, Kenichi, Die Pandektenwissenschaft und ihre historischen Hintergründe, Savigny Zeitschrift für Rechtsgeschichte (germ. Abt.) 136 (2019) 368–463.
Müller, Max, Prehistoric Antiquities of the Indo-Europeans (review of Jhering, Vorgeschichte der Indoeuropäer, 1894), Cosmopolis 1896, 619–644
Nicholas, Barry, An Introduction to Roman Law (Oxford 1962)
Nörr, Knut Wolfgang, Eher Hegel als Kant. Zum Privatrechtsverständnis des 19. Jahrhunderts (Paderborn etc. 1991)
Novick, Sheldon, Honorable Justice. The Life of Oliver Wendell Holmes (Boston 1989)
Nussbaum, Arthur, Die Rechtstatsachenforschung (Tübingen 1914)
Oestmann, Peter, Aktenversendung, Handwörterbuch zur Deutschen Rechtsgeschichte vol. I (2d ed. Albrecht Cordes et al. eds., Berlin 2008) 128–132
Olivecrona, Karl, Jherings Rechtspositivismus im Lichte der heutigen Wissenschaft, in: Franz Wieacker and Christian Wollschläger (eds.), Jherings Erbe (Göttingen 1970) 65–76
Patterson, Edwin, Equitable Relief for Unilateral Mistake, Columbia Law Review 28 (1928) 859–904
– Review of Roscoe Pound, The Spirit of the Common Law, Michigan Law Review 20 (1922) 809–813
Peterson, Jens, Von der Interessenjurisprudenz zur Wertungsjurisprudenz (Tübingen 2001)
Pietscher, August, Jurist und Dichter, Versuch einer Studie über Jhering's "Kampf ums Recht" und Shakespeares "Kaufmann von Venedig". Ein Vortrag (Dessau 1881)
Pleister, Wolfgang, Persönlichkeit, Wille und Freiheit im Werke Jherings (Ebelsbach 1982)
Pohlman, Harry, Justice Oliver Wendell Holmes and Utilitarian Jurisprudence (Lanham, Maryland 1984)
Post, Albert Hermann, Review of Jhering, Vorgeschichte der Indo-Europäer, Newspaper Clip, unknown origin, Niedersächsische Universitäts- und Staatsbibliothek, Göttingen, Cod. Ms Jhering 13:1,9

Pound, Roscoe, The Call for a Realist Jurisprudence, Harvard Law Review 44 (1931) 697–711
– Fifty Years of Jurisprudence, Harvard Law Review 51 (1938) 557–582
– Jurisprudence (5 vols., St. Paul, Minn., 1959)
– Law in Books and Law in Action, American Law Review 44 (1910) 12–36
– Liberty of Contract, Yale Law Journal 18 (1919) 454–487
– 'Mechanical Jurisprudence,' Columbia Law Review 8 (1908) 605–623
– The Need for a Sociological Jurisprudence, Green Bag 19 (1907) 607–615
– The Scope and Purpose of Sociological Jurisprudence, Harvard Law Review 24 (1911), 591–619; 25 (1912), 140–168, 489–516.
– The Spirit of the Common Law (Boston 1921)
Puchta, Georg Friedrich, Cursus der Institutionen (2 vols. 1841–1842)
– Das Gewohnheitsrecht (2 vols., 1828–1837)
– Lehrbuch der Pandekten (Leipzig 1838)
Rabban, David, Jhering's Influence on American Legal Thought, in: Stefan Meder and Eric-Christoph Mecke (eds.), Jhering Global (Göttingen 2023) 147–166
– Law's History (New York 2013)
Radbruch, Gustav, Vorschule der Rechtsphilosophie (Willsbach 1947)
Radin, Max, Handbook of Roman Law (St. Paul/Minn. 1927)
– Law as Logic and Experience (New Haven 1940)
Rea-Frauchinger, Maria, Der amerikanische Rechtsrealismus: Karl N. Llwellyn, Jerome Frank, Underhill More (Berlin 2006)
Reich, Norbert, Soziologische Rechtstheorie und legal realism im Rechtsdenken Amerikas (Heidelberg 1967)
Reichel, Hans, Geleitwort, in: Harry Lange, Die Wandlungen Jherings in seiner Auffassung vom Recht (Berlin-Grunewald 1927) III–V.
Reimann, Mathias, Comparative Law. An Overview of the Discipline, International Encyclopedia of Comparative Law vol. II (chapter 4) (Leiden 2020)
– Historical Jurisprudence, in: Markus Dubber and Christopher Tomlins (eds.), The Oxford Handbook of Legal History (Oxford 2018) 397–417
– Historische Schule und Common Law (Berlin 1993)
– Holmes's *Common Law* and German Legal Science, in: Robert Gordon (ed.), The Legacy of Oliver Wendell Holmes (Stanford 1992) 72–114
– Jhering's "Geist des römischen Rechts" as a Study of Ancient Social Order: A Comparative Perspective, in: Nils Jansen et al. (eds.), Iurium Itinera (Tübingen 2022) 221–244
– "In Such Forests Liberty was Nurtured" – von den germanischen Wurzeln der angloamerikanischen Freiheit, in: Gerhard Köbler and Hermann Nehlsen (eds.), Wirkungen europäischer Rechtskultur (München 1997) 933–951
– Interessenjurisprudenz, in: David Clark (ed.), Encyclopedia of Law and Society II (London 2008) 868
– Nineteenth Century German Legal Science, Boston College Law Review 1 (1990) 837–897
Rempel, Michael Norbert, Jherings juristisches Kabinett. Das kasuistische Element der Juristenausbildung bei Rudolf von Jhering (Hamburg 2018)
Riesenfeld, Stefan, The Impact of German Legal Ideas and Institutions on Legal Thought and Institutions in the United States, in: Mathias Reimann (ed.), The Reception of Continental Ideas in the Common Law World 1870–1920 (Berlin 1993) 89–97

Rivier, Alphonse, Rudolf von Jhering and Bernhard Windscheid, The Juridical Review 5 (1893) 1–12

Robinson, Edward, Law and the Lawyers (New York 1935)

Rose, U.M., Controversies of Modern Continental Jurists (part IV), Southern Law Review 2 (1876) 551–575

Ross, Edward, Social Control. A Study in the Foundations of Order (New York 1932)

Rousseau, Jean-Jacques, Du contrat social (Amsterdam 1762)

Rudokvas, Anton, Jhering's Influence on Russian Legal Thought, in: Stephan Meder and Christoph-Eric Mecke (eds.), Jhering Global (Göttingen 2023) 97–111

Rudorff, Adolf August Friedrich, Römische Rechtsgeschichte (2 vols. Leipzig 1857–1859)

Rückert, Joachim, Der Geist des Rechts in Jherings "Geist" und Jherings "Zweck," Rehtsgeschichte 5 (2004) 128–149; 6 (2005) 122–142

– Friedrich Carl von Savigny. Leben und Wirken (1779–1861) (forthcoming, München 2025)

– Idealismus, Jurisprudenz und Politik bei Friedrich Carl von Savigny (Ebelsbach 1984)

– Das Methodenorakel Rudolf von Jhering (1818–1892), Archiv für die civilistische Praxis 219 (2019) 457–487

– Religion und Recht bei Savigny, Zeitschrift der Savigny Stiftung für Rechtsgeschichte 139 (2020) 234–271

– Windscheid – verehrt, verstoßen, vergessen, rätselhaft?, Juristenzeitung 2017, 662–670

Rümelin, Max, Das neue schweizerische Zivilgesetzbuch und seine Bedeutung für uns (Tübingen 1908)

– Rudolf von Jhering (Tübingen 1922)

– Werturteile und Willensentscheidungen im Civilrecht (Freiburg 1891)

Sacco, Rodolfo, Legal Formants, American Journal of Comparative Law 39 (1991) 1–34, 343–401

Savigny, Friedrich Carl von, Juristische Methodenlehre (G. Wesenberg ed., Stuttgart 1951, orig. 1802/03)

– Das Recht des Besitzes (Gießen 1803)

– Stimmen für und wider neue Gesetzbücher, in: Thibaut und Savigny (Hans Hattenhauer ed., München 1973) 231–254 (orig. 1816)

– System des heutigen römischen Rechts (8 vols., Berlin 1840–1849)

– Über Zweck dieser Zeitschrift, Zeitschrift für geschichtliche Rechtswissenschaft 1 (1815) 1–12

– Vom Beruf unserer Zeit für Gesetzgebung und Rechtswissenschaft (Heidelberg 1814)

Schanze, Erich, Culpa in Contrahendo bei Jhering, in Helmut Coing (ed.), Ius Commune VII (Frankfurt/M. 1978)

Schelsky, Helmut, Das Jhering-Modell des sozialen Wandels durch Recht, in Manfred Rehbinder and Helmut Schelsky (eds.), Zur Effektivität des Rechts, Jahrbücher für Rechtssoziologie und Rechtstheorie 3 (1972) 47–86

Schild, Wolfgang, Der rechtliche Kampf gegen das Unrecht, in Gerhard Luf and Werner Ogris (eds.), Der Kampfs ums Recht (Berlin 1995) 31–56

Schiller, Friedrich, Was heist und zu welchem Ende studiert man Universalgeschichte? (Jena 1789)

Schlegel, John Henry, American Legal Realism and Empirical Social Science (Chapel Hill 1995)

Schmidt, Folke, Jherings Tradition im schwedischen Sachenrecht, in: Franz Wieacker and Christian Wollschläger (eds.), Jherings Erbe (Göttingen 1970) 207–210

Schmitt, Carl, Gesetz und Urteil (München 1969, orig. Berlin 1912)
– Der Führer schützt das Recht, Deutsche Juristen-Zeitung 39 (1934) 945–950
– Über die drei Arten des rechtswissenschaftlichen Denkens (Hamburg 1934)
Schmoeckel, Mathias (ed.), Psychologie als Argument in der juristischen Literatur des Kaiserreichs (Baden-Baden 2009)
Schober, Reinhold, Politische Jurisprudenz. Eine Würdigung ihres Wegbereiters Rudolf von Jhering (Köln 1933)
– Die Rechts- und Staatsphilosophie Iherings in ihrem geschichtlichen Zusammenhang (Berlin 1933)
Schröder, Jan, Recht als Wissenschaft (2 vols., 3d ed. München 2020)
– Rudolf von Jhering, in: Gerd Kleinheyer and Jan Schröder (eds.), Deutsche und Europäische Juristen aus neun Jahrhunderten (6th ed. Tübingen 2017) 233–239
Schulz, Fritz, Prinzipien des römischen Rechts (Berlin 1957, orig. 1934), (engl.: Principles of Roman Law, Marguerite Wolff transl. Oxford 1936)
Schwatz, Andreas, John Austin and the German Jurisprudence of His Time, Politica 1 (1934) 178–199
Science of Legal Method. Select Essays by Various Authors (Ernest Bruncken and Layton Register transl., Modern Legal Philosophy Series vol. X, Boston 1917)
Seagle, William, Men of Law. From Hammurabi to Holmes (New York 1947)
– Rudolf von Jhering or Law as a Means to an End, University of Chicago Law Review 13 (1945) 71–89 (reprinted in id., Men of Law (New York 1947) 306–330).
Sellnow, Werner, Gesellschaft – Staat – Recht (Berlin 1963)
Shakespeare, William, The Merchant of Venice (London 1600)
Sinha, Surya Prakash, Jurisprudence. Legal Theory (St. Paul/Minn. 1993)
Smith, Adam, A Theory of Moral Sentiment (Edinburgh 1759)
– The Wealth of Nations (London 1776)
Smith, Munroe, Four German Jurists. Bruns, Windscheid, Jhering, Gneist, Political Science Quarterly 10 (1895) 664–692; II: 11 (1896) 278–309, III: 12 (1897) 21–62
– Review of Rudolph von Ihering, Law as a Means to an End, Columbia Law Review 15 (1915) 470–471
Somek, Alexander, Die Kaserne des Egoismus. Jheringe Genealogie der Moralität, in Gerhard Luf and Werner Ogris (eds.) Der Kampf ums Recht (Berlin 1995) 57–93
– Legal Formality and Freedom of Choice. A Moral Perspective on Jhering's Constructivism, Ratio Juris 15 (2002) 52–62
Spencer, Herbert, Principles of Biology (London 1864)
– Principles of Ethics vol. II (London 1879)
– Principles of Psychology (London 1855)
Spengler, Oswald, Der Untergang des Abendlandes (2 vols., Wien 1918, München 1922)
Stahl, Friedrich Julius, Die Philosophie des Rechts nach geschichtlicher Ansicht (2 vols., Heidelberg 1830–37)
Stein, Peter, Legal Evolution. The Story of an Idea (Cambridge etc. 1980)
– Logic and Experience in Roman and Common Law, Boston University Law Review 59 (1979) 433–451
Stinzing, Roderich, and Landsberg, Ernst, Geschichte der deutschen Rechtswissenschaft III.2. (München und Berlin 1910)
Stolleis, Michael (ed.), Hermann Conring 1606–1681 (Berlin 1983)
Stone, Julius, The Province and Function of Law (Sydney 1946)
Streitberg, Wilhelm, Review of Jhering, Vorgeschichte der Indo-Europäer, newpaper clip, unknown origin, Niedersächsische Universitäts- und Staatsbibliothek Göttingen Cod. Ms Jhering 13:1,4

Stürner, Rolf, Das Zivilrecht der Moderne und die Bedeutung der Rechtsdogmatik, Juristenzeitung 67 (2012) 10–24
Summers, Robert, Instrumentalism and American Legal Theory (Ithaca and London 1982)
– Pragmatic Instrumentalism in Twentieth Century American Legal Thought, Cornell Law Review 66 (1980–81) 861–948
– Rudolf von Jhering's Influence on American Legal Theory, in: Okko Behrens (ed.), Jherings Rechtsdenken (Göttingen 1996) 61–76
Tamanaha, Brian, Law as a Means to an End. Threat to the Rule of Law (New York etc. 2006)
– A Realistic Theory of Law (Cambridge/UK and New York 2017)
Taylor, Isaac, Origin of the Aryan (New York 1890)
Teubner, Gunther, Rechts als autopoietisches System (Frankfurt 1989)
Thibaut, Anton Friedrich Justus, Über die Notwendigkeit eines allgemeinen bürgerlichen Rechts für Deutschland (Heidelberg 1814)
Tiedemann, Christopher, Methods of Legal Education, Yale Law Journal 1 (1891) 139–161
– The Unwritten Constitution of the United States (New York 1890)
Tönnies, Ferdinand, Gemeinschaft und Gesellschaft (Leipzig 1887)
Treitschke, Heinrich von, Die Freiheit (Leipzig 1861)
Twining, William, Karl Llewellyn and the Realis Movement (London 1973, 2d ed. Cambridge 2012)
Tyler, Edward, Primitive Culture (London 1871)
Vano, Cristina, Itinerari italiani di Rudolf von Jhering, in: Okko Behrends (ed.), Rudolf von Jhering, Beiträge und Zeugnisse (2d. ed. Göttingen 1993) 121–126
Vesco, Stephan, Die Erfindung der ökonomischen Rechtswissenschaft (Weilewists 2021)
Viehweg, Theodor, Rechtsdogmatik und Rechtszetetik bei Jhering, in Franz Wieacker and Manfred Wollschläger (eds.), Jherings Erbe (Göttingen 1970) 211–216
Vinogradoff, Paul, Outlines of Historical Jurisprudence (2 vol. 1920–22)
Vogenauer, Stefan, An Empire of Light, Cambridge Law Journal 46 (1005) 481–500
Walder, Rudolf, Das Wesen der Gesellschaft bei Adam Smith und Rudolf von Jhering. Zur Geschichte des rechtsphilosophischen und soziologischen Positivismus (Ph.D. thesis Kiel 1943)
Watson, Alan, Legal Transplants (Charlottesville, Ga. 1974, 2d ed. Athens, Ga. 1993)
– Rome of the Twelve Tables: Persons and Property (Princeton 1975)
– The Spirit of Roman Law (Athens and London 1995)
Weber, Max, Economy and Society (Guenther Roth and Claus Wittich eds., 2 vols., Berkeley, Los Angeles, London 1978, German orig. Tübingen 1922)
– Politik als Beruf (München and Leipzig 1919)
Welzel, Hans, Naturrecht und materiale Gerechtigkeit (4th ed., Tübingen 1964, orig. 1951)
White, G. Edward, Justice Oliver Wendell Holmes and the Inner Self (New York 1995)
White, Morton, Social Thought in America: The Revolt Against Formalism (New York 1949)
Whitman, James, Jhering parmi les Français, in: La science juridique française et la science juridique allemande de 1870 à 1918 (Strasbourg 1997) 151–164
– The Legacy of Roman Law in the German Romantic Era (Princeton 1990)
Wieacker, Franz, Rudolph von Jhering, in: id., Gründer und Bewahrer (Göttingen 1959) 197–211
– Jhering und der Darwinismus, in: Festschrift für Karl Larenz (G. Paulus et al., eds, München 1973) 63–92

– Privatrechtsgeschichte der Neuzeit (2[d] ed. Göttingen 1967) (engl.: A History of Private Law in Europe, Tony Weir transl, Oxford 1995)
– Römische Rechtsgeschichte I (München 1988)
– Rudolf von Jhering (Leipzig 1942)
– Rudolph von Jhering, Zeitschrift der Savigny-Stiftung für Rechtsgeschichte (rom. Abt.) 86 (1969) 1–36

Wieacker, Franz, and Wollschläger, Christian (eds.), Jherings Erbe (Göttingen 1970)

Wiedemann, Franz, Hegel (Reinbek 1965)

Wilhelm, Walter, Zur juristischen Methodenlehre im 19. Jahrhundert (Frankfurt 1958)

Windscheid, Bernhard, Die Aufgaben der Rechtswissenschaft, in Gesammelte Reden und Abhandlungen (Paul Oertmann ed., Leipzig 1904) 101–116 (orig. 1884)
– Die Actio des römischen Civilrechts vom Standpunkte des heutigen Rechts (Düsseldorf 1856)
– Lehrbuch des Pandektenrechts (3 vols., Düsseldorf 1862–1870)
– Die Lehre des römischen Rechts von der Voraussetzung (Düsseldorf 1850)

Wolf, Erik, Große Rechtsdenker der deutschen Geistesgeschichte (Tübingen 1939, 4th ed. 1963)

Wurmnest, Wolfgang, Contract Law, in: Joachim Zekoll and Gerhard Wagner (eds.), Introduction to German Law (Alphen an den Rijn 2018) 199–268

Zimmer, Heinrich, Altindisches Leben. Die Cultur der vedischen Arier nach den Sanhita dargestellt (Berlin 1879)

Zimmermann, Reinhard, Juristische Methodenlehre in Deutschland, Rabels Zeitschrift 83 (2019) 241–287
– Roman Law, Contemporary Law, European Law. The Civilian Tradition Today (Oxford 2001)

Zweig, Stefan, Die Welt der Sicherheit, in: id., Die Welt von Gestern (Köln 2013, orig. 1942) 1–51

Zweigert, Konrad, Jherings Bedeutung für die Entwicklung der rechtsvergleichenden Methode, in: Franz Wieacker und Christian Wollschläger (eds.), Jherings Erbe (Göttingen 1970) 240–251

Zweigert, Konrad, und Kötz, Hein, Einführung in die Rechtsvergleichung auf dem Gebiete des Privatrechts (2 vols. Tübingen 1969–1971, 3 ed. 1996); engl. Introduction to Comparative Law (Tony Weir transl., 3d ed. Oxford 1998)

Zweigert, Konrad and Siehr, Kurt, Jhering's Influence on the Development of Comparative Legal Method, American Journal of Comparative Law 19 (1971) 215–231

Index

(Works by Jhering in *Italics*)